23rd Annual

KNIVES 2003

THE WORLD'S GREATEST KNIFE BOOK

Edited by Joe Kertzman

KNIVES 2003 STAFF

Joe Kertzman, Editor

Editorial Comments and Suggestions

We're always looking for feedback on our books. Please let us know what you like about this edition. If you have suggestions for articles you'd like to see in future editions, please contact

Joe Kertzman/Knives
700 East State St.
Iola, WI 54990
email: kertzmanj@krause.com

The Cover Knives

To say the blades on the cover of *Knives 2003* are splendiferous specimens might sound superlative but it's the least one can say about the fine craftsmanship gracing the front of the newest edition of everything sharp. At top and leading the way is a Stephen Schwarzer traditional *aikuchi* (a *tanto* without a guard) dagger—Japanese style, of course—born from 5160 steel with the ever-present armor-piercing point and *hamon*, or temper line. The handle is white stingray skin with a carved *menuki* (a pin form for decoration) and a carved copper *habaki* (blade collar). Parallel to the piece and directly below it is a Scott Sawby self-locking folding knife sporting a Devin Thomas ladder-pattern-damascus blade, a black-lip-pearl handle and Chris Meyer bolster engraving of cougars in their natural habitat. The fancy dagger at left is from none other than Buster Warenski and features a matrix-opal handle, an abundance of gold inlay work by Julie Warenski and a shapely 440C blade. The "Howler" at bottom right was masterminded by Tom Anderson and incorporates a gray BG-42 blade, a three-tone, blued-titanium handle and a blue collar around the head of the pivot screw. All leave a lasting impression.

Published by

krause publications

700 E. State Street • Iola, WI 54990-0001
Telephone: 715/445-2214
Web: www.krause.com

Please call or write for our free catalog of publications.
Our toll-free number to place an order or obtain a free catalog is 800-258-0929
or please use our regular business telephone 715-445-2214.

Library of Congress Catalog Number: 80-67744

ISBN: 0-87349-448-2

INTRODUCTION

The knives are spread out here before you and you realize a simplistic art form. Envision a dark-blue chamois cloth, showing a trace of white lint, the fibers frayed slightly at the ends. Selected knives seem to slice through the cloth, but really they are splayed out atop it. The edges, so sharp to the touch, lie dangerously close to delicate woven threads. Bevels blend into the thickness of the blades—blades that are squared at their spines, but oh so pointed at their termini. Trace line from the guard along the swooping edge to a point that hangs there, one molecule jutting out beyond all the rest in Limbo.

That's the raw beauty.

It's easy to become lost in the romance of knives. Yet, no knifemaker with the stamina to trade sweat for success is an idealistic romantic. Those who strive for the glory of gain first learn the lessons of pain. Hours of study and days of deliverance turn into weeks and months of minuscule manipulation until a knife turns out just right. Until oil spread evenly among the pores of the blade creates a glistening liquid sheen, revealing no pits, imperfections or flaws, just a perfectly smooth surface.

There is a science to it, you know. No matter the exterior, there lies an internal uprising, a perplex steel composition that pleads to be addressed. It is within that lies the mystery, the intrigue of carbides on top of carbides, spread out like multiplying eggs. It's in the heat treat they say, that strength is formed, where molecules and cells are bonded together until nearly impenetrable.

Hulking knifemakers with hands like leather and faces like stone force blades in vises, place steel pipes over their tips and edges, and heave with all their might until the sharpened steel buckles under the pressure. Like introspective inventors, they study the mangled billets, spying imperfections, places where the steel folded, where it broke its metallurgical bond. Such steel is a menace and should be rid of before it spreads disease to the rest of Steel City.

They became lost in their work. The knives within the pages of this book are offspring of such passion. Flowing forms speak to the inner souls, and that is only accomplished through inspiration. The knives, themselves, also inspire. They provoke thought, and stories are told.

Read Joe Szilaski's account of early forging and follow his train of thought through a historical overview of the craft. Greg Bean warns you to beware of beastly battle-axes and dares you to feel the terror of the havoc they once wreaked. Linda Moll Smith shares an enthralling story of the knives she's loved and lost. James Ayres takes you halfway around the world to an outdoor European market where a Frenchman sells sword canes. Find out why the knives that gave U.S. servicemen the edge in World War II are the hottest cutlery collectibles. Get lost in the scenes and patterns of powdered-mosaic-damascus steel.

Trends in edged tools include phenomenal folding knives, tomahawks, S-curved blades, folders with locks and switches, drop-point hunters, bang-up bowies, an alliance of stately swords, fighters, dirks, daggers and more. Artistic outlets in knives involve scrimshaw, incredible inlays, overlays, inserts and spacers, carved handles, guards, blades and bolsters, dazzling damascus and ingenious engraving.

The knifemakers are physically drained. They lie down to sleep, but not before putting their blades to bed. They pick up the hefty handles, bulging like swollen thumbs so sore they're ready to burst. They run rough fingers along smooth steel, and somehow feeling a cold steel exterior spreads warmth within them. They tuck their steel creations under chamois-cloth covers, careful not to let the edges penetrate the fibers, for fibers, too, hold everything together.

Joe Kertzman

Knives 2003
CONTENTS

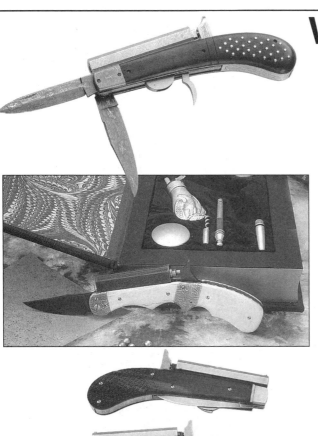

WOODEN SWORD AWARDS: 2003

It was necessary to award three makers Wooden Sword Awards this year in light of the phenomenal pistol knife creations that Wade Colter, Ron Newton and Bruce Bump labored over lovingly for long days and endless nights. From Colter (bottom photo) and Newton (top) come Unwin Roger pistol knife replicas—Colter's with two antique-finished 1084 blades, nickel-silver bolsters, a checkered-ebony handle and a hand-forged .32-caliber barrel with hammer and folding trigger. Like Colter and Bump, sole authorship is Newton's claim, meaning he alone built the pistol knife from start to finish, including ebony handle with silver studs, damascus blade with mosaic images of cowboys panning for gold, 24k-gold inlays, leaf-pattern engraving and, oh yeah, an Unwin Rodgers Saloon Pistol. Bump fashioned his War and Peace Pistol Knife (center) with a black-niter-blued O-1 blade, mosaic-damascus bolsters, a pre-ban elephant-ivory handle and a black-powder muzzle-loading pistol with all necessary tools. It stores in a book safe with ostrich leather exterior and padded black-velvet interior. (Point-Seven (top) and BladeGallery.com photos)

More Than Just Theater Knives, They're Freedom Fighters!

The knives that gave U.S. servicemen the edge in World War II could be the hottest cutlery collectibles

By Richard D. White

Richard D. White photos

Either of the two knives would be the centerpiece of any theater knife collection. At left is a large (almost 13 inches in overall length) sheath knife incorporating a poured-aluminum handle with integral guard, and a clip-point, bowie-style blade. The other is a double-edged fighter with brass guard and pinned, Bakelite® handle. The sheaths for both knives are precision stitched and unusually heavy.

THE JAPANESE ATTACK of Pearl Harbor on Dec. 7, 1941, brought with it an immediate call-out for additional armed forces personnel. It also resulted in tremendous shortages in essential supplies to support a massive military buildup. Almost overnight, there was endless demand for military clothing, weapons, medical supplies, munitions, food, vehicles and thousands of other items necessary to keep the military machine moving closer to an ultimate victory.

Switching U.S. factory production from a peacetime to wartime mode on such a massive scale caused an immediate depletion of crucial military supplies. This phenomenon was most painfully evident in the ability of American cutlery companies to outfit millions of servicemen with the single most essential combat weapon: the fighting knife.

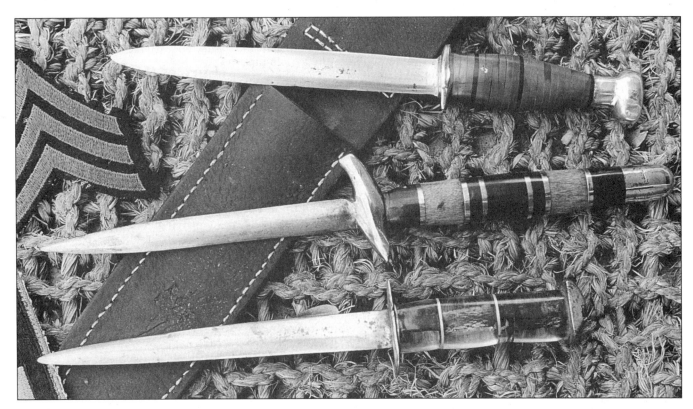

Creative GIs and friends of the soldiers alternately stacked leather handle spacers, or married leather with Bakelite® sections, aluminum, Plexiglas®, wood and brass, as evidenced by three dagger-style theater knives. This created colorful and individual handle spacers and designs. The top knife enlists alternating grip sections of red Bakelite and leather. The middle dagger, with unique brass guard and pommel, showcases interspersed spacers of red Bakelite, brass and walnut. The third dagger employs clear Plexiglas spacer material with alternating brass sections surrounding a red, painted center shaft.

Theater knives are often styled after the bowie knife, like the top piece that features red-and-black Bakelite handle spacers and a curved, brass guard. Front and center is a custom-designed bowie with clear Plexiglas spacers that clearly reveal a red, painted shaft. This knife has a large aluminum pommel and guard. The bottom knife incorporates clear Plexiglas spacers with a single, brown spacer in the center. It has a machined, aluminum pommel and familiar bowie-shaped blade.

The problem of filling the void in combat knives was addressed, in part, with a campaign that originated in California through the efforts of Frank Martinelli, a San Francisco nightclub owner. Martinelli discovered, while talking to wounded GIs who had served in the South Pacific, that the most pressing edged-weapon needs for combat soldiers were large, fixed-blade knives.

Martinelli was so moved by their stories that he formed a citizens committee with the intent of collecting unused knives from ordinary American citizens. The committee slogan was: "Save a Life with a Knife." Martinelli's efforts unearthed thousands of knives donated from people across the U.S. who wished to assist "their boys" fighting in the Pacific Theater.

The news of Martinelli's campaign broke in the Feb. 8, 1943, issue of LIFE magazine, which featured a particularly striking black-and-white photograph of two Air Force privates inventorying and classifying hundreds of knives that surrounded them. In addition to the dramatic photo, the article pinpointed the various styles of knives those same soldiers considered valuable tools for overseas fighting soldiers.

Responding to Martinelli's call-out, private citizens sent all types of knives to military outposts and various collection sites. Hunting knives, bowies, large sheath knives, daggers and all types of homemade knives turned up in the warehouses of military bases. The pull-together-for-victory knives were then sent to U.S. troops stationed in the South Pacific.

There were thousands of hand-made knives fashioned for soldiers, or by soldiers themselves who were stationed in the South Pacific or en-route aboard ships traveling to the Pacific Islands. The deeply historic, meaningful and impressive knives made by GIs have since been classified as "theater knives" because they were constructed by hand during service in or on passage to the Pacific Theater of military operations.

Lure of the Theater Knife

The collecting of theater knives is presently the hottest and most alluring segment of cutlery collecting, even more so than accumulating non-knife-related military collectibles.

One note of interest is that, until recently, theater knives were generally overlooked for their lack of tang stamps or other marks identifying the makers of the knives. In addition, compared to regular production knives, theater knives are often crudely fashioned from materials servicemen had at hand. What was once the turnoff is now the allure!

Resulting from a recent upsurge in military collecting; the publication of several well-illustrated books on the subject; and a much greater appreciation of the craftsmanship that went into theater knives, collectors and dealers have

Theater knives couldn't come in more creative packages, or designs, as these two fixed blades. The top knife was most likely made in a machine shop, a conclusion drawn by two handle halves, or slabs, that were pinned together. The knife was equipped with a sharp clip blade and a metal sheath. Below it is a somewhat crude version of a knuckle knife. The formidable fighting knife comes complete with a double-edge, saw-cut blade and a heavy metal guard to protect the fingers. The blade is stamped "EP" and "DO," in all probability, the maker's and/or user's initials.

experienced an almost frantic search for the historically relevant handmade knives.

The initial fashioning of theater knives was an interesting process that involved talented soldiers or sailors with time on their hands. The "hurry up and wait" philosophy seemingly present in the military meant that time was certainly not at a premium.

Sailors making the trek between the U.S. and the South Pacific had weeks of travel time with little to do during off-hours.

The massive aircraft carriers, troop transports, destroyers and battleships housed complete machine shops for the production of almost any part or tool for the self-sustaining ship, or for any aircraft it served. Trained machinists could operate lathes and mills, or temper steels, and had access to other metalworking tools in the onboard machine shops.

While transporting hundreds of soldiers and pilots to their ultimate destinations, sailors would frequently produce uniquely crafted fighting knives in return for cash, cigarettes or out of pure kindness, knowing beforehand what the soldiers faced in the near future.

Seabee Steel

Many soldiers who had machinist and other tool-making skills were stationed as "permanent party" on the islands designated as supply and equipment depots, first aid stations, temporary aircraft landing sites and repair stations.

Although quite busy when planes made emergency landings, GIs stationed on the islands had time to build knives that could be used in the war effort. This seemed to be especially true of the thousands of Seabees sent to various islands throughout the South Pacific.

Even though Seabees were generally the first to land on enemy islands, and whose role it was to provide bridges, runways, water systems, roads and buildings, they spent months and sometimes years on the same island, providing for the expansion and repair of various facilities. These talented engineers were some of the first to utilize the equipment available to them to produce theater knives in their spare time.

Hundreds of front-line soldiers who were issued a commercially produced sheath knife frequently wanted their knives personalized. While retaining the basic blade configuration, they exchanged the standard handle materials for customized, colorful spacers.

While in the resting areas behind the combat lines, tired and tattered soldiers needed to take their minds off the rigors and travesties of war, and took the time to work on modifying their regular-issue knives.

Of necessity for making theater knives was a cheap and plentiful source of materials, especially steel for the blades, handle materials of various types, and leather for sheaths. Fortunately, all three were plentiful.

▶The handles of the two handmade theater knives are made from the same material used on early KA-BAR and Hoffritz utility knives. Are they theater knives? The brass rivets holding the handle material on would suggest they are. One has threaded rivets that were ground off to form a smooth surface.

In addition to old, worn-out files, knifemaking soldiers used parts and pieces from downed enemy aircraft, primarily Japanese planes. Plexiglas® from windshields (in several different colors) was a favorite handle material.

Plane Blades?

Plexiglas could be cut and alternately stacked with leather, Bakelite® from electrical components, aluminum sections and brass, creating colorful and individual handle spacers and designs.

High-carbon steels from wing struts and other engine parts were annealed and later tempered to make blades in a variety of shapes. Aluminum, a major component of most planes, was also plentiful, and was used to make spacers and pommels, or was melted down and cast into guards for knuckle knives.

Brass from wiring and other internal parts was pounded into rivets and guards, and leather from seat belts was generally used to make high-quality sheaths.

There remained a significant demand for theater knives by members of the armed forces.

The sheath knife was by far the most important piece of equipment for most soldiers. In addition to its obvious use as a weapon, it was employed for opening cans and boxes, locating land mines, rescu-

ing fellow soldiers, digging foxholes, cutting leather and cloth, skinning animals, killing snakes, hacking through brush and grasses, notching sticks, and pounding anything that needed a good smack.

Although some serious cutlery collectors are well ahead of the game with regard to amassing theater knives, others are just now discovering not only the craftsmanship evident in these knives, but the history attached to the makers and the soldiers who carried them into battle.

As such, theater knives appeal not only to the cutlery collector, but to the military historian as well. Serious collectors once considered themselves lucky just to find a few

Here's a handsome group of stacked-spacer-handle theater knives. Notice the differences in spacer thickness, guard shapes and blade styles. Unlike factory production knives, these are "one-of-a-kind" edged weapons and tools, and each is a historical combat artifact with a unique story behind it. It represents either a GI who fought in the Pacific Theater, or some thoughtful individual who fashioned the knife for a soldier friend.

of the knives. Today, the same collectors have begun to specialize in the various types and styles of theater knives and their accompanying sheaths in the marketplace.

Whether it's a simple knife design that mimics a production model, a wavy-shaped kris style, a heavy-duty fighting knife with colorful spacers, or a double-edged dagger with "knuckle buster" guard, collectors are slowly refining the unique cutlery collectibles.

Name, Rank and Serial Number

With new discoveries comes heightened interest and significant research into the oral histories of the men who carried theater knives. Many examples are etched with the names of soldiers, their ranks and the islands where the knives were used. With that information, collectors and enthusiasts can begin to complete the personal sides of the handcrafted edged weapons.

In the author's opinion, the world of knives will experience a rapid increase in prices and interest for the once-overlooked theater knives. Military knives, in general, will grow in popularity.

Those living veterans who served a noble cause are reaching the twilight of their lives, prompting military knife enthusiasts to hold on to the knives that played such important roles in the struggle.

The rapid and sudden interest in theater knives is multi-faceted. Treasure troves of examples are certainly awaiting discovery, stored for years in footlockers, or misidentified as merely handmade knives. With each, there is a story. Some theater knives can be identified by names etched into the blades or sheaths, while others are traced through letters and photographs.

Still more are unmarked monuments to those men who fought and died in the South Pacific. Theater knives are a salute to their bravery and ultimate sacrifice. ●

Poured aluminum handles were frequently used on theater knives, no matter the size. The smaller piece looks to be a hunting knife, with guard and pommel poured integrally to the handles. The sheaths are also handmade and well designed.

The Lure of Sword Canes Lingers Today

An outdoor European market offers sword canes sufficient for 'setting upon a band of ruffians'

By James Ayres

HAVE YOU EVER wanted to own a sword cane, a real sword cane, and not some tacky imitation from a novelty store, but one with a true rapier blade? Perhaps you would like an antique sword cane, one that was once used by a gentleman to fight off a gang of brute rogues, one with a blade of damascus steel, sheathed in ebony.

When I was a boy, I read novels by Kipling and others about the British Empire and its days of glory. In these novels, it seemed that a gentleman was often "set upon by a band of ruffians." Inevitably, the gentleman would drive them off with the aid of his ever-present sword cane. He would usually manage to do so without inflicting serious injury due to his superior skill at fencing.

Photos by Justin Ayres

During an extended trip to Europe, the author found sword canes in a number of antique shops, yet nowhere did he find a collection to match this one of Gerard Fustier.

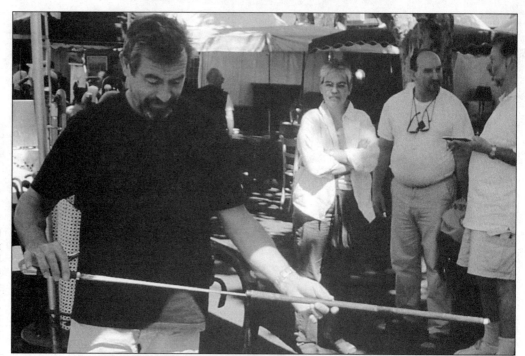

All of Gerard Fustier's sword canes are works of art. Most have shafts of rare and durable woods, such as this one that employs *mallaca*, a tough wood from Malaysia and a favorite choice for gentlemen's canes, sword and otherwise, for over a hundred years.

Sometimes, there was a lady in distress and he was coming to her aid, but always there was a sword cane and a spirited defense.

I have not read any such books for more than three decades, but the memory and the romance lingers, as does a fascination with the sword cane as a tangible piece of the past. Recently, during an extended trip to Europe, I found sword canes in a number of antique shops, yet nowhere did I find a collection to match that of Gerard Fustier.

I was in Aix en Provence on a weekend, where I had the pleasure of seeing some of the most wonderful sword canes, those only dreamed about while deeply engrossed in a Kipling novel. I happened by an outdoor antique market set up under white canopies by a fountain at the Cours Mirabeau.

The grand fountain is the focal point (literally the heart) of the charming town of Aix en Provence. Aix is an ancient town, built by the Romans, and the first capitol of Provence. The street leading to the fountain is lined with plane trees. The tall, rough-barked trees interlock their branches, making dappled shade for the sidewalks and outdoor cafes. The broad walkways are crowded in summer with people from all around the world who come to sample the many charms of Aix.

Fustier was displaying his wares under one of those white awnings and can be found there each Friday and Saturday with

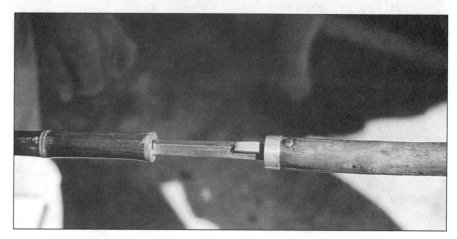

In some cases, the joining of handle to shaft in a well-built sword cane is so fine it cannot be seen without close examination. The locking mechanisms that hold the blades in the shafts of most of Gerard Fustier's canes are concealed in bands of silver, some plain, while others are carved or etched.

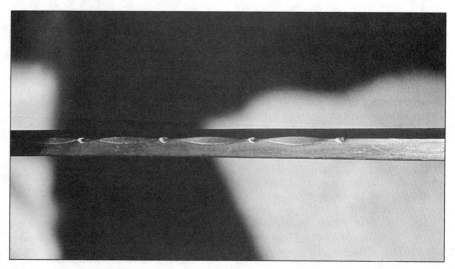

Many of the featured sword canes have decorative notches and dimples forged into the blades, serving dual roles as decorations and stress relievers.

Gerard Fustier displays the ornate sterling silver handle of an impressive sword cane.

his epee from its resting place in the ebony cane and, with stick in one hand and epee in the other, he would have sent the scoundrels running, or maybe not.

Sword canes seem so long ago. Men haven't carried sticks as personal accoutrements since World War I. They seem to have no practical place in today's world. But if you have a sense of nostalgia for a past you can only imagine, then a handsome sword cane becomes a powerful object of the imagination.

Fustier took the time to explain a small part of the history of these fascinating arms from the past. He said that in all European countries, the sword cane became the gentleman's preferred weapon of defense after it was no longer fashionable to openly carry a rapier. There were many schools in the past 200 years that taught the art of fencing with the sword cane. It seems that there were some specifics to the use of sword cane that varied from the standard rapier.

One distinguishing factor revealed itself in the blade of the typical sword cane, which was considerably shorter than the standard rapier. A classic sword cane blade ranges from 12 to 18 inches, whereas a typical rapier blade stretches nearly 30 to 36 inches in length. Therefore, the fencer would have had to work closer to his opponent using the blade of a sword cane.

The wooden sheath of the cane was retained in the off hand for use in parrying and as an impact weapon. In fact, a proper gentleman did not draw the blade of a sword cane until it was determined that a strike with the cane itself would not serve for defense.

Like all edged weapons, sword canes were made obsolete by the widespread availability of factory-made repeating firearms. Today, sword canes are only a relic of a romantic past.

Cane Mutiny?

In France, as in other countries, sword canes have, from time to time, been made illegal. The French government outlawed the walking sticks with sharpened steel cores at least five times over the years. Each time, the law was totally ignored by the gentlemen of the era, and on such occasions, after sufficient time had passed with no one adhering to the new law, it was repealed.

Fustier said sword canes have once again, just this year, been outlawed, unless in the possession of

his collection of sword canes. He also has a marvelous collection of turn-of-the-century walking canes in every material from which a cane can be fashioned. An erudite man, he instructs on the history and construction of each cane and will demonstrate the correct way to extract and deploy the epee or rapier.

Fustier is a handsome, dark-haired man who moves with the balance and grace of an athlete. On a warm, sunny morning, with a breeze cooled by the fountain, I asked him to show me one of his sword canes. It was a particularly striking piece with a silver band at the grip.

Parry the Thrust

He deftly, with a small flourish, drew the damascus blade from its ebony sheath. Retaining the stick in his left hand, he held the blade first *en garde*, and then, with a subtle movement, he shifted into *quarte*. With a flick of his wrist, he parried the thrust of an imagined opponent and riposted with skill and economy of motion.

Clearly, Fustier had studied the art of fencing. I imagined him as a long-ago gentleman, walking the narrow streets of Macao and being set upon by the mythical band of ruffians. He would have whipped

collectors and not being used on the streets. Collectors may possess any number of sword canes, and it seems anyone can become a collector by declaring to be one.

Why any government would outlaw such an antique, I cannot imagine. I doubt that there has been an outbreak of banditry conducted at the points of sword canes. But it seems that all governments become uncomfortable with the notion of citizens, or subjects, being in possession of weapons of any kind, ancient, modern or imagined.

Even today, adherence to such laws varies from country to country. In Great Britain, for example, its subjects are apparently in complete conformance with all such laws concerning sword canes. However, in France, the country of "Liberty, Equality and Fraternity," the citizens seem to be quite independent of this new government edict. It appears that, if the citizenry finds these new restrictions undemocratic, they ignore them. If a majority ignores the new rule, the government, faced with noncompliance by the majority, is expected to respond by retracting its regulations. If the majority does comply, then the new rule becomes law, resulting in total compliance. As I understand it, this unofficial process serves as a citizens' referendum.

In the meantime, reasonable men behave reasonably. While I was standing in Fustier's booth under the white awnings, the proper gentleman sold two handsome sword canes to collectors. Obviously they must have been collectors, otherwise they would not have purchased items restricted to collectors. Besides, I could see that they were collectors by the way they walked away down the broad sidewalk, passing from sunlight to shade, swinging their sticks gracefully at their sides.

All of Fustier's sword canes are works of art. Most have shafts of rare and durable woods, such as ebony or *mallaca*. Ebony is a dense hardwood from Africa, and *mallaca* is a tough wood from Malaysia, the latter a favorite choice for gentlemen's canes, sword and otherwise, for over a hundred years. One had a shaft of rattan, which is durable and flexible. The blades were, with only one exception, of damascus steel.

Steadfast Damascus

The forging of damascus might have been a lost art in America for many years but, in Europe, several

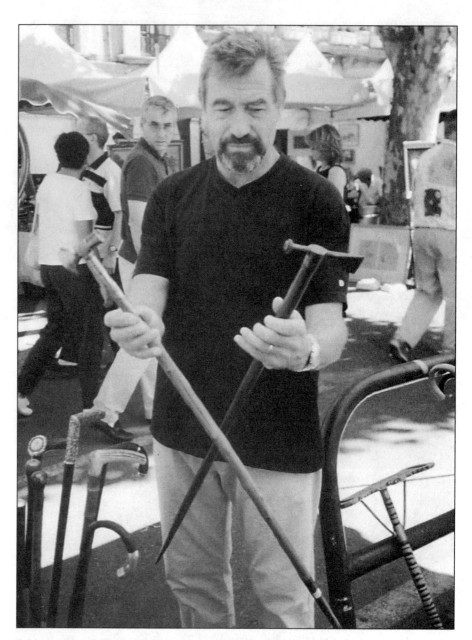

Held at arm's length are two axe canes used by foresters to mark trees.

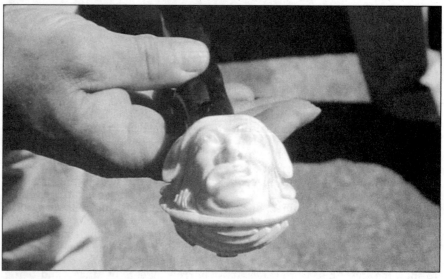

A carved ivory head starkly contrasts the ebony shaft of a sword cane found in the collection of European collector Gerard Fustier.

generations of layered steel has remained in continuous use from ancient times until present. These blades display none of the elaborate high-art techniques used by modern American smiths. They are simple pattern-welded blades meant for hard service.

Fustier allowed me to handle all of his swords and, in the course of doing so, I discovered that the blades all had a small degree of flex, yet they sprang back to true without hesitation. Some blades were triangular in cross section—true epees designed for contact with only the point.

Others had two edges in the manner of a rapier. Many had what appeared to be file work on the spines of the blades, but Fustier told me that the decorative notches and dimples were forged into the blade. He said the notches served as stress relievers, as well as being decorative.

The fit and finish of his sword canes was of the highest level of craft. In some cases, the joining of handle to shaft was so fine it could not be seen without close examination. The locking mechanism that held the blade in the shaft was usually concealed in a band of silver. Some silver bands were plain, while others were carved or etched. To the casual eye, it was not at all apparent that a foot-and-a-half of fine damascus steel was resting within the handsome wood shaft.

There would seem to be little use for a sword cane for the thrashing of scoundrels in today's world, but if you love fine steel, and if you have an ounce of romance in your soul, one of these relics of a distant past will be a welcome addition to your collection. ●

Gerard Fustier's treasures fall in the $200-$500 price range. He willingly responds to letters or phone calls and is always pleased to hear from U.S. collectors or other interested persons. He has photos of all of his sword canes and will send them on request.

To purchase a sword cane, contact: Gerard Fustier, La Sauvagine-Quartier BELLIN, Les Pinchinats, France. Phone: 33 (0) 4 42 21 37 57.

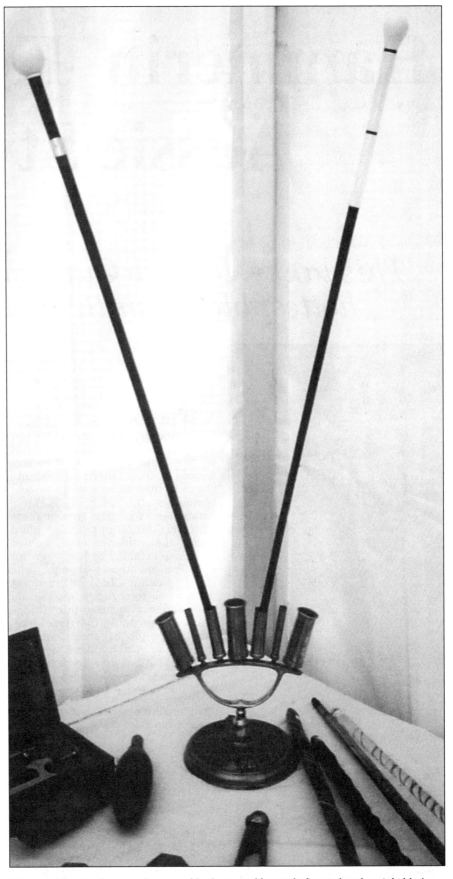

Here are two slender sword canes with ebony and ivory shafts, and rapier-style blades.

Hammerin' Hot Steel Aussie Style

This lanky, laconic Queenslander is the hottest blade smith 'down under'

By Keith Spencer

WE'VE GOT A lot of good blade smiths in Oz (Australia). Not so many years ago, you could count on one hand the blokes who preferred to forge their knives into shape rather than use the stock-removal method of blade making. Nowadays, you get tyro makers who start out forging blades, often under the guidance of a mentor who is an established blade smith.

There are those, though, who simply pick up a book or video, set up a basic forge, then recycle old files and car springs into things that cut. Inevitably, they meet like-minded people at shows, on the Internet or via a phone network that links Australian knifemakers. Their work becomes more refined, and then one day they win a show award, get mentioned in a knife article and so become a part of a rich tapestry in the world of knives.

We do not have the luxury of a blade smith's society on the big island we call Australia, but I suspect it's because the fellows that forge haven't found time yet to organize. Most are part-time blade makers, so they are forced to choose finishing forged-to-shape blade blanks as opposed to lengthy sessions spent at the fire and anvil.

In addition to fulfilling day-to-day orders for knives, makers need to rack up blade ware to offer buyers at six annual custom knife shows in Australia and New Zealand. There are no dull moments down under in the knife business these days.

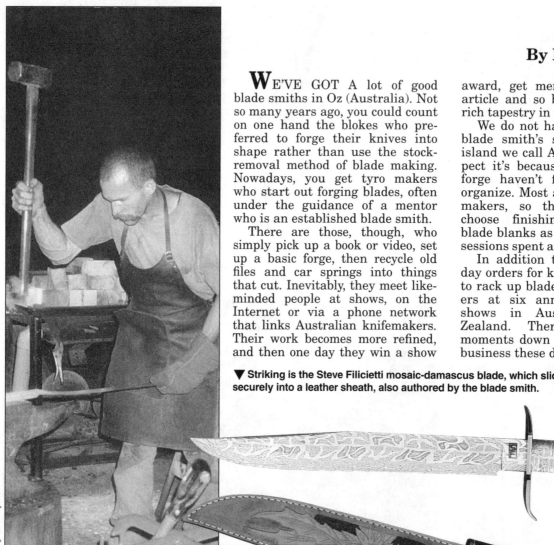

Photos by Keith Spencer

▼ Striking is the Steve Filicietti mosaic-damascus blade, which slides effortlessly but securely into a leather sheath, also authored by the blade smith.

▲ Australia's hottest knifemaker (weather aside), Steve Filicietti is hard at work on the Coraki farm near the south Queensland border.

▲ ▶Australian knifemaker Steve Filicietti did Japan proud with his version of a Japanese *wakizashi*. The long, stout-but-slender piece features a 10,000-layer, clay-quenched and water-hardened 1095, W1 and wrought-iron blade with discernable *harmon* (temper) line, complemented by a copper *habaki* (blade collar), and a scabbard of ringed *gidgee* (a wood native to Australia).

▲ Working with horses led Steve Filicietti to teach himself saddlery and general leatherwork on the family farm at Coraki. Learning saddlery, in turn, manifests in the artistic sheaths that accompany most Filicietti blade ware.

Many, however, have become members of blacksmith societies scattered around the states and territories. Maybe a blade smith's society can be structured under the auspices of a blacksmith's organization already in existence. Hammer-ins amongst pockets of blade smiths and groups of medieval re-enactors already take place. . . fun days, creative days, days of sharing and learning, followed by a barbecue and a few beers. One day there will be a collision of brain cells and "hey presto," a national body of blade smiths will appear. That'll be the day!

By winding back the clock, we discover that Australian black-smiths made knives from the time of settlement. Old records stored on microfiche sheets in state libraries reveal lists of black-smiths and ironmongers in the 18th and 19th centuries.

I have an old bowie-style knife forged by Tom Brammer, the father of the late Frank Brammer, who custom crafted fighting bowies for American soldiers who stopped over in Australia during World War II. Tom, who emigrated from England, forged throwing knives for performers in traveling circuses.

Huge numbers of all sorts of blade ware imported from Sheffield fulfilled the needs of pioneers and settlers, essentially by mail order out of port cities located on the perimeter of this vast continent.

For about 100 years (1875-1975), cutlery was manufactured in Australia, much of which was forged in factories in the southeast corner of the continent. The best-known manufacturers were Gregory Steel Products (Melbourne), W T Whittingslowe (Adelaide) and Thomas Chapman & Sons (Sydney).

Not a lot is known about custom knifemakers before 1975, but a Queenslander named George Lee Sye emerged as the pioneer of custom knifemaking in the modern era. Although not a blade smith, George made crossings to America and communicated with well-known makers, including Bob Loveless. George died in December 1982, but not before sharing much of what he knew about knifemaking via his column in a national hunting magazine and letters to some of the handful of makers scattered around the continent.

During the 1980s, a few of the fledgling group of knifemakers began gathering at gun shows to air their wares, and some of them were blade smiths. Although we now know that, at the time, there were a few damascus forgers already plying their trade in quiet corners of the commonwealth, Eric Gillard is attributed with being the maker who introduced damascus at a Melbourne militaria expo in 1985. This was 12 years after Bill Moran unveiled damascus blades at a Kansas City knife show. Two years later, Gillard, from the island-state of Tasmania, introduced cable damascus at another mainland show.

Nestled amongst Australian gum tree leaves and blossoms is a Steve Filicietti bowie with a 1095 and L-6 mosaic-damascus blade.

heavy hammers. Some work at night when it's cooler. Others have acquired power hammers to ease the discomfort and speed up the process of producing damascus steel and forging blade blanks to shape.

One knifemaker, Mike Petersen, actually smelts his own steel from iron sand in tataras (Japanese-style furnaces) that he constructs on his farm in the southern highlands. Some of Mike's steel and *mokumé* appear on the knives of award-winning Australian knifemaker, Glenn Waters, who resides in Japan.

The hottest blade smith at the moment, however, is Steve Filicietti, who, as it happens, lives in the heat above the 26th parallel in Queensland. Filicietti is a natural-born blade smith. Experienced blade forgers marvel at Steve's matter-of-fact capacity to comprehend complex forging techniques, as well as his ability to wrought a mixture of metals into an edged objet d'art.

This is not to imply that Steve is in any way conceited, but quite the contrary. In fact, he sometimes wonders what all the fuss is about when collectors "ooh and ah," and fellow makers stroke their chins whilst eyeing his spectacular blade patterns. But then, Steve's education before the forge began at age 10 when he inherited his grand-dad's blacksmithing equipment, which was passed on to him by his father, who encouraged the fledgling Filicietti.

Light the Forge, Read the Fire

Long before enrolling in high school, Steve knew how to light his forge and read the fire. Left to his devices, he forged files and rasps

Blade Smith Bug

Since then, the blade smith bug has bitten knifemakers everywhere. In the days when Moran reintroduced pattern-welded blade ware, the word "damascus" carried an air of mystique, and the formula for making this special steel was draped in mystery. Nowadays, the drapes have been drawn away and some tyro makers fashion their first knives from their own forge-welded steel.

The technology is readily available in books and videos, and the rest is practice and refinement through experimentation.

The editor of *Knives 2003* has a habit of phoning me and asking, "Who are the hottest Australian knifemakers at the moment?" If I wanted to be a smart aleck, I would reply, "Those that live above the 26th parallel in Australia." The top half of this country is hot for half the year and bloody hot for the other half. The "Top End," as we call it, also gets hellishly humid during the wet season, the monsoon period when scary cyclones come wandering across the coastline.

It's not a pleasant time for blade smiths slaving over fires and banging away at red-hot metal with

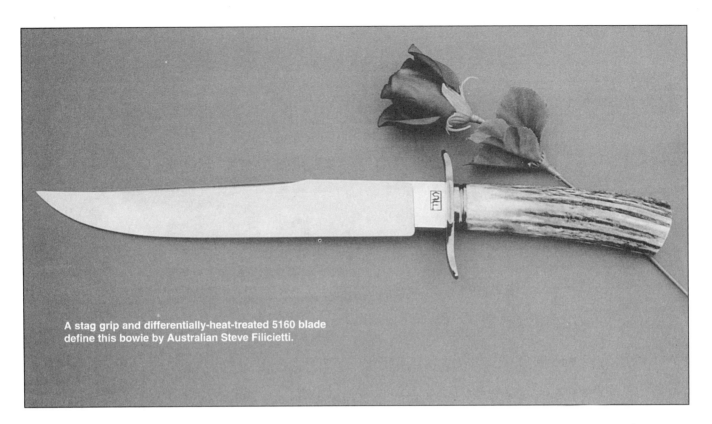

A stag grip and differentially-heat-treated 5160 blade define this bowie by Australian Steve Filicietti.

and transformed them into working knives. "I would make, use and lose knives, then make some more," said Steve.

Before turning 17, he was producing practical working knives and learning the art of forge-welding damascus steel. His dad taught Steve what he knew about blending metals and he read all he could scavenge on the subject. On Sunday mornings, he would spend time in the local country pub chatting over a beer with the village elders about iron sands, fluxes and pattern-welding techniques.

Now in his early 30s, Filicietti is a full-time blade smith who has mastered the art of producing mosaic-damascus blades that capture the hearts of discerning collectors across the globe (he has an agent in the U.S.). This lanky, laconic Queenslander made four visits to the podium at the 2001 Australian Knifemakers Guild show in Melbourne, taking away awards in the categories of Best Forged Knife, Best Damascus Knife, Best Utility Knife and Best Bush Knife.

Never one to be idle, Steve organized the first custom knife show held in Brisbane in February 2002, which proved to be a successful event. Ever mindful of what the industry has been able to do for him, Steve does what he can to further its interests. For example, he serves as mentor to no less than four aspiring blade smiths, teaching them what they need to know to

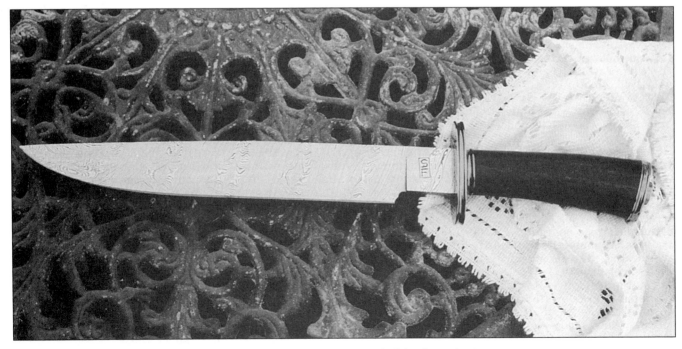

Black handle, blued fittings and black-gray-and-white blade add up to a colorful collage of cut.

Typical of the size and comfort-grip of Steve Filicietti's knives is this bowie with a stag handle and mosaic-damascus blade.

help them realize their own creative potential at the forge. Steve has earned the respect of his knifemaking colleagues and knife collectors and is a credit to the Australian custom knife industry.

But he hasn't exactly led a sheltered life. Steve's done some hard living along the way. At 20, for example, he took to rodeo riding, tackling bulls and horses for the excitement and money he could make. But he paid a penalty for living wild—66 broken bones in just a few years. A smashed hand and the fact no insurance company would carry him saw Steve give up riding wild-eyed creatures, although he did a stint as a rodeo clown. "You need to be fit and understand bulls...know where to be and where to go," he grins.

Working with horses led Steve to teach himself saddlery and general leatherwork on the family farm at Coraki a little south of the Queensland/New South Wales border. He received awards for leatherwork at regional shows. The legacy of learning saddlery manifests in the artistic sheaths that accompany most Filicietti blade ware.

You can be forgiven for thinking Filicietti's knives are too pretty to be practical. Forget it. He cut his teeth making blade ware for pig hunters and professional kangaroo

shooters, dependable knives for demanding conditions. Steve encouraged them to try damascus blades but found it difficult to convince outback users that blended metals provided them with tougher blades.

Undaunted, Steve continued to experiment with pattern-welding technology, and he concedes it took five years before being satisfied with his own results. He collected his own cutlery and gave some small hunting knives away for his mates to try. Steve paid to learn. "Damascus has to be able to chop things," he said, "not just look good." So, he forged tomahawks and axe heads, which were rigorously tested.

After reading numerous American knife magazines, Steve set his sights on producing "bigger and flashier working knives." American collectors took to them, but so too were Aussie knife enthusiasts captivated by Filicietti's mosaic-damascus magic. And South East Asian knife broker Tyron Tan not only purchased from Filicietti's show table, but also commissioned him to make Japanese-style swords. It was three years ago that Steve decided to become a full-time blade smith.

Preferring to live in Cleveland, Queensland, with his wife Lee and three children (two are sons keen to follow in their dad's forging footsteps), Steve drives south to his father's farm and forging facilities. He forges every night for a week. Then, he fishes and hunts for a week before making the four-hour drive back home. During the next two weeks, he completes the forged-to-shape mosaic damascus (and other) blanks. It's a hell of a life, but someone's got to do it!

Keith Spencer is the editor of Knives Australia, *a quarterly newsstand publication, and author of* Australian Custom Knifemakers 1991, Australaian Custom Knifemakers 2nd Edition *and* Edgemaster-50 Australian Knife Stories. *He has also worked as a columnist for* Edgemaster Australian Shooter *magazine since 1988, as well as being a respected knife designer and maker himself.* ●

Knives I Have Loved and Lost

One savvy lady shares anecdotes of adventures and misadventures with her favorite edged tools

By Linda Moll Smith

About the author: Linda Moll Smith is a former newspaper and magazine editor, now working in rural health systems and community development. She is an amateur photographer and an active member of the Texas State Guard. After losing nearly every knife she's ever loved, she now carries, and hopes to keep, a red Leatherman Juice C2 and a Leatherman Micra.

I Lose My Edge

"**N**OW BOARDING ROWS 15-30." It is the call for our American Airlines flight, departing Dallas-Ft. Worth, February 2, 2002, non-stop to Kansas City. I heave a big sigh of relief. Finally!

It is only the second time I've flown since last year's 9/11 terrorist attacks, and the first time since enhanced security measures have been instituted at air terminals across the country. But I am a seasoned traveler, and standing alongside my husband in the boarding-pass check line, I feel confident, even smug. "Look," I nudge my husband, "a random search."

Sure enough, a female security agent has pulled an elderly gentleman out of the line for a luggage check. "He doesn't look very threatening to me," my husband says, and I agree, but add, "The airlines are now required to conduct random searches—none of us look like terrorists, do we?"

I have just gotten those words out of my mouth, when the security agent beckons to me. Me? ME? Yes, me, darn it!

The author holds a bowie knife, finally, like the one she coveted from her older brother, and one he never allowed her to touch.

I follow the agent to the table. Off go my overcoat, shoes, jacket, while she frisks me using a hand-held X-ray wand. Next, she painstakingly searches my carry-on luggage.

Then she turns to my tote bag. Her explorations reveal my typical travel survival gear, including a water bottle, protein bars, a change of underwear, cosmetics, contact lens solution, first-aid and sewing kits, a compact camera, and-Oh my!

The security agent and I gaze at each other in equally stunned shock. Reaching into a zipped pocket, deep inside my bag, she has withdrawn my never-leave-home-without-it Spyderco Delica. It's Zytel® handle, the color of bubble gum, suddenly screams pink too loudly, and I feel my face flushing to match. My baby!

"No!" I manage to blurt out, before babbling that I always travel with my Spyderco, that it was formerly legal to carry on air flights, that I had forgotten it because . . . "Because I was tired and in a hurry to pack, and whatever you do, you can't take that knife. It's special, it's a collector's item."

The security agent says nothing, but gingerly grasping my 4-inch Spyderco with two fingers, as though it is an 8 1/2-inch, double-edged damascus dagger dripping blood, she surrenders my knife to the two women ticket agents. The three whisper, exchanging horrified looks, and I overhear, "What do we do now?"

The senior agent recovers to act as gatekeeper. She addresses me severely, "We have to confiscate this knife, you know." I can't respond before the junior agent interrupts rhetorically asking, "This got through X-ray?"

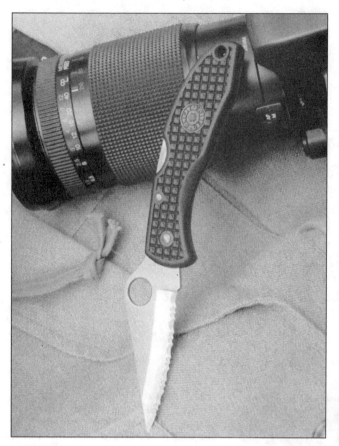

The author feels sick to her stomach when she thinks of her favorite folding knife, a Spyderco Delica model similar to that shown, being confiscated from her carry-on bag by airport security while traveling after the 9/11 terrorist attacks. She had forgotten it was in a zippered pocket deep within the bag.

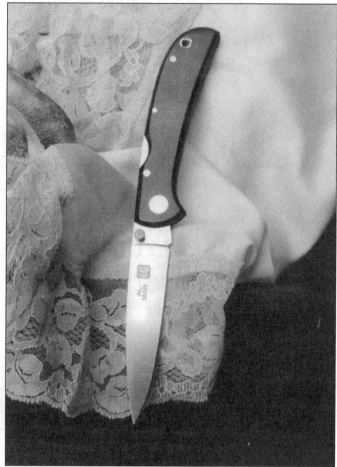

Small town life turned ugly when a neighbor boy lit off with the author's Al Mar Hawk Ultralight during a mid-day panty raid.

I am feeling sick to my stomach by now, afraid not of being arrested, but of losing my knife, a 40th birthday gift from a dear friend, who is a well-known knife expert and writer.

I turn and present an earnest case to the agents, all three of whom are now staring at me accusingly. "Look, I just forgot to take it out of my bag," I explain, "and I'll be flying back tomorrow. Can you keep it, put my name on it, and I'll take it back home with me then? Please? I'll pay you!"

The junior agent has turned pale, as innocent knife turns into awful weapon in her mind. She eyes me and asks, "But WHY would you ever need to carry a knife?"

A thousand replies fly by. Why? For cutting green apples, slicing through packaging tape, trimming garden stakes, paring thorns from Mr. Lincoln roses. Why? For snipping loose threads, for boring a notch in a dog collar, for splicing wires, or for clutching tightly while negotiating dark streets. Or better yet, for counterattacking terrorist hijackers! Why carry my Spyderco? Why indeed?

Pity this agent and her narrow suburban insularity, she doesn't have a clue. Has she never used a knife while camping, drawn out a blade to cut twine off hay bales, wielded a honed edge to trim branches for a weenie roast? I shake my head, and manage to say only, "If you were a photojournalist, you'd understand."

The senior agent hardens, replying, "We have to keep your knife. Everything we confiscate during a search, we throw away." With a sinking feeling, I watch as she places my beloved Spyderco in a drawer and closes it firmly. "You need to go board, NOW," she orders me.

Staring out the window as our jet takes flight, I am beset by rage and grief. Rage at myself, for not remembering to tuck my Spyderco into my checked luggage, and grief over losing a knife that was a fitting gift from a true friend.

The life of my late, great knife passes in front of my eyes, and I can envision it, as if in my hand, with its mid-lock, a sturdy pocket clip and plain edge of G-2 steel. How I admired the distinctive, bird's-eye thumb hole that made the blade easy to open and close with one hand, or thumb, and lent the blade's clip-point profile the look of an ever-hungry crane. My favorite photojournalist job for it was slashing the leader of hand-rolled, black-and-white film at an angle so the film would spool evenly into the camera.

To lose my favorite cutting edge after its splendid history was an unseemly fate for a brave little knife. In mourning my Spyderco, I stare out at the clouds and ponder all the other knives I've loved and lost.

My Pocketknife Passion Goes Unrequited

The year was 1958. Lloyd "Shorty" Rollins was named NASCAR Rookie of the Year, the Atomic Energy Commission met to discuss weapons test limitations, and sales of the 1958 model Corvette reached 9,168, enough to turn a profit from the sports car for the first time.

For me, 1958 was the year I fell in love for the first time. I was just 4 years old, and the moment would be the measure by which all later loves would be found wanting. For, on one late-May afternoon, my grandpa presented me with my very first knife.

He called me over to him, as we rested after picking strawberries in the shade of an old mulberry tree. "Look here," he said. Out of his left overall pocket, he drew a small knife. It was a petite replica of his own. Nearly every Kansas farmer I knew carried a similar pocketknife, most featuring brown, jigged-bone handle scales. The one I'd seen him use countless times stood out with its imitation ivory handle, worn to a buffed smoothness. It was a "good usin' knife," probably made by Colonial or Imperial.

The knife he showed me glowed softly with a mother-of-pearl handle. "This," my grandpa said, "is a fine little knife for a fine little lady like you." While I didn't know any ladies who carried knives, I was thrilled beyond words. It was the first gift he'd ever given me, beyond the odd stick of Wrigley's Juicy Fruit gum.

"Let me show you," he offered in his kind, quiet way, "how to work this knife." He explained that my knife, like his, was a jackknife because it had two blades, with both opening from one end. It was better than a penknife, he said, which had two blades, but with one opening from either end. He said to stick with jackknives because, "You never get mixed up which end of the knife you're holding, and that's important in emergencies."

"What kind of emergencies?" I wanted to know.

He gave me a serious look. "Like when the old boar hog is after you, and you need to scare him off," Grandpa replied. (He and my grandma were perpetually worried that I would slip in the hog pen and be trampled. I didn't tell him I had already escaped other hazards, such as nearly being crushed by a crazed cow. Yes sir, a knife would come in handy.)

Then, my grandpa drew one blade lightly across the surface of his arm, mowing down forearm hairs like a scythe cutting cane. "See how sharp this is?" he asked. "You need to keep it this sharp. Some other time I'll show you how, but for now, come to me when the blade gets dulled.

"In the meantime," he said, "do this." He drew out his own knife, hunched down and repeatedly stabbed the larger of the two blades into the sand in a nearby sandbox. The steel blade came out looking shiny, even before he wiped it off on his overalls. I was familiar with this routine—we always sunk our garden hoes into the sand a few times to clean them after use.

As usual, I resisted naptime that afternoon, but I remember

The author's favorite kitchen knife was her mother's paring knife. Part of a set, it was a petite 5 1/2 inches long, with a slim blade of 2 3/4 inches. Its sleek build was similar to a Chicago Cutlery 102S or a Granny Lamson paring knife (made by Lamson & Goodnow), and it even had a slightly concave shape worn on the cutting edge, similar to the Granny Lamson's "new used" blade. The full-tang, high-carbon-steel blade was secured, by two brass rivets, to a dark-brown-wood handle turned black with frequent use.

becoming drowsy with my hand still on my new knife ensconced in my pocket. In seemingly the next moment, my brother was shouting at me, "Get up, Lazybones, and come play cowboys and Indians!"

It was our favorite game, and this time the venue was the Grange Hall across the road from our farmhouse. I had just run behind the building to set up my "Indian camp," when I remembered my knife. I plunged my hand into my pocket. Nothing. I tried the other pocket. It, too, was empty. I stood alone in the hot sunshine, while the world slowly turned dark with anguish.

I spent the next half hour retracing my steps, strip-searching the bed and removing my clothes to check, all to no avail. My knife was gone, and I was crushed.

Bereft, I never told anyone, least of all my grandpa, that I had lost my knife, because I felt like a fail-ure. I just knew that I was being punished for my carelessness. Whenever I thought of it, I searched the grassy back lawn of the Grange Hall for my missing jewel. With each budding of spring daffodils, the wan hope that I would recover my knife or its rusted skeleton would bloom anew. Sadly, I never found a trace of it.

But once, probably 20 years later, my mother asked me to get something out of her "bedroom drawer." This was where she tucked important papers and other essentials, like jewelry, red lipstick and bobby pins. While rummaging through the drawer, I ran across a pearl-handled pocketknife. It seemed smaller than the one I remembered, so I barely noticed.

Only recently, after recalling that incident, have I concluded that I never lost the knife at all. More likely, my mother, bless her worried soul, took it out of my pocket while I was napping, thinking I was too young to handle a knife, and thinking also that I would never miss it. She must have told my grandpa she was holding it for safekeeping, because I thought it odd he never asked me about my knife.

Wannabe Keeper of My Brother's Bowie

Meanwhile, life did go on, eventually. My brother, older than me by 10 1/2 months, got to start school, while I sulked that entire year over staying home. It was excruciating for me to lose my playmate while he regaled us nightly with tales of newfound friends and their escapades.

One of his new friends was Tommy Green. It was a short-lived relationship — my mother heard Tommy casually say, "damn sonuvabitch," and forbade us to consort with "that foul-mouthed devil child" again. But, on his one visit to our house, he brought along his knife, which he let my brother keep.

Compared to my lost pocketknife, it was a REAL knife and I was in awe! My brother called it a bowie knife, named for the courageous frontiersman who fought in Texas' Battle of the Alamo. (We knew all about American history, especially about heroes like Davy Crockett, Jim Bowie and Teddy Roosevelt.)

My brother would lecture to me about the merits of his "Booo-eee" knife, even while tantalizing me with glimpses of it. He'd lovingly withdraw it from its sturdy leather sheath to expose the fearsome 6-inch clip point blade. It was a standard 1095 blade, complete with blood groove and similar to the classic bowie shape of a pre-World War II Marble's Ideal. It featured a Bakelite® butt cap, leather-washer handle and solid brass guard.

While I played Indian scout to his Lone Ranger, my brother never allowed me to carry his knife. Instead, I made do with a rubber knife strapped to my waist or thigh. He reserved his knife for "real" events, like skinning the bark from pear tree shoots to make arrows. He was obsessed, for a time, with hide tanning, and tried using the knife to scrape the inner side of a rabbit skin, but succeeded only in slicing it up.

My brother often whittled, rather aimlessly, with his knife, copying some of the adults we knew. He also used it to clean and scrape the scales from the bluegills and crappies we caught from the pond. And, it clung to his side when we swung across the creek on wild grapevines, pretending to be Tarzan and Jane.

But, the most famous use of my brother's knife came when we finally captured a giant bullfrog we had been stalking for years. He was huge, painted an inky, almost-black green, and his bellow was the throatiest of all his fellows. As kingpin of the pond, we called him simply, "The Big Bullfrog."

Early that summer morning, I had picked a bushel of green beans, and was about to begin canning them, when I heard excited shouting. My brothers, who should have been hoeing, burst in. Both were covered in mud but grinning triumphantly. "We caught The Big Bullfrog!" they screamed in unison. I ran outside, and sure enough, there he was ka-thumping around the bottom of a five-gallon bucket topped by a window screen.

My mother, alerted by the cacophony, examined our catch. "What are you going to do with him?" she asked. My brothers and I were baffled. In our presumptions of his non-capture, we had never discussed the fate of our frog king if we nabbed him.

My older brother, with sudden bravado, blurted out, "Eat his frog legs, that's for sure." My mother shrugged. "I'll cook them if you fix them." So, my brother used his Bowie to butcher the frog.

I was a scrappy 9-year-old and game for any dare. But I secretly mourned the loss of our amphibian nemesis, and refused to take one bite of the frog's legs, which, when fried, looked somehow both small and sad. My brothers, saying the taste was like chicken, ate them, but said little, as if they, too, were deflated.

My brother went on to other interests, but he never once let me actually use his beloved knife. He used to wipe the blade with motor oil to prevent rust and brittleness, and told me it would get my hands dirty.

Cut the Fluff

As part of our Midwestern farm life, we not only raised our own food, we helped kill and cut it up. Filling the freezer with fryers was a part of that food chain, to which everyone contributed. When I was 8 or 9 years old, having observed the process each year, I asked to help cut up the chickens.

In retrospect, I am amazed that I was allowed to handle the sharp boning knives we used. These were Old Hickory style, regular-sized boning knives, full-tang, with hickory handles. Their 1095 carbon steel

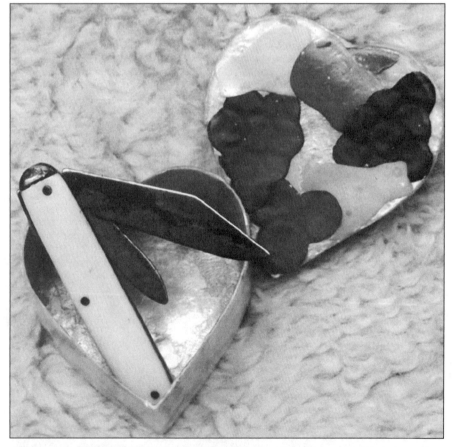

The only pocketknife the author remembers seeing her grandpa use was a two-blade folder with an imitation ivory handle, worn to a buffed smoothness. It was a "good usin' knife," probably made by Colonial or Imperial.

blades were as simple as steel gets, and nearly frontier in their simplicity. Not only were the 5-inch blades of these knives regularly honed to the extreme by my father's roller sharpener, they were the size of swords in my child's hand.

Somehow, I not only managed, I showed a real knack for cutting up chickens (probably missing a calling as a general surgeon). In a four-hour stretch, I cut up and bagged 14 chickens.

Those two boning knives disappeared. One was left on a picnic table on a camping trip to Texas, and the other was mysteriously burned in our trash barrel. All that was rescued was a charcoaled piece of handle and the blade.

Boning knives aside, my favorite kitchen knife was my mother's paring knife. It was part of a set, a wedding shower gift from her parents. It was a petite 5 1/2 inches long, with a slim blade of 2 3/4 inches. Its sleek build was similar to a Chicago Cutlery 102S or a Granny Lamson paring knife (made by Lamson & Goodnow). My mother's paring knife even had a slightly concave shape worn on the cutting edge, similar to the Granny Lamson's "new used" blade. It was full-tang high carbon steel, secured by two brass rivets, and its dark-brown wood handle had turned black with frequent use.

I used it constantly. It was the best tool ever to ease stubborn pin-

feathers from the wings of the aforementioned chickens. It also made easy work of slicing fresh-from-the-vine squash or cucumbers, or paring green summer apples.

One of my assigned chores was slicing vegetables for salad using the pad of my thumb as a mobile chopping block. This worked well, except when my father had been plying his skills on the roller sharpener. Then the salad would very nearly end up with extra protein in it from thumb shavings.

My brothers would sneak off with that paring knife to perform boy tasks, such as carving candles soft from recent flame, or using the tip to scrape off glue applied too liberally to model planes. Occasionally, the knife would stray, without a trace, from its off-duty berth in the cutlery drawer.

It struck fear into our hearts when my mother would ominously ask, "Has anyone seen my black-handled paring knife?"

But, as a lucky knife, it was always found again. In the nerve-wracking interim, we surreptitiously prayed for divine direction in its rediscovery and supernatural intervention to soothe my mother's wrath.

My Al Mar Falls Prey to a Panty Raider

A few years ago, a friend gave me a knife I valued from my first

glimpse of it. It was a gorgeous Al Mar black Micarta®-handled folder, the Hawk Ultralight model. The straight, nearly 3-inch blade of 8A stainless steel effortlessly held a fine edge and was branded with the Al Mar Chinese (horse) glyph. It featured a thumb stud for ease in opening the blade, and an ever-useful reversible pocket clip. In my relationships with knives, it was the second love of my life.

The knife was so beautiful, with its slim, drop-point blade, I didn't want to use it. I kept it boxed, in mint condition, in my lingerie drawer.

We live in a small, rural town and know all our neighbors, so we're relaxed about locking our doors. Our three boys and friends create a constant stream of visitors through our house. It was unnerving when I arrived home from work one afternoon to discover the aftermath of an unexpected guest. My husband, who was already home, met me at the door wearing an odd look.

"You'd better check your things in the bedroom," he said. He explained that he'd surprised a neighbor boy bursting out of our bedroom. The boy acted rattled, saying he'd seen an intruder enter our home, followed him into our bedroom, and chased him out the window. Then, before my husband could question him further, the boy rushed out. My husband checked to find his guns and other valuables still intact.

Sure enough, when I walked in, the bedroom window was standing wide open. I instantly felt violated. I instinctively opened my lingerie drawer, and gasped. My neatly folded panties were thrown into complete disarray but I discovered, after a "brief" inventory, that the only items missing were two pairs of pink underwear.

It wasn't until a few weeks later that I realized, with a horrendous jolt, that my Al Mar knife was also missing. Love's labor and a perfect knife, gone again.

Fortunately, the panty raider in question joined the armed services soon thereafter and moved away. How could I have faced him, all the while wondering if he was wearing my panties and pocketing my knife? I do hope, though, that after he's completed active duty, this same panty raider will enlist in our Texas State Guard battalion. As clerk of Company B, I will look him in the eye, and ask, "Social Security number, please, and by the way, sir, do you carry an Al Mar knife and wear pink thongs underneath your uniform?" ●

The author's brother tantalized her with glimpses of his bowie knife that he never let her use. He'd lovingly withdraw it from its sturdy leather sheath to expose a fearsome, 6-inch, clip point blade. It was a standard 1095 blade, complete with blood groove and similar to the classic bowie shape of a pre-World War II Marble's Ideal. It featured a Bakelite® butt cap, leather-washer handle and solid brass guard.

Knife Lover Seeks Single, Shapely, Sharp Blade with Medium Build

The author contends that knives with blades 5 to 6 inches long are often an ideal size, and for more than just shelter building

By Jack Collins

WE ARE ALL familiar with the virtues of small knives. I have even extolled them myself in "Dances With Deer," a story I wrote for *Knives 2001*. There is also much to be said for large knives. They can do many things that simply can't be accomplished with smaller knives.

During one of Bill Moran's seminars at the BLADE Show a couple of years ago, just after lopping off a sapling a little larger than my wrist with one swipe, Bill said,

"Try that with your 3-inch drop point hunter!" He was, of course, demonstrating one of his justly famous camp knives. Right on, Bill!

There are some things you simply can't do with the ideal deer knife with a 3-to 4-inch blade, at

The way the knives are pictured here clearly defines size differences, with medium-sized knives (having blades 5-to-6 inches long), in the middle, surrounded by small knives on either side, and large pieces above and below. From left in the center are knives by Wayne Hendrix, Jones Knives, Ricky Fowler, two from Charlie Douane, Randall Made Knives, Chris Reeve and Jones Knives. At top is a Busse Battle Mistress, and at bottom is a Becker Magnum Camp.

Most mid-sized knives, with blades 5 to 6 inches long, come with various types of belt sheaths. Whatever carrying difficulties a person imagines having with a mid-size fixed blade, they can be readily overcome by appropriate sheath selection. Pick your poison. Want the knife to ride high? Got it. Want your knife to hang lower? It's a piece of cake.

least I can't. In the real world where most of us live, we can carry our small deer knives and feel righteous among our peers, many of whom would accuse us of having a "Rambo complex" were we to show up carrying a blade longer than the accepted standard of 4 inches. We

can leave that 8-inch blade in camp or cabin for the few times it becomes necessary.

Be that as it may, there are times when a large blade becomes the ideal, and for more than just shelter building and land clearing. There have been at least two occa-

sions, approximately 30 years apart, when my having a big knife saved the day. No, neither one involved derring-do or adventure on my part. In each case, while away from home, a turkey was roasted for dinner, and while all of the trimmings had been planned

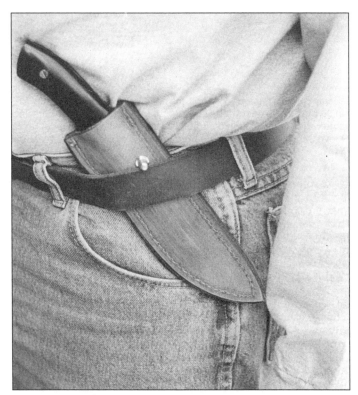

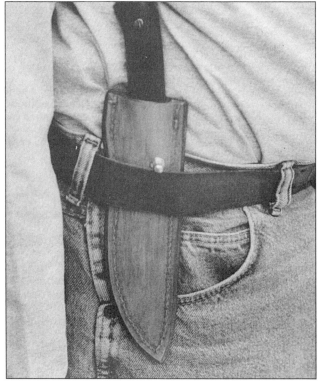

A studded sheath by Charlie Douane allows a variety of carry positions, including these shown here, as well as insertion into the top of a boot.

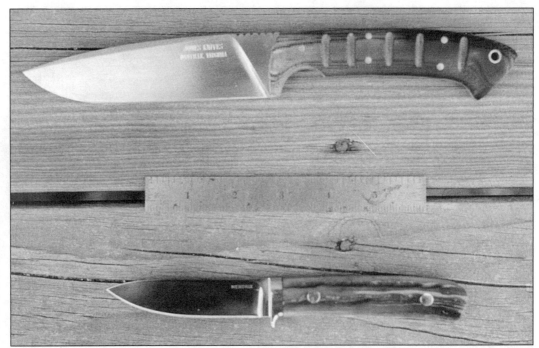

Different utilitarian capabilities come to mind in eyeing and comparing a general-purpose knife by Jones Knives (top) and a classic deer knife by Wayne Hendrix. A 6-inch scale is shown for size comparison.

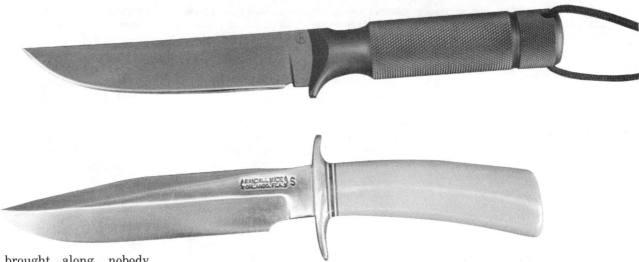

The writer's earliest attempt at purchasing a general-purpose knife is a 6-inch, circa-1970 Randall #1 (bottom). In 30-plus years of cutting, it has become evident to the author that a double guard and double edges are less than desirable for all-around use. His most recent acquisition, a Chris Reeve Sable, addresses some of those issues and embodies features dictated by experience.

for and brought along, nobody thought of a carving knife!

The first time we used my 7 1/2-inch Randall Model 14. Not the ideal knife, to be sure, but it did the job. The second time we used a similar blade. Suffice to say, no one chides me anymore for carrying a knife wherever I go.

I am not one to disparage the use of large knives, but I will address the intermediate blade length and its many and varied uses. I have read that a .22 LR semi-automatic handgun is the ideal gun for "woods bums," a category widely applicable to those of us who just like to be outdoors. The thrust of the article was to encourage readers to at least consider that a medium-sized blade is the cutlery counterpart to that worthy sidearm.

As in the article, we are looking at blades of about 5 to 6 inches in length. Shorter than that, and we are back into the deer knife cate-gory. Unless one is planning to dress game (and in many cases, even if one is), most cutting needs can be served with a medium-sized blade without any degradation of utility. When I plan to be in the woods, the knives I most often select (from among the 150 or more available) fall into the mid-sized range, unless there is a mission-specific reason to choose otherwise.

While admittedly more burden-some than a typical drop-point hunter, the weight difference between a medium-sized blade and a hunting knife is not that great. The average weight of five deer knives covered herein is 7 ounces (including sheath). The average weight of the mid-sized knives examined is 12 ounces (again, including sheath), with a high of 14 ounces and a low of 10 ounces. I submit that five ounces is a small price to pay for the increased func-tionality of the medium blade.

We may be talking about less than 4 ounces. The heaviest of the deer knives weighs 9 ounces, so depending on our starting point, we may be only penalized 1 ounce in order to carry a 5-inch blade. By comparison, seven folders (three Benchmades, one Spyderco, one R.E.K.A.T., one Kershaw and one Tom Anderson handmade) average 5 ounces. Think about it. Is that small weight increase too much to pay for the increased utility? Not for me.

Hang 'Em Up Without Hang-Up

If carrying ease is a hang-up, I suggest that whatever carrying difficulties a person imagines having with a mid-size fixed blade, they can be readily overcome by appropriate sheath selection. Note the illustration that shows the knives on the belt. Pick your poison. Want the knife to ride high? Got it. Want your knife to hang lower? It's a piece of cake.

What can one do with a medium sized blade that can't be done with a smaller one? Well nothing, really, if you don't care how long the task takes. You can cut a walking stick with any knife, but if you don't want to get left behind, you'll be much better off if you can cut your stick with just a couple of whacks than if you have to whittle it. Where I hunt deer, we usually use a readily available stick to prop open the abdominal cavity after

cleaning to promote more rapid cooling. Too small a stick, and it bends or breaks.

One you can break off by hand will often not provide the necessary strength. It's nice to cut the size you want and easy if your knife is up to the job. If you have a couple of twigs poking you in the back, tipping your hat, or obstructing your view, with a mid-ranged blade, the problem is simply and quickly resolved. Of course, any knife is better than no knife, but I submit that in this case, bigger is better up to a point (sorry about that).

With the proper blade design, you can perform all of the minor surgery you care to on yourself or others by simply choking up on the blade. No, I don't mean appendectomy or amputation. I was thinking more along the lines of splinter removal or blister opening. Personally, I carry a needle in my waterproof match case for such an operation, but to each his or her own.

Kitchen or camp chores are handily performed with a medium blade, more neatly in my experience than with a camp knife, which is usually taken to mean a blade of

7 inches or more. Try to slice almost any meat or bread product, dip the last bit of peanut butter or mayonnaise from a jar, or cut up vegetables for whatever purpose, and I believe you will find the additional length is well worth whatever penalty it imposes.

Depending upon the style of guard on your knife, and of course the shape of your blade, the rocking motion used in dicing, ala using chef's knives, may well be a useful technique in the preparation of camp stews.

Never let anyone say you can't dress game with a knife of medium size. While it isn't my first choice, I have cleaned deer with each of the three mid-sized knives pictured on page 30, and I find that I do, in fact, stay cleaner and less bloody than when I use the conventional deer knife. Small game the size of squirrels can be handled easily, their dressing consisting mostly of making that first incision, and then a lot of pulling.

As in other sizes, almost any point configuration is available. Admittedly, caping is more easily performed with a smaller knife,

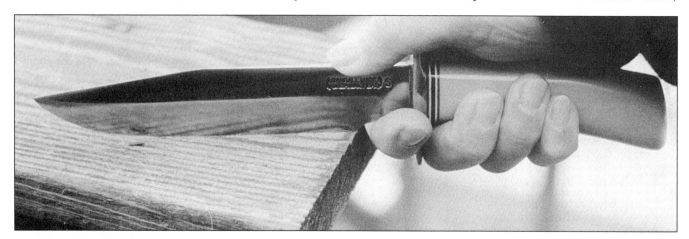

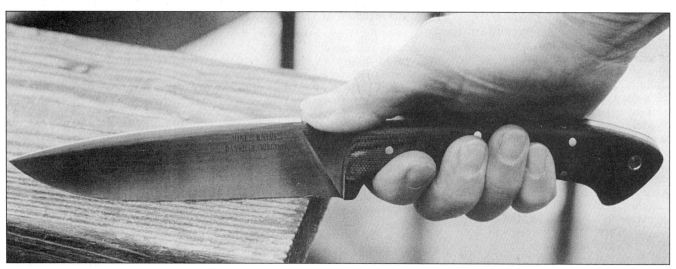

It seems to the author that direct pressure with a knife blade can be applied just as easily without a choil, or with a sharpened edge reaching all the way to the guard (below), as with a choil, an unsharpened portion of the blade between the edge and the guard.

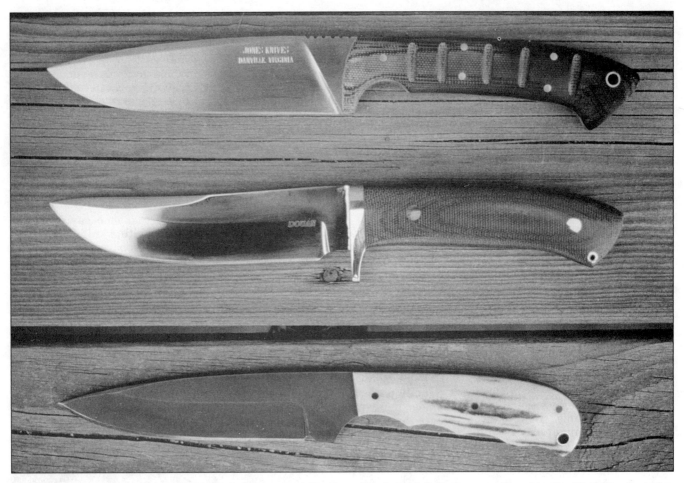

Each of the three medium-sized, fixed-blade knives was used by the author to field dress deer, and though not an ideal size, the writer found the task to be no more difficult, and in some respects easier, than if he had chosen shorter, more appropriately sized and shaped deer-skinning knives.

but I suggest this is seldom done in the field at the point of kill, but more likely back in camp (or at home), where most have access to several blade sizes.

Johnny Cut Lately

I have been critical in the past (*Knives '98*) of Chris Reeve knives, opining that they lacked features I found desirable. Mea culpa, mea culpa! I just didn't consider the wide spectrum of his production! Come on, I am not naive enough to think for a moment he would change anything because some Johnny-come-lately thinks it would be a good idea!

I now possess one of his Sable models, and it's perfect! The 5 1/2-inch blade is long enough that the knurled handle doesn't have to get blood on it in dressing a deer, so cleaning it isn't a problem. I am not generally in favor of round knife handles because of their tendency to rotate in the hand, but the knurling on Chris Reeve knives will not slip with any reasonable grip.

There are good, maybe excellent, tactile reference points to orient the knife in one's hand without

visual confirmation, and if one uses the knife every day, corrosion just isn't a problem. If the knife doesn't see daily use, just oil it before putting it away. You can even use olive oil if you want to avoid cleaning the knife before cutting food. The weight, which may seem too much in a smaller knife, seems just right in one with a medium blade.

I have no use for a *choil*, an unsharpened portion of the blade between the edge and the guard, on any knife. While I am forced to agree that a large choil allows the user to choke up on the knife to apply pressure more directly to the blade, it is my contention that, were the sharpened edge merely extended through the space required for the choil, direct pressure could be applied just as easily.

I don't like choils because they allow the knife to become trapped within whatever is being cut! I have experienced this several times while cleaning deer, and it frustrates me no end. But, lo, a longer blade can tolerate a choil because, with more cutting length to use, one is not forced to insert the blade its full length in order to perform a significant cut. We live and learn.

We do not like to think of having to use our knives as defensive tools, but should that situation arise, I believe you will be thankful for any increment of added length you have.

Of the knives used to illustrate this article, four are handmade and two, the Randall #1 and the Chris Reeve Sable, are properly considered to be factory knives, although one will have to look far and wide to find better knives.

The point is, of course, that a good knife is a good knife, regardless of the method of manufacture. We may each have our prejudices, and they will be served, but no matter what bias we carry, it does not prevent us from using a mid-ranged knife.

All of the mid-size knives shown reflect my own personal preferences. They each have what I consider desirable characteristics, for me. You pay your money and you make your choice. Your knife must please you. Make your own decision as far as the knife you carry, but whatever knife you decide upon, I suggest you give some serious consideration to a mid-size blade. •

Now Playing:
The Powdered-Mosaic-Damascus Revue

It was only a matter of time before someone figured out how to 'can' damascus steel

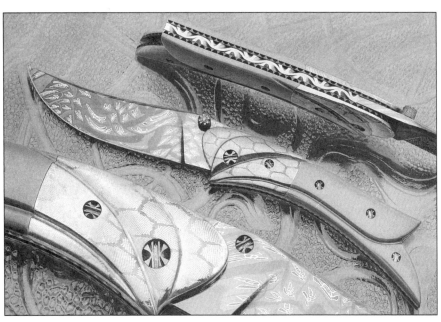

Knifemaker Barry Gallagher practiced the powdered-mosaic-damascus process to achieve hornets swarming across a blade and toward a honeycomb bolster. (BladeGallery.com photo)

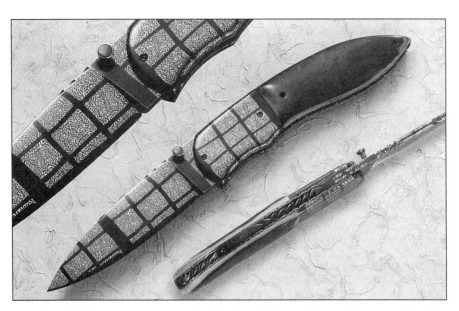

Steve Schwarzer named his folding knife "Windows" for its multi-paneled construction. The blade and bolsters were made with a mixture of powder and solid forms. (PointSeven photo)

By Peter Martin

IN THE EARLY 1970s, respected blade smith Bill Moran showed up at a knife show with what was referred to as "damascus steel." He rediscovered the pattern-welding process for the custom knife world, but it was not a new idea for steel.

In the early 1980s, Daryl Meier created a mosaic-damascus blade with his name in the steel using block letters. Again, a very new idea for the custom knife world, but not groundbreaking in the use of damascus steel. Block letter initials appeared in twist-damascus shotgun barrels in the late 1800s.

In the early part of 1992, knifemakers Stephen Schwarzer and Joe Hytovick created a billet of steel with Schwarzer's name in it, only it was done with pure nickel and it was written in script! Through the use of powdered nickel, a wire electrical discharge machine and forging techniques, Steve and Joe made the first "powdered"-steel-mosaic-damascus knife blade, a breakthrough for the custom knife world.

Powdered steel has been employed in the industrial sector for years. For instance, it can be sprayed out of a gun to rebuild worn parts, among other uses. Hot-pressed together in a machine called a hydraulic isothermal press, or H.I.P. machine, to make odd-shaped pieces that would otherwise be too costly to forge or machine shape, is another example.

Schwarzer experimented with his version of the poor man's H.I.P. machine. He used a heavy steel can to hold hard steel parts in one place, filled the empty areas around the parts with pure nickel powder, welded a lid on the can and then forge-welded the whole thing together. One can only imagine the delight on his face when he cut it open and found that it had worked out like he planned. He had put countless hours and a lot of money in other failed attempts.

That was the start of a whole new world for the forged-mosaic-damascus knife blade. Now, many damascus steel makers have joined Steve in the "canned" steel craze.

The canister is used to keep oxygen off the steel elements during the heating and forge-welding process. It is also a convenient way to hold all the parts together long enough to get the welding done. Often times, a maker will put quite a number of steel elements in one canister. One good example of this method is a checkerboard pattern, which incorporates 64 bars of square steel and, surrounding each of them, is pure-nickel sheet stock,

The blade and bolster of Don Hanson's folder are forged from powder and bar stock (center), including 48 bars, all starting out as powder elements (bottom).

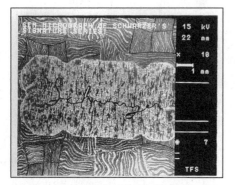

In the early part of 1992, knifemakers Stephen Schwarzer and Joe Hytovick created a billet of steel with Schwarzer's name in it. The phenomenon was achieved by using pure nickel powder to write the name in script! Here is a scanning electron microscope (SEM) picture of the first powder metal known to have been used in the construction of a damascus knife blade.

putting the total number of pieces at 121.

As Schwarzer has demonstrated, the canned steel process is not limited to hard steel elements. Powdered steel can be compacted and welded in the same manner.

To start a powdered steel billet, one needs a container suitable for the job. A steel, square tube cut to the desired length is the usual choice. A heavy steel plate is welded on to one end, forming the bottom of the can. Then a figure is made from pure-nickel sheet stock the same height as the inside of the can. This pure nickel figure resembles a cookie cutter, which most of us have used at least once to cut Christmas cookies.

Powder Fills Voids

Once the figure is placed in the can, powdered steel is poured around it and packed down, or vibrated down into the can to fill all the small voids. A heavy steel lid is placed on top and welded on, leaving one small pinhole for the gases to escape during heat treating.

The can is set in the forge and brought up to welding temperature, and soaked at this temperature for 20-to-30 minutes to make sure all the particles of steel and nickel components are at welding temperature. The next step is pressing or hammering the can from all four sides, gently at first, being careful not to distort the canister too much, too fast.

There Comes A Time In Every Man's Life...

When He Will Call Upon The Equipment He Has Chosen.

BUSSE COMBAT

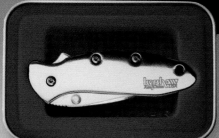

When the can reaches about half its original size, which usually takes several heats to accomplish, the maker will feel the billet getting harder under the hammer or press. Now, he or she can forge it more aggressively, reducing the can down to about one-third its original size to make sure it is properly welded through and through and, if the billet was reduced evenly on all four sides, the pattern should remain relatively uniform to the original nickel figure, only smaller.

After welding and "drawing" down the billet (reducing the heat temperature), it can be treated to the usual damascus blade pattern manipulation. Typical patterns and mosaic-damascus-making methods that work well with powdered steel

This series of photographs demonstrates various stages of powder-mosaic-damascus making by knifemaker, blade smith and author of this breakthrough article, Peter Martin. From top are powdered steel elements before layout; powder and elements in a square can before the top is welded on and the entire can is forged; a forged bar ready to use with other bars; blade stock forged from a combination of mosaic-damascus bars (the possibilities are endless); and a latch-release folding knife by Peter Martin featuring a powdered-steel-mosaic-damascus blade.

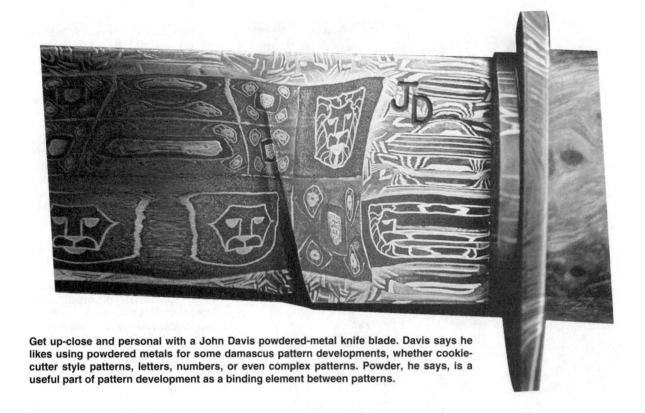

Get up-close and personal with a John Davis powdered-metal knife blade. Davis says he likes using powdered metals for some damascus pattern developments, whether cookie-cutter style patterns, letters, numbers, or even complex patterns. Powder, he says, is a useful part of pattern development as a binding element between patterns.

The American flag is the subject of a powder-mosaic-damascus blade forged up by Gary House for use on a Lloyd McConnell knife. Both makers deserve a salute. (PointSeven photo)

Knifemaker Ed Schempp made the Talon concept knife for Spyderco, Inc., incorporating powdered-mosaic-damascus bolsters showcasing the company's bug logo. (PointSeven photo)

include twist-damascus patterns, ladder patterns, cutting and stacking processes, or accordion patterns.

Another favorite of the smith's, is to add a number of previously welded mosaic bars into the canister along with a nickel figure, filling in with powdered steel to create spectacular pattern arrangements.

There are numerous types of steel available in powdered form, from high-carbon tool steels to low-carbon/high-nickel content mixtures including pure nickel and plain powdered iron.

Each steel type etches differently in acid, giving a wide range of colors from coal black to shiny chrome, giving the blade smith many options for color and contrast. With the vast choices of steels, patterns, shapes and techniques at the disposal of the blade smith, the only limiting factor is the imagination.

Many of the damascus steel makers believe powdered steel will open doors to unlimited patterns and figural layouts otherwise not feasible, or too costly to achieve any other way. The cost of wire E.D.M. work for one billet or figure can run into the thousands of dollars, and there is no guarantee it will weld up properly. With the cost of powdered steel and the accompanying materials, the cash outlay is only a fraction by comparison, with the same risk factor.

Cliff Parker shows his dexterity by holding the powdered-metal elements he forged together to make bar stock for the blade of his "Butterflies and Flowers" folding knife. (BladeGallery.com photo)

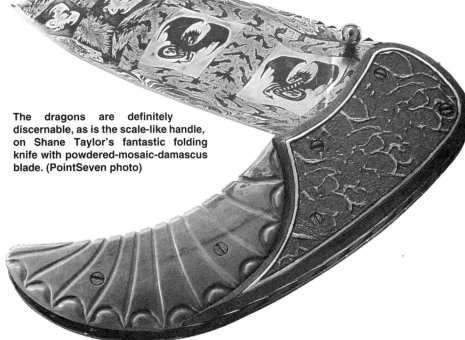

The dragons are definitely discernable, as is the scale-like handle, on Shane Taylor's fantastic folding knife with powdered-mosaic-damascus blade. (PointSeven photo)

Powdered steel is a great addition to the world of damascus steel, but it will not replace the traditional pattern-welded materials. Flowing lines and the controlled distortion of the layered materials are patterns that are only achieved through careful manipulation of laminated damascus steel by competent and creative blade smiths.

It is the ability of the blade smith that controls the outcome of the pattern in the steel. It is the talent to think outside the box (no pun intended) that will create the next chapter in pattern-welded steel for the handmade knife industry.

Ed Schempp, a talented smith involved with powder, had this to say: "Powdered steel is here to stay. Technologically speaking, the free flow of information among blade smiths, in addition to the imagination and creativity of those motivated enough to experiment with powdered steels, furthers its development. To optimize the visual and performance effects of powdered steel, pattern development of mosaic-damascus components, rather than limiting ourselves to the development of the patterns themselves, is another direction that powder has been taking."

I say, hang on to your hat, this is only the beginning. ●

She's a Battle-Axe

Political correctness has never played a role in bearing the brunt of a barbaric battle-axe

By Greg Bean

BATTLE-AXE! IT'S A term of terror more likely to conjure visions of barbarians and bottom-feeders than the chivalrous, the civilized and the elite, assuming you don't first think of mothers-in-law, head librarians and women CEOs. Political correctness was never part of barbarianism.

Battle-axes are usually associated with primitive terrorists committing ruin, rape and pillage, whether overrunning Rome, Paris or the American colonies. Two of these peoples, the Franks and the Vikings, were significant in the shaping of Europe, not just influencing war craft, but politics, economics, languages, trade, clothing and, in a word, culture.

With a growing modern appreciation of the Celts, their barbarous reputation has been tempered by knowledge of their creative and positive contributions. But to a village being overrun by axe-bearing soldiers, there would have been little time for appreciation.

Axes have been used for as long as humans have made tools. Stone knives and stone axes are among the earliest implements that archeologists have found in the primitive sites of man. The Stone Age precedes recorded history so knowledge of the earliest cultures is as much guesswork as science. The age of metals and the recording of history both happened at about the same time, so we know more of the metalworking cultures, making research easier and more reliable.

The axe has always been used in combat, if for no other reason than it is cheap, effective and available. In some instances, an axe has become a defining symbol for the culture that used it. Most often we think of the hulking barbarian, but in the oldest instance and the most recent, the axe has been a part of the most advanced culture and technology of its day.

One of the earliest great civilizations, the Minoan, on the island of Crete, used a double-headed metal axe as its national symbol. Minoan technology, predating the Egyptian, was probably limited to copper. Copper didn't make great weapons and

The double-headed axe was less common than the single head in early warfare, but its distinctive appearance induced terror on sight.

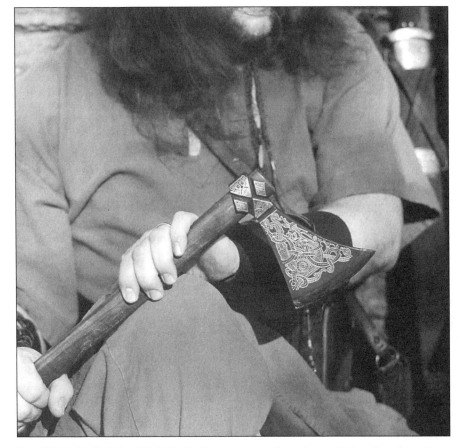

Beautiful but lethal, the C.A.S. Iberia Mammen axe mixes form with function. The silver-inlaid engraving announces the wealth and status of its bearer, a statement likely of little comfort on the receiving end of a well-aimed throw.

This warrior at ready displays a C.A.S. Iberia double-headed axe, a weapon with sufficient heft to use two-handed, but short enough to use one-handed, if the hand is backed by enough brawn.

the axe may have been used primarily for its symbolism, as European royalty would later use a mace or scepter as a symbol.

While the Minoans consciously chose the axe as a symbol for their oft-violent culture, in some instances, the axe was chosen for its utility. Eventually the axe became aristocratic during the age of chivalry and today is a status symbol with the American Special Forces deployed in Afghanistan.

At one point in history, the axe was a symbol of technology, tactics and culture for a group of northern European Celts known as the Franks. The land they wrested from Rome, Byzantium and other barbarian tribes became known as France. Their weapon of distinction was a thrown axe the Romans called a francisca.

The francisca was a short-handled iron axe with a narrow cutting edge and a long body between the haft and the edge. The length of the head frequently curved in an upswept fashion, and the edge flared a little, so it created a slight crescent at its edge. This upward curve created a point at the top of the cutting edge, and the crescent shape increased its cutting surface.

The design produced a better throwing weapon. With the axe spinning, it had a greater chance of striking with its cutting edge or the point at the top of the cutting edge.

Francisca the Fierce

The francisca may have been as plain as a woodsmen's hatchet or decorated enough to accompany a wealthy tribal chief into the afterlife. The francisca's use continued long after the Franks became literate and civilized.

Many historians write that the Franks are named for their weapon, the francisca, as many name the weapon for the tribe. Either way, modern France's name is righteously linked to this barbarian weapon.

The Franks used their axes as artillery has always been used, even to this day. In contemporary warfare, we bomb the stuffing out of an enemy's position, then send in the ground troops. This was done in the Roman and Frankish wars with spears, arrows and the francisca.

The Roman and Byzantine observers of the Franks in combat always commented on their accuracy, and a weapon like this would have been effective through helm or mail. A shield may have deflected it, but a bouncing and spinning axe

It may be a moment of rest, but with C.A.S. Iberia Danish axe in hand, Will Snodgrass displays the vigilance needed when raiding in hostile territory.

flying through the ranks was still to be feared. Even the blunt end would have bludgeoned the recipient. After both sides exchanged their preferred artillery, the pitched battle would begin. The Romans would try to make it a battle that hinged on discipline, tactics and training. The Franks would try to create an anarchic melee of one-on-one combats.

The early Franks often fought with little or no armor. Most of their warriors fought on foot, though they did have some mounted fighters using spears and swords. They depended on mobility and ferociousness. As time went on and they became more "Latinized," they took on the technology of the Romans. Eventually, the Franks became the one-man tanks of the medieval mounted knight.

The Franks were a group of tribes that wove in and out of Roman history during its decline. They first enter the recorded world as they were allowed to settle in northern Gaul. Rome used the Franks to provide a buffer against other more warlike Germanic tribes. While this was intended to spare Roman Gaul from northern

The francisca was a short-handled iron axe with a narrow cutting edge and a long body between the haft and the edge. This example, built by custom knife and tomahawk maker Ryan Johnson, shows the aesthetic as well as the aggressive side of the Celt tribe of the Franks. With an iron body and a steel edge, the axe's curves add more than looks and distinction. The upswept edge creates a point that increases the thrown axe's capabilities.

The C.A.S. Iberia bearded axe shows the extended cutting edge of this specialized weapon. The bearded axe was the first step in the evolution from agricultural axe to the point-ended Danish axe.

predation, it did not always work to Rome's advantage.

The writer Sidonius Apollinaris wrote of the Franks, "From childhood, war is their passion. They are overcome only by sheer weight of numbers or because of a hopeless situation, and if death should bring them low, it is not through fear." Ultimately, the Franks contributed more to Rome's downfall than to its preservation.

The Franks were not known for their patience or their tactics. Frank tactics were limited primarily to a group of individual conflicts. They attacked all at once with a screaming frenzy. They rarely had any reserve troops and put little effort or thought into where or when the battle took place. They usually had no fallback plans. They would never retreat, but instead chose to win all or lose all in their initial blast.

If they could add the element of surprise, like when the Romans were on march or camping without their usual fortifications, the Romans didn't stand a chance. If they could break through the Roman lines, and if the Romans had no reinforcements, the Franks might prevail.

Their individual, undisciplined style of fighting was well suited to the chaos that occurred when the ranks were broken and the armies were mingled. When the Romans were prepared, though, their superior technology, tactics and discipline usually prevailed.

Long Battle-Axe Brawls

The Byzantines, or the Eastern Roman Empire, taught tactics against the Franks based on their temperaments. Generals were taught methods to get the Franks to fight at the Byzantines' own time and place of choosing.

They would devise long campaigns against the Franks, instead of trying for a quick decisive victory. The Franks would become impatient after a couple weeks without a pitched battle and the ranks would be thinned from deserters going home or onto other battlefronts.

Or the Franks would start an ill-timed battle, perhaps fighting uphill or while crossing a river or a marsh. Another tactic was to engage the Franks, then retreat. The Franks, through lack of discipline, could be drawn out to pursue the retreating army. By having their ranks spread, they were easy to cut down with an enveloping counterattack.

It's just another day at the office, Viking style. The report of a Viking raid often caused a hasty evacuation. The sight of an actual Viking, advancing with an axe at the ready and mayhem in mind, would have caused panic if not paralysis.

Looking like a trove from a burial site, this trio of battle-axes from C.A.S. Iberia exhibits some of the variety to be found in a well-equipped war band.

The military and political history of the Franks, the other Germanic tribes such as the Goths and Vandals, and both the Eastern and Western Roman Empire is quite twisted and takes a dedicated soul to untwine.

Eventually, the Franks did become the dominant power in Gaul, and in the 6th century A.D., the Frank's leader, the Eastern Emperor, recognized Clovis as the official ruler of the Northern Roman Empire. The Franks and their francisca lent their name to northern Gaul to become known as Frankland, and eventually France.

Clovis' descendants, Charles Martel and Charlemagne, managed to affect history in less destructive ways. They rose above being base barbarians to become better barbarians. In fact, they became the entrenched civilized people who were being terrorized by a group of screaming, axe-wielding northern barbarians.

The first of the Norse raiders were Danish. As Charlemagne subjugated the Saxons in the north of France and Germany, putting thousands to death, the Norse tribes of Jutland, now Denmark, felt threatened. The Norsemen considered their early raids defensive, to counter the expansion of Charlemagne. The Dane's raids didn't stay defensive and they didn't stay local.

The Viking age, from the 8th to the 11th centuries, was an explosive force that left Europe reeling and reshaped nations. The Viking ship and the great two-handed Danish axe are enduring visual symbols of this dynamic time.

The Danes were the primary explorers and conquerors of Northern Europe, and since the Danes were the first to make their presence felt, their battle-axe became known as the Danish axe, much as extortion to be left in peace was called a Danegeld.

The earliest axe developed specifically for war was a type called a bearded axe, with a squared-off lower edge but a jutting and pointed upper edge.

The battle-axe developed from its use as a tool. For cutting wood, the blade needed support behind the cutting edge, so a farming axe was straight sided, like a modern axe.

The first axes to be specialized as weapons had an extended cutting surface created by dropping the lower edge, called a beard. This also created a hook, good for catching a shield and yanking it down and out of the way. Initially squared off, the thicker support at

And then one day the axe just fell. This was the last sight for many an innocent victim, as well as seasoned warriors.

Looking bored as only a Norseman can, this warrior has the great Danish battle-axe ready at hand.

the lower edge would have been strong enough to use the axe as a camp tool.

Bearded Battle-Axes?

Bearded axes were next developed where the top edge swept up to a point. A downward swing into an opponent's shield would break the shield or the axe would embed into the shield. Then, a quick upward levering movement would embed the point into the opponent. The upswept cutting edge turned the axe into a thrusting weapon and fueled its development into a strictly combat instrument.

Its next evolution was to create a point for the bottom part of the edge. This thrusting weapon in reverse could hook a shield to pull it down, exposing the shield bearer. It could also hook an arm or leg. Placing the haft on someone's shoulder and yanking back would have embedded the point into a victim's neck.

What came to be called the Danish axe was a broad-bladed weapon. The head had a narrow socket for the haft, and it spread out to make a crescent-shaped cutting edge. The haft may have been a couple feet long and intended for one-hand combat, or 4-to-6 feet long and used as a two-handed weapon. There were single- and double-headed versions.

The single hand, single head version was the most common, as evidenced by the great numbers found in archeological sites. Carried in the belt, the axe may have been a warrior's only weapon, or part of an ensemble that could include shield, sword and spear.

The throwing axe, inherited from the Franks, never went away, but did become a simpler shape. One of the best-known, and best-decorated examples of a throwing axe comes from a burial in Mammen, Denmark. The Mammen Axe, as it's known, is decorated with silver-inlaid engraving in a fairly typical Celtic manner.

The two-handed Danish axe was a heavy and intimidating piece of war craft, easily cleaving shield, helm, mail and man. There was no defense against a powerful swing from a blood-frenzied giant armed with one of these axes, except not to be in its way.

Using the axe as a two-handed weapon, though, left the Norseman vulnerable to attack or counterattack. He wouldn't be able to defend with a shield. This didn't seem to be a problem, perhaps due to the aggression and ferocity of a Viking raid. The concept that the best defense is a good offense predated college football.

One modern writer, Paddy Griffith, summed up the use of the axe, penning, "It was a highly uncompromising weapon that maybe epitomizes the whole essence of Viking combat."

Some battle-axes were forged with the same care and attention that was given to swords. They may have been engraved and decorated, as the Mammen Axe was. They were often named, and passed on from generation to generation. Legends grew up around some axes and their warriors, legends that reflected the Norse passion for the axe.

As professional fighters, the Vikings used as much tech as was available, whether innovating or adapting. One of the perks of their jobs were taking the arms of the fallen. So they benefited from all of the available weapons and technical advances.

A well-turned Viking band was likely to be outfitted in mail and armored helms with their own design in shields. They would be armed with spears, swords, bows and arrows, and axes. Their transportation included the best ships in the world, and overland they were competent on horseback and used iron-shod horses and saddles, stirrups and spurs.

While the Danes scourged Northern Europe, they were not the only Norsemen to go a-calling. The Norwegians explored the north Atlantic and contributed to the colonizing of Iceland and Greenland, which was essential for Leif Erikson to make his way to the North American coast in 1000 A.D.

The Swedes directed their efforts inland, into the river systems of Russia and Eastern Europe. There is speculation that this is the same path on which the earlier Scandinavian tribes descended into Europe and the international scene. The Swedes

Will Snodgrass shoulders a C.A.S. Iberia Danish axe and carries his shield. When in transit, he would have carried the shield on his back and worn the axe through his belt.

are credited with naming Russia, their early colony being known as the kingdom of Rus.

They made their way as far south as Constantinople, formerly Byzantium. The Swedes assaulted Constantinople several times, though they were quite undermanned for the task and not successful. The emperor was impressed nonetheless and tamed them enough to make them part of his elite troops and personal bodyguards, known as the Varangian Guard.

Hang An Axe, Not Your Head

Anna Comnena, daughter of one of the emperors, described the Norsemen as, "men who hung their swords and axes from their shoulders and regard their loyalty to the emperor and his protection as a sacred duty, an inheritance to be handed from father to son."

The axe became a common weapon in most of the countries the Vikings raided or conquered and settled, not just the British Isles and Ireland, but also the lands of Charlemagne's empire, Russia and the Balkan Peninsula.

These countries, in turn, developed the axe, with their variations of the axe becoming motifs for the countries, just as it did for the Franks and the Norse.

The Irish began to use the war axe, though making it smaller and with less iron. This made sense, since they were smaller than their Teutonic invaders and theirs was an iron-poor country.

The Scots used the axe much as the Danes but also developed and evolved it into the poleax known as the Lochaber axe, a distinctively Scots weapon named for Lochaber Scotland.

The 14th century Scot, Robert the Bruce, kicked off his reign with a battle won with an axe. Bruce and the English knight Sir Humphry de Bohun fought at the start of the battle of Bannockburn. Both were armored and mounted knights. The Englishman had a lance, and Bruce, a great axe. As they made a pass, Bruce deflected the lance blow and rose in his stirrups to bring a crashing blow to de Bohun, splitting his helmet and his head.

The Scots went on to crush the English nearly as thoroughly, and

France is named for the Franks and their francisca axe, an ironic beginning for a nation that prides itself on culture and civilization.

Robert the Bruce established himself as the undisputed high king of Scotland. The English eventually acknowledged this themselves and Bruce oversaw one of the few periods of Scottish unity and independence.

He may have not gotten a movie out of the deal, but Robert the Bruce certainly had a greater impact on Scotland's history than his contemporary and compatriot William Wallace.

When William the Conqueror invaded England, he had to deal with their elite troops, the Saxon and Norse-descended housecarls, infamous for their use of a 4-foot great axe. William knew of their threat and dealt with them through superior tactics and archers shooting from a safe distance.

William won, but witnessed at close range the effectiveness of the housecarls and their axes. He lost three horses to having their skulls split by axes.

The development of the axe continued. Generally, it got longer and more specialized. The Swiss mercenaries and German Landsnecht were famous for their use of the axe-based poleax. Heavy cavalry, wearing plate armor, developed an armor-piercing axe, short handled to facilitate its use on horseback.

As with swords and armor, axes gave way when firearms became the dominant technology. Battleaxes may be history now but they live well in legend and myth. Gimli the Dwarf, of the hit movie Fellowship of the Ring, will gladly demonstrate. ●

The Whole Knife Kit 'n' Cuttin' Caboodle

Knife kits are steppingstones to mastering the craft of knifemaking

By Dexter Ewing

THE NEWEST KNIFE kits on the market offer enthusiasts hands-on experiences in finishing-out and assembling folders and fixed blades, and the best part is, the resulting knives exhibit the most high-tech of materials and designs.

The kits will give neophytes a taste of what knifemakers do on a regular basis, and are also a good barometer to measure the desire, or lack thereof, to learn more about the technical aspects of knifemaking.

Some established knifemakers got their starts in the business assembling knife kits. Think of knifemaking kits as the steppingstones to becoming a knifemaker.

"I believe the primary advantage of kit knives is learning fit and finish," states knifemaker Dave Cole of DC Knives. "Since fit and finish of the handle scales, pins, guards and bolsters are so important to custom knifemaking,

kit knives allow the emphasis to be placed there."

Making sure all the parts fit flush and tight, polishing up parts and sanding up rough edges are certainly some of the most important skills a knifemaker must acquire, and these kits come with everything needed to take on the challenge.

"It is not easy to fit and finish a knife at all," agrees knifemaker Darrel Ralph, "especially when you don't have experience."

With a knife kit, the handle scales are pre-cut, the blade is already ground and heat-treated, and included are the necessary pins, screws and miscellaneous parts for complete assembly. Cole estimates that he put together 15 knife kits from such vendors as

Texas Knifemakers Supply, Jantz Supply and Sheffield Knifemakers Supply.

By the same token, custom maker Bobby Branton also got his feet wet in the knifemaking pool with kit knives. After reading a book on knifemaking by David Boye, Branton decided to purchase a kit and try his hand at the craft.

"I took on the project as a challenge," said Branton. When asked how his first kit turned out, he confessed, "Not too good! Even though I do not think that it is a pretty knife now, I had taken that first step and there was no turning back."

Perfectly symmetrical is KnifeKits.Com's GX6 folding dagger. It features an AUS-8, cryogenically treated blade, stainless steel bolsters and a hidden pivot. There are several options for handle materials, one of which is carbon fiber, as on the one pictured here. (Whetsell photo)

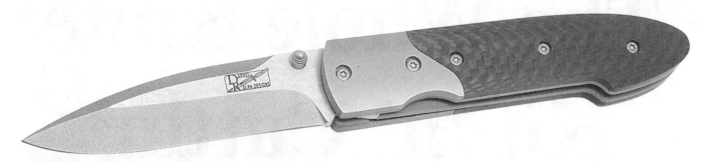

Gentlemen's folders are hot patterns these days, so KnifeKits.Com is offering the GPC-1000 folder. The stylish 2 3/4-inch AUS-8 blade is a spear point shape and set into a cornucopia-style handle. The bolsters are stainless steel and, as with all KnifeKit.Com folders, the GPC-1000 comes with several choices of handle materials, including carbon fiber. (Whetsell photo)

Ralph's first knife made from a kit turned out exactly like Branton's: "It was pretty bad," Ralph admits. He chalks it up to inexperience, as he did not know many knifemakers at the time from whom he could ask for advice. Ralph initially tackled a fixed-blade hunting knife kit from Koval Knives.

One of the most frequently asked questions in preparation for working on a knife kit is, "What kind of tools will I need?" Since the kits already come with blades that are fully ground and sharpened, and sometimes handle scales that are pre-cut to the right shape, you certainly don't need to invest in a heavy-duty slack belt grinder like a Burr King or a Bader.

In terms of power tools, a Dremel® tool, or some other equivalent like the Black & Decker RTX, will certainly prove its worth.

You can make use of various attachments like an abrasive cut-off wheel and sanding drums, especially when it comes time to assemble the handle of your knife. A power belt sander is not necessary but nice to have. Delta Machinery makes a 1-inch-by-30-inch belt sander that can be useful in contouring handle-scale material or bolsters for folders.

Cole warns that power tools are somewhat unforgiving in the hands of novices. The rest of the tools and supplies will consist of files, sandpaper and clamps. "Most, if not all, knifemakers use files and sandpaper at one or more points in mak-

The Koval Knives 605 Special was designed by Darrel Ralph and is the first high-quality, locking-liner folding knife kit on the market. The two completed knives shown are examples of how one can make his or her 605 truly custom by having a choice of handle scales. (Hoffman photo)

ing a knife, so filing and sanding are skills that need to be learned," Cole remarks.

Clamps will come in handy to provide constant pressure after handles have been glued onto frames or tangs with epoxy. Any of these tools can be readily purchased at local hardware stores or home centers.

So Ya Wanna Make Knives, Huh?

So, you've decided to put together a knife. Where can you find a suitable kit? In this day and age of the Internet, knifemaking suppliers have on-line catalogs for viewing selections of knifemaking machinery, tools and parts, as well as to glean information about them.

Texas Knifemakers Supply (www.texasknife.com) offers a good selection of kits. The Sam Houston Skinner Kit has a 3 5/8-inch, AUS-6, drop-point blade, 8 1/4 inches overall, and Dyamondwood® handle scales in a variety of color choices. Also included with this kit are a sewn-leather sheath, brass

pins and a tube of 30-minute epoxy. The entire package sells for $26.45!

If folders are more your desire, there is no lack of folder kits for your selection! Koval Knives (www.kovalknives.com) markets the Grizzly Folding Hunter Kit. The traditional lock-back folding hunter measures 5 inches closed, and has a Buck 110 style build with double brass bolsters and a stabilized-hardwood handle. The kit will be delivered to your door for $21.95.

If multi-blade pocketknives get your blood pumping, Koval has the Cinnamon Bear Stockman Folding Knife Kit for $16.95. If you've wondered how a slip-joint multi-blade pocketknife comes together, this kit is for you.

While the two Koval kits are basic, the supplier also offers the 605 Special folding knife kit, designed by Ralph. The 605 has been wildly successful for Koval, and the company claims it is the first high-quality locking-liner folding knife kit on the market. It has already spun off the Mini 605, a scaled-down version along the line of a small gent's folder.

Speaking of high-quality knife kits, Ralph has filled·that niche with offerings at www.Knife-Kits.com. A quick surfing of the site uncovers custom-designed kits made from high-quality materials, one of which is the GPC-1000 (Gents Personal Carry) folding knife kit. Featuring a 2 3/4-inch AUS-8 wharncliffe-style blade, the GPC-1000 measures a little over 6 inches overall. Base kit includes pre-cut black, green, maroon and ivory-Micarta® handle scales, and there is an upgrade available with carbon fiber grips.

The GPC-1000 is delivered with stainless-steel bolsters, and Knife-Kit.com includes a template with each kit that enables the knife assembler to effectively put an "S" curve in the bolsters. Prices for the GPC-1000 start at $39.95.

KnifeKits.com also offers the GDX-1000, a dagger-style folding knife with an AUS-8 blade, mated with a symmetrical handle that has stainless steel bolsters and a hidden pivot. Overall length of the GDX-1000 is just over 6 inches, making it a nice, eye-catching folder. Expect to pay $39.95 for the

Knifekits.com's TRAK neck knife features a 3-inch D-2 blade and black G-10 handle scales. Each kit comes with a custom molded Kydex sheath with neck chain. The one pictured here was finished out and put together by the author. (Hoffman photo)

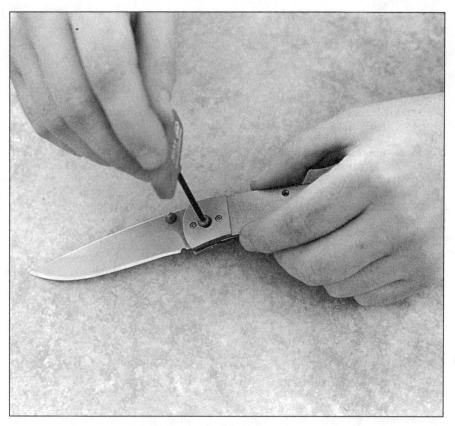

Knifemaking kits offer the enthusiast the experience of finishing out and assembling folders and fixed blades, with minimal investment in materials and tools. Anyone with the desire to learn the technical aspect of knives will succeed at putting together any knife kit. (Hoffman photo)

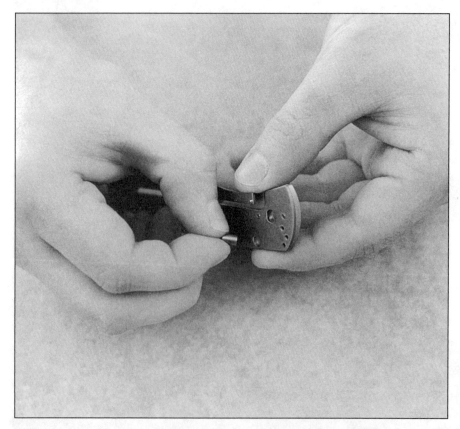

In spite of the fact that folder kits have numerous parts—much more so than a fixed blade kit—they are easy to assemble. Here, the stop pin is being inserted into the liner on a Koval Knives 605 Special locking-liner kit. (Hoffman photo)

GDX-1000 base kit and, like the GPC-1000, it comes with the same choices of handle material, including an upgrade to carbon fiber.

Neither the GPC-1000 nor the GDX-1000 comes with pocket clips, but KnifeKits.com offers a kit for installing a clip on the bolster of either knife. The Web site also features the TRAK fixed-blade neck knife kit involving a 2.95-inch D-2 blade and a black G-10 handle. Thong tubes and epoxy are also included, as is a custom-molded Kydex® sheath with neck chain. The TRAK sells for $79.95. Look for other high-quality knife kit designs coming from top knifemakers in the future.

Grohmann Knives is probably the first commercial knife manufacturer to offer some of their knives in kit form, ready to be assembled. These kit knives, cleverly referred to as the "You-Make-It Knife Kits," assemble into fixed blades that have been fully finished (including the contouring and profiling of handle scales). The Grohmann Web site points out that one can save up to 25 percent by purchasing a knife in kit form and assembling it, as compared to buying the same knife already assembled.

Each kit comes with a top-quality leather sheath and detailed instructions. If one chooses, handle-scale materials of his or her own choice may be substituted for the standard rosewood grips. Prices for the You-Make-It Knife Kits vary, so it is best to contact your favorite Grohmann dealer for pricing information.

Author Tackles First Kit

How easy is it for a knife enthusiast to put together one of these kits? For my inaugural attempt, I ordered a TRAK neck knife kit from KnifeKits.com. This was a first for me, and after consulting with several knifemaker friends about hand-rubbing a satin finish, I opted to attempt this with my blade. Over the course of a couple weekends, I heeded advice and labored to put it together, taking my time and not rushing any step of this process.

After hand-rubbing the blade up to a 240-grit satin finish, I put the thong tubes in place in the tang, glued the G-10 scales and clamped the scales down overnight to allow the glue to set. The next day, I cut the thong tubes using a Dremel tool with a cut-off wheel, and then I switched to a drum sander to grind the tubes flush with the handle. The

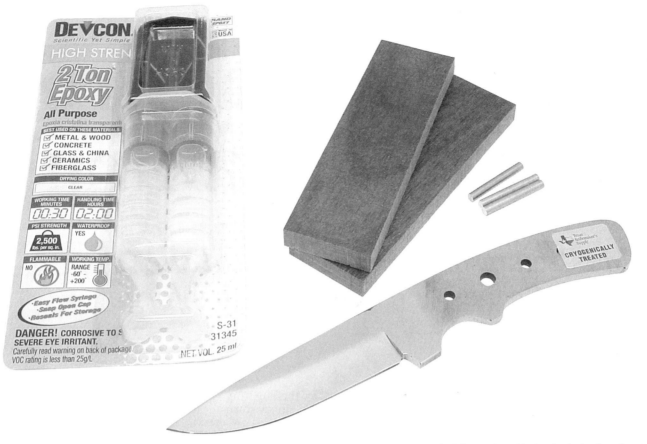

Exclusively available from Texas Knifemakers Supply, the Sam Houston Skinner kit is a typical fixed-blade kit that includes handle-scale material, blade blank, pins and epoxy. (Whetsell photo)

final step was hand-rubbing the G-10 scales for a smooth touch.

Overall, the entire experience was rewarding. It was the first time I accomplished a hand-rubbed finish, and it came out looking real good. Most of all, I got a taste of what most knifemakers go through on a daily basis. I now have come away from this experience with a little knowledge about hand rubbing satin finishes and general fit and finish. It has left me with a desire to pursue more knife kits in the future, hopefully resulting in highly useful and functional cutting tools.

Knifemakers are a special bunch of folks. On the surface, they seem to be a competitive lot, but deep down, they are willing to share tips and advice with each other or with knife enthusiasts. So, during the process of laboring to assemble your kit, don't be afraid to pick up the phone and give your favorite knifemaker a call.

If you have access to the Internet, BladeForums.com, KnifeForums.com, or the Custom Knife Directory Forum at www.custom-knifedirectory.com are set up specifically for fielding inquiries about custom knifemaking. Don't feel shy, log on and post your questions! They will be answered by more experienced knifemakers, some of them well known.

As we have seen, knife kits are great educational tools allowing novices to engage in knifemaking without the investment of machinery and boxfuls of tools. They are the perfect step up for enthusiasts who wish to learn more about the technical side of knives. There is a wide range of fixed-blade and folding knife kits out there, so no doubt you will find one or more of them to your liking.

Who knows? One day you might even wind up with a shop full of equipment to make your own custom knives! If not, you will come away from your experience with a cutting tool you have finished out and put together yourself. •

Meet the Maestros of Steel Making

Mysticism meets magic amid the lapping flames of a blacksmith's forge

By Joseph Szilaski

EARLY MAN FIGURED out, over time, how to work with fire. The ability to take advantage of fire was a revolutionary change for mankind. We are not just talking about using fire to fry cave-bear steak or heat the cave. Our ancestors figured out how to dig for ore and extract copper using fire. Then, they figured out how to cast and hammer the extracted ingots with stone hammers to create certain shapes.

The discovery that copper became harder in the process of hammering was probably astonishing, and could be compared to the excitement modern Americans felt watching astronauts land on the moon for the first time. And so forging began.

I don't want to get into the art of forging during the different time periods, such as the copper age, the Bronze Age, and so on. Not because these subjects do not deserve writing about, but because you could fill a library with such material. Instead, I would like to delve into blacksmithing that began with the Iron Age, the period of human cul-

ture characterized by the smelting of iron circa-1000 B.C. in western Egypt and Asia.

The discovery of iron was another revolutionary step for mankind. Iron is a non-hardening alloy until carbon is added to it. Carbon is the main and most important element in creating steel. It only takes a small amount of carbon to make steel. Too much carbon and you end up with cast iron, too small of an amount, and you have wrought iron.

Early blacksmiths worked, and, essentially, most continue to work, with four powerful elements, namely fire, air, iron and water. Air was traditionally used to fan the flames, increasing its heat to temperatures that could forge the iron extracted from the earth. Water was used to cool or temper man's cre-

ation. In some people's eyes, blacksmiths were mystical and magical.

The ancient Greeks and Romans had a god of blacksmithing. In some European countries, it was believed that a blacksmith's presence at a wedding would ensure the new couple's marriage would be strong, like the bond between iron and steel.

Blacksmiths were well-respected people throughout the world. In Japan, blacksmiths and sword smiths are highly regarded, and their techniques are held as strict family secrets. The knowledge and experience passed down dates back thousands of years. These families are national treasures.

In the 1970s, Bill Moran re-introduced the practically lost art of forging damascus steel. Everybody was amazed at the creative beauty of damascus, and collectors and makers went nutty trying to get or make a damascus blade. We have come a long way since then, as evidenced by this hunting knife by the author, Joe Szilaski, with a multi-bar, nickel-damascus blade forged with scrolling guard. The titanium liners are fileworked, and the ivory handle is carved extensively. (L. Szilaski photo)

In pioneer American towns and villages, the town fathers left a vacant land lot in hopes that a blacksmith would want to settle down. It was vital for the town to have a good blacksmith, as he would produce various household items, including pots and pans, forks, knives, spoons, cleavers, axes, horseshoes, spurs, wagon wheels, door hinges, locks and keys, and so on.

He also manufactured various medical and dental instruments, and all tools needed by various other craftsmen. For the carpenter, he made planes, chisels and hammers; for the woodsman, he made axes and hatchets; and for the hunters, he made knives, animal traps and guns.

Full Steam Ahead

Trade ships on voyage to the New World invariably had a couple of blacksmiths aboard. Ship blacksmiths were invaluable for repairing chains, pulleys, hooks, cannons and other instruments essential for a long voyage.

Literature is readily available documenting the importance of the blacksmith in the Lewis and Clark Expedition. Not only would the portable shops of the blacksmiths Lewis and Clark employed handle necessary repairs on the trail, but the smiths could also make a few items such as knives and tomahawks for trade with the local Indians.

Our blacksmith ancestors, in my opinion, were geniuses. They were forced through necessity to figure out and work out every dilemma in tool making, weapons manufacture, and so on.

In visiting any museum of history and studying the armor made for kings and knights, one is amazed at the precision of workmanship on every moving part. The intricate moving parts of armored steel gloves is impressive, considering most were crafted in the 15th and 16th centuries. The imagination and craftsmanship

Perhaps no single event in history helped fuel the fire of blacksmith and blade smith romanticism as the movie *The Iron Mistress*. James Black, as portrayed by David Wolfe, forges the Iron Mistress knife blade from a meteorite in a scene from the movie. Photo courtesy Joe Musso)

was a mechanical marvel of engineering at the time.

In Hungary, back in 1963, I was an apprentice for a blacksmith. My teacher was a third- or fourth-generation general blacksmith by the name of Stefan Stefanovics.

His shop was part of a textile factory, and when machinery in the factory would break down, it was the blacksmith who forged to shape the parts that would be finished by the machine shop. These parts usually included gears and crankshafts that required the additional strength of forged steel.

Discovering the freedom of what a person could and can do with fire and steel was an amazing experience for me. My first lesson came in making the fire. It was my responsibility to have that fire ready bright and early for the workday. I learned another important lesson watching Stefan make tenterhook nails.

Knifemaker Steve Schwarzer experiments with damascus and mosaic damascus, often with beautiful results, which would include this 13 1/2–inch damascus fixed blade with carved guard and oosic handle. (PointSeven photo)

The following day, he put 20 pieces of steel into the fire and it was my turn to make the nails. By the time I finished with three nails, the rest of the steel melted away into blobs, and I burned up a lot more steel before I could make a full batch of nails in one heat.

Later on, we made gears, shafts and other machine parts. After work, on his own time, he taught me how to make knives, cleavers, tomahawks, hatchets and much more. Believe me, this was more fun than making gears. I was glad to work for him, he was a very patient and good teacher.

I learned not to be afraid of experimenting with new ideas, and it did not matter if the results were good or bad, I gained a new experience. Still today, I love experi-

menting with different alloys and techniques. My curiosity sometimes gets me into trouble, or maybe keeps me out of trouble, one or the other.

Blacksmithing is a fascinating subject. When you start exploring blacksmithing, you find logic and an important ground breaking for

the developments of our highly sophisticated modern world.

Over time, various specialties developed within the blacksmithing field. Besides general practice blacksmiths, there developed individual professions of farrier, gunsmith,

The romance of steel making is alive and kicking, or at least pounding, thanks to knifemakers like Al Dippold, who has devoted himself to kicking out such magical steel patterns as this mosaic-bladed wonder with a carved-mammoth-ivory grip and opal thumb stud.

A focused and dedicated blade smith is Jay Hendrickson, who has spent many weekends away from home teaching techniques of forging and sharing his experiences with all others who would like to learn. It would take years of practice for novices to match this knife with a satin-finished 5160 steel blade, brass guard, and curly maple and stag handle with brass wire inlay. (BladeGallery.com photo)

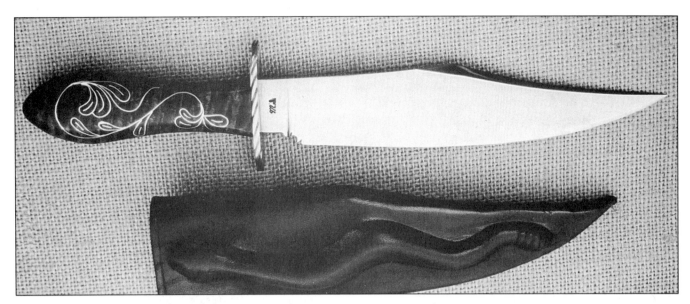

When it comes to blade smithing, most everybody has heard of James Black, William Scagel, Rudy Ruana and Bill Moran. Moran made this small bowie with comfortable curly-maple handle featuring silver-wire inlay and a distinctive Spanish notch on the blade. (Holter photo)

armorer, locksmith, ornamental ironworker and blade smith.

Bubbling Voodoo Brew

Thousands of years experimenting with iron, and the addition of carbon and other elements in the blacksmith's voodoo kitchen, have created the different types of steels and alloys that modern man's lifestyle demands. But this does not mean the kitchen is closed, not by a long shot. For some of us, it is a new challenge to experiment with the modern tools and steels available today.

Modern technology allows us to have a practically endless supply of different types of steel, so blade smiths and stock-removal knifemakers have a chance to experiment with the best materials available.

When it comes to blade smithing, most everybody has heard of James Black, William Scagel, Rudy Ruana and Bill Moran. Bill is the founder of the American Bladesmith Society and, back in the 1970's, he re-introduced the practically lost art of forging damascus steel. Everybody was amazed at the creative beauty of damascus, and collectors and makers went nutty trying to get or make a damascus blade. We have come a long way since then.

There are innumerable dedicated blade smiths and makers out there, but when it comes to the high-performance working knife, Ed Fowler comes to mind. Wayne Goddard introduced Ed to 52100 ball bearing steel 20 years ago. Since that day, Ed has been experimenting with 52100, putting in

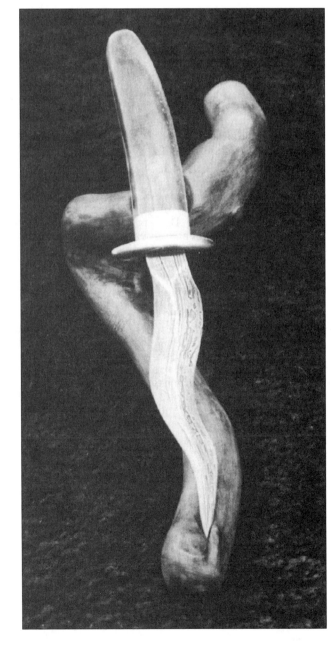

Wayne Goddard achieved this wavy-blade dagger using wire damascus. The guard is copper-nickel, the handle of fossil ivory. The display base is a branch from a "corkscrew" willow tree. (Goddard photo)

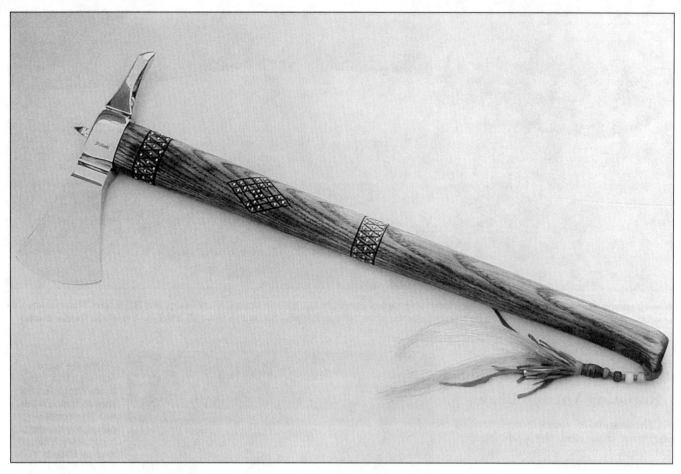

Author Joe Szilaski forged the head of the spike tomahawk from WI tool steels. The haft is hickory, checkered, adorned with brass tacks, and complemented by a horsehair tassel and glass beads. (L. Szilaski photo)

endless hours in the shop to find the best possible technique to forge the steel in order to get the best results from the heat-treating process. This shows dedication, not to mention the hours he spends writing and sharing his experience and his results. In my opinion, Ed will always be experimenting.

Another focused and dedicated blade smith is Jay Hendrickson, who has spent many weekends away from home teaching techniques of forging and sharing his experiences with all others who would like to learn. Goddard has written much on the subject of blade smithing. Al Pendray's

research on how to make *Wootz damascus* is well known, as are the efforts of other blade smiths like Rick Dunkerley, Al Dippold and Steve Schwarzer, the latter of whom experiments with mosaic damascus. Daniel Winkler strives to preserve the legacy and tradition of making early American knife styles, primitive knives, if you will, and tomahawks.

Blacksmithing is a unique and individual art form. Each blacksmith develops quite different techniques and style, and the differences among them can be seen in their individual work. Thousands of years of experience

working with fire and metal have given us a personal freedom. With forge and hammer we are able to both recreate the past, and build the present.

I only mentioned a few names, but the truth is that there are thousands of smiths out there, both past and present, that I would like to thank. Their contributions have made and continue to make a big difference in the wonderful art of blade smithing. I feel safe in knowing there are those determined to keep the art alive, for us and for future generations. Bless us all as a strong nation. ●

Building Blades in a South Boston Distillery

It will be a party of three who take you through their distillery and the knives made there

By Durwood Hollis

IMAGINE TWO KNIFEMAKERS living together under one roof, feeding off each other's creativity, sharing ideas, indulging in friendly competition, outdoing each other at every turn. Wouldn't potential for the steel output, the quality of workmanship, the style, grace and beauty of the knives be greater than that of a solitary knifemaker? Now imagine three knifemakers, all with high skill levels, living under one roof! Welcome to South Boston.

The city of Boston itself, a locale that gained historical significance during the Revolutionary War and, particularly, the Boston Tea Party, isn't a setting that springs to mind when one thinks of creative knife design. However, three knifemak-

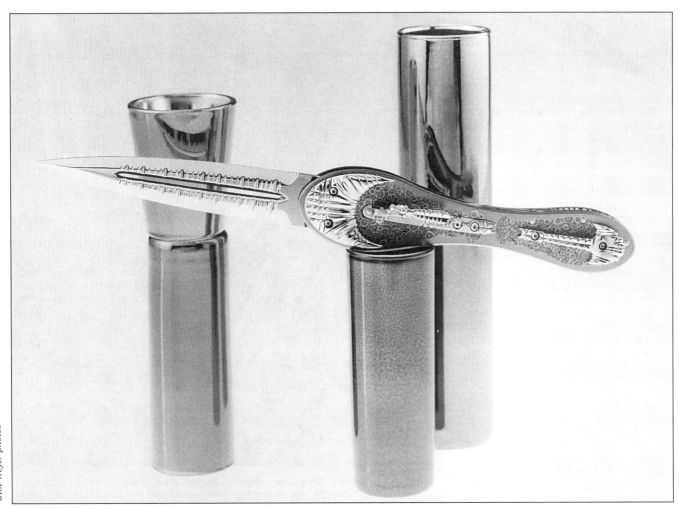

South Boston knifemakers Romas Banaitis and Scott Richter claim they borrowed from classic dagger designs in combination with organic, aquatic forms to come up with Atlantis, a spontaneous action, dual-position-lever folding knife with side locking mechanism. Among other things, it's carved, colorful and creative.

Jim Weyer photos

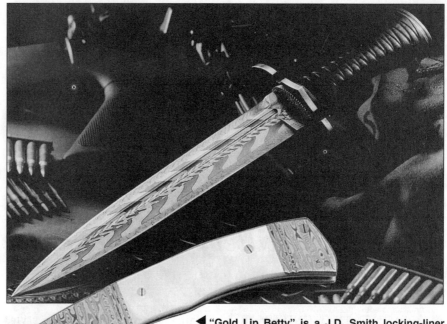

▶ Working out of The Distillery in South Boston, American Bladesmith Society master smith J.D. Smith built "The Black Moor" dagger with alternating light and dark chevron patterns of damascus, steel and bronze fittings and an African-blackwood hilt.

ers—J. D. Smith, Scott Richter and Romas Banaitis—all have workshops at the same location in the city of South Boston.

It wasn't exactly fortuitous happenstance, nor was it thoughtful planning that all three ended up in the same building, the site of a former distillery called, what else, "The Distillery." The story is more interesting than either of those scenarios suggests.

The old building is a Boston historic landmark. Rum and other spirits were distilled at this location beginning in the mid-19th century and continuing until the early 1940s. The distillery was subsequently turned into artists' workshops, and it currently houses a number of sculptors, metal smiths and other creative sorts.

◀ "Gold Lip Betty" is a J.D. Smith locking-liner folder with mokume front and rear bolsters, a gold-lip-pearl handle and a 1095 and 203E damascus blade with opal thumb stud.

Actually, Smith has been at the location since 1989. He started his career in knifemaking in 1982 as an apprentice to American Bladesmith Society (ABS) master smith Steve Nichols. Smith made his first blade, which he still has in his possession, under Nichols' direction. A short while later, Smith was forging damascus steel blades from castoff files and wrought iron.

During the period of 1986-1988, he worked with knifemakers Jot Singh Khalsa and Jimmy Fikes as he further refined his knifemaking skills. Smith opened his own shop and joined The Knifemakers' Guild, as well as the ABS. He became a voting Guild member, and eventually an ABS master smith.

Over the years, Smith has garnered a number of knifemaking awards (23 at last count, but who's counting?). In 1992, his work took the East Coast Custom Knife Show's "Judges Award," and in 1998, he was nominated as a candidate for the ABS "Best Master Smith" award. Of course, there have been many more accomplishments, including winning a few *BLADE Magazine* BLADEhandmade Awards®.

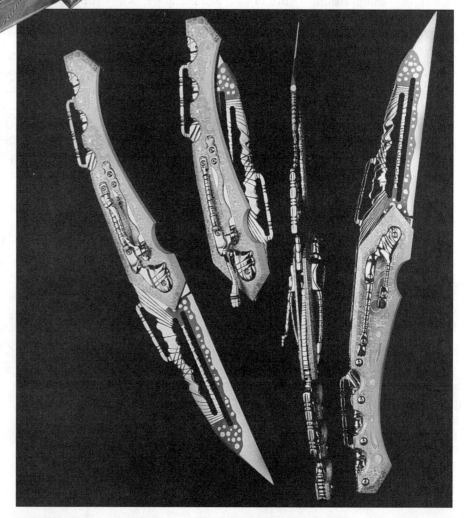

High-art knives like the "Spawn" are often "spawned" from an artistic vision, as is true in this case. The knifemaking duo of Scott Richter and Romas Banaitis envisioned uniting high-tech with an organic mask through the use of carving, polishing, grinding, milling, piercing, sand blasting, etching and anodizing techniques. The blade is ATS-34, the fittings are stainless, the frame is titanium, as is the lock. The look fuses organic and machine-like qualities.

Smith works his trade in traditional knife designs, concentrating his efforts on bowie knives, fighters, Persian pieces, swords and locking folders. His true specialty can be found in manipulating damascus patterns, as well as the shapes of bronze, steel and sterling-silver fittings.

In addition, Smith teaches blade smith work at the Massachusetts College of Art, Peter's Valley and Penland Craft Schools. His students are instructed on basic blade smith work, steel stock removal, and knife fitting, finishing and design. His classes are built around increasing each student's basic knifemaking skill level. According to Smith, "My classes are well attended and there's always a waiting list."

Banaitis first became interested in metal work and artistic design in high school. Upon graduation, he was accepted into the Massachusetts College of Art. However, the appeal of clay and cast forms didn't last long.

In a recent conversation, Romas told me, "Cast artwork didn't make any sense. I had to explore greater depth and was drawn into different mediums. It didn't really all come together until I met J. D. Smith. Through Smith's instruction, I learned to combine my artistic concepts with functional designs."

Master and Apprentice

Banaitis became Smith's cutlery apprentice and worked under him from 1996 to 1997. Banaitis learned from Smith what he termed "an artistic approach to knifemaking." Full of natural talent, Romas's skill flourished under the veteran smith's direction.

Eventually, Banaitis joined forces with Richter and, together, both men moved into a work studio of their own in The Distillery. Romas favors ATS-34 in his blade work. As well, he likes to work with titanium, stainless steel, aluminum and other metals for handles and fittings. While he is able to forge his own blades, he spends

most of his efforts in stock-removal projects. He often collaborates with his work studio partner on various knife pursuits.

Richter graduated from Northeast University in Boston, with a major in biology. His interest in life forms, as well as his uncanny understanding of mechanics, both can be seen in the phantasmagoric reality of his knives. He first got interested in knives in the early 1990s, working in a cutlery store. Believing he could ply the trade, he began making knives in the basement of his home.

Admittedly, his first attempts were rather crude, but he kept at it. Over time, his work exhibited dramatic improvement and, after meeting Smith in the cutlery store, his efforts in steel got even better. Smith offered some pointers and even suggested the workshop location in The Distillery.

Richter regards himself as a self-taught knifemaker, but willingly admits that that close proximity of Smith's workshop has had

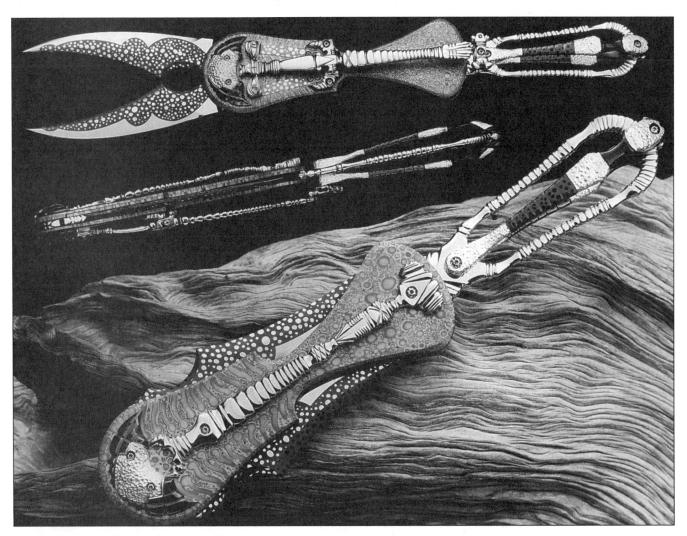

South Boston is a safer place to live now that Scott Richter and Romas Banaitis have created the Ancus Aquatic, a fantastic knife with two blades folding into one wild handle. Inspired by an elephant-herding tool exhibited at the Museum of Fine Arts in Boston, the knifemakers' quest was to recreate the natural beauty and powerful magic of this ceremonial tool. They succeeded!

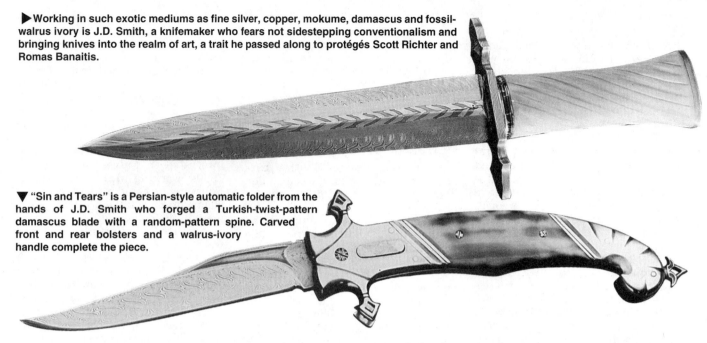

► Working in such exotic mediums as fine silver, copper, mokume, damascus and fossil-walrus ivory is J.D. Smith, a knifemaker who fears not sidestepping conventionalism and bringing knives into the realm of art, a trait he passed along to protégés Scott Richter and Romas Banaitis.

▼ "Sin and Tears" is a Persian-style automatic folder from the hands of J.D. Smith who forged a Turkish-twist-pattern damascus blade with a random-pattern spine. Carved front and rear bolsters and a walrus-ivory handle complete the piece.

a strong influence on his work. Scott's specialty is high-tech automatic folders in ATS-34. He also likes to work with Damasteel (powdered metal damascus made in Sweden). His handles and fittings are usually metal, with a strong emphasis on titanium and anodized aluminum.

Apparently, there are many advantages for these three makers that come from working at the same location. The fact that they get to pick each others' brains for ideas, share tools and hardware ("Can I borrow a cupful of handle rivets?"), and socialize from time to time (after all, they do work in an old distillery) obviously has its benefits.

Smith told me recently that, "Working so close together brings about a certain synergy." Not that this wouldn't probably happen naturally, but proximity brings it all to fruition.

Richter and Banaitis collaborate on some of the most awe-inspiring, futuristic and fantastic edged wonders that exist in the world of knives. A review of their work in *artsMEDIA* by Matthew Murphy is posted on the knifemakers' Web site: www.centipede-arms.com. The following excerpt from that review says it all:

"Acting like switch hitters in baseball, the artists use every machine in the workshop, from belt sanders to 4-inch files . . . It is the melding of their two visions that forges a powerful, ever-evolving style. Their recent work has altered the way craft and kinetic art intersect.

A hairpin mechanism summons a silent flinch and, suddenly, a silken, polished, silver blade reflects the room. Veering from art deco to gaudy Rococo, to slick Cadillac, Richter and Banaitis flex their ambidextrous talents at will. Are these weapons or toys? Sacrificial implements or Transformers?

Because these artists make the dangerous look High Society and the solid appear liquid, it's a fair assumptions that the final destinations of these knives will be not the cutlery rack, but the museum display cases. These one-of-a-kind creations are symbols of intense patience."

Unless the urban area is large enough to have a sizeable customer base, the presence of multiple knifemakers in the same city is a rarity. Even more unusual is the fact that all three of these men work in the same building, share tools, equipment and ideas.

The love of the craft and the artistic expressionism that knifemaking brings forth has given rise to this brotherhood. The knives that these men produce are a strong testimony to the fact that close proximity is no drawback to creative genius, and each man is quite obviously all of that — and more! ●

J.D. Smith is currently in the process of moving his workshop to another location. However, he, as well as Romas Banaitis and Scott Richter, can all be reached at The Distillery, 516 E. 2nd St., South Boston, MA 02127.

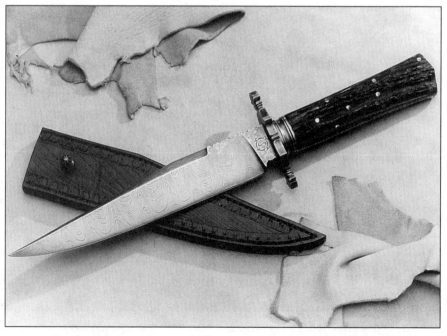

This handsome J.D. Smith bowie sports a 1095, O-1 and mild steel damascus blade in a ladder pattern, silver and copper mokume fittings, and a coffin-style stag handle.

TRENDS

The Trends section is where the author takes no credit. This is the place to say job well done and deny any and all responsibility. This part of the book is 100 percent dependent on there actually being trends in knives. What if the makers didn't come up with anything new in knives and when they did, if they didn't share it with their fellow professionals, if they all went their own ways and ignored all breakthroughs for the sake of individuality and sole propriety? No trends, no trends section.

Let's start with a generalization: tomahawks are hot. How about a few more? Boot and neck knives haven't seen any decline in popularity. Fighters are fighting back. Titanium is holding its own. Knifemakers are becoming more and more creative in naming their knives. They're building bowies better than ever. Pistol knives, the types actually made and worn in the Wild West for self-protection and preservation during high-stakes poker games, are seeing a comeback (see "Wooden Sword Award," page 5).

Blades have more curves than the Indianapolis 500. Makers of folding knives are finding more and unusual ways to lock them up, so as to eliminate all possibility of injury due to an unrestrained blade. Dropped-point hunters are still the preferred tool of the in-season crowd, though knives called such things as "buffalo skinner," "large-game hunter," "semi-skinner," "gut hook," "stubby skinner," and even "muskrat skinner" are making headway.

Not only are there trends in knives, but most of the trends are toward the betterment of the industry. When knifemakers try new things, they stick with them; they don't toss them aside and move on to the next potential moneymaking endeavor. Instead, they stay true to their trade. They take what has been learned and build upon it. They keep remaking a knife pattern until they have mastered it, until they can build it better than it has been built in the past.

Some makers specialize in reproducing patterns made popular by the masters who came before them. Some make exact replicas, others put their own twists on old models. They build, build and build some more.

One knifemaker wouldn't take credit for a development in knives, claiming there was another knifemaker on the other side of the country thinking along the same lines at the same time, so both should be credited for the advancement in knife technology. No matter who was first, it started a trend in knives, and that kind of unselfishness is admirable. That's just what the knife industry needs—trendsetters.

Joe Kertzman

Culture Shockers

THIS ONE SWEEPS upward like the wooden shoes of a Hollander. Check this out: the handle curls like a Greek cornucopia. And, hey, doesn't that one have a tilt like the Leaning Tower of Pisa? You couldn't find a finer example of an ornamental Chinese chopstick than that edged instrument over there. Now why do you suppose that knife ebbs and flows like the Nile River?

Why wouldn't the greater and lesser wonders of the world influence knife designs? Where else would knifemakers borrow ideas but from the landscape surrounding them, or, better yet, from exotic lands they once visited, whether in person or through the magic of books, movies and fairy tales?

Why do knives so closely resemble the cultural icons of even the most diverse and remote groups of people? For one, knives are an inherent part of any country's cultural heritage. If antique knives could talk, the histories of nations would unfold like the pointed blades of folding Italian stilettos. Knife designs often represent the very things associated with certain groups of people.

Who hasn't recognized the same precise workmanship exhibited in fine Swiss watches in the similarly intricate Swiss Army knives? Don't the engraved bolsters of a few chosen German pocketknives resemble the distinctive designs of Bavarian costumes, buildings and beer steins? Look at the carved wood handle of a Scottish dirk and tell me you haven't recognized similar patterns in the architecture along Whitehall, Thames or the Scotland Yard.

It's amazing how the stepped bolsters of knifemaker Koji Hara's folding and fixed-blade knives mimic the terraced land and farms near his Japanese home. South African Chris Reeve gives his knives Zulu names and borrows a few natural shapes and forms from his homeland. The silver filigree work of Russian Zaza Revishvili is a delicate, lace like ornamentation wholly un-American.

Such foreign influence is as refreshing as a cup of latte in a French café, don't you agree?

Joe Kertzman

◀ **VINCE EVANS: Great Scot!** (Weyer photo)

◀ **RICHARD MIZE:** The *sgian dubh* is Scottish. The carved handle is oak. The knife is AOK.

MICHAEL WATTELET: Fixtures on the Mexican bowie include blood stone set in sterling silver, 14k-gold, brass and a sterling-silver skull carved into the butt cap. The handle is gemsbok; the sheath is cowhide with sterling silver wire lacing; and the leather belt includes a sterling hand-stamped slide on the buckle. Nothing exotic, really.

▼ JERRY HOSSOM: The 154CM blade of the Persian short sword snakes around like a scythe with similar results. You couldn't get more gorgeous than the California buckeye burl handle. (BladeGallery.com photo)

PHILL HARTSFIELD: Standing at the ready is a 7 1/2-inch tanto with an A-2 tool steel blade, a copper *habaki* (blade collar) and *tsuba* (guard), and a brown leather-lined *saya* (sheath). (BladeGallery.com photo)

▲ ANDERS HOGSTROM: *Kwaikens* cut through cultural boundaries using Jim Ferguson high-contrast-damascus and carbon-steel blades. A kwaiken is a small tanto-style blade between 3 and 7 inches designed for concealment under clothing, sometimes with a double edge (top knife). Both of these examples are handled in ivory and with care. (BladeGallery.com photo)

◀ STEVE SCHWARZER: He calls it "Eastern Wind," and he doesn't mean off the rocky coast of Maine. (PointSeven photo)

DON POLZIEN: Don achieved that wavy temper line we've all grown to love. Then, he hand carved and lacquered the *saya* (sheath) and gave it an antiqued-red, distressed finish.

▲ MARDI MESHEJIAN: Mardi's middle name is "Imagination," and that's why he has taken a traditional Japanese *wakazashi* design and added such things as titanium, pink ivory and a garnet. (Weyer photo)

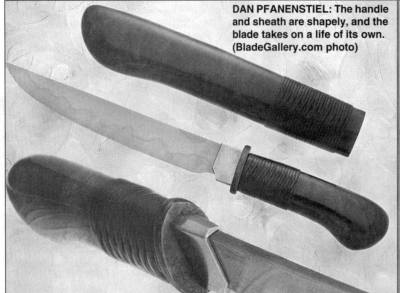

DAN PFANENSTIEL: The handle and sheath are shapely, and the blade takes on a life of its own. (BladeGallery.com photo)

▲ RICHARD MIZE: One, two, three *sgian dubhs* at the old blade game.

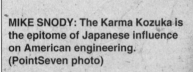

MIKE SNODY: The Karma Kozuka is the epitome of Japanese influence on American engineering. (PointSeven photo)

▲ MIKE MCRAE: He carved the briar handle of the *sgian dubh* in a thistle motif, added a carved-sterling-silver lion to the back of the handle, or pommel, and called it a day. (Hoffman photo)

◀ VINCE EVANS: Vince just wants to show you the ray-skin-and-antiqued-brass hilt and steel basket of the 31 3/4-inch Scottish sword. (Chan photo)

▼HEATHER SHOEBOTHAM and KEVIN HARVEY: The biltong is a traditional South African knife designed for cutting beef jerky. Recessed giraffe shin bone handle scales make it exotic and exciting. (BladeGallery.com photo)

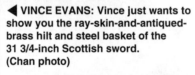

NOBUYUKI UEKAMA: Thin and stately is the traditional Japanese costume knife.

▼WILLIAM DEAN MITCHELL: The 11-inch blade has a Talwar flavor, though I wouldn't try tasting it if I were you.

▼KEVIN CASHEN: Goodness gracious, it's a Saxon dagger looking menacing in African *blackwood* and a powerfully patterned damascus blade that contrasts and lambastes. (Weyer photo)

◄SCOTT SLOBODIAN: Don't stand within striking distance but admire from afar.

▲ KEVIN HARVEY: Here's a traditional African dagger done up like we'd imagine it looking worn at a tribal gathering. The handle alone is intriguing in its makeup of jigged black ivory and wild *saringa* wood. The random-pattern damascus blade is by Heather Shoebotham. (BladeGallery.com photo)

◄DAVID GOLDBERG: Goldberg borrowed dragons, insects and ebony from Japanese lore, culture and surroundings. (PointSeven photo)

▼CHRISTOPH DERINGER: Mediterranean dirks are popular this year and, admittedly, the long, sleek style is attractive. Deringer dared to blend a mammoth-ivory grip with nickel-silver spacer and the side-exposed full tang of an O-1 carbon blade. It's as cool as the sea and twice as salty. (BladeGallery.com photo)

WENDELL BARNES: From chain or chord strung loosely around the neck hangs a ray-skin sheath holding a Japanese-influenced neck knife with twist-pattern damascus blade. It's imperial. (BladeGallery.com photo)

BRUCE BUMP: A French dagger does an eight-bar damascus twist to the accompaniment of a wire-wrapped eel-skin grip. The dagger is heavily engraved by Tom Moro. (BladeGallery.com photo)

▶ **DAVID SCHLUETER:** Finesse is what the *aikuchi* (knife without a guard) exudes. The 1050 blade is clay-coated and water-quenched in traditional Japanese style. The blade style is *hira-zukuri* (without ridge lines) and has *bo-hi* (fullers) on both sides. Handle charms (*menuki*) are branches plated in 24-k gold. (Scherzi photo)

▶ **PETER DEL RASO:** Black linen Micarta® wasn't available on original Japanese tantos, nor is it a staple in Japan today, but this is the here and now.

▼ **BILL BEHNKE:** The Mediterranean called to Bill before he built this small bowie. Africa got a word in through the continent's own black ivory wood. (Weyer photo)

STEVE LELAND: Don't see the foreign influence? This is a temple builder's knife, a design taken from a fixed-blade temple carpenter's knife in Japan (I didn't know until I read the back of the photo, either). (Weyer photo)

▲ **WALLY HAYES:** The 27-inch blade of the *katana* was hardened in water and, as Wally demonstrates, it cuts through solids as well as liquids.

▲ **JAY HENDRICKSON:** Jay's version of a Mediterranean dirk more than passes muster with his use of fine silver inlay, an integral guard and a mirror-polished L-6 blade. (BladeGallery.com photo)

▲ **KEVIN HARVEY:** The Mediterranean dirk is smooth in more ways than one, from the hand-rubbed, satin-finished blade and hand-filed, antique-copper bolster, to the *mopani* wood handle with wire wrap. (BladeGallery.com photo)

Hawk Heaven

I'T'S GOT TO be one of the fiercest weapons. Before Mel Gibson ever galloped across the screen wielding a tomahawk in "The Patriot," the world was exposed to images of American Rangers defending freedom, or Native Americans leaping off the backs of horses, attired in buckskins and little else, raising arms above heads and with shrill Indian cries and whole fell swoops at a time, well, you know the rest. It's gory, gruesome and gut wrenching.

There's a reason why kids continue to play cowboys and Indians to this day. There's a strange appeal to barbaric fighting tactics, to scalping and burning at the stake. It's not that all tomahawks are weapons of war. In fact, many true tomahawk artifacts were used for chopping, smoking, throwing, severing, fending off wild animals and even skinning them in a pinch.

The tomahawk is fascinating in that it's primitive. Tomahawks were used for good or evil and, in the darkest hours of true horror and bloodshed, they were thrown with deadly precision or swung from long hafts and aimed dead center at targets in full run. They dealt the ultimate blows.

There has been a huge resurgence in tomahawk popularity as of late. It is the one category in the world of edged tools and weaponry that fits neatest into the "Trends" section of the book. Not only are custom knifemakers building them better than ever before, but entire knife companies, including but not limited to the American Tomahawk Co., are being built

around the tomahawk. Patriotism is at an all-time high these days, and the tomahawk exudes passion, honor, glory and bravery.

The ghost of a soldier past clings onto his tomahawk, and for the honor of his country, swings it one last time before disappearing into the history books. The tomahawk is released, whistling through the air, sinking into its target with a thud, and a hawk flies from a tree, living to see another day.

Joe Kertzman

▼JAMES BARRY III: A fully functional pipe tomahawk with stimulating wood haft perches on a stag stand and pink-ivory base. Original, circa-1800 trade beads and a deer-hide pouch add authenticity. (Moya photo)

▶LONNIE HANSEN: The damascus head of the spike tomahawk reigns over an African blackwood haft and two-color artificial sinew. (BladeGallery.com photo)

FRED BRUNER JR.: The tomahawk head is filed and features a raised half moon and wooden haft. With knife, it's classic and dramatic.

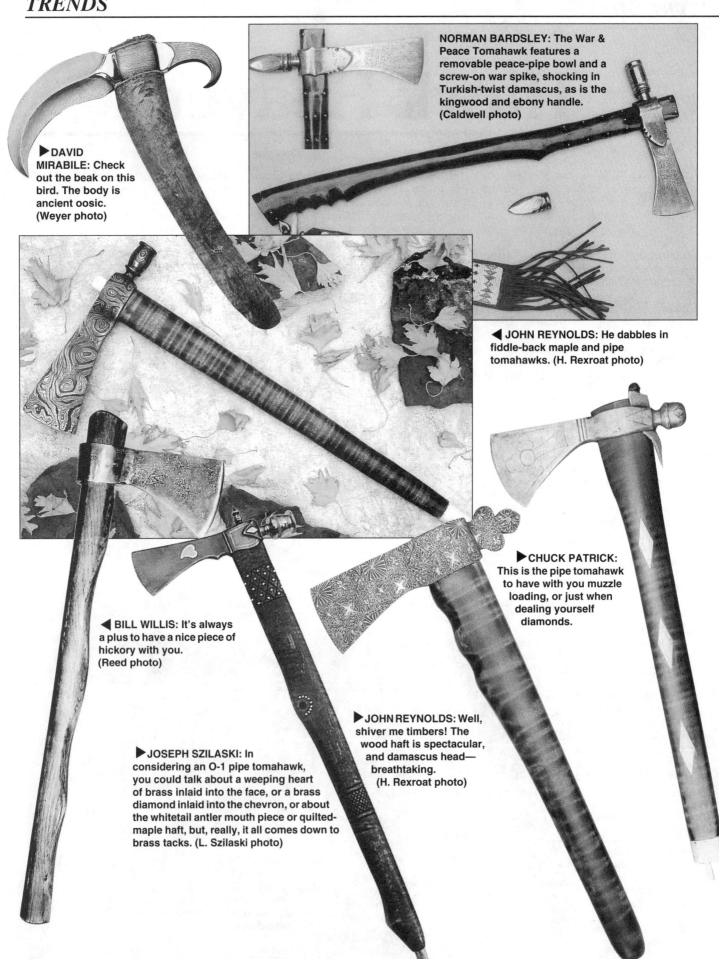

DAVID MIRABILE: Check out the beak on this bird. The body is ancient oosic. (Weyer photo)

NORMAN BARDSLEY: The War & Peace Tomahawk features a removable peace-pipe bowl and a screw-on war spike, shocking in Turkish-twist damascus, as is the kingwood and ebony handle. (Caldwell photo)

JOHN REYNOLDS: He dabbles in fiddle-back maple and pipe tomahawks. (H. Rexroat photo)

CHUCK PATRICK: This is the pipe tomahawk to have with you muzzle loading, or just when dealing yourself diamonds.

BILL WILLIS: It's always a plus to have a nice piece of hickory with you. (Reed photo)

JOSEPH SZILASKI: In considering an O-1 pipe tomahawk, you could talk about a weeping heart of brass inlaid into the face, or a brass diamond inlaid into the chevron, or about the whitetail antler mouth piece or quilted-maple haft, but, really, it all comes down to brass tacks. (L. Szilaski photo)

JOHN REYNOLDS: Well, shiver me timbers! The wood haft is spectacular, and damascus head—breathtaking. (H. Rexroat photo)

Dirks and Daggers

A DIRK IS a short, straight dagger. Now a dagger, well, a dagger is something else altogether. What isn't a dagger? A dagger is not curvy, complicated or wishy-washy in any way. It doesn't stray from a straightforward course. It never veers off to the side or blocks passageways. Traditionally, it hasn't even folded, but some versions fold up like a Depression-era bank.

Daggers are long, slender, sharp and pointed. The points seem so much more pointed than other blade tips. There's a reason. The curves of both edges of a dagger from guard to tip are more gradual. In fact, there's

▼**J.L. JACKSON:** This dagger was actually made from debris salvaged from the Windsor Castle after the Great Fire of 1992. The handle is English oak and is from one of the burnt roof timbers. J.L. is armourer to Her Majesty, the Queen.

little curve to them, but more like two long, graduating lines eventually ending at the tiptop of the pointy point. It's perfect and proper and how a knife should be.

Even the name is cool, "Dagger," or better yet, the shorter version, "Dirk." The name "Dirk" is dark and dastardly, funny and friendly, silly and sly, all rolled into one. The knife is much the same. It's fun to look at and hold in your hand. When you palm it, your forefinger tends to effortlessly slide up the spine of the handle and point toward the tip as if showing you how neat, pointy and sharp it is, just a pinprick of a point at the end of that long, steel sticker. But it is a sticker. Remember that. Don't try to push it into the palm of your hand or run your finger along the edge. It will bite. It's an untrained dog, wild and savage.

Knifemakers have learned the pattern well. They relish its simplicity and wallow in its wake. The dirks and daggers herein are so diverse and satisfying to we knife nuts that one begins to wonder just how simple the design can be. How can so much go on in such a confined space? How can you tell

▶**YASUTAKA WADA:** If this dagger doesn't do it for you, nothing will. It's so sleek, sharp and classic in styling and materials.

knifemakers to build long, slender, sharp, pointy knives without any gimmicks, gadgets, bulky guards or swooping, curving, craning, twisting, bending blades and end up with so many different versions of the same type of knife? It's confounding!

Knifemakers are the type of people who build knives because they find it enjoyable, not because they are going to get rich at it or famous or save the world with their steel and solid masses of cut. The pride in their work comes through like the tip of a dagger through a cellophane wrapper.

Creativity cuts as deeply as any dirk or dagger. Knife dimensions are drawn, not with pad and paper, but in the mind, and the hands of the craftsmen do the rest. Dirks and daggers are stylish and trendy, old and historic, antique and collectible, fine and presentable. Presenting Dirk and Dagger. Don't get them mixed up, now. Try to stay within the lines and maybe you'll get to the point.
Joe Kertzman

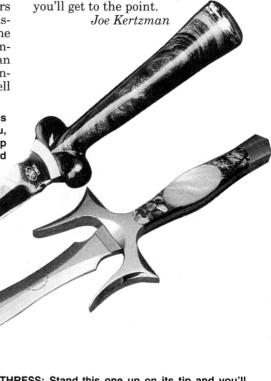

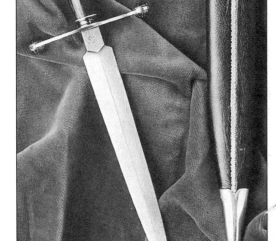

▲**JOHN POYTHRESS:** Stand this one up on its tip and you'll have a fine soldier with paua shell and pearl dress uniform. The piece won Best Art Dagger at the 2001 Southeastern Custom Knife Show.

▼WOLFE LOERCHNER: Slight, graceful curves collectively form a shapely dagger in plain and damascus steel. (Weyer photo)

JOSEPH SZILASKI: Here ye, here ye, the Quillion Dagger requests your presence at the royal ball. (L. Szilaski photo)

▶RALPH FREER: Ralph carried out the pointed theme from Robert Eggerling damascus blade to rear bolster, adding fluted mother-of-pearl handle scales between the two tips.

◀ MARVIN SOLOMON: A leaf-shaped blade sprouts from a green-Malitite handle. (Ward photo)

JOHN LEWIS JENSEN: John didn't get it. It took him two knives to make one dagger. It was actually the idea of a collector who wanted two versions of a knife similar to these so he could display them side-by-side as a mirrored pair, or a symmetrical entity, or as a dagger.

▲ FRED OTT: A 6-inch dagger blade descends from a carved stellar-sea-cow-bone handle.

JACK CRAIN: The African-trade-amber grip holds tight to a carved guard and lengthy blade.

MICHAEL VAGNINO: Giraffe bone handle scales were just the thing to complement the tight pattern of the Bob Eggerling damascus blade and bolsters.

▶**PETER DEL RASO:** This integral dagger is all D-2 steel stock, hollow ground, satin finished, engraved and inset with garnets and cabochons.

▶**PHILIP BOOTH:** Talk about damascus patterns adding to the overall effect of a knife design. This one with a Bob Eggerling damascus blade does just that. (Hoffman photo)

▲**EDWARD KALFAYAN:** Starring on a folding dagger are a mokume bolster made by Mike Sakmar, a Devin Thomas vines-and-roses damascus blade, and a bark-mammoth-ivory handle that is as impressive as the cast of characters before it. (Weyer photo)

◀**JAMES SCROGGS:** The blade grind alone is worth the investment, and the wood doubles as the presentation box.

▼**TIM HANCOCK:** A pinup girl, and she's gorgeous. (PointSeven photo)

▶**RENDON GRIFFIN:** Pearl and damascus are as different as day and night. (Weyer photo)

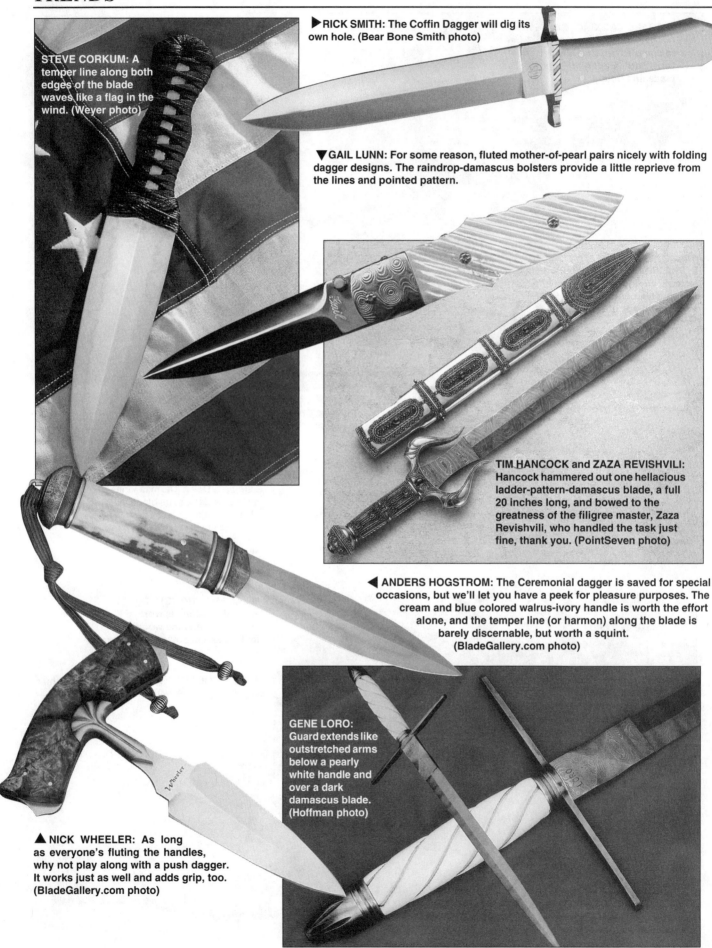

RICK SMITH: The Coffin Dagger will dig its own hole. (Bear Bone Smith photo)

STEVE CORKUM: A temper line along both edges of the blade waves like a flag in the wind. (Weyer photo)

GAIL LUNN: For some reason, fluted mother-of-pearl pairs nicely with folding dagger designs. The raindrop-damascus bolsters provide a little reprieve from the lines and pointed pattern.

TIM HANCOCK and ZAZA REVISHVILI: Hancock hammered out one hellacious ladder-pattern-damascus blade, a full 20 inches long, and bowed to the greatness of the filigree master, Zaza Revishvili, who handled the task just fine, thank you. (PointSeven photo)

ANDERS HOGSTROM: The Ceremonial dagger is saved for special occasions, but we'll let you have a peek for pleasure purposes. The cream and blue colored walrus-ivory handle is worth the effort alone, and the temper line (or harmon) along the blade is barely discernable, but worth a squint. (BladeGallery.com photo)

GENE LORO: Guard extends like outstretched arms below a pearly white handle and over a dark damascus blade. (Hoffman photo)

NICK WHEELER: As long as everyone's fluting the handles, why not play along with a push dagger. It works just as well and adds grip, too. (BladeGallery.com photo)

▼MICHAEL IRIE: This one had a hold of me long before I imagined what it would be like to hold it.

▲ EDWARD KALFAYAN: An elephant ivory handle and sharkstooth-damascus blade will bring out the animal in anyone. Edward's 18-inch dagger also showcases a Mike Sakmar mokume guard and butt cap. (Weyer photo)

▲STEVE HILL: The automatic folding dagger is decked out in sculpted and hot-blued Daryl Meier damascus bolsters, carved gold-lip-pearl handle and damascus blade. (PointSeven photo)

▲ SCOTT SLOBODIAN: The Grove Dagger cuts roses for empresses using a Robert Ferguson damascus blade, a cat's-eye-quartz pommel, gold fittings and a Thuya-burl handle.

▲ GLENN MARSHALL: This is not a dagger, but a mountain man dirk from the hills of Virginia and Tennessee by way of British seaman. Similar models saw a lot of action in the Rocky Mountains by early mountain men, but they were probably without the silver inlaid grizzly in an Amazonian rosewood handle, or the guard and bolster engraving by Don Henderson.

JOE OLSON: The Tribal Dagger wears a high-contrast John Davis damascus blade and fluted African blackwood handle with equal panache. (BladeGallery.com photo)

▲ MICHAEL MCCLURE: Here's a dagger with a single edge, well, two—it's also a strikingly beautiful design. (BladeGallery.com photo)

The Name Game

ONE OF MY favorite parts of walking through an art museum is looking at a painting, imagining what I would call it, then looking at the tag on or near the frame to find out what the artist named it. More often than not, what I see in a painting is completely different from the painter's vision. In speaking with artists, it becomes clear that they do not take exception to other viewpoints, but welcome them. Art is not only what the creator of the piece sees, but how others interpret it.

The name game becomes more fun as the titles of the works become increasingly funky. In the wacky world of knives, Twilight Tanto might Moon Dance with Seahawk and accidentally step on Little Bug underneath the Cheyenne Star, careful not to wake Sweeping Beauty, of course. Some names are nonsensical until you look up definitions of certain words, and then their meanings become all too clear.

Often the knives don't conjure up any images, but when you look at what the knifemakers named them, you see exactly what they saw, whether it be the shape of a knife, its inherent beauty or its startling darkness. All becomes clear when you open your mind. The name game is fun to play, and the more players the merrier.

Joe Kertzman

GRASS FIRE BOWIE: Neil McKee didn't even try to extinguish the flames spreading across the 5160 bowie blade. (BladeGallery.com photo)

BOUNTY HUNTER: What Jeff Hall is trying to say is that the S30V chisel-ground tanto blade, thick titanium liners and synthetic blade and bolsters could handle any job. (PointSeven photo)

►MORAY: In all honesty, this one by Paolo Scordia is as close to artwork as any, with a snakewood handle splayed out like an eel whipping through the water.

▶LITTLE BUG: Like a leech suctioning onto a garbage fish, Joe Olson's Little Bug sucks as much life as possible out of the confining space of a knife. (BladeGallery.com photo)

▲ ▶FLIGHT: Winged and ready is Gerard Hurst's Damasteel folder with 14k-gold pins.

◀MOON DANCER: This one by C. Lyle Brunckhorst wears moon boots for a guard and a long, damascus-nose-cone of a blade. (BladeGallery.com photo)

◀SEAHAWK: Tom Anderson put a bead-blasted BG-42 beak on this one. (PointSeven photo)

▶BOBCAT: A stainless steel guard keeps you from getting scratched by the 440C blade while holding Lynn Maxfield's babinga-and-curly-maple-handled Bobcat.

◀BATTLE ZONE: This isn't just an edged weapon, it is the entire battle zone. The Mike Snody knife was originally designed by Edmund Davidson. (PointSeven photo)

▶TWILIGHT TANTO: As the sun begins to set, Tom Ferry's tanto arches its back and sips in the last of the rays. (BladeGallery.com photo)

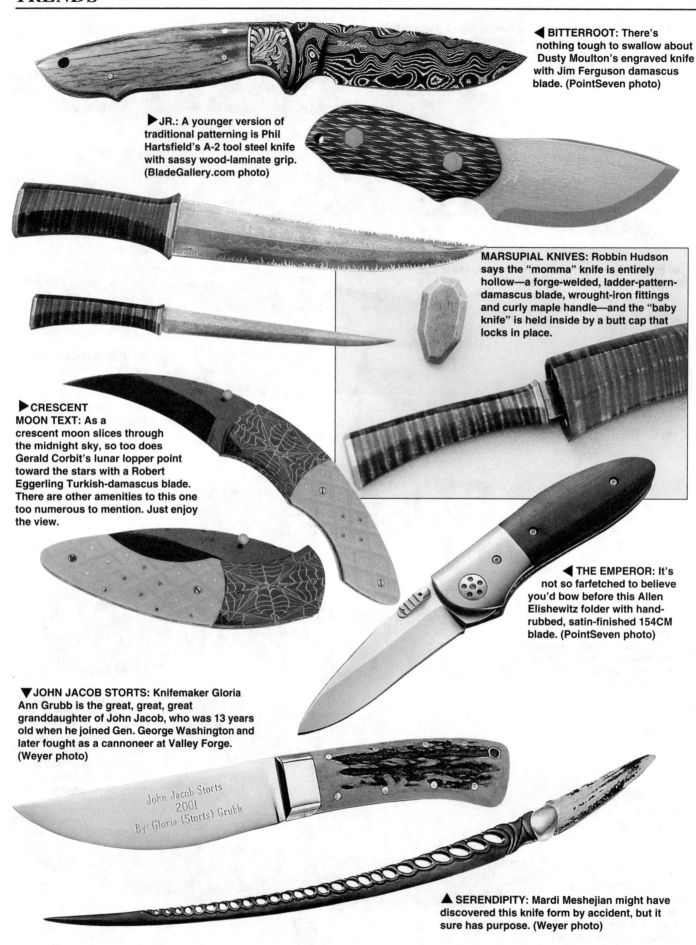

◄ BITTERROOT: There's nothing tough to swallow about Dusty Moulton's engraved knife with Jim Ferguson damascus blade. (PointSeven photo)

► JR.: A younger version of traditional patterning is Phil Hartsfield's A-2 tool steel knife with sassy wood-laminate grip. (BladeGallery.com photo)

MARSUPIAL KNIVES: Robbin Hudson says the "momma" knife is entirely hollow—a forge-welded, ladder-pattern-damascus blade, wrought-iron fittings and curly maple handle—and the "baby knife" is held inside by a butt cap that locks in place.

► CRESCENT MOON TEXT: As a crescent moon slices through the midnight sky, so too does Gerald Corbit's lunar lopper point toward the stars with a Robert Eggerling Turkish-damascus blade. There are other amenities to this one too numerous to mention. Just enjoy the view.

◄ THE EMPEROR: It's not so farfetched to believe you'd bow before this Allen Elishewitz folder with hand-rubbed, satin-finished 154CM blade. (PointSeven photo)

▼ JOHN JACOB STORTS: Knifemaker Gloria Ann Grubb is the great, great, great granddaughter of John Jacob, who was 13 years old when he joined Gen. George Washington and later fought as a cannoneer at Valley Forge. (Weyer photo)

John Jacob Storts
2001
By: Gloria (Storts) Grubb

▲ SERENDIPITY: Mardi Meshejian might have discovered this knife form by accident, but it sure has purpose. (Weyer photo)

►SWEEPING BEAUTY: Thomas Haslinger can "sweep" soundly tonight in the knowing of a job well done.

►CHIMERA: Trace Rinaldi creates a fire-breathing she-monster from Micarta® and BG-42. (Hoffman photo)

▼EAGLE: Reese Weiland's bird of prey shows a Thunderforged-damascus talon and carved-pearl feathers. (Doggett photo)

►HAWG MILLENIUM FIGHTER: Mike Franklin was hunkered down with this one in his bunker when 2001 rolled around. (Hoffman photo)

▲ MISSISSIPPI QUEEN: It's all frills and a lot of fuss for the Al Dippold knife showered with pearl, diamond, gold and damascus. (PointSeven photo)

▲ CHEYENNE STAR: James Luman might have named the piece after the Cheyenne-star-pattern damascus blade, but he also seasoned it with turquoise and maple burl for a native flavor. (BladeGallery.com photo)

►NIGHT SHADOW: Buffalo horn and black leather supplement the steely look of a Scott Slobodian tanto.

S-Curved Blades

DANGEROUS CURVES AHEAD! *Proceed with caution.* Whether you refer to them as "S-curved blades," "re-curved blades" or "compound edges," blades with sharp S-shaped bevels, when traced from tip to tang, have a certain appeal, and many believe they cut as good as they look.

One part of a re-curved edge is concave in relation to the spine, and one part is convex, creating a wavy blade effect. In most examples of re-curved or S-shaped edges, the first curve immediately extends outward just past the tip in a convex fashion, and then inward in a concave curve near the center of the blade. The "S" shape is completed as the blade edge curves back out again toward the handle.

The function lies in the added weight of the wider or outer-facing curve. In rope cutting, the inside, or concave curve, catches the rope, and the extended portion of the blade can be pulled through the fibers with relative ease. In a slashing motion, the S-curved blade is a winner in that there is more edge in the chop.

It doesn't take a dramatically pronounced re-curve to help a blade bite deeper into a branch in a chopping motion, and there's more cutting surface along an S-shaped edge than on a blade of the same length with a straight edge. There is a drawback, of course. Imagine grinding and sharpening one of these puppies.

Machines can cut the "S" shapes out, but to apply a hollow or flat grind, the blade has to be put through an "S" maneuver in the grinder. Imagine being a custom knifemaker in his garage machine shop with blade in hand and arms moving forward toward the grinding wheel. To follow the compound curves of a re-curved blade, and to match the left and right sides of the grind is rather like drawing a perfect circle freehand. It takes a true artist, and one with skill levels above those of his or her peers.

Persian knives and swords are great examples of S-curves, as are *kris* daggers with successive curves sloping in opposite directions. Knifemaker Larry Harley believes re-curved blades benefit from Persian influence and that Persian blades emulate animal horns. If that is the case, then knifemakers once again borrow from their surroundings, from shapes that are natural and true. The blades are definitely serpentine and snakelike in shape and form, with a slithering look and a bite to match.

Joe Kertzman

▼**STEPHEN OLSZEWSKI:** It wasn't a tough decision to include a snake figural knife in the "S-Curved Blades" section of the book, though it would have also fit in among the "Dazzling Damascus" and "Carved, Sculpted and Cool" categories.

▶**KEN ONION:** There's an alphabet of "S's" in the Mike Norris damascus and mother-of-pearl handles. (Weyer photo)

JOHN LEWIS JENSEN: The Barracuda Chromosome stretches 10 inches open, but is neither "X" nor "Y" chromosome, but "S" chromosome on the double helix of knife.

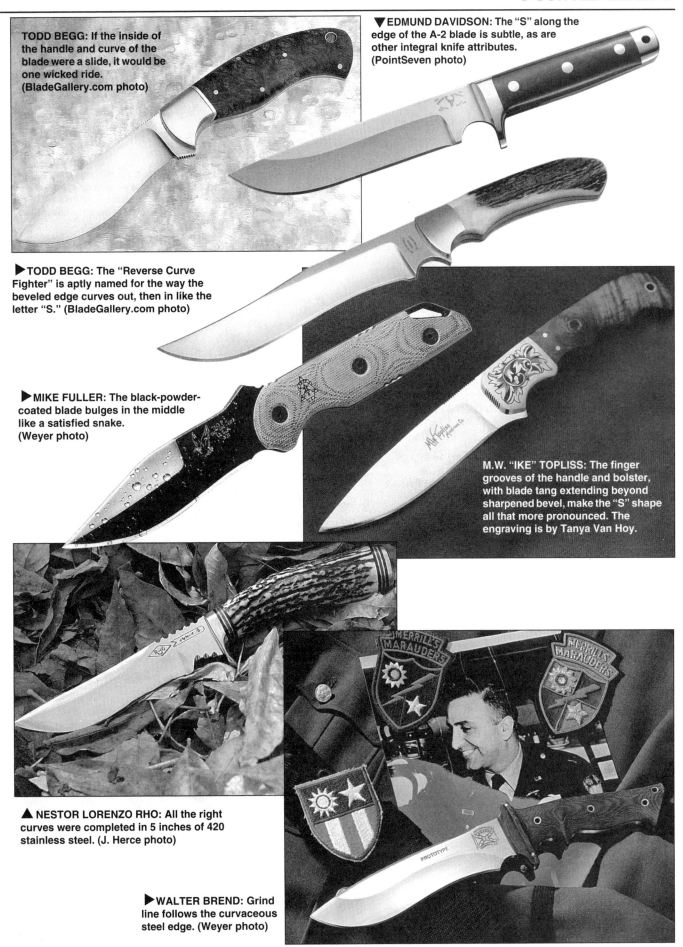

TODD BEGG: If the inside of the handle and curve of the blade were a slide, it would be one wicked ride. (BladeGallery.com photo)

EDMUND DAVIDSON: The "S" along the edge of the A-2 blade is subtle, as are other integral knife attributes. (PointSeven photo)

TODD BEGG: The "Reverse Curve Fighter" is aptly named for the way the beveled edge curves out, then in like the letter "S." (BladeGallery.com photo)

MIKE FULLER: The black-powder-coated blade bulges in the middle like a satisfied snake. (Weyer photo)

M.W. "IKE" TOPLISS: The finger grooves of the handle and bolster, with blade tang extending beyond sharpened bevel, make the "S" shape all that more pronounced. The engraving is by Tanya Van Hoy.

NESTOR LORENZO RHO: All the right curves were completed in 5 inches of 420 stainless steel. (J. Herce photo)

WALTER BREND: Grind line follows the curvaceous steel edge. (Weyer photo)

◄ **GAETAN BEAUCHAMP:** Gaetan built it with toothy spine and smiley blade.

ED FOWLER: Ed used a modified Michael Price grind on the side geometry of the blade, meaning it's thinner ahead of the *ricasso* and swells slightly toward the first third of the blade. This, he surmises, adds toughness and strength. It's a big camp knife, too. (BladeGallery.com photo)

▼ **TODD BEGG:** An integral push dagger is sharp in more ways than one, from fossil-ivory grip with mosaic pins, to *skeletonized* blade tang, and from integral dovetailed bolsters to S-shaped blade. (BladeGallery.com photo)

► **TAS KERLEY:** Tas set out to make a utility knife with simple 440C blade, then he flat ground it with a top *swedge*. He added satin blade bevels with blasted flats, and darned if the thing didn't take on a few curvy characteristics of its own.

► **WILBUR STEGNER:** It's his own cable damascus, so he can make it curve any way he wants. (Wolfdeckner photo)

► **GREG LIGHTFOOT:** Greg's emblem is a swimming shark, and the knife creates the waves.

► **ALFREDO KEHIAYAN:** They say the "S curve" cuts better in drawing it back after hooking the cutting medium with the hump of the blade. This particular model has many other facets for follow-through motions.

Bang-Up Bowies

BRINGING THE BOWIE to light is not a difficult task. The makers—now they have it rough—but not this writer, not him. His job is easy. Make these bowies look good on the pages of the book. Describe them for people, for the readers, so that while gazing at the photos, they feel as if they are actually holding the knives. That's the task before him. Bring the bowies to light. Make them shine. There. It's done. That's it. All it took was to show the pictures.

You already feel like you're holding the big bowies. The strength is in the design, in the size, the treatment, the forging and the building of the bang-up blades. It's in the rounded, contoured, bent, form-fitting handles; in the finger *choils*; the gargantuan guards; the flared butts; thick spines; the double edges; the piercing, clipping, upswept points; the high grinds; scary-sharp edges; the heft; the balance; and the style.

It's the very last one, you know. The writer was teasing you with the others. The secret of the bowie knife is in the style. It is the most copied, emulated, interpreted knife design in the world. The bowie knife's strength is in its identifying features. Defining a bowie—now, that task is tougher.

These bang-up bowies are so varied, so different, yet so similar. Look at them long enough and some subtle similarities form in your mind. Overall, it's the blade shape itself, where it humps and where it dips, how it rolls and how it clips. The sweeping edge meets tip at just the right time. More than anything, the myth and legend behind the bowie knife define it as such. When you delve into the bowie, it sweeps you off your feet. No, bringing the bowie to light is not a preposterous proposition. Building one, well, that's a different story altogether.

Joe Kertzman

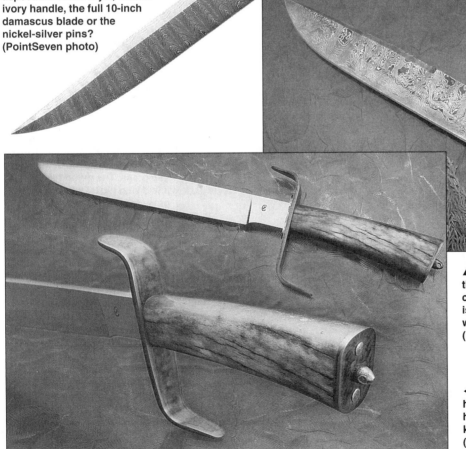

▶TIM HANCOCK: Is your favorite aspect the coffin-style, walrus-ivory handle, the full 10-inch damascus blade or the nickel-silver pins? (PointSeven photo)

▲ BOB BIZZELL: It's the least dramatic that oft holds the most interest. Neither curly-maple handle nor damascus blade is forged wrought iron from a circa-1900 wagon wheel rim, but the guard is. (BladeGallery.com photo)

◀ JON CHRISTENSEN: With case-hardened guard and pommel and edge-hardened 5160-steel blade, it's a tough knife, and holy cow-bone handle. (BladeGallery.com photo)

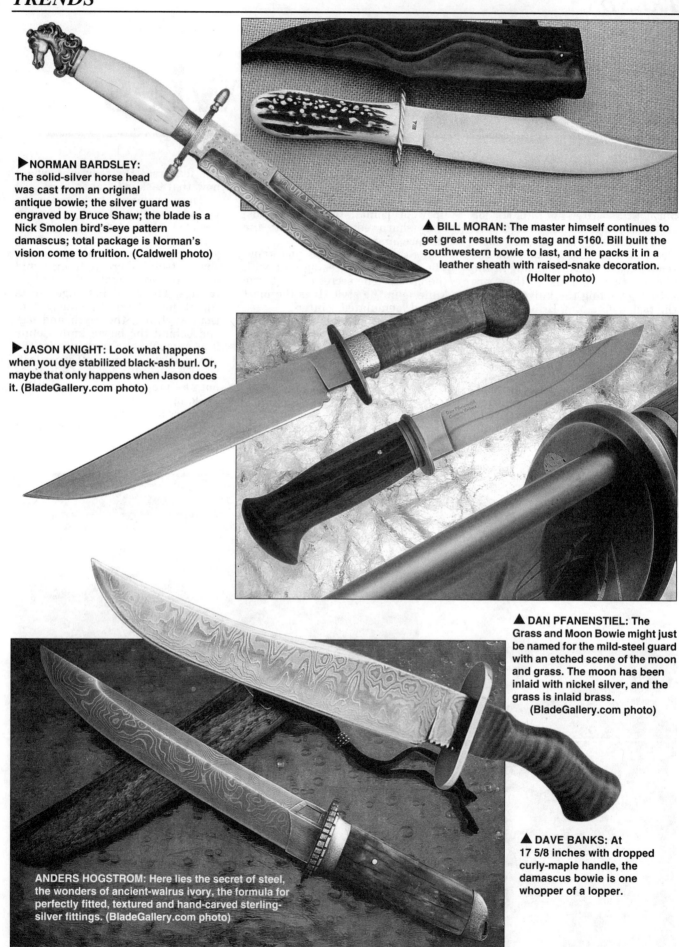

►NORMAN BARDSLEY: The solid-silver horse head was cast from an original antique bowie; the silver guard was engraved by Bruce Shaw; the blade is a Nick Smolen bird's-eye pattern damascus; total package is Norman's vision come to fruition. (Caldwell photo)

▲ BILL MORAN: The master himself continues to get great results from stag and 5160. Bill built the southwestern bowie to last, and he packs it in a leather sheath with raised-snake decoration. (Holter photo)

►JASON KNIGHT: Look what happens when you dye stabilized black-ash burl. Or, maybe that only happens when Jason does it. (BladeGallery.com photo)

▲ DAN PFANENSTIEL: The Grass and Moon Bowie might just be named for the mild-steel guard with an etched scene of the moon and grass. The moon has been inlaid with nickel silver, and the grass is inlaid brass. (BladeGallery.com photo)

ANDERS HOGSTROM: Here lies the secret of steel, the wonders of ancient-walrus ivory, the formula for perfectly fitted, textured and hand-carved sterling-silver fittings. (BladeGallery.com photo)

▲ DAVE BANKS: At 17 5/8 inches with dropped curly-maple handle, the damascus bowie is one whopper of a lopper.

▶MICHAEL MOONEY: Blade shape and oosic handle make this one more of a trendsetter than follower. (BladeGallery.com photo)

▶MIKE FELLOWS: If shapes, style and long blades are your thing, Mike made one for you with candlewood handle, elephant-ivory butt cap, gemsbok-horn spacers and a 10-inch satin-finished 440C blade. It swings.

▶TODD BEGG: The Preacher Man Bowie seems suitable for clearing land for a new church. (BladeGallery.com photo)

▲ JIM WALKER: You don't tug on Superman's cape. You don't spit in the wind. You don't pull the mask off the old Lone Ranger, and you don't mess around with Jim, or his 11 1/4-inch damascus bowie. (Lyrics borrowed from Jim Croce's "You Don't Mess Around With Jim," 1972.)

▶PETER DEL RASO: Peter took what is beautifully inherent in the bowie design and polished it.

▲ BUB WORRELL: It took 640 layers of damascus, a white African elephant and Bub to make this bowie. (Weyer photo)

▶GARY RODEWALD: If you're ever down on Canyon Creek, this is the bowie to take with you. (BladeGallery.com photo)

▶RICHARD MIZE: The long, thin red-stag handle is so smart against guard and blade.

◀ TERRY PRIMOS: Ten-and-a-half inches of forged bowie blade bring things into perspective. (Zolas photo)

▲ FRED OTT: Stalking its prey is a pointed L-6 blade, with giraffe-bone handle not far behind, and carved, blued-steel pommel taking up the rear.

▲ GLENN SMIT: This one can almost stand alone on its mule-deer-crown-antler handle and fend for itself.

▲ JACK CRAIN: His Model 96 bowie with blackwood handle and stainless blade shimmers in the light and lurks in the dark.

▶ROBERT LAY: A multi-faceted Dress Bowie is adorned with a California-buckeye and big-horn-sheep handle, engraved guard and butt and a 440C blade. (BladeGallery.com photo)

▶RICH MCDONALD: The aged finish of the 1084, the stag handle and the Mexican double-loop sheath by Jeanne McDonald would make any caballero swell with pride.

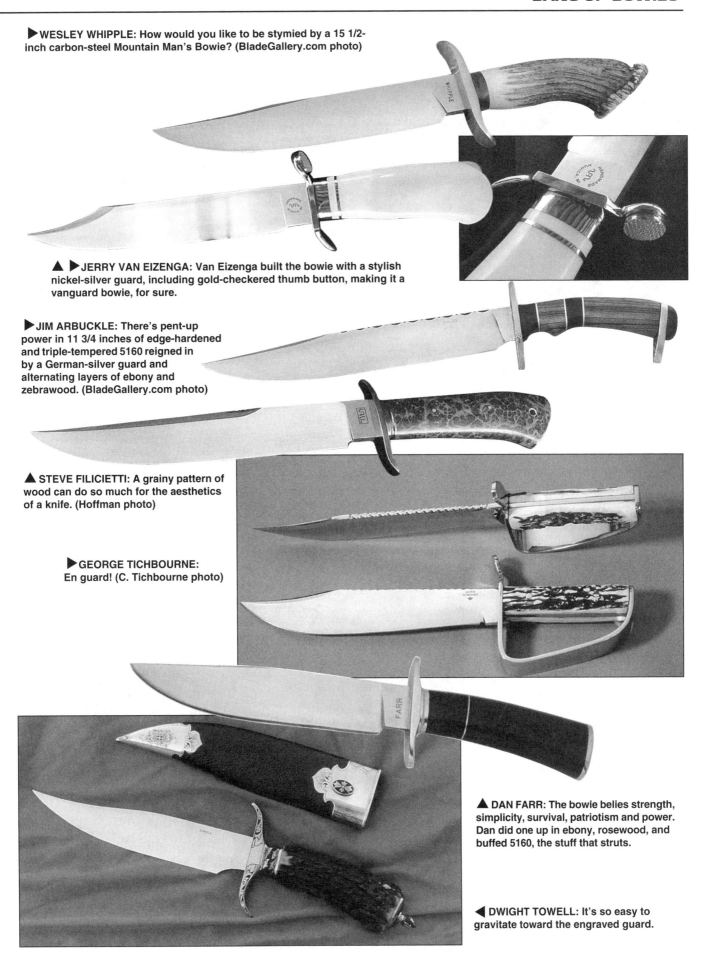

▶WESLEY WHIPPLE: How would you like to be stymied by a 15 1/2-inch carbon-steel Mountain Man's Bowie? (BladeGallery.com photo)

▲ ▶JERRY VAN EIZENGA: Van Eizenga built the bowie with a stylish nickel-silver guard, including gold-checkered thumb button, making it a vanguard bowie, for sure.

▶JIM ARBUCKLE: There's pent-up power in 11 3/4 inches of edge-hardened and triple-tempered 5160 reigned in by a German-silver guard and alternating layers of ebony and zebrawood. (BladeGallery.com photo)

▲ STEVE FILICIETTI: A grainy pattern of wood can do so much for the aesthetics of a knife. (Hoffman photo)

▶GEORGE TICHBOURNE: En guard! (C. Tichbourne photo)

▲ DAN FARR: The bowie belies strength, simplicity, survival, patriotism and power. Dan did one up in ebony, rosewood, and buffed 5160, the stuff that struts.

◀ DWIGHT TOWELL: It's so easy to gravitate toward the engraved guard.

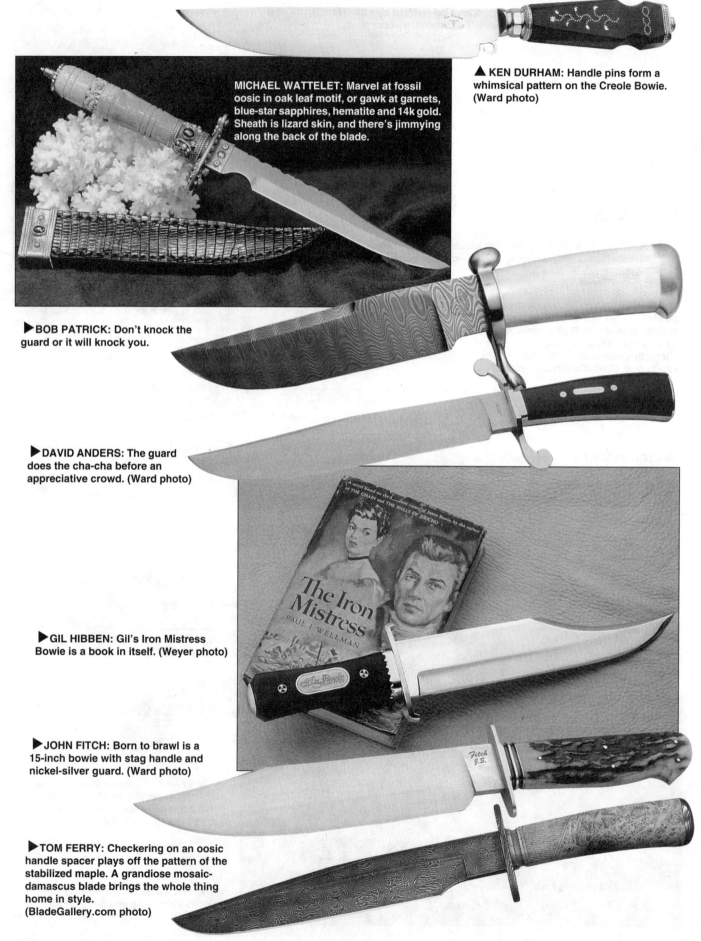

▲ **KEN DURHAM:** Handle pins form a whimsical pattern on the Creole Bowie. (Ward photo)

MICHAEL WATTELET: Marvel at fossil oosic in oak leaf motif, or gawk at garnets, blue-star sapphires, hematite and 14k gold. Sheath is lizard skin, and there's jimmying along the back of the blade.

▶ **BOB PATRICK:** Don't knock the guard or it will knock you.

▶ **DAVID ANDERS:** The guard does the cha-cha before an appreciative crowd. (Ward photo)

▶ **GIL HIBBEN:** Gil's Iron Mistress Bowie is a book in itself. (Weyer photo)

▶ **JOHN FITCH:** Born to brawl is a 15-inch bowie with stag handle and nickel-silver guard. (Ward photo)

▶ **TOM FERRY:** Checkering on an oosic handle spacer plays off the pattern of the stabilized maple. A grandiose mosaic-damascus blade brings the whole thing home in style. (BladeGallery.com photo)

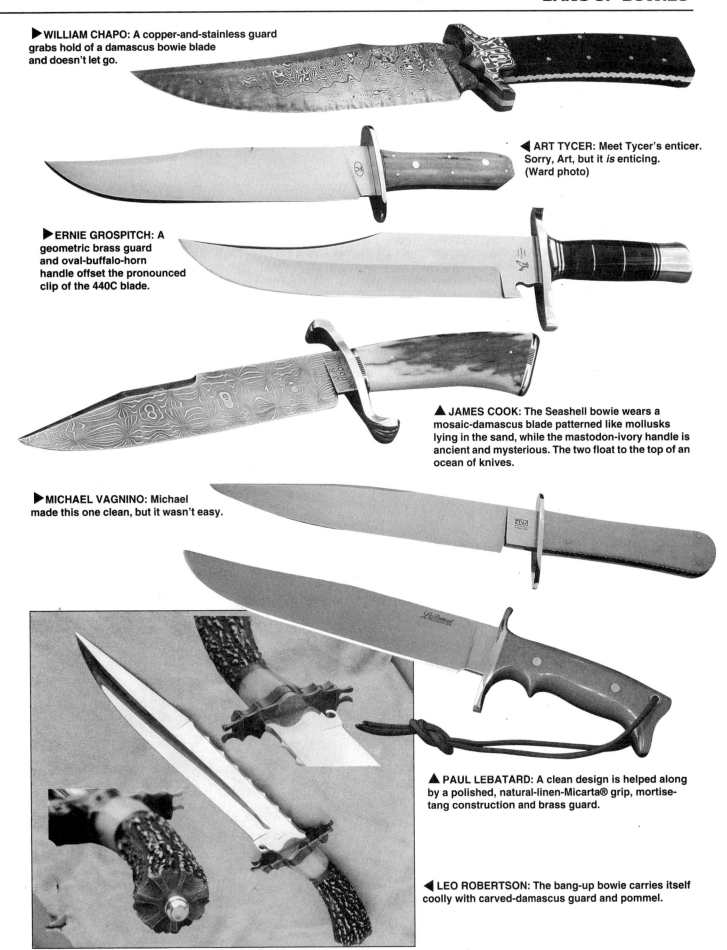

▶**WILLIAM CHAPO:** A copper-and-stainless guard grabs hold of a damascus bowie blade and doesn't let go.

◀**ART TYCER:** Meet Tycer's enticer. Sorry, Art, but it *is* enticing. (Ward photo)

▶**ERNIE GROSPITCH:** A geometric brass guard and oval-buffalo-horn handle offset the pronounced clip of the 440C blade.

▲**JAMES COOK:** The Seashell bowie wears a mosaic-damascus blade patterned like mollusks lying in the sand, while the mastodon-ivory handle is ancient and mysterious. The two float to the top of an ocean of knives.

▶**MICHAEL VAGNINO:** Michael made this one clean, but it wasn't easy.

▲**PAUL LEBATARD:** A clean design is helped along by a polished, natural-linen-Micarta® grip, mortise-tang construction and brass guard.

◀**LEO ROBERTSON:** The bang-up bowie carries itself coolly with carved-damascus guard and pommel.

Micro Managers

THE TITLE IS a play on words in more ways than one. The term is used in reference to miniature knives, but the makers of tiny cutlery are also micro managers. They have to be. They watch over *their own* shoulders and under their fingertips and behind their wrists, between digits, under nails, or sandwiched within the crevices of their knuckles, joints and palms.

Those are the areas where tenths-of-thousandths-of-inch screws, springs and pivot pins become lodged and lost. Better shave those long, hairy hands or you're likely to lose a gold or sterling silver screw. Think I'm joking? Just ask the manipulators of miniature blades, guards, handles and frames.

As in just about any field of miniature working-model manufacture, the workplace includes a microscope or magnifier of some type, and the finished edged tool or weapon is under the scrutiny of loupe-toting collectors who pay high dollar for the prized pieces.

One knife-show scene that's fun to witness is of an unassuming but distinguished gentleman with loupe held firmly up to one eye, squinting with the other, scrutinizing a miniature knife as the proud maker looks on, having studied it himself many times and eliminated any imperfections.

The micro managers in the knife industry are not ashamed of their titles. They manage in miniature what few have perfected in the full-size world.

Joe Kertzman

▼**S.R. JOHNSON:** Even in miniature, the Bob Loveless influence is plain to see and easy on the eyes. (PointSeven photo)

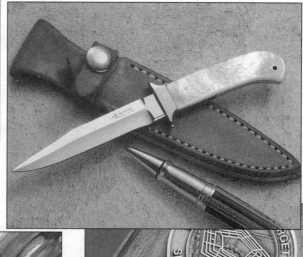

▲ **MICHAEL WATTELET:** When he says "Small Gentleman's Dress Knife," Michael doesn't mean the gentleman is small, he refers to the stainless damascus blade and jewel-encrusted handle.

▼**MIKE MERCER:** Small billboard, huge message—in tribute to those who died in the 9-11 terrorist attacks, Mike forged a 1 3/4-inch "In God We Trust" mosaic damascus blade and commissioned Gary Williams to scrimshaw a tiny ivory handle with an American flag and the Statue of Liberty. (Weyer photo)

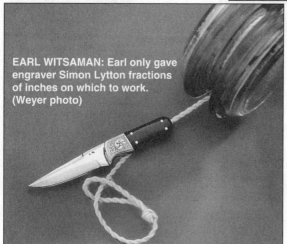

EARL WITSAMAN: Earl only gave engraver Simon Lytton fractions of inches on which to work. (Weyer photo)

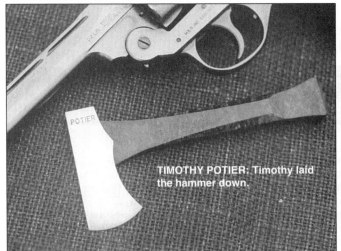

TIMOTHY POTIER: Timothy laid the hammer down.

ANDREW MCLURKIN: It's a head turner.

▲ FRANCIS FARRELL: From Francis of Swaziland comes a Bertie Rietveld pattern-welded and forged blade hidden within a gecko charm, held by a silver clasp and dangling from a sterling-silver choker. (BladeGallery.com photo)

DON HETHCOAT: Batteries included. (Ward photo)

►DOUGLAS NOREN: In the William Scagel style, the knife is named a "String Cutter" for its small stature. (Ward photo)

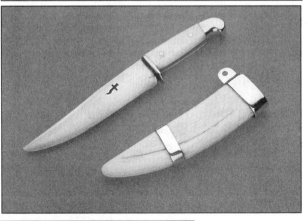

LORA SUE BETHKE: A chip off the old block, Lora does a nice job reproducing the knives of the Michigan master, William Scagel. (Ward photo)

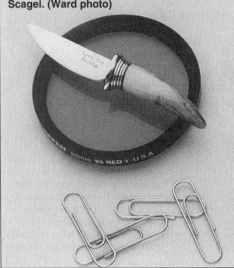

◄ JOSEPH SZILASKI: Are *miniature* switchblades considered a source of gang violence? (L. Szilaski photo)

Phenomenal Folders

YOU USED TO be able to call them pocketknives. "Yes," said some knifemakers, "I make a few pocketknives and a few hunting knives, but that's about it." There are still some guys and gals who say such things. There are some who take the craft that lightly, sort of nonchalantly, as if making knives to pass the time of day.

Yet, most makers either want or are forced to remain competitive and, to stay on top of their games, they have to make spectacular fixed blades and phenomenal folders, not pocketknives and a few hunting knives.

What is a phenomenal folder? It's one that melts in your hand, not in your sun room. It could be one with a gold-lip, black-lip or mother-of-pearl handle and dark, contrasting bolsters, or a fine piece with a stag grip and clean ATS-34 blade with long nail nick. A folder with a sterling silver shield and bolsters and a blade that pops open with a good tug and stays there during the cut is a good example.

Phenomenal folders are clean with bolsters flush against handles, no gaps between materials, blades that are stiff and sturdy and line up perfectly in and out of the frames and liners. There's embellishment but not too much. There's "eye candy" hidden in a few select places, like gemstones planted in thumb studs or file work along the spine of the blade or back of the liners.

Maybe the knifemaker signed his or her name inside the liner, or there is a clear, legible tang stamp. Pristine, strong, sturdy, reliable folders feel good in the hand and fit perfectly in the pocket. There are no rough edges, weak areas, unsafe angles or wobbly parts. Springs are stiff. Handles or bolsters might be carved or engraved. Blades are pattern-welded or plain steels buffed and sanded to satin or glossy finishes.

The best part of the stag horn is used for a grip, or a powerfully patterned antique-walrus-ivory handle is strategically fitted to a traditional folder. Even bead-blasted blades and Micarta® handles fit if done with a little class and a lot of care.

Pride of workmanship is the most important prerequisite to being named a phenomenal folder. I bet there's not a single maker of any of the following knives who is ashamed of the results. Nor should they be. These aren't just pocketknives, you know.

Joe Kertzman

▼**KAJ EMBRETSEN:** This is more than four blades and a corkscrew, it's four pattern-welded implements brought to a fine finish, a curlycue of a cork extractor and a pristine pearl handle highlighted by file work. (PointSeven photo)

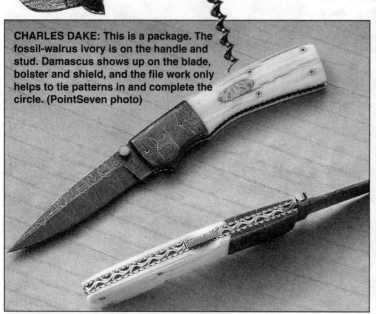

CHARLES DAKE: This is a package. The fossil-walrus ivory is on the handle and stud. Damascus shows up on the blade, bolster and shield, and the file work only helps to tie patterns in and complete the circle. (PointSeven photo)

BARRY DAVIS: It's the tight patterns of the damascus, the carved bolsters, the carved black-lip pearl, the file work, the gold bails, the highly figured mastodon ivory that set them apart. (PointSeven photo)

▶C. GRAY TAYLOR: Long and thin come to mind, but it's the care taken, the symmetrical, crisp, geometric and beveled blade shapes, the intricate carving, the polished look and the damascus that elevate these pieces to "phenomenal folders" status. (PointSeven photo)

▼LOYD MCCONNELL: All the curves move in synergy. (PointSeven photo)

TONY BOSE: Makes you want to nip and tuck doesn't it? (PointSeven photo)

▲ JOSH SMITH: Where the chocolate swirls of mastodon-ivory handle end, they pick up again on mosaic-damascus bolster, and all is sweet. (PointSeven photo)

▲ RICHARD ROGERS: The hump of the main blade projects upward like the snout of a bull shark, and the secondary edges take up the tail. (PointSeven photo)

▲ EDWARD KALFAYAN: These are slip joint folders. They don't lock open or closed. They just look fancy. (Weyer photo)

▶J.B. MOORE: A bone-handle trapper with shield embodies taste and tradition. (Weyer photo)

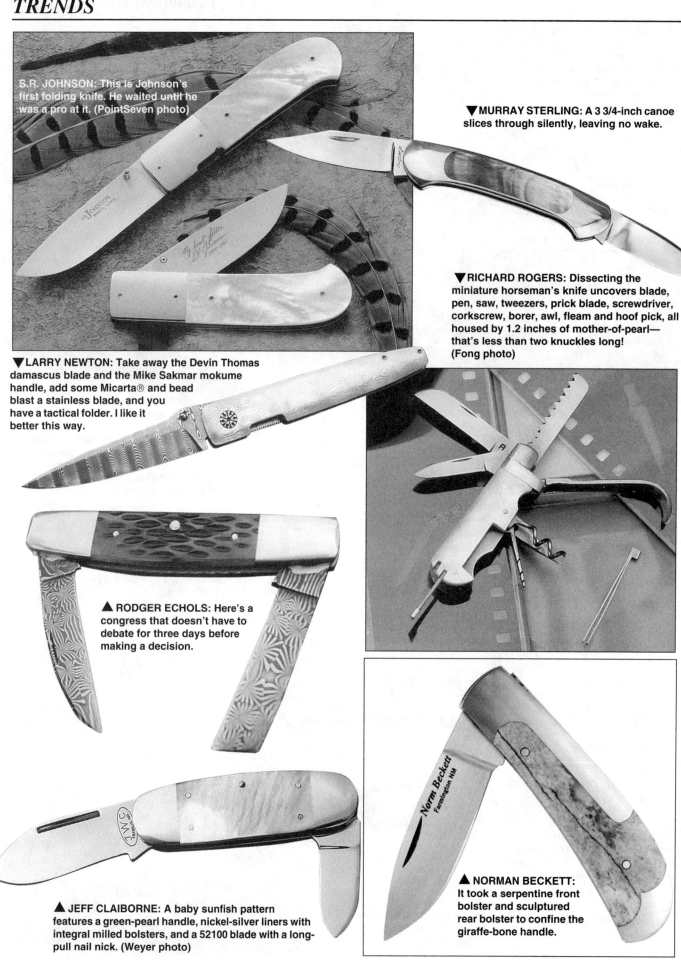

S.R. JOHNSON: This is Johnson's first folding knife. He waited until he was a pro at it. (PointSeven photo)

▼MURRAY STERLING: A 3 3/4-inch canoe slices through silently, leaving no wake.

▼RICHARD ROGERS: Dissecting the miniature horseman's knife uncovers blade, pen, saw, tweezers, prick blade, screwdriver, corkscrew, borer, awl, fleam and hoof pick, all housed by 1.2 inches of mother-of-pearl—that's less than two knuckles long! (Fong photo)

▼LARRY NEWTON: Take away the Devin Thomas damascus blade and the Mike Sakmar mokume handle, add some Micarta® and bead blast a stainless blade, and you have a tactical folder. I like it better this way.

▲ RODGER ECHOLS: Here's a congress that doesn't have to debate for three days before making a decision.

▲ NORMAN BECKETT: It took a serpentine front bolster and sculptured rear bolster to confine the giraffe-bone handle.

▲ JEFF CLAIBORNE: A baby sunfish pattern features a green-pearl handle, nickel-silver liners with integral milled bolsters, and a 52100 blade with a long-pull nail nick. (Weyer photo)

KENNETH PFEIFFER: Hey, when you have good stock, you breed it. (PointSeven photo)

▲ TONY BOSE: The doctor's knife is in, and its appointment book is full. (PointSeven photo)

▼ J.W. MCFARLIN: Usually jigged-bone handles are bolstered on each side and without a locking liner. It's nice to see bone taking up the whole handle without heavy conscience. (Weyer photo)

RICHARD ROGERS: It might be a gunstock pattern, but the ivory handle and polished bolsters make it look more like a presentation piece.

▶ RAYMOND MURSKI JR.: A folding bowie is neat. Add a locking liner and it gets interesting. Boya-burl handles are unusual. A state-of-the-art CPM-3V blade and titanium bolsters rocket it beyond "been done before."

▲ JOHN HOWSER: The split-back whittler is a super pattern, especially paired with an amber-Winterbottom-bone handle and integral stainless bolsters.

▼ TED MOORE: Imagine using this one to slice an apple. You wipe the blade down, close it into its handsome handle, brush a finger over the ivory one last time and slip it into your slacks pocket until another opportunity arises.

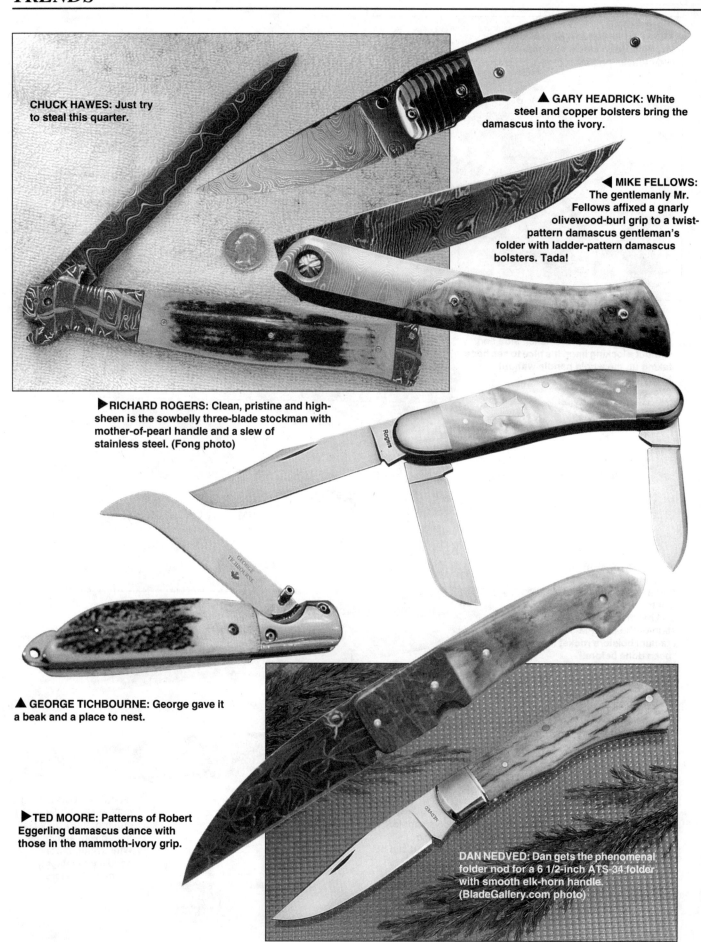

CHUCK HAWES: Just try to steal this quarter.

▲ GARY HEADRICK: White steel and copper bolsters bring the damascus into the ivory.

◀ MIKE FELLOWS: The gentlemanly Mr. Fellows affixed a gnarly olivewood-burl grip to a twist-pattern damascus gentleman's folder with ladder-pattern damascus bolsters. Tada!

▶RICHARD ROGERS: Clean, pristine and high-sheen is the sowbelly three-blade stockman with mother-of-pearl handle and a slew of stainless steel. (Fong photo)

▲ GEORGE TICHBOURNE: George gave it a beak and a place to nest.

▶TED MOORE: Patterns of Robert Eggerling damascus dance with those in the mammoth-ivory grip.

DAN NEDVED: Dan gets the phenomenal folder nod for a 6 1/2-inch ATS-34 folder with smooth elk-horn handle. (BladeGallery.com photo)

▶THOMAS HASLINGER: His Little Dove is at peace in desert ironwood, BG-42 stainless steel and titanium.

▶GARY CROWDER: Sheep horn never butted up against anything so strong. (Ward photo)

▶MICHAEL VAGNINO: A party girl she's not, but dignified and attractive.

▶JIM MAGEE: Jim knew when to stop the pattern and start the plain and pretty. (Ward photo)

▶ROBERT CAPDEPON: You sit the "average Joe" down with stag, titanium, pearl and steel, and he doesn't come anywhere close to this. (Mumford photo)

J.B. MOORE: Two trappers in bone handles lie in waiting. (Weyer photo)

▶DON HANSON III: Don used to make fancy sunfish-pattern folders, but never with the actual patterns of the fish in the folders, until now.

Emulating the Masters

TIM HANCOCK: The knife is dubbed "California Rose" and represents all that Michael Price and other West Coast knifemakers embodied during and after the Gold Rush era. Speaking of gold, the shields and buttons on the knife are of the 14k variety. Bryan Bridges is the engraver. I(PointSeven photo)

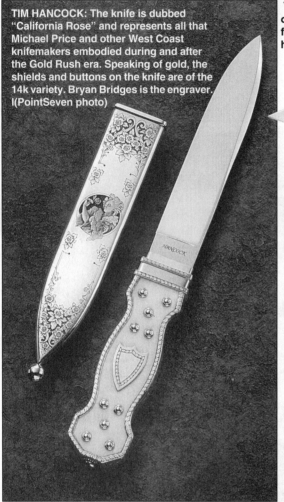

▼ETTORE BERTUZZI: Ron Lake's influence on knifemaking crossed the ocean to Bertuzzi's home in Italy where a Lake interframe folder was fashioned with a satin-finished ATS-34 blade and bark-mastodon-ivory handle inlay.

▼BRUCE BUMP and BRUCE EVANS: Two heads, hands and hearts were better than one in reproducing a Michael Price dagger. In his day, Michael didn't have the resources to create a powder-mosaic-damascus blade with so much character. (BladeGallery.com photo)

MIKE MCRAE: Mike was influenced by Daniel Searles and his bowies with silver pins, ebony handles, and hand-rubbed blades. That's the rub, anyway. (Hoffman photo)

▲ WALLY HAYES: This is an authorized copy of a Bill Moran ST-24 fighter, and that says a lot about both makers. (PointSeven photo)

WE'VE ALWAYS HAD teachers and classes. There have always been scholars, thinkers, philosophers, elders, advisors and statesmen. To this day, carpenters employ apprentices to whom they teach their craft. Veteran cops are often paired with rookies to show them the ropes. In the American Bladesmith Society, you must first test for your journeyman smith stamp before you can start preparing to become a master smith. The masters pass knowledge down to the novices. The inexperienced, the wet-behind-the-ears, the greenhorns have to prove themselves.

Becoming a master is more than taking tests, though. Those who have risen to the top of the knifemaking field have done it more through goal setting and achieving,

earnest work and results, creative aspirations and ultimate successes than they have through book learning and taking tests.

The masters make the knives better than anyone else. How hard can it be? You just have to concentrate, hone your skills and your knives, work hard, take a few chances, market yourself and your wares and advertise, right? Concentration alone never won anyone The Masters golf tournament. Tiger Woods doesn't take away more trophies than anyone else in the world just because he has better concentration skills, though it definitely helps. He wins because he has the

entire package, the skill, the will, the drive, the strength, the agility, the brains, the finesse, the discipline, concentration and the gift.

Michael Price, Bob Loveless, Bill Moran, Rudy Ruana, William Scagel, James Lile and D.E. Henry, to name a few, were gifted knifemakers. They leave legacies that continue to influence knife patterns and styles, knifemaking methods and techniques, and overall knife quality and value. They are the ones who aspiring knifemakers admire and emulate. Emulating the masters means the protégés strive to achieve what those before them achieved—greatness.

Joe Kertzman

▼DOUG NOREN: Doug tried a William Scagel hunter with quite excellent results. (Ward photo)

▶DOUG NOREN: Doug makes William Scagel-style knives, and when you do one thing for a long time, you become good at it. Here's a Scagel fighter reproduced in exacting detail from an original. (Ward photo)

▲ EDMUND DAVIDSON: Edmund is so enamored by the master he emulates, he etched "Loveless [Bob] Design" on all three BG-42 blades. He opted for Rocky Mountain sheep horn handles. (PointSeven photo)

▲ R.L. WELLING: Welling hand forged a William Scagel camp knife in 1095, nickel silver and whitetail crown stag. (Weyer photo)

◀ **S.R. JOHNSON:** This is an integral Bob Loveless-style dropped-point hunter. There is also a dropped-point hunter section in this book. Thanks, Bob. (PointSeven photo)

▶ **WOLFE LOERCHNER:** Wolfe has the decency to refer to this as a "Modern Price [Michael] Dagger," so as to separate it from the originals. Price would have been impressed. (Weyer photo)

◀ **JERRY VAN EIZENGA:** Matching the convex grind of a #5 Randall is quite an undertaking, and executed admirably here.

▶ **BOB PATRICK:** Bob took a liking to a Woodcraft model, and made his own to have and to hold.

◀ **DR. JAMES LUCIE:** The good doctor was William Scagel's personal physician and inherited many of Scagel's original spacers and other knife parts. Perhaps more importantly, Lucie makes a good Scagel repro, perhaps the best.

MARK HAYS: Hays is in the repair and restoration business, so maybe this one fits in the "Rebuilding the Masters" section, but it's a super example of a Randall Knives Model A with an 8-inch blade.

▲ **LORA SUE BETHKE:** Lora Sue lives in Michigan where William Scagel hailed from and where many makers build knives in the Scagel style. Lora has a knack for it. (Ward photo)

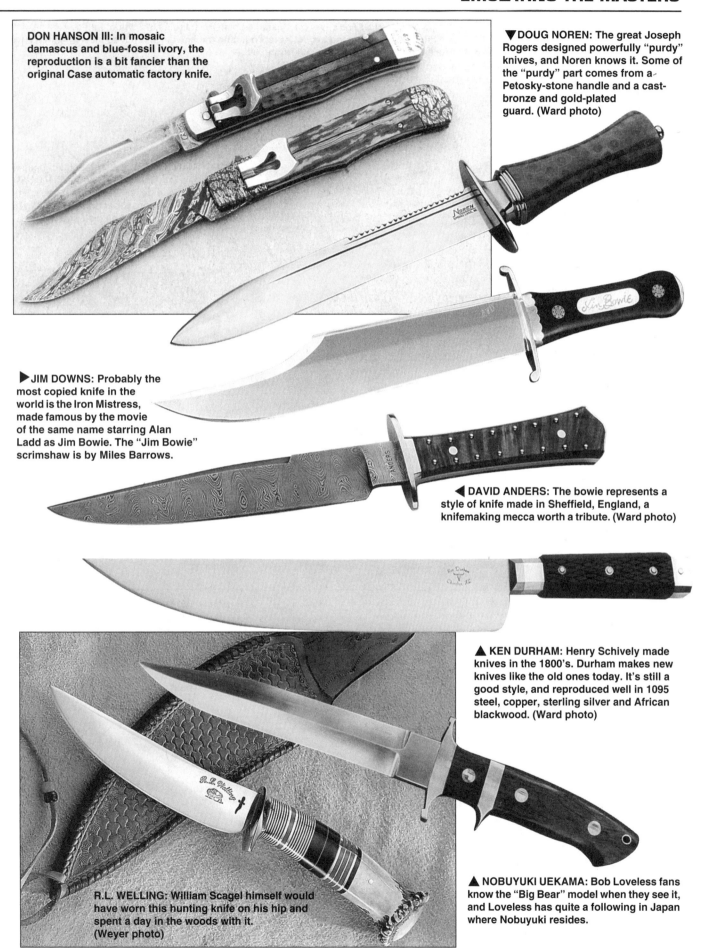

DON HANSON III: In mosaic damascus and blue-fossil ivory, the reproduction is a bit fancier than the original Case automatic factory knife.

▼**DOUG NOREN:** The great Joseph Rogers designed powerfully "purdy" knives, and Noren knows it. Some of the "purdy" part comes from a Petosky-stone handle and a cast-bronze and gold-plated guard. (Ward photo)

▶**JIM DOWNS:** Probably the most copied knife in the world is the Iron Mistress, made famous by the movie of the same name starring Alan Ladd as Jim Bowie. The "Jim Bowie" scrimshaw is by Miles Barrows.

◀**DAVID ANDERS:** The bowie represents a style of knife made in Sheffield, England, a knifemaking mecca worth a tribute. (Ward photo)

▲**KEN DURHAM:** Henry Schively made knives in the 1800's. Durham makes new knives like the old ones today. It's still a good style, and reproduced well in 1095 steel, copper, sterling silver and African blackwood. (Ward photo)

R.L. WELLING: William Scagel himself would have worn this hunting knife on his hip and spent a day in the woods with it. (Weyer photo)

▲**NOBUYUKI UEKAMA:** Bob Loveless fans know the "Big Bear" model when they see it, and Loveless has quite a following in Japan where Nobuyuki resides.

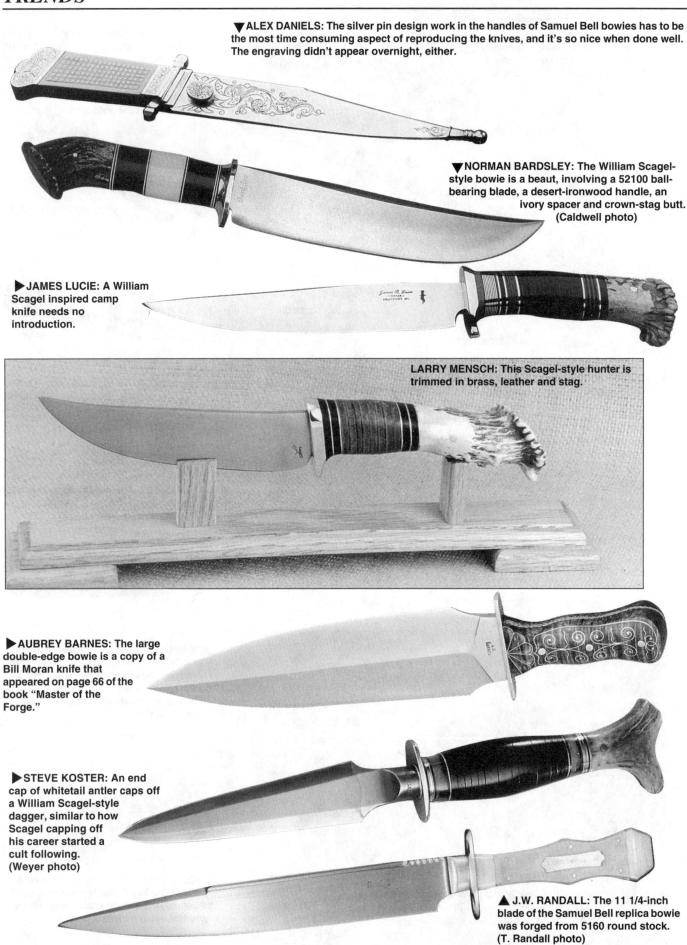

▼ALEX DANIELS: The silver pin design work in the handles of Samuel Bell bowies has to be the most time consuming aspect of reproducing the knives, and it's so nice when done well. The engraving didn't appear overnight, either.

▼NORMAN BARDSLEY: The William Scagel-style bowie is a beaut, involving a 52100 ball-bearing blade, a desert-ironwood handle, an ivory spacer and crown-stag butt. (Caldwell photo)

►JAMES LUCIE: A William Scagel inspired camp knife needs no introduction.

LARRY MENSCH: This Scagel-style hunter is trimmed in brass, leather and stag.

►AUBREY BARNES: The large double-edge bowie is a copy of a Bill Moran knife that appeared on page 66 of the book "Master of the Forge."

►STEVE KOSTER: An end cap of whitetail antler caps off a William Scagel-style dagger, similar to how Scagel capping off his career started a cult following. (Weyer photo)

▲ J.W. RANDALL: The 11 1/4-inch blade of the Samuel Bell replica bowie was forged from 5160 round stock. (T. Randall photo)

Drop-Point Hunters

WHAT THE CLIP-POINT blade is to a bowie knife, the drop-point blade is to American hunting knives. It always seemed a bit odd that Bob Loveless became so famous, achieving worldwide fame, mind you, for the drop-point hunting blade pattern. After all, it is just a blade shape. The question begged to be asked. What do people from all reaches of the world, especially the Japanese with their incredibly long cultural history in forging knives and swords, find so fascinating about the drop-point hunting knife?

There's no single answer, but possibly a twofold reason. First, the style and shape are both aesthetic and utilitarian, and a perfect shape for hunting and some camping chores. More importantly, though, is the man behind the design, a character

in and of himself. Loveless is not a typical American cowboy, folk hero or storyteller. He is a colorful character with a colorfully striped hat to match. He can light up a room or darken it, depending on his mood.

Though it's not politically correct to mention, there's the ever-present filter-less cigarette perched from between his lips and, speaking of politically incorrect, some of the sentences uttered from behind cigarette and lips are anything but softened. They are direct, matter-of-fact, and to the point. The knifemaker named Loveless is

intelligent and personable in his own right, yet he minces no words and not everything he has to say is positive or pleasant. He also has a memorable logo—a naked lady near the tang of each blade—and he's a master at his craft.

So, it's the soft, sexy blade shape and the rough, unrefined and memorable character behind the pattern that make it legendary in knife circles. Personally, I like the way the blade drops down at the point.

Joe Kertzman

▲ **TERRY PRIMOS:** The temper line on the blade drops at the same rate as the point, and at a similar rate to money falling onto a knife-show table after a collector sees this piece.

▶ **TIMOTHY POTIER:** Two wily woodsmen wait for the opportunity to cut.

▶ **W.J. MCDONALD:** Accompanying the dropped point are powerful materials used in the shapely handle, namely giraffe bone and cocobolo, with mosaic pins adding their own warmth. (S. McDonald photo)

▲ **BRAD RUTHERFORD:** Hunters will get into the elephant ivory handle and the way the mosaic handle pins look like miniature bull's-eyes. (Weyer photo)

TRENDS

MIKE DRAPER: Blade sprouts from a perfectly patterned, stabilized, spalted-maple handle. (BladeGallery.com photo)

▲ J.D. CLAY: Ivory Micarta® and bead-blasted handle give a drop-point hunter a good, tactical look and feel.

▼DICK FAUST: The blade is long enough for other chores, but dropped point, full tang, guard and wood handle prepare it for the hunt. (Ward photo)

▶BRUCE BERGLIN: The O-1 carbon steel blade, lightly file-worked spine, elk antler handle, red spacers and Loveless rivets define it as an outdoorsman's knife. The size and shape make it a drop-point hunter.

◀ DAN FARR: The drop-point hunter, in its most unadulterated form, remains attractive.

▶ANDREW MCLURKIN: This one reaches out like the nose of an anteater digging for tasty treats.

▶DANIEL EHRENBERGER: A green G-10 handle meets 224 layers of damascus at a nickel silver guard, and it's a party. (T. Ehrenberger photo)

It's Where You Wear 'Em

AS THE WORLD continues to become more and more politically correct, overprotective, sue happy and willing to submit to ever-increasing government regulations and control, it's nice to see the knife community moving at its own pace and often in the opposite direction.

Right now, you might be screaming, "What do you mean? Are you crazy? There are more knife laws than ever in history!" Well, that's true, but while switchblade carry has been outlawed in most states for quite some time,

easy-open, one-hand folders, some with spring-assisted openers that must be initiated with thumb movement, are ever increasing in popularity and taking over where switchblades left off. Knives that self-open when drawn from their sheaths are replacing gravity knives. And, there are thousands more makers of bowie knives, tantos, fighters, neck knives, tactical folders, small fixed blades and boot knives than ever in the United States and, for that matter, worldwide.

One neat continuation of the craft is in neck, boot, vest, hip, chest, small-of-the-back, leg and cross-draw knives and sheaths. Flooding the market are multi-carry sheath systems, as well as Kydex®, Concealex® and other form-fitting sheath materials.

These days, there's as much emphasis placed on "where you wear 'em" as on "what you carry."

Joe Kertzman

CHRISTOPH DERINGER: Here's a stocking stuffer (literally) made of ebony, nickel silver, brass and O-1 tool steel. (BladeGallery.com photo)

▲ WADE COLTER: The mother-of-pearl and damascus handle of the intriguing auto folder is shaped like a tuxedo vest to remind you where to wear it. (BladeGallery.com photo)

▶RAY KIRK: As he would handle a deck of playing cards, Ray cut the neck knife "thin to win." (Ward photo)

▲ ANDERS HOGSTROM: The leg dagger is adorned with a stunningly handsome birch handle and sheath, a Japanese-style, clay-tempered blade, removable handle, and antiqued and textured copper guard and butt cap. (BladeGallery.com photo)

▶LARRY RAMEY: There's something about the titanium neck knife with chord-wrap handle that brings you back to bare essentials and a sense of self-reliance. (Hawkinson photo)

▶WALLY HAYES: You might be clearing your throat often with the frog-skin handle dangling dangerously close to the Adam's apple from the neck sheath. (Tighe photo)

▶MIKE SNODY: Neck-in-neck are the Ronin and Compadre pieces. (Hoffman photo)

▼GLENN SMIT: Holes in the 5160-steel handle lighten the load for around-the-neck-and-dangling-down carry, against the chest, next to the heart.

▼DANIEL WINKLER: When drawn from the rawhide sheath, the boot knife stretches 8.62 inches and gives off an air of traditional elegance, including file-steel blade and mammoth-ivory handle. (BladeGallery.com photo)

JERRY LAIRSON: You might want to allow the fluted, black-pearl handle to stick out of the boot a little for show. (Ward photo)

▲ PETER DEL RASO: The "Chubby Boot Knife" was made for walking and it's going to walk all over you.

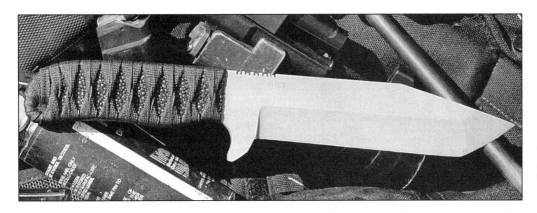

WALLY HAYES: It's fierce and formidable. (Goulet photo)

Fierce and Fantastic Fighters

THERE HAS BEEN discussion in the knife industry about how it might not be a good idea to call fighting knives "fighters." If those with anti-knife sentiments hear the term "fighter" or "fighting knife," that might be argument enough to get a grassroots movement under way to ban them, to outlaw the knives so that they can not be carried because they are "weapons." There's a fairly persuasive argument that we should not promote knives as weapons at all, but as tools. This angers makers of tactical-type knives.

I doubt fighters will ever be banned, and here's why: there is nothing about a fighting knife that identifies it as such. We already have laws in some states that ban the concealed carry of knives with blades under 3 or 2 1/2 inches. Most states have already outlawed the carry of switchblades, gravity knives and butterfly knives for anyone other than police and military, who have gotten exemptions in writing.

A fighter is a fixed blade, usually, but it can be a folder. The blade spines are likely thick, though thin ones do exist because they are more ergonomic, light and better for fine severing. Fighters tend to have tanto-type or clip-point blades, but some fighters incorporate spear-point and even drop-point blades. Some are long. Others are short. Some have practically indestructible, bulletproof handles, and others have full tangs and no handle slabs at all, or wood handles, or ray-skin grips with chord wraps, or bone or stag.

To ban fighters would be to ban knives. Not calling them "fighters" would put us in an amusing quandary. Do we call them "Tough Little Rascals," or "Choppers," or "Brawny Blades," or how about "Big, Ugly, Nasty Knives?" Nah, let's stick to "Fierce and Fantastic Fighters."

Joe Kertzman

▶**ART TYCER:** Most fighters don't have California-buckeye-burl handles or damascus blades, but we all have to wage our own battles. (Ward photo)

◀**PAUL LEBATARD:** The Survivor and Fighter would do well marooned on an island and might even attract a following of reality TV watchers.

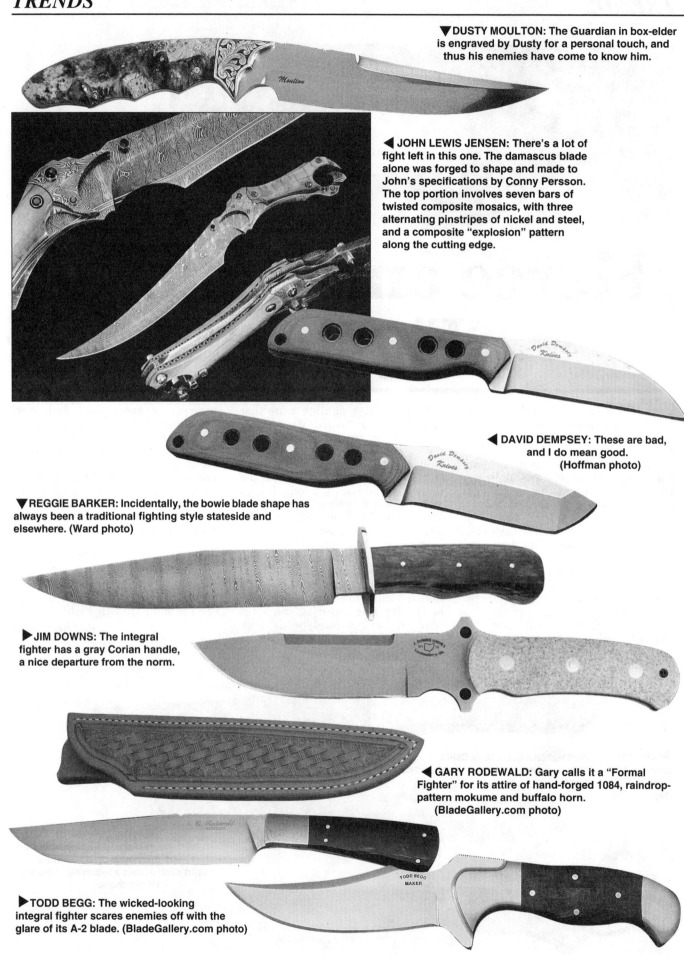

▼DUSTY MOULTON: The Guardian in box-elder is engraved by Dusty for a personal touch, and thus his enemies have come to know him.

◀JOHN LEWIS JENSEN: There's a lot of fight left in this one. The damascus blade alone was forged to shape and made to John's specifications by Conny Persson. The top portion involves seven bars of twisted composite mosaics, with three alternating pinstripes of nickel and steel, and a composite "explosion" pattern along the cutting edge.

◀DAVID DEMPSEY: These are bad, and I do mean good. (Hoffman photo)

▼REGGIE BARKER: Incidentally, the bowie blade shape has always been a traditional fighting style stateside and elsewhere. (Ward photo)

▶JIM DOWNS: The integral fighter has a gray Corian handle, a nice departure from the norm.

◀GARY RODEWALD: Gary calls it a "Formal Fighter" for its attire of hand-forged 1084, raindrop-pattern mokume and buffalo horn. (BladeGallery.com photo)

▶TODD BEGG: The wicked-looking integral fighter scares enemies off with the glare of its A-2 blade. (BladeGallery.com photo)

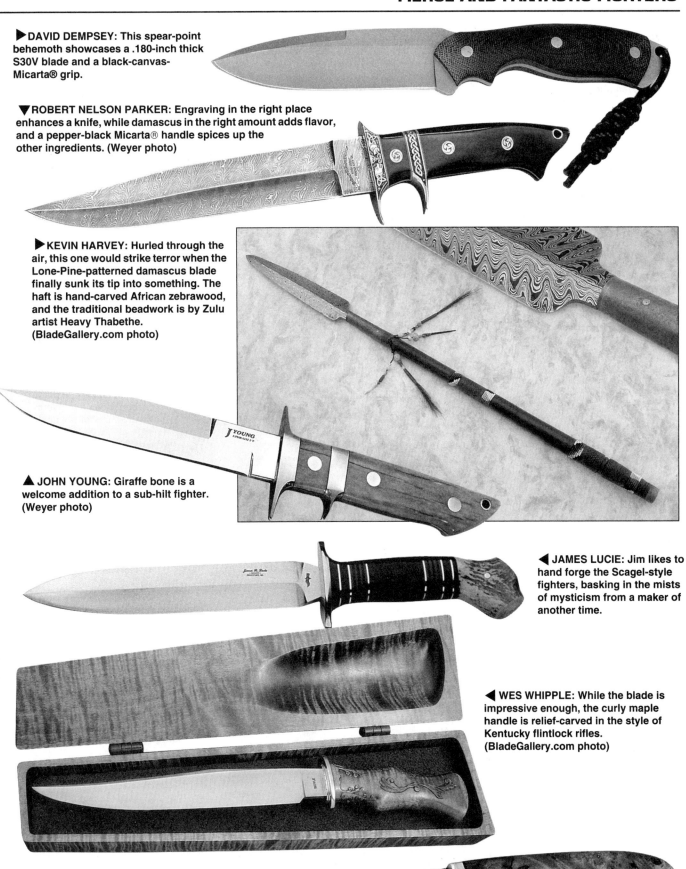

▶DAVID DEMPSEY: This spear-point behemoth showcases a .180-inch thick S30V blade and a black-canvas-Micarta® grip.

▼ROBERT NELSON PARKER: Engraving in the right place enhances a knife, while damascus in the right amount adds flavor, and a pepper-black Micarta® handle spices up the other ingredients. (Weyer photo)

▶KEVIN HARVEY: Hurled through the air, this one would strike terror when the Lone-Pine-patterned damascus blade finally sunk its tip into something. The haft is hand-carved African zebrawood, and the traditional beadwork is by Zulu artist Heavy Thabethe. (BladeGallery.com photo)

▲ JOHN YOUNG: Giraffe bone is a welcome addition to a sub-hilt fighter. (Weyer photo)

◀ JAMES LUCIE: Jim likes to hand forge the Scagel-style fighters, basking in the mists of mysticism from a maker of another time.

◀ WES WHIPPLE: While the blade is impressive enough, the curly maple handle is relief-carved in the style of Kentucky flintlock rifles. (BladeGallery.com photo)

▶JIM ARBUCKLE: A spalted-maple-burl grip sends shivers down the spine of the 440C blade with a long, tapered clip point. (BladeGallery.com photo)

▶ **WADE COLTER:** An overall blood-sucking vampire bat theme is carried out through blade steel, multi-piercing point, winged file work and carved thumb stud. (PointSeven photo)

◀ **GLENN WATERS:** Two blade steels instead of one are all the better for slaying dragons.

▶ **MARK MCCOUN:** Just in front of the stabilized-box-elder grip, the guard flares out like the neck of a python posed to strike.

◀ **TERRY PRIMOS:** Terry's temper line is a telltale sign of blade toughness and overall effectiveness of the design.

▶ **ERIC ERICKSON:** This one was two years in construction and a collaboration of sorts between Eric, Ron Bishop, who forged the blade steel, Bill Behnke, who provided the guard steel, and Larry Fleming, who designed the piece. (Weyer photo)

▶ **MIKE MCRAE:** One of five review knives for his American Bladesmith Society journeyman rating, the fighter features Sambar stag, 5160 steel and brass furniture. (Hoffman photo)

▲ **NICK WHEELER:** The Giraffe Bone Fighter is tall and lean, almost spike-like in appearance. (BladeGallery.com photo)

Tipping the Titanium Scales

IN CELEBRATION OF the birth of his first and only child, a co-worker who's an avid bicycler went to the local bike shop and bought a brand-new mountain bike. The story goes that, to this day, he teases his wife that they need to have another baby so he can get a better bike, and he claims he has gotten her to agree that when and if they have a third child, he gets to buy that titanium bike he's always wanted.

▼**KEVIN HOFFMAN: The titanium frames are barely discernable under embossed and reticulated sterling-silver handle scales.**

Ask a golfer what kind of club heads he or she would prefer if money were no object. Again, titanium will probably rear its "head." Aside from being high-tech, titanium is strong and lightweight. In knifemaking circles, lightweight is a primary consideration. What do knifemakers say again? "That knife is so heavy it feels like an anvil in your pocket." That's it. Only a knifemaker would say something so colorful.

Actually, knives aren't that far removed from mainstream trends and product developments. Cell phones, pagers, laptop computers, video cameras, digital videodisc (DVD) players and global positioning systems (GPS's) are all becoming lightweight, portable and advanced. So are knives.

Knives are also becoming prettier than ever, and titanium can take much of the credit in that regard. The material is easily anodized, like aluminum, into a rainbow of colors, or into one bright, beautiful, almost fluorescent color. Seems like titanium not only acts cutting edge but looks it, too.

New to knives is Timascus, the creation and collaboration of knifemakers Tom Ferry, Bill Cottrell and Chuck Bybee, whose goal it was to create a corrosion-resistant, non-magnetic, lightweight damascus that would lend itself to adding an upscale look to a knife without the disadvantages of steel damascus. Timascus consists of two or more titanium alloys laminated and patterned to resemble steel damascus.

Primarily bolster, blade, frame and liner materials, titanium and Timascus are sensational additions to the wealth of materials available to knifemakers who wish to build the best blades cutting.

Joe Kertzman

ROGER DOLE, TOM MAYO and PHIL BOGUSZEWSKI: "Timascus times four" describes the foursome of folders by Roger (bottom), Phil (two top models) and Tom. Three handles and one bolster are patterned with two or more titanium alloys to resemble damascus and, in these cases, it worked! (BladeGallery.com photo)

▲ **MIKE FRANKLIN: The Serenghetti Tactical Tanto wears a titanium frame with G-10 spacers like a knight wears a suit of armor, and atop it are two "extra" blades that swing down for multiple cutting options. (Hoffman photo)**

►TOM FERRY: Timascus raindrops spill over the handle of Tom's locking-liner folder with jellyroll-damascus blade. (BladeGallery.com photo)

►PAT and WES CRAWFORD: Two different applications of titanium bolsters give a pair of similar knife patterns different looks altogether. The damascus sort of dresses up the bottom one, too, doesn't it? (PointSeven photo)

JEFF HALL: This as a 6AL4V titanium frame lock floating off the page like a helium balloon. (BladeGallery.com photo)

▼TOM ANDERSON: Titanium frames work well with bead-blasted blades, and G-10 would definitely be the bulletproof overlay material of choice. (PointSeven photo)

▼ROGER DOLE: The open back-bar, or spine, of the knife reduces weight, as do the titanium bolsters and liners, thus a heavy-duty knife is lightweight and fast. (BladeGallery.com photo)

▼LARRY RAMEY: The no-frills titanium neck knife is 6 1/2 inches long and costs 50 bucks. (Hawkinson photo)

▲ DES HORN: If a Grade-S titanium handle doesn't ignite the afterburners, a couple Gibeon-Meteorite inlays will send it into orbit. (PointSeven photo)

Feel-Good Fixed Blades

LEAVE THE SHARP edges to the blade, not the grip. Just because a knife is a tool doesn't mean it has to feel like a square chunk of steel in the palm of your hand. It doesn't have to be uncomfortable to hold. In fact, it shouldn't be. Helmets are made for heads and few of them are square (although, maybe some should be). Shoes are fitted for the feet and few are triangular.

So, when building a beefed-up fixed blade for anything from hard-core cutting to delicate detailing, the handle should mold to your hand and the blade should feel like an extension of your fingers. The grip should feel good in the regular, choked-up and even some reverse or backward holds. The blade should be easily indexed, even when you can't keep an eye on it and the cutting medium at the same time. The guard should do its job without getting in the way. The piece, as a whole, should be large enough to feel right and small enough to maneuver.

Maybe that's asking a whole lot. These are knifemakers, not massage therapists. The knives have to cut, not tickle your palm and make you giddy. They have to be safe to use, not nice to hold. Knives are tools, not clothing accessories that should feel good next to your skin.

By looking at the examples built by conscientious, exacting professionals today, it's hard to tell they're toolmakers, not anatomists. These guys want to hand you something you can smile about and hold for days without knowing it's there. They want your cutting experience to be pleasurable. They want you to feel pampered like a puffed-up, powdered and towel-dried vacationer exiting a spa. Whew! It's getting steamy.

Joe Kertzman

▼**PAOLO SCORDIA:** It feels good just to look at the Latin Stiletto.

◀**ROBERT BEATY:** Photography captures as best it can the three-dimensional rounded look and feel of the handle, and a photo is worth 1,000 words. (BladeGallery.com photo)

GENO DENNING: To help you feel good, or to make the knife feel good in your hand, Geno uses horn with indentations for fingers and palm to grip onto while cutting. (Hoffman photo)

▲ **ED FOWLER:** Fowler is a bit renowned in the knife industry for sheep-horn handles made for cradling and cupping. (BladeGallery.com photo)

DICK FAUST: The curved and dropped handle allows the fingers to slide between it and guard and rest soundly in their places. The box elder, itself, however, is at constant unrest.

PAT MULLER: The sub-hilt is designed for a non-slip grip, but the maker ensured comfort in his smooth application, interpretation and ultimate manifestation of the style. (Ward photo)

BERNARD BERTHOLUS: His treatment of the wood handle, how he carved it with a slight lip near the top and a groove down the center, makes it easy to grab onto and hold.

JASON KING: In case you couldn't figure out where the handles flare out for grasping, Jason used California buckeye burl patterned in just the right places. (H. King photo)

WILLIAM ENGLE: William lent a hand to this design. (PointSeven photo)

MARVIN SOLOMON: As if the mammoth ivory wasn't funky enough, Marvin detailed the bolster and made the blade wave to its spectators. (Ward photo)

TAKAO MAE: The contoured handle complements the complicated convex grind lines of the blade.

Deer Hunters, Buffalo Skinners and Game Processors

THERE'S NOT A hunting knife following these words that wouldn't be fantastic to own. There's not a knifemaker in the group who wouldn't be fun to hunt with and watch in action. The skills these makers exhibit are humbling, really. There's a talented group of guys and gals out there who make good, down-to-earth, standup knives for others to use, feel safe using and get the job done. These knifemakers are sending their brethren into the woods packing good pieces of steel, patting them on the backs and wishing them safe and prosperous journeys. That's commendable. It's forthright, it's honest and it's heartwarming.

Not one of the knives, not one of the makers is likely to gain notoriety other than right here, right now. This is their forum. Here's where the blades shine and the knives do the talking. It feels good to help provide the platform, because worthiness as a prerequisite for print has been met a thousand times over. These knives are worthy of our worship.

The amazing thing, too, is that they weren't stamped out at some factory, that a person with some metalworking skills, a good eye and strong will is able to stop catching the bus and riding to work every day to punch a clock and make someone else rich. These makers took a chance, at least some of them, quit their jobs, outfitted their shops, bought their own insurance and went to work, hoping to sell enough knives to feed and clothe themselves and their families. After all, when you get right down to the heart of the matter, that's what hunting and gathering is all about.

Joe Kertzman

▶MARVIN SOLOMON: The pattern is as spirited as the damascus, and begs for a hunter's cold hand to cup it and cut with it. (Ward photo)

ED BAUMGARDNER: There he stood, ramrod straight, with spine of steel, decorated uniform—a knife in sheep-horn clothing. (PointSeven photo)

▼LEO ROBERTSON: Get a load of this gut hook with grand ironwood grip.

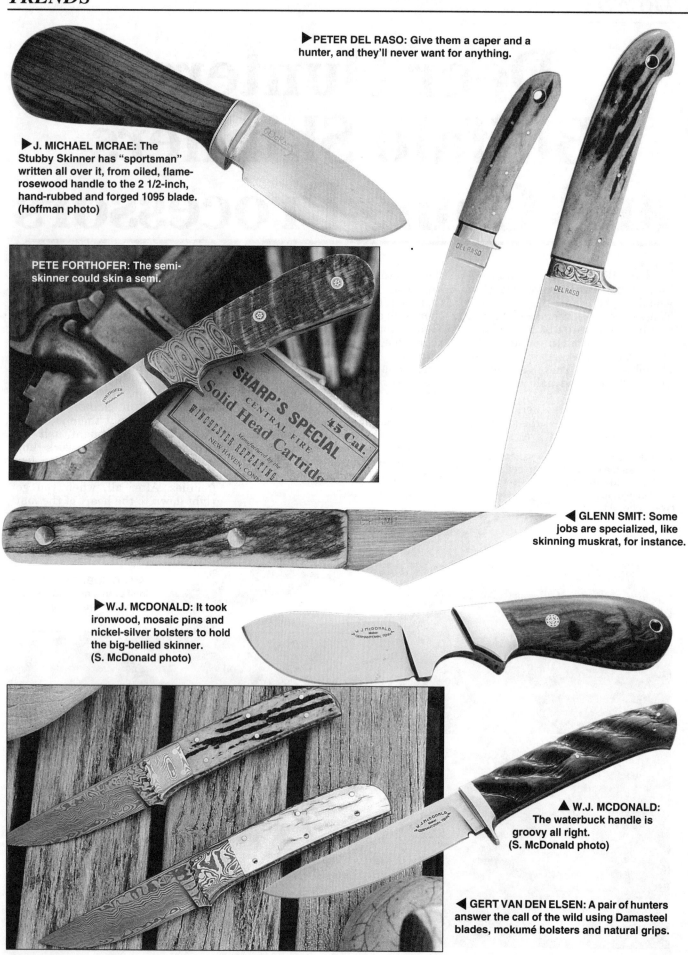

J. MICHAEL MCRAE: The Stubby Skinner has "sportsman" written all over it, from oiled, flame-rosewood handle to the 2 1/2-inch, hand-rubbed and forged 1095 blade. (Hoffman photo)

PETER DEL RASO: Give them a caper and a hunter, and they'll never want for anything.

PETE FORTHOFER: The semi-skinner could skin a semi.

GLENN SMIT: Some jobs are specialized, like skinning muskrat, for instance.

W.J. MCDONALD: It took ironwood, mosaic pins and nickel-silver bolsters to hold the big-bellied skinner. (S. McDonald photo)

W.J. MCDONALD: The waterbuck handle is groovy all right. (S. McDonald photo)

GERT VAN DEN ELSEN: A pair of hunters answer the call of the wild using Damasteel blades, mokumé bolsters and natural grips.

▶M.W. "IKE" TOPLISS: A personalized hunting knife might garner a little envy at camp. The engraving is by Tanya Van Hoy.

▶LLOYD PENDLETON: Lloyd went stag, but he didn't stagger. Check out those blades and bolsters. (PointSeven photo)

◀NICK WHEELER: The maker sculpted a myrtle-wood handle and stainless steel bolsters, adding mosaic pins and fancy filework. (BladeGallery.com photo)

▶NICK WHEELER: Stainless steel pins stand out in contrast to the milky-white ivory grip. (BladeGallery.com photo)

◀WILLARD PATRICK: The Pro-Skinner goes to work using a vine-pattern-fileworked ATS-34 blade and a stabilized-elephant-bone handle. (BladeGallery.com photo)

▶T.D. OLIVER: The twist-pattern damascus hunter is crowned with a crown-stag handle.

◀AUDRA DRAPER: The sheep-horn handle makes this one a heavy hitter. (BladeGallery.com photo)

▶**LOYD THOMSEN: A** trailing-point skinner is outfitted with a 320-layer damascus blade and a stabilized black ash handle.

GENO DENNING: Kudos for the little semi-skinner with Kudo-wood handle. (Hoffman photo)

▼**DICK FAUST:** Fillet of fish anyone?

▶**BILL SOWELL:** Imagine extracting this one from the sheath, feeling the grooves in the sheep-horn grip and allowing the light to refract off the mokumé bolster. (Hoffman photo)

◀**GEORGE COUSINO:** Stabilized maple and stag sure group together nicely on a grip. (Weyer photo)

▼**TOM LEWIS:** There's something about the big-bellied blades, especially in damascus, that bring out those hunter and gatherer instincts.

▶**CHUCK PATRICK:** Chuck just did what he does best in building a damascus hunter with thick, stitched-leather sheath for toting purposes.

◀ **LYNN MAXFIELD:** The lock-back folder was designed for field dressing deer and elk. The Montana-elk-antler handle helps it blend into its surroundings.

◀ **JOHN WALKER:** His and hers? John says they're short and heavy with plenty of thumb purchase using the exaggerated *choils*.

◀ **TAS KERLEY:** Let's throw a Bilby Hunter into the mix.

▶ **WESLEY WHIPPLE:** A length of 52100 ball bearing steel slides neatly into a steel bolster and becomes one with a French walnut handle. (BladeGallery.com photo)

▲ **JON CHRISTENSEN:** A caping knife is saddled with a horse-shin-bone handle. (BladeGallery.com photo)

▶ **JOHN HOLLAND:** Blade and screws are treated with a titanium-nitride coating, gold in color to capture the essence of the curly-maple handle. (Hodge photo)

◀ **STEVE LELAND:** A small hunter, or bird-and-trout knife, is brought to life by a bark-elephant-ivory grip. (Weyer photo)

◀ **BOB LAY:** You don't see maple burl and elk antler together often, unless in the woods. (Weyer photo)

▶ **LOWELL LOCKETT:** A fancy one in redwood burl and mosaic pins is for showing to your pals, and a straightforward stag hunter with brass pins is for getting dirty.

◀ **J.P. HOLMES:** Sometimes knives are all about artistic lines rather than materials. This one's about both. (BladeGallery.com photo)

▶ **PHIL WILSON:** Phil's become quite good at fillet knives, specializing in powder metallurgical steel blades that hold an edge and bend just enough for the fishy stuff.

◀ **JARRELL LAMBERT:** Beefy in build, simple in style, perfect in execution. (Ward photo)

GREG LIGHTFOOT and TOM JOHANNING: Two 7-inch fillet blades equal one 14-inch keeper.

▶LYNN MAXFIELD: The Badger knife was bred for hunting North American big game.

▼ART TYCER: Little touches like a trailing point and finger notches on blade spine make this damascus skinner all that and more. (Ward photo)

JOHN YOUNG: This one constituted the use of a reconstituted stone handle. (Weyer photo)

▼RUSS SUTTON: It will clean bird or trout equally well, but it would be a shame to get it dirty.

▶CHRIS BOWLES: A soft curve begins at the back of the handle and continues along the spine to the tip of the blade. (Ward photo)

JAY HENDRICKSON: The piggyback part of a piggyback knife set refers to how they both ride in the sheath, like two pigs in a poke. (BladeGallery.com photo)

▲ THOMAS BROOME: This one's built.

Locks and Switches

IN THE KNIFE industry, there are these traditional animals, these history-buff-like beings harkening for days past, ever fashioning, fondling and playing with neoclassical slip-joint folding knives, pulling blades open with two fingers, gazing at their intrinsic forms and features, closing them, smiling, pulling them open again, cutting something and enjoying. They enjoy.

A slip joint has folding blades but no locks to hold them in position. Imagine, no locks! Rather, spring tension is trusted to keep the remarkable cutting contraptions in working order. Don't shy away. Lay your eyes and hands on a pristine,

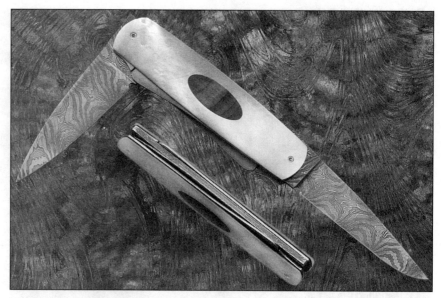

W.E. ANKROM: This is a fine knife in many ways. The mother-of-pearl grip inlaid with black-lip pearl is powerful, as is the double-locking liner that holds both blades open. (BladeGallery.com photo)

exacting, highly fit, finished and embellished slip joint made by one of the masters of the old school. It has an appeal, but does not fit in or belong with this, a small section dealing with the intruders, a wholly different network of knives, those with joints that do more than slip!

To hunt down the intruders and investigate their modern motives, we enter the grounds of the gadget geeks, those people who need locks and switches. Locks-and-switches folk crave gadgets to get them into ghoulish grooves so wicked they laugh insanely as they whet their insatiable appetites on locks, bolts, springs, push buttons, bushings, ball bearings, pivots, pins, cams, shafts and triggers. These are the wild-eyed makers of switchblades, C-Locks, E-Locks, BladeLocks® (Michael Walker), locking liners and

instruments with blades that project and flail around wildly, but within controlled environs.

The locking folders are supposedly safer. They won't accidentally fold up on fingers. They are positively engaged. How far they evolve is up to the vivid imaginations of guys and gals with engineering degrees in knife design. These folks hold tolerances within tens-of-thousandths of inches. Blades nestle snugly in handles waiting for a push of a thumb stud, or for a switch to go off, slamming a spring into steel and sending edged delight into half orbit, nothing holding it within its own atmosphere but a pivot pin attached to a frame and handle slabs.

They are the future. They are the magnanimous, the noble of heart and mind, the makers of knives with locks and switches and everything bewitching that amuse the masses and make folders far out and fun.

Joe Kertzman

▼**CHUCK HAWES:** Chuck designs two butterfly knives, one with big wings and one with small, but both incorporating a lock to keep the handles closed around the blade in the pocket, pack or purse.

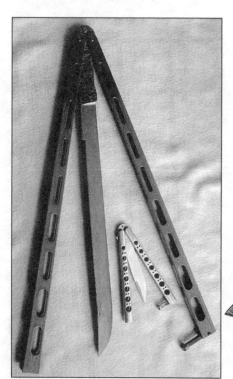

▼**ALLEN ELISHEWITZ:** The Kaiser incorporates an "E-Lock" mechanism, and that most likely stands for "essential and easy to use every day." By the way, the blade is Damasteel and the rocker is Devin Thomas damascus. (PointSeven photo)

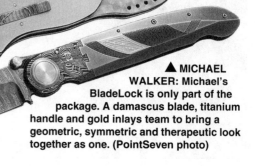

▲ **MICHAEL WALKER:** Michael's BladeLock is only part of the package. A damascus blade, titanium handle and gold inlays team to bring a geometric, symmetric and therapeutic look together as one. (PointSeven photo)

►**CAPTAIN KOYAMA:** Captain's C-Lock engages, doesn't it? The blued titanium and carbon fiber aren't bad, either. (PointSeven photo)

►**JAMES HARRISON:** An ordinary locking-liner folder is made extraordinary through the use of pearl, nickel silver and style. (Weyer photo)

TIM HANCOCK: It's only a lock-back, but I like the way Tim carved the mechanism to look like a seashell, file-worked the liners and let the damascus speak for itself. (PointSeven photo)

▼**AL DIPPOLD:** Before releasing the latch, make sure you palm the mammoth ivory and rub the damascus a little for good luck. (Ward photo)

►**MICHAEL VAGNINO, TIM HANCOCK and BOYD BRITT:** Here's a triple action from a trio of magnificent knifemakers. (PointSeven photo)

▼**RUSS SUTTON:** The locking liner is easily accessed and recessed where ruby thumb stud slides into the Bob Eggerling mosaic-damascus bolster. Tiger coral grip and Devin-Thomas-damascus blade stand up to be counted.

▲ **DON HANSON III:** A reproduction of an old Case Cutlery automatic knife in mosaic damascus and blue-fossil ivory, this one is embellished with a gold release, a touch of class for the gents or ladies.

The Sword Alliance

IT TRULY IS an alliance. Sword makers are a breed of men to be reckoned with and respected.

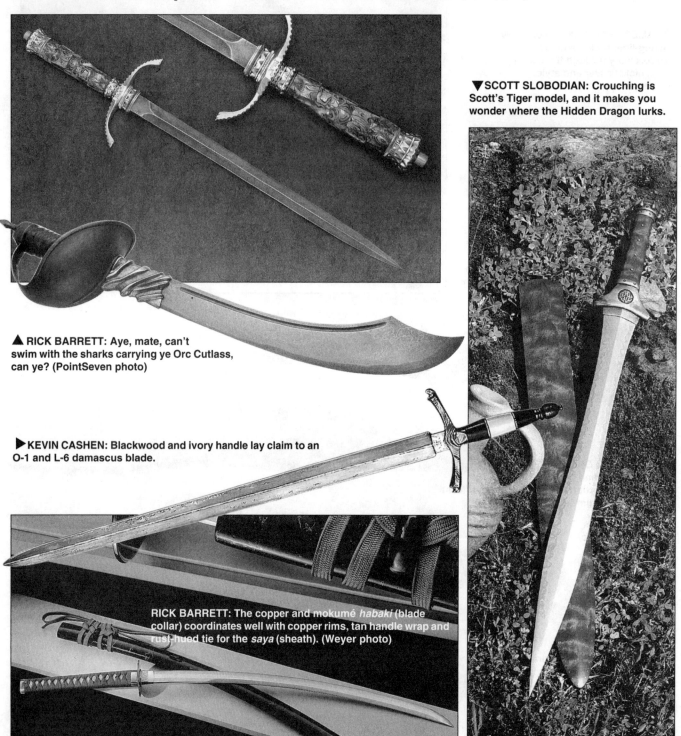

BILLY KOJETIN: File-worked nickel silver, mosaic paua shell and Heather Harvey "ladder-and-flash" damascus play off each other until a circle of light appears above the blade and blesses all who use it. (BladeGallery.com photo)

SCOTT SLOBODIAN: Crouching is Scott's Tiger model, and it makes you wonder where the Hidden Dragon lurks.

▲ **RICK BARRETT:** Aye, mate, can't swim with the sharks carrying ye Orc Cutlass, can ye? (PointSeven photo)

▶**KEVIN CASHEN:** Blackwood and ivory handle lay claim to an O-1 and L-6 damascus blade.

RICK BARRETT: The copper and mokumé *habaki* (blade collar) coordinates well with copper rims, tan handle wrap and rust-hued tie for the *saya* (sheath). (Weyer photo)

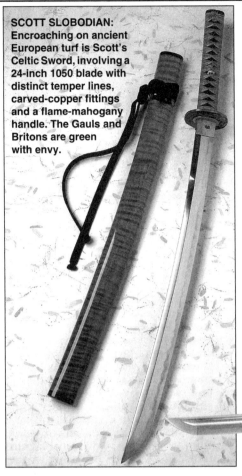

SCOTT SLOBODIAN: Encroaching on ancient European turf is Scott's Celtic Sword, involving a 24-inch 1050 blade with distinct temper lines, carved-copper fittings and a flame-mahogany handle. The Gauls and Britons are green with envy.

EDWARD KALFAYAN: The Bill Behnke damascus blade stretches 37 inches on a two-handed Norman sword, as if a warrior wouldn't be able to tell he needed two hands to heft it. (Weyer photo)

DAVID GOLDBERG: To make the practice katana, Goldberg practiced the art of katana making, often. (PointSeven photo)

▼**STEVE SCHWARZER, WALLY HAYES and DON FOGG:** Three of the best traditional-style, Japanese-sword-making minds team on a 28 1/4-inch piece, with Don's 1086 blade waving its temper line all over town. (PointSeven photo)

▶**DAVID SCHLUETER:** The *shinogi-zukuri* blade has *bo-hi* (fullers) on both sides, while the handle reveals *menuki* (handle charms) of silver alligators with frogs sitting on their backs, all wrapped in lacquered, leather lacing.

▼**KEVIN HARVEY:** The Young Prince's Sword is an exciting piece with a Heather Harvey raindrop damascus blade, carved rosewood-burl handle, and a wrought-iron guard forged from an old ox-wagon wheel. (BladeGallery.com photo)

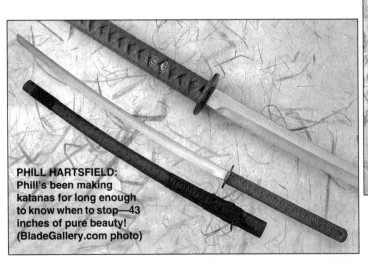

PHILL HARTSFIELD: Phill's been making katanas for long enough to know when to stop—43 inches of pure beauty! (BladeGallery.com photo)

▼**WALLY HAYES:** Wally achieved a splendid double temper line on 15 inches of blade, adding a stingray handle and chord wrap. (PointSeven photo)

On the Edge of the Frontier

THE MODERN WORLD is so far removed from its original natural state. People used to move and be as one with the air, waves, moon and sun. Hunters lied low under cape buffalo robes, faces blackened, tools in hand but reflecting no light, quiet and motionless. Those on horseback listened more than they talked, and rode more *with* the horse than on or against it.

Chores came first at camp and play later. We rose with the sun, sang with the rain and danced with the moon. We weren't afraid to get wet or dirty. We cooked what we caught or killed.

▼NORMAN BARDSLEY: A tip-off of the frontier influence on the Native American Dagger is the beaded-deer-leg-bone handle, copper guard and re-heat-treated saw blade material from a Southwestern ghost town. (Caldwell photo)

Modern re-enactors and rendez-vous goers aren't "escaping" as many might believe. They are remembering, cherishing and honoring tradition because nature is the only truth to them. The knives they bring along, the ones they make using traditional methods, reflect their attitudes, goals and heritage.

Fur trade daggers were hawked for furs. Stag and bone was used for handles. Beads were the ornamentation. Leather smelled as good as it felt. Some knives were forged from the steel of old gun barrels. Brass was malleable enough for guards, bolsters and pommels.

More than anything, the knives had to be sharp. Skinning animals was more motion than work with a sharp knife. Cutting tent stakes was nothing more, nothing less,

than a cutting motion. Steak was sliced. Slits were cut in willow branches. Clothing patterns were traced with steady hand, and it was all motion. Muscle and brawn were saved for wrestling cattle and roping horses. More motion.

The modern world moves at a far different pace, but if you have time, and if you can escape, pack some beef jerky, pick up a patch knife or strap a bowie to your hip, slip on those buckskins you rarely wear and take a drive past the concrete and steel to a place where the wind whips through nothing but trees and bushes. Look out at the horizon and let your instincts take over. Listen to the spirits that call you there and return to a natural state. It's right there waiting for you, on the edge of the frontier.

Joe Kertzman

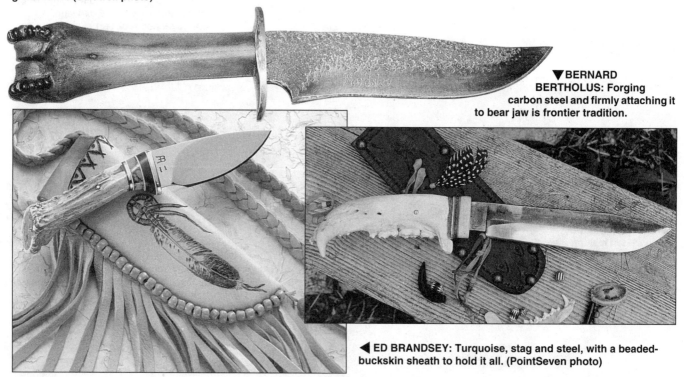

▼BERNARD BERTHOLUS: Forging carbon steel and firmly attaching it to bear jaw is frontier tradition.

◀ED BRANDSEY: Turquoise, stag and steel, with a beaded-buckskin sheath to hold it all. (PointSeven photo)

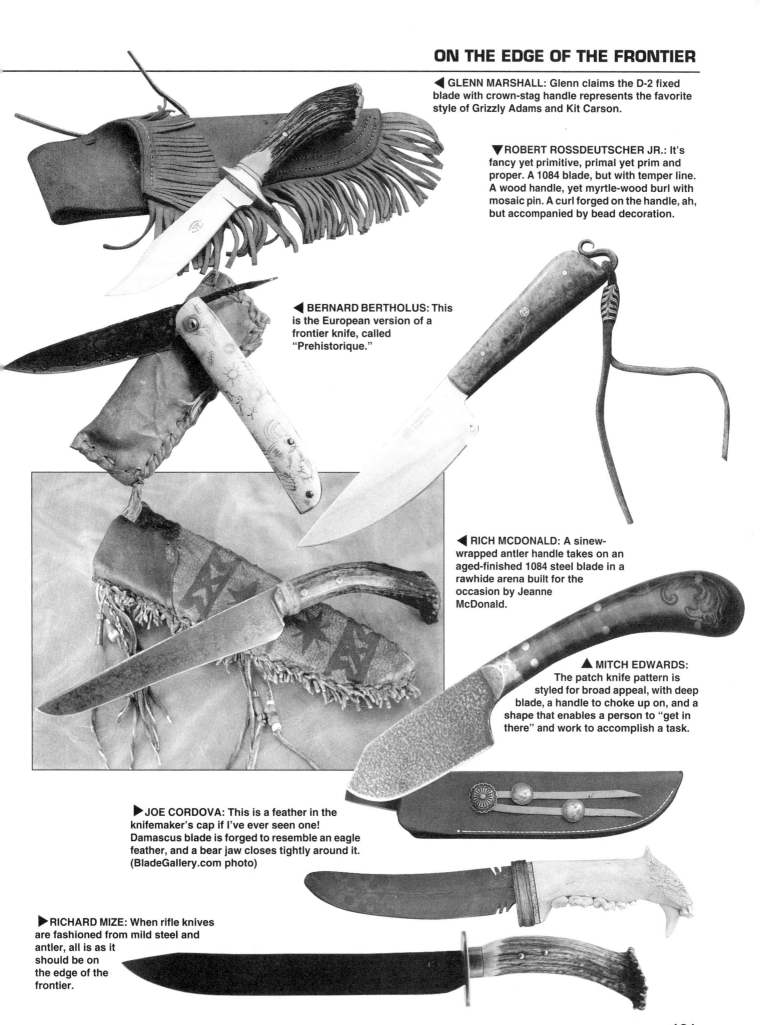

ON THE EDGE OF THE FRONTIER

◄ GLENN MARSHALL: Glenn claims the D-2 fixed blade with crown-stag handle represents the favorite style of Grizzly Adams and Kit Carson.

▼ ROBERT ROSSDEUTSCHER JR.: It's fancy yet primitive, primal yet prim and proper. A 1084 blade, but with temper line. A wood handle, yet myrtle-wood burl with mosaic pin. A curl forged on the handle, ah, but accompanied by bead decoration.

◄ BERNARD BERTHOLUS: This is the European version of a frontier knife, called "Prehistorique."

◄ RICH MCDONALD: A sinew-wrapped antler handle takes on an aged-finished 1084 steel blade in a rawhide arena built for the occasion by Jeanne McDonald.

▲ MITCH EDWARDS: The patch knife pattern is styled for broad appeal, with deep blade, a handle to choke up on, and a shape that enables a person to "get in there" and work to accomplish a task.

► JOE CORDOVA: This is a feather in the knifemaker's cap if I've ever seen one! Damascus blade is forged to resemble an eagle feather, and a bear jaw closes tightly around it. (BladeGallery.com photo)

► RICHARD MIZE: When rifle knives are fashioned from mild steel and antler, all is as it should be on the edge of the frontier.

▼R. BOYES: The primitive-style bowie knife sports a modern-Micarta® handle, but a more traditional brass bolster and pins, and a fringed-leather sheath by Doug Bandl.

▶JEFF CLAIBORNE: Forged from a 50-caliber Hawken barrel, the blade was then fire blued and attached to a maple wood handle for "tomahawkin' with a Hawken."

DANIEL WINKLER: A cowboy bowie rides high in the rawhide saddle, with fringed beads, tin cones and horse hair trailing behind it. (BladeGallery.com photo)

▶MICK WARDELL: The appreciation for a carbon-damascus, drop-point hunter with stag handle hasn't escaped this English maker.

▲ GIL GUIGNARD: The rustic finish on the 5160 blade sells it as a primitive piece of workmanship, bedecked also in brass and stag for good measure.

▶BILL HART: One of the prettier versions of a forged rifleman's knife has a stylishly upswept blade, a curlicue guard and a dropped stag handle for getting a firm grip on the situation.

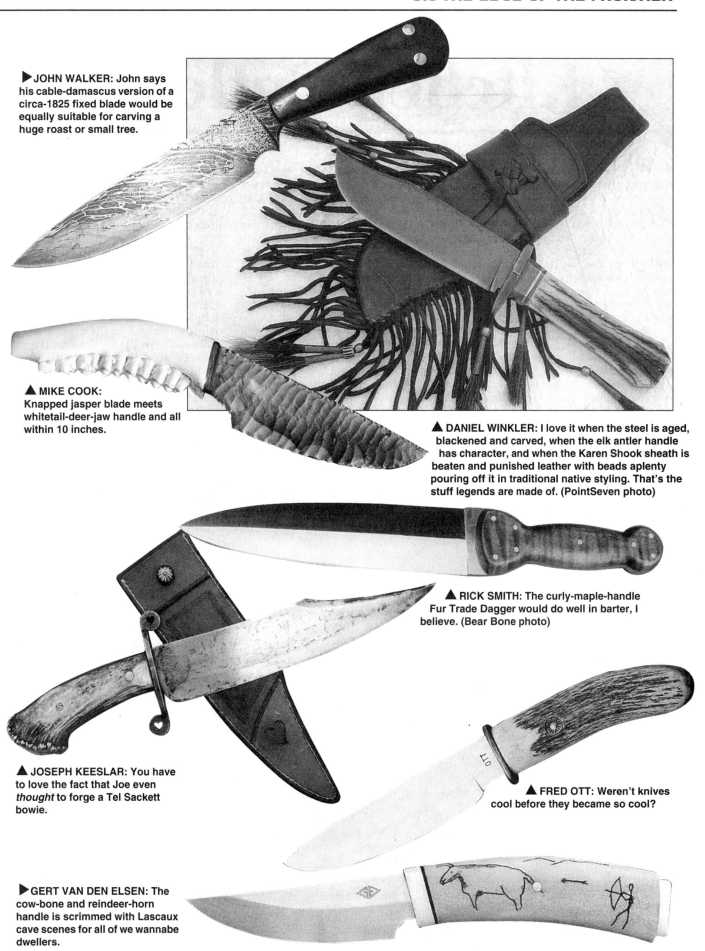

▶JOHN WALKER: John says his cable-damascus version of a circa-1825 fixed blade would be equally suitable for carving a huge roast or small tree.

▲ MIKE COOK: Knapped jasper blade meets whitetail-deer-jaw handle and all within 10 inches.

▲ DANIEL WINKLER: I love it when the steel is aged, blackened and carved, when the elk antler handle has character, and when the Karen Shook sheath is beaten and punished leather with beads aplenty pouring off it in traditional native styling. That's the stuff legends are made of. (PointSeven photo)

▲ RICK SMITH: The curly-maple-handle Fur Trade Dagger would do well in barter, I believe. (Bear Bone photo)

▲ JOSEPH KEESLAR: You have to love the fact that Joe even *thought* to forge a Tel Sackett bowie.

▲ FRED OTT: Weren't knives cool before they became so cool?

▶GERT VAN DEN ELSEN: The cow-bone and reindeer-horn handle is scrimmed with Lascaux cave scenes for all of we wannabe dwellers.

Kitchen Cutlery

WHEN KNIFEMAKERS BREAK out the kitchen cutlery, it's unlike any other homebrewed chef withdrawing a few select paring knives and cleavers from the butcher block. Have you ever wondered what a knifemaker cuts her or his steak with, or garden vegetables, or mangos? It's downright amazing, actually; yet, at the same time, it's not all that surprising that knifemakers fashion kitchen cutlery out of anything from Micarta® handles to oosic and oak grips, and from BG-42 steel to damascus blades.

Knifemakers make sure their kitchen knives cut as well as their working knives. You see, to a fellow who builds blades for a living, knives are tools, and why should chef's knives be any different? While the average American might view kitchen cutlery as utensils with which to prepare dinner, the typical knifemaker is thinking, "OK, my

truck breaks down on the way back from hunting camp and there's not a gas station for miles. It's a two-day hike, and I have no tent. I brought my meat cleaver along for processing game, and it's a good thing I fixed it up with a BG-42 blade because it should bite well into small limbs for shelter building."

There's a term called "overbuilding" and like any car or body shop mechanic worth his salt, a knifemaker overbuilds knives. They bring edges to hair-splitting sharpness and handles to 1,000-pound-pressure holding wickedness. When finished, not only can the steel cut, the knives look like edged art.

The forged tableware coming from some smithies' shops is a far

cry from the pieces Grandma brought out on special occasions. These things are for hearty meals eaten by men built to lumberjack-like proportions. Nothing but pewter, wood, copper and steel are good enough for cutting up pork roast or carving off the first turkey drumstick.

Do these knives serve toward the betterment of society? Well, maybe not, but it's nice to see artists so involved in their work that even they, the knifemakers, become eccentric. You don't have to be president of a Fortune 500 company to take pride in your work, and even CEO's don't eat this good!

Joe Kertzman

▼**PAT MULLER:** The oosic-handle cleaver comes right at you with dramatic damascus chopping blade.

▲ **JOE SZILASKI:** Joe wants to have a forged tableware party.

◄ **JIM ARBUCKLE:** This 8-inch chef's knife showcases a deep finger *choil* to make it easy to grip with wet or slippery hands. (Blade Gallery.com photo)

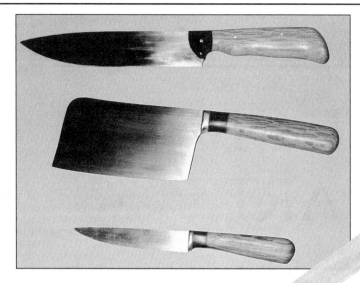

◀ THOMAS GERNER: Horn and she-oak handles give character to a chef's knife, cleaver and paring knife.

▼ RICH MCDONALD: Rich gave them an aged finish, curly-maple handles and pewter bolsters for an overall antique patina that pleases the palate.

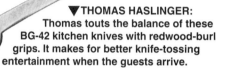

▼ THOMAS HASLINGER: Thomas touts the balance of these BG-42 kitchen knives with redwood-burl grips. It makes for better knife-tossing entertainment when the guests arrive.

▲ TRACE RINALDI: This is about as tactical as a kitchen knife gets, so here's hoping no one burned dinner. (Hoffman photo)

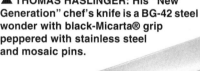

▲ THOMAS HASLINGER: His "New Generation" chef's knife is a BG-42 steel wonder with black-Micarta® grip peppered with stainless steel and mosaic pins.

◀ PETE FORTHOFER: Mammoth ivory, mokumé and mosaic make for a great meal.

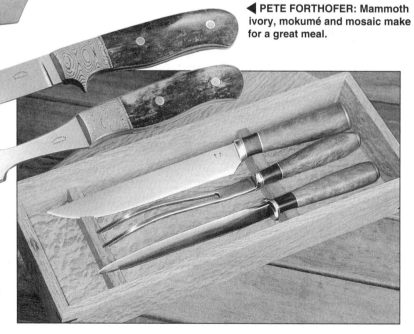

▶ THOMAS GERNER: Lace she-oak, red-ebony spacers and nickel-silver fittings put this carving set past the "Get out the fine silver" status.

STATE OF
THE ART

Why do people attend art shows? Is there something *in it* for them? Appreciation for art takes many forms, probably the foremost of which is being deeply moved by the talent and insight of another. Some folks just like looking at pretty pictures, but others try to decide what the artist's thoughts were when he or she created a particular work. Self-appointed aficionados become engrossed in movements, styles, patterns and themes. Novices get more into the mood than the meaning or interpretation

Art is history; it's romance; it can be cultural; sensual; disruptive; disgusting; appealing; awe-inspiring; surreal; all too real; pompous; practical; forgiving; revealing; scene-stealing; dark; dry; morbid; vivid; or alive. It can also be much more. Art can be all engrossing and encompassing.

When art and knives cross paths, there's more than entertainment value at stake. There is another dimension, not just artist and audience, but artist, audience and *function*. Knives are cutting implements. They have purpose and usefulness. They are not for entertainment or display only. These are tools that can come through in a pinch. They can save lives or open mail with equal aptitude and panache. Add an art element to cutlery and you have sharp cutting tools in more ways than one. These are scintillating loppers, eye poppers and woodchoppers, all rolled into one.

This makes being artist much more challenging than lounging around in the studio, playing classical music and waiting for inspiration. Design and utility are prerequisites to boldness and beauty. There are no wine-and-cheese-tasting or "opening night at the exhibit" parties for knife artists. No, they attend knife shows.

"That piece doesn't do anything for me, personally," or, "That's the best overall representative work in the exhibition," are meaningless, nonsensical observances or statements. They don't matter. Art is subjective. As they say, "To each his or her own." Maybe that is the appeal.

Why do people attend art shows? There is something *in it* for everyone. Enjoy the art *and* knife show.

Joe Kertzman

Incredible Inlays, Overlays, Inserts and Spacers

KNIFEMAKERS ARE CREATING major inroads in handle inlays, overlays, inserts and spacers. It used to be that a stacked-leather knife grip with stag or ebony spacers marked a complex design. Add a red liner or some red and black synthetic spacers, and it was considered exquisite. Now, knifemakers with art, jewelry, machining, blacksmithing, metallurgy and gemology backgrounds are marrying a myriad of materials. Mother-of-pearl, gold, silver, precious stones, wood, ivory, bone, stag and the colorful and curly horns of the most exotic animals are combined with steel, aluminum, titanium or cast metal. It is all very exhilarating and aesthetically pleasing.

Smooth lines, carving, engraving, gold- and silver-wire inlay so exquisite it belongs in museums, are the rule and not the exception. With so many natural stones and gems in a rainbow of colors from which to choose, and with gun bluing, etching, metal fusing, and colorful blade heat-treating capabilities, knives exude vivid themes from grip to tip.

There are even some sly blade smiths encrusting steel blades with gold. Add some inlays in a few select places, or a thumb-stud inlay and handle spacers, and there's enough to look at while fumbling through your wallet for a few Ben Franklins.

Pearls come in black, green, pink, yellow and blue hues, not just white mother-of-pearl. While the world has gotten smaller, the variety of materials has become more vast. African blackwood makes a striking handle inlay on the right knife, and Swedish birch is pleasant on another. Abalone radiates with color, while turquoise brings one back to earth tones.

Life is full of little surprises, so why not knives? Even back spacers—the area of knives between the two handle slabs and opposite the blade edge—is a favorite place to park a little pearl or ivory spacer. Inside the handle of a folding knife is a good spot for precious stone inlays that catch the eye. Seems knives are sparkling from all ends these days, or is that just the sparkle reflecting off the makers' eyes?

Joe Kertzman

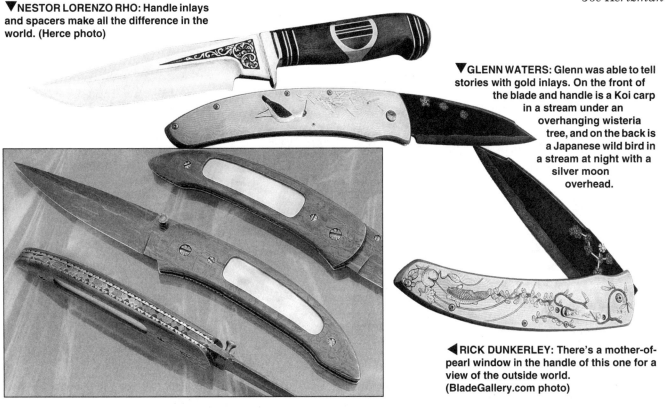

▼**NESTOR LORENZO RHO:** Handle inlays and spacers make all the difference in the world. (Herce photo)

▼**GLENN WATERS:** Glenn was able to tell stories with gold inlays. On the front of the blade and handle is a Koi carp in a stream under an overhanging wisteria tree, and on the back is a Japanese wild bird in a stream at night with a silver moon overhead.

◄**RICK DUNKERLEY:** There's a mother-of-pearl window in the handle of this one for a view of the outside world. (BladeGallery.com photo)

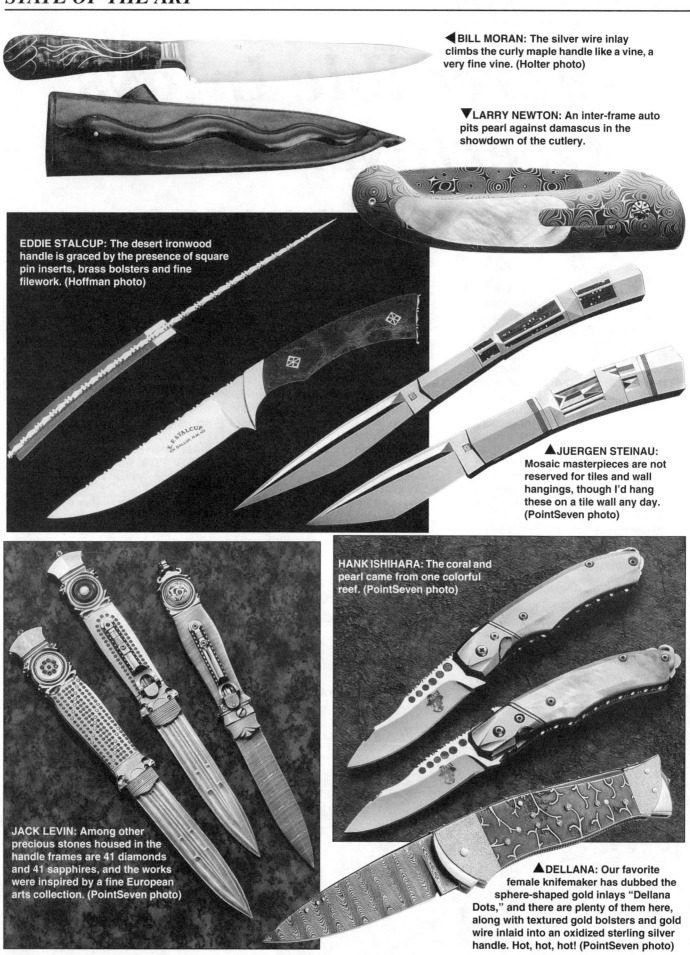

BILL MORAN: The silver wire inlay climbs the curly maple handle like a vine, a very fine vine. (Holter photo)

LARRY NEWTON: An inter-frame auto pits pearl against damascus in the showdown of the cutlery.

EDDIE STALCUP: The desert ironwood handle is graced by the presence of square pin inserts, brass bolsters and fine filework. (Hoffman photo)

JUERGEN STEINAU: Mosaic masterpieces are not reserved for tiles and wall hangings, though I'd hang these on a tile wall any day. (PointSeven photo)

HANK ISHIHARA: The coral and pearl came from one colorful reef. (PointSeven photo)

JACK LEVIN: Among other precious stones housed in the handle frames are 41 diamonds and 41 sapphires, and the works were inspired by a fine European arts collection. (PointSeven photo)

DELLANA: Our favorite female knifemaker has dubbed the sphere-shaped gold inlays "Dellana Dots," and there are plenty of them here, along with textured gold bolsters and gold wire inlaid into an oxidized sterling silver handle. Hot, hot, hot! (PointSeven photo)

HANK ISHIHARA: Exoticism might be defined as ammonite and green-onyx handle inlays accompanied by brass and mokumé blade inlays. (PointSeven photo)

JAY HENDRICKSON: Once the squirrel in you finds the nickel-silver nut, then you can admire the silver-wire inlay while nibbling on it. (BladeGallery.com photo)

DERYK MUNROE: Blued damascus envelops a black-lip-pearl handle insert like a hard outer shell. (PointSeven photo)

BILL MORAN: The renowned knifemaker allows his customers to decide whether this one is a large bowie or a southwestern camp knife. As he tends to do, Bill inlaid some silver wire as a perk. (Holter photo)

STEVE JERNIGAN: OK, so we have the violet oyster pearl and the 24k-gold wire, now we need to inlay them in the form of flowers and stems. So, who wants to go first? (PointSeven photo)

HOWARD HITCHMOUGH: Black-lip pearl and damascus entangle on the dance floor. (PointSeven photo)

ZAZA REVISHVILI: Who needs to see the blade? The silver filigree and garnet insets will cut through anything in their paths. (Weyer photo)

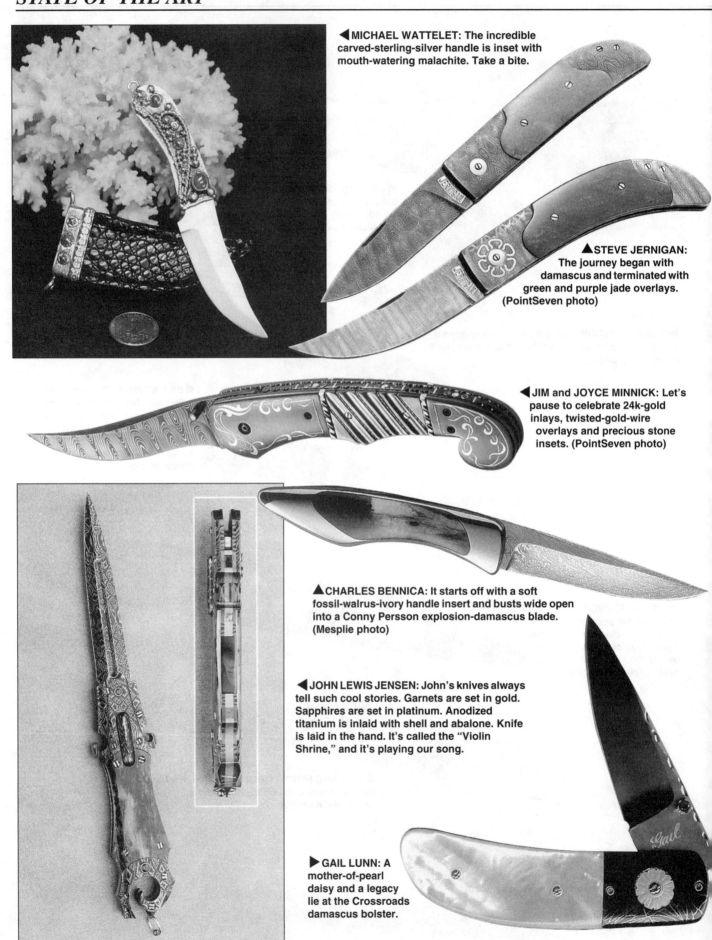

MICHAEL WATTELET: The incredible carved-sterling-silver handle is inset with mouth-watering malachite. Take a bite.

STEVE JERNIGAN: The journey began with damascus and terminated with green and purple jade overlays. (PointSeven photo)

JIM and JOYCE MINNICK: Let's pause to celebrate 24k-gold inlays, twisted-gold-wire overlays and precious stone insets. (PointSeven photo)

CHARLES BENNICA: It starts off with a soft fossil-walrus-ivory handle insert and busts wide open into a Conny Persson explosion-damascus blade. (Mesplie photo)

JOHN LEWIS JENSEN: John's knives always tell such cool stories. Garnets are set in gold. Sapphires are set in platinum. Anodized titanium is inlaid with shell and abalone. Knife is laid in the hand. It's called the "Violin Shrine," and it's playing our song.

GAIL LUNN: A mother-of-pearl daisy and a legacy lie at the Crossroads damascus bolster.

▶CHARLES BENNICA: The blade and body are integral and embellished only with black pearl.

◀GERT VAN DEN ELSEN: The fancy Masur-birch handle is sandwiched by moose horn in a happy unison of sorts.

▶BRUCE BUMP: His Fire Blade Dagger is spittin' mad, restrained only by copper and steel wire wrapping around a black goat-leather grip. (BladeGallery.com photo)

▶J.W. RANDALL: When ebony is introduced to ivory, silver and abalone, the four form a coalition. (Ward photo)

▲BARRY GALLAGHER: An abalone inlay flows like lava under an earthen crust of damascus. (BladeGallery.com photo)

▲JAY HENDRICKSON: Inlays enliven. (BladeGallery.com photo)

▶BARRY GALLAGHER: Heat-colored mosaic damascus makes room for black lip mother-of-pearl inlays. (BladeGallery.com photo)

Get a 'Lode' of These Golden Nuggets

▶ **REINHARD TSCHAGER:** He engraved it, gold inlaid it, lavished it with diamonds and gave it a lapis lazuli grip.

▶ **D.C. MUNROE:** The damascus handle is forged from 1084 and 15N20 with 18k- and 24k-gold applied using the *samaradok* technique. (BladeGallery.com photo)

▶ **LOYD MCCONNELL:** The damascus blade and bolster are 14k-gold plated and complemented by a gold thumb stud. (PointSeven photo)

▶ **DELLANA:** Dellana engraved and textured the 14-karat yellow gold in a way only she could. (PointSeven photo)

▲ **DWIGHT TOWELL:** The 24k-gold inlay workmanship on a Devin Thomas damascus blade is the type of embellishment that sells a knife, no questions asked. (PointSeven photo)

▶ **KEN STEIGERWALT:** The gold bolsters shine like beacons on either end of a black lip pearl grip, and the gold pins are like the light shimmering off ocean waves. Ken credits Jerry Rados for the Turkish damascus. (PointSeven photo)

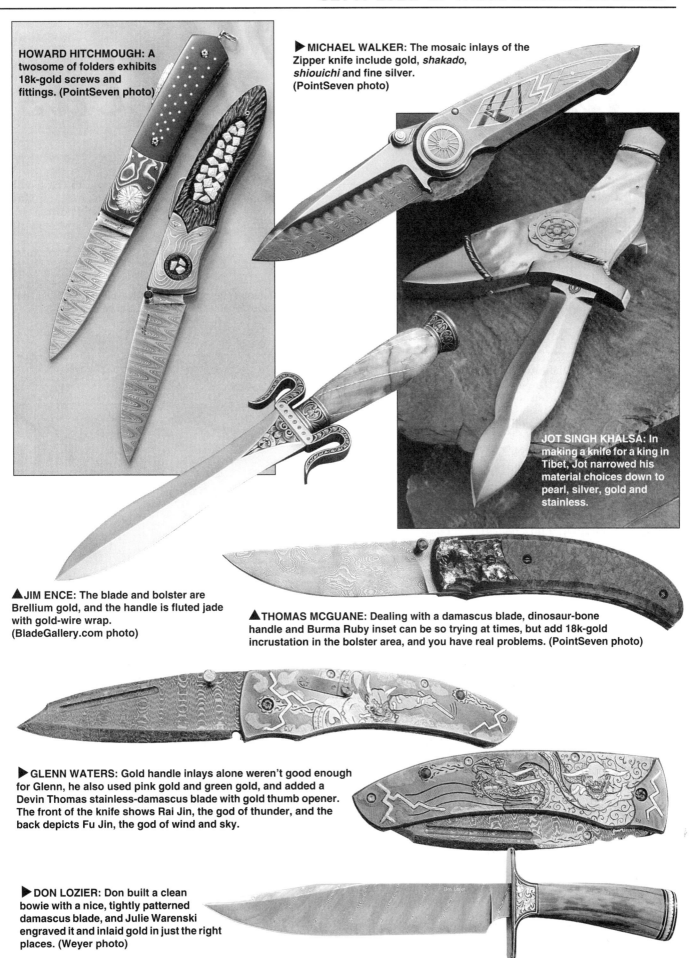

HOWARD HITCHMOUGH: A twosome of folders exhibits 18k-gold screws and fittings. (PointSeven photo)

►**MICHAEL WALKER:** The mosaic inlays of the Zipper knife include gold, *shakado*, *shiouichi* and fine silver. (PointSeven photo)

JOT SINGH KHALSA: In making a knife for a king in Tibet, Jot narrowed his material choices down to pearl, silver, gold and stainless.

▲**JIM ENCE:** The blade and bolster are Brellium gold, and the handle is fluted jade with gold-wire wrap. (BladeGallery.com photo)

▲**THOMAS MCGUANE:** Dealing with a damascus blade, dinosaur-bone handle and Burma Ruby inset can be so trying at times, but add 18k-gold incrustation in the bolster area, and you have real problems. (PointSeven photo)

►**GLENN WATERS:** Gold handle inlays alone weren't good enough for Glenn, he also used pink gold and green gold, and added a Devin Thomas stainless-damascus blade with gold thumb opener. The front of the knife shows Rai Jin, the god of thunder, and the back depicts Fu Jin, the god of wind and sky.

►**DON LOZIER:** Don built a clean bowie with a nice, tightly patterned damascus blade, and Julie Warenski engraved it and inlaid gold in just the right places. (Weyer photo)

Dazzling Damascus

STEP BACK FROM the knife industry a moment. Pretend you've never experienced the world of knives. Imagine being an average American who remembers Granddaddy's three-blade trapper folding knife, who owns a Swiss Army knife, who uses kitchen knives and who has a knife or two in the toolbox, tackle box, garden shed or hunting pack.

Now, imagine being exposed to damascus for the first time. It's a great feeling, isn't it? It's that sense of awe that those who have come to know damascus felt the first few times and now feel on occasion when a breathtaking damascus blade, bolster, handle or knife is laid before them.

But knifemakers weren't satisfied with awing the general populace.

Damascus is no longer limited to a few layers of steel, some nickel and hours upon hours of forging, pounding, folding, and heating, pounding, folding and forging again until a desired pattern is accomplished.

Several steel manipulators created their own damascus patterns. Others delved into powder and "canned" or "canister" steels. Canister steel is made in cans, tubes or canisters. (See "Now Playing: The Powdered-Mosaic-Damascus Revue" on page 31.)

By using a canister to hold hard steel figures together—examples would include puppy dog profiles, smiley faces or flowers—the empty areas around the figures are filled in with pure nickel powder, which is usually poured in and shook

down. A lid is welded onto the end of the canister, and the whole thing is forge-welded together.

The next step is pressing or hammering the can from all four sides. After welding and "drawing down" (reducing the heat temperature) the

billet, it can be treated to the usual damascus blade pattern manipulation, and a knife blade is born.

Funny, we're all in awe again. It's a great feeling, isn't it?

Joe Kertzman

▼LARRY NEWTON: Although from different sources, the Damasteel blade and Devin Thomas raindrop-pattern damascus bolsters pool together as one. (PointSeven photo)

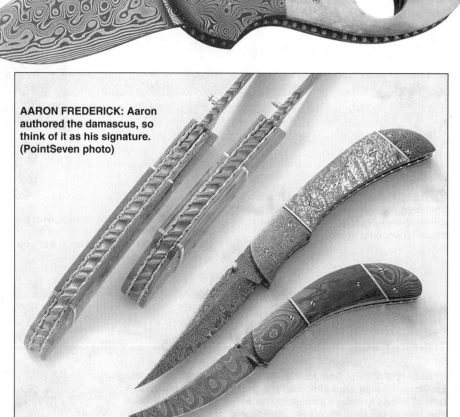

AARON FREDERICK: Aaron authored the damascus, so think of it as his signature. (PointSeven photo)

▼BARRY GALLAGHER: The network of lines and dots on the heat-colored, mosaic damascus blade isn't just chance, it's a planned pattern begun with an idea and brought forth by inspiration and perspiration. (BladeGallery.com photo)

◀ **WILLIAM HERNDON:** He heavily etched the 5160 and L-6 damascus blade to achieve the desired effect.

▶ **SHANE TAYLOR:** Either he had a little person walk across the blade while he was bluing it, or Shane purposely forged the mosaic damascus. The handle is Celtic Circles mosaic damascus. (BladeGallery.com photo)

▲ **STEVE SCHWARZER:** The father of modern mosaic damascus, Steve forges dramatic windows-pattern mosaic damascus for blade, bolsters and us. (PointSeven photo)

▶ **ED SCHEMPP:** A Celtic-Knot-pattern blade reminds of a quilt, with each square connected and each having its own history and meaning. (BladeGallery.com photo)

◀ **JIM WALKER:** Mosaic damascus has its way with a big ole bowie knife.

▶ **ED SCHEMPP:** Ed designed this conceptual folding knife for Spyderco, incorporating the company's patented bug logo into the bolster steel. (PointSeven photo)

▶ **CLIFF PARKER:** The steel and powdered-steel elements that compose the face, lines and spaces around the puppy head are nothing short of artistic creativity, foresight and ingenious manipulation of steel. (PointSeven photo)

▼HENRI VIALLON: A Celtic damascus pattern is repeated along the length of the 12.9-inch blade. The dirk also showcases an ebony handle carved by Serge Raoux. (Crohas photo)

◄GERARD HURST: Like momma and baby birds, the Guardian (left) and Flight models are winged and ready, feathers smoothed and soft.

►DANIEL WINKLER: That's some sly damascus patterning on a stunning bowie that purrs, prowls, pounces and preys. Mike Isenhour engraved the blade collar and sheath. (PointSeven photo)

►JOE OLSON: Joe calls the damascus pattern "Nightlife," and it's fun. (BladeGallery.com photo)

►STEVE FILICIETTI: A Wood-Grain damascus pattern is equally spaced along an 11 1/2-inch bowie blade. (Hoffman photo)

►JEFF HALL: Jeff used two patterns of Robert Eggerling damascus and combined them with a pearl handle in a gentlemanly manner. We thank him for that. (PointSeven photo)

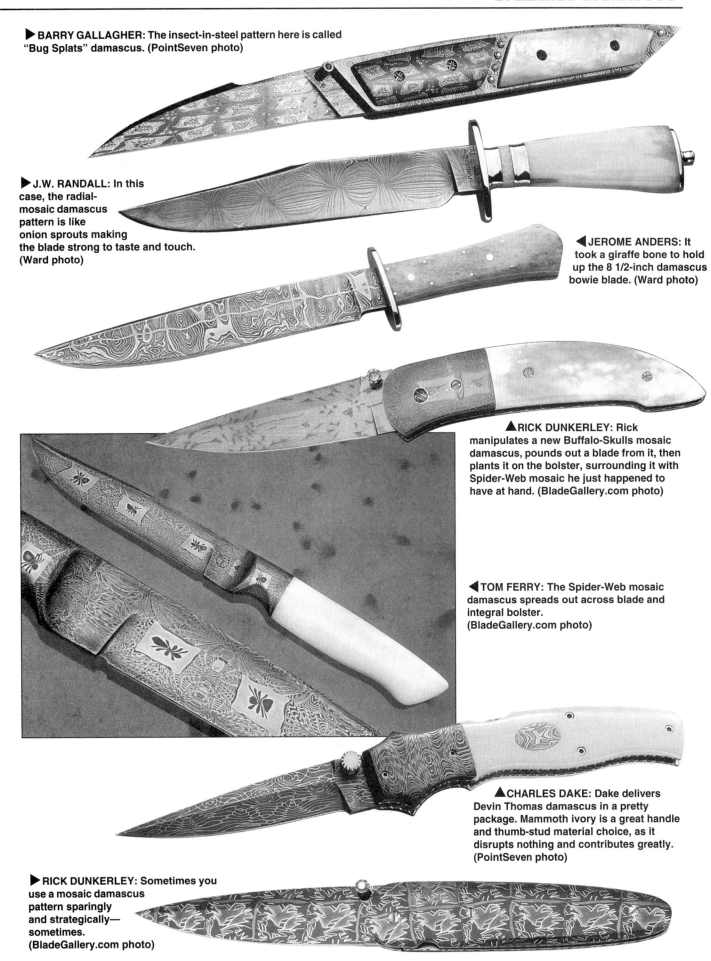

▶BARRY GALLAGHER: The insect-in-steel pattern here is called "Bug Splats" damascus. (PointSeven photo)

▶J.W. RANDALL: In this case, the radial-mosaic damascus pattern is like onion sprouts making the blade strong to taste and touch. (Ward photo)

◀JEROME ANDERS: It took a giraffe bone to hold up the 8 1/2-inch damascus bowie blade. (Ward photo)

▲RICK DUNKERLEY: Rick manipulates a new Buffalo-Skulls mosaic damascus, pounds out a blade from it, then plants it on the bolster, surrounding it with Spider-Web mosaic he just happened to have at hand. (BladeGallery.com photo)

◀TOM FERRY: The Spider-Web mosaic damascus spreads out across blade and integral bolster. (BladeGallery.com photo)

▲CHARLES DAKE: Dake delivers Devin Thomas damascus in a pretty package. Mammoth ivory is a great handle and thumb-stud material choice, as it disrupts nothing and contributes greatly. (PointSeven photo)

▶RICK DUNKERLEY: Sometimes you use a mosaic damascus pattern sparingly and strategically—sometimes. (BladeGallery.com photo)

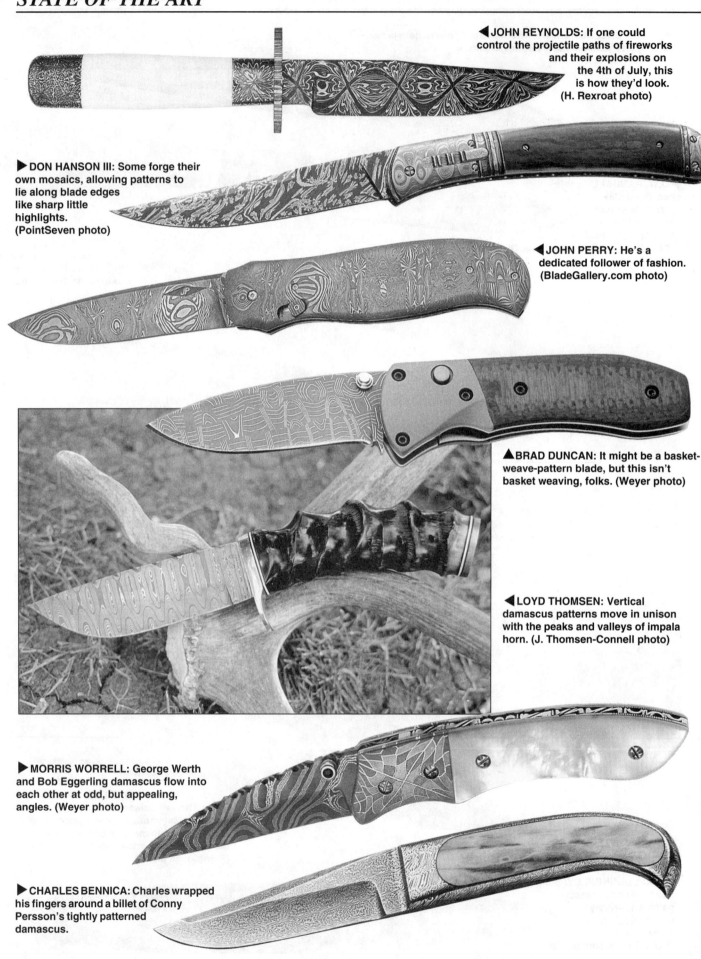

◀JOHN REYNOLDS: If one could control the projectile paths of fireworks and their explosions on the 4th of July, this is how they'd look. (H. Rexroat photo)

▶DON HANSON III: Some forge their own mosaics, allowing patterns to lie along blade edges like sharp little highlights. (PointSeven photo)

◀JOHN PERRY: He's a dedicated follower of fashion. (BladeGallery.com photo)

▲BRAD DUNCAN: It might be a basket-weave-pattern blade, but this isn't basket weaving, folks. (Weyer photo)

◀LOYD THOMSEN: Vertical damascus patterns move in unison with the peaks and valleys of impala horn. (J. Thomsen-Connell photo)

▶MORRIS WORRELL: George Werth and Bob Eggerling damascus flow into each other at odd, but appealing, angles. (Weyer photo)

▶CHARLES BENNICA: Charles wrapped his fingers around a billet of Conny Persson's tightly patterned damascus.

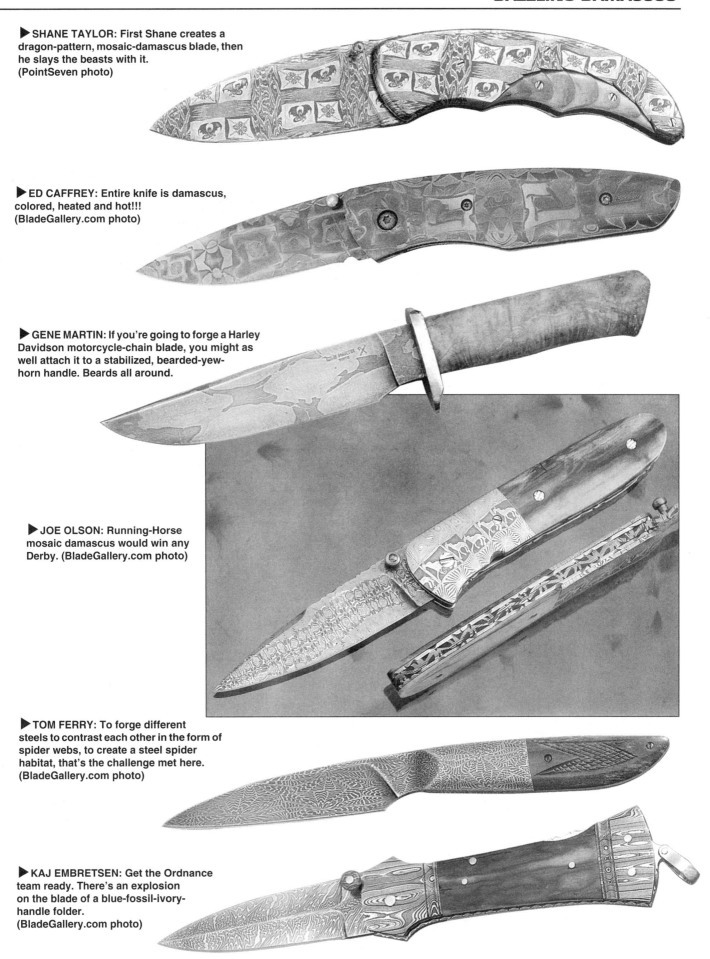

▶SHANE TAYLOR: First Shane creates a dragon-pattern, mosaic-damascus blade, then he slays the beasts with it. (PointSeven photo)

▶ED CAFFREY: Entire knife is damascus, colored, heated and hot!!! (BladeGallery.com photo)

▶GENE MARTIN: If you're going to forge a Harley Davidson motorcycle-chain blade, you might as well attach it to a stabilized, bearded-yew-horn handle. Beards all around.

▶JOE OLSON: Running-Horse mosaic damascus would win any Derby. (BladeGallery.com photo)

▶TOM FERRY: To forge different steels to contrast each other in the form of spider webs, to create a steel spider habitat, that's the challenge met here. (BladeGallery.com photo)

▶KAJ EMBRETSEN: Get the Ordnance team ready. There's an explosion on the blade of a blue-fossil-ivory-handle folder. (BladeGallery.com photo)

▶**T.R. OVEREYNDER:** One of the smoother applications of Devin Thomas Vines & Roses damascus is the combination of it with a curvaceously shaped mother-of-pearl handle and 18k-pink-gold pins and thumb stud. (PointSeven photo)

▶**JOSHUA SMITH:** It's amazing what is possible when you mix pure nickel and carbon steel. (BladeGallery.com photo)

▼**DON HETHCOAT:** Damascus deviates from light to dark, as does a lustrous mother-of-pearl handle. (Weyer photo)

▼**BILL LEVENGOOD:** Daryl Meier and Robert Eggerling provided the damascus, and the rest came to the maker as he put all the love he had into one pattern before going off on vacation to be rejuvenated (or at least taking a 10 minute break). (PointSeven photo)

◀**JIM THILL:** A mammoth damascus knife with exposed damascus tang is appropriately outfitted with a mammoth-ivory grip. (BladeGallery.com photo)

▲**ROGER DOLE:** The grind line running lengthwise down the center of the blade dissects the two sides of Tom Ferry's Spider Web damascus steel design. (BladeGallery.com photo)

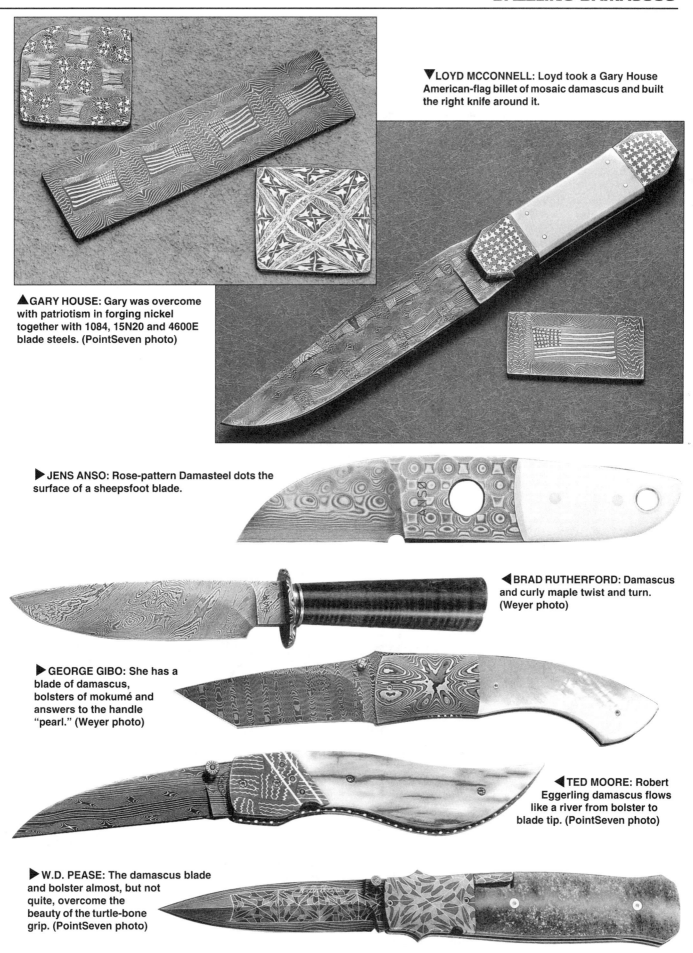

▼LOYD MCCONNELL: Loyd took a Gary House American-flag billet of mosaic damascus and built the right knife around it.

▲GARY HOUSE: Gary was overcome with patriotism in forging nickel together with 1084, 15N20 and 4600E blade steels. (PointSeven photo)

▶JENS ANSO: Rose-pattern Damasteel dots the surface of a sheepsfoot blade.

◀BRAD RUTHERFORD: Damascus and curly maple twist and turn. (Weyer photo)

▶GEORGE GIBO: She has a blade of damascus, bolsters of mokumé and answers to the handle "pearl." (Weyer photo)

◀TED MOORE: Robert Eggerling damascus flows like a river from bolster to blade tip. (PointSeven photo)

▶W.D. PEASE: The damascus blade and bolster almost, but not quite, overcome the beauty of the turtle-bone grip. (PointSeven photo)

Sheathing

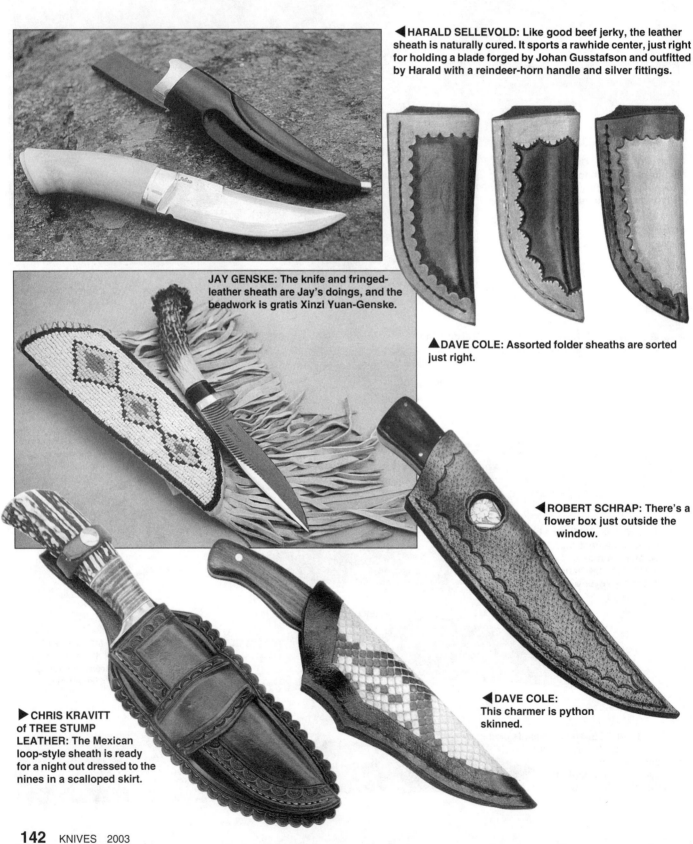

◀HARALD SELLEVOLD: Like good beef jerky, the leather sheath is naturally cured. It sports a rawhide center, just right for holding a blade forged by Johan Gusstafson and outfitted by Harald with a reindeer-horn handle and silver fittings.

JAY GENSKE: The knife and fringed-leather sheath are Jay's doings, and the beadwork is gratis Xinzi Yuan-Genske.

▲DAVE COLE: Assorted folder sheaths are sorted just right.

◀ROBERT SCHRAP: There's a flower box just outside the window.

▶CHRIS KRAVITT of TREE STUMP LEATHER: The Mexican loop-style sheath is ready for a night out dressed to the nines in a scalloped skirt.

◀DAVE COLE: This charmer is python skinned.

►CHRIS KRAVITT: The green iguana skin of the sheath matches the color of the scrimshawed dragon on the handle of the Mike Sakmar bowie.

►STEVE SCHWARZER: Steve had enough insight to beckon Wally Hostatter to work his lacquer magic on the scabbard and to fancy up some of the knife fittings. (PointSeven photo)

▼JAY HENDRICKSON: The leather sheath with feather tooling figures to turn a few heads. (BladeGallery.com photo)

◄R.D. "RICK" MILLER: The 8-ounce, hand-tooled, hand-sewn sheath employs a brass snap closure to secure an 11 1/2-inch bowie with an L-6 and reptile-pattern-damascus blade.

►KENNY ROWE: Depending on the mood, rattlesnake skin (left) might be called to duty, or acorns and oak leaves would be given the nod.

▲RICK BRUNER: A large skinning knife, a leather sheath and the sound of wind whistling through the trees, that's all anyone needs for a day away from the grind.

►RICK BRUNER: The brown whip snake had no clue he'd be sacrificed for the good of a buckskin sheath. Marv Palmer made the lucky knife to be housed in this beauty.

◀RICK BRUNER: Happy in their leather digs with a few fringes, some beads, rattlesnake inserts, brass thimbles and other extras, neck knives take the high ride.

▼BARNEY FOLEY: The Western side-by-side sheath cradles two Rudy Ruana fixed blades.

▼KENNY ROWE: Kenny packs one in rattlesnake hide with basket-weave decor, a touch of tooling, and a frog button to boot.

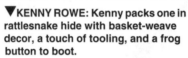

▲PEGGY PATRICK: When you're beading a bowie knife sheath, you bead it big.

◀BARNEY FOLEY: Lee Reeves made the knife and was mighty proud when Barney did up a Mexican loop sheath with kangaroo-skin lacing.

▲JUDY CHOATE: When Milton Choate makes a stag-handle hunter, Judy dresses it in leather.

A Most Brilliant Collection of Cutters

I**T'S THE FEELING.** The experience is real, and everything has become crystal clear. To know how a collector feels when, after spending half of his or her life accumulating custom knives and guns, the opportunity arises to display them publicly. To have people see the collection that has absorbed and drained every ounce of energy in the collector's body, a hobby that has occupied every waking moment in search of that one special piece, that rare knife or antique gun that has eluded them their whole lives.

Perhaps the feeling is not that intense. Maybe being given the opportunity to show, for the first time in 23 years of the annual "Knives" book, a collection of custom blades in color is not equivalent to displaying your hard-earned knife or gun collection. But it does give a person an inkling of how it feels.

The experience is so rewarding, not necessarily because the honor was earned or endowed upon anyone, but because the knifemakers have worked so hard, toiled so many hours on the knives, and now there arises the chance to reward efforts with a complete color display in a book that has historically been offered only in black and white.

Sure, knives have been paraded in all their colorful glory in other books and magazines. *The Knives Points of Interest* books by Jim Weyer are prime examples of fabulous coffee table offerings showcasing the sharpest of sharp instruments. Magazines like BLADE® feature knives in a rainbow of colors for readers to admire on a regular basis. Yet, here there are no interruptions or advertisements within the color section. Among photos, there is little text. The knives are allowed to tell their stories, and what stories they tell. They are enthralling, insightful and colorful—colorful, that is, as an engraved inter-frame folder with a blued-damascus blade, anodized liners and a jewel-encrusted thumb stud.

Joe Kertzman

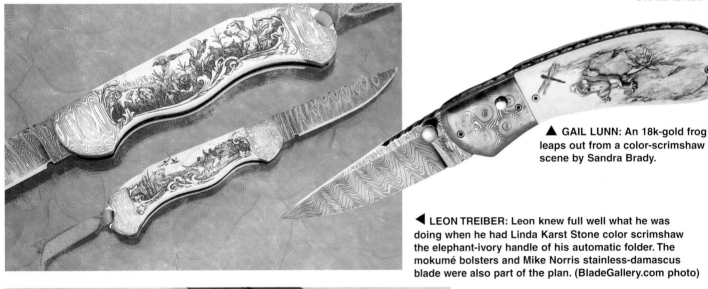

▲ **GAIL LUNN:** An 18k-gold frog leaps out from a color-scrimshaw scene by Sandra Brady.

◄ **LEON TREIBER:** Leon knew full well what he was doing when he had Linda Karst Stone color scrimshaw the elephant-ivory handle of his automatic folder. The mokumé bolsters and Mike Norris stainless-damascus blade were also part of the plan. (BladeGallery.com photo)

◄ **DERYK MUNROE:** You only used to hear phrases like "nitre-blued," "Tribal-pattern mosaic damascus" and "18-karat, reticulated-red-gold pocket inlays" when talking about high-end art forms other than knifemaking. Watch out world! (BladeGallery.com photo)

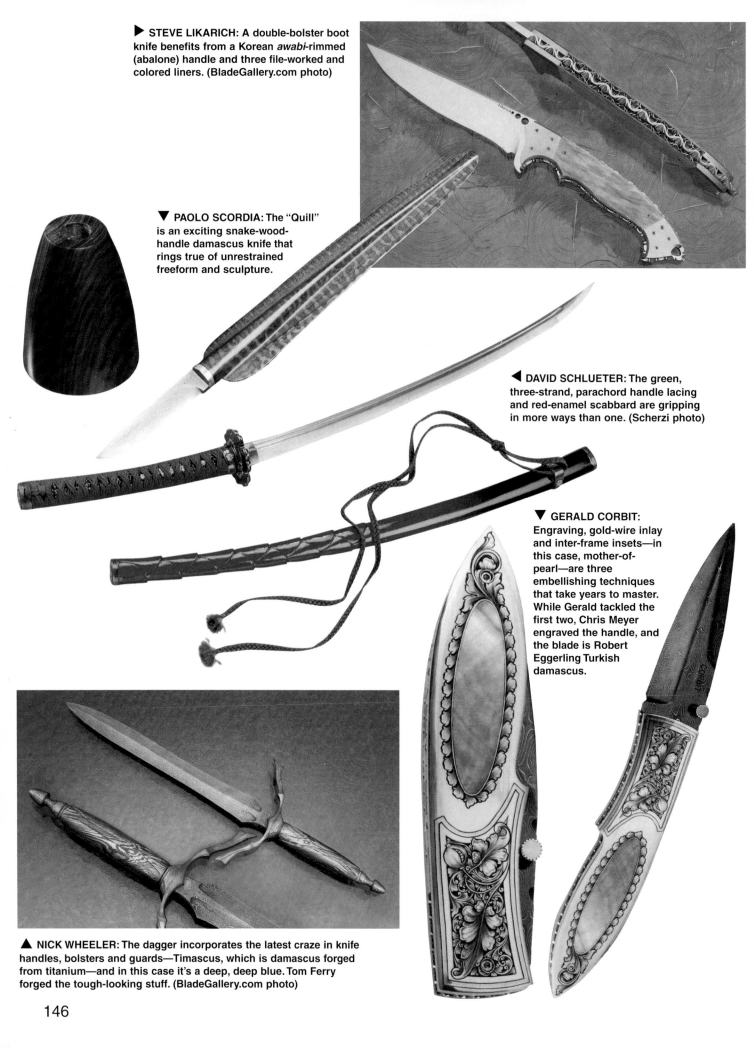

▶ STEVE LIKARICH: A double-bolster boot knife benefits from a Korean *awabi*-rimmed (abalone) handle and three file-worked and colored liners. (BladeGallery.com photo)

▼ PAOLO SCORDIA: The "Quill" is an exciting snake-wood-handle damascus knife that rings true of unrestrained freeform and sculpture.

◀ DAVID SCHLUETER: The green, three-strand, parachord handle lacing and red-enamel scabbard are gripping in more ways than one. (Scherzi photo)

▼ GERALD CORBIT: Engraving, gold-wire inlay and inter-frame insets—in this case, mother-of-pearl—are three embellishing techniques that take years to master. While Gerald tackled the first two, Chris Meyer engraved the handle, and the blade is Robert Eggerling Turkish damascus.

▲ NICK WHEELER: The dagger incorporates the latest craze in knife handles, bolsters and guards—Timascus, which is damascus forged from titanium—and in this case it's a deep, deep blue. Tom Ferry forged the tough-looking stuff. (BladeGallery.com photo)

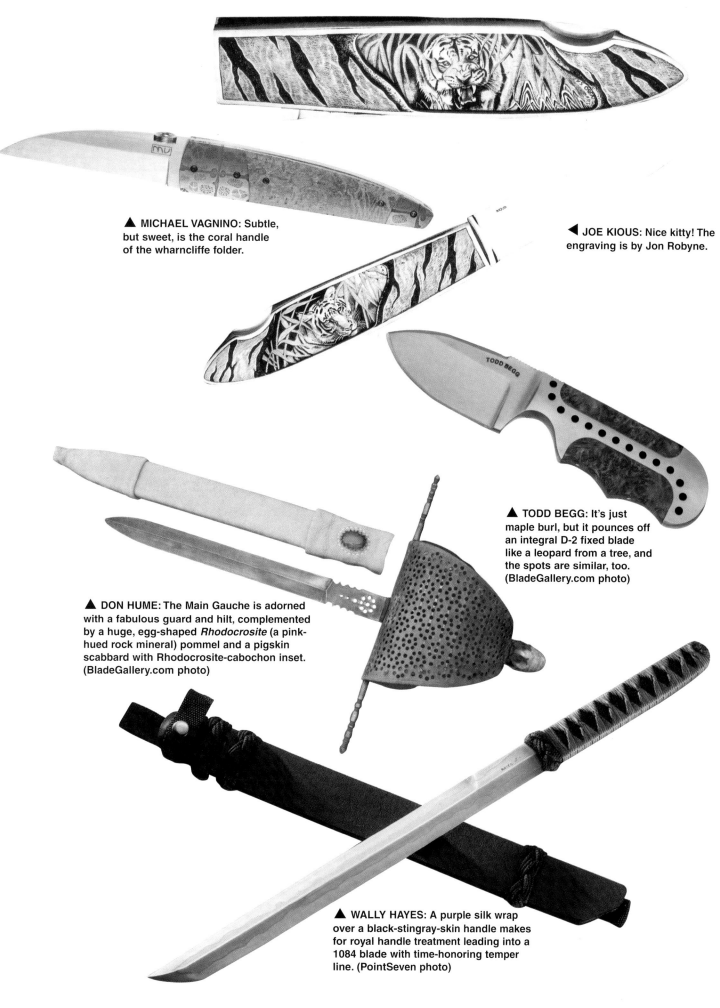

▲ MICHAEL VAGNINO: Subtle, but sweet, is the coral handle of the wharncliffe folder.

◀ JOE KIOUS: Nice kitty! The engraving is by Jon Robyne.

▲ TODD BEGG: It's just maple burl, but it pounces off an integral D-2 fixed blade like a leopard from a tree, and the spots are similar, too. (BladeGallery.com photo)

▲ DON HUME: The Main Gauche is adorned with a fabulous guard and hilt, complemented by a huge, egg-shaped *Rhodocrosite* (a pink-hued rock mineral) pommel and a pigskin scabbard with Rhodocrosite-cabochon inset. (BladeGallery.com photo)

▲ WALLY HAYES: A purple silk wrap over a black-stingray-skin handle makes for royal handle treatment leading into a 1084 blade with time-honoring temper line. (PointSeven photo)

147

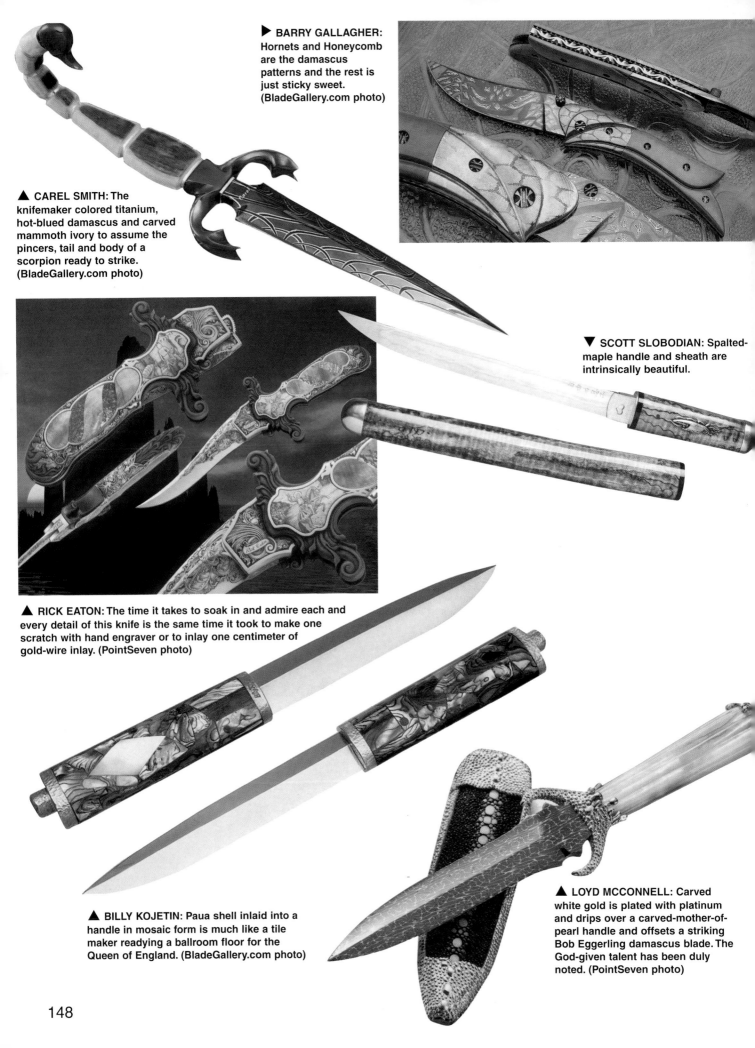

BARRY GALLAGHER: Hornets and Honeycomb are the damascus patterns and the rest is just sticky sweet. (BladeGallery.com photo)

▲ **CAREL SMITH:** The knifemaker colored titanium, hot-blued damascus and carved mammoth ivory to assume the pincers, tail and body of a scorpion ready to strike. (BladeGallery.com photo)

▼ **SCOTT SLOBODIAN:** Spalted-maple handle and sheath are intrinsically beautiful.

▲ **RICK EATON:** The time it takes to soak in and admire each and every detail of this knife is the same time it took to make one scratch with hand engraver or to inlay one centimeter of gold-wire inlay. (PointSeven photo)

▲ **BILLY KOJETIN:** Paua shell inlaid into a handle in mosaic form is much like a tile maker readying a ballroom floor for the Queen of England. (BladeGallery.com photo)

▲ **LOYD MCCONNELL:** Carved white gold is plated with platinum and drips over a carved-mother-of-pearl handle and offsets a striking Bob Eggerling damascus blade. The God-given talent has been duly noted. (PointSeven photo)

◀ HOWARD HITCHMOUGH: Anodized titanium and rose damascus rally together for a good cause. (PointSeven photo)

▲ LARRY FUEGEN: The carved-mammoth-ivory grip is caramel-brown colored, highlighted by French-gray fittings and 14k-gold spacers. (PointSeven photo)

▶ RUSS SUTTON: If mammoth ivory this blue still exists today, and it does, then the woolly creatures were drop-dead gorgeous in more ways than one.

◀ JOT SINGH KHALSA: Crazy lace agate is the stone behind which a Ron Skaggs leopard lays in waiting. The prize might be the oxblood-coral accents or the Bob Eggerling braided-damascus blade.

▶ TOM FERRY: Tom was instrumental in introducing the custom knife scene to Timascus, a damascus forged from titanium in titillating fashion. (BladeGallery.com photo)

▲ GLENN WATERS: This is Glenn's specialty, making all who gaze upon his knives stare in wide wonder. Eye candy includes stainless damascus, gold and silver inlays, mammoth ivory, twisted gold wire, engraving, mother-of-pearl inlays and fancy file work.

◄ EDMUND DAVIDSON: Leapin' lizards, this is one powerful interpretation of a Bob Loveless chute knife in BG-42 blade steel, with color and black-and-white scrimshaw by Linda Karst Stone and engraving by Jere Davidson. All is well in fantasyland. (PointSeven photo)

▼ RUSS KOMMER: Both the palettes and paintings are pretty, the former by Russ and the latter by scrimshaw artist Mary Muller. (PointSeven photo)

▲ MATT DISKIN: The wine steward will be walking tall tonight. (PointSeven photo)

► JURGEN STEINAU: Jurgen shocks us with a futuristic folder and a stellar handle. (PointSeven photo)

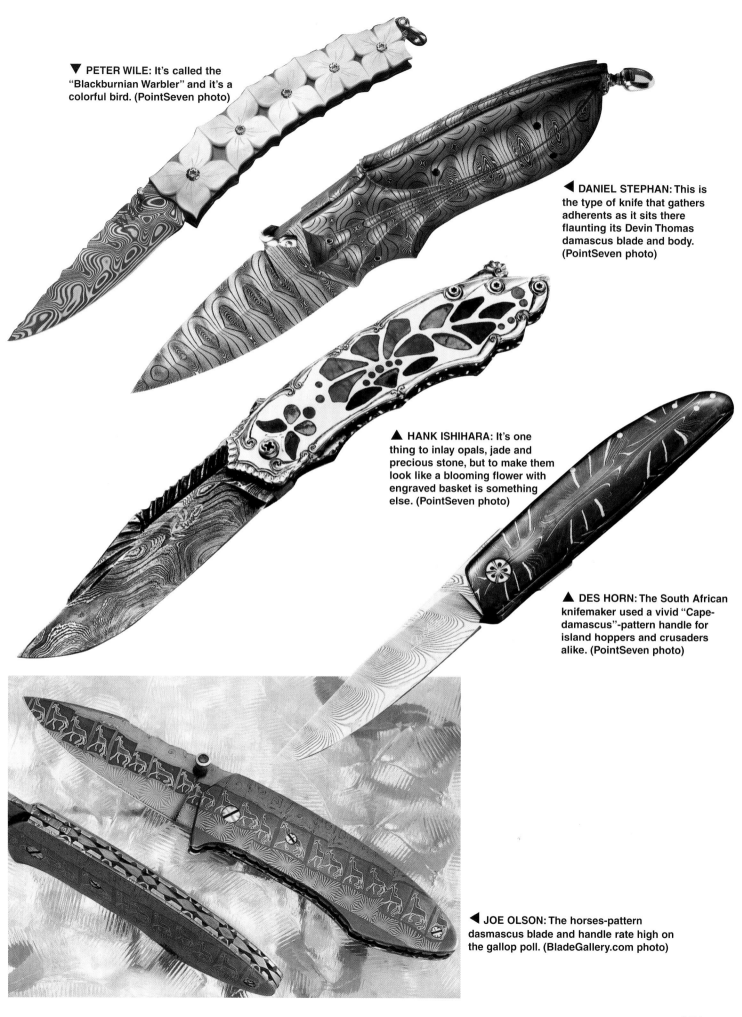

▼ PETER WILE: It's called the "Blackburnian Warbler" and it's a colorful bird. (PointSeven photo)

◄ DANIEL STEPHAN: This is the type of knife that gathers adherents as it sits there flaunting its Devin Thomas damascus blade and body. (PointSeven photo)

▲ HANK ISHIHARA: It's one thing to inlay opals, jade and precious stone, but to make them look like a blooming flower with engraved basket is something else. (PointSeven photo)

▲ DES HORN: The South African knifemaker used a vivid "Cape-damascus"-pattern handle for island hoppers and crusaders alike. (PointSeven photo)

◄ JOE OLSON: The horses-pattern dasmascus blade and handle rate high on the gallop poll. (BladeGallery.com photo)

► HARUMI HIRAYAMA: Three dimensional inlays bring the feline subjects above the surface, revealing their material makeup of mastodon tusk, wood, shell, coral, stone and gold. They're purr-r-r-fect.

► PAUL JARVIS: The lapis stone handle is honored by bold bolsters, awarded with a damascus blade and crowned with a cherry-red garnet. (PointSeven photo)

▲ STEVE SCHWARZER: Sometimes the most traditional of methods brings forth the best results. (PointSeven photo)

▲ DON HANSON III: Rose gold and black-lip mother-of-pearl compose a duo of deep-hued handle materials, and to marry them with a stark-black and snow-white damascus blade is vivid treatment of the subject. (PointSeven photo)

▲ THOMAS MCGUANE: The Nemo Abyss is delivered with blue damascus nearly too deep for measurement. (PointSeven photo)

Ingenious Engraving

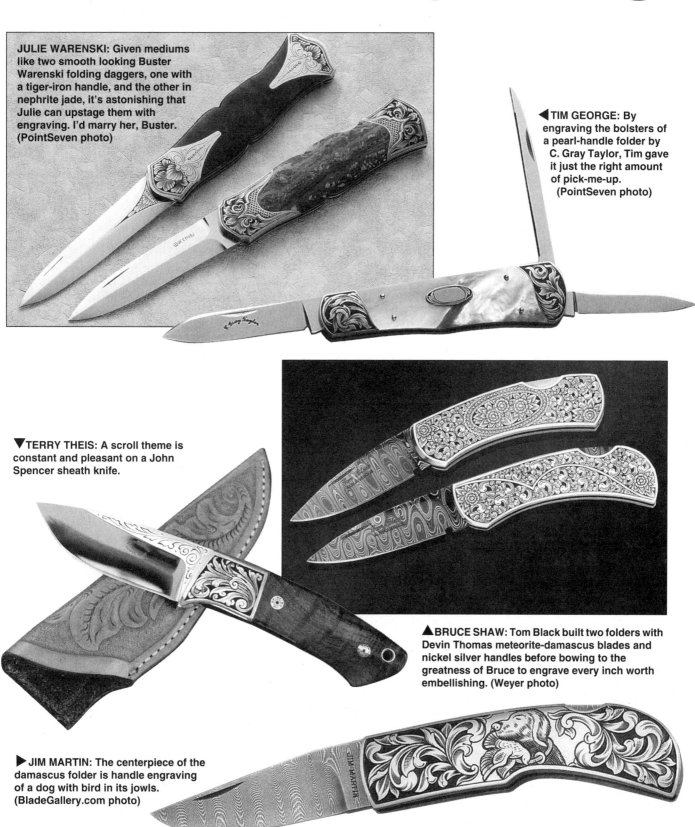

JULIE WARENSKI: Given mediums like two smooth looking Buster Warenski folding daggers, one with a tiger-iron handle, and the other in nephrite jade, it's astonishing that Julie can upstage them with engraving. I'd marry her, Buster. (PointSeven photo)

◄TIM GEORGE: By engraving the bolsters of a pearl-handle folder by C. Gray Taylor, Tim gave it just the right amount of pick-me-up. (PointSeven photo)

▼TERRY THEIS: A scroll theme is constant and pleasant on a John Spencer sheath knife.

▲BRUCE SHAW: Tom Black built two folders with Devin Thomas meteorite-damascus blades and nickel silver handles before bowing to the greatness of Bruce to engrave every inch worth embellishing. (Weyer photo)

►JIM MARTIN: The centerpiece of the damascus folder is handle engraving of a dog with bird in its jowls. (BladeGallery.com photo)

T.R. OVEREYNDER: Scroll engraving creates a ripple effect down a damascus blade. (PointSeven photo)

DUSTY MOULTON: Three engraved guards are thrice as nice. (PointSeven photo)

FRED HARRINGTON: Fred's engraving and scrimshaw highlight an Edward Kalfayan Natchez bowie, patterned after two knives carried by a Texas Ranger in the 1930s-'40s. The scrimshaw image is of the *Natchez*, a 19th century rear-wheel riverboat. (Weyer photo)

BRYAN BRIDGES: A flower for the lovely lady.

BILLY BATES: Bulldog Brand released a pristine, pearl-handle, lock-back folder with fabulous swirling-damascus blade, and Billy brought it to an even higher level with ingenious engraving.

NESTOR LORENZO RHO: The resin-phenol handle is gripping in its own right. Add an engraved blade and this one busts out all over. (Herce photo)

▶BRYAN BRIDGES: The engraved bolster is the life of the party on a Tim Hancock damascus fixed blade with ironwood grip. (PointSeven photo)

◀JOHN W. SMITH: Engraving envelops the mother-of-pearl and abalone handle inserts and sends a damascus blade out to play awhile. (PointSeven photo)

▶JULIE WARENSKI: Scroll engraving so powerful, it became three dimensional in the form of a carved guard and blade. We are truly the beneficiaries. Buster Warenski built the canvas on which Julie's art appears. (PointSeven photo)

▲LLOYD PENDLETON: Tusk, tusk, tusk: saber-tooth tiger, hulking mastodon and ivory handles. (PointSeven photo)

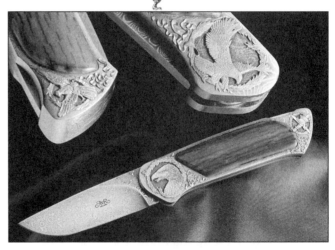

▲DANY HERMINE: White, yellow and pink-gold eagles are the featured performers on Aad Van Rijswijk inter-frame folder.

▶SHAWN and SHARLA HANSEN: At home in a royal henchman's treasure chest or a modern collector's display case, a folding dagger showcases a black lip mother-of-pearl handle inset and Turkish damascus blade. It's fully file-worked and engraved with a chivalrous scene of knight in shining armor slaying a fire-breathing dragon and highlighted by scroll engraving in gold, silver and black. (PointSeven photo)

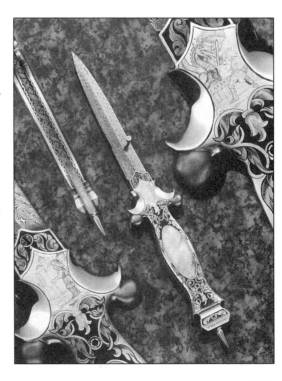

▲SIMON LYTTON: The mysteries of the Orient are uncovered within the confines of a Scott Sawby folding knife. (PointSeven photo)

STEVEN RAPP: This reminds me of the upscale engraving and silverwork witnessed on fine Mexican saddles, conchos, spurs and buckles. (PointSeven photo)

▼**JULIE WARENSKI:** Smack-dab in the middle of scroll engraving is a golden dragonfly taking to the air on diamond wings, proving that dreams really do come true, at least on a Howard Hitchmough folder. (PointSeven photo)

►**RICARDO VELARDE:** Stag and tasteful engraving grant two fixed blades passage into another realm of cut. (PointSeven photo)

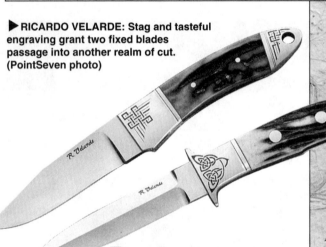

CHRIS MEYER: A wholly mammoth trumpets loudly from the engraved bolster of a W.D. Pease folder with carved-mammoth-ivory handle. (PointSeven photo)

▼**JOHN W. SMITH:** John couldn't keep this woman or these flower petals under wrap much longer, so he brought them out for public viewing. (PointSeven photo)

▼**SIMON LYTTON:** Knifemaker Kaj Embretsen polished up a couple pearl-handle, damascus folding knives, providing gold bolsters on which his friend Simon could show off his handiwork. (PointSeven photo)

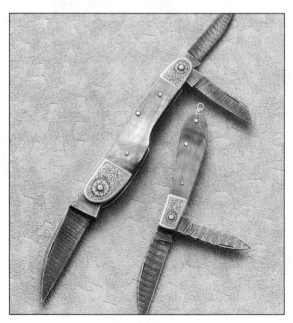

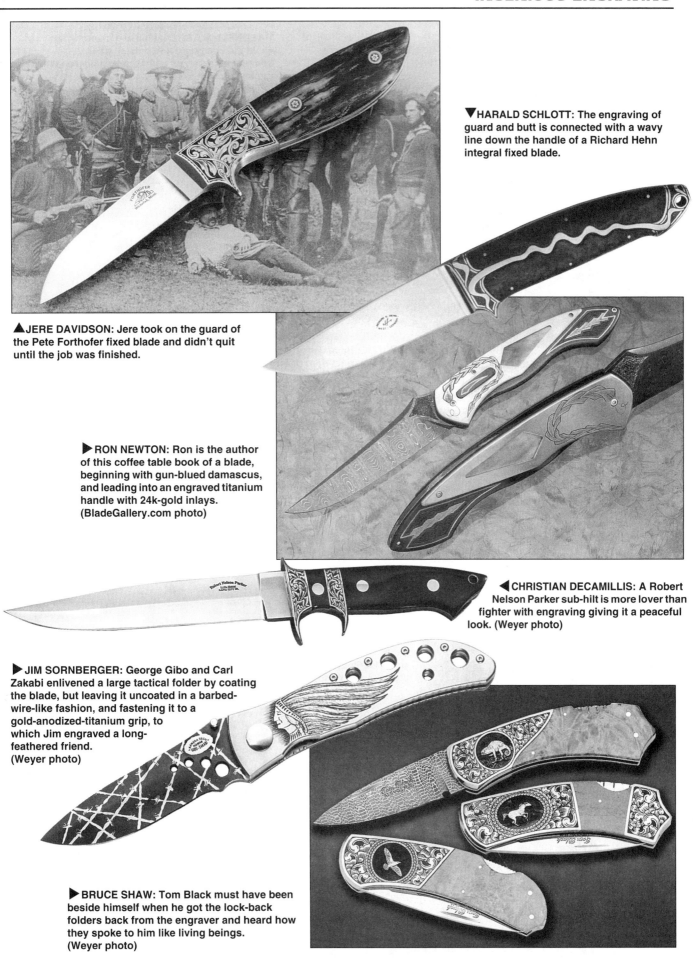

▼HARALD SCHLOTT: The engraving of guard and butt is connected with a wavy line down the handle of a Richard Hehn integral fixed blade.

▲JERE DAVIDSON: Jere took on the guard of the Pete Forthofer fixed blade and didn't quit until the job was finished.

▶RON NEWTON: Ron is the author of this coffee table book of a blade, beginning with gun-blued damascus, and leading into an engraved titanium handle with 24k-gold inlays. (BladeGallery.com photo)

◀CHRISTIAN DECAMILLIS: A Robert Nelson Parker sub-hilt is more lover than fighter with engraving giving it a peaceful look. (Weyer photo)

▶JIM SORNBERGER: George Gibo and Carl Zakabi enlivened a large tactical folder by coating the blade, but leaving it uncoated in a barbed-wire-like fashion, and fastening it to a gold-anodized-titanium grip, to which Jim engraved a long-feathered friend. (Weyer photo)

▶BRUCE SHAW: Tom Black must have been beside himself when he got the lock-back folders back from the engraver and heard how they spoke to him like living beings. (Weyer photo)

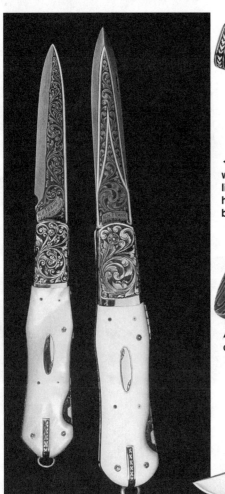

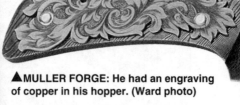

KENNETH WARREN: Fine use of engraving would include guard and bolster areas that stimulate the senses and wrap up a bowie knife package like this Bob Lay piece, also scrimshawed by Guy Dahl. (Weyer photo)

HENRY FRANK: He does exquisite work, concentrating on gold bolsters, liners, pins, inlays and toothpick; ivory handles; and engraving that garnishes but never tarnishes.

MULLER FORGE: He had an engraving of copper in his hopper. (Ward photo)

BERNARD SPARKS: Bernard runs sled dogs during the Idaho winters and across blades in the Idaho springs, summers and falls.

GENE BASKETT: File work and engraving share billing on a fabulous folder.

HENRY FRANK: It's an honor to bring you a few high art, engraved folders from the maker who's been impressing the knife public with his work since 1965. (PointSeven photo)

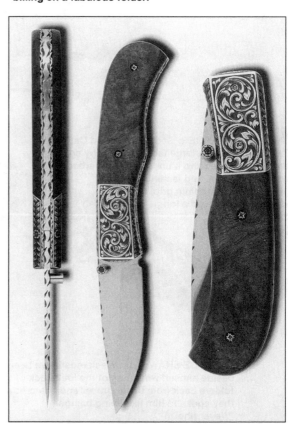

▶TANYA VAN HOY: John Walker couldn't figure out what his dagger was missing, so Tanya showed him.

▶JERE DAVIDSON: The engraved bolsters of an Edmund Davidson integral skinning knife are like snapshots in time that will never fade from memory. (PointSeven photo)

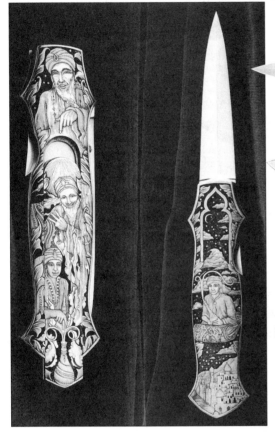

▲DWIGHT TOWELL: Inter-frame folding daggers are fine places for engraving around handle inlays.

▲TIM HERMAN: Tim's no novice at picking up a few files and engravers and fancying a few inches of steel around the old lapis stone. (PointSeven photo)

▼CHRIS MEYER: Capturing the essence and dominating the domain are two totally different things. Consider this Gerald Corbit folder captured by Chris. The blade is Robert Eggerling mosaic damascus.

◀JOE KIOUS: A magic carpet ride of incredible Arabic engraving begins with a genie or sultan, whichever you choose, pointing toward a hidden door, which can be engraved with any secrets you have.

▼RICHARD SPINALE: This is that old "seeing is believing" thing ringing true again. (Weyer photo)

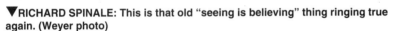

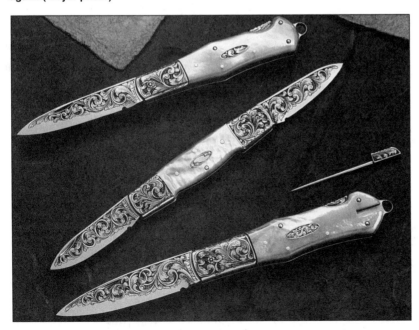

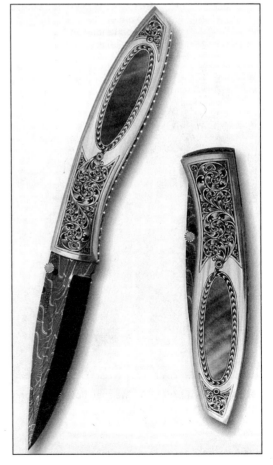

Carved, Sculpted and Cool

◀LARRY FUEGEN: File work is carving. Texturing gold bands is carving, and carving mammoth ivory, that's carving, too. (PointSeven photo)

▶CHARLES ROULIN: Meet the pierced blade and bolster master, the one who has just fashioned the most fancy of fishing knives.

▶WADE COLTER: Wade must have felt like the first man on the moon after carving the blued damascus. The meteorite handle is from the Gibeon landfall in Namibia. (BladeGallery.com photo)

▼JAY FISHER: To give some idea of proportion, "Dragonslayer-The Taste of Steel" sports a 54-inch, double-hollow-ground 440C blade (that's 4 1/2 feet), and the base is a 400-lb. bronze dragon sculpted with aventurine and blue-tiger-eye inlays. It's monstrous.

▲BARRY GALLAGHER: The lines flow in unison with the knife. (BladeGallery.com photo)

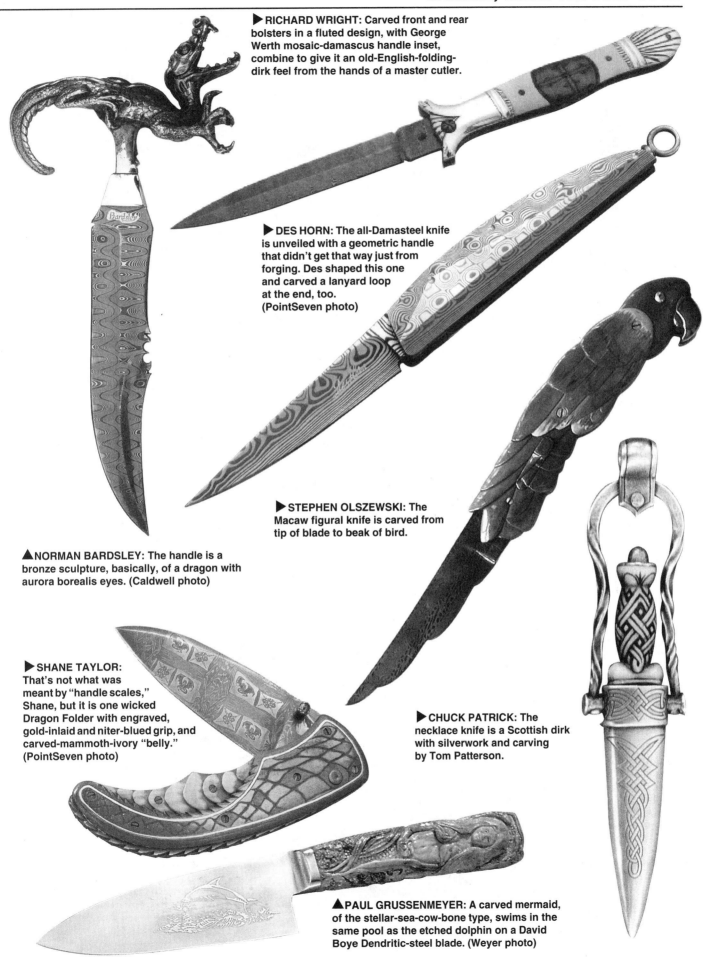

▶RICHARD WRIGHT: Carved front and rear bolsters in a fluted design, with George Werth mosaic-damascus handle inset, combine to give it an old-English-folding-dirk feel from the hands of a master cutler.

▶DES HORN: The all-Damasteel knife is unveiled with a geometric handle that didn't get that way just from forging. Des shaped this one and carved a lanyard loop at the end, too. (PointSeven photo)

▲NORMAN BARDSLEY: The handle is a bronze sculpture, basically, of a dragon with aurora borealis eyes. (Caldwell photo)

▶STEPHEN OLSZEWSKI: The Macaw figural knife is carved from tip of blade to beak of bird.

▶SHANE TAYLOR: That's not what was meant by "handle scales," Shane, but it is one wicked Dragon Folder with engraved, gold-inlaid and niter-blued grip, and carved-mammoth-ivory "belly." (PointSeven photo)

▶CHUCK PATRICK: The necklace knife is a Scottish dirk with silverwork and carving by Tom Patterson.

▲PAUL GRUSSENMEYER: A carved mermaid, of the stellar-sea-cow-bone type, swims in the same pool as the etched dolphin on a David Boye Dendritic-steel blade. (Weyer photo)

MIKE FELLOWS: Artistic is the sub-hilt fighter with carved *habaki* (blade collar), and turned and filed damascus guard and butt cap. Hand-filed spheres trail off the guard and pommel like axis-spinning planets.

J. MICHAEL MCRAE: The Chief's Dirk qualifies as such mainly because of the ivory and sterling silver carved in thistle and knot-work motifs. (Hoffman photo)

DON POLZIEN: The carved teakwood handle and *saya* (sheath) are breathtaking.

PAUL GRUSSENMEYER: Daniel Winkler fashioned this spectacular knife blade from a file, and Paul carved a dragon sentinel to look over it and protect it from harm. (Weyer photo)

WADE COLTER: The master smith proves why he can stay and play with the best of 'em. (BladeGallery.com photo)

SHANE TAYLOR: While dragons fly with fantastical wings across the mosaic-damascus blade, they leave their scaly bodies behind in the form of carved-steel guard and sculpted fossil-walrus-ivory grip. (BladeGallery.com photo)

REX ROBINSON: The carving tools and files knew no difference between damascus and mother-of-pearl, but instead shaped everything to their liking. (PointSeven photo)

▶BARRY GALLAGHER: The textured walrus ivory gives the right feel to this damascus folder. (BladeGallery.com photo)

▼AUDRA DRAPER: Fluted brass acts as a shapely waist between stabilized-giraffe-bone grip and Mike Draper twist-pattern damascus blade. (BladeGallery.com photo)

▼LARRY FUEGEN: While carved pearl caresses the hand, carved steel allows fingers to index it for feel, flow and fun. (PointSeven photo)

▶JOHN W. SMITH: Diamond-pattern mother-of-pearl buddies up to two fluted bolsters. (PointSeven photo)

▼LARRY FUEGEN: Crown stag is already highly figured. To make a monster emerge from it, to carve the bolster and blade thematically is a sign of insight more powerful than foresight and hindsight combined. (PointSeven photo)

▲ROBERT WEINSTOCK: The Daryl Meier steel was sculpted in such an appealing manner. (PointSeven photo)

▼DAN WILKERSON: This is intricately carved by an artist and knifemaker of the highest caliber. It swallows you up and spits you out. (PointSeven photo)

▶TAYLOR PALMER: An entire theme runs the length of the knife, namely the joining of the Union Pacific and Central Pacific railroads, and the piece features Taylor's lost-wax castings of a railroad-track-and-spike guard, two trains, a water tower and an old railroad lantern.

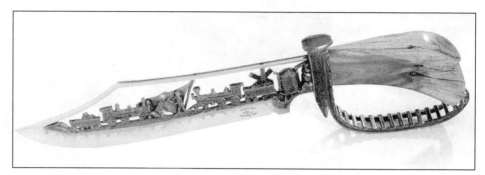

▶JAY GENSKE: The carved snake coils itself around a Peter Martin damascus blade.

▶PETER MARTIN: The whole blasted bug is carved in one way or another, with a pearl and damascus body on one side and ancient ivory on the other. It's so easy to be bitten by this one. (PointSeven photo)

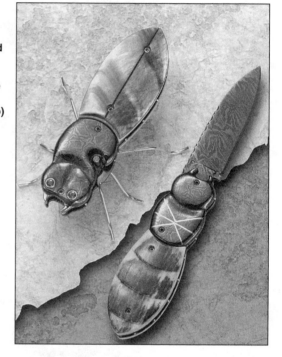

▶LARRY FUEGEN: The carved walrus ivory is in a class by itself. (PointSeven photo)

▶AL DIPPOLD: Carved pearl and steel fan out like the fingers that will eventually feel for the knife. (Ward photo)

▼HARUMI HIRAYAMA: The baby swan and parents are far from being ugly ducklings, that's for sure.

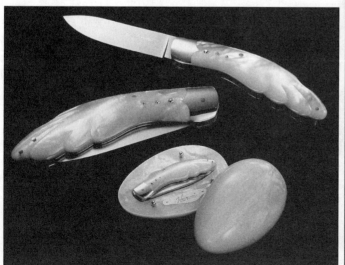

BARRY DAVIS: It takes so long to take in the checkering and carving by Daniel Stephan, you almost miss the 14k-gold pins, liners, escutcheon and buttons. (PointSeven photo)

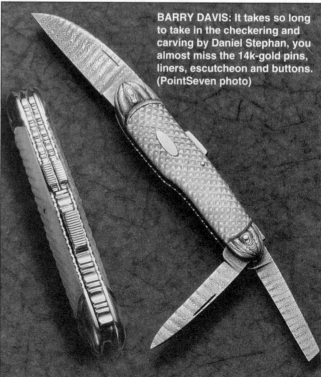

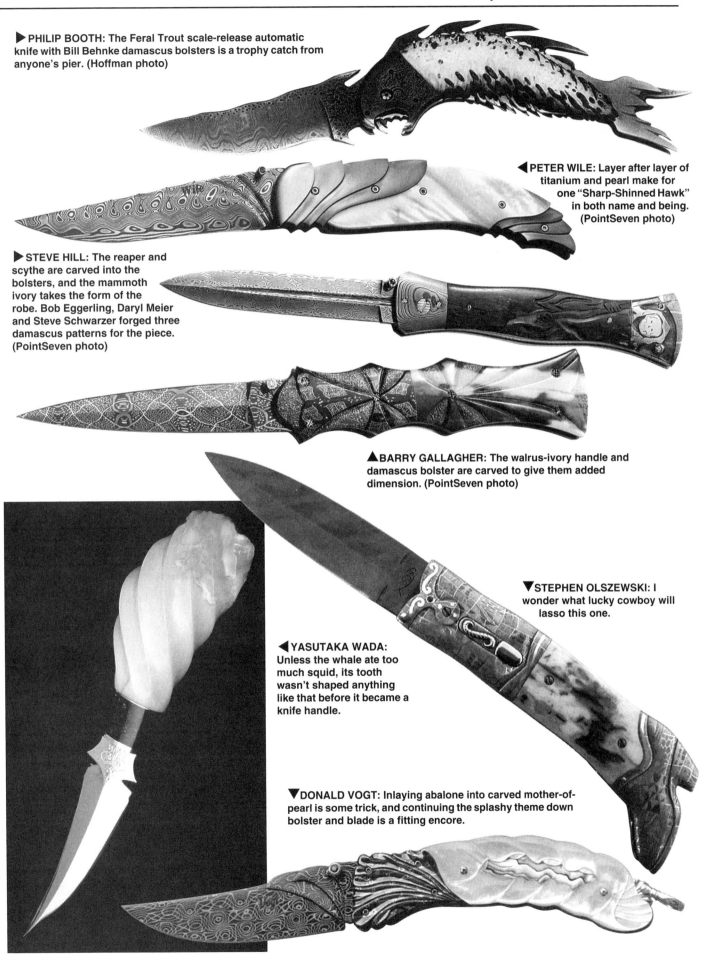

▶PHILIP BOOTH: The Feral Trout scale-release automatic knife with Bill Behnke damascus bolsters is a trophy catch from anyone's pier. (Hoffman photo)

◀PETER WILE: Layer after layer of titanium and pearl make for one "Sharp-Shinned Hawk" in both name and being. (PointSeven photo)

▶STEVE HILL: The reaper and scythe are carved into the bolsters, and the mammoth ivory takes the form of the robe. Bob Eggerling, Daryl Meier and Steve Schwarzer forged three damascus patterns for the piece. (PointSeven photo)

▲BARRY GALLAGHER: The walrus-ivory handle and damascus bolster are carved to give them added dimension. (PointSeven photo)

▼STEPHEN OLSZEWSKI: I wonder what lucky cowboy will lasso this one.

◀YASUTAKA WADA: Unless the whale ate too much squid, its tooth wasn't shaped anything like that before it became a knife handle.

▼DONALD VOGT: Inlaying abalone into carved mother-of-pearl is some trick, and continuing the splashy theme down bolster and blade is a fitting encore.

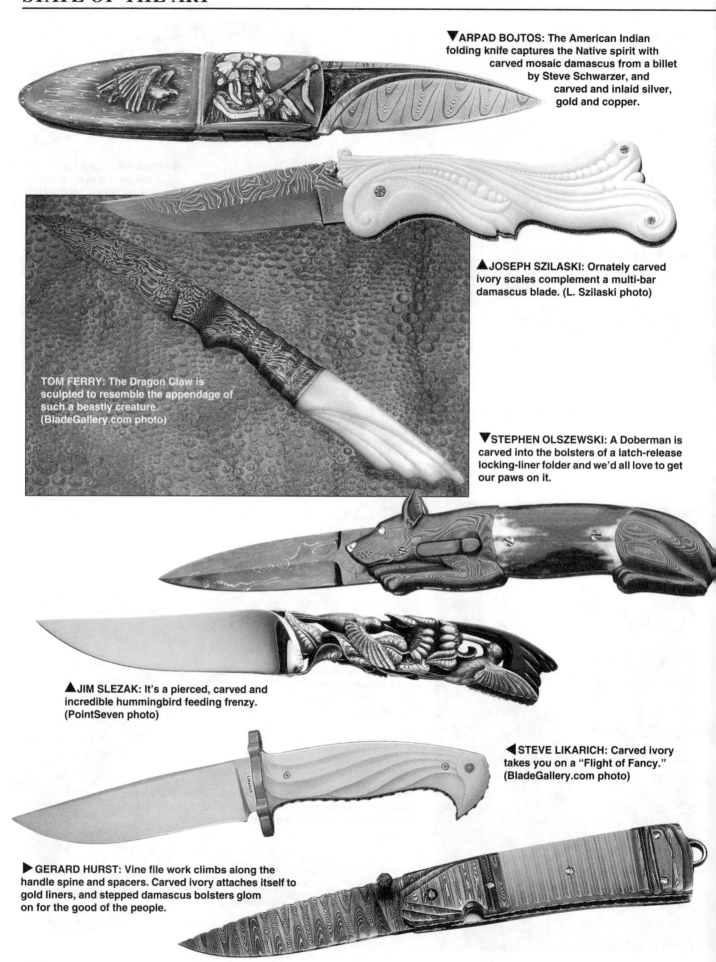

▼ARPAD BOJTOS: The American Indian folding knife captures the Native spirit with carved mosaic damascus from a billet by Steve Schwarzer, and carved and inlaid silver, gold and copper.

▲JOSEPH SZILASKI: Ornately carved ivory scales complement a multi-bar damascus blade. (L. Szilaski photo)

TOM FERRY: The Dragon Claw is sculpted to resemble the appendage of such a beastly creature. (BladeGallery.com photo)

▼STEPHEN OLSZEWSKI: A Doberman is carved into the bolsters of a latch-release locking-liner folder and we'd all love to get our paws on it.

▲JIM SLEZAK: It's a pierced, carved and incredible hummingbird feeding frenzy. (PointSeven photo)

◀STEVE LIKARICH: Carved ivory takes you on a "Flight of Fancy." (BladeGallery.com photo)

▶ GERARD HURST: Vine file work climbs along the handle spine and spacers. Carved ivory attaches itself to gold liners, and stepped damascus bolsters glom on for the good of the people.

Scrimshaw Showcase

DEEP, DETAILED, TOTALLY engrossing: a trio of adjectives that attempt to put to words the complexity and raw beauty of each scrimshawed knife handle. To say some of the human faces stippled in the pores of ivory exude character can be likened to describing Col. James Bowie as an "interesting chap." Native American faces are favored subjects, perhaps for their naturally stoic and stately appearances, with deep lines telling stories of pain, suffering and wisdom brought forth during years

of war and survival. Animals are presented in their natural surroundings, with distinctive markings captured by the skilled hands of scrimshaw artists with eyes for the unusual.

Uncommon beauty: a phrase most often used to describe an entrancing woman, but here to tell the tale of artists at work. Scrimshaw is much more gorgeous in person than it is on paper, so imagine holding a smooth, palpable ivory handle with the most fantastic color scrimshaw work

sunk beneath the surface of the porous material but brought forth like oil on canvas.

Captured: a moment in time, a beast in the wild, or a lady in waiting. Photographs capture such things. Scrimshaw is more masterpiece than technological wonder. Brought to life are subjects that have been dead for years or lost in the history books forever. Here, paraded before us are the bold, the brave, the fierce and the fantastic. These artists love their work, and we love to look at it.

Blown away, knocked over and stunned: the ones who view such intimate work and are deeply touched by its powerful message.

Joe Kertzman

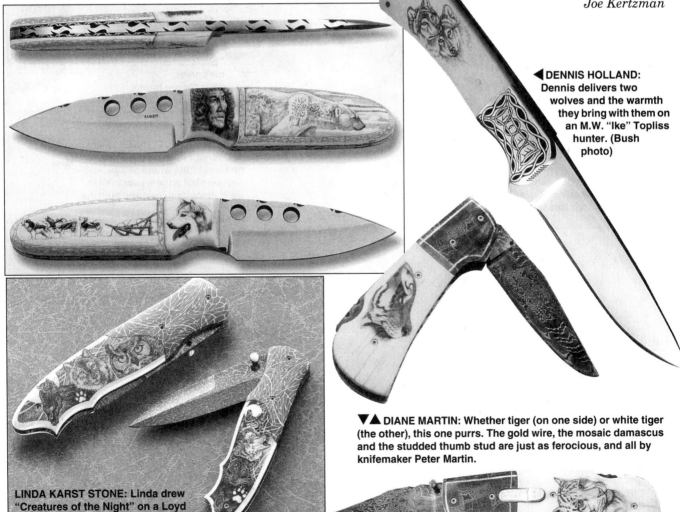

▼**GARY WILLIAMS:** The origin of an Alaskan drop-point hunter (by Gene Baskett) is revealed through Gary's needle and ink, and what a gorgeous effect he created.

◄**DENNIS HOLLAND:** Dennis delivers two wolves and the warmth they bring with them on an M.W. "Ike" Topliss hunter. (Bush photo)

LINDA KARST STONE: Linda drew "Creatures of the Night" on a Loyd McConnell folder, and we'll all have wild dreams tonight. (PointSeven photo)

▼▲ **DIANE MARTIN:** Whether tiger (on one side) or white tiger (the other), this one purrs. The gold wire, the mosaic damascus and the studded thumb stud are just as ferocious, and all by knifemaker Peter Martin.

STATE OF THE ART

◄MARY MUELLER: "Secretary, cancel my appointments, and hold all my calls." Did Mary do a fine job on a Tom Ferry presentation dagger, or what?! (BladeGallery.com photo)

◄JOHN STAHL: An eagle is close up and in flight on a Howard Hitchmough sheath knife. (PointSeven photo)

◄JOHN STAHL: Howard Hitchmough has a good thing going if John plans to scrim wolves on all his knives. (PointSeven photo)

►RICHARD HUTCHINGS: Even if it weren't reverse scrim (white on black), this would still be anything but ordinary scrimshaw. Ed Wallace designed and built the candidly cool cutter. (PointSeven photo)

▲JOHN STAHL: When John saw the slab of elephant ivory, he envisioned a goshawk attacking a mink, something no one else could see until the piece was complete. (PointSeven photo)

▼JOHN STAHL: The letter opener would never get used in my office. (PointSeven photo)

LINDA KARST STONE: Could you please rub my temple tiger? A Dennis Friedly damascus dagger is all the better for asking. (PointSeven photo)

▲SHARON BURGER: Ready for a knife is a rectangular-elephant-ivory-handle inset with black stipple of a baby elephant with herd.

▶LINDA KARST STONE: With gold-plated Gary House damascus in patriotic theme, Linda had no option but to stipple the Loyd McConnell folder red, white and blue. The result is amazing. (PointSeven photo)

JOHN STAHL: A ruffed grouse shows why Mother Nature can't be fooled. Howard Hitchmough builds the knives that make the whole world sing. (PointSeven photo)

◀LINDA KARST STONE: The range of material Linda is able to cover with ink, needle and steady hand is fabulous. She saw what she saw in a Leon Treiber lock-back folding knife, and it looks like she was right. (BladeGallery.com photo)

▶GAETAN BEAUCHAMP: Three Eagles of the Nez Perce tribe appears stoic and proud.

▼RICK LUDWIG: Rick fought fires for 26 years in Manhattan, Brooklyn and the greater New York area, and he built a commemorative knife for his fallen comrades with the Emerald Society, Fire Department New York logo scrimshawed on an ivory handle insert.

▶SHARON BURGER: While a whimsical fairy emerges from within the pores of the warthog-ivory handle of a Mackrill & Son knife, a group of gnomes makes their presence known on the other side of the grip.

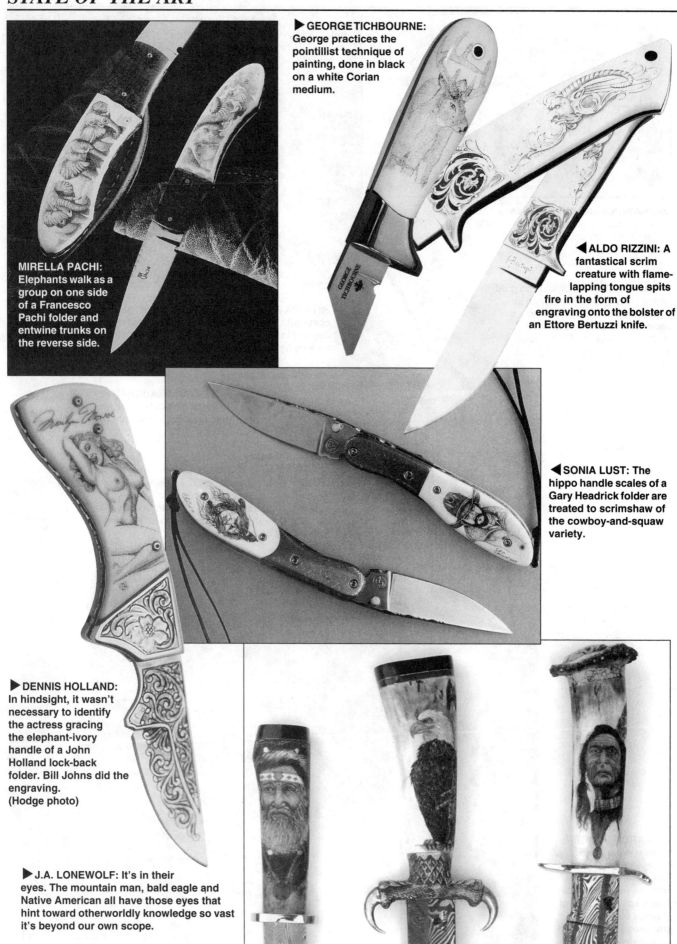

GEORGE TICHBOURNE: George practices the pointillist technique of painting, done in black on a white Corian medium.

MIRELLA PACHI: Elephants walk as a group on one side of a Francesco Pachi folder and entwine trunks on the reverse side.

ALDO RIZZINI: A fantastical scrim creature with flame-lapping tongue spits fire in the form of engraving onto the bolster of an Ettore Bertuzzi knife.

SONIA LUST: The hippo handle scales of a Gary Headrick folder are treated to scrimshaw of the cowboy-and-squaw variety.

DENNIS HOLLAND: In hindsight, it wasn't necessary to identify the actress gracing the elephant-ivory handle of a John Holland lock-back folder. Bill Johns did the engraving. (Hodge photo)

J.A. LONEWOLF: It's in their eyes. The mountain man, bald eagle and Native American all have those eyes that hint toward otherworldly knowledge so vast it's beyond our own scope.

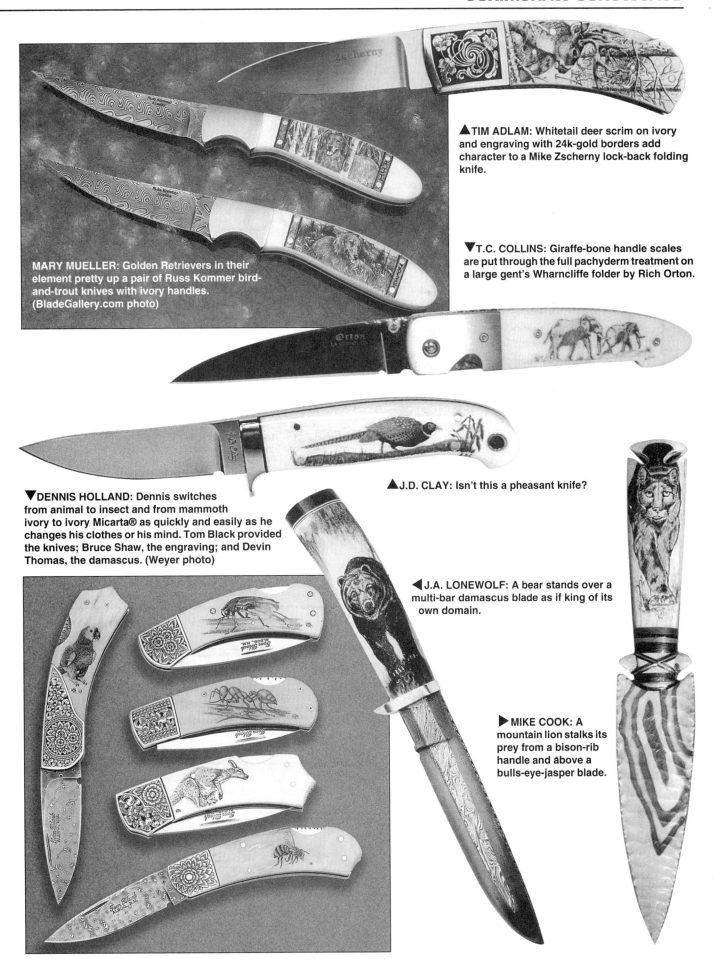

▲TIM ADLAM: Whitetail deer scrim on ivory and engraving with 24k-gold borders add character to a Mike Zscherny lock-back folding knife.

MARY MUELLER: Golden Retrievers in their element pretty up a pair of Russ Kommer bird-and-trout knives with ivory handles. (BladeGallery.com photo)

▼T.C. COLLINS: Giraffe-bone handle scales are put through the full pachyderm treatment on a large gent's Wharncliffe folder by Rich Orton.

▼DENNIS HOLLAND: Dennis switches from animal to insect and from mammoth ivory to ivory Micarta® as quickly and easily as he changes his clothes or his mind. Tom Black provided the knives; Bruce Shaw, the engraving; and Devin Thomas, the damascus. (Weyer photo)

▲J.D. CLAY: Isn't this a pheasant knife?

◀J.A. LONEWOLF: A bear stands over a multi-bar damascus blade as if king of its own domain.

▶MIKE COOK: A mountain lion stalks its prey from a bison-rib handle and above a bulls-eye-jasper blade.

FACTORY TRENDS

Can we produce that custom knife design? Can we anodize and inset titanium, build frame locks, *skeletonize* handles, design spring-assisted-opening folding knives? Can we grind that super steel? These questions and more are on the lips of many knife manufacturers, engineers, sales managers and chief executive officers across the board in the cutlery industry.

Three dimensional designing, open knife frames with no back bars, knives you can actually look into and through, fancy spacers, thumb studs, pocket clips, multi-carry-option sheaths and lightweight fixed blades and folders are fast becoming realities.

Speedy folders, with blades that pop out faster than the eye can see, are hot. Neck knives are so light you can barely feel them suspended from breakaway bead chains under your shirt and against your chest. Tough tactical folders with a softened look and feel have replaced black handles, gray blades and bead blasting throughout the design of each bullet-proof offering.

Locking liners continue to remain popular, but watch out for frame-locking folders. With a frame lock, there's less to produce and a great deal of strength in a folder that is propped open by its own frame. No liner means few extra parts. Speaking of parts, they are all included. Some knives come with wrenches to adjust pivot tensions, and others, specifically tool knives, incorporate wrenches into their designs. Wrenches for skateboards, snowboards, mountain bikes and scooters are the latest craze.

Could you please pass me the clip-point bowie knife? I have a sliver to extract. Oh, no bowie, well the spear point will do, or the *tanto* if necessary. Knives are coming in shapes, sizes, materials and designs that are just plain useful, fun and beautiful to behold. They're light to the touch, easy to handle and they cut like mad. Can we make that? You bet we can, boss. In fact, we just did.

Joe Kertzman

Knife Pros Sing the Praises of a Cutlery Giant

A.G. Russell is an entrepreneur, major influence in the field

By Mac Overton

IN THE HILLS of northwestern Arkansas resides a man that has had more influence on the modern knife business—both handmade and production knives—than anyone else. A catalyst in the knife boom of the late 1960s and early 1970s, A.G. Russell's influence continues strong today!

Custom knifemakers and heads of production companies credit A.G. with helping them along. I personally remember a phone conversation I had with him in 1972 or '73. I called him with questions I had about knives, and even though he had never met me, he spent at least an hour on the phone politely responding to my inquiries.

He has been of immeasurable influence on others, too. B.R. "Bill" Hughes, one of the most noted and prolific writers in the field of knives, and an influence on the business in his own right, credits A.G. with helping him get a start in penning articles about man's oldest tool.

Bill was writing gun and hunting articles for *GUNSport* magazine. After Ken Warner, who was editor and had written some well-received articles about knives for that magazine, left to start another magazine,

A.G. Russell (left) and company president and CEO Goldie Russell are the brains, brawn, backbone and lifeblood of A.G. Russell Knives.

the publisher asked if anyone on the staff knew anything about knives.

Bill volunteered and quickly called A.G. who gave him a crash course on knives, knifemakers and knifemaking. "Thanks to A.G.'s help, I made it all right," Bill said. "That's how my career as a knife writer started."

"I have felt for a long time that A.G. has not gotten the recognition that he deserves," said Wally Gardiner, president of the Imperial Schrade Co. "He was the first to suggest and arrange a custom/factory knife collaboration [between Schrade and Bob Loveless in the early 1970s], and he was the first to produce lightweight lock-back knives."

The A.G. Russell-designed (and much copied) Woodswalker has been a hit since he introduced it as a non-folding pocketknife with wallet sheath in the 1970s. Today, with a Kydex® neck sheath, it is enjoying a resurgence in popularity. Price is moderate: $25 with Kydex® sheath, $20 with leather wallet sheath, or $10 for the knife alone.

"He was the first to successfully create popular-priced commemoratives that started the whole collector segment of the business," Gardiner added.

A.G. founded the Knife Collector's Club in the early 1970s, offering members the Kentucky Rifle, a large stockman folding knife made by Schrade with ivory-colored Delrin® handles. Other club knives included the Camillus Cutlery Granddaddy Barlow, the Luger Pistol knife from Puma and six Hen & Rooster models. In fact, in the 1970s, A.G. bought the German Bertram firm that carried the Hen & Rooster trademark when it was on the brink of bankruptcy, keeping it afloat for five years.

"He is a marketing genius with an entrepreneur's enthusiasm for the cutlery business," Gardiner said. "With the exception of Albert M. Baer, he is the most knowledge-able person in the knife business I've had the pleasure of knowing. He deserves far more credit than he has been given."

Born in southeast Arkansas in 1933, A.G. knew the value of a sharp knife. He got his start in the knife business shortly after visiting hardware stores in the area to purchase a natural Arkansas whetstone. "I went into every hardware store in a 50-mile radius," he said. "None of them had anything but Carborundum [silicon carbide abrasive]."

Whetstone Awareness

He recognized a market for whetstones and began buying and

The all-steel knife is A.G. Russell's innovative Hocho folding cook's knife, and the two pieces below it are different sizes of chef's knives from his exclusive kitchen knife series.

selling them, placing ads in gun magazines to market the sharpening stones. Knives were next in his inventory when he bought some German pocketknives and Swedish kitchen knives from the widow of a small importer.

He often featured custom knives in his ads, giving exposure to makers who would not have otherwise reached a wide knife-buying audience. "I did run those ads until another knifemaker told me it was his turn," A.G. said. "It seemed it had become an entitlement."

A.G. believes his company was the only knife mail-order business in the mid-1960s. "It was tiny," he noted, "but now I feel that we are a mid-size mail-order company."

While he classes his mail-order business as mid-sized, he distributes three catalogs with a combined circulation of more than 4 million copies a year. These include *The A.G. Russell® Catalog of Knives, Russell's for Men®* and *Cutting Edge®*, an aftermarket catalog. The A.G. Russell Co. has more than 100 online domains, including the four sites Russell considers most important: http://agrussell.com; http://russellsformen.com; http://cuttingedge.com; and http://knifedigest.org.

In 2000, A.G. said, the Internet accounted for about one-twelfth of his business, and a year later, it had grown to one-sixth of total sales.

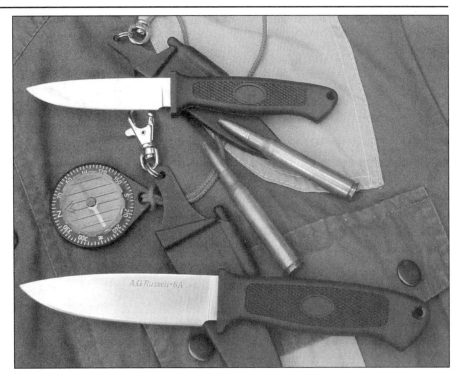

The A.G. Russell Deer Hunter and smaller Bird and Trout Knife are engineered as a package and are ground from extremely thin stock.

Early on, A.G. helped co-found The Knifemakers' Guild because, "I felt there was a need for banding together for publicity and friendship. Every one of the 12 to 15 makers I knew then hated all other knifemakers. I talked R.W. [Bob] Loveless and Dan Dennehy into helping me form the Guild."

Spencer Frazer, founder and president of SOG Specialty Knives, termed A.G. "a giant in our industry."

"He has been influential in the growth of the knife business on a custom knifemaker level, as a mail order/Internet power, as a historian, and I probably missed a few others," Frazer said. "A.G. was instrumental

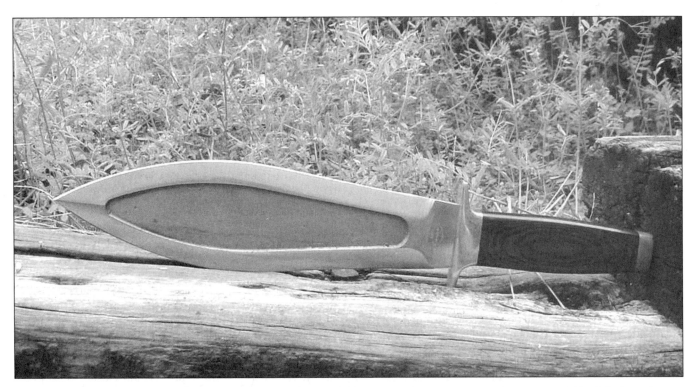

This massive, double-edged, 10-inch-blade "utility knife," the Assagi, was inspired by a traditional African tribal knife. A.G. Russell commissioned it to be made in Solingen, Germany, and it has not been in his catalog for some time.

in helping us at SOG get into business. We contacted him and he gave freely of his advice and introduced us to overseas contacts.

"Today, if I have a question about an old knife pattern or, for that matter, a brand-new product concept, A.G. is one of the first people I ask," Frazer said.

The One Hand Knife

A.G. has many knife designs to his credit, some of which have been widely copied. Among these is the One Hand Knife, which he terms "the easiest opening and closing knife you can buy." It features a handle machined out of a solid piece of stainless steel, and a lock bar integral to the handle frame.

"In the more than 40 years that I have been making, designing and collecting knives, I have never seen a knife that excites me more than that one does," A.G. stated.

In the mid 1990s, A.G. introduced a variation of the One Hand Knife in an ultra-lightweight version. It has a fiberglass-reinforced-nylon (similar to Zytel®) handle, an 8A steel blade, and weighs 1.5 ounces (the all-steel version is 2.4 ounces). The price tag is about one-quarter that of the standard steel version, and it's available with a choice of a general-purpose blade (my favorite—it's great for digging out splinters), or a clip-point blade for those wanting a more traditional profile.

Around the same time, A.G. Russell Knives introduced the Deer Hunter and Bird and Trout fixed-blade knives of extremely thin stock. The Deer Hunter showcases a 4-inch drop-point blade .080-inches thick, and the Bird and Trout model features a 3-inch drop-point blade of .060-inch stock.

A.G. believes that thin blades cut well, and that the actual utility knives of the legendary mountain men of the early 19th century were of thin blade stock, somewhat like Old Hickory or Russell-Harrington butcher knives. His reasoning: mountain men carried hundreds of pounds of equipment with them on their long journeys and, if thick blades were better, they wouldn't have minded sacrificing a few ounces of weight in other gear to carry them.

One of A.G.'s first commercial designs was the Woodswalker, a non-folding pocketknife that can be carried in a special hip-pocket blade wallet. He introduced it in the 1970s as a small-game and light

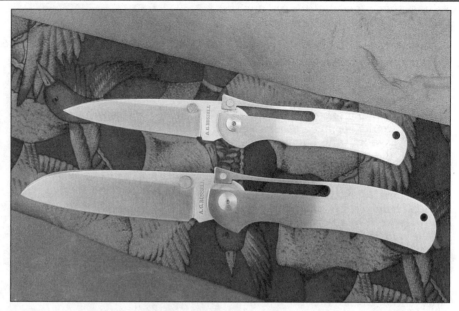

A.G. has many knife designs to his credit, and among these is the One Hand Knife, which he terms "the easiest opening and closing knife you can buy." It features a handle machined out of a solid piece of stainless steel, and a lock bar integral to the handle frame.

Lightweight versions of the One Hand Knife, the A.G. Russell FeatherLites showcase fiberglass-reinforced-nylon handles, molded as solid pieces. Each is checkered and shaped, not only to fit the hand with comfort when working, but also to fit in a pocket without wearing holes in the lining.

utility knife. It looks like an efficient paring knife, and A.G. says four or more of them would make a fine steak knife set. He recently introduced a Kydex® sheath on a bead chain, expanding the uses of the model to a neck knife.

A.G. has, indeed, contributed his skills to the kitchen cutlery field. In the late 1970s, he unveiled a line of forged kitchen knives made for him in Solingen, Germany. They resembled Sabatier, Wusthof and other traditional European forged knives, but A.G. said he used superior steel. One testimony to the quality of the line, now discontinued, is that several custom makers bought sets for their wives to use in their own kitchens.

A.G. said, "Those were the finest forged-bolster knives in the world. The company that did that special work for us has closed, and when we sell the remaining knives from that source, there will be no more."

When A.G. Russell turns his thoughts to Gent's Knives, here are three of the results. The two-blade piece is a whittler model.

Two versions of A.G. Russell's Sting fixed-blade tactical knife are shown, as well as the folding camp knife version of his exclusive StrikeForce series.

Tungsten in Check

More recently, he has introduced a kitchen cutlery line of his own design. While not revealing the steel, he said that it is "a very special high-carbon, stainless tool steel, containing enough tungsten to assure real edge holding."

The offset handles allow them to be used for hours without becoming uncomfortable, and they fit both large and small hands. They are lightweight, and like the Deer Hunter and Bird and Trout models, have thin blades with just enough stiffness. "I have always admired the forged-bolster look of traditional European-style kitchen cutlery, but I have always had problems with weight, balance and the fact that great modern steels cannot be easily forged," he noted. While they are not cheap, prices are much lower than forged blades designed for the same function.

A.G.'s ability to think "outside the box" is perhaps no more evident than in his development of what, as far as I know, is the only folding cook's knife in existence. The Hocho features a 4 1/4-inch blade with a very slight curve to the edge and a hardness rating of 60-61RC on the Rockwell Hardness Scale. It measures 5 1/8 inches closed and is made entirely of ATS-34 stainless steel for easy sterilizing. The Hocho is ground with a thin edge on a thin blade.

"It is designed to be a personal knife for those who want the finest possible tool for slicing, dicing and otherwise preparing vegetables and meats," A.G. stated. "It is not a camp knife or a hunting knife but, when preparing a meal is the task at hand, it works equally well in the kitchen of a New York City apartment, or in a Wyoming hunt camp."

There's more, much more to the A.G. story, such as how he purchased the Morseth Knives trademark in the early 1970s and kept that historic trademark alive, still using the same laminated Norwegian steel that founder Harry Morseth used.

But that and other aspects of A.G.'s career, which has benefited knife lovers everywhere, have been covered elsewhere. His achievements, and the influence he has had on the knife business, are not bad for someone who started out only wanting to find a better stone to sharpen his own knives! ●

For more information, contact A.G. Russell Knives, 1920 N. 26th St., Lowell, AR 72754-8489; phone: (800) 255-9034; fax: (479) 631-8493.

The Softening of Tactical Folders

WILLIAM HENRY KNIVES: The inter-frame folder is inset with abalone for a striking first impression.

◀ **WILLIAM HENRY KNIVES:** The look doesn't get much softer than the Mardi Gras, qualifying as a tactical folder for its locking liner, thumb stud and strong design, but aesthetically superior with a Mike Norris raindrop-pattern, stainless-damascus blade, and a silver-granulated handle. (PointSeven photo)

▲ **SPYDERCO:** Spyderco gives a choice of a vibrant-blue, shell-inlaid handle or a black fiberglass-reinforced grip on the Frank Centofante Vesuvius C66.

▼ **FROST CUTLERY:** Frost's Quicksilver lock-back folders showcase mother-of-pearl or combinations of abalone and pearl handles.

▲ **CHRIS REEVE KNIVES:** You can count on Chris Reeve Knives to soften the look of tactical-type folders, but don't count on the company to scrimp on strength. (PointSeven photo)

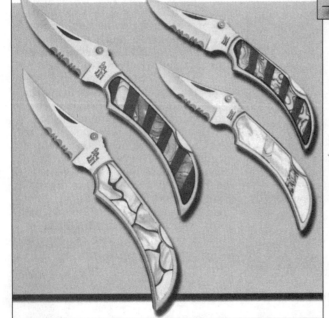

▲ ▼ **DELTA Z:** Fresh from Delta Z are locking-liner folders with plain and semi-serrated 420 stainless-steel clip-point blades, aluminum bolsters and maple-burl

MEYERCO: The Meyerco Speedster is aptly named for the speed of which the blade rotates on a bronze bushing.

►GERBER LEGENDARY BLADES: The slim G-10 grip of the Gerber/Fred Carter Utility I features four milled slots to lighten the load and give the knife a sporty appearance.

▲ BEAR CUTLERY: Black, ruby, sapphire and clear are the color choices for the Zytel® handle, and straight or serrated are the blade configurations.

▼KELLAM KNIVES: It locks, it cuts and it looks hot in an amboyna handle and damascus blade.

Spear, Clip and *Tanto* Tips

▲ TOPS KNIVES: A *skeletonized* tactical folder, the TOPS CQT-Thunder Hawke comes in a *tanto* or "hunter" blade.

◄ MASTERS OF DEFENSE: The spear-point blade is re-curved and multi-faceted, with a double edge on the first third nearest the tip, serrations near the multi-purpose hilt, and thumb notches on top.

▲ TOPS KNIVES: TOPS regards the blade shape as a Mexican bowie style, and with 1/4 inch of steel thickness to backup the company's claim, who's to argue?

►**SOG SPECIALTY KNIVES:** New versions of the SOG Vision folders include those with G-10 or Zytel handles and partially serrated ATS-34 *tanto* blades.

►**KA-BAR:** It's not called a thorn because the blade is wavy. This Bob Dozier-designed knife is spear pointed all the way.

◄**TIMBERLINE:** The Butch Vallotton-designed Discovery Lock boasts partial blade serrations on a black, Teflon®-coated, chisel-ground, AUS-8 blade.

►**SPYDERCO:** Lightweight and utilitarian are two characteristics of a new breed of clip-point bowies. This one is the Fred Perrin FB04 model, and it embodies those two traits and more.

◄**TAYLOR CUTLERY:** The Smith & Wesson H.R.T. is a Darrel Ralph and Mike Lamprey design incorporating a spear-point, bead-blasted 440C blade and a magnesium handle.

►**CAMILLUS:** The clip-point CUDA MAXX bowie is one of the largest production folders to date. The massive 5 1/4-inch D-2 blade folds into an anodized-titanium handle with integral frame lock.

▲ **MASERIN:** A safety ensures the spear-point blades of the locking-liner folding knives won't close accidentally.

Foxy Folders

DELTA Z: From the tip of the Mike Norris stainless-damascus blade to the "American-flame-red" maple-burl handle, the DZ-7111-MR Collector's Osprey from Delta Z is one sharp instrument.

XIKAR: When Xikar pairs G-10 (handle) with aircraft aluminum (frame), the result is a slim, trim frame-lock folder with a one-hand-opening, stainless steel blade.

TIGERSHARP TECHNOLOGIES: The Neon is a utility folder with replaceable GIN-5 blade in a drop-point configuration and complemented by aircraft-aluminum handle material anodized barn red, royal blue or silver.

KERSHAW KNIVES: The Black Chive is one nifty boron-coated folding knife with one of those blades that pops into position at the speed of light thanks to its Speed-Safe assisted-opening mechanism.

SHEPHERD HILLS CUTLERY: The Case Seahorse Whittler from Shepherd Hills shines forth with a Vintage Bone handle and stainless-steel pen, coping and Wharncliffe blades.

IMPERIAL SCHRADE: Production knives in stainless damascus include the special-edition Schrade Kious. Schrade introduced the two-blade gentleman's pocketknife at the 2002 S.H.O.T. (Shooting Hunting Outdoor Trade) Show. It is designed by Joe Kious.

▶SOG SPECIALTY KNIVES: Flash me a steel blade, SOG.

◀BUCK KNIVES: A departure from old-style pocketknives, the Ecco has a glass-filled nylon handle and 420 HC spear-point and sheepsfoot blades. It's available in two sizes and overall weights of 2.6 and 2.9 ounces.

▼AL MAR KNIVES: Al Mar has reintroduced the 1/2-ounce Osprey front-lock folders with 1 1/4-inch AUS-8 blades.

Handy Fixed Blades

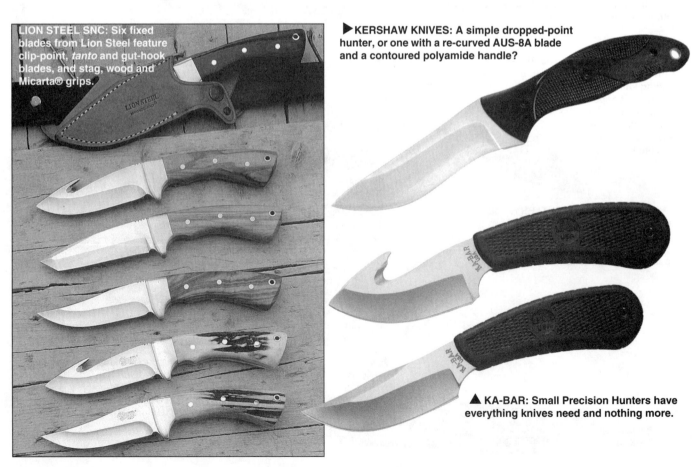

LION STEEL SNC: Six fixed blades from Lion Steel feature clip-point, *tanto* and gut-hook blades, and stag, wood and Micarta® grips.

▶KERSHAW KNIVES: A simple dropped-point hunter, or one with a re-curved AUS-8A blade and a contoured polyamide handle?

▲ KA-BAR: Small Precision Hunters have everything knives need and nothing more.

►BUCK KNIVES: Buck offers limited-edition pieces with wily wood grips and gorgeous blades, bolsters and guards.

▲ COLD STEEL: The checkered grips of the Pendleton Hunters (Lloyd Pendleton designs) are precursors to the quality hollow-ground blades, and cunning contours and cross sections of the knives.

▲ BERETTA: Beretta allows customers to choose from a selection of four full-tang, fixed-blade International Guide Knives.

◄ BUCK KNIVES: High-carbon, martensitic-stainless-steel blades and Kraton® handles hold their own on the Diamondbacks from Buck.

Rescue Knives and Tools

▲ BENCHMADE: Designed to cut rope, safety belts, clothing and other fibrous materials quickly and effectively is the Model 5 Rescue Hook, and that's an honorable profession.

▼UNITED CUTLERY: Fire engine red is the United Fire Fighter, and useful are the laser-cut blade serrations for cutting people out of trouble.

FACTORY TRENDS

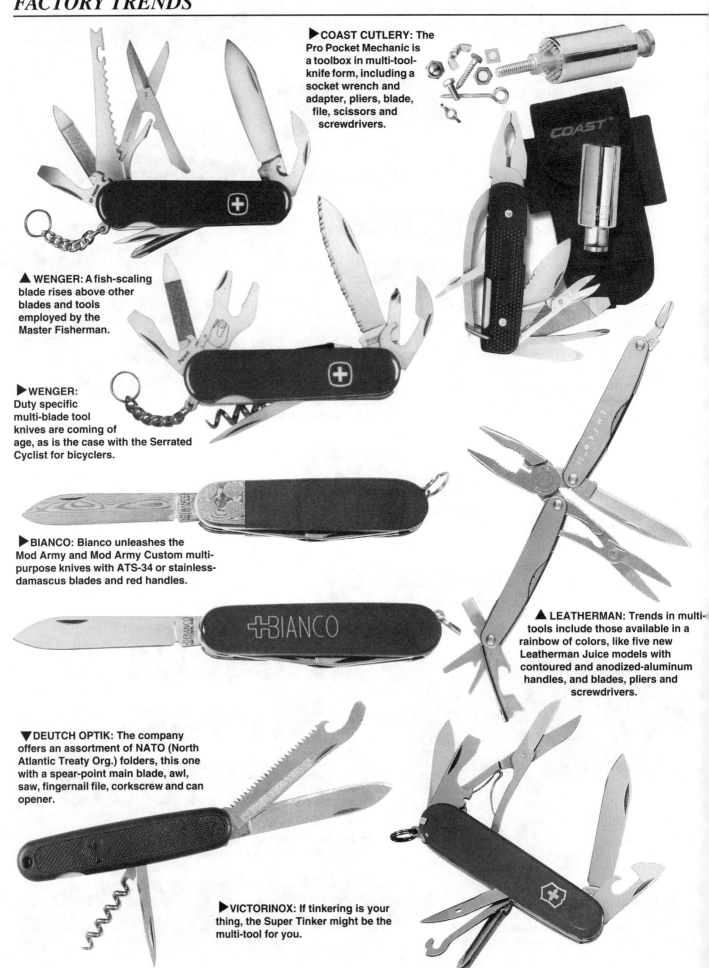

▶COAST CUTLERY: The Pro Pocket Mechanic is a toolbox in multi-tool-knife form, including a socket wrench and adapter, pliers, blade, file, scissors and screwdrivers.

▲ WENGER: A fish-scaling blade rises above other blades and tools employed by the Master Fisherman.

▶WENGER: Duty specific multi-blade tool knives are coming of age, as is the case with the Serrated Cyclist for bicyclers.

▶BIANCO: Bianco unleashes the Mod Army and Mod Army Custom multi-purpose knives with ATS-34 or stainless-damascus blades and red handles.

▲ LEATHERMAN: Trends in multi-tools include those available in a rainbow of colors, like five new Leatherman Juice models with contoured and anodized-aluminum handles, and blades, pliers and screwdrivers.

▼DEUTCH OPTIK: The company offers an assortment of NATO (North Atlantic Treaty Org.) folders, this one with a spear-point main blade, awl, saw, fingernail file, corkscrew and can opener.

▶VICTORINOX: If tinkering is your thing, the Super Tinker might be the multi-tool for you.

GERBER LEGENDARY BLADES: For high visibility and safety, the E-Z Out Utility and E-Z Rescue come in yellow nylon handles and blunt-tipped stainless steel blades.

UNITED CUTLERY: If you're a modern connoisseur of fine knives, the Colt Police Task Force might tickle your fancy with the blue-anodized and machined, aircraft-aluminum grip, rounded pocket clip and biting *tanto*-style blade.

IMPERIAL SCHRADE: How far have tool knives come? The Schrade i-Quip is equipped with a computer module that activates an altimeter, digital compass and digital clock. The "implement pod" incorporates screwdrivers, blade, scissors, saw, cap lifter, can opener, corkscrew. A signal mirror, survival whistle, lighter, belt clip and LED flashlight complete the package.

RICHARTZ: Fresh from Richartz is the Quadro pocketknife with a combination of black-coated and gray implements, including two blades, scissors, cap lifter, corkscrew, screwdriver and can opener.

A Gripping Group of Knives

BUCK KNIVES: A pronounced finger notch on a sculpted and slotted handle allows one to choke up on the Buck NXT Lockblade.

UNITED CUTLERY: The latest Gil Hibben design from United includes a bead-blasted 6061-T6 aluminum handle that's *skeletonized* and color anodized for feel and flavor.

▲ COLUMBIA RIVER KNIFE & TOOL: The contoured G-10 handle of the Howard Viele-designed Wasp allows for positive hand purchase, and the AUS 118 blade will do the rest.

▲ BOKER: Black Kraton is inset into lightweight, durable and shapely ABS handles in a variety of colors.

▶COLUMBIA RIVER KNIFE & TOOL: When Michael Walker designed the BladeLock, he did so with a raised Zytel® handle panel and a blade that locks open and closed via the thumb stud. (PointSeven photo)

▼SPYDERCO: Peter Herbst designed the Spyderco C53 locking-liner folder to integrate a contoured and lightweight titanium handle.

▼BENCHMADE: The textured, lightweight handle of the Griptilian handle is molded of Noryl GTX for strength and durability. The handle is shaped to nest naturally in the open palm of an adult's hand.

▲ TAYLOR CUTLERY: There's nothing more stealth, lightweight, handy and hot than an all-black Smith & Wesson locking-liner folder with a *skeletonized* grip and partially serrated, modified-*tanto* blade.

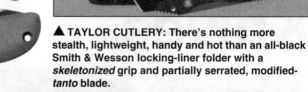

▶COLUMBIA RIVER KNIFE & TOOL: From the mind of Peter Marzitelli is the Prowler folder with a checkered-Zytel® grip and AUS-6M blade.

Neck and Key Chain Knives

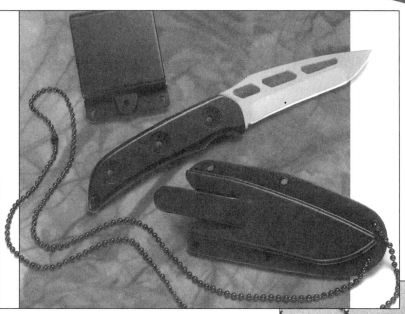

▲ EMERSON KNIVES: A claw-like knife from noted French knifemaker Fredric Perrin, the La Griffe is all 154 CM steel with a black-oxide finish and a Kydex® neck sheath for discrete carry.

▲ OUTDOOR EDGE: Here's a fixed blade—the Outdoor Edge G-Force—with a multi-option sheath designed for neck, belt or pocket carry.

▶CAMILLUS: The simplicity of the one-piece Arclite CUDA belies its utilitarian advantages as a neck knife with an integral, *skeletonized* grip to reduce weight. (PointSeven photo)

▼IMPERIAL SCHRADE: The Schrade Simon is a key chain or belt-loop knife sporting a plunger-like clip, a 2 1/4-inch stainless steel blade with one-hand opener, an anodized-aluminum grip and a frame lock.

▼COLD STEEL: Cold Steel's Spike neck knife weighs less than 3 ounces and is available with a cord-wrapped handle and a choice of a spear-point or *tanto* 420 blade.

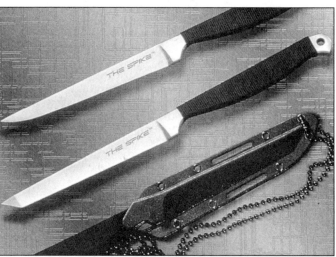

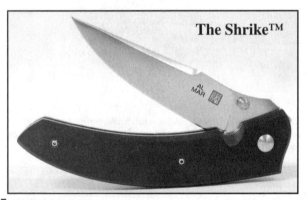
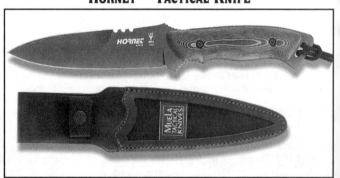

KNIVES MARKETPLACE

SHARPEN YOUR KNIFE THE PROFESSIONAL WAY

You've seen them demonstrated at knife, gun and craft shows, State Fairs, sharpening booths in your local gun and pawn shops, major sporting retailers and by friends in their workshops. These knife wheels have been designed to help professional knifemakers to put a perfect edge on any knife, old or new. Perfected by Jantz Supply, these wheels are now the perfect size and grit to bring you the ultimate sharpening system available. In just seconds you can restore an old rusty knife to an unbelievably sharp useful tool. The two wheel set includes everything needed to start sharpening with your buffer or grinder. Each wheel is 8 x 3/4" and can be used on a 1/2" or 5/8" shaft. Complete sharpening outfits are available which include a Baldor buffer or Delta grinder along with the wheels and compounds necessary to set up a professional sharpening center in your shop.

Visit their showroom located at 309 West Main, Davis, OK. Call 1-800-351-8900 to order yours today. Dealers inquire.

JANTZ SUPPLY
P.O. Box 584
Davis, OK 73030-0584
Phone: 580-369-2316 • Fax: 580-369-3082
Web: www.knifemaking.com

Established in 1992, Arizona Custom Knives (AZCK) has become a market leader in bringing you the finest handmade knives. From one-of-a-kind, investment-grade knives to your everyday carry knife, Arizona Custom Knives tries to "custom fit" the customer with the right knife at the right price. The company brings to you the best of the top makers, along with the latest from the up-and-comers. Years of established relationships with hundreds of custom knifemakers assures you of obtaining those rare gems you seek.

Your collection is their first priority!

ARIZONA CUSTOM KNIVES
Jay & Karen Sadow
8617 E. Clydesdale Trail, Scottsdale, AZ 85258
Phone: 480-951-0699 • Fax: 480-951-0699
Web: http://www.arizonacustomknives.com
Email: sharptalk@aol.com

GARY LEVINE FINE KNIVES
A DEALER OF HANDMADE KNIVES

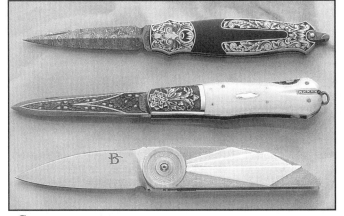

Gary's goal is to offer the collector the best custom knives available, in stock and ready for delivery. He has the best makers as well as the rising stars at fair prices. Gary enjoys working with collectors who want to enhance their collections, as well as someone who just wants a great knife to carry. Gary is also always on the lookout for collections, as well as single custom knives to purchase. Please stop by his website.

GARY LEVINE FINE KNIVES
P.O. Box 382, Chappaqua, NY 10514
Phone: 914-238-5748 • Fax: 914-238-6524
Web: http://www.levineknives.com
Email: gary@levineknives.com

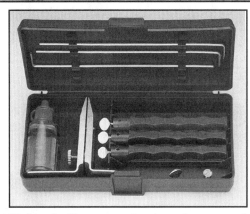

Since 1979, **Lansky Sharpeners has been known as the World Leader in sharpening system technology. Lansky's** fixed-angle sharpening system has been designed, developed and manufactured in America by professionals in the knife industry to satisfy the most critical requirements of sportsmen, hobbyists and household knife users. Lansky makes knife sharpening as easy as 1, 2, 3. Supplied in a colorful, lightweight, impact-resistant molded plastic carry-case, the Lansky Standard Knife Sharpening System revolves around the fixed angle knife clamp. which provides four different sharpening angle guide holes. A fully illustrated instruction brochure explains the simple sharpening procedure. For more information and a free color catalog, contact:

LANSKY SHARPENERS
P.O. Box 50830, Dept. KSK • Henderson, NV 89016
Phone: 702-361-7511 • Fax: 702-896-9511
Web: www.lansky.com • Email: bkufahl@lansky.com

KNIVES MARKETPLACE

XIKAR XI KNIVES

XIKAR knives utilize high tech materials and processes by the best knife makers in the world. Designed as slim, lightweight, ergonomic cutting instruments.

Xi 118 Elan. These gentlemen's jewelry knives are constructed of polished stainless frames with AUS-8 stainless blades hardened to HRC 57. Handles of carbon fiber or Chinese quince wood adorn the knife. Made in Seki, Japan. Total weight 1.3 oz!

Xi 138 Excel. These functional everyday knives are constructed of aircraft aluminum and have Z60CDV14 stainless blades hardened to HRC 57. Handles of G10 compliment the aluminum frame anodized in your choice of silver, black, or blue. Made in Maniago, Italy. Total weight 1.5 oz!

Xi 158 Excursion. These awesome gentlemen's knives are constructed of titanium and have Z60CDV14 stainless blades hardened to HRC 57. Handles of bead blasted carbon figer compliment the titanium frame anodized in your choice of silver, blue or champagne. Made in Maniago, Italy. Total weight 1.8 oz!

XIKAR, INC.
Cutler to the Trade
Phone Toll Free: 888-266-1193• Web: www.xikar.com

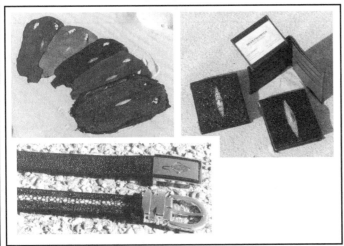

GATCO 5-STONE SHARPENING SYSTEM

The GATCO 5-Stone Sharpening System is the only fixed-angle sharpening kit needed to restore a factory perfect edge on even the most well-used knives.

Instructions are permanently mounted inside the storage case to make the job easy.

Just secure the blade in the polymer vise, select the proper angle guide, insert one of the five hone-stone angle guide bars into the guide slot, then put a few drops of mineral oil on the stone and start sharpening.

The GATCO 5-Stone Sharpening System includes extra coarse, coarse, medium and fine honing stones that are made from high-density aluminum oxide for long wear. The fifth, triangular-shaped hone is used for serrated blades.

All stones are mounted in color-coded grips.

To locate a GATCO dealer, call 1-800-LIV-SHARP.

GATCO SHARPENERS

P.O. Box 600, Getzville, NY 14068-0600
Phone: 716-877-2200 • Fax: 716-877-2591
E-mail: gatco@buffnet.net • www.gatcosharpeners.com

CUSTOM KNIVES

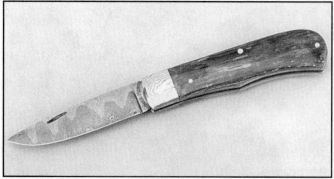

Knife pictured has Damascus blade made of 480 layers of 1095-203E steels in Mr. Hawes' shimmed ladder pattern. Bolster made of mokume from Sakmar. Handles are mammoth ivory. Truly a one-of-a-kind gem that will also function as a utility knife if you desire.

Hawes Forge specializes in high carbon, Damascus steel that are not just for show, they are made to stand up to use and will hold a superior edge. Let Hawes Forge provide you with a knife you can be proud of from their designs or yours.

HAWES FORGE

P.O. Box 176, Weldon, IL 61882
Phone: 217-736-2479

WWW.KNIFEMAKING.COM

They have it! Pre-shaped hardened and tempered blades, blade stock, brass, nickel silver, guards, pommels, rivets, handle materials, finishing supplies and equipment for sharpening, finishing, drilling, sanding, measuring, and much more. They stock what they sell and ship daily. Their customer service department is rated #1. They offer only the best quality merchandise available and sell to you with confidence.

Don't have access to the web yet? No problem. They offer a complete catalog of their supplies and have a showroom located right off I-35 in Davis, OK, for your convenience.

Shop the web for all your knifemaking supplies, tools, and equipment.

Visit their showroom located at 309 West Main, Davis, OK.

Call 1-800-351-8900 to order yours today. Dealers inquire.

JANTZ SUPPLY

P.O. Box 584
Davis, OK 73030-0584
Phone: 580-369-2316 • Fax: 580-369-3082
Web: www.knifemaking.com

A.G. RUSSELL™ KNIVES

The oldest mail order knife company, A.G. Russell Knives has a tradition of offering the finest quality knives and accessories worldwide. Lines include Randall, Dozier, William Henry, Leatherman, Case, Gerber, SOG, Ka-Bar, Kershaw, Columbia River, Al Mar, Klotzli, Boker, Marble's, Schatt & Morgan, A.G. Russell, and more. Call for a free catalog, or shop online to see the entire inventory of products at agrussell.com.

A.G. RUSSELL KNIVES

1920 North 26th Street, Dept. KA03
Lowell, AR 72745-8489
Phone: 479-571-6161 • Fax: 479-631-8493
Email: ag@agrussell.com • Web: agrussell.com

KNIVES MARKETPLACE

THE RELENTLESS PURSUIT OF PERFECTION!

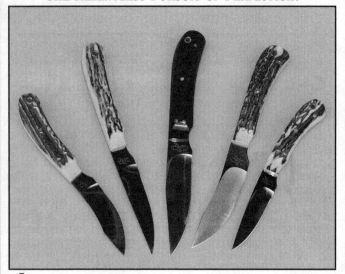

If you are looking for a handcrafted knife that is not only elegant, but is also designed to be used in the field, then a Dunn Knife is for you. Each knife is designed with the sportsman in mind, from the 440V steel (six to ten deer without resharpening is normal) to the finger recesses in the handle. "Your satisfaction is our goal," pledges company president Steve Greene.

Call or write:

DUNN KNIVES

P.O. Box 204, Rossville, KS 66533

Phone: 800-245-6483

MNANDI...A ZULU WORD MEANING NICE

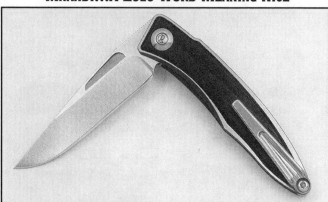

The **Mnandi** from Chris Reeve Knives is an elegant gentleman's folding knife. Hi-tech titanium combines with the natural warmth of wood to make this 2.75 inch bladed folder discreet and easy to carry. Weighing only 1.25 oz., the Mnandi features the Integral Lock©, tight tolerances and sharp cutting edge always associated with CRK. A removable clip provides a choice of carry style. Available in left and right hand models, the Mnandi has a Ziricote inlay on both sides of the handle.

The Mnandi is the newest addition to the legacy started by the One Piece Range and then the Sebenza Integral Lock Folding Knives.©

CHRIS REEVE KNIVES

11624 W. President Dr., #B, Boise, ID 83713

Phone: 208-375-0367

Web: http://www.chrisreeve.com

HAWKS!

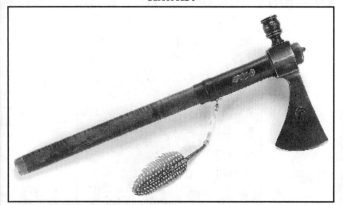

Ryan and Bob Johnson have been working together as a father and son team forging knives and tomahawks for over 16 years. Each tomahawk they craft is forged from mild steel with a slice of 1095 high carbon steel for the cutting edge. Most RMJ Forge tomahawks have curly maple hafts, pewter fittings, and are wrapped with leather near the head. Ryan and Bob research tomahawks of the 18th and 19th centuries and incorporate these design elements into their own style of tomahawk. RMJ Forge crafts pipe tomahawks, spike tomahawks, hammer poll tomahawks, and trade axes, offering over 30 different styles on their website. The website is the best place to learn about RMJ Forge.

RMJ FORGE

7620 Foster Hixon Cemetery Road, Hixson, TN 37343

Phone: 423-842-9323

E-mail: ryan@rmjforge.com • Web: www.rmjforge.com

Draper Knives
Mike & Audra Draper
#10 Creek Dr. Riverton, Wyoming. 82501
(307) 856-6807
(307) 851-0426
adraper@wyoming.com

KNIVES MARKETPLACE

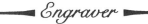
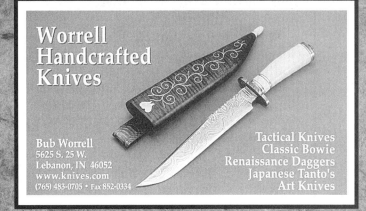

DIRECTORY

Browsing through this book, it's almost certain you will find a couple—or a couple dozen, more likely—creations that you would like to see in your pocket, under your Christmas tree or otherwise tucked in your knife collection.

Now comes the time to find the artisan, call or write that person, and make the deal.

Or perhaps you are a knifemaker yourself, searching for a chunk of mammoth ivory, or stag, or mother-of-pearl or other materials for your project.

Maybe you just want to call a commercial cutlery company for a catalog. Or write to *Blade* magazine or some other knife publication for a subscription.

Whatever your interest in the world of knives, we'll to help you make the connection with this directory. We don't play favorites when it comes to these lists. Most of the listings here were developed following a massive annual mailing that goes to custom knifemakers, companies and other organizations. Each knifemaking organization typically supplies the names of its members to us.

If you weren't listed, or if the listing has erroneous information, please write to Knives Annual at Krause Publications, 700 E. State St., Iola, WI 54990-0001, and we will list you or correct the mistake next year.

If you are a custom knifemaker, feel free to submit complete information about your specialties (using the listings in the book as a guide), along with sample photos of a few of your best works.

Thanks for helping us to make this the best source book—the only complete handbook—of the world's most dazzling, creative cutlery for 23 straight years.

a

ABBOTT, WILLIAM M., Box 102A, RR #2, Chandlerville, IL 62627, Phone: 217-458-2325
Specialties: High-grade edged weapons. **Patterns:** Locking folders, Bowies, working straight knives, kitchen cutlery, minis. **Technical:** Grinds D2, ATS-34, 440C and commercial Damascus. Heat-treats; Rockwell tests. Prefers natural handle materials. **Prices:** $100 to $1,000. **Remarks:** Part-time maker; first knife sold in 1984. **Mark:** Name.

ABEGG, ARNIE, 5992 Kenwick CR, Huntington Beach, CA 92648, Phone: 714-848-5697

ABERNATHY, PAUL J., 3033 Park St., Eureka, CA 95501, Phone: 707-442-3593
Specialties: Period pieces and traditional straight knives of his design and in standard patterns. **Patterns:** Miniature daggers, fighters and swords. **Technical:** Forges and files SS, brass and sterling silver. **Prices:** $100 to $250; some to $500. **Remarks:** Part-time maker. Doing business as Abernathy's Miniatures. **Mark:** Stylized initials.

ACKERSON, ROBIN E, 119 W Smith St, Buchanan, MI 49107, Phone: (616) 695-2911

ADAMS, WILLIAM D., 9318 Cole Creek Dr., Houston, TX 77040, Phone: 713-855-5643, Fax:713-855-5638
Specialties: Hunter scalpels and utility knives of his design. **Patterns:** Hunters and utility/camp knives. **Technical:** Grinds 1095, 440C and 440V. Uses stabilized wood and other stabilized materials. **Prices:** $100 to $200. **Remarks:** Part-time maker; first knife sold in 1994. **Mark:** Last name in script.

ADAMS, LES, 6413 NW 200 St., Hialeah, FL 33015, Phone: 305-625-1699
Specialties: Working straight knives of his design. **Patterns:** Fighters, hunters and fillet knives. **Technical:** Grinds ATS-34, 440C and D2. Offers scrimshawed handles. **Prices:** $100 to $200; some to $290. **Remarks:** Part-time maker; first knife sold in 1989. **Mark:** First initial, last name, Custom Knives.

ADAMS, BILL, P O Box 666, Conyers, GA 31078, Phone: 912-836-4195

ADKINS, RICHARD L., 138 California Ct, Mission Viejo, CA 92692-4079

AIDA, YOSHIHITO, 26-7 Narimasu 2-chome, Itabashi-ku, Tokyo 175-0094, JAPAN, Phone: 81-3-3939-0052, Fax:81-3-3939-0058
Specialties: High-tech working straight knives and folders of his design. **Patterns:** Bowies, lockbacks, hunters, fighters, fishing knives, boots. **Technical:** Grinds CV-134, ATS-34; buys Damascus; works in traditional Japanese fashion for some handles and sheaths. **Prices:** $400 to $900; some higher. **Remarks:** Full-time maker; first knife sold in 1978. **Mark:** Initial logo and Riverside West.

AKAHORI, YOICHIRO, Fuzieda 1-5-4, Shizuoka-ken, 426-0006, JAPAN, Phone: 81 54 641-4830, Fax:81 54 641 4830
Specialties: Classic & traditional straight knives of his design. **Patterns:** Bowies, hunters & utility/camp knives. **Technical:** Forges Japanese carbon steels; his own Damascus. Prices: $250 to $750; some to $1500. **Remarks:** Full-time maker; first knife sold in 1990. **Mark:** SAEMON in Japanese Kanji.

ALBERICCI, EMILIO, 19 via Masone, 24100, Bergamo, ITALY, Phone: 01139-35-215120
Specialties: Folders and Bowies. **Patterns:** Collector knives. **Technical:** Uses stock removal with extreme lavoration accuracy; offers exotic and high-tech materials. **Prices:** Not currently selling. **Remarks:** Part-time maker. **Mark:** None.

ALDERMAN, ROBERT, 2655 Jewel Lake Rd., Sagle, ID 83860, Phone: 208-263-5996
Specialties: Classic and traditional working straight knives in standard patterns or to customer specs and his design; period pieces. **Patterns:** Bowies, fighters, hunters and utility/camp knives. **Technical:** Casts, forges and grinds 1084; forges and grinds L6 and O1. Prefers an old appearance. **Prices:** $100 to $350; some to $700. **Remarks:** Full-time maker; first knife sold in 1975. Doing business as Trackers Forge. **Mark:** Deer track. **Other:** Starting April 2000 I am starting a knife making school. It's a 2 week course for beginners; will cover forging, stock removal, hardening, tempering, case making. All materials supplies - $1,250.

ALDRETE, BOB, P O Box 1471, Lomita, CA 90717, Phone: (310) 326-3041

ALEXANDER, DARREL, Box 381, Ten Sleep, WY 82442, Phone: 307-366-2699
Specialties: Traditional working straight knives. **Patterns:** Hunters, boots and fishing knives. **Technical:** Grinds D2, 440C, ATS-34 and 154CM.

Prices: $75 to $120; some to $250. **Remarks:** Full-time maker; first knife sold in 1983. **Mark:** Name, city, state.

ALEXANDER, JERED, 213 Hogg Hill Rd, Dierks, AR 71833, Phone: (870) 286-2981

ALEXANDER, EUGENE, Box 540, Ganado, TX 77962-0540, Phone: (512) 771-3727

ALLEN, MIKE "WHISKERS", 12745 Fontenot Acres Rd., Malakoff, TX 75148, Phone: 903-489-1026
Specialties: Working and collector-quality lockbacks, liner locks and automatic folders to customer specs. **Patterns:** Hunters, tantos, Bowies, swords and miniatures. **Technical:** Grinds Damascus, 440C & ATS-34, engraves. **Prices:** $200 and up. **Remarks:** Full-time maker; first knife sold in 1984. **Mark:** Whiskers and date.

ALLRED, BRUCE F., 1764 N Alder, Layton, UT 84041, Phone: 801-825-4612
Specialties: Knives are custom utility knives. **Patterns:** Several knives are designed by myself they include a unique grind line and thumb notches, many of my knives include mosaic pins and /or brass thumb guards. **Technical:** ATS34, 154CM and 440C. **Remarks:**The handle material include but not limited to Micarta (in various colors), natural woods and reconstituted stone.

ALVERSON, TIM (R. V.), 215 111 St, Orofino, ID 83544, Phone: 208-476-3999
Specialties: Fancy working knives to customer specs; other types on request. **Patterns:** Bowies, daggers, folders and miniatures. **Technical:** Grinds 440C, ATS-34; buys some Damascus. **Prices:** Start at $175. **Remarks:** Full-time maker; first knife sold in 1981. **Mark:** R. V. A. around rosebud.

AMERI, MAURO, Via Riaello No. 20, Trensasco St. Olcese, 16010 Genova, ITALY, Phone: 010-8357077
Specialties: Working and using knives of his design. **Patterns:** Hunters, Bowies and utility/camp knives. **Technical:** Grinds 440C, ATS-34 and 154CM. Handles in wood or Micarta; offers sheaths. **Prices:** $200 to $1,200. **Remarks:** Spare-time maker; first knife sold in 1982. **Mark:** Last name, city.

AMES, MICKEY L., 1521 N Central Ave, Monett, MO 65708-1104, Phone: 417-235-5941
Specialties: Traditional working and using straight knives of his design and to customer specs. **Patterns:** Bowies, hunters and utility/camp knives. **Technical:**Forges 5160, 1084, 1095 and makes own Damascus. Filework; silver wire inlay. **Prices:** Start at $100. **Remarks:** Part-time maker; first knife sold in 1990. Doing business as Ames Forge. **Mark:** Last name.

AMMONS, DAVID C., 8710 N Hollybrook Ave, Tucson, AZ 85742

AMOR JR., MIGUEL, 485-H Judie Lane, Lancaster, PA 17603, Phone: 717-468-5736
Specialties: Working and fancy straight knives in standard patterns; some to customer specs. **Patterns:** Bowies, hunters, fighters and tantos. **Technical:** Grinds 440C, ATS-34, carbon steel and commercial Damascus; forges some in high carbon steels. **Prices:** $125 to $500; some to $1,500 and higher. **Remarks:** Part-time maker; first knife sold in 1983. **Mark:** Last name. On collectors' pieces: last name, city, state.

AMOUREUX, A. W., PO Box 776, Northport, WA 99157, Phone: 509-732-6292
Specialties: Heavy-duty working straight knives. **Patterns:** Bowies, fighters, camp knives and hunters for world-wide use. **Technical:** Grinds 440C, ATS-34 and 154CM. **Prices:** $80 to $2,000. **Remarks:** Full-time maker; first knife sold in 1974. **Mark:** ALSTAR.

ANDERS, JEROME, 157 Barnes Dr, Center Ridge, AR 72027, Phone: (501) 893-2294

ANDERS, DAVID, 157 Barnes Dr., Center Ridge, AR 72027, Phone: 501-893-2294
Specialties: Working straight knives of his design. **Patterns:** Bowies, fighters and hunters. **Technical:** Forges 5160, 1080 and Damascus. **Prices:** $225 to $3200. **Remarks:** Part-time maker; first knife sold in 1988. Doing business as Anders Knives. **Mark:** Last name/MS.

ANDERSEN, HENRIK LEFOLII, Jagtvej 8, Groenholt, 3480, Fredensborg, DENMARK, Phone: 0011-45-48483026
Specialties: Hunters and matched pairs for the serious hunter. **Technical:** Grinds A2; uses materials native to Scandinavia. **Prices:** Start at $250. **Remarks:** Part-time maker; first knife sold in 1985. **Mark:** Initials with arrow.

ANDERSON, TOM, 955 Canal Road Extd., Manchester, PA 17345, Phone: 717-266-6475
Specialties: High-tech one-hand folders and fixed blades. **Patterns:** Fighters, utility, and dress knives. **Technical:** Grinds BG-42 and stainless damascus. Uses titanium, carbon fiber and select natural handle materials. **Prices:** Start at $275. **Remarks:**First knife sold in 1996. **Mark:** Stylized A over T logo with maker's name.

custom knifemakers

ANDERSON, GARY D., RD 2, Box 2399C, Spring Grove, PA 17362-9802, Phone: 717-229-2665
Specialties: From working knives to collectors quality blades, some folders. **Patterns:** Traditional and classic designs; customer patterns welcome. **Technical:** Forges Damascus carbon & stainless steels. Offers silver inlay, mokume, filework, checkering. **Prices:** $250 and up. **Remarks:** Full-time maker; first knife sold in 1985. **Mark:** GAND, MS. **Other:** Some engraving, scrimshaw and stone work.

ANDERSON, MEL, 1718 Lee Lane, Cedaredge, CO 81413, Phone: 970-856-6465, Fax:970-856-6463
Specialties: Full-size, miniature and one-of-a-kind straight knives and folders of his design. **Patterns:** Bowies, daggers, fighters, hunters and pressure folders. **Technical:** Grinds 440C, 5160, D2, 1095 and Damascus; offers antler, ivory and wood carved handles. **Prices:** Start at $145. **Remarks:** Full-time maker; first knife sold in 1987. **Mark:** Scratchy Hand.

ANDRESS, RONNIE, 415 Audubon Dr. N., Satsuma, AL 36572, Phone: 251-675-7604
Specialties: Working straight knives in standard patterns. **Patterns:** Boots, Bowies, hunters, friction folders and camp knives. **Technical:** Forges 1095, 5160, O1 and his own Damascus. Offers filework and inlays. **Prices:** $125 to $500. **Remarks:** Part-time maker; first knife sold in 1983. Doing business as Andress Knives. **Mark:** Last name, J. S. **Other:** Jeweler, goldsmith, gold work, stone setter. Not currently making knives.

ANDREWS, DON, N. 5155 Ezy St., Coeur D'Alene, ID 83814, Phone: 208-765-8844
Specialties: Plain and fancy folders and straight knives. **Technical:** Grinds D2, 440C, ATS-34; does lost wax casting for guards and pommels. **Prices:** Moderate to upscale. **Remarks:** Full-time maker; first knife sold in 1983. Not currently making knives. **Mark:** Name.

ANDREWS, ERIC, 132 Halbert Street, Grand Ledge, MI 48837, Phone: 517-627-7304
Specialties: Traditional working and using straight knives of his design. **Patterns:** Full-tang hunters, skinners and utility knives. **Technical:** Forges carbon steel; heat-treats. All knives come with sheath; most handles are of wood. **Prices:** $80 to $160. **Remarks:** Part-time maker; first knife sold in 1990. Doing business as The Tinkers Bench.

ANDREWS II, E R (RUSS), 131 S Sterling Av, Sugar Creek, MO 64054, Phone: (816) 252-3344

ANGELL, JON, 22516 East C R 1474, Hawthorne, FL 32640, Phone: (352) 475-5380

ANKROM, W. E., 14 Marquette Dr., Cody, WY 82414, Phone: 307-587-3017, Fax:307-587-3017
Specialties: Best quality folding knives of his design. **Patterns:**Lock backs, liner locks, single 2 blade. **Technical:** ATS 34 commercial damascus. **Prices:** $500 and up. **Remarks:** Full-time maker; first knife sold in 1975. **Mark:** Name or name, city, st.

ANSO, JENS, GL. Skanderborgveo, 116, 8472 Sporvp, DENMARK, Phone: 45 86968826
Specialties: Working knives of my own design. **Patterns:** Hunters and tacticals. Folders and straight blades. Tantos, drop point, Sheepfoot. **Technical:** Grinds RWL-34 Damasteel ATS-34, B6-42. I use hand rubbed finish on all blades. **Price:** $100 to $400, some up to $1000. **Remarks:** Part-time maker. First knife sold 1997. Doing business as ANSOKNIVES. **Mark:** ANSO. **Other:** Full-time maker since January 2002.

ANTONIO JR., WILLIAM J., 6 Michigan State Dr, Newark, DE 19713-1161, Phone: 302-368-8211
Specialties: Fancy working straight knives of his design. **Patterns:** Hunting, survival and fishing knives. **Technical:** Grinds D2, 440C and 154CM; offers stainless Damascus. **Prices:** $125 to $395; some to $900. **Remarks:** Part-time maker; first knife sold in 1978. **Mark:** Last name, city, state.

AOUN, CHARLES, 69 Nahant St, Wakefield, MA 01880, Phone: 781-224-3353
Specialties: Classic and fancy straight knives of his design. **Patterns:** Fighters, hunters and personal knives. **Technical:** Grinds W2, 1095, ATS-34 and Damascus. Uses natural handle materials; embellishes with silver and semi-precious stones. **Prices:** Start at $290. **Remarks:** Part-time maker; first knife sold in 1995. Doing business as Galeb Knives. **Mark:** G stamped on ricasso or choil.

APPLETON, RAY, 244 S Fetzer St, Byers, CO 80103-9748
Specialties: One-of-a-kind folding knives. **Patterns:** Unique folding multi-locks and high-tech patterns. **Technical:** All parts machined; D2, S7, 440C, and 6a14v. **Prices:** Start at $8,500. **Remarks:** Spare-time maker; first knife sold in 1986. **Mark:** Initials within arrowhead, signed & dated.

ARBUCKLE, JAMES M, 114 Jonathan Jct, Yorktown, VA 23693, Phone: (757) 867-9578
Specialties: One-of-a-kind of his design; working knives. **Patterns:** Mostly chefs knives & hunters. **Technical:** Forged & stock removal blades using exotic hardwoods, natural materials, Micarta and stabilized woods. Forge 5160, 1084 & 01; stock remove D2, ATS-34, 440C. Make own pattern welded steel. **Prices:** $150 to $700. **Remarks:** Forge, grind, heat-treat, finish and embellish all knives myself. Do own leatherwork and wood work. Part-time maker. **Mark:** J. Arbuckle or Arbuckle with maker below it. **Other:** ABS member; ASM member.

ARCHER, RAY & TERRI, PO Box 129, Medicine Bow, WY 82329, Phone: 307-379-2567
Specialties: High finish working straight knives and small one of a kind. **Patterns:** Hunters/skinners, camping. **Technical:** Flat grinds ATS-34, 440C, D2; buys Damascus. **Price:** $100 to $500. **Remarks:** Make own sheaths; first knife sold 1994. **Mark:** Last name over city and state. **Other:** Member of PKA.

ARDWIN, COREY, 4700 North Cedar, North Little Rock, AR 72116, Phone: 501-791-0301, Fax:501-791-2974

ARNOLD, JOE, 47 Patience Cres., London, Ont., CANADA N6E 2K7, Phone: 519-686-2623
Specialties: Traditional working and using straight knives of his design and to customer specs. **Patterns:** Fighters, hunters and Bowies. **Technical:** Grinds 440C, ATS-34 and 5160. **Prices:** $75 to $500; some to $2,500. **Remarks:** Part-time maker; first knife sold in 1988. **Mark:** Last name, country.

ARROWOOD, DALE, 556 Lassetter Rd., Sharpsburg, GA 30277, Phone: 404-253-9672
Specialties: Fancy and traditional straight knives of his design and to customer specs. **Patterns:** Bowies, fighters and hunters. **Technical:** Grinds ATS-34 and 440C; forges high-carbon steel. Engraves and scrimshaws. **Prices:** $125 to $200; some to $245. **Remarks:** Part-time maker; first knife sold in 1989. **Mark:** Anvil with an arrow through it; Old English "Arrowood Knives".

ASHBY, DOUGLAS, 10123 Deermont, Dallas, TX 75243, Phone: 214-238-7531
Specialties: Traditional and fancy straight knives of his design or to customer specs. **Patterns:** Hunters, fighters and utility/camp knives. **Technical:** Grinds 440C, ATS-34 and commercial Damascus. **Prices:** $75 to $200; some to $500. **Remarks:** Part-time maker; first knife sold in 1990. **Mark:** Name, city.

ASHWORTH, BOYD, 3135 Barrett Ct., Powder Springs, GA 30127, Phone: 770-943-4963
Specialties: Fancy Damascus locking folders. **Patterns:** Fighters, hunters and gents. **Technical:** Forges own Damascus; offers filework; uses exotic handle materials. **Prices:** $500 to $2,500. **Remarks:** Part-time maker; first knife sold in 1993. **Mark:** Last name.

ATKINSON, DICK, General Delivery, Wausau, FL 32463, Phone: 850-638-8524
Specialties: Working straight knives and folders of his design; some fancy. **Patterns:** Hunters, fighters, boots; locking folders in interframes. **Technical:** Grinds A2, 440C and 154CM. Likes filework. **Prices:** $85 to $300; some exceptional knives. **Remarks:** Full-time maker; first knife sold in 1977. **Mark:** Name, city, state.

AYARRAGARAY, CRISTIAN L., Buenos Aires 250, (3100) Parana-Entre Rios, ARGENTINA, Phone: 043-231753
Specialties: Traditional working straight knives of his design. **Patterns:** Fishing and hunting knives. **Technical:** Grinds and forges carbon steel. Uses native Argentine woods and deer antler. **Prices:** $150 to $250; some to $400. **Remarks:** Full-time maker; first knife sold in 1980. **Mark:** Last name, signature.

b

BABCOCK, RAYMOND G., Rt. 1 Box 328A, Vincent, OH 45784, Phone: 614-678-2688
Specialties: Plain and fancy working straight knives. I will make knives to my design and to custom specifications. I also make folding knives of my design. **Patterns:** Hunting knives, bowies and folders. **Technical:** Hollow grinds L6. **Prices:** $95 to $500. **Remarks:** Part-time maker; first knife sold in 1973. **Mark:** First initial & last name; R. Babcock.

BACHE-WIIG, TOM, N-5966, Eivindvik, NORWAY, Phone: 4757784290, Fax:4757784122
Specialties: High-art and working knives of his design. **Patterns:** Hunters, utility knives, hatchets, axes and art knives. **Technical:** Grinds Uddeholm Elmax, powder metallurgy tool stainless steel. Handles made of rear burls of Nordic woods stabilized with vacuum/high-pressure technique. **Prices:** $430 to $900; some to $2,300. **Remarks:** Part-time maker; first knife sold 1988. **Mark:** Etched name and eagle head.

BACON, DAVID R, 906 136th St E, Bradenton, FL 34202-9694, Phone: (813) 996-4289

BAGLEY, R KEITH, Old Pine Forge, 4415 Hope Acres Dr, White Plains, MD 20695, Phone: 301-932-0990
Specialties: High carbon Damascus with semi-precious stones set in exotic wood handle; tactical and skinner knives. **Technical:** Use ATS-34, 5160, 01, 1085, 1095. **Patterns:** Various patterns; prefer all Tool-Steel and Nickel Damascus. **Price:** Damascus from $250 to $500; stainless from $100 to $225. **Remarks:** Furrier for 25 years, blacksmith for 25 years, knife maker for 10 years.

BAILEY, JOSEPH D., 3213 Jonesboro Dr., Nashville, TN 37214, Phone: 615-889-3172
Specialties: Working and using straight knives; collector pieces. **Patterns:** Bowies, hunters, tactical, folders. **Technical:** 440C, ATS-34, Damascus and wire Damascus. Offers scrimshaw. **Prices:** $85 to $1,200. **Remarks:** Part-time maker; first knife sold in 1988. **Mark:** Joseph D Bailey Nashville Tennessee.

BAILEY, KIRBY C., 2055 F. M. 2790 W., Lytle, TX 78052, Phone: 830-772-3376
Specialties: All kinds of knives folders, fixed blade, fighters. **Patterns:** Hunters, folders, fighters, bowies, miniatures. **Technical:** I do all my own work; heat treating, file work etc. **Prices:** $200 to $1,000. **Remarks:** I build any kind of hand cutlery. Have made knives for 45 years; sold knives for 28 years. **Mark:** K. C. B. & serial #. **Other:** Have sold knives in Asia & all states in US.

BAILEY, RYAN, 4185 S St Rt 605, Galena, OH 43021, Phone: 614-577-1040
Specialties: Fancy, high-art, high-tech, collectible straight knives and folders of his design and to customer specs; unique mechanisms, some disassemble. **Patterns:** Daggers, fighters and swords. **Technical:** Does own Damascus & forging from high carbon. Embellishes with file work & gold work. **Prices:** $200 to $2500. **Remarks:** Full-time maker; first knife sold in 1999. Doing business as Briar Knives. **Mark:** RLB.

BAKER, WILD BILL, Box 361, Boiceville, NY 12412, Phone: 914-657-8646
Specialties: Primitive knives, buckskinners. **Patterns:** Skinners, camp knives and Bowies. **Technical:** Works with L6, files and rasps. **Prices:** $100 to $350. **Remarks:** Part-time maker; first knife sold in 1989. **Mark:** Wild Bill Baker, Oak Leaf Forge, or both.

BAKER, RAY, P. O. Box 303, Sapulpa, OK 74067, Phone: 918-224-8013
Specialties: High-tech working straight knives. **Patterns:** Hunters, fighters, Bowies, skinners and boots of his design and to customer specs. **Technical:** Grinds 440C, 1095 spring steel or customer request; heat-treats. Custom-made scabbards for any knife. **Prices:** $125 to $500; some to $1,000. **Remarks:** Full-time maker; first knife sold in 1981. **Mark:** First initial, last name.

BAKER, VANCE, 574 Co. Rd. 675, Riceville, TN 37370, Phone: 423-745-9157
Specialties: Traditional working straight knives of his design and to customer specs. Prefers drop-point hunters and small Bowies. **Patterns:** Hunters, utility and kitchen knives. **Technical:** Forges Damascus, cable, L6 and 5160. **Prices:** $100 to $250; some to $500. **Remarks:** Part-time maker; first knife sold in 1985. **Mark:** Initials connected.

BAKER, HERB, 14104 NC 87 N, Eden, NC 27288, Phone: 336-627-0338

BALBACH, MARKUS, Heinrich - Worner - Str. 3, 35789 Weilmunster-Laubuseschbach/Ts., GERMANY 06475-8911, Fax:912986
Specialties: High-art knives and working/using straight knives and folders of his design and to customer specs. **Patterns:** Hunters and daggers. **Technical:** Stainless steel, one of Germany's greatest Smithies. Supplier for the forges of Solingen. **Remarks:** Full-time maker; first knife sold in 1984. Doing business as Schmiedewerkstatte M. Balbach. **Mark:** Initials stamped inside the handle.

BALDWIN, PHILLIP, P. O. Box 563, Snohomish, WA 98290, Phone: 425-334-5569
Specialties: One-of-a-kind elegant table cutlery; exotics. **Patterns:** Elegant or exotic knives. Likes the challenge of axes, spears and specialty tools. **Technical:** Forges W2, W1 and his own pattern welded steel and mokume-gane. **Prices:** Start at $1,000. **Remarks:** Full-time maker; first knife sold in 1973. **Mark:** Last initial marked with chisel.

BALL, KEN, 127 Sundown Manor, Mooresville, IN 46158, Phone: 317-834-4803
Specialties: Classic working/using straight knives of his design and to customer specs. **Patterns:** Hunters and utility/camp knives. **Technical:** Flat-grinds ATS-34. Offers filework. **Prices:** $150 to $400. **Remarks:** Part-time maker; first knife sold in 1994. Doing business as Ball Custom Knives. **Mark:** Last name.

BALLESTRA, SANTINO, via D. Tempesta 11/17, 18039 Ventimiglia (IM), ITALY 0184-215228
Specialties: Using and collecting straight knives. **Patterns:** Hunting, fighting, skinners, Bowies, medieval daggers and knives. **Technical:** Forges ATS-34, D2, O2, 1060 and his own Damascus. Uses ivory and silver. **Prices:** $500 to $2,000; some higher. **Remarks:** Full-time maker; first knife sold in 1979. **Mark:** First initial, last name.

BALLEW, DALE, P. O. Box 1277, Bowling Green, VA 22427, Phone: 804-633-5701
Specialties: Miniatures only to customer specs. **Patterns:** Bowies, daggers and fighters. **Technical:** Files 440C stainless; uses ivory, abalone, exotic woods and some precious stones. **Prices:** $100 to $800. **Remarks:** Part-time maker; first knife sold in 1988. **Mark:** Initials and last name.

BANKS, DAVID L., 99 Blackfoot Ave, Riverton, WY 82501, Phone: 307-856-3154/Cell:307-851-4365
Specialties: Heavy-duty working straight knives. **Patterns:** Hunters, Bowies and camp knives. **Technical:** Forges Damascus 1084-15N20, L-6-W1 pure nickel, 5160, 52100 and his own Damascus; differential heat treat and tempers. Handles made of horn, antlers and exotic wood. Hand-stitched harness leather sheaths. **Prices:** $300 to $2000. **Remarks:** Part-time maker. **Mark:** Initials connected Blackfoot forge Dave Banks, Banks Riverton Leyo.

BARBER, ROBERT E., 1828 Franklin Dr., Charlottesville, VA 22911-8513, Phone: 804-295-4036
Specialties: Working straight knives and trapper pocket knives, some fancy with filework. **Patterns:** Hunters, skinners, combat knives/fighters and Bowies. **Technical:** Grinds ATS-34, 440C, D2, A2 and CPM 420V. **Prices:** $45 to $1,000. **Remarks:** Part-time maker; member North Carolina Custom Knife Makers Guild; first knife sold in 1984;. **Mark:** Initials within rebel hat logo.

BARDSLEY, NORMAN P., 197 Cottage St., Pawtucket, RI 02860, Phone: 401-725-9132
Specialties: Working and fantasy knives. **Patterns:** Fighters, boots, fantasy, renaissance & native American in upscale and presentation fashion. **Technical:** Grinds all steels and Damascus. Uses exotic hides for sheaths. **Prices:** $100 to $15,000. **Remarks:** Full-time maker. **Mark:** Last name in script with logo.

BAREFOOT, JOE W., 117 Oakbrook Dr., Liberty, SC 29657
Specialties: Working straight knives of his design. **Patterns:** Hunters, fighters and boots; tantos and survival knives. **Technical:** Grinds D2, 440C and ATS-34. Mirror finishes. Uses ivory and stag on customer request only. **Prices:** $50 to $160; some to $500. **Remarks:** Part-time maker; first knife sold in 1980. **Mark:** Bare footprint.

BARKER, REGGIE, 603 S Park Dr., Springhill, LA 71075, Phone: (318) 539-2958
Specialties: Camp knives & hatchets. **Patterns:** Bowie, skinning, hunting, camping, kitchen or customer design. **Technical:** Forges carbon steel and own pattern welded steels. Prices $150 to $2,000. **Remarks:** Part-time maker. Winner of 1999 & 2000 Spring Hammerin Cutting contest. Winner of Best Value of Show 2001; Arkansas Knife Show. **Mark:** Barker. **Other:** Border Guard Forge.

BARKER, ROBERT G., 2311 Branch Rd., Bishop, GA 30621, Phone: 706-769-7827
Specialties: Traditional working/using straight knives of his design. **Patterns:** Bowies, hunters and utility knives, ABS Journeyman Smith. **Technical:** Hand forged carbon & Damascus. Forges to shape high-carbon 5160, cable and chain. Differentially heat-treats. **Prices:** $200 to $500; some to $1,000. **Remarks:** Spare-time maker; first knife sold in 1987. **Mark:** BARKER/J. S.

BARLOW, JANA POIRIER, 3820 Borland Cir, Anchorage, AK 99517, Phone: (907) 243-4581

BARNES, MARLEN R, 904 Crestview Dr S, Atlanta, TX 75551-1854, Phone: (903) 796-3668
Specialties: Hammer forges random & mosaic Damascus. **Patterns:** Hatchets, straight & folding knives. **Technical:** Hammer forges carbon steel using 5160, 1084 & 52100 with 15N20 & 203E nickel. **Prices:** $150 and up. **Remarks:** Part-time maker; first knife sold 1999. **Mark:** Script M. R. B., other side J. S.

BARNES, GARY L., Box 138, New Windsor, MD 21776-0138, Phone: 410-635-6243, Fax:410-635-6243
Specialties: Ornate button lock damascus folders. **Patterns:** Barnes original. **Technical:** Forges own Damascus. **Prices:** Average $2,500. **Remarks:** ABS Master Smith since 1983. **Mark:** Hand engraved logo of letter B pierced by dagger.

custom knifemakers

BARNES, JACK, P. O. Box 1315, Whitefish, MT 59937-1315, Phone: 406-862-6078

BARNES, ERIC, H C 74 Box 41, Mountain View, AR 72560, Phone: (501) 269-3358

BARNES, AUBREY G., 11341 Rock Hill Road, Hagerstown, MD 21740, Phone: 301-223-4587
Specialties: Classic working and using knives of his design, to customer specs and in standard patterns. **Patterns:** Bowies, hunters, fighters, daggers and utility/camping knives. **Technical:** Forges 5160, 1085, L6 and Damascus, Silver wire inlays. **Prices:** $300 to $2,500. **Remarks:** Full-time maker; first knife sold in 1992. Doing business as Falling Waters Forge. **Mark:** First and middle initials, last name, M. S.

BARNES, WILLIAM, P O Box 383, Middlefield, CT 06455, Phone: (860) 349-0443

BARNES, WENDELL, 2160 Oriole Dr, Missoula, MT 59808, Phone: 406-721-0908
Specialties: Working straight knives. **Patterns:** Hunters, folders, neck knives. **Technical:** Grinds 440C, ATS-34, D2 and Damascus. **Prices:** Start at $75. **Remarks:** Spare-time maker; first knife sold in 1996. **Mark:** First initial and last name around broken heart.

BARNES, GREGORY, 266 W. Calaveras St, Altadena, CA 91001, Phone: (626) 398-0053

BARNES JR, CECIL C, 141 Barnes Dr, Center Ridge, AR 72027, Phone: (501) 893-2267

BARNETT, VAN, Barnett Int'l Inc, 1135 Terminal Way Ste #209, Reno, NV 89502, Phone: 866 ARTKNIFE or 304-727-5512, Fax:775-201-0038
Specialties: Collector grade one of a kind / embellished high art daggers and art folders. **Patterns:** Art daggers and folders. **Technical:** Forges and grinds own Damascus. **Prices:** Upscale. **Remarks:** Designs and makes one of a kind highly embellished art knives using high karat gold, diamonds and other gemstones, pearls, stone and fossil ivories, carved steel guards and blades, all knives are carved and or engraved, does own engraving, carving and other embellishments, sole authorship; full-time maker since 1981. **Mark:** V. H. Barnett or Van Barnett in script. **Other:** Does one high art collaboration a year with Dellana. Voting Member of Knifemakers Guild. Member of ABS.

BARNEY, RICHARD, 1137 Neptune Way, Mt. Shasta, CA 96967

BARNGROVER, JERRY, RR #4, Box 1230, Afton, OK 74331, Phone: 918-257-5076

BARR, A. T., P. O. Box 828, Nicholasville, KY 40340-0828, Phone: 859-885-1042, Fax:859-887-5400
Specialties: Working and collector grade liner lock folders. **Patterns:** Liner lock folders. **Technical:** Flat-grinds ATS-34, BG 42, Damascus, D2, A2 and O1; hand-rubbed, satin or tumbled finish. **Prices:** Start at $300. **Remarks:** Full time maker, first knife sold in 1979, web design and hosting. **Mark:** Full name.

BARR, JUDSON C, 1905 Pickwick Circle, Irving, TX 75060, Phone: (972) 790-7195
Specialties: Bowies. **Patterns:** Sheffield & Early American. **Technical:** Forged carbon steel and Damascus. Also stock removal. **Remarks:** Associate member of ABS. **Mark:** Barr.

BARRETT, RICK L (TOSHI HISA), 18943 CR 18, Goshen, IN 46528, Phone: 574-533-4297
Specialties: Japanese style blades from sushi knives to katana and fantasy pieces. **Patterns:** Swords, axes, spears/lances, hunter and utility knives. **Technical:**Forges and grinds damascus and carbon steels, occasionally uses stainless. **Prices:**$250-$4000+. **Remarks:**Full time bladesmith, jeweler. **Mark:**Japanese mei on Japanese pieces and stylized initials.

BARRETT, CECIL TERRY, 2514 Linda Lane, Colorado Springs, CO 80909, Phone: 719-473-8325
Specialties: Working and using straight knives and folders of his design, to customer specs and in standard patterns. **Patterns:** Bowies, hunters, kitchen knives, locking folders and slip-joint folders. **Technical:** Grinds 440C, D2 and ATS-34. Wood and leather sheaths. **Prices:** $65 to $500; some to $750. **Remarks:** Full-time maker. **Mark:** Stamped middle name.

BARRON, BRIAN, 123 12th Ave., San Mateo, CA 94402, Phone: 650-341-2683
Specialties: Traditional straight knives. **Patterns:** Daggers, hunters and swords. **Technical:** Grinds 440C, ATS-34 and 1095. Sculpts bolsters using an S-curve. **Prices:** $130 to $270; some to $1,500. **Remarks:** Part-time maker; first knife sold in 1993. **Mark:** Diamond Drag "Barron".

BARRY III, JAMES J., 115 Flagler Promenade No, West Palm Beach, FL 33405, Phone: 561-832-4197
Specialties: High-art working straight knives of his design also high art tomahawks. **Patterns:** Hunters, daggers and fishing knives. **Technical:**

Grinds 440C only. Prefers exotic materials for handles. Most knives embellished with filework, carving and scrimshaw. Many pieces designed to stand unassisted. **Prices:** $500 to $5000. **Remarks:** Part-time maker; first knife sold in 1975. **Mark:** Branded initials as a J & B together.

BARTH, J D, 101 4th St, PO Box 186, Alberton, MT 59820, Phone: 406-722-4557
Specialties: Working and fancy straight knives of his design. **Technical:** Grinds ATS-34, 440-C, stainless and carbon Damascus. Uses variety of natural handle materials and Micarta. Likes dovetailed bolsters. Filework on most knives, full and tapered tangs. Makes custom fit sheaths for each knife. **Mark:** Name over maker, city & state.

BARTLOW, JOHN, 5078 Coffeen Ave, Sheridan, WY 82801, Phone: 307 673-4941
Specialties: New liner locks. **Patterns:** Working hunters, skinners, capers, bird and trout knives. **Technical:** Working on 6 new liner lock designs. **Prices:** $150 to $1,500. **Remarks:** Full-time maker; first knife sold in 1979. Field-tests knives. **Mark:** Last name.

BARTRUG, HUGH E., 2701 34th St. N., #142, St. Petersburg, FL 33713, Phone: 813-323-1136
Specialties: Inlaid straight knives and exotic folders; high-art knives and period pieces. **Patterns:** Hunters, Bowies and daggers; traditional patterns. **Technical:** Diffuses mokume. Forges 100 percent nickel, wrought iron, mosaic Damascus, shokeedo and O1 tool steel; grinds. **Prices:** $210 to $2,500; some to $5,000. **Remarks:** Retired maker; first knife sold in 1980. **Mark:** Ashley Forge or name.

BASKETT, LEE GENE, 427 Sutzer Ck. Rd., Eastview, KY 42732, Phone: 270-862-5019
Specialties: Fancy working knives and fantasy pieces, often set up in desk stands. **Patterns:** Fighters, Bowies and survival knives; locking folders and traditional styles. **Technical:** Liner locks. Grinds O1, 440C; buys Damascus. Filework provided on most knives. **Prices:** Start at $135. **Remarks:** Part-time maker; first knife sold in 1980. **Mark:** Last name.

BATLEY, MARK S, P O Box 217, Wake, VA 23176, Phone: (804) 776-7794

BATSON, JAMES, 176 Brentwood Lane, Madison, AL 35758, Phone: 205-971-6860
Specialties: Forged Damascus blades and fittings in collectible period pieces. **Patterns:** Integral art knives, Bowies, folders, American-styled blades and miniatures. **Technical:** Forges 52100, 5160 and his Damascus. **Prices:** $150 to $1,800; some to $4,500. **Remarks:** Full-time maker; first knife sold in 1978. **Mark:** Name, bladesmith with horse's head.

BATSON, RICHARD G., 6591 Waterford Rd., Rixeyville, VA 22737, Phone: 540-937-5932
Specialties: Military, utility and fighting knives in working and presentation grade. **Patterns:** Daggers, combat and utility knives. **Technical:** Grinds O1, 1095 and 440C. Etches and scrimshaws; offers polished, Parkerized finishes. **Prices:** $200 to $450. **Remarks:** Semi-retired, limit production. First knife sold in 1958. **Mark:** Bat in circle, hand-signed and serial numbered.

BATTLE AXE, THE, 722 Greenwood, Wichita, KS 67211, Phone: 316-264-0171
Specialties: Fantasy & replica. **Patterns:** Battle axes. **Technical:** Forge and grind. **Remarks:** First knife sold in 1994.

BATTS, KEITH, 450 Manning Rd, Hooks, TX 75561, Phone: 903-832-1140
Specialties: Working straight knives of his design or to customer specs. **Patterns:** Bowies, hunters, skinners, camp knives and others. **Technical:** Forges 5160 and his Damascus; offers filework. **Prices:** $245 to $895. **Remarks:** Part-time maker; first knife sold in 1988. **Mark:** Last name.

BAUCHOP, PETER, c/o Beck's Cutlery Specialties, 107 Edinburgh S #109, Cary, NC 27511, Phone: 919-460-0203, Fax:919-460-7772
Specialties: Working straight knives and period pieces. **Patterns:** Fighters, swords and survival knives. **Technical:** Grinds O1, D2, G3, 440C and AST-34. Scrimshaws. **Prices:** $100 to $350; some to $1500. **Remarks:** Full-time maker; first knife sold in 1980. **Mark:** Bow and axe (BOW-CHOP).

BAUCHOP, ROBERT, P. O. Box 330, Munster, Kwazulu-Natal 4278, SOUTH AFRICA, Phone: +27 39 3192419
Specialties: Fantasy knives; working and using knives of his design and to customer specs. **Patterns:** Hunters, swords, utility/camp knives, diver's knives and large swords. **Technical:** Grinds Sandvick 12C27, D2, 440C. Uses South African hardwoods red ivory, wild olive, African blackwood, etc. --on handles. **Prices:** $200 to $800; some to $2,000. **Remarks:** Full-time maker; first knife sold in 1986. Doing business as Bauchop Custom Knives and Swords. **Mark:** Viking helmet with Bauchop (bow and chopper) crest.

BAUM, RICK, 435 North Center St, Lehi, UT 84043, Phone: (801) 431-7290

BEAM, JOHN R., 1310 Foothills Rd., Kalispell, MT 59901, Phone: 406-755-2593
Specialties: Classic, high-art and working straight knives of his design. Patterns: Bowies and hunters. Technical: Grinds 440C, Damascus and scrap. Prices: $175 to $600; some to $3,000. Remarks: Part-time maker; first knife sold in 1950. Doing business as Beam's Knives. Mark: Beam's Knives.

BEASLEY, GENEO, P O Box 339, Wadsworth, NV 89442, Phone: (775) 575-2584

BEATTY, GORDON H., 121 Petty Rd., Seneca, SC 29672, Phone: 864-882-6278
Specialties: Working straight knives, some fancy. Patterns: Traditional patterns, mini-skinners and letter openers. Technical: Grinds 440C, D2 and ATS-34; makes knives one at a time. Prices: $75 to $450; some to $450. Remarks: Part-time maker; first knife sold in 1982. Mark: Name.

BEATY, ROBERT B, Cutler, 1995 Big Flat Rd, Missoula, MT 59804, Phone: 406-549-1818
Specialties: Plain & fancy working knives & collector pieces; will accept custom orders. Patterns: Hunters, Bowies, utility, kitchen & camp knives; locking folders. Technical: Grinds D-2, ATS-34, Dendritie D-2, makes all tool steel Damascus, forges 1095, 5160, 52100. Prices: $100 to $450; some to $1,100. Remarks: Full-time maker; first knife sold 1995. Mark: Stainless: First name, middle initial, last name, city & state. Carbon: Last name stamped on Ricasso.

BEAUCHAMP, GAETAN, 125, de la Rivire, Stoneham, PQ, CANADA G0A 4P0, Phone: 418-848-1914, Fax:418-848-6859
Specialties: Working knives and folders of his design and to customer specs. Patterns: Hunters, fighters, fantasy knives. Technical: Grinds ATS-34, 440C, Damascus. Scrimshaws on ivory; specializes in buffalo horn and black backgrounds. Offers a variety of handle materials. Prices: Start at $125. Remarks: Full-time maker; first knife sold in 1992. Mark: Signature etched on blade.

BECKER, STEVE, 201 1st Ave NW, Conrad, MT 59425, Phone: (406) 278-7753

BECKER, FRANZ, AM Kreuzberg 2, 84533, Marktl/Inn, GERMANY 08678-8020
Specialties: Stainless steel knives in working sizes. Patterns: Semi- and full-integral knives; interframe folders. Technical: Grinds stainless steels; likes natural handle materials. Prices: $200 to $2,000. Mark: Name, country.

BECKETT, NORMAN L., 1501 N. Chaco Ave., Farmington, NM 87401, Phone: 505-325-4468, Fax:505-325-4468
Specialties: Fancy, traditional and working folders & straight knives of his design. Patterns: Bowies, fighters, folders & hunters. Technical: Grinds ATS-34, 440C, CPM 440V and Damascus. File works blades; hollow and flat grinds. Prefers mirror finish; satin finish on working knives. Uses exotic handle material, stabilized woods & Micarta. Hand-tooled or inlaid sheaths. Prices: $125 to $900; some to $2,500 and up. Remarks: Full-time maker; first knife sold in 1993. Doing business as Norm Beckett Knives. Mark: First and last name, maker, city and state.

BEERS, RAY, 2501 Lakefront Dr., Lake Wales, FL 33853, Phone: Winter 863-696-3036, Fax:863-696-9421 (fax)

BEERS, RAY, 8 Manorbrook Rd., Monkton, MD 21111, Phone: Summer 410-472-2229, Fax:410-472-9136 Fax

BEETS, MARTY, 390 N 5TH Ave, Williams Lake, BC, CANADA V2G 2G4, Phone: 250-392-7199
Specialties: Working and collectable straight knives of my own design. Patterns: Hunter, skinners, bowies and utility knives. Technical: Grinds 440C-I do all of my own work including heat treating Uses a variety of handle material specializing in exotic hardwoods, antler and horn. Price: $125-$400. Remarks: Wife, Sandy does handmade/hand stitched sheaths. First knife sold in 1988. Business name Beets Handmade Knives.

BEHNKE, WILLIAM, 931 W Sanborn Rd, Lake City, MI 49651-7600, Phone: 231-839-3342
Specialties: Hunters, belt knives and folders. Patterns: Traditional styling in moderate-sized straight and folding knives. Technical: Forges his own Damascus, cable, saw chain and 5160; likes brass and natural materials. Prices: $150 to $2000. Remarks: Part-time maker. Mark: Bill Behnke Knives.

BELL, DONALD, 2 Division St., Bedford, Nova Scotia, CANADA B4A 1Y8, Phone: 902-835-2623
Specialties: Fancy knives; working/using straight knives and folders of his design. Patterns: Hunters, locking folders, jewelry knives. Technical: Grinds Damascus and ATS-34; forges and grinds O1; pierces and carves blades. Prices: $150 to $650; some to $1,200. Remarks: Spare-time maker; first knife sold in 1993. Mark: Bell symbol with first initial inside.

BELL, MICHAEL, 88321 N Bank Lane, Coquille, OR 97423, Phone: 541-396-3605
Specialties: Full line of traditional Japanese swords. Patterns: Complete Japanese line; Tanto, Katana etc. Technical: All forged, cable & hand-made steel. Prices:Swords from $4000 to $20,000. Remarks: Full-time maker; first knife sold in 1972. Served apprenticeship with Japanese sword maker. Doing business as Dragonfly Forge. Mark: Dragonfly in shield or tombo Kuni Mitsu.

BENDIK, JOHN, 7076 Fitch Rd, Olmsted Falls, OH 44138

BENFIELD JR, ROBERT O, 532 Bowie, Forney, TX 75126

BENJAMIN JR., GEORGE, 3001 Foxy Lane, Kissimmee, FL 34746, Phone: 407-846-7259
Specialties: Fighters in various styles to include Persian, Moro and military. Patterns: Daggers, skinners and one-of-a-kind grinds. Technical: Forges O1, D2, A2, 5160 and Damascus. Favors Pakkawood, Micarta, and mirror or Parkerized finishes. Makes unique para-military leather sheaths. Prices: $150 to $600; some to $1,200. Remarks: Doing business as The Leather Box. Mark: Southern Pride Knives.

BENNETT, BRETT C, 1922 Morrie Ave, Cheyenne, WY 82001, Phone: 307-432-0985

BENNETT, PETER, P. O. Box 143, Engadine N. S. W. 2233, AUSTRALIA, Phone: 02-520-4975 (home), Fax:O2-528-8219 (work)
Specialties: Fancy and embellished working and using straight knives to customer specs and in standard patterns. Patterns: Fighters, hunters, bird/trout and fillet knives. Technical: Grinds 440C, ATS-34 and Damascus. Uses rare Australian desert timbers for handles. Prices: $90 to $500; some to $1,500. Remarks: Full-time maker; first knife sold in 1985. Mark: First and middle initials, last name; country.

BENNETT, GLEN C, 5821 S Stewart Blvd, Tucson, AZ 85706

BENNICA, CHARLES, Chemin du Salet, 34190 Moules et Baucels, FRANCE, Phone: (+33) 4 67 73 42 40
Specialties: Fixed blades and folding knives; the latter with slick closing mechanisms with push buttons to unlock blades. Unique handle shapes, signature to the maker. Technical: 416 stainless steel frames for folders and ATS34 blades. Also specializes in Damascus.

BENSON, DON, 2505 Jackson St., #112, Escalon, CA 95320, Phone: 209-838-7921
Specialties: Working straight knives of his design. Patterns: Axes, Bowies, tantos and hunters. Technical: Grinds 440C. Prices: $100 to $150; some to $400. Remarks: Spare-time maker; first knife sold in 1980. Mark: Name.

BENTLEY, C L, 2405 Hilltop Dr, Albany, GA 31707, Phone: (912) 432-6656

BER, DAVE, 656 Miller Rd, San Juan Island, WA 98250, Phone: 206-378-7230
Specialties: Working straight and folding knives for the sportsman; welcomes customer designs. Patterns: Hunters, skinners, Bowies, kitchen and fishing knives. Technical: Forges and grinds saw blade steel, wire Damascus, O1, L6, 5160 and 440C. Prices: $100 to $300; some to $500. Remarks: Full-time maker; first knife sold in 1985. Mark: Last Name.

BERG, LOTHAR, 37 Hillcrest Ln, Kitchener ON, CANADA NZK 1S9, Phone: 519-745-3260 519-745-3260

BERG, STEVEN, The Pen and the Sword Ltd, 1833 E 12th St Ste 2D, Brooklyn, NY 11229, Phone: 718-382-4847, Fax:718-376-5745

BERGER, MAX A., 5716 John Richard Ct., Carmichael, CA 95608, Phone: 916-972-9229
Specialties: Fantasy and working/using straight knives of his design. Patterns: Fighters, hunters and utility/camp knives. Technical: Grinds ATS-34 and 440C. Offers fileworks and combinations of mirror polish and satin finish blades. Prices: $200 to $600; some to $2,500. Remarks: Part-time maker; first knife sold in 1992. Mark: Last name.

BERGH, ROGER, PL1137, 83070 NRA, SWEDEN, Phone: +46 613 12046, Fax:+46 613 12046

BERGLIN, BRUCE D., 17441 Lake Terrace Place, Mount Vernon, WA 98274, Phone: 360-422-8603
Specialties: Working and using straight knives of his own design. Patterns: Hunters, boots, bowies, utility/camp knives and period pieces, some made to look old. Technical: Forges and grinds carbon steels. Prefers natural handle material. Prices: Start at $200. Remarks: Part-time maker since 1998. Mark: First initial, middle initial and last name, sometimes surrounded with an oval

BERTHOLUS, BERNARD, Atelier Du Brute, De Forge 21, rue Fersen 06600, Antibes, FRANCE, Phone: 04 93 34 95 90
Specialties: Traditional working and using straight knives of his design. Patterns: Bowies, daggers and hunters. Technical: Forges ATS-34, 440,

custom knifemakers

D2 and carbon steels. **Prices:** $120 to $150; some to $400. **Remarks:** Full-time maker; first knife sold in 1990. **Mark:** City and last name.

BERTUZZI, ETTORE, Via Partigiani 3, 24068 Seriate (Bergamo), ITALY, Phone: 035-294262, Fax:035-294262
Specialties: Classic straight knives and folders of his design, to customer specs and in standard patterns. **Patterns:** Bowies, hunters and locking folders. **Technical:** Grinds ATS-34, D3, D2 and various Damascus. **Prices:** $300 to $500. **Remarks:** Part-time maker; first knife sold in 1993. **Mark:** Name etched on ricasso.

BESEDICK, FRANK E., RR 2, Box 802, Ruffsdale, PA 15679, Phone: 724-696-3312
Specialties: Traditional working and using straight knives of his design. **Patterns:** Hunters, utility/camp knives and miniatures; buckskinner blades and tomahawks. **Technical:** Forges and grinds 5160, O1 and Damascus. Offers filework and scrimshaw. **Prices:** $75 to $300; some to $750. **Remarks:** Part-time maker; first knife sold in 1990. **Mark:** Name or initials.

BETHKE, LORA SUE, 13420 Lincoln St., Grand Haven, MI 49417, Phone: 616-842-8268, Fax:616-844-2696
Specialties: Classic and traditional straight knives of her design. **Patterns:** Boots, Bowies and hunters. **Technical:** Forges 5160. **Prices:** Start at $300. **Remarks:** Part-time maker; first knife sold in 1997. **Mark:** Full name - JS on reverse side. **Other:** Journeyman bladesmith, American Bladesmith Society.

BEUKES, TINUS, 83 Henry St., Risiville, Vereeniging 1939, SOUTH AFRICA, Phone: 27 16 423 2053
Specialties: Working straight knives. **Patterns:** Hunters, skinners and kitchen knives. **Technical:** Grinds D2, 440C and chain, cable and stainless Damascus. **Prices:** $80 to $180. **Remarks:** Part-time maker; first knife sold in 1993. **Mark:** Full name, city, logo.

BEVERLY II, LARRY H., P. O. Box 741, Spotsylvania, VA 22553, Phone: 540-898-3951
Specialties: Working straight knives, slip-joints and liner locks. Welcomes customer designs. **Patterns:** Bowies, hunters, guard less fighters and miniatures. **Technical:** Grinds 440C, A2 and O1. **Prices:** $125 to $1000. **Remarks:** Part-time maker; first knife sold in 1986. **Mark:** Initials or last name in script.

BEZUIDENHOUT, BUZZ, 30 Surlingham Ave., Malvern, Queensburgh, Natal 4093, SOUTH AFRICA, Phone: 031-4632827, Fax:031-3631259
Specialties: Traditional working and using straight knives of his design and to customer specs. **Patterns:** Boots, hunters, kitchen knives and utility/camp knives. **Technical:** Grinds 12C27, 440C and ATS-34. Uses local hardwoods, horn - kudu, impala, buffalo - giraffe bone and ivory for handles. **Prices:** $150 to $200; some to $1500. **Remarks:** Spare-time maker; first knife sold in 1988. **Mark:** First name with a bee emblem.

BIGGERS, GARY, Ventura Knives, 1278 Colina Vista, Ventura, CA 93003, Phone: 805-658-6610, Fax:805-658-6610
Specialties: Fixed blade knives of his design. **Patterns:** Hunters, boots/fighters, Bowies and utility knives. **Technical:** Grinds ATS-34, 01 and commercial Damascus. **Prices:** $150 to $550. **Remarks:** Part-time maker; first knife sold in 1996. Doing business as Ventura Knives. **Mark:** First and last name, city and state.

BILLGREN, PER, Stallgatan 9, S815 76 Soderfors, SWEDEN, Phone: +46 293 17480, Fax:+46 293 30124
Specialties: Damasteel, stainless Damascus steels. **Patterns:** Rose twist, Odin's eye, Vinland, Hakkapelliitta. **Technical:** Modern Damascus steel made by patented powder metallurgy method. **Prices:** $100 to $200. **Remarks:** Damasteel is available through distributors around the globe.

BIRDWELL, IRA LEE, P O Box 1135, Bagdad, AR 86321, Phone: (520) 633-2516

BIRNBAUM, EDWIN, 9715 Hammocks Blvd I 206, Miami, FL 33196

BISH, HAL, 9347 Sweetbriar Trace, Jonesboro, GA 30236, Phone: (770) 477-2422

BIZZELL, ROBERT, 145 Missoula Av, Butte, MT 59701, Phone: 406-782-4403
Specialties: Damascus. **Patterns:** Composite, mosaic & traditional. **Technical:** Only fixed blades at this time. **Prices:** Start at $150. **Mark:** Hand signed.

BLACK, SCOTT, 27100 Leetown Rd, Picayune, MS 39466, Phone: 601-799-5939
Specialties: Friction folders; fighters. **Patterns:** Bowies, fighters, hunters, smoke hawks, friction folders, daggers. **Technical:** All forged, all work done by me, own hand-stitched leather work; own heat-treating. **Prices:** $100 to $2200. **Remarks:** ABS Journeyman Smith. **Mark:** Hot Mark - Copperhead Snake. **Other:** Cabel / Damascus/ High Carbone.

BLACK, SCOTT, 570 Malcom Rd., Covington, GA 30209
Specialties: Working/using folders of his design. **Patterns:** Daggers, hunters, utility/camp knives and friction folders. **Technical:** Forges pattern

welded, cable, 1095, O1 and 5160. **Prices:** $100 to $500. **Remarks:** Part-time maker; first knife sold in 1992. Doing business as Copperhead Forge. **Mark:** Hot mark on blade, copperhead snake.

BLACK, TOM, 921 Grecian NW, Albuquerque, NM 87107, Phone: 505-344-2549
Specialties: Working knives to fancy straight knives of his design. **Patterns:** Drop-point skinners, folders, using knives, Bowies and daggers. **Technical:** Grinds 440C, 154CM, ATS-34, A2, D2 and Damascus. Offers engraving and scrimshaw. **Prices:** $185 to $1,250; some over $8,500. **Remarks:** Full-time maker; first knife sold in 1970. **Mark:** Name, city.

BLACK, EARL, 3466 South, 700 East, Salt Lake City, UT 84106, Phone: 801-466-8395
Specialties: High-art straight knives and folders; period pieces. **Patterns:** Boots, Bowies and daggers; lockers and gents. **Technical:** Grinds 440C and 154CM. Buys some Damascus. Scrimshaws and engraves. **Prices:** $200 to $1,800; some to $2,500 and higher. **Remarks:** Full-time maker; first knife sold in 1980. **Mark:** Name, city, state.

BLACKTON, ANDREW E., 12521 Fifth Isle, Bayonet Point, FL 34667, Phone: 727-869-1406
Specialties: Straight and folding knives, some fancy. **Patterns:** Hunters, Bowies and daggers. **Technical:** Grinds D2, 440C and 154CM. Offers some embellishment. **Prices:** $125 to $450; some to $2,000. **Remarks:** Full-time maker. **Mark:** Last name in script.

BLANCHARD, G. R. (GARY), 5917 Negril Ave, Las Vegas, NV 89130, Phone: 702-645-9774
Specialties: Fancy folders and high-art straight knives of his design. **Patterns:** Boots, daggers and locking folders. **Technical:** Grinds 440C and ATS-34 and Damascus. Engraves knives. **Prices:** $1,500 to $18,000 or more. **Remarks:** Full-time maker; first knife sold in 1989. **Mark:** First and middle initials, last name.

BLASINGAME, ROBERT, 2906 Swanson Lane, Kilgore, TX 75662, Phone: 903-984-8144
Specialties: Classic working and using straight knives and folders of his design and to customer specs. **Patterns:** Bowies, daggers, fighters and hunters; one-of-a-kind historic reproductions. **Technical:** Hand-forges P. W. Damascus, cable Damascus and chain Damascus. **Prices:** $150 to $1,000; some to $2,000. **Remarks:** Full-time maker; first knife sold in 1968. **Mark:** 'B' inside anvil.

BLAUM, ROY, 319 N. Columbia St., Covington, LA 70433, Phone: 504-893-1060
Specialties: Working straight knives and folders of his design; lightweight easy-open folders. **Patterns:** Hunters, boots, fishing and woodcarving/whittling knives. **Technical:** Grinds A2, D2, O1, 154CM and ATS-34. Offers leatherwork. **Prices:** $40 to $800; some higher. **Remarks:** Full-time maker; first knife sold in 1976. **Mark:** Engraved signature or etched logo.

BLOOMER, ALAN T., 116 E 6th St, Maquon, IL 61458, Phone: 309-875-3583
Specialties: All Damascus folders, making own Damascus. **Patterns:** Bowies, Folders, chef etc. **Technical:** Does own heat treating. **Prices:** $400 to $1000. **Remarks:** Part-time maker; Guild member. **Mark:** Stamp Bloomer. **Other:** No orders.

BLOOMQUIST, R GORDON, 6206 Tiger Tail Dr, Olympia, WA 98512, Phone: (360) 352-7162

BLUM, CHUCK, 743 S. Brea Blvd., #10, Brea, CA 92621, Phone: 714-529-0484
Specialties: Art and investment daggers and Bowies. **Technical:** Flatgrinds; hollow-grinds 440C, ATS-34 on working knives. **Prices:** $125 to $8,500. **Remarks:** Part-time maker; first knife sold in 1985. **Mark:** First and middle initials and last name with sailboat logo.

BLUM, KENNETH, 1729 Burleson, Brenham, TX 77833, Phone: 979-836-9577
Specialties: Traditional working straight knives of his design. **Patterns:** Camp knives, Hunters and Bowies. **Technical:** Forges 5160; grinds 440C and D2. Uses exotic woods and Micarta for handles. **Prices:** $150 to $300. **Remarks:** Part-time maker; first knife sold in 1978. **Mark:** Last name on ricasso.

BOARDMAN, GUY, 39 Mountain Ridge R., New Germany 3619, SOUTH AFRICA, Phone: 031-726-921
Specialties: American and South African styles. **Patterns:** Bowies, American and South African hunters, plus more. **Technical:** Grinds Bohler steels, some ATS-34. **Prices:** $100 to $600. **Remarks:** Part-time maker; first knife sold in 1986. **Mark:** Name, city, country.

BOATRIGHT, BASEL, 11 Timber Point, New Braunfels, TX 78132, Phone: 210-609-0807
Specialties: Working and using knives of his design. **Patterns:** Hunters, skinners and utility/camp knives. **Technical:** Grinds and hand-tempers 5160. **Prices:** $75 to $300. **Remarks:** Part-time maker. **Mark:** Stamped BBB.

BOCHMAN, BRUCE, 183 Howard Place, Grants Pass, OR 97526, Phone: 503-471-1985
Specialties: Working straight knives in standard patterns. **Patterns:** Bowies, hunters, fishing and bird knives. **Technical:** 440C; mirror or satin finish. **Prices:** $140 to $250; some to $750. **Remarks:** Part-time maker; first knife sold in 1977. **Mark:** Custom blades by B. Bochman.

BODEN, HARRY, Via Gellia Mill, Bonsall Matlock, Derbyshire DE4 2AJ, ENGLAND, Phone: 0629-825176
Specialties: Traditional working straight knives and folders of his design. **Patterns:** Hunters, locking folders and utility/camp knives. **Technical:** Grinds Sandvik 12C27, D2 and O1. **Prices:** £70 to £150; some to £300. **Remarks:** Full-time maker; first knife sold in 1986. **Mark:** Full name.

BODNER, GERALD "JERRY", 4102 Spyglass Ct., Louisville, KY 40229, Phone: 502-968-5946
Specialties: Fantasy straight knives in standard patterns. **Patterns:** Bowies, fighters, hunters and micro-miniature knives. **Technical:** Grinds Damascus, 440C and D2. Offers filework. **Prices:** $35 to $180. **Remarks:** Part-time maker; first knife sold in 1993. **Mark:** Last name in script and JAB in oval above knives.

BODOLAY, ANTAL, Rua Wilson Soares Fernandes #31, Planalto, Belo Horizonte MG-31730-700, BRAZIL, Phone: 031-494-1885
Specialties: Working folders and fixed blades of his design or to customer specs; some art daggers and period pieces. **Patterns:** Daggers, fighters, locking folders, utility knives and Khukris. **Technical:** Grinds D6, high carbon steels and 420 stainless. Forges files on request. **Prices:** $30 to $350. **Remarks:** Full-time maker; first knife sold in 1965. **Mark:** Last name in script.

BOEHLKE, GUENTER, Parkstrasse 2, 56412 Grossholbach, GERMANY 2602-5440
Specialties: Classic working/using straight knives of his design. **Patterns:** Hunters, utility/camp knives and ancient remakes. **Technical:** Grinds Damascus, CPM-T-440V and 440C. Inlays gemstones and ivory. **Prices:** $220 to $700; some to $2,000. **Remarks:** Spare-time maker; first knife sold in 1985. **Mark:** Name, address and bow and arrow.

BOGUSZEWSKI, PHIL, P. O. Box 99329, Lakewood, WA 98499, Phone: 253-581-7096
Specialties: Working folders--some fancy--mostly of his design. **Patterns:** Folders, slip-joints and lockers; also makes anodized titanium frame folders. **Technical:** Grinds BG42 & Damascus; offers filework. **Prices:** $450 to $2,500. **Remarks:** Full-time maker; first knife sold in 1979. **Mark:** Name, city and state.

BOJTOS, ARPA D, Dobsinskeho 10, 98403 Lucenec, Slovakia, Phone: 00421-47 4333512
Specialties: Fantasy and high-art knives. **Patterns:** Daggers, fighters and hunters. **Technical:** Grinds ATS-34. Carves on steel, handle materials and sheaths. **Prices:** $2,000 to $5,000; some to $8,000. **Remarks:** Full-time maker; first knife sold in 1990. **Mark:** Stylized initials.

BOLD, STU, 63 D'Andrea Tr., Sarnia, Ont., CANADA N7S 6H3, Phone: 519-383-7610
Specialties: Traditional working/using straight knives in standard patterns and to customer specs. **Patterns:** Boots, Bowies and hunters. **Technical:** Grinds ATS-34, 440C and Damascus; mosaic pins. Offers scrimshaw and hand-tooled leather sheaths. **Prices:** $140 to $500; some to $2,000. **Remarks:** Part-time maker; first knife sold in 1983. **Mark:** Name, city, province.

BOLEWARE, DAVID, P. O. Box 96, Carson, MS 39427, Phone: 601-943-5372
Specialties: Traditional and working/using straight knives of his design, to customer specs and in standard patterns. **Patterns:** Bowies, hunters and utility/camp knives. **Technical:** Grinds ATS-34, 440C and Damascus. **Prices:** $85 to $350; some to $600. **Remarks:** Part-time maker; first knife sold in 1989. **Mark:** First and last name, city, state.

BOLTON, CHARLES B., P. O. Box 6, Jonesburg, MO 63351, Phone: 636-488-5785
Specialties: Working straight knives of his design. **Patterns:** Hunters, skinners, boots and fighters. **Technical:** Grinds 440C and ATS-34. **Prices:** $100 to $300; some to $600. **Remarks:** Full-time maker; first knife sold in 1973. **Mark:** Last name.

BONASSI, FRANCO, Via Superiore 14, Pordenone 33170, ITALY, Phone: 434-550821
Specialties: Fancy and working one-of-a-kind straight knives of his design. **Patterns:** Hunters, skinners, utility and liner locks. **Technical:** Grinds CPM, ATS-34, 154CM and commercial Damascus. Uses only titanium foreguards and pommels. **Prices:** Start at $250. **Remarks:** Spare-time maker; first knife sold in 1988. Has made cutlery for several celebrities; Gen. Schwarzkopf, Fuzzy Zoeller, etc. **Mark:** FRANK.

BOOCO, GORDON, 175 Ash St., P. O. Box 174, Hayden, CO 81639, Phone: 970-276-3195
Specialties: Fancy working straight knives of his design and to customer specs. **Patterns:** Hunters and Bowies. **Technical:** Grinds 440C, D2 and A2. Heat-treats. **Prices:** $150 to $350; some $600 and higher. **Remarks:** Part-time maker; first knife sold in 1984. **Mark:** Last name with push dagger artwork.

BOOS, RALPH, 5107 40 Ave., Edmonton, Alberta, CANADA T6L 1B3, Phone: 780-463-7094
Specialties: Classic, fancy and fantasy miniature knives and swords of his design or to customer specs. **Patterns:** Bowies, daggers and swords. **Technical:** Hand files O1, stainless and Damascus. Engraves and carves. Does heat bluing and acid etching. **Prices:** $125 to $350; some to $1,000. **Remarks:** Part-time maker; first knife sold in 1982. **Mark:** First initials back to back.

BOOTH, PHILIP W., 301 S. Jeffery Ave., Ithaca, MI 48847, Phone: 989-875-2844
Specialties: Folding knives, various mechanisms, maker of the "minnow" series small folding knife. **Patterns:** Auto lock backs, liner locks, classic pattern multi-blades. **Technical:** Grinds ATS-34, 440C, 1095 and commercial Damascus. Prefers natural materials, offers file work and scrimshaw. **Prices:** $200 and up. **Remarks:** Full-time maker; first knife sold in 1991. **Mark:** Last name or name with city and map logo.

BORGER, WOLF, Benzstrasse 8, 76676 Graben-Neudorf, GERMANY, Phone: 07255-72303, Fax:07255-72304
Specialties: High-tech working and using straight knives and folders, many with corkscrews or other tools, of his design. **Patterns:** Hunters, Bowies and folders with various locking systems. **Technical:** Grinds 440C, ATS-34 and CPM. Uses stainless Damascus. **Prices:** $250 to $900; some to $1,500. **Remarks:** Full-time maker; first knife sold in 1975. **Mark:** Howling wolf and name; first name on Damascus blades.

BOSE, REESE, PO Box 61, Shelburn, IN 47879, Phone: 812-397-5114
Specialties: Traditional working and using knives in standard patterns and multi-blade folders. **Patterns:** Multi-blade slip-joints. **Technical:** ATS-34, D2 and CPM 440V. **Prices:** $275 to $1,500. **Remarks:** Full-time maker; first knife sold in 1992. Photos by Jack Busfield. **Mark:** R. Bose.

BOSE, TONY, 7252 N. County Rd., 300 E., Shelburn, IN 47879-9778, Phone: 812-397-5114
Specialties: Traditional working and using knives in standard patterns; multi-blade folders. **Patterns:** Multi-blade slip-joints. **Technical:** Grinds commercial Damascus, ATS-34 and D2. **Prices:** $400 to $1200. **Remarks:** Full-time maker; first knife sold in 1972. **Mark:** First initial, last name, city, state.

BOSSAERTS, CARL, Rua Albert Einstein 906, 14051-110, Ribeirao Preto, S. P. BRAZIL, Phone: 016 633 7063
Specialties: Working and using straight knives of his design, to customer specs and in standard patterns. **Patterns:** Hunters, fighters and utility/camp knives. **Technical:** Grinds ATS-34, 440V and 440C; does filework. **Prices:** 60 to $400. **Remarks:** Part-time maker; first knife sold in 1992. **Mark:** Initials joined together.

BOST, ROGER E, 30511 Cartier Dr, Palos Verdes, CA 90275-5629, Phone: (310) 541-6833
Specialties: Hunters, fighters, boot, utility. **Patterns:** Loveless style. **Technical:** ATS-34, 60-61RC, stock removal & forge. **Prices:** $200 & up. **Remarks:** First knife sold in 1990. **Mark:** Diamond with initials inside and Palos Verdes California around outside. **Other:** Cal. Knifemakers Assn, ABS.

BOSWORTH, DEAN, 329 Mahogany Dr., Key Largo, FL 33037, Phone: 305-451-1564
Specialties: Free hand hollow ground working knives with hand rubbed satin finish, filework and inlays. **Patterns:** Bird & Trout, hunters, skinners, filet, Bowies, miniatures. **Technical:** Using 440C, ATS-34, D2, Meier Damascus, custom wet formed sheaths. **Prices:** $250 & up. **Remarks:** Part-time maker; first knife made in 1985. **Mark:** BOZ stamped in block letters. **Other:** Member: Florida Knifemakers Assoc.

BOURBEAU, JEAN YVES, 15 Rue Remillard, Notre Dame, Ile Perrot, Quebec, CANADA J7V 8M9, Phone: 514-453-1069
Specialties: Fancy/embellished and fantasy folders of his design. **Patterns:** Bowies, fighters and locking folders. **Technical:** Grinds 440C, ATS-34 and Damascus. Carves precious wood for handles. **Prices:** $150 to $1000. **Remarks:** Part-time maker; first knife sold in 1994. **Mark:** Interlaced initials.

BOUSE, D. MICHAEL, 1010 Victoria Pl., Waldorf, MD 20602, Phone: 301-843-0449
Specialties: Traditional and working/using straight knives of his design. **Patterns:** Daggers, fighters and hunters. **Technical:** Forges 5160 and Damascus; grinds D2; differential hardened blades; decorative handle pins. **Prices:** $125 to $350. **Remarks:** Spare-time maker; first knife sold in

1992. Doing business as Michael's Handmade Knives. **Mark:** Etched last name.

BOWEN, TILTON, Rt. 1, Box 225A, Baker, WV 26801, Phone: 304-897-6159
Specialties: Straight, stout working knives. **Patterns:** Hunters, fighters and boots; also offers buckskinner and throwing knives. All my D2-blades since 1st of year, 1997 are Deep Cryogenic processed. **Technical:** Grinds D2 and 4140. **Prices:** $60 to $275. **Remarks:** Full-time maker; first knife sold in 1982-1983. Sells wholesale to dealers. **Mark:** Initials and BOWEN BLADES, WV.

BOWLES, CHRIS, PO Box 985, Reform, AL 35481, Phone: 205-367-8245
Specialties: Working/using straight knives, one-of-a-kind pieces and period pieces. **Patterns:** Hardcore skinners, bowies, fighters, tactical and camp/utility, elegant hunters, neck knives & period pieces. **Technical:** Grinds 01, 440C, 154CM, BG-42, Damascus. Forges 01, 1095, L-6. **Prices:** $75 to $600, depending on style and embellishments. **Remarks:** Part-time maker. Doing business as Chris Bowles Custom Made Knives. **Mark:** First & last name etched in script or tang stamped.

BOXER, REX, Legend Forge, 965 N River Rd, Sylva, NC 28779, Phone: 828-508-5839
Specialties: Handmade hunting knives hand cut from saw blades and rasp files. All are antler handled. Also, hand forge Damascus steel with some stainless steel Damascus. **Patterns:** Hunters and Bowies. **Technical:** Uses hi-carbon steel from older saw blades and rasp files. **Prices:** $150 to $1500 on some very exceptional Damascus knives. **Remarks:** Full-time furrier and maker. **Mark:** The name "Legend Forge" hand engraved on every blade. **Additional:** Makes his own custom leather sheath stamped with maker stamp. Leather work is hand tooled primarily hunting scenes. His knives are used by the outdoorsman of the Smoky Mountains, North Carolina, and the Rockies of Montana.

BOYD, FRANCIS, 1811 Prince St., Berkeley, CA 94703, Phone: 510-841-7210
Specialties: Folders and kitchen knives; Japanese swords. **Patterns:** Push-button sturdy locking folders; San Francisco-style chef's knives. **Technical:** Forges and grinds; mostly uses high-carbon steels. **Prices:** Moderate to heavy. **Remarks:** Designer. **Mark:** Name.

BOYE, DAVID, P. O. Box 1238, Dolan Springs, AZ 86441, Phone: 800-853-1617
Specialties: Folders, hunting and kitchen knives. Forerunner in the use of dendritic steel and dendritic cobalt for blades. **Patterns:** Boye Basics sheath knives, lockback folders, kitchen knives and hunting knives. **Technical:** Casts blades in stainless 440Cand cobalt. **Prices:** From $79 to $500. **Remarks:** Full-time maker; author of *Step-by-Step Knife making* **Mark:** Name.

BOYER, MARK, 10515 Woodinville Dr., #17, Bothell, WA 98011, Phone: 206-487-9370
Specialties: High-tech and working/using straight knives of his design. **Patterns:** Fighters and utility/camp knives. **Technical:** Grinds 1095 and D2. Offers Kydex sheaths; heat-treats. **Prices:** $45 to $120. **Remarks:** Part-time maker; first knife sold in 1994. Doing business as Boyer Blades. **Mark:** Eagle holding two swords with name.

BOYSEN, RAYMOND A, 125 E St Patrick, Rapid City, SD 57701, Phone: (605) 341-7752

BRACK, DOUGLAS D., 119 Camino Ruiz, #71, Camirillo, CA 93012, Phone: 805-987-0490
Specialties: Working straight knives of his design. **Patterns:** Heavy-duty skinners, fighters and boots. **Technical:** Grinds 440C, ATS-34 and 5160; forges cable. **Prices:** $90 to $180; some to $300. **Remarks:** Part-time maker; first knife sold in 1984. **Mark:** tat.

BRADBURN, GARY, 1714 Park Pl., Wichita, KS 67203, Phone: 316-269-4273
Specialties: Straight knives of his design and to customer specs. **Patterns:** Bowies, fighters, hunters and miniatures. **Technical:** Forges 5160 and his own Damascus; grinds D2. **Prices:** $50 to $350; some to $800. **Remarks:** Full-time maker; first knife sold 1991. **Mark:** Last name or last initial inside a shamrock.

BRADFORD, GARRICK, 582 Guelph St, Kitchener ON, CANADA N2H-5Y4, Phone: (519) 576-9863

BRADLEY, JOHN, P. O. Box 37, Pomona Park, FL 32181, Phone: 904-649-4739
Specialties: Fixed-blade using knives. **Patterns:** Skinners, bowies, camp knives and Sgian Dubhs. **Technical:** Hand forged from 52100, 1095 and own Damascus. **Prices:** $125 to $500; some higher. **Remarks:** Part-time maker; first knife sold in 1988. **Mark:** Last name.

BRADLEY, DENNIS, 2410 Bradley Acres Rd., Blairsville, GA 30512, Phone: 706-745-4364
Specialties: Working straight knives and folders, some high-art. **Patterns:** Hunters, boots and daggers; slip-joints and two-blades. **Technical:** Grinds

ATS-34, D2, 440C and commercial Damascus. **Prices:** $100 to $500; some to $2,000. **Remarks:** Part-time maker; first knife sold in 1973. **Mark:** BRADLEY KNIVES in double heart logo.

BRADSHAW, BAILEY, 17800 Dickerson St, Ste 112, Dallas, TX 75252, Phone: 972-381-0558, Fax:972-381-1255
Specialties: Traditional folders and contemporary front lock folders. **Patterns:** Single or multi-blade folders, bowies. **Technical:** Grind CPM 3V, CPM 440V, CPM 420V, Forge Damascus, 52100. **Prices:** $250 to $3,000. **Remarks:** I engrave, carve and do sterling silver sheaths. **Mark:** Tori arch over initials back to back.

BRANDON, MATTHEW, 4435 Meade St, Denver, CO 80211, Phone: (303) 458-0786
Specialties: Hunters, Skinners, Full Tang Bowies. **Prices:** $100-$250. **Remarks:** Satisfaction or full refund. **Mark:** MTB.

BRANDSEY, EDWARD P., 335 Forest Lake Dr, Milton, WI 53563, Phone: 608-868-9010
Specialties: Large bowies. **Patterns:** Hunters, fighters, Bowies and daggers, some buckskinner styles. Native American influence on some. **Technical:** ATS-34, 440-C, 0-1, and some Damascus. **Prices:** $200 to $400; some to $3,000. **Remarks:** . Full-time maker. First knife sold in 1973. **Mark:** Initials connected - registered Wisc. Trademark since March 1983.

BRANDT, MARTIN W, 833 Kelly Blvd, Springfield, OR 97477, Phone: (541) 747-5422

BRANTON, ROBERT, 4976 Seewee Rd., Awendaw, SC 29429, Phone: 843-928-3624
Specialties: Working straight knives of his design or to customer specs; throwing knives. **Patterns:** Hunters, fighters and some miniatures. **Technical:** Grinds ATS-34, A2 and 1050; forges 5160, O1. Offers hollow- or convex-grinds. **Prices:** $25 to $400. **Remarks:** Part-time maker; first knife sold in 1985. Doing business as Pro-Flyte, Inc. **Mark:** Last name; or first and last name, city, state.

BRATCHER, BRETT, 11816 County Rd 302, Plantersville, TX 77363, Phone: (936) 894-3788, Fax:(936) 894-3790
Specialties: Hunting and skinning knives. **Patterns:** Clip & Drop Point. Hand forged. **Technical:** Material 5160, D2, 1095 & Damascus. **Price:** $200 to $500. **Mark:** Bratcher.

BRAY JR., W. LOWELL, 6931 Manor Beach Rd., New Port Richey, FL 34652, Phone: 727-846-0830
Specialties: Traditional working and using straight knives and folders of his design. **Patterns:** Hunters, kitchen knives and utility knives. **Technical:** Grinds 440C & ATS34; forges high carbon. **Prices:** $70 to $300. **Remarks:** Spare-time maker; first knife sold in 1992. **Mark:** Lowell Bray Knives in shield.

BREED, KIM, 733 Jace Dr, Clarksville, TN 37040, Phone: 931-645-9171
Specialties: High end thru folders, working straight knives. **Patterns:** Hunters, fighters, daggers, bowies, his designer customers. Likes one of a kind designs. **Technical:** Makes own Mosiand and regular Damascus, but will use stainless steels offers filework and sculpted material. **Prices:** $150-$1200. **Remarks:** Part-time maker. First knife sold in 1990. **Mark:** Last name.

BRENNAN, JUDSON, P. O. Box 1165, Delta Junction, AK 99737, Phone: 907-895-5153, Fax:907-895-5404
Specialties: Period pieces. **Patterns:** All kinds of Bowies, rifle knives, daggers. **Technical:** Forges miscellaneous steels. **Prices:** Upscale, good value. **Remarks:** Muzzle-loading gunsmith; first knife sold in 1978. **Mark:** Name.

BRESHEARS, CLINT, 1261 Keats, Manhattan Beach, CA 90266, Phone: 310-372-0739, Fax:310-372-0739
Specialties: Working straight knives and folders. **Patterns:** Hunters, Bowies and survival knives. Folders are mostly hunters. **Technical:** Grinds 440C, 154CM and ATS-34; prefers mirror finishes. **Prices:** $125 to $750; some to $1800. **Remarks:** Part-time maker; first knife sold in 1978. **Mark:** First name.

BREUER, LONNIE, P. O. Box 877384, Wasilla, AK 99687-7384
Specialties: Fancy working straight knives. **Patterns:** Hunters, camp knives and axes, folders and Bowies. **Technical:** Grinds 440C, AEB-L and D2; likes wire inlay, scrimshaw, decorative filing. **Prices:** $60 to $150; some to $300. **Remarks:** Part-time maker; first knife sold in 1977. **Mark:** Signature.

BRIDWELL, RICHARD A., Rt. 2, Milford Ch. Rd., Taylors, SC 29687, Phone: 803-895-1715
Specialties: Working straight knives and folders. **Patterns:** Boot and fishing knives, fighters and hunters. **Technical:** Grinds stainless steels and D2. **Prices:** $85 to $165; some to $600. **Remarks:** Part-time maker; first knife sold in 1974. **Mark:** Last name logo.

BRIGHTWELL, MARK, 21104 Creekside Dr., Leander, TX 78641, Phone: 512-267-4110
Specialties: Fancy and plain folders of his design. **Patterns:** Fighters, hunters and gents, some traditional. **Technical:** Hollow- or flat- grinds ATS-34, D2, custom Damascus; elaborate filework; heat-treats. Extensive choice of natural handle materials; no synthetics. **Prices:** $300 to $1,500. **Remarks:** Full-time maker. **Mark:** Last name.

BRITTON, TIM, 5645 Murray Rd, Winston-Salem, NC 27106, Phone: 336-922-9582 336-922-9582
Specialties: Small and simple working knives, sgian dubhs and special tactical designs. **Technical:** Forges and grinds stainless steel. **Prices:** $110 to $600. **Remarks:** Veteran knife maker. **Mark:** Etched signature.

BROADWELL, DAVID, P. O. Box 4314, Wichita Falls, TX 76308, Phone: 940-692-1727, Fax:940-692-4003
Specialties: Sculpted high-art straight and folding knives. **Patterns:** Daggers, sub-hilted fighters, folders, sculpted art knives and some Bowies. **Technical:** Grinds mostly Damascus; carves; prefers natural handle materials, including stone. Some embellishment. **Prices:** $350 to $3,000; some higher. **Remarks:** Full-time maker; first knife sold in 1982. **Mark:** Stylized emblem bisecting "B"/with last name below.

BROCK, KENNETH L., P. O. Box 375, 207 N. Skinner Rd., Allenspark, CO 80510, Phone: 303-747-2547
Specialties: Custom designs, Full-tang working knives and button lock folders of his design. **Patterns:** Hunters, miniatures and minis. **Technical:** Flat-grinds D2 and 440C; makes own sheaths; heat-treats. **Prices:** $50 to $500. **Remarks:** Part-time maker; first knife sold in 1978. **Mark:** Last name, city, state and serial number.

BROMLEY, PETER, 1408 S Bettman, Spokane, WA 99212, Phone: (509) 534-4235
Specialties: Period bowies. **Patterns:** Boot knives, hunting, bowies, folders. **Technical:** High carbon steel. **Prices:** $100 to $700. **Remarks:** Member of Montana Knifemakers Assoc., Oregon Knife Coll., A. B. S. **Mark:** Bromley-Spokane WA.

BROOKER, DENNIS, Rt. 1, Box 12A, Derby, IA 50068, Phone: 515-533-2103
Specialties: Fancy straight knives and folders of his design. **Patterns:** Hunters, folders and boots. **Technical:** Forges and grinds. Full-time engraver and designer; instruction available. **Prices:** Moderate to upscale. **Remarks:** Part-time maker. Takes no orders; sells only completed work. **Mark:** Name.

BROOKS, BUZZ, 2345 Yosemite Dr, Los Angles, CA 90041, Phone: (323) 256-2892

BROOKS, MICHAEL, 4645 52nd St Apt F4, Lubbock, TX 79414-3802
Specialties: Working straight knives of his design or to customer specs. **Patterns:** Tantos, swords, Bowies, hunters, skinners and boots. **Technical:** Grinds 440C, D2 and ATS-34; offers wide variety of handle materials. **Prices:** $40 to $800. **Remarks:** Part-time maker; first knife sold in 1985. **Mark:** Initials.

BROOKS, STEVE R., 1610 Dunn Ave, Walkerville, MT 59701, Phone: 406-782-5114
Specialties: Working straight knives and folders; period pieces. **Patterns:** Hunters, Bowies and camp knives; folding lockers; axes, tomahawks and buckskinner knives; swords and stilettos. **Technical:** Forges O1, Damascus and mosaic Damascus. Some knives come embellished. **Prices:** $150 to $2,000. **Remarks:** Full-time maker; first knife sold in 1982. **Mark:** Lazy initials.

BROOME, THOMAS A., 1212 E. Aliak Ave., Kenai, AK 99611-8205, Phone: 907-283-9128
Specialties: Working hunters & folders **Patterns:** Traditional & custom orders. **Technical:** Grinds ATS-34, BG-42, CPM-S30V. **Prices:** $175 to $350. **Remarks:** Full-time maker; first knife sold in 1979. Doing business as Thom's Custom Knives. **Mark:** Full name, city, state. **Other:** Doing business as: Alaskan Man O; Steel Knives.

BROTHERS, ROBERT L., 989 Philpott Rd., Colville, WA 99114, Phone: 509-684-8922
Specialties: Traditional working and using straight knives and folders of his design to customer specs. **Patterns:** Bowies, fighters and hunters. **Technical:** Grinds D2; forges Damascus. Makes own Damascus from saw steel wire rope and chain; part-time goldsmith and stone-setter. **Prices:** $100 to $400; some higher. **Remarks:** Part-time maker; first knife sold in 1986. **Mark:** Initials and year made.

BROWER, MAX, 2016 Story St., Boone, IA 50036, Phone: 515-432-2938
Specialties: Working/using straight knives. **Patterns:** Bowies, hunters and boots. **Technical:** Grinds 440C & ATS-34. **Prices:** Start at $125. **Remarks:** Spare-time maker; first knife sold in 1981. **Mark:** Last name.

BROWN, TROY L., 22945 W867 Rd, Park Hill, OK 74451, Phone: 918-457-4128
Specialties: Working and using knives and folders. **Patterns:** Bowies, hunters, folders & scagel style. **Technical:** Forges 5160, 52100, 1084; makes his own Damascus. Prefers stag, wood and Micarta for handles. Offers engraved bolsters and guards. **Prices:** $150 to $750. **Remarks:** Full-time maker; first knife sold in 1994. Knives. **Mark:** Troy Brown. **Other:** Doing business as Elk Creek Forge.

BROWN, HAROLD E., 3654 NW Hwy. 72, Arcadia, FL 34266, Phone: 863-494-7514
Specialties: Fancy and exotic working knives. **Patterns:** Folders, slip-lock, locking several kinds. **Technical:** Grinds D2, 440C and ATS-34. Embellishment available. **Prices:** $175 to $1000. **Remarks:** Part-time maker; first knife sold in 1976. **Mark:** Name and city with logo.

BROWN, ROB E., P. O. Box 15107, Emerald Hill 6011, Port Elizabeth, SOUTH AFRICA, Phone: 27-41-3661086, Fax:27-41-4511731
Specialties: Contemporary-designed straight knives and period pieces. **Patterns:** Utility knives, hunters, boots, fighters and daggers. **Technical:** Grinds 440C, D2, ATS-34 and commercial Damascus. Knives mostly mirror finished; African handle materials. **Prices:** $100 to $1,500. **Remarks:** Full-time maker; first knife sold in 1985. **Mark:** Name and country.

BROWN, DENNIS G, 1633 North 197th Place, Shoreline, WA 98133, Phone: (206) 542-3997

BROWN, JIM, 1097 Fernleigh Cove, Little Rock, AR 72210

BROWNE, RICK, 980 West 13th St., Upland, CA 91786, Phone: 909-985-1728
Specialties: Sheffield pattern pocket knives. **Patterns:** Hunters, fighters and daggers. No heavy-duty knives. **Technical:** Grinds ATS-34. **Prices:** Start at $450. **Remarks:** Part-time maker; first knife sold in 1975. **Mark:** R. E. Nrowne, Upland, CA

BROWNING, STEVEN W, 3400 Harrison Rd, Benton, AR 72015, Phone: (501) 316-2450

BROYLES-SEBENICK, LISA, P O Box 21070, Chattanooga, TN 37424, Phone: 423-892-5007, Fax:423-899-9456

BRUNCKHORST, LYLE, Country Village, 23706 7th Ave SE, Ste B, Bothell, WA 98021, Phone: 425-402-3484
Specialties: Traditional working and using straight knives and folders of his design. **Patterns:** Bowies, hunters and locking folders. **Technical:** Grinds ATS-34; forges 5160 and his own Damascus. Iridescent RR spike knives. Offers scrimshaw, inlays and animal carvings in horn handles. **Prices:** $225 to $750; some to $3,750. **Remarks:** Full-time maker; first knife sold in 1976. Doing business as Bronk's Knife works. **Mark:** Bucking horse.

BRUNER, RICK, 7756 Aster Lane, Jenison, MI 49428, Phone: 616-457-0403
Specialties: Sheath Making

BRUNER JR, FRED, BRUNER BLADES, E10910W Hilldale Dr, Fall Creek, WI 54742, Phone: 715-877-2496

BRUNETTA, DAVID, P. O. Box 4972, Laguna Beach, CA 92652, Phone: 714-497-9611
Specialties: Straights and folders and art knives. **Patterns:** Bowies, camp/hunting, folders, fighters. **Technical:** Grinds ATS-34, D2, BG42. forges O1, 52100, 5160, 1095, makes own Damascus. **Prices:** $300 to $9000. **Mark:** Circle DB logo with last name straight or curved.

BRYAN, TOM, 14822 S Gilbert Rd, Gilbert, AZ 85296, Phone: (480) 812-8529
Specialties: Straight & folding knives. **Patterns:** Drop-point hunter fighters. **Technical:** ATS-34, 154CM, 440C & A2. **Prices:** $150 to $800. **Remarks:** Part-time maker; sold first knife in 1994. **Mark:** T. Bryan. **Other:** DBA as T. Bryan Knives.

BUCHMAN, BILL, 63312 South Rd., Bend, OR 97701, Phone: 503-382-8851
Specialties: Working straight knives. **Patterns:** Hunters, Bowies, fighters and boots. Makes full line of leather craft & saddle maker knives. **Technical:** Forges 440C and Sandvik 15N20. Prefers 440C for saltwater. **Prices:** $95 to $400. **Remarks:** Full-time maker; first knife sold in 1982. **Mark:** Initials or last name.

BUCHNER, BILL, P. O. Box 73, Idleyld Park, OR 97447, Phone: 541-498-2247
Specialties: Working straight knives, kitchen knives and high-art knives of his design. **Technical:** Uses W1, L6 and his own Damascus. Invented "spectrum metal" for letter openers, folder handles and jewelry. Likes sculpturing and carving in Damascus. **Prices:** $40 to $3,000; some higher. **Remarks:** Full-time maker; first knife sold in 1978. **Mark:** Signature.

custom knifemakers

BUCHOLZ, MARK A., 9197 West Parkview Terrace Loop, Eagle River, AK 99577, Phone: 907-694-1037
Specialties: Liner lock folders. **Patterns:** Hunters and fighters. **Technical:** Grinds ATS-34. **Prices:** Upscale. **Remarks:** Full-time maker; first knife sold in 1976. **Mark:** Name, city and state in buffalo skull logo or signature.

BUCKBEE, DONALD M., 243 South Jackson Trail, Grayling, MI 49738, Phone: 517-348-1386
Specialties: Working straight knives, some fancy, in standard patterns; concentrating on kitchen knives. **Patterns:** Kitchen knives, hunters, Bowies. **Technical:** Grinds D2, 440C, ATS-34. Makes ultra-lights in hunter patterns. **Prices:** $100 to $250; some to $350. **Remarks:** Part-time maker; first knife sold in 1984. **Mark:** Antlered bee--a buck bee.

BUCKNER, JIMMIE H., P. O. Box 162, Putney, GA 31782, Phone: 912-436-4182
Specialties: Camp knives, Bowies (1 of a kind), liner lock folders, tomahawks, camp axes, neck knives for law enforcement and hide out knives for body guards and professional people. **Patterns:** Hunters camp knives, Bowies. **Technical:** Forges 1084, 5160 and Damascus (own), own heat treats. **Prices:** $195 to $795 and up. **Remarks:** Full-time maker; first knife sold in 1980, ABS Mastersmith. **Mark:** Name over spade.

BUEBENDORF, ROBERT E., 108 Lazybrooke Rd., Monroe, CT 06468, Phone: 203-452-1769
Specialties: Traditional and fancy straight knives of his design. **Patterns:** Hand-makes and embellishes belt buckle knives. **Technical:** Forges and grinds 440C, O1, W2, 1095, his own Damascus and 154CM. **Prices:** $200 to $500. **Remarks:** Full-time maker; first knife sold in 1978. **Mark:** First and middle initials, last name and MAKER.

BULLARD, BILL, Rt. 5, Box 35, Andalusia, AL 36420, Phone: 334-222-9003
Specialties: Traditional working and using straight knives and folders of his design. **Patterns:** Hunters, slip-joint folders and utility/camp knives and folders to customer specs. **Technical:** Forges Damascus, cable. Offers filework. **Prices:** $100 to $500; some to $1,500. **Remarks:** Part-time maker; first knife sold in 1974. Doing business as Five Runs Forge. **Mark:** Last name stamped on ricasso.

BULLARD, TOM, 117 MC 8068, Flippin, AR 72634, Phone: 870-453-3421
Specialties: Armadillo handle material on hunter and folders. **Patterns:** Bowies, hunters, lockback folders. **Technical:** Grinds 440-C, ATS-34, commercial Damascus. **Prices:** $150 to $500. **Remarks:** Offers filework and engraving. I do not make screw together knives. **Mark:** Tbullard.

BULLARD, RANDALL, 7 Mesa Dr., Canyon, TX 79015, Phone: 806-655-0590
Specialties: Working/using straight knives and folders of his design or to customer specs. **Patterns:** Hunters, locking folders and slip-joint folders. **Technical:** Grinds O1, ATS-34 and 440C. Does file work. **Prices:** $125 to $300; some to $500. **Remarks:** Part-time maker; first knife sold in 1993. Doing business as Bullard Custom Knives. **Mark:** First and middle initials, last name, maker, city and state.

BUMP, BRUCE D, 1103 Rex Lane, Walla Walla, WA 99362, Phone: (509) 522-2219
Specialties: Pattern welded Damascus, two knife sets, folders & fixed. **Patterns:** Mosaic, ladder, raindrop, combinations. **Technical:** Forge welded mosaic bolsters, mastodon ivory. **Prices:** $350 to $2500. **Remarks:** I make my own Damascus. I use only natural handle materials on custom knives. **Mark:** Bruce D. Bump Walla Walla WA or Bruce D. Bump Custom Walla Walla WA. **Remarks:** American Bladesmith Society "Journeyman Smith".

BURAK, CHET, Knife Services Photographer, PO Box 14383, E Providence, RI 02914, Phone: 401-431-0625, Fax:401-434-9821

BURDEN, JAMES, 405 Kelly St., Burkburnett, TX 76354

BURGER, FRED, Box 436, Munster 4278, Kwa-Zulu Natal, SOUTH AFRICA, Phone: 27 393216
Specialties: Sword canes and tactical walking sticks. **Patterns:** 440C & carbon steel blades. **Technical:** Double hollow ground and Poniard style blades. **Prices:** $190 to $600. **Remarks:** Full-time maker with son, Barry, since 1987. **Mark:** Last name in oval pierced by a dagger. **Other:** Member South African Guild.

BURGER, PON, 12 Glenwood Ave., Woodlands, Bulawayo, Zimbabwe 75514
Specialties: Collectors items. **Patterns:** Fighters, locking folders of traditional styles, buckles. **Technical:** Scrimshaws 440C blade. Uses polished buffalo horn with brass fittings. Cased in buffalo hide book. **Prices:** $450 to $1100. **Remarks:** Full-time maker; first knife sold in 1973. Doing business as Burger Products. **Mark:** Spirit of Africa.

BURKE, DAN, 22001 Ole Barn Rd., Edmond, OK 73034, Phone: 405-341-3406, Fax:405-340-3333
Specialties: Slip joint folders. **Patterns:** Traditional folders. **Technical:** Grinds D2 and BG-42. Prefers natural handle materials; heat-treats. **Prices:** $440 to $1900. **Remarks:** Full-time maker; first knife sold in 1976. **Mark:** First initial and last name.

BURKE, BILL, 315 Courthouse Dr, Salmon, ID 83467, Phone: (208) 756-3797
Specialties: Hand forged working knives. **Patterns:** Fowler pronghorn, clip point & drop point hunters. **Technical:** Forges 52100 & 5160. Makes own Damascus from 15N20 and 1084. **Prices:** $250 to $2000. **Remarks:** I am dedicated to fixed blade high performance knives. **Mark:** Initials connected. **Other:** Also make "Ed Fowler" miniatures.

BURNETT, MAX, 537 Old Dug Mtn. Rd., Paris, AR 72855, Phone: 501-963-2767
Specialties: Forging with coal/charcoal; some stock removal. **Patterns:** Hunters, Bowies, camp, tactical, neck knives & kydex sheaths. **Technical:** Steels used: 1084, 1095, 52100, 5160, L6, 01 & others available. **Prices:** $50 & up for neck knives/Bowies $250 & up. **Remarks:** Full-time since March 2000. **Mark:** M. OGG & omega symbol.

BURROWS, STEPHEN R., 3532 Michigan, Kansas City, MO 64109, Phone: 816-921-1573
Specialties: Fantasy straight knives of his design, to customer specs and in standard patterns; period pieces. **Patterns:** Fantasy, bird and trout knives, daggers, fighters and hunters. **Technical:** Forges 5160 and 1095 high-carbon steel, O1 and his Damascus. Offers lost wax casting in bronze or silver of cross guards and pommels. **Prices:** $65 to $600; some to $2,000. **Remarks:** Full-time maker; first knife sold in 1983. Doing business as Gypsy Silk. **Mark:** Etched name.

BUSFIELD, JOHN, 153 Devonshire Circle, Roanoke Rapids, NC 27870, Phone: 252-537-3949, Fax:252-537-8704
Specialties: Investor-grade folders; high-grade working straight knives. **Patterns:** Original price-style and trailing-point interframe and sculpted-frame folders, drop-point hunters and semi-skinners. **Technical:** Grinds 154CM and ATS-34. Offers interframes, gold frames and inlays; uses jade, agate and lapis. **Prices:** $275 to $2,000. **Remarks:** Full-time maker; first knife sold in 1979. **Mark:** Last name and address.

BUSSE, JERRY, 11651 Co. Rd. 12, Wauseon, OH 43567, Phone: 419-923-6471
Specialties: Working straight knives. **Patterns:** Heavy combat knives and camp knives. **Technical:** Grinds D2, A2, INFI. **Prices:** $1,100 to $3,500. **Remarks:** Full-time maker; first knife sold in 1983. **Mark:** Last name in logo.

BUTLER, JOHN R, 20162 6th Av NE, Shoreline, WA 98155, Phone: (206) 362-3847

BUTLER, BART, 822 Seventh St, Ramona, CA 92065, Phone: (760) 789-6431

BUTLER, JOHN, 777 TYRE RD, HAVANA, FL 32333, Phone: (850) 539-5742
Specialties: Hunters, Bowies, period. **Technical:** Damascus, 52100, 5160, L6 steels. **Prices:** $80 and up. **Remarks:** Making knives since 1986. **Mark:** JB. **Other:** Journeyman (ABS).

BUTTON-INMAN, DEE, 3705 Artic Blvd 111, Anchorage, AK 99503, Phone: (907) 562-2597

BYBEE, BARRY J., 795 Lock Rd. E., Cadiz, KY 42211-8615
Specialties: Working straight knives of his design. **Patterns:** Hunters, fighters, boot knives, tantos and Bowies. **Technical:** Grinds ATS-34, 440C. Likes stag and Micarta for handle materials. **Prices:** $125 to $200; some to $1,000. **Remarks:** Part-time maker; first knife sold in 1968. **Mark:** Arrowhead logo with name, city and state.

BYRD, WESLEY L, 189 Countryside Dr, Evansville, TN 37332, Phone: (423) 775-3826

C

CABE, JERRY (BUDDY), 62 McClaren Lane, Hattieville, AR 72063, Phone: (501) 354-3581

CABRERA, SERGIO B, 25711 Frampton Av Apt 113, Harbor City, CA 90710

CAFFREY, EDWARD J., 2608 Central Ave. West, Great Falls, MT 59404, Phone: 406-727-9102
Specialties: Working/using knives and collector pieces; will accept some customer designs. **Patterns:** Hunters, fighters, camp/utility, folders, hawks and hatchets. **Technical:** Forges 5160, 52100, his Damascus, cable and chain Damascus. **Prices:** Start at $125. **Remarks:** ABS mastersmith,Part-time maker; first knife sold in 1989. **Mark:** Last name or engraved initials.

CAIRNES JR, CARROLL B, RT 1 Box 324, Palacios, TX 77465, Phone: (369) 588-6815

CALDWELL, BILL, 255 Rebecca, West Monroe, LA 71292, Phone: 318-323-3025
Specialties: Straight knives and folders with machined bolsters and liners. **Patterns:** Fighters, Bowies, survival knives, tomahawks, razors and push knives. **Technical:** Owns and operates a very large, well-equipped blacksmith and bladesmith shop extant with six large forges and eight power hammers. **Prices:** $400 to $3,500; some to $10,000. **Remarks:** Full-time maker and self-styled blacksmith; first knife sold in 1962. **Mark:** Wild Bill & Sons.

CALLAHAN, ERRETT, 2 Fredonia, Lynchburg, VA 24503
Specialties: Obsidian knives. **Patterns:** Modern styles and Stone Age replicas. **Technical:** Flakes and knaps to order. **Prices:** $100 to $3,400. **Remarks:** Part-time maker; first flint blades sold in 1974. **Mark:** Blade--engraved name, year and arrow; handle--signed edition, year and unit number.

CALLAHAN, F. TERRY, P. O. Box 880, Boerne, TX 78006, Phone: 210-981-8274, Fax:210-981-8274
Specialties: Custom hand-forged edged knives, collectible and functional. **Patterns:** Bowies, folders, daggers, hunters, camp knives and swords. **Technical:** Forges 5160, 1095 and his own Damascus. Offers filework and handmade sheaths. **Prices:** $125 to $2,000. **Remarks:** First knife sold in 1990. **Mark:** Initials inside a keystone symbol. **Other:**ABS/Journeyman Bladesmith.

CALVERT JR, ROBERT W (BOB), 911 Julia, PO Box 858, Rayville, LA 71269, Phone: (318) 728-4113, Fax:(318) 728-0000
Specialties: Using & hunting knives; your design or mine. Since 1990. **Patterns:** Forges own Damascus; all patterns. **Technical:** 5160, D2, 52100, 1084. Prefers natural handle material. **Prices:** $150 & up. **Remarks:** TOMB Member ABS, Journeyman Smith. **Mark:** Calvert (Block) J S.

CAMERON, RON G., P. O. Box 183, Logandale, NV 89021, Phone: 702-398-3356
Specialties: Fancy and embellished working/using straight knives and folders of his design. **Patterns:** Bowies, hunters and utility/camp knives. **Technical:** Grinds ATS-34, 440C and Devin Thomas Damascus or my own Damascus. Does filework, fancy pins, mokume fittings. Uses exotic hardwoods, stag and Micarta for handles. **Prices:**$150-$500 some to $1000. **Remarks:** Part-time maker; first knife sold in 1994. Doing business as Cameron Handmade Knives. **Mark:** Last name, town, state or last name.

CAMPBELL, DICK, 20000 Silver Ranch Rd., Conifer, CO 80433, Phone: 303-697-0150
Specialties: Working straight knives, period pieces. **Patterns:** Hunters, fighters, boots; 19th century bowies. **Technical:** Grinds 440C, 154CM. **Prices:**$200 to $2500. **Remarks:** Full-time maker. First knife sold in 1975. **Mark:** Name.

CAMPBELL, COURTNAY M, P O Box 23009, Columbia, SC 29224, Phone: (803) 787-0151

CAMPOS, IVAN, R. XI de Agosto, 107, Tatui, SP, BRAZIL 18270-000, Phone: 00-55-15-2518092, Fax:00-55-15-2594368
Specialties: Brazilian handmade and antique knives.

CANDRELLA, JOE, 1219 Barness Dr., Warminster, PA 18974, Phone: 215-675-0143
Specialties: Working straight knives, some fancy. **Patterns:** Daggers, boots, Bowies. **Technical:** Grinds 440C and 154CM. **Prices:** $100 to $200; some to $1,000. **Remarks:** Part-time maker; first knife sold in 1985. Does business as Franjo. **Mark:** FRANJO with knife as J.

CANNADY, DANIEL L., Box 301, Allendale, SC 29810, Phone: 803-584-2813
Specialties: Working straight knives and folders in standard patterns. **Patterns:** Drop-point hunters, Bowies, skinners, fishing knives with concave grind, steak knives and kitchen cutlery. **Technical:** Grinds D2, 440C and ATS-34. **Prices:** $65 to $325; some to $500. **Remarks:** Full-time maker; first knife sold in 1980. **Mark:** Last name above Allendale, S. C.

CANNON, RAYMOND W., P. O. Box 1412, Homer, AK 99603, Phone: 907-235-7779
Specialties: Fancy working knives, folders and swords of his design or to customer specs; many one-of-a-kind pieces. **Patterns:** Bowies, daggers and skinners. **Technical:** Forges and grinds O1, A6, 52100, 5160, his combinations for his own Damascus. **Prices:** First knife sold in 1984. **Mark:** Cannon Alaska or "Hand forged by Wes Cannon".

CANNON, DAN, 9500 Leon, Dallas, TX 75217, Phone: 972-557-0268
Specialties: Damascus, hand forged. **Patterns:** Bowies, hunters, folders. **Prices:** $300. **Remarks:** Full-time maker. **Mark:** CANNON D

CANOY, ANDREW B, 14040 Reed Rd, Byron, MI 48418, Phone: (810) 266-6039

CANTER, RONALD E., 96 Bon Air Circle, Jackson, TN 38305, Phone: 731-668-1780
Specialties: Traditional working knives to customer specs. **Patterns:** Beavertail skinners, Bowies, hand axes and folding lockers. **Technical:** Grinds A1, 440C and 154CM. **Prices:** $65 to $250; some $500 and higher. **Remarks:** Spare-time maker; first knife sold in 1973. **Mark:** Three last initials intertwined.

CANTRELL, KITTY D, 19720 Hiway 78, Ramona, CA 92076, Phone: (760) 788-8304

CAPDEPON, ROBERT, 829 Vatican Rd., Carencro, LA 70520, Phone: 337-896-8753, Fax:318-896-8753
Specialties: Traditional straight knives and folders of his design. **Patterns:** Boots, hunters and locking folders. **Technical:** Grinds ATS-34, 440C and D2. Hand-rubbed finish on blades. Likes natural horn materials for handles, including ivory. Offers engraving. **Prices:** $250 to $750. **Remarks:** Full-time maker; first knife made in 1992. **Mark:** Last name.

CAPDEPON, RANDY, 553 Joli Rd., Carencro, LA 70520, Phone: 318-896-4113, Fax:318-896-8753
Specialties: Straight knives and folders of his design. **Patterns:** Hunters and locking folders. **Technical:** Grinds ATS-34, 440C and D2. **Prices:** $200 to $600. **Remarks:** Part-time maker; first knife made in 1992. Doing business as Capdepon Knives. **Mark:** Last name.

CAREY JR., CHARLES W., 1003 Minter Rd., Griffin, GA 30223, Phone: 770-228-8994
Specialties: Working and using knives of his design and to customer specs; period pieces. **Patterns:** Fighters, hunters, utility/camp knives and forged-to-shape miniatures. **Technical:** Forges 5160, old files and cable. Offers filework; ages some of his knives. **Prices:** $35 to $400. **Remarks:** Part-time maker; first knife sold in 1991. **Mark:** Knife logo.

CARLISLE, FRANK, 5930 Hereford, Detroit, MI 48224, Phone: 313-882-8349
Specialties: Fancy/embellished and fantasy folders of his design. **Patterns:** Hunters, locking folders and swords. **Technical:** Grinds Damascus and stainless. **Prices:** $80 to $300. **Remarks:** Full-time maker; first knife sold in 1993. Doing business as Carlisle Cutlery. **Mark:** Last name.

CARLISLE, JEFF, P O Box 282 12753 Hwy 200, Simms, MT 59477, Phone: (406) 264-5693

CARLSSON, MARC BJORN, Pileatraede 42, 1112 Copenhagen K, DENMARK, Phone: +45 33 91 15 99, Fax:+45 33 91 17 99
Specialties: High-tech knives and folders. **Patterns:** Skinners, tantos, swords, folders and art knives. **Technical:** Grinds ATS-34, Elmax and D2. **Prices:** Start at $250. **Remarks:** Doing business as "Mememto Mori", Professional jeweler and knife maker. Doing business as Metal Point. **Mark:** First name in runic letters within Viking ship.

CARNAHAN, CHARLES A, 10700 Wayfarer Rd, Germantown, MD 20876, Phone: 301-916-2893
Specialties: Hand forged fixed blade knives. **Patterns:** Bowies and hunters. **Technical:** Steels used; 5160, 1095, 1085, L6 and A023-E. **Prices:** $300 - $2000. **Remarks:** Part-time maker. First knife sold in 1991. Knives all made by hand forging, no stock removal. **Mark:** Last name.

CAROLINA CUSTOM KNIVES, SEE TOMMY MCNABB,

CARPENTER, RONALD W, RT 4 Box 323, Jasper, TX 75951, Phone: (409) 384-4087

CARR, TIM, 3660 Pillon Rd, Muskegon, MI 49445, Phone: (231) 766-3582
Specialties: Hunters, camp knives. **Patterns:** Mine or yours. **Technical:** Hand forged 52100 and Damascus. **Prices:** $125 to $700. **Remarks:** Part-time maker. **Mark:** The letter combined from my initials TRC.

CARROLL, CHAD, 12182 McClelland, Grant, MI 49327, Phone: (616) 834-9183

CARSON, HAROLD J. "KIT", 1076 Brizendine Lane, Vine Grove, KY 40175, Phone: 270 877-6300, Fax:270 877 6338
Specialties: Military fixed blades and folders; art pieces. **Patterns:** Fighters, D handles, daggers, combat folders and Crosslock styles, tactical folders, tactical fixed blades. **Technical:** Grinds Stellite 6K, Talonite, CPM steels, Damascus. **Prices:** $400 to $750; some to $5,000. **Remarks:** Full-time maker; first knife sold in 1973. **Mark:** Name stamped or engraved.

CARTER, FRED, 5219 Deer Creek Rd., Wichita Falls, TX 76302, Phone: 817-723-4020
Specialties: High-art investor-class straight knives; some working hunters and fighters. **Patterns:** Classic daggers, Bowies; interframe, stainless and blued steel folders with gold inlay. **Technical:** Grinds a variety of steels. Uses no glue or solder. Engraves and inlays. **Prices:** Generally upscale. **Remarks:** Full-time maker. **Mark:** Signature in oval logo.

CARTER, MURRAY M, 2506 Toyo Oka, Ueki Kamoto, Kumamoto, JAPAN 861-0163, Phone: 81-96-272-6759 **Specialties:** Traditional Japanese cutlery, utilizing San soh ko (3 layer) or Kata-ha (two layer) blade construction. **Patterns:** Works from over 200 standard Japanese and North American designs. **Technical:** Forges or grinds Hitachi white steel #1, Hitachi blue super steel or Hitachi ZDP247 stainless steel exclusively. Forges own Damascus. **Prices:** $30 to $3000. **Remarks:** Full-time maker. First knife sold in 1989. Owner & designer of "Muteki" brand knives. **Mark:** Name with Japanese character on forged pieces. "Muteki" with Japanese characters on stock-removal blades.

CASH, TERRY, 113 Sequoyah Circle, Canton, GA 30115, Phone: (770) 345-2031 **Specialties:** Railroad spike knives, traditional straight knives, working/using knives. **Patterns:** Bowies, hunters, utility, camp knives; standard, own design or to customer spec. **Technical:** Forges 5160, 1095, 52100, heat treatment, makes leather sheaths, presentation boxes & makes own Damascus. **Prices:** $125 to $800. **Remarks:** Full-time maker,; first knife sold 1995. **Mark:** First initial and last name. **Other:** Doing business as Cherokee Forge.

CASHEN, KEVIN R., 5615 Tyler St., Hubbardston, MI 48845, Phone: 989-981-6780 **Specialties:** Working straight knives, high art pattern welded swords, traditional renaissance and ethnic pieces. **Patterns:** Hunters, bowies, utility knives, swords, daggers. **Technical:** Forges 1095, 1084 and his own O1/L6 Damascus. **Prices:** $100 to $4,000+. **Remarks:** Full-time maker; first knife sold in 1985. Doing business as Matherton Forge. **Mark:** Black letter Old English initials and master smith stamp.

CASTEEL, DIANNA, P. O. Box 63, Monteagle, TN 37356, Phone: 931-723-0851, Fax:931-723-1856 **Specialties:** Small, delicate daggers and miniatures; most knives one of a kind. **Patterns:** Daggers, boot knives, fighters and miniatures. **Technical:** Grinds 440C; makes her own Damascus. **Prices:** Start at $350; miniatures start at $250. **Remarks:** Full-time maker. **Mark:** Di in script.

CASTEEL, DOUGLAS, P. O. Box 63, Monteagle, TN 37356, Phone: 931-723-0851, Fax:931-723-1856 **Specialties:** One-of-a-kind collector-class period pieces. **Patterns:** Daggers, Bowies, swords and folders. **Technical:** Grinds 440C; makes his own Damascus. Offers gold and silver castings. **Prices:** Upscale. **Remarks:** Full-time maker; first knife sold in 1982. **Mark:** Last name.

CATOE, DAVID R, 4024 Heutte Dr, Norfolk, VA 23518, Phone: 757-480-3191 **Technical:** Does own forging, Damascus and heat treatments. **Price:** $200 to $500; some higher. **Remarks:** Part-time maker; trained by Dan Maragni 1985-1988; first knife sold 1989. **Mark:** Leaf of a camillia.

CAUDELL, RICHARD M., P. O. Box 602, Lawrenceville, IL 62439, Phone: 618-943-5278 **Specialties:** Classic working/using straight knives in standard patterns. **Patterns:** Boots, fighters, combat fighters and utility/camp knives. **Technical:** Hollow-grinds 440C, ATS-34 and A2. **Prices:** $115 to $600; some to $1,200. **Remarks:** First knife sold in 1994. Doing business as Caudell's Custom Knives. **Mark:** Last name.

CAWTHORNE, CHRISTOPHER A, P O Box 604, Wrangell, AK 99929

CENTOFANTE, FRANK, P. O. Box 928, Madisonville, TN 37354-0928, Phone: 423-442-5767 **Specialties:** Fancy working folders. **Patterns:** Lockers and liner locks. **Technical:** Grinds ATS-34; hand-rubbed satin finish on blades. **Prices:** $500 to $1200. **Remarks:** Full-time maker; first knife sold in 1968. **Mark:** Name, city, state.

CHAFFEE, JEFF L., 14314 N Washington St., P. O. Box 1, Morris, IN 47033, Phone: 812-934-6350 **Specialties:** Fancy working and utility folders and straight knives. **Patterns:** Fighters, dagger, hunter and locking folders. **Technical:** Grinds commercial Damascus, 440C, ATS-34, D2 and O1. Prefers natural handle materials. **Prices:** $350 to $2,000. **Remarks:** Part-time maker; first knife sold in 1988. **Mark:** Last name.

CHAMBERLAIN, JON A., 15 S. Lombard, E. Wenatchee, WA 98802, Phone: 509-884-6591 **Specialties:** Working and kitchen knives to customer specs; exotics on special order. **Patterns:** Over 100 patterns in stock. **Technical:** Prefers ATS-34, D2, L6 and Damascus. **Prices:** Start at $50. **Remarks:** First knife sold in 1986. Doing business as Johnny Custom Knifemakers. **Mark:** Name in oval with city and state enclosing.

CHAMBERLAIN, CHARLES R., P. O. Box 156, Barren Springs, VA 24313-0156, Phone: 703-381-5137

CHAMBERLAIN, JOHN B., 1621 Angela St., Wenatchee, WA 98801, Phone: 509-663-6720 **Specialties:** Fancy working and using straight knives mainly to customer specs, though starting to make some standard patterns. **Patterns:** Hunt-

ers, Bowies and daggers. **Technical:** Grinds D2, ATS-34, M2, M4 and L6. **Prices:** $60 to $190; some to $2,500. **Remarks:** Full-time maker; first knife sold in 1943. **Mark:** Name, city, state.

CHAMBERLIN, JOHN A., 11535 Our Rd., Anchorage, AK 99516, Phone: 907-346-1524, Fax:907-562-4583 **Specialties:** Art and working knives. **Patterns:** Daggers and hunters; some folders. **Technical:** Grinds ATS-34, 440C, A2, D2 and Damascus. Uses Alaskan handle materials such as oosic, jade, whale jawbone, fossil ivory. **Prices:** Start at $100. **Remarks:** Does own heat treating and cryogenic deep freeze. Full-time maker; first knife sold in 1984. **Mark:** Name over English shield and dagger.

CHAMBLIN, JOEL, 296 New Hebron Church Rd., Concord, GA 30206, Phone: 770-884-9055 **Specialties:** Fancy & working folders. **Patterns:** Fancy locking folders, traditional, multi-blades and utility. **Technical:** Grinds ATS-34, 440V, BG-42 and commercial Damascus. Offers filework. **Prices:** Start at $300. **Remarks:** Full-time maker; first knife sold in 1989. **Mark:** Last name.

CHAMPAGNE, PAUL, 48 Brightman Rd., Mechanicville, NY 12118, Phone: 518-664-4179 **Specialties:** Rugged, ornate straight knives in the Japanese tradition. **Patterns:** Katanas, wakizashis, tantos and some European daggers. **Technical:** Forges and hand-finishes carbon steels and his own Damascus. Makes Tamahagane for use in traditional blades; uses traditional heat-treating techniques. **Prices:** Start at $750. **Remarks:** Has passed all traditional Japanese cutting tests. Doing business as Twilight Forge. **Mark:** Three diamonds over a stylized crown.

CHAMPION, ROBERT, 1806 Plateau Ln, Amarillo, TX 79106, Phone: 806-359-0446 **Specialties:** Traditional working straight knives. **Patterns:** Hunters, skinners, camp knives, Bowies, daggers. **Technical:** Grinds 440C & D2. **Prices:** $100 to $600. **Remarks:** Part-time maker; first knife sold in 1979. **Mark:** Last name with dagger logo, city and state. **Other:** Stream-line hunters.

CHAPO, WILLIAM G., 45 Wildridge Rd., Wilton, CT 06897, Phone: 203-544-9424 **Specialties:** Classic straight knives and folders of his design and to customer specs; period pieces. **Patterns:** Boots, Bowies and locking folders. **Technical:** Forges stainless Damascus. Offers filework. **Prices:** $750 and up. **Remarks:** Full-time maker; first knife sold in 1989. **Mark:** First and middle initials, last name, city, state.

CHARD, GORDON R., 104 S. Holiday Lane, Iola, KS 66749, Phone: 316-365-2311 **Specialties:** High-tech locking folders. **Patterns:** Titanium side lock folders, push-button locking folders, interframe lockbacks and some art knives. **Technical:** Flat- and hollow-grinds mostly ATS-34, some Damascus; hand-finishes blades. **Prices:** $135 to $2,500. **Remarks:** Full-time maker; first knife sold in 1983. **Mark:** Name, city and state in wheat logo.

CHASE, JOHN E., 217 Walnut, Aledo, TX 76008, Phone: 817-441-8331 **Specialties:** Straight high-tech working knives in standard patterns or to customer specs. **Patterns:** Hunters, fighters, daggers and Bowies. **Technical:** Grinds D2, 01, 440C; offers mostly satin finishes. **Prices:** Start at $235. **Remarks:** Part-time maker; first knife sold in 1974. **Mark:** Last name in logo.

CHASE, ALEX, 208 E Pennsylvania Ave, DeLand, FL 32724, Phone: 904-734-9918 **Specialties:** Historical steels, classic and traditional straight knives of his design and to customer specs. **Patterns:** Art, fighters and hunters. **Technical:** Forges O1-L6 Damascus, meteoric Damascus, 52100, 5160; uses fossil walrus & mastodon ivory etc. **Prices:** $150 to $1,000; some to $3,500. **Remarks:** Part-time maker; first knife sold in 1990. Doing business as Confederate Forge. **Mark:** Stylized initials-A. C.

CHASTAIN, WADE, Rt. 2, Box 137-A, Horse Shoe, NC 28742, Phone: 704-891-4803 **Specialties:** Fancy fantasy and high-art straight knives of his design; period pieces. Known for unique mounts. **Patterns:** Bowies, daggers and fighters. **Technical:** Grinds 440C, ATS-34 and O1. Engraves; offers jeweling. **Prices:** $400 to $1,200; some to $2,000. **Remarks:** Full-time maker; first knife sold in 1984. Doing business as The Iron Master. **Mark:** Engraved last name.

CHAUVIN, JOHN, 200 Anna St., Scott, LA 70583, Phone: 318-237-6138, Fax:318-237-8079 **Specialties:** Traditional working and using straight knives of his design, to customer specs and in standard patterns. **Patterns:** Bowies, fighters, and hunters. **Technical:** Grinds ATS-34, 440C and O1 high carbon. Paul Bos heat treating. Uses ivory, stag, oosic and stabilized Louisiana swamp maple for handle materials. Makes sheaths using alligator and ostrich. **Prices:** $125 to $200; Bowies start at $500. **Remarks:** Part-time maker; first knife sold in 1995. **Mark:** Full name, city, state.

CHAVAR, EDWARD V, 1830 Richmond Ave, Bethlehem, PA 18018, Phone: 610-865-1806
Specialties: Working straight knives to his or customer design specifications, folders, high art pieces and some forged pieces. **Patterns:** Fighters, hunters, tactical, straight and folding knives and high art straight and folding knives for collectors. **Technical:** Grinds ATS-34, 440C, L6, Damascus from various makers and uses Damascus Steel and Mokume of his own creation. **Prices:** Standard models range from $95 to $1500, custom and specialty up to $3000. **Remarks:** Full-time maker; first knife sold in 1990. **Mark:** Name, city, state or signature.

CHEATHAM, BILL, P. O. Box 636, Laveen, AZ 85339, Phone: 602-237-2786
Specialties: Working straight knives and folders. **Patterns:** Hunters, fighters, boots and axes; locking folders. **Technical:** Grinds 440C. **Prices:** $150 to $350; exceptional knives to $600. **Remarks:** Full-time maker; first knife sold in 1976. **Mark:** Name, city, state.

CHELQUIST, CLIFF, P. O. Box 91, Arroyo Grande, CA 93421, Phone: 805-489-8095
Specialties: Highly polished sportsman's knives. **Patterns:** Bird knives to Bowies. **Technical:** Grinds D2 and ATS-34. **Prices:** $75 to $150; some to $400. **Remarks:** Spare-time maker; first knife sold in 1983. **Mark:** Last initial.

CHERRY, FRANK J, 3412 Tiley Ne, Albuquerque, NM 87110, Phone: (505) 883-8643

CHOATE, MILTON, 1665 W County 17-1/2, Somerton, AZ 85350, Phone: 520-627-7251
Specialties: Classic working and using straight knives of his design, to customer specs and in standard patterns. **Patterns:** Bowies, hunters and utility/camp knives. **Technical:** Grinds 440C; grinds and forges 1095 and 5160. Does filework on top and guards on request. **Prices:** $150 to $600. **Remarks:** Part-time maker; first knife made in 1990. All knives come with handmade sheaths by Judy Choate. **Mark:** JC.

CHRISTENSEN, JON P., 7814 Spear Dr, Shepherd, MT 59079, Phone: (406) 373-0253
Specialties: Patch knives, hunter/utility knives, bowies, tomahawks. **Technical:** All blades forged, do all my own work including sheaths. **Prices:** $80 on up. **Remarks:** First knife sold in 1999. **Mark:** First and middle initial surrounded by last initial.

CHURCHMAN, T. W., 7402 Tall Cedar, San Antonio, TX 78249, Phone: 210-690-8641
Specialties: Fancy and traditional straight knives and single blade liner locking folders. Bird/trout knives of his design and to customer specs. **Patterns:** Bird/trout knives, fillet, Bowies, daggers, fighters, boot knives, some miniatures. **Technical:** Grinds 440C and D2. Offers stainless fittings, fancy filework, exotic and stabilized woods and hand sewed lined sheaths. **Prices:** $80 to $650; some to $1,500. **Remarks:** Part-time maker; first knife made n 1981 after reading "KNIVES" "81". Doing business as "Custom Knives Churchman Made". **Mark:** Last name, dagger.

CLAIBORNE, RON, 2918 Ellistown Rd., Knox, TN 37924, Phone: 615-524-2054
Specialties: Working and using straight knives; period pieces. **Patterns:** Hunters, daggers, folders. **Technical:** Forges Damascus: mosaic, powder mosaic. Prefers bone and natural handle materials; some exotic woods. **Prices:** $125 to $2,500. **Remarks:** Part-time maker; first knife sold in 1979. Doing business as Thunder Mountain Forge Claiborne Knives. **Mark:** Claiborne.

CLAIBORNE, JEFF, 1470 Roberts Rd, Franklin, IN 46131, Phone: 317-736-7443
Specialties: All one of a kind by hand--no jigs or fixtures-- swords, straight knives, period pieces, multi-blade folders. Handle--uses ivory, stag, pearl, oosic, bone or exotic wood. **Technical:** Forges cable Damascus, grinds O1, D2, 1095, 5160, 52100. **Prices:** $100 and up. **Remarks:** Part-time maker; first knife sold in 1989. **Mark:** Stylized initials in an oval.

CLARK, PETER, 1624 Juneau Dr, Anchorage, AK 99501

CLARK, D. E. (LUCKY), 126 Woodland St., Mineral Point, PA 15942, Phone: 814-322-4725
Specialties: Working straight knives and folders to customer specs. **Patterns:** Customer designs. **Technical:** Grinds D2, 440C, 154CM. **Prices:** $100 to $200; some higher. **Remarks:** Part-time maker; first knife sold in 1975. **Mark:** Name on one side; "Lucky" on other.

CLARK, DAVE, 82 Valley View Manor Dr, Andrews, NC 28901, Phone: 828-321-8067
Specialties: Folders to customer specs. **Patterns:** Locking folders. **Technical:** Grinds 440C, D2 and stainless Damascus. **Prices:** $400 to $1,500. **Remarks:** Full-time maker; first knife sold in 1988. **Mark:** Name.

CLARK, HOWARD F., 115 35th Pl., Runnells, IA 50237, Phone: 515-966-2126
Specialties: Currently Japanese style swords. **Patterns:** Katana. **Technical:** Forges 1086, L6, 52100 and his own all tool steel Damascus; bar stock; forged blanks. **Prices:** $500 to $3,000. **Remarks:** Full-time maker; first knife sold in 1979. Doing business as Morgan Valley Forge. **Prior Mark:** Block letters and serial number on folders; anvil/initials logo on straight knives. **Current Mark:** Two character kanji "Big Ear".

CLARK, NATE, 501 Churchill Dr, Oakland, OR 97462, Phone: 541-459-6036
Specialties: Automatics (Push button & hidden release) ATS-34 mirror polish or satin finish, most Damascus, Pearl, Ivory, Abalone, Woods, Bone, Micarta, G-10, filework and carving. Engraving available by Dane Clark. **Prices:** $500. 00-$2500. 00. **Remarks:** Fulltime knife maker since 1996. **Mark:** Nate Clark.

CLARK, ROGER, Rt. 1, Box 538, Rockdale, TX 76567, Phone: 512-446-3388
Specialties: Traditional working and using straight knives of his design or to customer specs. **Patterns:** Hunters, Bowies and camp knives; primitive styles for black powder hunters. **Technical:** Forges 1084, O1 and Damascus. Sheaths are extra. **Prices:** Primitive styles start at $100; shiny blades start at $150; Damascus start at $250. **Remarks:** Full-time maker; first knife sold in 1989. **Mark:** First initial, last name.

CLASSIC CUTLERY, 230 S Main St Apt 1, Franklin, NH 03235-1565, Phone: 603-226-0885, Fax:same as phone #
Specialties: Custom knives, gemstones, high quality factory knives.

CLAY, WAYNE, Box 125B, Pelham, TN 37366, Phone: 931-467-3472, Fax:931-467-3076
Specialties: Working straight knives and folders in standard patterns. **Patterns:** Hunters and kitchen knives; gents and hunter patterns. **Technical:** Grinds ATS-34. **Prices:** $125 to $500; some to $1,000. **Remarks:** Full-time maker; first knife sold in 1978. **Mark:** Name.

CLAY, J. D., 5050 Hall Rd., Greenup, KY 41144, Phone: 606-473-6769
Specialties: Long known for cleanly finished, collector quality knives of functional design. **Patterns:** Practical hunters and locking folders. **Technical:** Grinds 440C - high mirror finishes. **Prices:** Start at $95. **Remarks:** Full-time maker; first knife sold in 1972. **Mark:** Name stamp in script on blade.

CLICK, JOE, U-344 Rd. 2, Liberty Center, OH 43532, Phone: 419-875-6199, Fax:419-875-5736
Specialties: Fancy/embellished and traditional working/using straight knives of his design, to customer specs and in standard patterns. **Patterns:** Bowies, hunters and utility/camp knives. **Technical:** Grinds and forges A2, D2, 5160 and Damascus. Does fancy filework; triple temper. Uses ivory for handle material. **Prices:** $75 to $300; some to $700. **Remarks:** Doing business as Click Custom Knives. **Mark:** Full name.

COCKERHAM, LLOYD, 1717 Carolyn Av, Denham Springs, IA 70726, Phone: (225) 665-1565

COFER, RON, 188 Ozora Road, Loganville, GA 30052
Specialties: Fancy working and using straight knives of his design. **Patterns:** Hunters, Bowies and fighters. **Technical:** Grinds 440C and ATS-34. Heat-treats. Some knives have carved stag handles or scrimshaw. Makes leather sheath for each knife and walnut and deer antler display stands for art knives. **Prices:** $125 to $250; some to $600. **Remarks:** Spare-time maker; first knife sold in 1991. **Mark:** Name, serial number.

COFFMAN, DANNY, 541 Angel Dr S, Jacksonville, AL 36265-5787, Phone: 256-435-1619
Specialties: Straight knives and folders of his design. Now making liner locks for $650 to $1,200 with natural handles and contrasting Damascus blades and bolsters. **Patterns:** Hunters, locking and slip-joint folders. **Technical:** Grinds Damascus, 440C and D2. Offers filework and engraving. **Prices:** $100 to $400; some to $800. **Remarks:** Spare-time maker; first knife sold in 1992. Doing business as Customs by Coffman. **Mark:** Last name stamped or engraved.

COHEN, TERRY A., P. O. Box 406, Laytonville, CA 95454
Specialties: Working straight knives and folders. **Patterns:** Bowies to boot knives and locking folders; mini-boot knives. **Technical:** Grinds stainless; hand rubs; tries for good balance. **Prices:** $85 to $150; some to $325. **Remarks:** Part-time maker; first knife sold in 1983. **Mark:** TERRY KNIVES, city and state.

COHEN, N. J. (NORM), 2408 Sugarcone Rd., Baltimore, MD 21209, Phone: 410-484-3841
Specialties: Working class knives. **Patterns:** Hunters, skinners, bird knives, push daggers, boots, kitchen and practical customer designs. **Technical:** Stock removal 440C, ATS-34. Uses Micarta, Corian. Some woods in handles. **Prices:** $50 to $250. **Remarks:** Part-time maker; first knife sold in 1982. **Mark:** Etched initials or NJC MAKER.

custom knifemakers

COIL, JIMMIE J., 2936 Asbury Pl., Owensboro, KY 42303, Phone: 270-684-7827
Specialties: Traditional working and using straight knives of his design. **Patterns:** Hunters, Bowies and fighters. **Technical:** Grinds 440C, ATS-34 and D2. Blades are flat-ground with brush finish; most have tapered tang. Offers filework. **Prices:** $65 to $250; some to $750. **Remarks:** Spare-time maker; first knife sold in 1974. **Mark:** Name.

COLE, WELBORN I., 3284 Inman Dr. NE, Atlanta, GA 30319, Phone: 404-261-3977
Specialties: Traditional straight knives of his design. **Patterns:** Hunters. **Technical:** Grinds 440C, ATS-34 and D2. Good wood scales. **Prices:** NA. **Remarks:** Full-time maker; first knife sold in 1983. **Mark:** Script initials.

COLE, JAMES M, 505 Stonewood Blvd, Bartonville, TX 76226, Phone: (817) 430-0302

COLE, DAVE, 620 Poinsetta Dr, Satellite Beach, FL 32937, Phone: 321-773-1687
Specialties: Working straight knives of his design or customer specs. **Patterns:** Utility, hunters. **Technical:** Grinds 01, ATS-34, Damascus; prefers natural handle materials, handmade sheaths. **Prices:** $100 and up. **Remarks:** Part-time maker, member of FKA; first knife sold in 1991. **Mark:** None, DC, or Cole.

COLEMAN, KEITH E., 5001 Starfire Pl NW, Albuquerque, NM 87120-2010, Phone: 505-899-3783
Specialties: Affordable collector-grade straight knives and folders; some fancy. **Patterns:** Fighters, tantos, combat folders, gents folders and boots. **Technical:** Grinds ATS-34 and Damascus. Prefers specialty woods; offers filework. **Prices:** $150 to $700; some to $1,500. **Remarks:** Full-time maker; first knife sold in 1980. **Mark:** Name, city and state.

COLLINS, HAROLD, 503 First St., West Union, OH 45693, Phone: 513-544-2982
Specialties: Traditional using straight knives and folders of his design or to customer specs. **Patterns:** Hunters, Bowies and locking folders. **Technical:** Forges and grinds 440C, ATS-34, D2, O1 and 5160. Flat-grinds standard; filework available. **Prices:** $75 to $300. **Remarks:** Full-time maker; first knife sold in 1989. **Mark:** First initial, last name, Maker.

COLLINS, A. J., 9651 Elon Ave., Arleta, CA 91331, Phone: 818-762-7728
Specialties: Working dress knives of his design. **Patterns:** Street survival knives, swords, axes. **Technical:** Grinds O1, 440C, 154CM. **Prices:** Start at $100. **Remarks:** Full-time maker; first knife sold in 1972. Doing business as Kustom Krafted Knives--KKK. **Mark:** Name.

COLLINS, LYNN M., 138 Berkley Dr., Elyria, OH 44035, Phone: 440-366-7101
Specialties: Working straight knives. **Patterns:** Field knives, boots and fighters. **Technical:** Grinds D2, 154CM and 440C. **Prices:** Start at $150. **Remarks:** Spare-time maker; first knife sold in 1980. **Mark:** Initials, asterisks.

COLTER, WADE, P. O. Box 2340, Colstrip, MT 59323, Phone: 406-748-4573
Specialties: Fancy and embellished straight knives, folders and swords of his design; historical and period pieces. **Patterns:** Bowies, swords and folders. **Technical:** Hand forges 52100 ball bearing steel and L6, 1090, cable and chain Damascus from 5N20 & 1084. Carves and makes sheaths. **Prices:** $250 to $3500. **Remarks:** Part-time maker; first knife sold in 1990. Doing business as "Colter's Hell" Forge. **Mark:** Initials on left side ricasso.

COLTRAIN, LARRY D, P O Box 1331, Buxton, NC 27920

COMAR, ROGER N, RT 1 Box 485, Marion, NC 28752, Phone: (828) 652-2448

COMBS, ROGER, P O 68040, Anaheim, CA 92817-9800

COMPTON, WILLIAM E., 106 N. Sequoia Ct., Sterling, VA 20164, Phone: 703-430-2129
Specialties: Working straight knives of his design or to customer specs; some fancy knives. **Patterns:** Hunters, camp knives, Bowies and some kitchen knives. **Technical:** Also forges 5160, 1095 and make my own Damascus. **Prices:** $150. 00 to $750. 00, some to &1,500. 00. **Remarks:** Part-time maker, ABS journeyman smith. first knife sold in 1994. Doing business as Comptons Custom Knives. **Mark:** Stock removal; first and middle initials, last name, city & state. Forged; first & middle initials, last name, city & state, anvil in middle.

COMUS, STEVE, P O Box 68040, Anaheim, CA 92817-9800

CONKEY, TOM, 9122 Keyser Rd., Nokesville, VA 22123, Phone: 703-791-3867
Specialties: Classic straight knives and folders of his design and to customer specs. **Patterns:** Boots, hunters and locking folders. **Technical:** Grinds ATS-34, O1 and commercial Damascus. Lockbacks have jeweled scales and locking bars with dovetailed bolsters. Folders utilize unique 2-piece bushing of his design and manufacture. Sheaths are handmade. Pre-

sentation boxes made upon request. **Prices:** $100 to $500. **Remarks:** Part-time maker; first knife sold in 1991. Collaborates with Dan Thomas. **Mark:** Last name with "handcrafted" underneath.

CONKLIN, GEORGE L., Box 902, Ft. Benton, MT 59442, Phone: 406-622-3268, Fax:406-622-3410
Specialties: Designer and manufacturer of the "Brisket Breaker. " **Patterns:** Hunters, utility/camp knives and hatchets. **Technical:** Grinds 440C, ATS-34, D2, 1095, 154CM and 5160. Offers some forging and heat-treats for others. Offers some jewelling. **Prices:** $65 to $200; some to $1,000. **Remarks:** Full-time maker. Doing business as Rocky Mountain Knives. **Mark:** Last name in script.

CONLEY, BOB, 1013 Creasy Rd., Jonesboro, TN 37659, Phone: 423-753-3302
Specialties: Working straight knives and folders. **Patterns:** Lockers, two-blades, gents, hunters, traditional styles, straight hunters. **Technical:** Grinds 440C, 154CM and ATS-34. Engraves. **Prices:** $250 to $450; some to $600. **Remarks:** Full-time maker; first knife sold in 1979. **Mark:** Full name, city, state.

CONN JR., C. T., 206 Highland Ave., Attalla, AL 35954, Phone: 205-538-7688
Specialties: Working folders, some fancy. **Patterns:** Full range of folding knives. **Technical:** Grinds O2, 440C and 154CM. **Prices:** $125 to $300; some to $600. **Remarks:** Part-time maker; first knife sold in 1982. **Mark:** Name.

CONNELL, STEVE, 217 Valley St, Adamsville, AL 35005-1852, Phone: 205-674-0440

CONNELLEY, LARRY, 10020 West Markham St, Little Rock, AR 72205, Phone: (501) 221-1616

CONNER, ALLEN L, 6399 County Rd 305, Fulton, MO 65251, Phone: (573) 642-9200

CONNOLLY, JAMES, 2486 Oro-Quincy Hwy., Oroville, CA 95966, Phone: 916-534-5363
Specialties: Classic working and using knives of his design. **Patterns:** Boots, Bowies and daggers. **Technical:** Grinds ATS-34; forges 5160; forges and grinds O1. **Prices:** $100 to $500; some to $1,500. **Remarks:** Full-time maker; first knife sold in 1980. Doing business as Gold Rush Designs. **Mark:** First initial, last name, Handmade.

CONNOR, MICHAEL, Box 502, Winters, TX 79567, Phone: 915-754-5602
Specialties: Straight knives, period pieces, some folders. **Patterns:** Hunters to camp knives to traditional locking folders to Bowies. **Technical:** Forges 5160, O1, 1084 steels and his own Damascus. **Prices:** Moderate to upscale. **Remarks:** Spare-time maker; first knife sold in 1974. **Mark:** Last name, M. S. **Other:** ABS Master Smith 1983.

CONNOR, JOHN W, P O Box 12981, Odessa, TX 79768-2981, Phone: (915) 362-6901

CONTI, JEFFREY D., 4640 Feigley Rd. W., Port Orchard, WA 98367, Phone: 360-405-0075
Specialties: Working straight knives. **Patterns:** Fighters and survival knives; hunters, camp knives and fishing knives. **Technical:** Grinds D2, 154CM and O1. Engraves. **Prices:** Start at $80. **Remarks:** Part-time maker; first knife sold in 1980. **Mark:** Initials, year, steel type, name and number of knife.

COOGAN, ROBERT, 1560 Craft Center Dr., Smithville, TN 37166, Phone: 615-597-6801
Specialties: One-of-a-kind knives. **Patterns:** Unique items like ooloo-style Appalachian herb knives. **Technical:** Forges; his Damascus is made from nickel steel and W1. **Prices:** Start at $100. **Remarks:** Part-time maker; first knife sold in 1979. **Mark:** Initials or last name in script.

COOK, LOUISE, 475 Robinson Ln., Ozark, IL 62972, Phone: 618-777-2932
Specialties: Working and using straight knives of her design and to customer specs; period pieces. **Patterns:** Bowies, hunters and utility/camp knives. **Technical:** Forges 5160. Filework; pin work; silver wire inlay. **Prices:** Start at $50/inch. **Remarks:** Part-time maker; first knife sold in 1990. Doing business as Panther Creek Forge. **Mark:** First name and journeyman stamp on one side; panther head on the other.

COOK, MIKE A., 10927 Shilton Rd., Portland, MI 48875, Phone: 517-647-2518
Specialties: Fancy/embellished and period pieces of his design. **Patterns:** Daggers, fighters and hunters. **Technical:** Stone bladed knives in agate, obsidian and jasper. Scrimshaws; opal inlays. **Prices:** $60 to $300; some to $800. **Remarks:** Part-time maker; first knife sold in 1988. Doing business as Art of Ishi. **Mark:** Initials and year.

COOK, JAMES R., 3611 Hwy. 26 W., Nashville, AR 71852, Phone: 870 845 5173
Specialties: Working straight knives and folders of his design or to customer specs. **Patterns:** Bowies, hunters and camp knives. **Technical:**

Forges 1084 and high carbon Damascus. **Prices:** $195 to $5,500. **Remarks:** Part-time maker; first knife sold in 1986. **Mark:** First and middle initials, last name.

COOK, MIKE, 475 Robinson Ln, Ozark, IL 62972, Phone: 618-777-2932
Specialties: Traditional working and using straight knives of his design and to customer specs. **Patterns:** Bowies, hunters and utility/camp knives. **Technical:** Forges 5160. Filework; pin work. **Prices:** Start at $50/inch. **Remarks:** Spare-time maker; first knife sold in 1991. **Mark:** First initial, last name and journeyman stamp on one side; panther head on the other.

COOMBS JR., LAMONT, 546 State Rt 46, Bucksport, ME 04416, Phone: 207-469-3057, Fax:207-469-3057
Specialties: Classic fancy and embellished straight knives; traditional working and using straight knives. Knives of his design and to customer specs. **Patterns:** Hunters, folders and utility/camp knives. **Technical:** Hollow- and flat-grinds ATS-34, 440C, A2, D2 and O1; grinds Damascus from other makers. **Prices:** $100 to $500; some to $3,500. **Remarks:** Full-time maker; first knife sold in 1988. **Mark:** Last name on banner, handmade underneath.

COON, RAYMOND C., 21135 SE Tillstrom Rd., Gresham, OR 97080, Phone: 503-658-2252
Specialties: Working straight knives in standard patterns. **Patterns:** Hunters, Bowies, daggers, boots and axes. **Technical:** Forges high carbon steel and Damascus. **Prices:** Start at $135. **Remarks:** Full-time maker; does own leatherwork, makes own Damascus, daggers; first knife sold in 1995. **Mark:** First initial, last name.

COOPER, TODD A, 8208 N Pine Haven PT, Crystal River, FL 34428, Phone: (352) 795-6219

COPELAND, THOM, 171 County Line Rd South, Nashville, AR 71852
Specialties: Hand forged fixed blades; hunters, Bowies & camp knives. **Mark:** Copeland. **Other:** Member of ABS and AKA (Arkansas Knifemakers Association)

COPELAND, GEORGE STEVE, 220 Pat Carr Lane, Alpine, TN 38543, Phone: 931-823-5214
Specialties: Traditional and fancy working straight knives and folders. **Patterns:** Friction folders, Congress two- and four-blade folders, button locks and one- and two-blade automatics. **Technical:** Stock removal of 440C, ATS-34 and A2; heat-treats. **Prices:** $180 to $950; some higher. **Remarks:** Full-time maker; first knife sold in 1979. Doing business as Alpine Mountain Knives. **Mark:** G. S. Copeland (HANDMADE); some with four-leaf clover stamp.

CORBIT, GERALD E., 1701 St. John Rd., Elizabethtown, KY 42701, Phone: 270-765-7728
Specialties: Investment grade art folders and automatics. **Patterns:** Rocker release automatics and liner lock folders. **Technical:** Hollow grinds, high contras nickel Damascus. Finishes are hot glued or etched. **Prices:** $1200-$3500. **Remarks:** Part-time maker. First knife sold in 1991. **Mark:** Last name stamped. **Other:** Heat treats, fileworks blades, spacer & liners. Most knives are inlayed with gold and gem stones.

CORBY, HAROLD, 218 Brandonwood Dr., Johnson City, TN 37604, Phone: 615-926-9781
Specialties: Large fighters and Bowies; self-protection knives; art knives. Along with art knives and combat knives, Corby now has a all new automatic MO. PB1, also side lock MO LL-1 with titanium liners G-10 handles. **Patterns:** Sub-hilt fighters and hunters. **Technical:** Grinds 154CM, ATS-34 and 440C. **Prices:** $200 to $6,000. **Remarks:** Full-time maker; first knife sold in 1969. Doing business as Knives by Corby. **Mark:** Last name.

CORDOVA, JOSEPH G., P. O. Box 977, Peralta, NM 87042, Phone: 505-869-3912
Specialties: One-of-a-kind designs, some to customer specs. **Patterns:** Fighter called the 'Gladiator', hunters, boots and cutlery. **Technical:** Forges 1095, 5160; grinds ATS-34, 440C and 154CM. **Prices:** Moderate to upscale. **Remarks:** Full-time maker; first knife sold in 1953. **Mark:** Cordova made.

CORKUM, STEVE, 34 Basehoar School Rd, Littlestown, PA 17340, Phone: 717-359-9563

CORRADO, JIM, 255 Rock View Lane, Glide, OR 97443, Phone: 503-496-3951, Fax:503-496-3595
Specialties: 2 blade pen knife with tip bolsters and inlay - cast silver knives with engraving. **Patterns:** Slip joint folders, multi-blade folders, lock backs. **Technical:** Small, accurate, home-made screws & photo etching. **Prices:** $300 to $4000. Re**Mark:** Close attention to detail & contouring. **Mark:** Etched "CORRADO". **Other:** Rare art knife called "The Wing".

CORRIGAN, DAVID P, HCR 65 Box 67, Bingham, ME 04920, Phone: (207) 672-4879

COSBY, E. BLANTON, 2954 Pierpont Ave., Columbus, GA 31904, Phone: 706-323-0327
Specialties: Traditional working & using straight knives, folders & autos of his design or to customer specs. **Patterns:** Hunters, Bowies, boots and switchblades. **Technical:** Grinds 440C, 12C27, ATS-34 and commercial Damascus. **Prices:** $125 to $350; some to $700. **Remarks:** Full-time maker; first knife sold in 1988. **Mark:** Engraved initials and year.

COSGROVE, CHARLES G., 2314 W Arbook Blvd, Arlington, TX 76015, Phone: 817-472-6505
Specialties: Traditional fixed or locking blade working knives. **Patterns:** Hunters, Bowies and locking folders. **Technical:** Stock removal using 440C, ATS-34 and D2; heat-treats. Makes heavy, hand-stitched sheaths. **Prices:** $250 to $2,500. **Remarks:** Full-time maker; first knife sold in 1968. No longer accepting customer designs. **Mark:** First initial, last name, or full name over city and state.

COSTA, SCOTT, 409 Coventry Rd, Spicewood, TX 78669, Phone: 830-693-3431
Specialties: Working straight knives. **Patterns:** Hunters, skinners, axes, trophy sets, custom boxed steak sets, carving sets and bar sets. **Technical:** Grinds D2, ATS-34, 440 and Damascus. Heat-treats. **Prices:** $225 to $2,000. **Remarks:** Full-time maker; first knife sold in 1985. **Mark:** Initials connected.

COSTELLO, DR. TIMOTHY L, 30883 Crest Forest, Farmington Hills, MI 48331, Phone: (248) 592-9746

COTTRILL, JAMES I., 1776 Ransburg Ave., Columbus, OH 43223, Phone: 614-274-0020
Specialties: Working straight knives of his design. **Patterns:** Caters to the boating and hunting crowd; cutlery. **Technical:** Grinds O1, D2 and 440C. Likes filework. **Prices:** $95 to $250; some to $500. **Remarks:** Full-time maker; first knife sold in 1977. **Mark:** Name, city, state, in oval logo.

COUGHLIN, MICHAEL M, #74 Mainstreet North, Woodbury, CT 06798, Phone: 203-263-4181
Specialties: One of a king large folders and daily carry knives. **Remarks:** Likes customer input and involvement.

COURTNEY, ELDON, 2718 Bullinger, Wichita, KS 67204, Phone: 316-838-4053
Specialties: Working straight knives of his design. **Patterns:** Hunters, fighters and one of a kinds. **Technical:** Grinds and tempers L6, 440C and spring steel. **Prices:** $100 to $500; some to $1,500. **Remarks:** Full-time maker; first knife sold in 1977. **Mark:** Full name, city and state.

COURTOIS, BRYAN, 3 Lawn Avenue, Saco, ME 04072, Phone: 207-282-3977
Specialties: Working straight knives; prefers customer designs, no standard patterns. **Patterns:** Functional hunters; everyday knives. **Technical:** Grinds 440C or customer request. Hollow-grinds with a variety of finishes. Specializes in granite handles and custom skeleton knives. **Prices:** Start at $75. **Remarks:** Part-time maker; first knife sold in 1988. Doing business as Castle Knives. **Mark:** A rook chess piece machined into blade using electrical discharge process.

COUSINO, GEORGE, 7818 Norfolk, Onsted, MI 49265, Phone: 517-467-4911, Fax:517-467-4911
Specialties: Working straight knives. **Patterns:** Hunters, Bowies, buckskinners, folders and daggers. **Technical:** Grinds 440C. **Prices:** $95 to $300. **Remarks:** Part-time maker; first knife sold in 1981. **Mark:** Last name.

COVER, RAYMOND A., Rt. 1, Box 194, Mineral Point, MO 63660, Phone: 314-749-3783
Specialties: High-tech working straight knives and folders in standard patterns. **Patterns:** Bowies and boots; two-bladed folders. **Technical:** Grinds D2, 440C and 154CM. **Prices:** $135 to $250; some to $400. **Remarks:** Part-time maker; first knife sold in 1974. **Mark:** Name.

COWLES, DON, 1026 Lawndale Dr., Royal Oak, MI 48067, Phone: 248-541-4619
Specialties: Straight, non-folding pocket knives of his design. **Patterns:** Gentlemen's pocket knives. **Technical:** Grinds ATS-34, CPM440V, CPM 420V, Talonite. Scrimshaws; pearl inlays in some handles. **Prices:** $300 to $1,200. **Remarks:** Part-time maker; first knife sold in 1994. **Mark:** Full name with oak leaf.

COX, SAM, 1756 Love Springs Rd., Gaffney, SC 29341, Phone: 864-489-1892, Fax:864-489-0403
Specialties: Classic high-art working straight knives of his design. Duck knives copyrighted. **Patterns:** Diverse. **Technical:** Grinds 154 CM. **Prices:** $300 to $1,400. **Remarks:** Full-time maker; first knife sold in 1983. **Mark:** Cox Call, Sam, Sam Cox, unique 2000 logo

custom knifemakers

COX, COLIN J., 107 N. Oxford Dr., Raymore, MO 64083, Phone: 816-322-1977
Specialties: Working straight knives and folders of his design; period pieces. **Patterns:** Hunters, fighters and survival knives. Folders, two-blades, gents and hunters. **Technical:** Grinds D2, 440C, 154CM and ATS-34. **Prices:** $125 to $750; some to $4,000. **Remarks:** Full-time maker; first knife sold in 1981. **Mark:** Full name, city and state.

CRAFT, RICHARD C., 3045 Longwood Dr., Jackson, MS 39212, Phone: 601-373-4046
Specialties: Fancy working knives. **Patterns:** Offers chopping knife and block for kitchen, bird knives and steak knives with presentation case. **Technical:** Grinds O1, L6 and 440C. Cases made of cherry or mahogany. **Prices:** $275 and up. **Remarks:** Part-time maker; first knife sold in 1985. **Mark:** Last name.

CRAFT III, JOHN M., PO Box 278, Peoria, AZ 85380, Phone: 602-284-2280
Specialties: Renaissance rapiers, swords, daggers, Japanese forms. **Patterns:** Swept hilt rapiers from sparring to high art grades. **Technical:** ATS-34 and springs steels by stock removal; forges own damascus. **Prices:** $150 to $400 and up. **Remarks:** Full-time maker; first knife sold in 1985. **Mark:** Runic "M" in pommel. Scottie armory logo on blade. **Other:** AKA Provost Master Malolm The Scot.

CRAIG, ROGER L., 2815 Fairlawn Rd, Topeka, KS 66614, Phone: 785-233-9499
Specialties: Working and camp knives, some fantasy; all his design. **Patterns:** Fighters, hunter . **Technical:** Grinds 1095 and 5160. Most knives have file work. **Prices:** $50 to $250. **Remarks:** Part-time maker; first knife sold in 1991. Doing business as Craig Knives. **Mark:** Last name-Craig.

CRAIN, FRANK, 1127 W. Dalke, Spokane, WA 99205, Phone: 509-325-1596

CRAIN, JACK W., PO Box 212, Granbury, TX 76048, Phone: 817-599-6414
Specialties: Fantasy and period knives; combat and survival knives. **Patterns:** One-of-a-kind art or fantasy daggers, swords and Bowies; survival knives. **Technical:** Forges Damascus; grinds stainless steel. Carves. **Prices:** $350 to $2,500; some to $20,000. **Remarks:** Full-time maker; first knife sold in 1969. Designer and maker of the knives seen in the films *Dracula 2000,Executive Decision, Demolition Man, Predator I* and *II, Commando, Die Hard I* and *II, Road House, Ford Fairlane* and *Action Jackson,* and television shows *War of the Worlds, Air Wolf, Kung Fu: The Legend Cont.* and *Tales of the Crypt.* **Mark:** Stylized crane.

CRAWFORD, PAT & WES, 205 N Center, West Memphis, AR 72301, Phone: 870-732-2452
Specialties: Stainless steel Damascus. High-tech working self-defense and combat types and folders. **Patterns:** Folding patent locks & inter-frames. **Technical:** Grinds ATS-34, D2 and 154CM. **Prices:** $125 to $2,000. **Remarks:** Full-time maker; first knife sold in 1973. **Mark:** Last name.

CRAWLEY, BRUCE R., 16 Binbrook Dr., Croydon 3136 Victoria, AUSTRALIA
Specialties: Folders. **Patterns:** Hunters, lockback folders and Bowies. **Technical:** Grinds 440C, ATS-34 and commercial Damascus. Offers file-work and mirror polish. **Prices:** $160 to $3500. **Remarks:** Part-time maker; first knife sold in 1990. **Mark:** Initials.

CRENSHAW, AL, Rt. 1, Box 717, Eufaula, OK 74432, Phone: 918-452-2128
Specialties: Folders of his design and in standard patterns. **Patterns:** Hunters, locking folders, slip-joint folders, multi blade folders. **Technical:** Grinds 440C, D2 and ATS-34. Does filework on back springs and blades; offers scrimshaw on some handles. **Prices:** $150 to $300; some higher. **Remarks:** Full-time maker; first knife sold in 1981. Doing business as A. Crenshaw Knives. **Mark:** First initial, last name, Lake Efaula, state stamped; first initial last name in rainbow; Lake Efaula across bottom with Okla. in middle.

CROCKFORD, JACK, 1859 Harts Mill Rd., Chamblee, GA 30341, Phone: 770-457-4680
Specialties: Lockback folders. **Patterns:** Hunters, fishing and camp knives, traditional folders. **Technical:** Grinds A2, D2, ATS-34 and 440C. Engraves and scrimshaws. **Prices:** Start at $175. **Remarks:** Part-time maker; first knife sold in 1975. **Mark:** Name.

CROSS, ROBERT, RMB 200B, Manilla Rd., Tamworth 2340, N. S. W AUSTRALIA, Phone: 067-618385

CROSSMAN, DANIEL C, Box 5236, Blakely Island, WA 98222, Phone: (360) 375-6542

CROWDER, ROBERT, Box 1374, Thompson Falls, MT 59873, Phone: 406-827-4754
Specialties: Traditional working knives to customer specs. **Patterns:** Hunters, Bowies, fighters and fillets. **Technical:** Grinds ATS-34, 154CM, 440C, Vascowear and commercial Damascus. **Prices:** $160 to $250; some to $2,500. **Remarks:** Part-time maker; first knife sold in 1985. **Mark:** First initial, last name.

CROWELL, JAMES L., 7181 Happy Hollow Rd, Mtn. View, AR 72560, Phone: 870-269-4215
Specialties: Bowie knives; fancy period pieces and working knives to customer specs. **Patterns:** Hunters to daggers, war hammers to tantos; locking folders and slip-joints. **Technical:** Forges 1084-5160-01 and his own Damascus. **Prices:** $325 to $3,500; some to $7500. **Remarks:** Part-time maker; first knife sold in 1980. Earned ABS Master blade Smith in 1986. **Mark:** A shooting star.

CROWTHERS, MARK F, P O Box 4641, Rolling Bay, WA 98061-0641, Phone: (206) 842-7501

CULPEPPER, JOHN, 2102 Spencer Ave., Monroe, LA 71201, Phone: 318-323-3636
Specialties: Working straight knives. **Patterns:** Hunters, Bowies and camp knives in heavy-duty patterns. **Technical:** Grinds O1, D2 and 440C; hollow-grinds. **Prices:** $75 to $200; some to $300. **Remarks:** Part-time maker; first knife sold in 1970. Doing business as Pepper Knives. **Mark:** Pepper.

CULVER, STEVE, 5682 94th st, Meriden, KS 66512, Phone: 785-484-0146
Specialties: Edged tools and weapons, collectible and functional. **Patterns:** Bowies, daggers, swords, hunters, folders and edged tools. **Technical:** Forges carbon steels and his own pattern welded steels. **Prices:** $200 to $500; some to $4,000. **Remarks:** Part-time maker; first knife sold in 1989. **Mark:** Last name, J. S.

CUMMING, R. J., CUMMING KNIVES, 35 Manana Dr, Cedar Crest, NM 87008, Phone: 505-286-0509
Specialties: Custom one-of-a-kind hunters and field knives in D2, ATS34 and 1095 Damascus, exotic handles. Custom leather work, Scrimshaw and engraving. **Prices:** $225 to $750; some higher. **Remarks:** Full-time maker; first knife sold in 1978 in Denmark; mentored by late Jim Nolen. Retired US Foreign Service Officer. Member PKA, NCCKG. **Mark:** Stylized CUMMING.

CUTCHIN, ROY D., 960 Hwy. 169 S., Seale, AL 36875, Phone: 334-855-3080
Specialties: Fancy and working folders of his design. **Patterns:** Locking folders. **Technical:** Grinds ATS-34 and commercial Damascus; uses anodized titanium. **Prices:** Start at $250. **Remarks:** Part-time maker. **Mark:** First initial, last name, city and state, number.

CUTE, THOMAS, State Rt. 90-7071, Cortland, NY 13045, Phone: 607-749-4055
Specialties: Working straight knives. **Patterns:** Hunters, Bowies and fighters. **Technical:** Grinds O1, 440C and ATS-34. **Prices:** $100 to $1,000. **Remarks:** Full-time maker; first knife sold in 1974. **Mark:** Full name.

d

DACONCEICAO, JOHN M., 138 Perryville Rd., Rehoboth, MA 02769, Phone: 508-252-9686
Specialties: One-of-a-kind straight knives of his design and to customer specs. **Patterns:** Boots, fighters and folders. **Technical:** Grinds O1, 1095 and commercial Damascus. All knives come with leather sheath; cross-draw and shoulder harnesses available. **Prices:** $90 to $200; some to $500. **Remarks:** Part-time maker; first knife sold in 1993. **Mark:** JMD Blades.

DAILEY, G. E., 577 Lincoln St., Seekonk, MA 02771, Phone: 508-336-5088
Specialties: One-of-a-kind exotic designed edged weapons. **Patterns:** Folders, daggers and swords. **Technical:** Reforges and grinds Damascus; prefers hollow-grinding. Engraves, carves, offers filework and sets stones and uses exotic gems and gold. **Prices:** Start at $1100. **Remarks:** Full-time maker. First knife sold in 1982. **Mark:** Last name or stylized initialed logo.

DAKE, C. M., 19759 Chef Menteur Hwy., New Orleans, LA 70129-9602, Phone: 504-254-0357, Fax:504-254-9501
Specialties: Fancy working folders. **Patterns:** Front-lock lockbacks, button-lock folders. **Technical:** Grinds ATS-34 and Damascus. **Prices:** $500 to $2500; some higher. **Remarks:** Full-time maker; first knife sold in 1988. Doing business as Bayou Custom Cutlery. **Mark:** Last name.

DAKE, MARY H, RT 5 Box 287A, New Orleans, LA 70129, Phone: (504) 254-0357

DALAND, B. MACGREGOR, RT 5 Box 196, Harbeson, DE 19951, Phone: (302) 945-2609

DALLYN, KELLY, 14695 Deerridge Dr S E, Calgary AB, CANADA T2J 6A8, Phone: (403) 278-3056

DAMLOVAC, SAVA, 10292 Bradbury Dr., Indianapolis, IN 46231, Phone: 317-839-4952
Specialties: Period pieces, Fantasy, Viking, Moran type all Damascus daggers. **Patterns:** Bowies, fighters, daggers, Persian style knives. **Technical:** Uses own Damascus, some stainless, mostly hand forges. **Prices:** $150 to $2,500; some higher. **Remarks:** Full-time maker; first knife sold in 1993. **Mark:** "Sava' stamped in Damascus or etched in stainless. **Other:** Specialty, Bill Moran all Damascus dagger sets, in Moran style wood case.

D'ANDREA, JOHN, 501 Penn Estates, East Stroudsberg, PA 18301, Phone: 570-420-6050
Specialties: Fancy working straight knives and folders with filework and distinctive leatherwork. **Patterns:** Hunters, fighters, daggers, folders and an occasional sword. **Technical:** Grinds ATS-34, 154CM, 440C and D2. **Prices:** $180 to $600; some to $1,000. **Remarks:** Part-time maker; first knife sold in 1986. **Mark:** First name, last initial imposed on samurai sword.

D'ANGELO, LAURENCE, 14703 NE 17th Ave., Vancouver, WA 98686, Phone: 360-573-0546
Specialties: Straight knives of his design. **Patterns:** Bowies, hunters and locking folders. **Technical:** Grinds D2, ATS-34 and 440C. Hand makes all sheaths. **Prices:** $100 to $200. **Remarks:** Full-time maker; first knife sold in 1987. **Mark:** Football logo--first and middle initials, last name, city, state, Maker.

DANIEL, TRAVIS E., 1655 Carrow Rd, Chocowinity, NC 27817, Phone: 252-940-0807
Specialties: Traditional working straight knives of his design or to customer specs. **Patterns:** Hunters, fighters and utility/camp knives. **Technical:** Forges and grinds ATS-34 and his own Damascus. **Prices:** $90 to $1,250; some to $2,000. **Remarks:** Full-time maker; first knife sold in 1976. **Mark:** Carolina Custom Knives or "TED"

DANIELS, ALEX, 1416 County Rd. 415, Town Creek, AL 35672, Phone: 256-685-0943
Specialties: Working and using straight knives and folders; period pieces, reproduction Bowies. **Patterns:** Mostly reproduction Bowies but offer full line of knives. **Technical:** Now also using BG-42 along with 440C and ATS-34. **Prices:** $200 to $2,500. **Remarks:** Full-time maker; first knife sold in 1963. **Mark:** First and middle initials, last name, city and state.

DARBY, RICK, 71 Nestingrock Lane, Levittown, PA 19054
Specialties: Working straight knives. **Patterns:** Boots, fighters and hunters with mirror finish. **Technical:** Grinds 440C and CPM440V. **Prices:** $125 to $300. **Remarks:** Part-time maker; first knife sold in 1974. **Mark:** First and middle initials, last name.

DARBY, DAVID T, 30652 S 533 Rd, Cookson, OK 74427, Phone: (918) 457-4868

DARBY, JED, 7878 E. Co. Rd. 50 N., Greensburg, IN 47240, Phone: 812-663-2696
Specialties: Traditional working/using straight knives of his design and to customer specs. **Patterns:** Bowies, hunters and utility/camp knives. **Technical:** Grinds 440C, ATS-34 and Damascus. **Prices:** $70 to $550; some to $1,000. **Remarks:** Full-time maker; first knife sold in 1992. Doing business as Darby Knives. **Mark:** Last name and year.

DARCEY, CHESTER L, 1608 Dominik Dr, College Station, TX 77840, Phone: 979-696-1656
Specialties: Lockback, liner lock and scale release folders. **Patterns:** Bowies, hunters and daggers. **Technical:** Stock removal on carbon and stainless steels, forge own Damascus. **Prices:** $200 to $1000. **Remarks:** Part-time maker, first knife sold in 1999. **Mark:** Last name in script.

DARPINIAN, DAVE, 15219 W 125th, Olathe, KS 66062, Phone: 913-397-8914
Specialties: Working knives and fancy pieces to customer specs. **Patterns:** Full range of straight knives including art daggers and short swords. **Technical:** Art grinds ATS-34, 440C, 154 CM, 5160, 1095. **Prices:** $200 to $1000. **Remarks:** First knife sold in 1996, part-time maker. **Mark:** Last name.

DAVENPORT, JACK, 36842 W. Center Ave., Dade City, FL 33525, Phone: 352-521-4088
Specialties: Titanium liner lock, button-lock and release. **Patterns:** Boots and double-ground fighters. **Technical:** Grinds ATS-34, 12C27 SS and Damascus; liquid nitrogen quench; heat-treats. **Prices:** $250 to $5,000. **Remarks:** Full-time maker; first knife sold in 1986. **Mark:** Last name.

DAVIDSON, EDMUND, 3345 Virginia Ave, Goshen, VA 24439, Phone: 540-997-5651
Specialties: Working straight knives; many integral patterns and upgraded models. **Patterns:** Heavy-duty skinners and camp knives. **Technical:** Grinds A2, ATS-34, BG-42, S7, 440C, CPM-T-440V. **Prices:** $75 to $1,500. **Remarks:** Full-time maker; first knife sold in 1986. **Mark:** Name in deer head or motorcycle logo.

DAVIS, DON, 8415 Coyote Run, Loveland, CO 80537-9665, Phone: 970-669-9016, Fax:970-669-8072
Specialties: Working straight knives in standard patterns or to customer specs. **Patterns:** Hunters, utility knives, skinners and survival knives. **Technical:** Grinds 440C, ATS-34. **Prices:** $75 to $250. **Remarks:** Full-time maker; first knife sold in 1985. **Mark:** Signature, city and state.

DAVIS, W. C., 19300 S. School Rd., Raymore, MO 64083, Phone: 816-331-4491
Specialties: Fancy working straight knives and folders. **Patterns:** Folding lockers and slip-joints; straight hunters, fighters and Bowies. **Technical:** Grinds A2, ATS-34, 154, CPM T490V and CPM 530V. **Prices:** $100 to $300; some to $1,000. **Remarks:** Full-time maker; first knife sold in 1972. **Mark:** Name.

DAVIS, JESSE W., 7398A Hwy. 3, Sarah, MS 38665, Phone: 601-382-7332
Specialties: Working straight knives and folders in standard patterns and to customer specs. **Patterns:** Boot knives, daggers. **Technical:** Grinds O1, A2, D2, 440C and commercial Damascus. **Prices:** $125 to $300. **Remarks:** Full-time maker; first knife sold in 1977. Former member Knife Makers Guild (in good standing). **Mark:** Name or initials.

DAVIS, VERNON M., 2020 Behrens Circle, Waco, TX 76705, Phone: 817-799-7671
Specialties: Presentation-grade straight knives. **Patterns:** Bowies, daggers, boots, fighters, hunters and utility knives. **Technical:** Hollow-grinds 440C, ATS-34 and D2. Grinds an aesthetic grind line near choil. **Prices:** $125 to $550; some to $5,000. **Remarks:** Part-time maker; first knife sold in 1980. **Mark:** Last name and city inside outline of state.

DAVIS, TERRY, Box 111, Sumpter, OR 97877, Phone: 541-894-2307
Specialties: Traditional and contemporary folders. **Patterns:** Multi-blade folders, whittlers and interframe multiblades; sunfish patterns. **Technical:** Flat-grinds ATS-34. **Prices:** $400 to $1,000; some higher. **Remarks:** Full-time maker; first knife sold in 1985. **Mark:** Name in logo.

DAVIS, GREG, PO Box 272, Fillmore, UT 84631, Phone: 435-896-7410

DAVIS, CHARLIE, ANZA Knives, P. O. Box 710806, Santee, CA 92072, Phone: 619-561-9445, Fax:619-390-6283
Specialties: Fancy and embellished working straight knives of his design. **Patterns:** Hunters, camp and utility knives. **Technical:** Grinds high-carbon files. **Prices:** $20 to $185 - custom depends. **Remarks:** Full-time maker; first knife sold in 1980. **Mark:** ANZA U. S. A. **Other:** we now offer custom.

DAVIS, BARRY L., 4262 U. S. 20, Castleton, NY 12033, Phone: 518-477-5036
Specialties: Collector-quality and Damascus interframe folders. **Patterns:** Traditional gentlemen's folders. **Technical:** Makes Damascus; uses only natural handle materials. **Prices:** $1,000 to $2,500; some to $6,000. **Remarks:** Part-time maker; first knife sold in 1980. **Mark:** Initials.

DAVIS, JOHN, 235 Lampe Road, Selah, WA 98942, Phone: 509-697-3845, Fax:509-697-8087
Specialties: Working and using straight knives of his own design, to customer specs and in standard patterns. **Patterns:** Boots, hunters, kitchen and utility/camp knives. **Technical:** Grinds ATS-34, 440C and commercial Damascus; makes own Damascus and mosaic Damascus. Embellishes with stabilized wood, mokume and nickel-silver. **Prices:** Start at $150. **Remarks:** Part-time maker; first knife sold in 1996. **Mark:** Name city and state on Damascus stamp initials.

DAVIS, STEVE, 3370 Chatsworth Way, Powder Springs, GA 30127, Phone: 770-427-5740
Specialties: Traditional Gents and Ladies folders of his design and to customer specs. **Patterns:** Slip-joint folders, locking-liner folders, lock back folders. **Technical:** Grinds ATS-34, 440C and Damascus. Offers filework; prefers hand-rubbed finishes and natural handle materials. Uses pearl, ivory, stag and exotic woods. **Prices:** $250 to $600; some to $1,500. **Remarks:** Part-time maker; first knife sold in 1988. Doing business as Custom Knives by Steve Davis. **Mark:** Name engraved on blade.

DAVISSON, COLE, 25939 Casa Loma Ct, Hemet, CA 92544, Phone: (909) 652-8588

DAWKINS, DUDLEY L., 221 NW Broadmoor Ave., Topeka, KS 66606-1254
Specialties: Stylized old or "Dawkins Forged" with anvil in center. New Tang Stamps. **Patterns:** Straight knives. **Technical:** Mostly carbon steel; some Damascus-all knives forged. **Prices:** $125 and up. **Remarks:** All

custom knifemakers

knives supplied with wood-lined sheaths. **Other:** ABS Member - sole authorship.

DAWSON, BARRY, 10A Town Plaza, Suite 303, Durango, CO 81301 **Specialties:** Samurai swords, combat knives, collector daggers, tactical, folding and hunting knives. **Patterns:** Offers over 60 different models. **Technical:** Grinds 440C, ATS 34, own heat-treatment. **Prices:** $75 to $1,500; some to $5,000. **Remarks:** Full-time maker; first knife sold in 1975. **Mark:** Last name, USA in print or last name in script.

DAWSON, LYNN, 10A Town Plaza #303, Durango, CO 81301, Fax:928-772-1729 **Specialties:** Swords, hunters, utility, and art pieces. **Patterns:** Over 25 patterns to choose from. **Technical:** Grinds 440C, ATS 34, own heat treating. **Prices:** $80 to $1000. **Remarks:** Custom work and my own designs. **Mark:** The name "Lynn" in print or script.

DE CASTRO, MARCO A M, Rua Bandeira Paulista, 600, Conj. 113, Sao Paulo Sp, BRAZIL 04532-001, Phone: (5511) 3842-6911, Fax:(5511) 3842-6029

DE MARIA JR, ANGELO, 12 Boronda Rd, Carmel Valley, CA 93924, Phone: 831 659-3381, Fax:831 659-1315

DE VILLIERS, ANDRE & KIRSTEN, Postnet suite 263, Private bag X6, Cascades 3202, SOUTH AFRICA, Phone: 27 31 785 1278, Fax:27031078501278

DEAN, HARVEY J., Rt. 2, Box 137, Rockdale, TX 76567, Phone: 512-446-3111, Fax:512-446-5060 **Specialties:** Collectible, functional knives. **Patterns:** Bowies, hunters, folders, daggers, swords, battle axes, camp and combat knives. **Technical:** Forges 1095, O1 and his Damascus. **Prices:** $300 to $8,000. **Remarks:** Full-time maker; first knife sold in 1981. **Mark:** Last name and MS.

DEBRAGA, JOSE C., 2276 Boul, Cardinal Villeneuve Quebec, CANADA G1L 3H6, Phone: 418-523-1144, Fax:418-948-0105 **Specialties:** Art knives, fantasy pieces and working knives of his design or to customer specs. **Patterns:** Knives with sculptured or carved handles, from miniatures to full-size working knives. **Technical:** Grinds and hand-files 440C and ATS-34. A variety of steels and handle materials available. Offers lost wax casting. **Prices:** Start at $300. **Remarks:** Full-time maker; wax modeler, sculptor and knife maker; first knife sold in 1984. **Mark:** Initials in stylized script and serial number.

DEFEO, ROBERT A., 403 Lost Trail Dr., Henderson, NV 89014, Phone: 702-434-3717 **Specialties:** Working straight knives and period pieces. **Patterns:** Hunters, fighters, daggers and Bowies. **Technical:** Grinds ATS-34 & Damascus. **Prices:** $250 to $500; some higher. **Remarks:** Part-time maker; first knife sold in 1982. **Mark:** Last name.

DEFREEST, WILLIAM G., P. O. Box 573, Barnwell, SC 29812, Phone: 803-259-7883 **Specialties:** Working straight knives and folders. **Patterns:** Fighters, hunters and boots; locking folders and slip-joints. **Technical:** Grinds 440C, 154CM and ATS-34; clean lines and mirror finishes. **Prices:** $100 to $700. **Remarks:** Full-time maker; first knife sold in 1974. **Mark:** GORDON.

DEL RASO, PETER, 28 Mayfield Dr, Mt. Waverly, Victoria, 3149, AUSTRALIA, Phone: 613-9807 6771 **Specialties:** Fixed Blades, some folders, art knives. **Patterns:** Daggers, Bowies, tactical, boot, personal and working knives. **Technical:** Grinds ATS-34, commercial Damascus and any other type of steel on request. **Prices:** $100 to $1500. **Remarks:** part time maker, first show in 1993. **Mark:** Makers surname stamped.

DELAROSA, JIM, 202 Macarthur Dr, Mukwonago, WI 53149, Phone: 262-363-9605 **Specialties:** Working straight knives and folders of my design or customer specs. **Patterns:** Hunters, skinners, fillets, utility and locking folders. **Technical:** Grinds ATS-34, 440-C, D2, 01 and commercial Damascus. **Prices:** $75. 00 to $450. 00; some higher. **Remarks:** Part-time maker. **Mark:** First and last name, city and state.

DELL, WOLFGANG, Am Alten Berg 9, D-73277 Owen-Teck, GERMANY, Phone: 49-7021-81802 **Specialties:** Fancy high-art straight of his design and to customer specs. **Patterns:** Fighters, hunters, bowies and utility/camp knives. **Technical:** Grinds ATS-34, RWL-34, Elmax, Damascus (Fritz Schneider). Offers high gloss finish and engraving. **Prices:** $500 to $1,000; some to $1,600. **Remarks:** Full-time maker; first knife sold in 1992. **Mark:** Hopi hand of peace. **Other:** Member of German Knife maker Guild since 1993. Member of the Italian Knife maker Guild since 2000.

DELLANA, Dellana Inc., 1135 Terminal Way Ste #209, Reno, NV 89502, Phone: 866 Dellana or 304-727-5512, Fax:775-201-0038 **Specialties:** Collector grade fancy/embellished high art folders and art daggers. **Patterns:** Locking folders and art daggers. **Technical:** Forges her own Damascus and W-2. Engraves, does stone setting, filework, carv-

ing and gold/platinum fabrication. Prefers exotic, high karat gold, platinum, silver, gemstone and mother of pearl handle materials. **Price:** Upscale. **Remarks:** Sole authorship, full-time maker, first knife sold in 1994. **Mark:** First name. **Other:** Also does one high art collaboration a year with Van Barnett. Member: Art Knife Invitational and ABS; voting member: Knifemakers Guild.

DELONG, DICK, 17561 E. Ohio Circle, Aurora, CO 80017, Phone: 303-745-2652 **Specialties:** Fancy working knives and fantasy pieces. **Patterns:** Hunters and small skinners. **Technical:** Grinds and files O1, D2, 440C and Damascus. Offers cocobolo and Osage orange for handles. **Prices:** Start at $50. **Remarks:** Part-time maker. **Mark:** Last name; some unmarked. **Other:** Member of Art Knife Invitational. Voting member of Knifemakers Guild. Member of ABS.

DEMENT, LARRY R., P O Box 1807, Prince Fredrick, MD 20678, Phone: (410) 586-9011

DEMPSEY, GORDON S., P. O. Box 7497, N. Kenai, AK 99635, Phone: 907-776-8425 **Specialties:** Working straight knives. **Patterns:** Pattern welded Damascus and carbon steel blades. **Technical:** Pattern welded Damascus and carbon steel. **Prices:** $80 to $250. **Remarks:** Part-time maker; first knife sold in 1974. **Mark:** Name.

DEMPSEY, DAVID, 103 Chadwick Dr, Macon, GA 31210, Phone: 912-474-4948 **Specialties:** Tactical, Utility, Working, Classic straight knives. **Patterns:** Fighters, Tantos, Hunters, Neck, Utility or Customer design. **Technical:** Grinds carbon steel and stainless including S30V. (differential heat treatment), Stainless Steels. **Prices:** Start at $135 for Neck Knives. **Remarks:** Full-time maker, full-time maker since 1998. First knife sold 1998. **Mark:** Last Name. **Other:** Member North Carolina Knifemakers Guild.

DENNEHY, DAN, P. O. Box 2F, Del Norte, CO 81132, Phone: 719-657-2545 **Specialties:** Working knives, fighting and military knives, throwing knives. **Patterns:** Full range of straight knives, tomahawks, buckle knives. **Technical:** Forges and grinds A2, O1 and D2. **Prices:** $200 to $500. **Remarks:** Full-time maker; first knife sold in 1942. **Mark:** First name and last initial, city, state and shamrock.

DENNING, GENO, Caveman Engineering, 135 Allenvalley Rd, Gaston, SC 29053, Phone: 803-794-6067 **Specialties:** Mirror finish. **Patterns:** Hunters, fighters, folders. **Technical:** ATS-34, 440V, S-30-V D-2. **Prices:** $100 and up. **Remarks:** Full-time maker since 96. Sole income since 99. **Mark:** Denning with year below. **Other:** A director of SCAK. South Carolina Association of knife makers.

DENT, DOUGLAS M., 1208 Chestnut St., S. Charleston, WV 25309, Phone: 304-768-3308 **Specialties:** Straight and folding sportsman's knives. **Patterns:** Hunters, boots and Bowies, interframe folders. **Technical:** Forges and grinds D2, 440C, 154CM and plain tool steels. **Prices:** $70 to $300; exceptional knives to $800. **Remarks:** Part-time maker; first knife sold in 1969. **Mark:** Last name.

DERINGER, CHRISTOPH, 1559 St. Louis #4, Sherbrooke, Quebec, CANADA J1H 4P7, Phone: 819-565-4260 **Specialties:** Traditional working/using straight knives and folders of his design and to customer specs. **Patterns:** Boots, hunters, folders, art knives, kitchen knives and utility/camp knives. **Technical:** Forges 5160, O1 and Damascus. Offers a variety of filework. **Prices:** Start at $250. **Remarks:** Full-time maker; first knife sold in 1989. **Mark:** Last name stamped/engraved.

DERR, HERBERT, 413 Woodland Dr, St Albans, WV 25177, Phone: 304-727-3866 **Specialties:** Damascus one-of-a-kind knives, carbon steels also. **Patterns:** Birdseye, Ladder back, Mosaics. **Technical:** All styles functional as well as artistically pleasing. **Prices:** $90 to $175 carbon, $175 to $600 Damascus. **Remarks:** All Damascus made by maker. **Mark:** H. K. Derr.

DES JARDINS, DENNIS, P. O. Box 1103, Plains, MT 59859, Phone: 406-826-3981 **Specialties:** Classic working/using straight knives of his design and to customer specs. **Patterns:** Bowies, hunters and utility/camp knives. **Technical:** Forges 5160 and L6, 203E and 1095 Damascus; fancy file work on all knives. **Prices:** $100 to $500; some to $1,000. **Remarks:** Full-time maker; first knife was sold in 1985. **Mark:** Initials, city and state.

DETMER, PHILLIP, 14140 Bluff Rd., Breese, IL 62230, Phone: 618-526-4834 **Specialties:** Working knives. **Patterns:** Bowies, daggers and hunters. **Technical:** Grinds ATS-34 and D2. **Prices:** $60 to $400. **Remarks:** Part-time maker; first knife sold in 1977. **Mark:** Last name with dagger.

custom knifemakers

DI MARZO, RICHARD, 2357 Center Pl., Birmingham, AL 35205, Phone: 205-252-3331

DICKERSON, GAVIN, P. O. Box 7672, Petit 1512, SOUTH AFRICA, Phone: +27 011-965-0988, Fax:+27 011-965-0988
Specialties: Straight knives of his design or to customer specs. **Patterns:** Hunters, skinners, fighters and Bowies. **Technical:** Hollow-grinds D2, 440C, ATS-34, 12C27 and Damascus upon request. Prefers natural handle materials; offers synthetic handle materials. **Prices:** $190 to $2,500. **Remarks:** Part-time maker; first knife sold in 1982. **Mark:** Name in full.

DICKERSON, GORDON S, 152 Laurel Ln, Hohenwald, TN 38462, Phone: (931) 796-1187
Specialties: Traditional working straight knives; Civil War era period pieces. **Patterns:** Bowies, hunters, tactical, camp/utility knives; some folders. **Technical:** Forges carbon steel; pattern welded and cable Damascus. **Prices:** $150 to $500; some to $3,000. **Mark:** Last name. **Other:** ABS member.

DICKISON, SCOTT S., Fisher Circle, Portsmouth, RI 02871, Phone: 401-419-4175
Specialties: Working and using straight knives and locking folders of his design and automatics. **Patterns:** Trout knives, fishing and hunting knives. **Technical:** Forges and grinds commercial Damascus and D2, O1. Uses natural handle materials. **Prices:** $400 to $750; some higher. **Remarks:** Part-time maker; first knife sold in 1989. **Mark:** Stylized initials.

DIEBEL, CHUCK, PO Box 13, Broussard, LA 70516-0013

DIETZ, HOWARD, 421 Range Rd., New Braunfels, TX 78132, Phone: 830-885-4662
Specialties: Lock back folders, working straight knives. **Patterns:** Folding hunters, high grade pocket knives. ATS-34, 440C, CPM 440V, D2 and stainless Damascus. **Prices:** $300 to $1,000. **Remarks:** Full-time gun & knife maker; first knife sold in 1995. **Mark:** Name, city, and state.

DIETZEL, BILL, P. O. Box 1613, Middleburg, FL 32068, Phone: 904-282-1091
Specialties: Forged straight knives and folders. **Patterns:** His interpretations. **Technical:** Forges his Damascus and other steels. **Prices:** Middle ranges. **Remarks:** Likes natural materials; uses titanium in folder liners. **Mark:** Name. **Other:** Master Smith (1997).

DIGANGI, JOSEPH M., Box 950, Santa Cruz, NM 87567, Phone: 505-753-6414, Fax:505-753-8144
Specialties: Kitchen and table cutlery. **Patterns:** French chef's knives, carving sets, steak knife sets, some camp knives and hunters. Holds patents and trademarks for "System II" kitchen cutlery set. **Technical:** Grinds ATS-34. **Prices:** $150 to $595; some to $1,200. **Remarks:** Full-time maker; first knife sold in 1983. **Mark:** DiGangi Designs.

DILL, DAVE, 7404 NW 30th St., Bethany, OK 73008, Phone: 405-789-0750
Specialties: Folders of his design. **Patterns:** Various patterns. **Technical:** Hand-grinds 440C, ATS-34. Offers engraving and filework on all folders. **Prices:** Starting at $450. **Remarks:** Full-time maker; first knife sold in 1987. **Mark:** First initial, last name.

DILL, ROBERT, 1812 Van Buren, Loveland, CO 80538, Phone: 970-667-5144, Fax:970-667-5144
Specialties: Fancy and working knives of his design. **Patterns:** Hunters, Bowies and fighters. **Technical:** Grinds 440C and D2. **Prices:** $100 to $800. **Remarks:** Full-time maker; first knife sold in 1984. **Mark:** Logo stamped into blade.

DILLUVIO, FRANK J., 13611 Joyce Dr., Warren, MI 48093, Phone: 810-775-1216
Specialties: Traditional working straight knives, some high-tech. **Patterns:** Hunters, Bowies, fishing knives, sub-hilts, liner lock™ folders and miniatures. **Technical:** Grinds D2, 440C, CPM; works for precision fits--no solder. **Prices:** $95 to $450; some to $800. **Remarks:** Full-time maker; first knife sold in 1984. **Mark:** Name and state.

DION, GREG, 3032 S. Jackson St., Oxnard, CA 93033, Phone: 805-483-1781
Specialties: Working straight knives, some fancy. Welcomes special orders. **Patterns:** Hunters, fighters, camp knives, Bowies and tantos. **Technical:** Grinds ATS-34, 154CM and 440C. **Prices:** $85 to $300; some to $600. **Remarks:** Part-time maker; first knife sold in 1985. **Mark:** Name.

DIPPOLD, AL, 90 Damascus Ln., Perryville, MO 63775, Phone: 573-547-1119
Specialties: Fancy one-of-a-kind locking folders. **Patterns:** Locking folders. **Technical:** Forges and grinds mosaic and pattern welded Damascus. Offers filework on all folders. **Prices:** $500 to $3,500; some higher. **Remarks:** Full-time maker; first knife sold in 1980. **Mark:** Last name in logo inside of liner.

DISKIN, MATT, P. O. Box 653, Freeland, WA 98249, Phone: 360-730-0451
Specialties: Damascus autos. **Patterns:** Dirks & daggers. **Technical:** Forges mosaic Damascus using 15N20, 1084, 02, 06, L6; pure nickel. **Prices:** Start at $500. **Remarks:** Full-time maker. **Mark:** Last name.

DIXON JR., IRA E., P. O. Box 2581, Ventura, CA 93002-2581, Phone: 805-659-5867
Specialties: Utilitarian straight knives of his design. **Patterns:** Camp, hunters, boot, fighters. **Technical:** Grinds ATS-34, 440C, D2, 5160. **Prices:** $150 to $400. **Remarks:** Part-time maker; first knife sold in 1993. **Mark:** First name, Handmade.

DOGGETT, BOB, 1310 Vinetree Dr, Brandon, FL 33510, Phone: 813-654-5075
Specialties: Clean, functional working knives. **Patterns:** Classic styled hunter, fighter and utility fixed blades; liner locking folders. **Technical:** Uses ATS-34 and commercial Damascus, 416 stainless for bolsters and hardware, hand-rubbed satin finish, top quality handle materials and titanium liners on folders Uses a variety of modern stainless steels and commercial Damascus. **Prices:** Start at $175. **Remarks:** Part-time maker; specializes in web design for knife makers. **Mark:** Last name

DOIRON, DONALD, 6 Chemin Petit Lac Des Ced, Messines PQ, CANADA JOX-2JO, Phone: (819) 465-2489

DOLAN, ROBERT L., 220--B Naalae Road, Kula, HI 96790, Phone: 808-878-6406
Specialties: Working straight knives in standard patterns, his designs or to customer specs. **Patterns:** Fixed blades and potter's tools, ceramic saws. **Technical:** Grinds O1, D2, 440C and ATS-34. Heat-treats and engraves. **Prices:** Start at $75. **Remarks:** Full-time tool and knife maker; first knife sold in 1985. **Mark:** Last name, USA.

DOMINY, CHUCK, P. O. Box 593, Colleyville, TX 76034, Phone: 817-498-4527
Specialties: Titanium liner lock folders. **Patterns:** Hunters, utility/camp knives and liner lock folders. **Technical:** Grinds 440C and ATS-34. **Prices:** $250 to $3,000. **Remarks:** Full-time maker; first knife sold in 1976. **Mark:** Last name.

DONOVAN, PATRICK, 1770 Hudson Dr., San Jose, CA 95124, Phone: 408-267-9825
Specialties: Working straight knives and folders; period pieces. **Patterns:** Hunters, boots and daggers; lockers and slip-joints. **Technical:** Grinds 440C. Embellishes. **Prices:** $75 to $475; some to $1,200. **Remarks:** Full-time maker; first knife sold in 1980. **Mark:** First name.

DOOLITTLE, MIKE, 13 Denise Ct., Novato, CA 94947, Phone: 415-897-3246
Specialties: Working straight knives in standard patterns. **Patterns:** Hunters and fishing knives. **Technical:** Grinds 440C, 154CM and ATS-34. **Prices:** $125 to $200; some to $750. **Remarks:** Part-time maker; first knife sold in 1981. **Mark:** Name, city and state.

DOTSON, TRACY, 1280 Hwy. C-4A, Baker, FL 32531, Phone: 850-537-2407
Specialties: Folding fighters and small folders. **Patterns:** Liner lock and lockback folders. **Technical:** Hollow-grinds ATS-34 and commercial Damascus. **Prices:** Start at $250. **Remarks:** Part-time maker; first knife sold in 1995. **Mark:** Last name.

DOUGLAS, JOHN J., 506 Powell Rd, Lynch Station, VA 24571, Phone: 804-369-7196
Specialties: Fancy and traditional straight knives and folders of his design and to customer specs. **Patterns:** Locking folders, swords and sgian dubhs. **Technical:** Grinds 440C stainless, ATS-34 stainless and customer's choice. Offers newly designed non-pivot uni-lock folders. Prefers highly polished finish. **Prices:** $160 to $1,400. **Remarks:** Full-time maker; first knife sold in 1975. Doing business as Douglas Keltic. **Mark:** Stylized initial. Folders are numbered; customs are dated.

DOURSIN, GERARD, Chemin des Croutoules, F 84210, Pernes les Fontaines, FRANCE
Specialties: Period pieces. **Patterns:** Liner locks and daggers. **Technical:** Forges mosaic Damascus. **Prices:** $600 to $4,000. **Remarks:** First knife sold in 1983. **Mark:** First initial, last name and I stop the lion.

DOUSSOT, LAURENT, 6262 De La Roche, Montreal, Quebec, CANADA H2H 1W9, Phone: 516-270-6992, Fax:516-722-1641
Specialties: Fancy and embellished folders and fantasy knives. **Patterns:** Fighters and locking folders. **Technical:** Grinds ATS-34 and commercial Damascus. Scale carvings on all knives; most bolsters are carved titanium. **Prices:** $350 to $3,000. **Remarks:** Part-time maker; first knife was sold in 1992. **Mark:** Stylized initials inside circle.

DOWELL, T. M., 139 NW St. Helen's Pl., Bend, OR 97701, Phone: 541-382-8924
Specialties: Integral construction in hunting knives. **Patterns:** Limited to featherweights, lightweights, integral built & funny folders. **Technical:**

custom knifemakers

Grinds D-2, BG-42 & Vasco wear. **Prices:** $185 and up. **Remarks:** Full-time maker; first knife sold in 1967. **Mark:** Initials logo.

DOWNIE, JAMES T., 10076 Estate Dr, Port Franks, Ont., CANADA NOM 2LO, Phone: 519-243-2290, Fax:519-243-1487
Specialties: Serviceable straight knives and folders; period pieces. **Patterns:** Hunters, Bowies, camp knives and miniatures. **Technical:** Grinds D2, 440C and ATS-34, Damasteel, stainless steel Damascus. **Prices:** $100 to $500; some higher. **Remarks:** Full-time maker, supplier; first knife sold in 1978. **Mark:** Signature of first and middle initials, last name. **Other:** Canadian supplier, free catalogue.

DOWNING, TOM, 2675 12th St, Cuyaho Falls, OH 44223, Phone: 330-923-7464
Specialties: Working straight knives; period pieces. **Patterns:** Hunters, fighters and tantos. **Technical:** Grinds 440C, ATs-34 and CPM-T-440V. Prefers natural handle materials. **Prices:** $150 to $900, some to $1500. **Remarks:** Part-time maker; first knife sold in 1979. **Mark:** First and middle initials, last name.

DOWNING, LARRY, 12268 Hwy. 181N, Bremen, KY 42325, Phone: 270-525-3523, Fax:270-525-3372
Specialties: Working straight knives and folders. **Patterns:** From mini-knives to daggers, folding lockers to interframes. **Technical:** Forges and grinds 154CM, ATS-34 and his own Damascus. **Prices:** $150 to $750; some higher. **Remarks:** Part-time maker; first knife sold in 1979. **Mark:** Name in arrowhead.

DOWNS, JAMES F., 35 Sunset Rd., Londonderry, OH 45647, Phone: 740-887-2099
Specialties: Working straight knives of his design or to customer specs. **Patterns:** Folders, bowies, boot, hunters, utility. **Technical:** Grinds 440C and other steels. Prefers stag, jigged bone, Micarta and stabilized woods. **Prices:** $75 to $1,200. **Remarks:** Full-time maker; first knife sold in 1980. Brochures $2. 00. **Mark:** Last name.

DOX, JAN, Zwanebloemlaan 27, B 2900 Schoten, BELGIUM, Phone: 32 3 658 77 43
Specialties: Working/using knives to swords, from kitchen to battlefield. **Patterns:** Own designs, some based on traditional ethnic patterns (Scots, Celtic, Scandinavian and Japanese) or to customer specs. **Technical:** Grinds 4034, 1. 2379(D2) and others on request. Most convex edges. **Handles:** wrapped in modern or traditional patterns, resin impregnated if desired. Natural or synthetic materials, some carved. Sends out for heat-treating by professionals. **Prices:** Start at 25 to 50 Euro (USD) and up. **Remarks:** Spare-time maker, first knife sold 2001. **Mark:** Name.

DOZIER, BOB, P. O. Box 1941, Springdale, AR 72765, Phone: 888-823-0023, Fax:501-756-9139
Specialties: Using knives (fixed blades and folders). **Patterns:** Some fine collector-grade knives. **Technical:** Uses D2. Prefers Micarta handle material. **Prices:** Using knives to $145 to $595. **Remarks:** Full-time maker; first knife sold in 1965. **Mark:** State, made, last name in a circle (for fixed blades); Last name with arrow through 'D' and year over name (for folders).

DRAPER, AUDRA, #10 Creek Dr, Riverton, WY 82501, Phone: 307-856-6807
Specialties: One of a kind straight and folders. **Patterns:** Design custom knives, using, Bowies, and mini's. **Technical:** Forge 52100 and Damascus; I heat-treat all my knives. **Prices:** Start at $60 for key chain knives; up to $3000 for art knives. **Remarks:** Full-time maker; journeyman in the ABS. Member of the PKA; first knife sold in 1995. **Mark:** Audra

DRAPER, MIKE, #10 Creek Drive, Riverton, WY 82501, Phone: 307-856-6807
Specialties: Hand forged working straight knives. **Patterns:** Hunters, bowies and camp knives. **Technical:** Forges 52100 and Damascus. **Prices:** Starting at $150. **Remarks:** Part-time maker; first knife sold in 1996. **Mark:** Initials M. J. D. or Name, city and state.

DRAW, GERALD, 2 Glenn Cable, Asheville, NC 28802, Phone: 828-299-7821
Specialties: Blade ATS 34 5 1/2". Handle Splated Maple. 10" OAL. **Price:** $125.

DRISCOLL, MARK, 4115 Avoyer Pl., La Mesa, CA 91941, Phone: 619-670-0695
Specialties: High-art, period pieces and working/using knives of his design or to customer specs; some fancy. **Patterns:** Swords, Bowies, Fighters, daggers, hunters and primitive (mountain man type styles). **Technical:** Forges 52100, 5160, O1, L6, 1095, and maker his own Damascus and mokume; also does multiple quench heat treating. Uses exotic hardwoods, ivory and horn, offers fancy file work, carving, scrimshaws. **Prices:** $150 to $550; some to $1,500. **Remarks:** Part-time maker; first knife sold in 1986. Doing business as Mountain Man Knives. **Mark:** Double "M".

DRISKILL, BERYL, P. O. Box 187, Braggadocio, MO 63826, Phone: 573-757-6262
Specialties: Fancy working knives. **Patterns:** Hunting knives, fighters, Bowies, boots, daggers and lockback folders. **Technical:** Grinds ATS-34.

Prices: Start at $200. **Remarks:** Part-time maker; first knife sold in 1984. **Mark:** Name.

DROST, MICHAEL B., Rt. 2, Box 49, French Creek, WV 26218, Phone: 304-472-7901
Specialties: Working/using straight knives and folders of all designs. **Patterns:** Hunters, locking folders and utility/camp knives. **Technical:** Grinds ATS-34, D2 and CPM-T-440V. Offers dove-tailed bolsters and spacers, filework and scrimshaw. **Prices:** $125 to $400; some to $740. **Remarks:** Full-time maker; first knife sold in 1990. Doing business as Drost Custom Knives. **Mark:** Name, city and state.

DROST, JASON D., Rt. 2 Box 49, French Creek, WV 26218, Phone: 304-472-7901
Specialties: Working/using straight knives of his design. **Patterns:** Hunters and utility/camp knives. **Technical:** Grinds 154 CM and D2. **Prices:** $125 to $5,000. **Remarks:** Spare-time maker; first knife sold in 1995. **Mark:** First and middle initials, last name, maker, city and state.

DROUIN, JOSEPH D, 3950 N E Hyak Way, Bremerton, WA 98311, Phone: (360) 692-9979

DUBLIN, DENNIS, 708 Stanley St., Box 986, Enderby, BC, CANADA V0E 1V0, Phone: 604-838-6753
Specialties: Working straight knives and folders, plain or fancy. **Patterns:** Hunters and Bowies, locking hunters, combination knives/axes. **Technical:** Forges and grinds high carbon steels. **Prices:** $100 to $400; some higher. **Remarks:** Full-time maker; first knife sold in 1970. **Mark:** Name.

DUFF, BILL, P. O. Box 694, Virginia City, NV 89440, Phone: 702-847-0566
Specialties: Working straight knives and folders. **Patterns:** Hunters and Bowies; locking folders and interframes. **Technical:** Grinds D2, 440C and 154CM. **Prices:** $175 to $3,500. **Remarks:** Part-time maker; first knife sold in 1976. **Mark:** Name, city, state and date.

DUFOUR, ARTHUR J., 8120 De Armoun Rd., Anchorage, AK 99516, Phone: 907-345-1701
Specialties: Working straight knives from standard patterns. **Patterns:** Hunters, Bowies, camp and fishing knives--grinded thin and pointed. **Technical:** Grinds 440C, ATS-34, AEB-L. Tempers 57-58R; hollow-grinds. **Prices:** $135; some to $250. **Remarks:** Part-time maker; first knife sold in 1970. **Mark:** Prospector logo.

DUGAN, BRAD M, 422 A Cribbage Ln, San Marcos, CA 92069, Phone: (760) 752-4417

DUGGER, DAVE, 2504 West 51, Westwood, KS 66205, Phone: 913-831-2382
Specialties: Working straight knives; fantasy pieces. **Patterns:** Hunters, boots and daggers in one of a kind styles. **Technical:** Grinds D2, 440C and 154CM. **Prices:** $75 to $350; some to $1,200. **Remarks:** Part-time maker; first knife sold in 1979. Not currently accepting orders. Doing business as Dog Knives. **Mark:** DOG.

DUNKERLEY, RICK, Box 111, Lincoln, MT 59639, Phone: 406-362-3097
Specialties: Mosaic damascus folders and carbon steel utility knives. **Patterns:**One of a kind folders, standard hunters and utility designs. **Technical:** Forges 52100, Damascus and mosaic Damascus. Prefers natural handle materials. **Prices:** $200 and up. **Remarks:** Full-time maker; first knife sold in 1984, ABS Mastersmith. Doing business as Dunkerley Custom Knives. **Mark:** Dunkerley, MS.

DUNN, CHARLES K., 17740 GA Hwy. 116, Shiloh, GA 31826, Phone: 706-846-2666
Specialties: Fancy and working straight knives and folders of his design and to customer specs. **Patterns:** Bowies, hunters and locking folders. **Technical:** Grinds 440C and ATS-34. Engraves; filework offered. **Prices:** $75 to $300. **Remarks:** Part-time maker; first knife sold in 1988. **Mark:** First initial, last name, city, state.

DUNN, MELVIN T., 5830 NW Carlson Rd., Rossville, KS 66533, Phone: 785-584-6856
Specialties: Traditional working straight knives and folders. **Patterns:** Locking folders, straight hunters, fishing and kitchen knives. **Technical:** D2, 440V, 420V & 440C. **Prices:** $60 to $500. **Remarks:** Full-time maker; first knife sold in 1972. **Mark:** Name in script with address & year of mfg.

DUNN, STEVE, 376 Biggerstaff Rd., Smiths Grove, KY 42171, Phone: 270-563-9830
Specialties: Working and using straight knives of his design; period pieces. **Patterns:** Hunters, skinners, Bowies, fighters, camp knives, folders, swords and battle axes. **Technical:** Forges his Damascus, O1, 5160, L6 and 1095. **Prices:** Moderate to upscale. **Remarks:** Full-time maker; first knife sold in 1990. **Mark:** Last name and MS.

DURAN, JERRY T., P. O. Box 80692, Albuquerque, NM 87198-0692, Phone: 505-873-4676
Specialties: Tactical folders, bowies, fighters, liner locks® and hunters. **Patterns:** Folders, bowies, hunters & tactical knives. **Technical:** Forges

own damascus and forges carbon steel. **Prices:** Moderate to upscale. **Remarks:** Full-time maker; first knife sold in 1978. **Mark:** Initials in elk rack logo.

DURHAM, KENNETH, Buzzard Roost Forge, 10495 White Pike, Cherokee, AL 35616, Phone: (256) 359-4287
Specialties: Bowies, dirks, hunters. **Patterns:** Traditional patterns. **Technical:** Forges 1095, 5160, 52100 and makes own Damascus. **Prices:** $85 to $1,250. **Remarks:** Began making knives about 1995. Received journeyman stamp 1999. **Mark:** Bulls head with Ken Durham above and Cherokee AL below.

DURIO, FRED, 144 Gulino St., Opelousas, LA 70570, Phone: 337-948-4831
Specialties: Folders. **Patterns:** Liner locks; plain & fancy. **Technical:** Makes own Damascus. **Prices:** Moderate to upscale. **Remarks:** Full-time maker. **Mark:** Last name-Durio.

DUVALL, FRED, 10715 Hwy. 190, Benton, AR 72015, Phone: 501-778-9360
Specialties: Working straight knives and folders. **Patterns:** Locking folders, slip joints, hunters, fighters and Bowies. **Technical:** Grinds D2 and CPM440V; forges 5160. **Prices:** $100 to $400; some to $800. **Remarks:** Part-time maker; first knife sold in 1973. **Mark:** Last name.

DUVALL, LARRY E., Rt. 3, Gallatin, MO 64640, Phone: 816-663-2742
Specialties: Fancy working straight knives and folders. **Patterns:** Hunters to swords, minis to Bowies; locking folders. **Technical:** Grinds D2, 440C and 154CM. **Prices:** $150 to $350; some to $2,000. **Remarks:** Part-time maker; first knife sold in 1980. **Mark:** Name and address in logo.

DYER, DAVID, 4531 Hunters Glen, Granbury, TX 76048, Phone: (817) 573-1198
Specialties: Working skinners & early period knives. **Patterns:** Customer designs, my own patterns. **Technical:** Coal forged blades; 5160 & 52100 steels. **Prices:** $150 for neck-knives & small (3" to 3-1/2"). To $600 for large blades & specialty blades. **Mark:** Last name DYER electro etched. **Other:** Grinds D-2, 1095, L-6.

DYESS, EDDIE, 1005 Hamilton, Roswell, NM 88201, Phone: 505-623-5599
Specialties: Working and using straight knives in standard patterns. **Patterns:** Hunters and fighters. **Technical:** Grinds 440C, 154CM and D2 on request. **Prices:** $85 to $135; some to $250. **Remarks:** Spare-time maker; first knife sold in 1980. **Mark:** Last name.

DYRNOE, PER, Sydskraenten 10, Tulstrup, DK 3400 Hilleroed, DENMARK, Phone: +45 42287041
Specialties: Hand-crafted knives with zirconia ceramic blades. **Patterns:** Hunters, skinners, Norwegian-style tolle knives, most in animal-like ergonomic shapes. **Technical:** Handles of exotic hardwood, horn, fossil ivory, etc. Norwegian-style sheaths. **Prices:** Start at $500. **Remarks:** Part-time maker in cooperation with Hans J. Henriksen; first knife sold in 1993. **Mark:** Initial logo.

e

EAKER, ALLEN L., 416 Clinton Ave., Dept Kl, Paris, IL 61944, Phone: 217-466-5160
Specialties: Traditional straight knives and folders of his design. **Patterns:** Hunters, locking folders and slip-joint folders. **Technical:** Grinds 440C; inlays. **Prices:** $125 to $325; some to $500. **Remarks:** Spare-time maker; first knife sold in 1994. **Mark:** Initials in tankard logo stamped on tang, serial number on back side.

EALY, DELBERT, PO Box 121, Indian River, MI 49749, Phone: 231-238-4705

EASLER JR., RUSSELL O., P. O. Box 301, Woodruff, SC 29388, Phone: 864-476-7830
Specialties: Working straight knives and folders. **Patterns:** Hunters, tantos and boots; locking folders and interframes. **Technical:** Grinds 440C, 154CM and ATS-34. **Prices:** $100 to $350; some to $800. **Remarks:** Part-time maker; first knife sold in 1973. **Mark:** Name or name with bear logo.

EATON, AL, P. O. Box 43, Clayton, CA 94517, Phone: 925-672-5351
Specialties: One-of-a-kind high-art knives and fantasy knives of his design, full size and miniature. **Patterns:** Hunters, fighters, daggers. **Technical:** Grinds 440C, 154CM and ATS-34; ivory and metal carving. **Prices:** $125 to $3,000; some to $5,000. **Remarks:** Full-time maker; first knife sold in 1977. **Mark:** Full name, city and state.

EATON, RICK, 9944 McCranie St, Shepherd, MT 59079 3126
Specialties: Interframe folders and one hand opening side locks. **Patterns:** Bowies, daggers, fighters and folders. **Technical:** Grinds 154CM, ATS-34, 440C and other maker's Damascus. Offers high-quality hand

engraving, Bulino and gold inlay. **Prices:** Upscale. **Remarks:** Full-time maker; first knife sold in 1982. **Mark:** Full name or full name and address.

EBISU, HIDESAKU, 3-39-7 Koi Osako Nishi Ku, Hiroshima City, JAPAN 733 0816

ECHOLS, ROGER, 46 Channing Rd, Nashville, AR 71852-8588, Phone: 870-451-9089
Specialties: Liner locks, auto-scale release, lock backs. **Patterns:** My own or yours. **Technical:** Autos. **Prices:** $500 to $1,700. **Remarks:** I like to use pearl, ivory & Damascus the most. **Mark:** My name. **Other:** Made first knife in 1984. **Remarks:** Part-time maker; tool & die maker by trade.

EDDY, HUGH E, 211 E Oak St, Caldwell, ID 83605, Phone: (208) 459-0536

EDEN, THOMAS, P O Box 57, Cranbury, NJ 08512, Phone: (609) 655-4995
Patterns: Fixed blade, working patterns, hand forged. **Technical:** Damascus. **Mark:** Eden (script). **Remarks:** ABS Smith.

EDGE, TOMMY, P. O. Box 156, Cash, AR 72421, Phone: 501-477-5210
Specialties: Fancy/embellished working knives of his design. **Patterns:** Bowies, hunters and utility/camping knives. **Technical:** Grinds 440C, ATS-34 and D2. Makes own cable Damascus; offers filework. **Prices:** $70 to $250; some to $1,500. **Remarks:** Part-time maker; first knife sold in 1993. **Mark:** Stamped first initial, last name and stenciled name, city and state in oval shape.

EDWARDS, MITCH, 303 New Salem Rd, Glasgow, KY 42141, Phone: 270-651-9257
Specialties: Period pieces. **Patterns:** Neck knives, camp, rifleman & Bowie knives. **Technical:** All hand forged, forges own Damascus 01, 1084, 1095, L-6, 15N20. **Prices:** $200 to $1000. **Remarks:** Journeyman smith. **Mark:** Broken heart.

EDWARDS, FAIN E., P. O. Box 280, Topton, NC 28781, Phone: 828-321-3127

EDWARDS, LYNN, 778 CR B91, W. Columbia, TX 77486, Phone: 979-345-4080, Fax:979-345-3472
Specialties: Traditional working and using straight knives of his design and to customer specs. **Patterns:** Bowies, hunters and utility/camp knives. **Technical:** Forges 5168 and O1; forges and grinds D2. Triple-hardens on request; offers silver wire inlay, stone inlays and spacers, filework. **Prices:** $100 to $395; some to $800. **Remarks:** Part-time maker; first knife sold in 1988. Doing business as E&E Emporium. **Mark:** Last name in script.

EHRENBERGER, DANIEL ROBERT, 6192 Hiway 168, Shelbyville, MO 63469, Phone: 573-633-2010
Specialties: Affordable working/using straight knives of his design & to custom specs. Patterns: 10" western bowie, fighters, hunting & skinning knives. **Technical:** Forges 1085, 1095, his own Damascus & cable Damascus. **Prices:** $80 to $500. **Remarks:** Full-time maker, first knife sold 1994. **Mark:** Ehrenberger JS.

EKLUND, MAIHKEL, Föne 1111, S-820 41 Farila, SWEDEN
Specialties: Collector-grade working straight knives. **Patterns:** Hunters, Bowies and fighters. **Technical:** Grinds ATS-34, Uddeholm and Dama steel. Engraves and scrimshaws. **Prices:** $150 to $700. **Remarks:** Full-time maker; first knife sold in 1983. **Mark:** Initials or name.

ELDER JR, PERRY B, 1321 Garrettsburg Rd, Clarksville, TN 37042-2516, Phone: (931) 647-9416

ELDRIDGE, ALLAN, 7731 Four Winds Dr, Ft Worth, TX 76133, Phone: 817-370-7778
Specialties: Fancy classic straight knives in standard patterns. **Patterns:** Hunters, Bowies, fighters, folders and miniatures. **Technical:** Grinds O1 and Damascus. Engraves silver-wire inlays, pearl inlays, scrimshaws and offers filework. **Prices:** $50 to $500; some to $1,200. **Remarks:** Spare-time maker; first knife sold in 1965. **Mark:** Initials.

ELISHEWITZ, ALLEN, 3960 Lariat Ridge, New Braunfels, TX 78132, Phone: 830-227-5325, Fax:830-899-4595
Specialties: Collectible high-tech working straight knives and folders of his design. **Patterns:** Working, utility and tactical knives. **Technical:** Grinds 154CM and stainless steel Damascus. All designs drafted and field-tested. **Prices:** $400 to $600. **Remarks:** Full-time maker; first knife sold in 1989. **Mark:** Last name with a Japanese crane.

ELKINS, R. VAN, P. O. Box 156, Bonita, LA 71223, Phone: 318-823-2124, Fax:318-283-6802
Specialties: High-art Bowies, fighters, folders and period daggers; all one-of-a-kind pieces. **Patterns:** Welcomes customer designs. **Technical:** Forges his own Damascus in several patterns, O1 and 5160. **Prices:** $250 to $2,800. **Remarks:** First knife sold in 1984. **Mark:** Last name.

ELLEFSON, JOEL, P. O. Box 1016, 310 S. 1st St., Manhattan, MT 59741, Phone: 406-284-3111
Specialties: Working straight knives, fancy daggers and one-of-a-kinds. **Patterns:** Hunters, daggers and some folders. **Technical:** Grinds A2,

custom knifemakers

440C and ATS-34. Makes own mokume in bronze, brass, silver and shibuishi; makes brass/steel blades. **Prices:** $75 to $500; some to $2,000. **Remarks:** Part-time maker; first knife sold in 1978. **Mark:** Stylized last initial.

ELLERBE, W. B., 3871 Osceola Rd., Geneva, FL 32732, Phone: 407-349-5818
Specialties: Period and primitive knives and sheaths. **Patterns:** Bowies to patch knives, some tomahawks. **Technical:** Grinds Sheffield O1 and files. **Prices:** Start at $35. **Remarks:** Full-time maker; first knife sold in 1971. Doing business as Cypress Bend Custom Knives. **Mark:** Last name or initials.

ELLIOTT, JERRY, 4507 Kanawha Ave., Charleston, WV 25304, Phone: 304-925-5045
Specialties: Classic and traditional straight knives and folders of his design and to customer specs. **Patterns:** Hunters, locking folders and Bowies. **Technical:** Grinds ATS-34, 154CM, O1, D2 and T-440-V. All guards silver-soldered; bolsters are pinned on straight knives, spot-welded on folders. **Prices:** $80 to $265; some to $1,000. **Remarks:** Full-time maker; first knife sold in 1972. **Mark:** First and middle initials, last name, knife maker, city, state.

ELLIOTT, MARCUS, Pen Dinas, Wyddfydd Rd., Great Orme, Llandudno Gwynedd, GREAT BRITAIN LL30 2QL, Phone: 01492-872747
Specialties: Fancy working knives. **Patterns:** Boots and small hunters. **Technical:** Grinds O1, 440C and ATS-34. **Prices:** $160 to $250. **Remarks:** Spare-time maker; first knife sold in 1981. Makes only a few knives each year. **Mark:** First name, middle initial, last name, knife maker, city, state.

ELLIS, WILLY B, Willy B Custom Sticks & Picks, 79 Derry Rd, Methuen, MA 01844 5605, Phone: 978-688-2785, Fax:SAME

ELLIS, WILLIAM DEAN, 8875 N. Barton, Fresno, CA 93720, Phone: 209-299-0303
Specialties: Classic and fancy knives of his design. **Patterns:** Boots, fighters and utility knives. **Technical:** Grinds ATS-34, D2 and Damascus. Offers tapered tangs and six patterns of filework; tooled multi-colored sheaths. **Prices:** $180 to $350; some to $1,300. **Remarks:** Part-time maker; first knife sold in 1991. Doing business as Billy's Blades. **Mark:** "B" in a five-point star next to "Billy," city and state within a rounded-corner rectangle.

ELLIS, DAVE/ABS MASTORSMITH, 3505 Camino Del Rio So Ste 334, San Diego, CA 92108, Phone: (619) 285-1305 Eves:(760) 945-7177, Fax:(619) 285-1326
Specialties: Bowies, utility & combat knives. **Patterns:** Using knives to art quality pieces. **Technical:** Forges 5160, L-6, 52100, cable and my own Damascus steels. **Prices:** $300 to $4,000. **Remarks:** Part-time maker. California's first ABS, Mastersmith. **Mark:** Dagger-Rose with name & M. S. mark.

ELLIS, ABS, MASTERSMITH, DAVID, 3505 Camino Del Rio S., #334, San Diego, CA 92108, Phone: 619-285-1305 days, Fax:760-945-7177 evenings
Specialties: Fighters and Bowies. **Patterns:** Utility knives. **Technical:** Forges and grinds 5160, O1, 1095; now working with pattern-welded Damascus. Most knives have hand-rubbed finish and single and double temper lines. Most knives are double or triple hardened and triple drawn. Prefers natural handle materials. **Prices:** $300 to $2,000; some to $5,000. **Remarks:** Part-time maker; first knife sold in 1988. "California's First ABS Mastersmith. " **Mark:** Last name with dagger and rose below & M. S. mark. **Other:** ABS-Mastersmith.

ELROD, ROGER R, RT 3 Box 353, Enterprise, AL 36330, Phone: (334) 347-1863

EMBRETSEN, KAJ, Faluvagen 67, S-82821 Edsbyn, SWEDEN, Phone: 46-271-21057, Fax:46-271-22961
Specialties: High quality folders. **Patterns:** Scandinavian style knives. **Technical:** Forges Damascus. Uses only his blades; natural materials. **Prices:** Upscale. **Remarks:** Full-time maker. **Mark:** Name.

EMERSON, ERNEST R., PO Box 4180, Torrance, CA 90510-4180
Specialties: High-tech folders and combat fighters. **Patterns:** Fighters, liner lock combat folders and SPECWAR combat knives. **Technical:** Grinds ATS-34 and D2. Makes folders with titanium fittings, liners and locks. Chisel grind specialist. **Prices:** $275 to $475; some to $3,000. **Remarks:** Full-time maker; first knife sold in 1983. **Mark:** Last name and Specwar knives.

ENCE, JIM, 145 S 200 East, Richfield, UT 84701, Phone: 435-896-6206
Specialties: High-art period pieces (spec in California knives) art knives. **Patterns:** Art, boot knives, fighters, bowies and occasional folders. **Technical:** Grinds 440C for polish & beauty boys'; makes own Damascus. **Prices:** Upscale. **Remarks:** Full-time maker; first knife sold in 1977. Does

own engraving, gold work & stone work. **Mark:** Ence, usually engraved. **Other:** Guild member since 1977. Founding member of the AKI.

ENGLAND, VIRGIL, 7133 Arctic Blvd #5, Anchorage, AK 99518, Phone: 907-274-9494
Specialties: Edged weapons and equipage, one of a kind only. **Patterns:** Axes, swords, lances and body armor. **Technical:** Forges and grinds as pieces dictate. Offers stainless and Damascus. **Prices:** Upscale. **Remarks:** A veteran knife maker. No commissions. **Mark:** Stylized initials.

ENGLE, WILLIAM, 16608 Oak Ridge Rd., Boonville, MO 65233, Phone: 816-882-6277
Specialties: Traditional working and using straight knives of his design. **Patterns:** Hunters, Bowies and fighters. **Technical:** Grinds 440C, ATS-34 and 154 CM. **Prices:** $250 to $500; some higher. **Remarks:** Part-time maker; first knife sold in 1982. All knives come with certificate of authenticity. **Mark:** Last name in block lettering.

ENGLEBRETSON, GEORGE, 1209 NW 49th St., Oklahoma City, OK 73118, Phone: 405-840-4784
Specialties: Working straight knives. **Patterns:** Hunters and Bowies. **Technical:** Grinds A2, D2, 440C and ATS-34. **Prices:** Start at $150. **Remarks:** Full-time maker; first knife sold in 1967. **Mark:** "By George," name and city.

ENGLISH, JIM, 14586 Olive Vista Dr., Jamul, CA 91935, Phone: 619-669-0833
Specialties: Traditional working straight knives to customer specs. **Patterns:** Hunters, Bowies, fighters, tantos, daggers, boot and utility/camp knives. **Technical:** Grinds 440C, ATS-34, commercial Damascus and customer choice. **Prices:** $130 to $350. **Remarks:** Part-time maker; first knife sold in 1985. In addition to custom line, also does business as Mountain Home Knives. **Mark:** Double "A," Double "J" logo.

ENNIS, RAY, 1220S 775E, Ogden, UT 84404, Phone: 800-410-7603, Fax:501-621-2683

ENOS III, THOMAS M, 12302 State Rd 535, Orlando, FL 32836, Phone: 407-239-6205
Specialties: Heavy-duty working straight knives; unusual designs. **Patterns:** Swords, machetes, daggers, skinners, filleting, period pieces. **Technical:** Grinds 440C, D2, 154CM. **Prices:** $75 to $1,500. **Remarks:** Full-time maker; first knife sold in 1972. **Mark:** Name in knife logo and year, type of steel and serial number. **Other:** No longer accepting custom requests. Will be making my own designs. Send SASE for listing of items for sale.

ENTIN, ROBERT, 127 Pembroke Street 1, Boston, MA 02118

EPTING, RICHARD, 4021 Cody Dr, College Station, TX 77845, Phone: 979-690-6496
Specialties: Folders and working straight knives. **Patterns:** Hunters, bowies, and locking folders. **Technical:** Forges high-carbon steel and his own damascus. **Prices:** $200 to $800; some to $1800. **Remarks:** Part-time maker, first knife sold 1996. **Mark:** Name in arch logo.

ERICKSON, L. M., P. O. Box 132, Liberty, UT 84310, Phone: 801-745-2026
Specialties: Straight knives; period pieces. **Patterns:** Bowies, fighters, boots and hunters. **Technical:** Grinds 440C, 154CM and commercial Damascus. **Prices:** $200 to $900; some to $5,000. **Remarks:** Part-time maker; first knife sold in 1981. **Mark:** Name, city, state.

ERICKSON, WALTER E., 22280 Shelton Tr, Atlanta, MI 49709, Phone: 989-785-5262
Specialties: Unusual survival knives and high-tech working knives. **Patterns:** Butterflies, hunters, tantos. **Technical:** Grinds ATS-34 or customer choice. **Prices:** $150 to $500; some to $1,500. **Remarks:** Full-time maker; first knife sold in 1981. **Mark:** Last name in depressed area on blade.

ERIKSEN, JAMES THORLIEF, dba Viking Knives, 3830 Dividend Dr, Garland, TX 75042, Phone: 972-494-3667, Fax:972-235-4932
Specialties: Heavy-duty working and using straight knives and folders utilizing traditional, Viking original and customer specification patterns. Some high-tech and fancy/embellished knives available. **Patterns:** Bowies, hunters, skinners, boot and belt knives, utility/camp knives, fighters, daggers, locking folders, slip-joint folders and kitchen knives. **Technical:** Hollow-grinds 440C, D2, ASP-23, ATS-34, 154CM, Vascowear. **Prices:** $150 to $300; some to $600. **Remarks:** Full-time maker; first knife sold in 1985. Doing business as Viking Knives. For a color catalog showing 50 different models, mail $5 to above address. **Mark:** VIKING or VIKING USA for export.

ESSEGIAN, RICHARD, 7387 E. Tulare St., Fresno, CA 93727, Phone: 309-255-5950
Specialties: Fancy working knives of his design; art knives. **Patterns:** Bowies and some small hunters. **Technical:** Grinds A2, D2, 440C and 154CM. Engraves and inlays. **Prices:** Start at $600. **Remarks:** Part-time maker; first knife sold in 1986. **Mark:** Last name, city and state.

ESSMAN, JUSTUS P, 201 Rialto Way Ne, St Petersburg, FL 33704, Phone: (727) 894-5327

ETZLER, JOHN, 11200 N. Island, Grafton, OH 44044, Phone: 440-748-2460
Specialties: High-art and fantasy straight knives and folders of his design and to customer specs. **Patterns:** Folders, daggers, fighters, utility knives. **Technical:** Forges and grinds nickel Damascus and tool steel; grinds stainless steels. Prefers exotic, natural materials. **Prices:** $250 to $1200; some to $6,500. **Remarks:** Full-time maker; first knife sold in 1992. **Mark:** Name or initials.

EVANS, RONALD B, 209 Hoffer St, Middleton, PA 17057-2723, Phone: (717) 944-5464

EVANS, CARLTON, P. O. Box 815, Aledo, TX 76008, Phone: 817-441-1363
Specialties: Fancy and working liner locks, full and narrow tang knives, slip-joint folders and locking folders. **Patterns:** Hunters, fighters, tactical and working straight knives. **Technical:** Use the stock removal method. Fancy file work on some knives. The materials I use are of the highest quality like O1, D2, ATS 34, 154 Cm and Damascus steel. Paul Bos heat treats my blades. **Prices:** Start at $200. **Remarks:** I made my first knife in 1967 (Slip-joint folder). Sold my first knife in 1970. I am a part time knife-maker.

EVANS, BRUCE A, 409 CR 1371, Booneville, MS 38829, Phone: (662) 720-0193
Specialties: Forges blades. **Patterns:** Hunters, Bowies, or will work with customer. **Technical:** 5160, cable Damascus, pattern welded Damascus. **Prices:** $100 and up. **Mark:** Bruce A. Evans.

EVANS, VINCENT K. & GRACE, 6301 Apache Trail, Show Low, AZ 85901, Phone: 928-537-9123
Specialties: Working straight knives; period pieces; swords. **Patterns:** Scottish and central Asian patterns; bowies, hunters. **Technical:** Forges 5160 and his own Damascus. **Prices:** $100 to $1,000; some to $5,000. **Remarks:** Full-time maker; first knife sold in 1983. **Mark:** Last initial with fish logo.

EWING, WYMAN, 55 Robertson Rd, Pueblo, CO 81001, Phone: (719) 544-9275

EWING, JOHN H., 3276 Dutch Valley Rd., Clinton, TN 37716, Phone: 615-457-5757
Specialties: Working straight knives, hunters, camp knives. **Patterns:** Hunters. **Technical:** Grinds 440, Forges 5160 52100; prefers forging. **Prices:** $150 to $2,000. **Remarks:** Part-time maker; first knife sold in 1985. **Mark:** First initial, last name, some embellishing done on knives.

EXTREME RATIO S. A. S, Mauro Chiostri / Maurizio Castrati, Viale Montegrappa 298, 59100 Prato, ITALY, Phone: 0039 0574 58 46 39, Fax:0039 0574 58 13 12
Specialties: Tactical/military knives and sheaths, blades and sheaths to customer's specs. **Patterns** Tactical fixed blade knives and folders. **Technical:** Grinds stainless cobalt steel. Coatings: Glass-beated, black polymorphic, striped. Handles in CFP, with scales made of high seizure pads. Tactical sheaths with double retention system and multiple anchorage points. **Prices:** $140 to $350. **Remarks:** Full-time maker; first knife sold in 1998. **Mark:** Name of company, steel and knife.

f

FAGAN, JAMES A, 109 S 17 Ave, Lake Worth, FL 33460, Phone: (561) 585-9349

FANT JR, GEORGE, 1983 CR 3214, Atlanta, TX 75551-6515, Phone: (903) 846-2938

FARID R., MEHR, 8 Sidney Close, Tunbridge Wells, Kent, ENGLAND TN2 5QQ, Phone: 011-44-1892 520345
Specialties: High-tech titanium folders. **Patterns:** Chisel ground liner lock and integral mechanism folders. **Technical:** Grinds modified 440C, CPM-T-440V, CPM-420V, CPM-15V and T-1 high speed steel and Vasco-max alloy and tool steel. **Prices:** $525 to $15,000. **Remarks:** Full-time maker; first knife sold in 1991. **Mark:** First name and country.

FARR, DAN, 285 Glen Ellyn Way, Rochester, NY 14618, Phone: 585-721-1388
Specialties: Hunting, camping, fighting & utility. **Patterns:** Fixed blades. **Technical:** Forged or stock removal. **Prices:** $150-$750.

FASSIO, MELVIN G., 420 Tyler Way, Lobo, MT 59847, Phone: 406-273-9143
Specialties: Working folders to customer specs. **Patterns:** Locking folders, hunters and traditional-style knives. **Technical:** Grinds 440C. **Prices:**

$125 to $350. **Remarks:** Part-time maker; first knife sold in 1975. **Mark:** Name and city, dove logo.

FAUCHEAUX, HOWARD J., P. O. Box 206, Loreauville, LA 70552, Phone: 318-229-6467
Specialties: Working straight knives and folders; period pieces. Also a hatchet with capping knife in the handle. **Patterns:** Traditional locking folders, hunters, fighters and Bowies. **Technical:** Forges W2, 1095 and his own Damascus; stock removal D2. **Prices:** Start at $200. **Remarks:** Full-time maker; first knife sold in 1969. **Mark:** Last name.

FAUST, JOACHIM, Kirchgasse 10, 95497 Goldkronach, GERMANY

FAUST, DICK, 624 Kings Hwy N, Rochester, NY 14617, Phone: 716-544-1948
Specialties: High performance working straight knives. **Patterns:** Hunters and utility/camp knives. **Technical:** Hollow grinds ATS-34, full tang. Exotic woods, stag and Micarta handles. Provides a custom leather sheath with each knife. **Prices:** From $100 to $500, some higher. **Remarks:** Full-time maker. **Mark:** Signature.

FECAS, STEPHEN J., 1312 Shadow Lane, Anderson, SC 29625, Phone: 864-287-4834, Fax:864-287-4834
Specialties: Front release lock backs, liner locks. Folders only. **Patterns:** Gents folders. **Technical:** Grinds ATS-34, Damascus-Ivories and pearl handles. **Prices:** $650 to $1200. **Remarks:** Full-time maker since 1980. First knife sold in 1977. **Mark:**Last name signature. **Other:** All knives hand finished to 1500 grit.

FEIGIN, B, Liir Corp, 3037 Holly Mill Run, Marietta, GA 30062, Phone: 770-579-1631, Fax:770-579-1199

FELIX, ALEXANDER, PO Box 4036, Torrance, CA 90510, Phone: (310) 891-0825
Specialties: Straight working knives, fancy ethnic designs. **Patterns:** Hunters, Bowies, daggers, period pieces. **Technical:** Carbon steel & Damascus; forged stainless & titanium jewelry, gold & silver casting. **Prices:** $110 & up. **Remarks:** Jeweler, part-time maker. **Mark:** Signature.

FELLOWS, MIKE, PO Box 166, Velddrie 7365, SOUTH AFRICA, Phone: 27 82 960 3868
Specialties: Miniatures, art knives, subhilt fighters and folders. **Patterns:** Original designs & client's specs. **Technical:** I use my own Damascus (L6 and nickel). **Other:** All my knives carry strong, reliable thru-tang handles screwed & bonded together. I use only indigenous materials for handles, i. e., various hard woods, selected horns, ivory, warthog tusk, hippo tooth, etc. Love to carve animal heads; my favorite-Roses. **Mark:** "Shin" letter from Hebrew alphabet in front of Hebrew word "Karat". **Prices:** R800 - R5500 ($100 to $700, + or -).

FERDINAND, DON, P. O. Box 1564, Shady Cove, OR 97539-1564, Phone: 503-560-3355
Specialties: One-of-a-kind working knives and period pieces; all tool steel Damascus. **Patterns:** Bowies, push knives and fishing knives. **Technical:** Forges high-carbon alloy steels L6, D2; makes his own Damascus. Exotic handle materials offered. **Prices:** $100 to $500. **Remarks:** Full-time maker since 1980. Does business as Wyvern. **Mark:** Initials connected.

FERGUSON, JIM, 32131 Via Bande, Temecula, CA 92592, Phone: 909-719-1552
Specialties: Nickel Damascus - Bowies - Daggers - Push Blades. **Patterns:** All styles. **Technical:** Forges Damascus & sells in US and Canada. **Prices:** $120 to $5,000. **Remarks:** 1200 Sq. Ft. commercial shop - 75 ton press. **Mark:** Jim Ferguson over push blade. Also make swords, battle axes & utilities.

FERGUSON, LEE, Rt. 2, Box 109, Hindsville, AR 72738, Phone: 501-443-0084
Specialties: Straight working knives and folders, some fancy. **Patterns:** Hunters, daggers, swords, locking folders and slip-joints. **Technical:** Grinds D2, 440C and ATS-34; heat-treats. **Prices:** $50 to $600; some to $4,000. **Remarks:** Part-time maker; first knife sold in 1977. **Mark:** Last name.

FERGUSON, JIM, P. O. Box 764, San Angelo, TX 76902, Phone: 915-651-6656
Specialties: Straight working knives and folders. **Patterns:** Working belt knives, hunters, Bowies and some folders. **Technical:** Grinds ATS-34, D2 and Vascowear. Flat-grinds hunting knives. **Prices:** $200 to $600; some to $1,000. **Remarks:** Full-time maker; first knife sold in 1987. **Mark:** First and middle initials, last name.

FERRARA, THOMAS, 122 Madison Dr., Naples, FL 33942, Phone: 813-597-3363, Fax:813-597-3363
Specialties: High-art, traditional and working straight knives and folders of all designs. **Patterns:** Boots, Bowies, daggers, fighters and hunters. **Technical:** Grinds 440C, D2 and ATS-34; heat-treats. **Prices:** $100 to $700; some to $1300. **Remarks:** Part-time maker; first knife sold in 1983. **Mark:** Last name.

custom knifemakers

FERRIER, GREGORY K, 3119 SIMPSON DR, RAPID CITY, SD 57702, Phone: (605) 342-9280

FERRIS, BILL, 186 Thornton Dr, Palm Beach Garden, FL 33418

FERRY, TOM, 16005 SE 322nd St, Auburn, WA 98092, Phone: 253-939-4468
Specialties: Damascus, fixed blades and folders. **Patterns:** Folders Damascus, and fixed blades. **Technical:** Specialize in Damascus and timascus™(Titanium Damascus). **Prices:** $400 to $2000. **Remarks:** Name Tom Ferry DBA: Soos Creek Ironworks. Mark: Combined T & F in a circle and / or last name on folders. Other: Co-developer of Timascus TM (Titanium Damascus).

FIKES, JIMMY L., P. O. Box 3457, Jasper, AL 35502, Phone: 205-387-9302, Fax:205-221-1980
Specialties: High-art working knives; artifact knives; using knives with cord-wrapped handles; swords and combat weapons. **Patterns:** Axes to buckskinners, camp knives to miniatures, tantos to tomahawks; spring less folders. **Technical:** Forges W2, O1 and his own Damascus. **Prices:** $135 to $3000; exceptional knives to $7000. **Remarks:** Full-time maker. **Mark:** Stylized initials.

FILIPPOU, IOANNIS-MINAS, 7 Krinis Str Nea Smyrni, Athens 17122, GREECE, Phone: (1) 935-2093

FINCH, RICKY D., 2446 HWY 191, West Liberty, KY 41472, Phone: 606-743-7151
Specialties: Traditional working/using straight knives of his design or to customer spec. **Patterns:** Hunters, skinners & utility/camp knives. **Technical:** Grinds 440C & ATS-34, hand rubbed stain finish, use Micarta, stag, stabilized wood - natural & exotic. **Prices:** $55 to $175; some $250. **Remarks:** Part-time maker, first knife made 1994. Doing business as Finch Knives. **Mark:** Last name inside outline of state of Kentucky.

FIORINI, BILL, 390 North St, PO Box 237, Dakota, MN 55925-0237, Phone: 507-643-7946
Specialties: Fancy working knives and lockbacks. **Patterns:** Hunters, boots, Japanese-style knives and kitchen/utility knives. **Technical:** Forges own Damascus. **Prices:** Full range. **Remarks:** Full-time metal smith researching pattern materials. **Mark:** Orchid crest with name KOKA in Japanese.

FISHER, THEO (TED), 8115 Modoc Lane, Montague, CA 96064, Phone: 916-459-3804
Specialties: Moderately priced working knives in carbon steel. **Patterns:** Hunters, fighters, kitchen and buckskinner knives, Damascus miniatures. **Technical:** Grinds ATS-34, L6 and 440C. **Prices:** $65 to $165; exceptional knives to $300. **Remarks:** First knife sold in 1981. **Mark:** Name in banner logo.

FISHER, JAY, 104 S Main St., P. O. Box 267, Magdalena, NM 87825, Phone: (505) 854-2118
Specialties: High-art, ancient and exact working and using straight knives of his design and client's designs. Military working and commemoratives. **Patterns:** Hunters, daggers, folding knives, museum pieces and high-art sculptures. **Technical:** Grinds 440C, ATS-34, 01and D2. Prolific maker of stone-handled knives and swords. **Prices:** $250 to $50,000; some higher. **Remarks:** Full-time maker; first knife sold in 1980. **Mark:** Very fine--JaFisher--Quality Custom Knives. **Other:** High resolution etching, computer and manual engraving.

FISK, JERRY, 145 N Park Ave, Lockesburg, AR 71846, Phone: 870-289-3240
Specialties: Edged weapons, collectible and functional. **Patterns:** Bowies, daggers, swords, hunters, camp knives and others. **Technical:** Forges carbon steels and his own pattern welded steels. **Prices:** $250 to $15,000. **Remarks:** National living treasure. **Mark:** Name, MS.

FISTER, JIM, 5067 Fisherville Rd., Simpsonville, KY 40067, Phone: 502-834-7841
Specialties: One of a kind collectibles and period pieces. **Patterns:** Bowies, camp knives, hunters, buckskinners, and daggers. **Technical:** Forges, 1085, 5160, 52100, his own Damascus, pattern and turkish. **Prices:** $150 to $2,500. **Remarks:** Part-time maker; first knife sold in 1982. **Mark:** Name & MS.

FITCH, JOHN S, 45 Halbrook Rd, Clinton, AR 72031-8910, Phone: (501) 893-2020

FITZGERALD, DENNIS M., 4219 Alverado Dr., Fort Wayne, IN 46816-2847, Phone: 219-447-1081
Specialties: One of a kind collectibles and period pieces. **Patterns:** Skinners, fighters, camp and utility knives; period pieces. **Technical:** Forges 1085, 1095, L6, 5160, 52100, his own pattern and Turkish Damascus. **Prices:** $100 to $500. **Remarks:** Part-time maker; first knife sold in 1985. Doing business as The Ringing Circle. **Mark:** Name and circle logo.

FLETCHER, MICHAEL J, 7415 E 77th St, Tulsa, OK 74133-3536, Phone: (918) 252-7816

FLINT, ROBERT, 2902 Aspen Dr, Anchorage, AK 99517, Phone: 907-243-6706
Specialties: Working straight knives and folders. **Patterns:** Utility, hunters, fighters and gents. **Technical:** Grinds ATS-34, BG-42, D2 and Damascus. **Prices:** $150 and up. **Remarks:** Part-time maker, first knife sold in 1998. **Mark:** Last name; stylized initials.

FLORES, HENRY, 1000 Kiely Blvd #115, Santa Clara, CA 95051-4819, Phone: (408) 246-0491

FLOURNOY, JOE, 5750 Lisbon Rd., El Dorado, AR 71730, Phone: 870-863-7208
Specialties: Working straight knives and folders. **Patterns:** Hunters, Bowies, camp knives, folders and daggers. **Technical:** Forges only high-carbon steel, steel cable and his own Damascus. **Prices:**$350 Plus. **Remarks:** First knife sold in 1977. **Mark:** Last name and MS in script.

FOGARIZZU, BOITEDDU, via Crispi, 6, 07016 Pattada, ITALY
Specialties: Traditional Italian straight knives and folders. **Patterns:** Collectible folders. **Technical:** forges and grinds 12C27, ATS-34 and his Damascus. **Prices:** $200 to $3,000. **Remarks:** Full-time maker; first knife sold in 1958. **Mark:** Full name and registered logo.

FOGG, DON, 40 Alma Road, Jasper, AL 35501-8813, Phone: 205-483-0822
Specialties: Swords, daggers, Bowies and hunting knives. **Patterns:** Collectible folders. **Technical:** Hand forged high carbon & Damascus steel. **Prices:** $200 to $5,000. **Remarks:** Full-time maker; first knife sold in 1976. **Mark:** 24K gold cherry blossom.

FONTENOT, GERALD J, 901 Maple Av, Mamou, LA 70554, Phone: (318) 468-3180

FORREST, BRIAN, Forrest Knives, PO Box 203, Descanso, CA 91916, Phone: 619-445-6343
Specialties: Working straight knives, some fancy made to customer order. **Patterns:** Traditional patterns, Bowies, hunters, skinners & daggers. **Technical:** Grinds 440C, files & rasps. **Prices:** $125 & up. **Remarks:** Member of California Knife maker Association. Full-time maker. First knife sold in 1971. **Mark:** Forrest USA.

FORSTALL, AL, 38379 Aunt Massey Rd, Pearl River, LA 70452, Phone: 504-863-2930
Specialties: Traditional working and using straight knives of his design or to customer specs. **Patterns:** Fighters, hunters and utility/camp knives. **Technical:** Grinds ATS-34, 440C, commercial Damascus and others upon request. **Prices:** $75 to $250. **Remarks:** Spare-time maker; first knife sold in 1991. **Mark:** Fleur Di Lis with name.

FORTHOFER, PETE, 5535 Hwy. 93S, Whitefish, MT 59937, Phone: 406-862-2674
Specialties: Interframes with checkered wood inlays; working straight knives. **Patterns:** Interframe folders and traditional-style knives; hunters, fighters and Bowies. **Technical:** Grinds D2, 440C, 154CM and ATS-34. **Prices:** $350 to $2,500; some to $1,500. **Remarks:** Part-time maker; full-time gunsmith. First knife sold in 1979. **Mark:** Name and logo.

FORTUNE PRODUCTS, INC., 205 Hickory Creek Rd, Marble Falls, TX 78654, Phone: 830-693-6111, Fax:830-693-6394
Specialties: Knife sharpeners.

FOSTER, NORVELL C, 619 Holmgreen Rd, San Antonio, TX 78220, Phone: (210) 333-1675
Specialties: Engraving; ivory handle carving. **Patterns:** American-large and small scroll-oak leaf and acorns. **Prices:** $25 to $400. **Mark:** N. C. Foster - S. A., TX & current year.

FOSTER, AL, 118 Woodway Dr, Magnolia, TX 77355, Phone: 936-372-9297
Specialties: Straight knives and folders. **Patterns:** Hunting, fishing, folders & bowies. **Technical:** Grinds 440-C, ATS-34 & D2. **Prices:** $100 to $1,000. **Remarks:** Full time maker; first knife sold in 1981. **Mark:** Scorpion logo & name.

FOSTER, R. L. (BOB), 745 Glendale Blvd., Mansfield, OH 44907

FOSTER, RONNIE E, 95 Riverview Rd, Morrilton, AR 72110, Phone: (501) 354-5389

FOSTER, TIMOTHY L, 723 Sweet Gum Acres Rd, El Dorado, AR 71730, Phone: (870) 863-6188

FOWLER, JERRY, 610 FM 1660 N., Hutto, TX 78634, Phone: 512-846-2860
Specialties: Using straight knives of his design. **Patterns:** A variety of hunting and camp knives, combat knives. Custom designs considered. **Technical:** Forges 5160, his own Damascus and cable Damascus. Makes sheaths. Prefers natural handle materials. **Prices:** Start at $150. **Remarks:** Part-time maker; first knife sold in 1986. Doing business as Fowler Forge Knife works. **Mark:** First initial, last name, date and J. S.

FOWLER, RICKY & SUSAN, Fowler Custom Knives, PO Box 339, 22080 9th St, Silverhill, AL 36576, Phone: 334-945-3289, Fax:334-945-3290
Specialties: Traditional working/using straight knives of his design or to customer specifications. **Patterns:** Skinners, fighters, tantos, bowies and utility/camp knives. **Technical:** Grinds O1, ATS-34, 440C, D2, A2 & commercial damascus. Forges 5160, Damascus, & other steels. **Prices:** Start at $150. **Remarks:** Full-time maker; first knife sold in 1994. Doing business as Fowler Custom Knives. **Mark:** Last name tang stamped & serial numbered.

FOWLER, ED A., Willow Bow Ranch, P. O. Box 1519, Riverton, WY 82501, Phone: 307-856-9815
Specialties: Height performance working and using straight knives. **Patterns:** Hunter, Camp, Bird, and Trout knives and Bowies. New model the gentleman's Pronghorn. **Technical:** Forges 52100 multiple quench heat treating, engraves all knives, all handles domestic sheep horn processed and aged at least 5 years. Makes heavy duty hand stitched waxed harness leather pouch type sheathes. **Prices:** $800-$6000. **Remarks:** Full-time maker. First knife sold in 1962. **Mark:** Initials connected.

FOWLER, CHARLES R, 226 National Forest Rd 48, Ft McCoy, FL 32134-9624, Phone: (904) 467-3215

FOX, JACK L., 7085 Canelo Hills Dr., Citrus Heights, CA 95610, Phone: 916-723-8647
Specialties: Traditional working/using straight knives of all designs. **Patterns:** Hunters, utility/camp knives and bird/fish knives. **Technical:** Grinds ATS-34, 440C and D2. **Prices:** $125 to $225; some to $350. **Remarks:** Spare-time maker; first knife sold in 1985. Doing business as Fox Knives. **Mark:** Stylized fox head.

FOX, PAUL, 4721 Rock Barn Road, Claremont, NC 28610, Phone: 828-459-2000, Fax:828-459-9200
Specialties: Hi-Tech. **Patterns:** Naibsek, Otnat, & Zorro (tactical) knives. **Technical:** Grinds ATS-34, 440C and D2. **Prices:** $500. **Remarks:** Spare-time maker; first knife sold in 1985. Doing business as Fox Knives. **Mark:** Laser engraved.

FOX, WENDELL, 1480 S 39th St, Springfield, OR 97478, Phone: 541-747-2126
Specialties: Large camping knives and friction folders of his design and to customer specs. **Patterns:** Hunters, locking folders, slip-joint folders and utility/camp knives. **Technical:** Forges and grinds high carbon steel only. **Prices:**$200 and up. **Remarks:** Full-time maker; first knife sold in 1952. **Mark:** Stamped name or logo. **Other:** All one-of-a-kind pieces. Specializing in early American.

FRALEY, D B, 1355 Fairbanks Ct, Dixon, CA 95620, Phone: 707-678-0393
Specialties: Traditional working/using straight knives and folders of his design and in standard patterns. **Patterns:** Fighters, hunters, utility/camp knives. **Technical:** Grinds ATS-34. Offers hand-stitched sheaths. **Prices:** Start at $100. **Remarks:** Part-time maker; first knife sold in 1990. **Mark:** First and middle initials, last name over buffalo.

FRAMSKI, WALTER P, 24 Rek Lane, Prospect, CT 06712, Phone: (203) 758-5634

FRANCE, DAN, Box 218, Cawood, KY 40815, Phone: 606-573-6104
Specialties: Traditional working and using straight knives of his design. **Patterns:** Hunters, Bowies and utility/camp knives. **Technical:** forges and grinds O1, 5160 and L6. **Prices:** $35 to $125; some to $350. **Remarks:** Spare-time maker; first knife sold in 1985. **Mark:** First name.

FRANCIS, VANCE, 2612 Alpine Blvd., Alpine, CA 91901, Phone: 619-445-0979
Specialties: Working straight knives. **Patterns:** Bowies and utility knives. **Technical:** Uses ATS-34, A2, D2 and Damascus; differentially tempers large blades. **Prices:** $175 to $600. **Remarks:** Part-time maker. **Mark:** First name, last name, city and state under feather in oval.

FRANK, HEINRICH H., 13868 NW Keleka Pl., Seal Rock, OR 97376, Phone: 541-563-3041, Fax:541-563-3041
Specialties: High-art investor-class folders, handmade and engraved. **Patterns:** Folding daggers, hunter-size folders and gents. **Technical:** Grinds 07 and O1. **Prices:** $4,800 to $16,000. **Remarks:** Full-time maker; first knife sold in 1965. Doing business as H. H. Frank Knives. **Mark:** Name, address and date.

FRANKL, JOHN M, 12 Holden St, CAMBRIDGE, MA 02138, Phone: 617-547-0359
Specialties: Hand forged tool steel and Damascus. **Patterns:** Camp knives, bowies, hunters and fighters. **Technical:** Forge own Damascus, 5160 and V 1084. **Prices:** $150-$1000. **Mark:** Last name "Frankl" on ricasso.

FRANKLAND, ANDREW, P. O. Box 256, Wilderness 6560, SOUTH AFRICA, Phone: 044-877-0260, Fax:044-877-0260
Specialties: Classic working and using straight knives and folders of his design and to customer specs. **Patterns:** Daggers, fighters, hunters and

utility/camp knives. **Technical:** Grinds 440C, D2 and ATS-34. All double-edge knives have broad spine. **Prices:** $250 to $400; some to $1,500. **Remarks:** full-time maker; first knife sold in 1979. **Mark:** Last name surrounded by mountain, lake, forest scene.

FRANKLIN, MIKE, 9878 Big Run Rd., Aberdeen, OH 45101, Phone: 937-549-2598
Specialties: High-tech tactical folders. **Patterns:** Tactical folders. **Technical:** Grinds CPM-T-440V, 440-C, ATS-34; titanium liners and bolsters; carbon fiber scales. Uses radical grinds and severe serrations. **Prices:** $275 to $600. **Remarks:** Full-time maker; first knife sold in 1969. **Mark:** Stylized boar with HAWG.

FRAPS, JOHN, 3810 Wyandotte Trail, Indianapolis, IN 46240-3422, Phone: 317-849-9419, Fax:317-842-2224
Specialties: Working and Collector Grade liner lock and slip joint folders. **Patterns:** Liner lock foldersand slip joint folders. **Technical:** Flat and hollow grinds ATS-34, Damascus, Talonite, CPM S30V, 154Cm, Stellite 6K; hand rubbed or mirror finish. **Prices:** Start at $175. **Remarks:** Full-time maker; first knife sold in 1997. **Mark:** Cougar Creek Knives and/or name.

FRAZIER, RON, 2107 Urbine Rd., Powhatan, VA 23139, Phone: 804-794-8561
Specialties: Classy working knives of his design; some high-art straight knives. **Patterns:** Wide assortment of straight knives, including miniatures and push knives. **Technical:** Grinds 440C; offers satin, mirror or sand finishes. **Prices:** $85 to $700; some to $3,000. **Remarks:** Full-time maker; first knife sold in 1976. **Mark:** Name in arch logo.

FRED, REED WYLE, 3149 X Street, Sacramento, CA 95817, Phone: 916-739-0237
Specialties: Working using straight knives of his design. **Patterns:** Hunting and camp knives. **Technical:** Forges any 10 series, old files and carbon steels. Offers initialing upon request; prefers natural handle materials. **Prices:** $30 to $300; some to $300. **Remarks:** Part-time maker; first knife sold in 1994. Doing business as R. W. Fred Knife maker. **Mark:** Engraved first and last initials.

FREDERICK, AARON, 1213 Liberty Rd, West Liberty, KY 41472, Phone: 606-743-3399

FREEMAN, JOHN, 160 Concession St., Cambridge, Ont., CANADA N1R 2H7, Phone: 519-740-2767, Fax:519-740-2785
Specialties: Working straight knives. **Patterns:** Hunters, skinners, utilities, backpackers. **Technical:** Grinds 440C and ATS-34. **Prices:** Start at $125. **Remarks:** Full-time maker; first knife sold in 1985. **Mark:** Last name, country, Handmade.

FREER, RALPH, 114 12th St, Seal Beach, CA 90740, Phone: 562-493-4925, Fax:same
Specialties: Exotic folders, liner locks, folding daggers, fixed blades. **Patters:** All original. **Technical:** Lots of Damascus, ivory, pearl, jeweled, thumb studs, carving ATS-34, 420V, 530V. **Prices:** $400-$2500 and up. **Mark:** Freer in German style text, also freer shield.

FREILING, ALBERT J., 3700 Niner Rd., Finksburg, MD 21048, Phone: 301-795-2880
Specialties: Working straight knives and folders; some period pieces. **Patterns:** Boots, Bowies, survival knives and tomahawks in 4130 and 440C; some locking folders and interframes; ball-bearing folders. **Technical:** Grinds O1, 440C and 154CM. **Prices:** $100 to $300; some to $500. **Remarks:** Part-time maker; first knife sold in 1966. **Mark:** Initials connected.

FREY, STEVE, 19103 131st Drive SE, Snohomish, WA 98296, Phone: 360-668-7351

FREY JR., W. FREDERICK, 305 Walnut St., Milton, PA 17847, Phone: 570-742-9576
Specialties: Working straight knives and folders, some fancy. **Patterns:** Wide range--boot knives to tomahawks. **Technical:** Grinds A2, O1 and D2; hand finishes only. **Prices:** $55 to $170; some to $600. **Remarks:** Spare-time maker; first knife sold in 1983. **Mark:** Last name in script.

FRIEDLY, DENNIS E., 12 Cottontail Ln. - E, Cody, WY 82414, Phone: 307-527-6811
Specialties: Fancy working straight knives and daggers, lock back folders and liner locks. **Patterns:** Hunters, fighters, short swords, minis and miniatures; new line of full-tang hunters/boots. **Technical:** Grinds 440C, commercial Damascus, mosaic damascus and ATS-34 blades; prefers hidden tangs. **Prices:** $135 to $900; some to $2,500. **Remarks:** Full-time maker; first knife sold in 1972. **Mark:** Name, city, state.

FRIGAULT, RICK, 3584 Rapidsview Dr, Niagara Falls ON, CANADA L2G 6C4, Phone: (905) 295-6695
Specialties: Fixed blades. **Patterns:** Hunting, tactical & large Bowies. **Technical:** Grinds ATS-34, 440-C, D-2 & Damascus. Use G-10, Micarta, ivory, antler, ironwood & other stabilized woods for handle material. Makes leather sheaths by hand. Tactical blades made by a Concealex sheath made by "On Scene Tactical". **Remarks:** Sold first knife in 1997. Member of Canadian Knifemakers Guild. **Mark:** RFRIGAULT.

custom knifemakers

FRITZ, JESSE, 900 S. 13th St, Slaton, TX 79364, Phone: 806-828-5083, Fax:915-530-0508
Specialties: Working and using straight knives in standard patterns. **Patterns:** Hunters, utility/camp knives and skinners with gut hook. **Technical:** Grinds 440C, O1 and 1095. Fline-napped steel design, blued blades, filework and machine jewelling. Inlays handles with turquoise, coral and mother-of-pearl. Makes sheaths. **Prices:** $85 to $275; some to $500. **Mark:** Crossed half ovals: handmade on top, last name in middle, city and state on bottom.

FRIZZELL, TED, 14056 Low Gap Rd., West Fork, AR 72774, Phone: 501-839-2516
Specialties: Swords, axes and self defense weapons. **Patterns:** Small skeleton knives to large swords. **Technical:** Grinds 5160 almost exclusively--1/4" to 1/2"-- bars some O1 and A2 on request. All knives come with Kydex sheaths. **Prices:** $45 to $1,200. **Remarks:** Full-time maker; first knife sold in 1984. Doing business as Mineral Mountain Hatchet Works. Wholesale orders welcome. **Mark:** A circle with line in the middle; MM and HW within the circle.

FRONEFIELD, DANIEL, 137 Catherine Dr, Hampton Cove, AL 35763-9732, Phone: (256) 536-7827
Specialties: Fixed and folding knives featuring meteorites and other exotic materials. **Patterns:** San-mai Damascus, custom Damascus. **Prices:** $500 to $3000.

FROST, DEWAYNE, 1016 Van Buren Rd, Barnesville, GA 30204, Phone: (770) 358-1426

FRUHMANN, LUDWIG, Stegerwaldstr 8, 84489 Burghausen, GERMANY
Specialties: High-tech and working straight knives of his design. **Patterns:** Hunters, fighters and boots. **Technical:** Grinds ATS-34, CPM-T-440V and Schneider Damascus. Prefers natural handle materials. **Prices:** $200 to $1,500. **Remarks:** Spare-time maker; first knife sold in 1990. **Mark:** First initial and last name.

FUEGEN, LARRY, 617 N. Coulter Circle, Prescott, AZ 86303, Phone: 928-776-8777
Specialties: High-art folders and classic and working straight knives. **Patterns:** Forged scroll folders, lockback folders and classic straight knives. **Technical:** Forges 5160, 1095 and his own Damascus. Works in exotic leather; offers elaborate filework and carving; likes natural handle materials, now offers my own engraving. **Prices:** $400 to $7000. **Remarks:** Full-time maker; first knife sold in 1975. **Mark:** Initials connected. Other: Sole authorship on all knives.

FUJIKAWA, SHUN, Sawa 1157 Kaizuka, Osaka 597 0062, JAPAN, Phone: 81-724-23-4032, Fax:81-726-23-9229
Specialties: Folders of his design and to customer specs. **Patterns:** Locking folders. **Technical:** Grinds his own steel. **Prices:** $450 to $2,500; some to $3,000. **Remarks:** Part-time maker.

FUJISAKA, STANLEY, 45-004 Holowai St., Kaneohe, HI 96744, Phone: 808-247-0017
Specialties: Fancy working straight knives and folders. **Patterns:** Hunters, boots, personal knives, daggers, collectible art knives. **Technical:** Grinds 440C, 154CM and ATS-34; clean lines, inlays. **Prices:** $150 to $1,200; some to $3,000. **Remarks:** Full-time maker; first knife sold in 1984. **Mark:** Name, city, state.

FUKUTA, TAK, 38-Umeagae-cho, Seki-City, Gifu-Pref, JAPAN, Phone: 0575-22-0264
Specialties: Bench-made fancy straight knives and folders. **Patterns:** Sheffield-type folders, Bowies and fighters. **Technical:** Grinds commercial Damascus. **Prices:** Start at $300. **Remarks:** Full-time maker. **Mark:** Name in knife logo.

FULLER, BRUCE A., 1305 Airhart Dr., Baytown, TX 77520, Phone: 713-427-1848
Specialties: One-of-a-kind working/using straight knives and folders of his designs. **Patterns:** Bowies, hunters, folders, and utility/camp knives. **Technical:** Forges high-carbon steel and his own Damascus. prefers El Solo Mesquite and natural materials. Offers filework. **Prices:** $200 to $500; some to $1,800. **Remarks:** Spare-time maker; first knife sold in 1991. Doing business as Fullco Forge. **Mark:** Fullco, M. S.

FULLER, JACK A., 7103 Stretch Ct., New Market, MD 21774, Phone: 301-798-0119
Specialties: Straight working knives of his design and to customer specs. **Patterns:** Fighters, camp knives, hunters, tomahawks and art knives. **Technical:** Forges 5160, O1, W2 and his own Damascus. Does silver wire inlay and own leather work, wood lined sheaths for big camp knives. **Prices:** $300 to $850. **Remarks:** Part-time maker. Master Smith in ABS; first knife sold in 1979. **Mark:** Fuller's Forge, MS.

FULTON, MICKEY, 406 S Shasta St, Willows, CA 95988, Phone: 530-934-5780
Specialties: Working straight knives and folders of his design. **Patterns:** Hunters, Bowies, lockback folders and steak knife sets. **Technical:** Hand-filed, sanded, buffed ATS-34, 440C and A2. **Prices:** $65 to $600; some to $1,200. **Remarks:** Full-time maker; first knife sold in 1979. **Mark:** Signature.

g

GADBERRY, EMMET, 82 Purple Plum Dr, Hattieville, AR 72063, Phone: (501) 354-4842

GADDY, GARY LEE, 205 Ridgewood Lane, Washington, NC 27889, Phone: 252-946-4359
Specialties: Working/using straight knives of his design; period pieces. **Patterns:** Bowies, hunters, utility/camp knives. **Technical:** Grinds ATS-34, 01; forges 1095**Prices:** $100 to $225; some to $400. **Remarks:** Spare-time maker; first knife sold in 1991. **Mark:** Quarter moon logo.

GAETA, ANGELO, R. Saldanha Marinho, 1295 Centro Jau, SP-17201-310, BRAZIL, Phone: 0146-224543, Fax:0146-224543
Specialties: Straight using knives to customer specs. **Patterns:** Hunters, fighting, daggers, belt push dagger. **Technical:** Grinds D6, ATS-34 and 440C stainless. titanium nitride golden finish upon request. **Prices:** $60 to $300. **Remarks:** Full-time maker; first knife sold in 1992. **Mark:** First initial, last name.

GAETA, ROBERTO, Rua Shikazu Myai 80, 05351 Sao Paulo, S. P., BRAZIL, Phone: 11-37684626
Specialties: Wide range of using knives. **Patterns:** Brazilian and North American hunting and fighting knives. **Technical:** Grinds stainless steel; likes natural handle materials. **Prices:** $100 to $250; some to $500. **Remarks:** Full-time maker; first knife sold in 1979. **Mark:** BOB'G.

GAGSTAETTER, PETER, Nibelungenschmiede, Bergstrasse 2, 9306 Freidorf TG, SWITZERLAND

GAINES, BUDDY, Gaines Knives, 155 Red Hill Rd, Commerce, GA 30530
Specialties: Collectable and working folders and straight knives. **Patterns:** Folders, hunters, Bowies, tactical knives. **Technical:** Forges own Damascus, grinds ATS-34, D2, commercial Damascus. Prefers Mother of Pearl and Stag. **Prices:** Start at $200. **Remarks:** Part-time maker, sold first knife in 1985. **Mark:** last name

GAINEY, HAL, 904 Bucklevel Rd., Greenwood, SC 29649, Phone: 864-223-0225
Specialties: Traditional working and using straight knives and folders. **Patterns:** Hunters, slip-joint folders and utility/camp knives. **Technical:** Hollow-grinds ATS-34 and D2; makes sheaths. **Prices:** $95 to $145; some to $500. **Remarks:** Full-time maker; first knife sold in 1975. **Mark:** Eagle head and last name.

GALLAGHER, SEAN, 24828 114th PL SE, Monroe, WA 98272-7685

GALLAGHER, BARRY, 135 Park St, Lewistown, MT 59457, Phone: 406-538-7056
Specialties: One of a kind Damascus folders. **Patterns:** Folders - utility to high art, some straight knives - hunter, Bowies, and art pieces. **Technical:** Forges own mosaic Damascus and carbon steel, some stainless. **Prices:** $400 to $5,000+. **Remarks:** Full-time maker; first knife sold in 1993. Doing business as Gallagher Custom Knives. **Mark:** Last name.

GAMBLE, ROGER, 2801 65 Way N., St. Petersburg, FL 33710, Phone: 727-384-1470
Specialties: Traditional working/using straight knives and folders of his design. **Patterns:** Liner locks & hunters. **Technical:** Grinds ATS-34 and Damascus. **Prices:** $100 to $1000. **Remarks:** Part-time maker; first knife sold in 1982. Doing business as Gamble Knives. **Mark:** First name in a fan of cards over last name.

GAMBLE, FRANK, 3872 Dunbar Pl., Fremont, CA 94536, Phone: 510-797-7970
Specialties: Fantasy and high-art straight knives and folders of his design. **Patterns:** Daggers, fighters, hunters and special locking folders. **Technical:** Grinds 440C and ATS-34; forges Damascus. Inlays; offers jewelling. **Prices** $150 to $10,000. **Remarks:** Full-time maker; first knife sold in 1976. **Mark:** First initial, last name.

GANSTER, JEAN-PIERRE, 18, Rue du Vieil Hopital, F-67000 Strasbourg, FRANCE, Phone: (0033) 388 32 65 61, Fax:(0033) 388 32 52 79
Specialties: Fancy and high-art miniatures of his design and to customer specs. **Patterns:** Bowies, daggers, fighters, hunters, locking folders and miniatures. **Technical:** Forges and grinds stainless Damascus, ATS-34, gold and silver. **Prices:** $100 to $380; some to $2,500. **Remarks:** Part-time maker; first knife sold in 1972. **Mark:** Stylized first initials.

GARCIA, MARIO EIRAS, R. Edmundo Scanapieco, 300 Caxingui, Sao Paulo SP-05516-070, BRAZIL, Fax:011-37214528
Specialties: Fantasy knives of his design; one of a kind only. **Patterns:** Fighters, daggers, boots and two-bladed knives. **Technical:** Forges car

leaf springs. Uses only natural handle material. **Prices:** $100 to $200. **Remarks:** Part-time maker; first knife sold in 1976. **Mark:** Two "B"s, one opposite the other.

GARCIA, TONY, 134 Gregory Place, West Palm Beach, FL 33405, Phone: 561-582-1291, Fax:561-585-9532
Specialties: Traditional working/using straight knives of his design and to customer specs. **Patterns:** Bowies, hunters, fillet and utility/camp knives. **Technical:** Grinds 440C, 440V and ATS-34. **Prices:** $125 to $250. **Remarks:** Part-time maker; first knife sold in 1992. **Mark:** Name, city, state; logo of fishing hook with arrow across it.

GARDNER, ROB, 387 Mustang Blvd., Port Aransas, TX 78373, Phone: 361-749-3597, Fax:361-749-3597
Specialties: High-art working and using knives of his design and to customer specs. **Patterns:** Daggers, hunters and ethnic-patterned knives. **Technical:** Forges Damascus, L6 and 10-series steels. Engraves and inlays. Handles and fittings may be carved. **Prices:** $175 to $500; some to $2,500. **Remarks:** Spare-time maker; first knife sold in 1987. Knives made by custom order only. **Mark:** Engraved or stamped initials.

GARNER, LARRY W, 13069 FM 14, Tyler, TX 75706, Phone: (903) 597-6045
Specialties: Fixed blade hunters & Bowies. **Patterns:** My designs or yours. **Technical:** Hand forges 5160. **Prices:** $200 to $500. **Remarks:** Apprentice blade smith Feb 1999. **Mark:** Last name.

GARNER JR., WILLIAM O., 2803 East DeSoto St., Pensacola, FL 32503, Phone: 850-438-2009
Specialties: Working straight and art knives. **Patterns:** Hunters and folders. **Technical:** Grinds 440C and ATS-34 steels. **Prices:** $235 to $600. **Remarks:** Full-time maker; first knife sold in 1985. **Mark:** First and last name in oval logo or last name.

GARRITY., TIMOTHY P, 217 S Grandview Blvd, Waukesha, WI 53188, Phone: (414) 785-1803

GARVOCK, MARK W, RR 1, Balderson, Ontario, CANADA K1G 1A0, Phone: 613-833-2545, Fax:613-833-2208
Specialties: Hunters, Bowies, Japanese, daggers & swords. **Patterns:** Cable Damascus, random pattern welded or to suit. **Technical:** Forged blades; hi-carbon. **Prices:** $250 to $900. **Remarks:** Also CKG member & ABS member. **Mark:** Big G with M in middle. **Other:** Shipping & taxes extra.

GASTON, RON, 330 Gaston Dr., Woodruff, SC 29388, Phone: 803-433-0807, Fax:803-433-9958
Specialties: Working period pieces. **Patterns:** Hunters, fighters, tantos, boots and a variety of other straight knives; single-blade slip-joint folders. **Technical:** Grinds ATS-34. Hand-rubbed satin finish is standard. **Prices:** $200 to $600; some to $1,000. **Remarks:** Full-time maker; first knife sold in 1980. **Mark:** Ron Gaston, Woodruff SC.

GASTON, BERT, P. O. Box 9047, North Little Rock, AR 72119, Phone: 501-372-4747
Specialties: Traditional working and using straight knives of his design. **Patterns:** Hunters, Bowies and fighters. **Technical:** Forges his Damascus, 5168 and L6. Only uses natural handle materials. **Prices:** $200 to $500; some to $1,500. **Remarks:** Part-time maker; first knife sold in 1989. **Mark:** Stylized last initial and M. S.

GAUDETTE, LINDEN L., 5 Hitchcock Rd., Wilbraham, MA 01095, Phone: 413-596-4896
Specialties: Traditional working knives in standard patterns. **Patterns:** Broad-bladed hunters, Bowies and camp knives; wood carver knives; locking folders. **Technical:** Grinds ATS-34, 440C and 154CM. **Prices:** $150 to $400; some higher. **Remarks:** Full-time maker; first knife sold in 1975. **Mark:** Last name in Gothic logo; used to be initials in circle.

GAULT, CLAY, #1225 PR 7022, Lexington, TX 78947, Phone: 979-773-3305
Specialties: Classic straight and folding hunting knives and multi-blade folders of his design. **Patterns:** Folders and hunting knives. **Technical:** Grinds BX-NSM 174 steel, custom rolled from billets to his specifications. Uses exotic leathers for sheaths, and fine natural materials for all knives. **Prices:** $325 to $600; some higher. **Remarks:** Full-time maker; first knife sold in 1970. **Mark:** Name or name with cattle brand.

GEISLER, GARY R., P. O. Box 294, Clarksville, OH 45113, Phone: 937-383-4055
Specialties: Period Bowies and such; flat ground. **Patterns:** Working knives usually modeled close after an existing antique. **Technical:** Flat grinds 440C, A2 & ATS-34. **Prices:** $300 and up. **Remarks:** Part-time maker; first knife sold in 1982. **Mark:** G. R. Geisler Maker; usually in script on reverse side because I'm left handed.

GENSKE, JAY, 283 Doty St, Fond Du Lac, WI 54935, Phone: 920-921-8019/Cell Phone 920-579-0144
Specialties: Working/using knives and period pieces of his design and to customer specs. **Patterns:** Bowies, fighters, hunters. **Technical:** Grinds ATS-34 and 440C, 01 and 1095 forges and grinds Damascus and 1095.

Offers custom-tooled sheaths, scabbards and hand carved handles. **Prices:** $95 to $500; some to $1,000. **Remarks:** Full-time maker; first knife sold in 1985. Doing business as Genske Knives. **Mark:** Stamped or engraved last name.

GEORGE, HARRY, 3137 Old Camp Long Rd., Aiken, SC 29805, Phone: 803-649-1963
Specialties: Working straight knives of his design or to customer specs. **Patterns:** Hunters, skinners and utility knives. **Technical:** Grinds ATS-34. Prefers natural handle materials, hollow-grinds and mirror finishes. **Prices:** Start at $70. **Remarks:** Part-time maker; first knife sold in 1985. Trained under George Herron. Member SCAK. Member Knifemakers Guild. **Mark:** Name, city, state.

GEORGE, LES, 1703 Payne, Wichita, KS 67203, Phone: 316-267-0736
Specialties: Classic, traditional and working/using straight knives of his design and to customer specs. **Patterns:** Fighters, hunters, swords and miniatures. **Technical:** Grinds D2; forges 5160 and Damascus. Uses mosaic handle pins and his own mokume-gane. **Prices:** $35 to $200; some to $800. **Remarks:** No orders taken at this time due to enlistment in the US Marine Corps. ; first knife sold in 1992. Doing business as George Custom Knives. **Mark:** Last name or initials stacked.

GEORGE, TOM, 6311 Shelton Ct, Magalia, CA 95954-9132, Phone: 530-873-3306
Specialties: Working straight knives, display knives and folders of his design. **Patterns:** Hunters, daggers and buckskinners and folders. **Technical:** Uses D2, 440C, ATS-34 and 154CM. **Prices:** $175 to $4,500. **Remarks:** First knife sold in 1981. Custom orders accepted. **Mark:** Name.

GEPNER, DON, 2615 E. Tecumseh, Norman, OK 73071, Phone: 405-364-2750
Specialties: Traditional working and using straight knives of his design. **Patterns:** Bowies and daggers. **Technical:** Forges his Damascus, 1095 and 5160. **Prices:** $100 to $400; some to $1,000. **Remarks:** Spare-time maker; first knife sold in 1991. Has been forging since 1954; first edged weapon made at 9 years old. **Mark:** Last initial.

GERNER, THOMAS, P O Box 30 Deep River Farm, Walpole, WESTERN AUSTRALIA 06398, Phone: 61 8 9840-1016, Fax:61 8 9840 1035
Specialties: Forged working knives; plain steel & pattern welded. **Patterns:** I try most patterns I hear or read about. **Technical:** 5160, L6, 01, 52100 steels; Australian hardwood handles. **Prices:** $120 & up. **Remarks:** Achieved ABS master smith rating in 2001. **Mark:** My mark is more like a standing arrow and a leaning cross (This is T>G> in the Runic (Viking) alphabet).

GERUS, GERRY, P. O. Box 2295, G. P. O. Cairns, Qld. 4870, Australia 070-341451, Phone: 019 617935
Specialties: Fancy working and using straight knives of his design. **Patterns:** Hunters, Bowies and fighters. **Technical:** Uses 440C, ATS-34 and commercial Damascus. **Prices:** $275 to $600; some to $1,200. **Remarks:** Part-time maker; first knife sold in 1988. **Mark:** Last name; or last name, Hand Made, city, country.

GEVEDON, HANNERS (HANK), 1410 John Cash Rd., Crab Orchard, KY 40419-9770
Specialties: Traditional working and using straight knives. **Patterns:** Hunters, swords, utility and camp knives. **Technical:** Forges and grinds his own Damascus, 5160 and L6. Cast aluminum handles. **Prices:** $50 to $250; some to $400. **Remarks:** Part-time maker; first knife sold in 1983. **Mark:** Initials and LBF tang stamp.

GIAGU, SALVATORE AND DEROMA MARIA ROSARIA, Via V. Emanuele 64, 07016 Pattada (SS), ITALY, Phone: 079-755918, Fax:079-755918
Specialties: Using and collecting traditional and new folders from Sardegna. **Patterns:** Folding, hunting, utility, skinners and kitchen knives. **Technical:** Forges ATS-34, 440, D2 and Damascus. **Prices:** $200 to $2,000; some higher. **Mark:** First initial, last name and name of town and muflon's head.

GIBO, GEORGE, PO Box 4304, HILO, HI 96720, Phone: 808-987-7002
Specialties: straight knives and folders. **Patterns:** hunters, bird and trout, utility, gentlemen and tactical folders. **Technical:** grinds ATS-34, BG-42, Talonite, Stainless Steel Damascus. **Prices:** $250 to $1000. **Remarks:** spare time maker first knife sold in 1995. **Mark:** name, city and state around Hawaiian "Shaka" sign.

GIBSON, JAMES HOOT, RR1, Box 177F, Bunnell, FL 32110, Phone: 904-437-4383
Patterns: Bowies, daggers and hunters. **Technical:** Grinds ATS-34, 440C and Damascus. **Prices:** $150 to $1,200; some to $2,500. **Remarks:** Part-time maker; first knife sold in 1965. Doing business as Hoot's Handmade Knives. **Mark:** Hoot.

custom knifemakers

GILBREATH, RANDALL, 55 Crauswell Rd., Dora, AL 35062, Phone: 205-648-3902
Specialties: Damascus folders and fighters. **Patterns:** Folders and fixed blades. **Technical:** Forges Damascus and & high carbon; stock removal stainless steel. **Prices:** $300 to $1,500. **Remarks:** Full-time maker; first knife sold in 1979. **Mark:** Name in ribbon.

GILJEVIC, BRANKO, 35 Hayley Crescent, Queanbeyan 2620, N. S. W., AUSTRALIA 0262977613
Specialties: Classic working straight knives and folders of his design. **Patterns:** Hunters, Bowies, skinners and locking folders. **Technical:** Grinds 440C. Offers acid etching, scrimshaw and leather carving. **Prices:** $150 to $1,500. **Remarks:** Part-time maker; first knife sold in 1987. Doing business as Sambar Custom Knives. **Mark:** Company name in logo.

GITTINGER, RAYMOND, 6940 S RT 100, Tiffin, OH 44883, Phone: (419) 397-2517

GLASSCOCK, JOHN, 18510 Lippizaner, Cypress, TX 77433, Phone: (713) 859-4060

GLOVER, RON, 7702 Misty Springs Ct, Mason, OH 45040, Phone: 513-398-7857
Specialties: High-tech working straight knives and folders. **Patterns:** Hunters to Bowies; some interchangeable blade models; unique locking mechanisms. **Technical:** Grinds 440C, 154CM; buys Damascus. **Prices:** $70 to $500; some to $800. **Remarks:** Part-time maker; first knife sold in 1981. **Mark:** Name in script.

GLOVER, WARREN D, d/b/a Bubba Knives, PO Box 475, Cleveland, GA 30528, Phone: 706-865-3998, Fax:706-348-7176
Specialties: Traditional and custom working and using straight knives of his design and to customer request. **Patterns:** Hunters, skinners, bird & fish, utility and kitchen knives. **Technical:** Grinds 440, ATS-34 and stainless steel Damascus. **Prices:** $75 to $400 and up. **Remarks:** Part-time maker; sold first knife in 1995. **Mark:** Bubba, year, name, state.

GODDARD, WAYNE, 473 Durham Ave., Eugene, OR 97404, Phone: 541-689-8098
Specialties: Working/using straight knives and folders. **Patterns:** Hunters and folders. **Technical:** Works exclusively with wire Damascus and his own-pattern welded material. **Prices:** $250 to $4000. **Remarks:** Full-time maker; first knife sold in 1963. Three-year backlog on orders. **Mark:** Blocked initials on forged blades; regular capital initials on stock removal.

GOERS, BRUCE, 3423 Royal Ct. S., Lakeland, FL 33813, Phone: 941-646-0984
Specialties: Fancy working and using straight knives of his design and to customer specs. **Patterns:** Hunters, fighters, Bowies and fantasy knives. **Technical:** Grinds ATS-34, some Damascus. **Prices:** $195 to $600; some to $1,300. **Remarks:** Part-time maker; first knife sold in 1990. Doing business as Vulture Cutlery. **Mark:** Buzzard with initials.

GOERTZ, PAUL S., 201 Union Ave. SE, #207, Renton, WA 98059, Phone: 425-228-9501
Specialties: Working straight knives of his design and to customer specs. **Patterns:** Hunters, skinners, camp, bird and fish knives, camp axes, some Bowies, fighters and boots. **Technical:** Grinds ATS-34, BG42, & CPM420V. **Prices:** $75 to $500. **Remarks:** Full-time maker; first knife sold in 1985. **Mark:** Signature.

GOFOURTH, JIM, 3776 Aliso Cyn. Rd., Santa Paula, CA 93060, Phone: 805-659-3814
Specialties: Period pieces and working knives. **Patterns:** Bowies, locking folders, patent lockers and others. **Technical:** Grinds A2 and 154CM. **Prices:** Moderate. **Remarks:** Spare-time maker. **Mark:** Initials interconnected.

GOGUEN, SCOTT, 166 Goguen Rd., Newport, NC 28570, Phone: 919-393-6013
Specialties: Classic and traditional working knives. **Patterns:** Kitchen, camp, hunters, Bowies & swords. **Technical:** Forges high carbon steel and own Damascus. Offers clay tempering and cord wrapped handles. **Prices:** $85 to $1,500. **Remarks:** Spare-time maker; first knife sold in 1988. **Mark:** Last name or name in Japanese characters.

GOLDBERG, METALSMITH, DAVID, 1120 Blyth Ct, Blue Bell, PA 19422, Phone: 215-654-7117
Specialties: Japanese style swords and fittings. **Patterns:** Kozuka to Dai-Sho, Naginata, Yari and sword canes. **Technical:** Forges and heat treats his own Damascus, cable Damascus, meteorite, and handmade steel from carbonized iron, straw ash and clay. Uses traditional materials, carves fittings, handles and cases. Sole author. **Prices:** Upon request. **Remarks:** Full-time maker; first knife sold in 1987. **Mark:** Last name in Japanese Kanji - "Kinzan". **Other:** Damascus metalsmithing teacher: C Robbin Hudson. Japanese swordsmithing teacher: Michael Bell; fittings etc self taught.

GOLDING, ROBIN, P. O. Box 267, Lathrop, CA 95330, Phone: 209-982-0839
Specialties: Working straight knives of his design. **Patterns:** Survival knives, Bowie extractions, camp knives, dive knives and skinners. **Technical:** Grinds 440C, 154CM and ATS-34. **Prices:** $95 to $250; some to $500. **Remarks:** Full-time maker; first knife sold in 1985. Up to 1-1/2 year waiting period on orders. **Mark:** Signature of last name.

GOLTZ, WARREN L., 802 4th Ave. E., Ada, MN 56510, Phone: 218-784-7721
Specialties: Fancy working knives in standard patterns. **Patterns:** Hunters, Bowies and camp knives. **Technical:** Grinds 440C and ATS-34. **Prices:** $120 to $595; some to $950. **Remarks:** Part-time maker; first knife sold in 1984. **Mark:** Last name.

GONZALEZ, LEONARDO WILLIAMS, Ituzaingo 473, Maldonado, CP 20000, URUGUAY, Phone: 598 4222 1617, Fax:598 4222 1617
Specialties: Classic high-art and fantasy straight knives; traditional working and using knives of his design, in standard patterns or to customer specs. **Patterns:** Hunters, Bowies, daggers, fighters, boots, swords and utility/camp knives. **Technical:** Forges and grinds high carbon and stainless Bohler steels. **Prices:** $100 to $2500. **Remarks:** Full-time maker; first knife sold in 1985. **Mark:** Willy, whale, R. O. U.

GOO, TAI, 5920 W Windy Lou Ln, Tucson, AZ 85742, Phone: 520-744-9777
Specialties: High-art, neo-tribal and fantasy knives. **Patterns:** Fighters, daggers, Bowies, buckskinners, edged fetishes and sculptures. **Technical:** Forges and grinds A6, 440C and his own Damascus with iron meteorites. **Prices:** $150 to $500; some to $10,000. **Remarks:** Full-time maker; first knife sold in 1978. **Mark:** Chiseled signature; mark in spacer and tang.

GOODE, BEAR, P. O. Box 6474, Navajo Dam, NM 87419, Phone: 505-632-8184
Specialties: Working/using straight knives of his design and in standard patterns. **Patterns:** Bowies, hunters and utility/camp knives. **Technical:** Grinds 440C, ATS-34, 154-CM; forges and grinds 1095, 5160 and other steels on request; uses Damascus. **Prices:** $60 to $225; some to $500 and up. **Remarks:** Part-time maker; first knife sold in 1993. Doing business as Bear Knives. **Mark:** First and last name with a three-toed paw print.

GOODLING, RODNEY W, 6640 Old Harrisburg Rd, York Springs, PA 17372

GORDON, LARRY B., 23555 Newell Cir W, Farmington Hills, MI 48336, Phone: 248-477-5483

GORENFLO, JAMES T. (JT), 9145 Sullivan Rd., Baton Rouge, LA 70818, Phone: 504-261-5868
Specialties: Traditional working and using straight knives of his design. **Patterns:** Bowies, hunters and utility/camp knives. **Technical:** Forges 5160, 1095, 52100 and his own Damascus. **Prices:** Start at $125. **Remarks:** Part-time maker; first knife sold in 1992. **Mark:** Last name or initials, J. S. on reverse.

GORENFLO, GABE, 9145 Sullivan Rd, Baton Rouge, LA 70818, Phone: (504) 261-5868

GOTTAGE, JUDY, 43227 Brooks Drive., Clinton Twp., MI 48038-5323, Phone: 810-286-7275
Specialties: Custom folders of her design or to customer specs. **Patterns:** Interframes or integral. **Technical:** Stock removal. **Prices:** $300 to $3,000. **Remarks:** Full-time maker; first knife sold in 1980. **Mark:** Full name, maker in script.

GOTTAGE, DANTE, 43227 Brooks Drive., Clinton Twp., MI 48038-5323, Phone: 810-286-7275
Specialties: Working knives of his design or to customer specs. **Patterns:** Large and small skinners, fighters, Bowies and fillet knives. **Technical:** Grinds O1, 440C and 154CM and ATS-34. **Prices:** $150 to $600. **Remarks:** Part-time maker; first knife sold in 1975. **Mark:** Full name in script letters.

GOTTSCHALK, GREGORY J., 12 First St. (Ft. Pitt), Carnegie, PA 15106, Phone: 412-279-6692
Specialties: Fancy working straight knives and folders to customer specs. **Patterns:** Hunters to tantos, locking folders to minis. **Technical:** Grinds 440C, 154CM, ATS-34. Now making own Damascus. Most knives have mirror finishes. **Prices:** Start at $150. **Remarks:** Part-time maker; first knife sold in 1977. **Mark:** Full name in crescent.

GOUKER, GARY B., P. O. Box 955, Sitka, AK 99835, Phone: 907-747-3476
Specialties: Hunting knives for hard use. **Patterns:** Skinners, semi-skinners, and such. **Technical:** Likes natural materials, inlays, stainless steel. **Prices:** Moderate. **Remarks:** New Alaskan maker. **Mark:** Name.

GOYTIA, ENRIQUE, 2120 E Paisano Ste 276, El Paso, TX 79905
GRAFFEO, ANTHONY I., 100 Riess Place, Chalmette, LA 70043, Phone: 504-277-1428
Specialties: Traditional working and using straight knives of his design, to customer specs and in standard patterns. **Patterns:** Hunters, utility/camp knives and fishing knives. **Technical:** Hollow- and flat-grinds ATS-34, 440C and 154CM. Handle materials include Pakkawood, Micarta and sambar stag. **Prices:** $65 to $100; some to $250. **Remarks:** Part-time maker; first knife sold in 1991. Doing business as Knives by: Graf. **Mark:** First and middle initials, last name city, state, Maker.
GRAHAM, GORDON, RT 3 Box 207, New Boston, TX 75570, Phone: (903) 628-6337
GRAVELINE, PASCAL AND ISABELLE, 38, rue de Kerbrezillic, 29350 Moelan-sur-Mer, FRANCE, Phone: 33 2 98 39 73 33, Fax:33 2 98 39 73 33
Specialties: French replicas from the 17th, 18th and 19th centuries. **Patterns:** Traditional folders and multi-blade pocket knives; traveling knives, fruit knives and fork sets; puzzle knives and friend's knives; rivet less knives. **Technical:** Grind 12C27, ATS-34, Damascus and carbon steel. **Prices:** $500 to $5,000; some to $2,000. **Remarks:** Full-time makers; first knife sold in 1992. **Mark:** Last name over head of ram.
GRAY, BOB, 8206 N. Lucia Court, Spokane, WA 99208, Phone: 509-468-3924
Specialties: Straight working knives of his own design or to customer specs. **Patterns:** Hunter, fillet and carving knives. **Technical:** Forges 5160, L6 and some 52100; grinds 440C. **Prices:** $100 to $600. **Remarks:** Part-time knife maker; first knife sold in 1991. Doing business as Hi-Land Knives. **Mark:** HI-L.
GRAY, DANIEL, Gray Knives, 686 Main Rd, Brownville, ME 04414, Phone: 207-965-2191
Specialties: Straight knives, Fantasy, folders, automatics and traditional of my own design. **Patterns:** Automatics, fighters, hunters. **Technical:** Grind 01, 154CM & D2. **Prices:** From $155 to $750. **Remarks:** Full-time maker; first knife sold in 1974. **Mark:** Gray Knives.
GREBE, GORDON S., P. O. Box 296, Anchor Point, AK 99556-0296, Phone: 907-235-8242
Specialties: Working straight knives and folders, some fancy. **Patterns:** Tantos, Bowies, boot fighter sets, locking folders. **Technical:** Grinds stainless steels; likes 1/4" inch stock and glass-bead finishes. **Prices:** $75 to $250; some to $2,000. **Remarks:** Full-time maker; first knife sold in 1968. **Mark:** Initials in lightning logo.
GRECO, JOHN, 100 Mattie Jones Road, Greensburg, KY 42743, Phone: 270-932-3335, Fax:270-932-2225
Specialties: Limited edition knives & swords. **Patterns:** Tactical, fighters, camp knives, short swords. **Technical:** Stock removal carbon steel. Also make Greco/Lile Knives in conjunction with Lile Knives based on Jimmy's old patterns. **Prices:** Moderate. **Remarks:** Full-time maker since1986. First knife sold in 1979. **Mark:** Greco or Greco/line. **Other:** Do custom limited edition knives for other designers complete with their logo.
GREEN, WILLIAM (BILL), 46 Warren Rd., View Bank Vic., AUSTRALIA 3084, Fax:03-9459-1529
Specialties: Traditional high-tech straight knives and folders. **Patterns:** Japanese-influenced designs, hunters, Bowies, folders and miniatures. **Technical:** Forges O1, D2 and his own Damascus. Offers lost wax castings for bolsters and pommels. Likes natural handle materials, gems, silver and gold. **Prices:** $400 to $750; some to $1,200. **Remarks:** Full-time maker. **Mark:** Initials.
GREEN, BILL, 706 Bradfield, Garland, TX 75042, Phone: 972-272-4748
Specialties: High-art and working straight knives and folders of his design and to customer specs. **Patterns:** Bowies, hunters, kitchen knives and locking folders. **Technical:** Grinds ATS-34, D2 and 440V. Hand-tooled custom sheaths. **Prices:** $70 to $350; some to $750. **Remarks:** Part-time maker; first knife sold in 1990. **Mark:** Last name.
GREEN, ROGER M., 4640 Co. Rd. 1022, Joshua, TX 76058, Phone: 817-641-5057
Specialties: 19th century period pieces. **Patterns:** Investor-grade Sheffield Bowies and dirks, fighters and hunters. **Technical:** Grinds 440C and tool steels; forges Damascus and occasionally carbon steel. Prefers flat grinds and hand-rubbed finishes. **Prices:** $350 to $3,500. **Remarks:** Full-time maker; first knife sold in 1984. **Mark:** First and middle initials, last name.
GREEN, RUSS, 6013 Briercrest Ave. Lakewood, CA 90713, Phone: 562-867-2305
Specialties: Sheaths & using knives. **Technical:** Knives 440C, ATS-34, 5160, 01, cable Damascus. **Prices:** Knives-$135 to $850; sheaths- $30 to $200. **Mark:** Russ Green & year.

GREEN, MARK, 1523 S Main St P O Box 20, Graysville, AL 35073, Phone: (205) 647-9353
GREENAWAY, DON, 3325 Dinsmore Trail, Fayetteville, AR 72704, Phone: (501) 521-0323
GREENE, CHRIS, 707 Cherry Lane, Shelby, NC 28150, Phone: 704-434-5620
GREENE, DAVID, 570 Malcom Rd., Covington, GA 30209, Phone: 770-784-0657
Specialties: Straight working using knives. **Patterns:** Hunters. **Technical:** Forges mosaic and twist Damascus. Prefers stag and desert ironwood for handle material.
GREENFIELD, G. O., 2605 15th St. #522, Everett, WA 98201, Phone: 425-258-1551
Specialties: High-tech and working straight knives and folders of his design. **Patterns:** Boots, daggers, hunters and one of a kinds. **Technical:** Grinds ATS-34, D2, 440C and T-440V. Makes sheaths for each knife. **Prices:** $100 to $800; some to $10,000. **Remarks:** Part-time maker; first knife sold in 1978. **Mark:** Springfield®, serial number.
GREGORY, MICHAEL, 211 Calhoun Rd., Belton, SC 29627, Phone: 864-338-8898
Specialties: Working straight knives and folders. **Patterns:** Hunters, tantos, locking folders and slip-joints, boots and fighters. **Technical:** Grinds 440C, 154CM and ATS-34; mirror finishes. **Prices:** $95 to $200; some to $1,000. **Remarks:** Part-time maker; first knife sold in 1980. **Mark:** Name, city in logo.
GREINER, RICHARD, 1073 E. County Rd. 32, Green Springs, OH 44836
GREISS, JOCKL, Obere Muhlstr. 5, 73252, Gutenberg, GERMANY, Phone: +49 0 7026 3224
Specialties: Classic and working using straight knives of his design. **Patterns:** Bowies, daggers and hunters. **Technical:** Uses only Jerry Rados Damascus. All knives are one of a kind made by hand; no machines are used. **Prices:** $700 to $2000; some to $3000. **Remarks:** Full-time maker; first knife sold in 1984. **Mark:** An "X" with a long vertical line through it.
GRENIER, ROGER, 540 Chemin De La Dague, Saint Jovite, Que., CANADA J0T 2H0, Phone: 819-425-8893
Specialties: Working straight knives. **Patterns:** Heavy-duty Bowies, fighters, hunters, swords and miniatures. **Technical:** Grinds O1, D2 and 440C. **Prices:** $70 to $225; some to $800. **Remarks:** Full-time maker; first knife sold in 1981. **Mark:** Last name on blade.
GREY, PIET, PO Box 363, Naboomspruit 0560, SOUTH AFRICA, Phone: 014-743-3613
Specialties: Fancy working and using straight knives of his design. **Patterns:** Fighters, hunters and utility/camp knives. **Technical:** Grinds ATS-34 and AEB-L; forges and grinds Damascus. Solder less fitting of guards. Engraves and scrimshaws. **Prices:** $125 to $750; some to $1,500. **Remarks:**Part-time maker; first knife sold in 1970. **Mark:** Last name.
GRIFFIN, THOMAS J., 591 Quevli Ave., Windom, MN 56101, Phone: 507-831-1089
Specialties: Period pieces and fantasy straight knives of his design. **Patterns:** Daggers and swords. **Technical:** Forges 1095, 52100 and L6. Most blades are his own Damascus; turned fittings and wire-wrapped grips. **Prices:** $250 to $800; some to $2,000. **Remarks:** Full-time maker; first knife sold in 1991. Doing business as Griffin Knives. **Mark:** Last name etched.
GRIFFIN, RENDON AND MARK, 9706 Cedardale, Houston, TX 77055, Phone: 713-468-0436
Specialties: Working folders and automatics of their designs. **Patterns:** Standard lockers and slip-joints. **Technical:** Most blade steels; stock removal. **Prices:** Start at $350. **Remarks:** Rendon's first knife sold in 1966; Mark's in 1974. **Mark:** Last name logo.
GRIFFIN JR., HOWARD A., 14299 SW 31st Ct., Davie, FL 33330, Phone: 305-474-5406
Specialties: Working straight knives and folders. **Patterns:** Hunters, Bowies, locking folders with his own push-button lock design. **Technical:** Grinds 440C. **Prices:** $100 to $200; some to $500. **Remarks:** Part-time maker; first knife sold in 1983. **Mark:** Initials.
GRIFFITH, LYNN, PO Box 876, Glenpool, OK 74033, Phone: 918-366-8303
Specialties: Flat ground, full tang tactical knives. **Patterns:** Neck & multi-carry knives, drop and clip points, tantos and Wharncliffes. **Technical:** Grinds ATS34 and Talonite. **Prices:** $125 to $400; some to $700. **Remarks:** Full-time knife maker; first knife sold in 1987. **Mark:** Last name over year made.

custom knifemakers

GROESBECK, BRAD, 478 N 650 W, American Fork, UT 84003, Phone: (801) 763-1689

GROSPITCH, ERNIE, 18440 Amityville Dr, Orlando, FL 32820, Phone: 407-568-5438
Specialties: Bowies, hunting, fishing, kitchen, lockback folders. **Patterns:** My design or customer. **Technical:** Stock removal using most available steels. **Prices:** $140. 00 and up. **Remarks:** Part-time maker, sold first knife in 1990. Mark: Etched name/maker city and state

GROSS, W. W., 325 Sherbrook Dr., High Point, NC 27260
Specialties: Working knives. **Patterns:** Hunters, boots, fighters. **Technical:** Grinds. **Prices:** Moderate. **Remarks:** Full-time maker. **Mark:** Name.

GROSSMAN, STEWART, 24 Water St., #419, Clinton, MA 01510, Phone: 508-365-2291; 800-mysword
Specialties: Miniatures and full-size knives and swords. **Patterns:** One of a kind miniatures--jewelry, replicas--and wire-wrapped figures. Full-size art, fantasy and combat knives, daggers and modular systems. **Technical:** Forges and grinds most metals and Damascus. Uses gems, crystals, electronics and motorized mechanisms. **Prices:** $20 to $300; some to $4,500 and higher. **Remarks:** Full-time maker; first knife sold in 1985. **Mark:** G1.

GRUSSENMEYER, PAUL G., 310 Kresson Rd, Cherry Hill, NJ 08034, Phone: 856-428-1088, Fax:856-428-8997
Specialties: Assembling fancy and fantasy straight knives with his own carved handles. **Patterns:** Bowies, daggers, folders, swords, hunters and miniatures. **Technical:** Uses forged steel and Damascus, stock removal and knapped obsidian blades. **Prices:** $250 to $4,000. **Remarks:** Spare-time maker; first knife sold in 1991. **Mark:** First and last initial hooked together on handle.

GUARNERA, ANTHONY R, 42034 Quail Creek Dr, Quartzhill, CA 93536, Phone: (661) 722-4032
Patterns: Hunters, camp, Bowies, kitchen, fighter knives. **Technical:** Forged and stock removal. **Prices:** $100 and up.

GUESS, RAYMOND L., 7214 Salineville Rd. NE, Mechanicstown, OH 44651, Phone: 330-738-2793
Specialties: Working straight knives and folders of his design or to customer specs. **Patterns:** Hunters, Bowies, fillet knives, steak and paring knife sets. **Technical:** Grinds 440C. Offers silver inlay work and mirror finishes. Custom-made leather sheath for each knife. **Prices:** $65 to $850; some to $700. **Remarks:** Spare-time maker; first knife sold in 1985. **Mark:** First initial, last name.

GUIDRY, BRUCE, 24550 Adams Av, Murrieta, CA 92562, Phone: (909) 677-2384

GUIGNARD, GIB, Box 3413, Quartzsite, AZ 85359, Phone: 520-927-4831
Specialties: Rustic finish on primitive bowies with stag or ironwood handles & turquoise inlay. **Patterns:** Very large in 5160 & ATS-34 - Small & med. size hunting knives in ATS-34. **Technical:** Forges 5160 and grind ATS-34. **Prices:** $100 to $1000. **Remarks:** Full-time maker; first knife sold in 1989. Doing business as Cactus Forge. **Mark:** Last name or G+ on period pieces and primitive.

GUILD, DON, Guild Knives, 320 Paani Place 1A, Paia, HI 96779, Phone: 808-877-3109

GUNDERSEN, D. F. "DOC", 5811 S Siesta Lane, Tempe, AZ 85283
Specialties: Small and medium belt knives, sword canes/staffs, kitchen cutlery, slip joint folders, throwers. **Patterns:** Utility, hunters, fighters and sailors' knives. **Technical:** Both forged and stock removal knives available in a variety of steels. Unique carvings available on many items. **Prices:** $65 to $250. **Remarks:** Full-time maker; first knife sold in 1988. Doing business as L & H Knife Works. **Mark:** L&H Knife Works.

GUNN, NELSON L., 77 Blake Road, Epping, NH 03042, Phone: 603-679-5119
Specialties: Classic and working/using straight knives of his design. **Patterns:** Bowies, fighters and hunters. **Technical:** Grinds O1 and 440C. Carved stag handles with turquoise inlays. **Prices:** $125 to $300; some to $700. **Remarks:** Part-time maker; first knife sold in 1996. Doing business as Nelson's Custom Knives. **Mark:** First and last initial.

GUNTER, BRAD, 13 Imnaha Road, Tijeras, NM 87059, Phone: 505-281-8080

GURGANUS, MELVIN H., 2553 N. C. 45 South, Colerain, NC 27924, Phone: 252-356-4831, Fax:252-356-4650
Specialties: High-tech working folders. **Patterns:** Leaf-lock and back-lock designs, bolstered and interframe. **Technical:** D2 and 440C; makes mokume. Wife Carol scrimshaws. Heat-treats, carves and offers lost wax casting. **Prices:** $300 to $3,000. **Remarks:** Part-time maker; first knife sold in 1983. **Mark:** First initial, last name and maker.

GURGANUS, CAROL, 2553 N. C. 45 South, Colerain, NC 27924, Phone: 252-356-4831, Fax:252-356-4650
Specialties: Working and using straight knives. **Patterns:** Fighters, hunters and kitchen knives. **Technical:** Grinds D2, ATS-34 and Damascus

steel. Uses stag, and exotic wood handles. **Prices:** $100 to $300. **Remarks:** Full-time maker; first knife sold in 1992. **Mark:** Female symbol, last name, city, state.

GUTHRIE, GEORGE B., 1912 Puett Chapel Rd., Bassemer City, NC 28016, Phone: 704-629-3031
Specialties: Working knives of his design or to customer specs. **Patterns:** Hunters, boots, fighters, locking folders and slip-joints in traditional styles. **Technical:** Grinds D2, 440C and 154CM. **Prices:** $105 to $300; some to $450. **Remarks:** Part-time maker; first knife sold in 1978. **Mark:** Name in state.

h

HAGEN, PHILIP L., P. O. Box 58, Pelican Rapids, MN 56572, Phone: 218-863-8503
Specialties: High-tech working straight knives and folders. **Patterns:** Defense-related straight knives; wide variety of folders. **Technical:** Automatics; 4 styles. **Prices:** $100 to $800; some to $3,000. **Remarks:** Part-time maker; first knife sold in 1975. **Mark:** DOC HAGEN in shield, knife, banner logo; or DOC.

HAGGERTY, GEORGE S., P. O. Box 88, Jacksonville, VT 05342, Phone: 802-368-7437
Specialties: Working straight knives and folders. **Patterns:** Hunters, claws, camp and fishing knives, locking folders and backpackers. **Technical:** Forges and grinds W2, 440C and 154CM. **Prices:** $85 to $300. **Remarks:** Part-time maker; first knife sold in 1981. **Mark:** Initials or last name.

HAGUE, GEOFF, The Malt House, Hollow Ln., Wilton Marlborough, Wiltshire, ENGLAND SN8 3SR, Phone: (+44) 01672-870212, Fax:(+44) 01672 870212
Specialties: Fixed blade and folding knives. **Patterns:** Locking and friction folders, hunters & small knives. **Technical:** Grinds ATS-34, RWL34 and Damascus; others by agreement. **Prices:** Start at $200. **Remarks:** Full-time maker. **Mark:** Last name. **Other:** British voting member of the Knife Makers Guild.

HAINES, JEFF, HAINES CUSTOM KNIVES, 302 N. Mill St, Wauzeka, WI 53826, Phone: 608-875-5002
Patterns: Hunters, skinners, camp knives, customer designs welcome. **Technical:** Forges 1095, 5160, & Damascus, grinds A2. **Prices:** $40 and up. **Remarks:** Part-time maker since 1995. **Mark:** Last name.

HALL, JEFF, PO Box 435, Los Alamitos, CA 90720, Phone: 562-594-4740
Specialties: Collectible and working folders of his design. **Technical:** Grinds ATS-34, 154CM, 440V and various makers' Damascus. **Patterns:** Fighters, gentleman's, hunters and utility knives. **Prices:** $300 to $500; some to $1000. **Remarks:** Full-time maker. First knife sold 1998. **Mark:** Last name.

HALLIGAN, ED, 14 Meadow Way, Sharpsburg, GA 30277, Phone: 770-251-7720, Fax:770-251-7720
Specialties: Working straight knives and folders, some fancy. **Patterns:** Liner locks, hunters, skinners, boots, fighters and swords. **Technical:** Grinds ATS-34; forges 5160; makes cable and pattern Damascus. **Prices:** $160 to $2,500. **Remarks:** Full-time maker; first knife sold in 1985. Doing business as Halligan Knives. **Mark:** Last name, city, state and USA.

HAMLET JR., JOHNNY, 300 Billington, Clute, TX 77531, Phone: 409-265-6929
Specialties: Working straight knives and folders. **Patterns:** Hunters, fighters, fillet and kitchen knives, locking folders. Likes upswept knives and trailing-points. **Technical:** Grinds 440C, D2, ATS-34. Makes sheaths. **Prices:** $55 to $225; some to $500. **Remarks:** Part-time maker; first knife sold in 1988. **Mark:** Hamlet's Handmade in script.

HAMMOND, JIM, P. O. Box 486, Arab, AL 35016, Phone: 256-586-4151, Fax:256-586-0170
Specialties: High-tech fighters and folders. **Patterns:** Proven-design fighters. **Technical:** Grinds 440C, 440V, ATS-34 and other specialty steels. **Prices:** $385 to $1,200; some to $8,500. **Remarks:** Full-time maker; first knife sold in 1977. Designer for Columbia River Knife & Tool. **Mark:** Full name, city, state in shield logo.

HANCOCK, TIM, 10805 N. 83rd St., Scottsdale, AZ 85260, Phone: 480-998-8849
Specialties: High-art and working straight knives and folders of his design and to customer preferences. **Patterns:** Bowies, fighters, daggers, tantos, swords, folders. **Technical:** Forges Damascus and 52100; grinds ATS-34. Makes Damascus. Silver-wire inlays; offers carved fittings and file work. **Prices:** $500 to $10,000. **Remarks:** Full-time maker; first knife sold in 1988. **Mark:** Last name or heart. **Other:** Mastersmith ABS

HAND, BILL, P. O. Box 773, 1103 W. 7th St., Spearman, TX 79081, Phone: 806-659-2967, Fax:806-659-5117
Specialties: Traditional working and using straight knives and folders of his design or to customer specs. **Patterns:** Hunters, Bowies, folders and fighters. **Technical:** Forges 5160, 52100 and Damascus. **Prices:** Start at $150. **Remarks:** Part-time maker; Journeyman Smith. Current delivery time twelve to sixteen months. **Mark:** Stylized initials.

HAND M. D., JAMES E., 1001 Mockingbird Ln., Gloster, MS 39638, Phone: 601-225-4197
Specialties: All types of straight knives. Also High-tec folders for $150. **Patterns:** Hunters, fighters, boots and collector knives. **Technical:** Grinds ATS-34 and commercial Damascus. All knives are handmade. **Prices:** $125 to $850; some to $1,200. **Remarks:** Full-time maker; first knife sold in 1985. **Mark:** Name and city.

HANKINS, R, 9920 S Rural Rd #10859, Tempe, AZ 85284, Phone: 480-940-0559
Specialties: Completely hand-made tactical, practical and custom Bowie knives. Use Damascus, ATS-34 and 440C stainless steel for blades. Stock removal method of grinding. Handle material varies from ivory, stag to Micarta, depending on application and appearance. Part-time maker applying for Knifemakers Guild Int'l membership in June 2001.

HANSEN, LONNIE, PO Box 4956, Spanaway, WA 98387, Phone: 253-847-4632
Specialties: Working straight knives of his design. **Patterns:** Tomahawks, tantos, hunters, filet. **Technical:** Forges 1086, 52100, grinds 440V, BG-42. **Prices:** Starting at $300. **Remarks:** Part-time maker since 1989. **Mark:** First initial and last name. Also first and last initial

HANSEN, ROBERT W., 35701 University Ave. N. E., Cambridge, MN 55008, Phone: 612-689-3242
Specialties: Working straight knives, folders and integrals. **Patterns:** From hunters to minis, camp knives to miniatures; folding lockers and slip-joints in original styles. **Technical:** Grinds O1, 440C and 154CM; likes file-work. **Prices:** $75 to $175; some to $550. **Remarks:** Part-time maker; first knife sold in 1983. **Mark:** Fish with last initial inside.

HANSON III, DON L, P O Box 13, Success, MO 65570-0013, Phone: (573) 674-3045
Specialties: One-of-a-kind Damascus folders. **Patterns:** Small, fancy pocket knives, large folding fighters. **Technical:** I forge my own pattern welded Damascus, file work & carving. **Prices:** $800 & up. **Remarks:** Full-time maker, first knife sold in 1984. **Mark:** Sunfish. **Other:** Member of ABS, ABANA, BAM.

HARA, KOUJI, 292-2 Ohsugi, Seki-City, Gifu-Pref. 501-32, JAPAN, Phone: 0575-24-7569, Fax:0575-24-7569
Specialties: High-tech and working straight knives of his design; some folders. **Patterns:** Hunters, locking folders and utility/camp knives. **Technical:** Grinds Cowry X, Cowry Y and ATS-34. Prefers high mirror polish; pearl handle inlay. **Prices:** $80 to $500; some to $1,000. **Remarks:** Full-time maker; first knife sold in 1980. Doing business as Knife House "Hara". **Mark:** First initial, last name in fish.

HARDY, SCOTT, 639 Myrtle Ave., Placerville, CA 95667, Phone: 530-622-5780
Specialties: Traditional working and using straight knives of his design. **Patterns:** Most anything with an edge. **Technical:** Forges carbon steels. Japanese stone polish. Offers mirror finish; differentially tempers. **Prices:** $100 to $1,000. **Remarks:** Part-time maker; first knife sold in 1982. **Mark:** First initial, last name and Handmade with bird logo.

HARDY, DOUGLAS E, 114 Cypress Rd, Franklin, GA 30217, Phone: (706) 675-6305

HARILDSTAD, MATT, 18627 68 Ave, Edmonton, AB, T5T 2M8, CANADA, Phone: 780-481-3165
Specialties: Working knives, fancy fighting knives, kitchen cutlery, letter openers. **Patterns:** Full range of straight knives in classic patterns. **Technical:** Grinds ATS-34, 440C, commercial damascus and some high carbon. **Prices:** $120 to $500 (US). **Remarks:** Part-time maker, first knife sold in 1997. **Mark:** Name, city province.

HARJU, GARY, Harju's Nordic Knife Supply, 5051 Saddleview Dr, Franklin, TN 30767, Phone: 615-595-9579, Fax:615-595-9579

HARKINS, J. A., P. O. Box 218, Conner, MT 59827, Phone: 406-821-1060
Specialties: Investment grade folders. **Patterns:** flush buttons, lockers. **Technical:** Grinds ATS-34 . Engraves; offers gem work. **Prices:** Start at $550. **Remarks:** Full-time maker and engraver; first knife sold in 1988. **Mark:** First and middle initials, last name.

HARLESS, WALT, P. O. Box 845, Stoneville, NC 27048-0820, Phone: 336-573-9768
Specialties: Traditional working straight knives. **Patterns:** Hunters, utility, combat and specialty knives; one of a kind historical interpretations. **Tech-**

nical: Grinds ATS-34 and 440C. **Prices:** $90 to $350; some to $1,200. **Remarks:** Full-time maker; first knife sold in 1978. Doing business as Arrow Forge. **Mark:** "A" with arrow; name, city, state.

HARLEY, LARRY W., 348 Deerfield Dr., Bristol, TN 37620, Phone: 423-878-5368 (shop), Fax:276-466-6771
Specialties: One of a kind Persian in one of a kind Damascus. **Patterns:** Anything. **Prices:** $500 and up. **Mark:** Pine tree.

HARM, PAUL W, 818 Young Rd, Attica, MI 48412, Phone: (810) 724-5582
Specialties: Early American working knives. **Patterns:** Hunters, skinners, patch knives, fighters, folders. **Technical:** Forges and grinds 1084, 01, 52100 and own Damascus. **Prices:** $75 to $1000. **Remarks:** First knife sold in 1990. **Mark:** Connected initials.

HARMON, JAY, 462 Victoria Rd., Woodstock, GA 30189, Phone: 770-928-2734
Specialties: Working straight knives and folders of his design or to customer specs; collector-grade pieces. **Patterns:** Bowies, daggers, fighters, boots, hunters and folders. **Technical:** Grinds 440C, 440V, ATS-34, D2 1095 and Damascus; heat-treats; makes own mokume. **Prices:** Start at $185. **Remarks:** Part-time maker; first knife sold in 1984. **Mark:** Last name.

HARRINGTON, ROGER, 3 Beech Farm Cottages, Bugsell Lane, East Sussex, ENGLAND TN 32 5 EN, Phone: 44 0 1580 882194
Specialties: Working straight knives to his or customer's designs, flat saber Norwegian style grinds on full tang knives. **Technical:** Grinds 01, D2. **Prices:** £100 to £400. **Remarks:** First knife made by hand in 1997 whilst traveling around the world. Mark: Bison with bison written under.

HARRIS, TEDD, 4419 W Redwood Dr, Cedar Hills, UT 84062, Phone: (801) 785-7651
Specialties: Hunters, fighters, Bowies, kitchen knives - all hand forged. **Technical:** 5160, 1084, L6 & 52100 steels. **Prices:** Start at $200 for kitchen knives; $250 for others. **Mark:** TFHarris Hand Forged Cedar Hills, UT.

HARRIS, RALPH DEWEY, 2607 Bell Shoals Rd., Brandon, FL 33511, Fax:813-654-8175
Specialties: Collector quality interframe folders. **Patterns:** High tech locking folders of his own design with various mechanisms. **Technical:** Grinds 440C, ATS-34 and commercial Damascus. Offers various frame materials including 416ss, and titanium; file worked frames and his own engraving. **Prices:** $400 to $3,000. **Remarks:** Full-time maker; first knife sold in 1978. **Mark:** Last name, or name and city.

HARRIS, JAY, 991 Johnson St., Redwood City, CA 94061, Phone: 415-366-6077
Specialties: Traditional high-tech straight knives and folders of his design. **Patterns:** Daggers, fighters and locking folders. **Technical:** Uses 440C, ATS-34 and CPM. **Prices:** $250 to $850. **Remarks:** Spare-time maker; first knife sold in 1980.

HARRIS, JEFFERY A, 705 Olive St Ste 325, St. Louis, MO 63101, Phone: (314) 241-2442
Remarks: Purveyor and collector of handmade knives.

HARRIS, CASS, 19855 Frasier Hill Lane, Bluemont, VA 20135, Phone: (540) 554-8774
Prices: $160 to $500.

HARRISON, JAMES, 721 Fairington View Dr, St Louis, MO 63129, Phone: 314-894-2525
Specialties: Liner lock folder. **Technical:** 440C

HARRISON, JIM (SEAMUS), 721 Fairington View Dr, St. Louis, MO 63129, Phone: 314-894-2525
Specialties: Gent's/tactical locking liner folders. Straight hunters & backpackers. **Patterns:** Hunters, folders & tacticals. **Technical:** Grinds 440-c, ATS-34, D2, pattern welded heat treats. **Prices:** Straight blades $150-$300 folders $200-$400. **Remarks:** Prefer knives to be minimum size for the purpose. **Mark:** Seamus.

HARSEY, WILLIAM H., 82710 N. Howe Ln., Creswell, OR 97426, Phone: 519-895-4941
Specialties: High-tech kitchen and outdoor knives. **Patterns:** Folding hunters, trout and bird folders; straight hunters, camp knives and axes. **Technical:** Grinds; etches. **Prices:** $125 to $300; some to $1,500. Folders start at $350. **Remarks:** Full-time maker; first knife sold in 1979. **Mark:** Full name, state, U. S. A.

HART, BILL, 647 Cedar Dr., Pasadena, MD 21122, Phone: 410-255-4981
Specialties: Fur-trade era working straight knives and folders. **Patterns:** Springbuck folders, skinners, Bowies and patch knives. **Technical:** Forges and stock removes 1095 and 5160 wire Damascus. **Prices:** $100 to $600. **Remarks:** Part-time maker; first knife sold in 1986. **Mark:** Name.

custom knifemakers

HARTGROVE, WM ANTHONY, P O Box 771482, EAGLE RIVER, AR 99577, Phone: (901) 696-0156

HARTMAN, ARLAN (LANNY), 340 Ruddiman, N. Muskegon, MI 49445, Phone: 616-744-3635
Specialties: Working straight knives and folders. **Patterns:** Drop-point hunters, coil spring lockers, slip-joints. **Technical:** Flat-grinds D2, 440C and ATS-34. **Prices:** $200 to $2,000. **Remarks:** Part-time maker; first knife sold in 1982. **Mark:** Last name.

HARTSFIELD, PHILL, P. O. Box 1637, Newport Beach, CA 92659-0637, Phone: 949-722-9792 & 714-636-7633
Specialties: Heavy-duty working and using straight knives. **Patterns:** Fighters, swords and survival knives, most in Japanese profile. **Technical:** Grinds A2. **Prices:** $350 to $20,000. **Remarks:** Full-time maker; first knife sold about 1966. Doing business as A Cut Above. **Mark:** Initials, chiseled character plus register mark.

HARVEY, Kevin's Custom Knives, Private Bag 1890, Gold Reef City 2159, Johannesburg, SOUTH AFRICA, Phone: +27 11 496 1600, Fax:+27 11 835 2932
Specialties: Large knives of presentation quality and creative art knives. **Patterns:** Fixed blades of Bowie, dagger and fighter styles. Carving and cutlery sets. My design or customized. **Technical:** I mostly stock remove but also forge carbon steel and my own Damascus. Indigenous African handle materials preferred. Stacked handles and file work often used. Shell mosaic and inlay. Own Scrimshaw. Ostrich, bullfrog, fish, crocodile and snake leathers used on unique sheaths. Surface texturing and heat coloring of materials. Work closely with jeweler, sculptor, engraver and case maker. **Prices:** $500 to $9,000. **Remarks:** Full-time maker. First knife sold 1984. Member of the Knife Makers Guild of Southern Africa since 1991. Work in living museum depicting the times of early gold mining in Johannesburg. **Mark:** First name in calligraphy, South Africa.

HARVEY, HEATHER & KEVIN, Heavin Forge, 68 Van Kraayenburg St., Belfast, SOUTH AFRICA, Phone: 27 13 253 0914
Specialties: Collectible, forged ABS Journeyman Smiths. **Patterns:** Historical pieces. **Technical:** Own traditional Damascus. **Prices:** $600-$2000. **Remarks:** Full-time, husband & wife team Kevin & Heather Harvey. **Mark:** Heavin with halo.

HARVEY, MAX, 14 Bass Rd., Bull Creek, Perth 6155, WESTERN AUSTRALIA, Phone: 09-332-7585
Specialties: Daggers, Bowies, fighters and fantasy knives. **Patterns:** Hunters, Bowies, tantos and skinners. **Technical:** Hollow-and flat-grinds 440C, ATS-34, 154CM and Damascus. Offers gem work. **Prices:** $250 to $4,000. **Remarks:** Part-time maker; first knife sold in 1981. **Mark:** First and middle initials, last name.

HASLINGER, THOMAS, 164 Fairview Dr SE, Calgary AB, CANADA T2H 1B3, Phone: 403-253-9628
Specialties: One-of-a-kind using, working & art knives including folders and signature sweeping gridlines. **Patterns:** No fixed patterns, likes to work with customers on design. **Technical:** Grinds BG42, Elmax, RWL 34, ATS 34 and Damascus, high end satin finish. Prefers natural handle materials, e. g., ancient ivory, stag, pearl abalone, stone and exotic woods. I do inlay work with stone, some sterling silver, niobium and gold wire work. Custom sheaths using matching woods or hand stitched with unique leather like salmon, Nile perch or carp. **Prices:** Starting at $150. **Remarks:** Full-time maker; first knife sold in 1994. Doing business as Haslinger Custom Knives. **Mark:** 2 marks used; high end work uses stylized initials, other uses elk antler with Thomas Haslinger, Canada, Handcrafted above

HATCH, KEN, RR 1 Box 83-A-5, Kooskia, ID 83539
Specialties: Indian & early trade knives. **Patterns:** Buckskinners and period Bowies. **Technical:** Forges and grinds 1095, O1, W2, ATS-34. Prefers natural handle materials. **Prices:** $85 to $400. **Remarks:** Part-time maker, custom leather & bead work; first knife sold in 1977. **Mark:** Last name or dragonfly stamp.

HAWES, CHUCK, Hawes Forge, PO Box 176, Weldon, IL 61882, Phone: 217-736-2479
Specialties: 95% of all work in own Damascus. **Patterns:**Slip-joints-Liner locks, hunters bowie's, swords anything in between. **Technical:** Forges everything use all high carbon steels-no stainless. **Prices:** $150-$4000. **Remarks:** Like to do custom orders-my style or yours sells Damascus. **Mark:** Small football shape. Chuck Hawes maker Weldon,IL. **Other:** Full-time maker sine 1995.

HAWK, GRANT, Box 401, Idaho City, ID 83631, Phone: 208-392-4911
Specialties: Cowboy fixed blades with horse hoof handles and rawhide laced sheaths; large folders with unique ambidextrous lock system. **Patterns:** Hunter/utility and tactical folders. **Technical:** Grinds ATS-34, zigzag finish, folder handles of 6061 aluminum or titanium. Handle overlays; horse hoof, exotic woods or other. Checkering of handle overlays available. **Prices:** Start at $325. **Remarks:** Full time maker, first knife sold in 1995. **Mark:** First initials and last name.

HAWK, JACK L., Rt. 1, Box 771, Ceres, VA 24318, Phone: 703-624-3878
Specialties: Fancy and embellished working and using straight knives of his design or to customer specs. **Patterns:** Hunters, Bowies and daggers. **Technical:** Hollow-grinds 440C, ATS-34 and D2; likes bone and ivory handles. **Prices:** $75 to $1,200. **Remarks:** Full-time maker; first knife sold in 1982. **Mark:** Full name and initials.

HAWK, JOEY K., Rt. 1, Box 196, Ceres, VA 24318, Phone: 703-624-3282
Specialties: Working straight knives, some fancy. Welcomes customer designs. **Patterns:** Hunters, fighters, daggers, Bowies and miniatures. **Technical:** Grinds 440C or customer preference. Offers some knives with jewelling. **Prices:** $100 to $250; some to $500. **Remarks:** Part-time maker; first knife sold in 1983. **Mark:** First and middle initials, last name stamped.

HAWK, GAVIN, Box 401, Idaho City, ID 83631, Phone: 208-392-4911
Specialties: Working straight knives with rawhide laced sheaths. **Patterns:** Hunter/utility. **Technical:** Grinds ATS-34 zigzag finish on blade flats; handle material horse hoof in combination with exotic wood or antler. **Prices:** Start at $175. **Remarks:** Part-time maker, 17 years old. Sold first knife in 1996. **Mark:** First and last name on butt cap.

HAWKINS, RADE, 110 Buckeye Rd., Fayetteville, GA 30214, Phone: 770-964-1177, Fax:770-306-2877
Specialties: Exotic steels, custom designs, one-of-a-kind knives. **Patterns:** All styles. **Technical:** Grinds CPM10V, CPM440V, Vascomax C-350, and Damascus. **Prices:** Start at $190. **Remarks:** Full-time maker; first knife sold in 1972. **Mark:** Rade Hawkins Custom Knives.

HAWKINS, BUDDY, P O Box 5969, Texarkana, TX 75505-5969, Phone: (903) 838-7917

HAYES, SCOTTY, Texarkana College, 2500 N Robinson Rd, Texarkana, TX 75501, Phone: 903-838-4541, x3236, Fax:903-832-5030
Specialties: ABS School of Bladesmithing.

HAYES, WALLY, 1026 Old Montreal Rd, Orleans, Ont., CANADA K4A-3N2, Phone: 613-824-9520
Specialties: Classic and fancy straight knives and folders. **Patterns:** Daggers, Bowies, fighters, tantos. **Technical:** Forges own Damascus and O1; engraves. **Prices:** $150 to $14,000. **Mark:** Last name, M. S. and serial number.

HAYES, DOLORES, P. O. Box 41405, Los Angeles, CA 90041, Phone: 213-258-9923
Specialties: High-art working and using straight knives of her design. **Patterns:** Art knives and miniatures. **Technical:** Grinds 440C, stainless AEB, commercial Damascus and ATS-34. **Prices:** $50 to $500; some to $2,000. **Remarks:** Spare-time maker; first knife sold in 1978. **Mark:** Last name.

HAYNIE, CHARLES, 125 Cherry Lane, Toccoa, GA 30577, Phone: 706-886-8665

HAYS, MARK, Hays Handmade Knives, 1008 Kavanagh Dr, Austin, TX 78748, Phone: 512-292-4410
Specialties: Working straight knives and folders. Patterns inspired by Randall & Stone. **Patterns:** Bowies, hunters and slip-joint folders. **Technical:** 440C stock removal. Repairs and restores Stone knives. **Prices:** Start at $200. **Remarks:** Part-time maker, brochure available, with Stone knives 1974-1983, 1990-1991. **Mark:** First initial, last name, state and serial number.

HAZEN, MARK, 9600 Surrey Rd, Charlotte, NC 28227, Phone: 704-573-0904, Fax:704-573-0052
Specialties: Working/using straight knives of his design and to customer specs. **Patterns:** Hunters/skinners, fillet, utility/camp, fighters, short swords. **Technical:** Grinds 154 CM, ATS-34, 440C. **Prices:** $75 to $450; some to $1,500. **Remarks:** Part-time maker. First knife sold 1982. **Mark:** Name with cross in it, stamped in blade.

HEADRICK, GARY, 122 Blvd Wilson, Juan Les Pins, FRANCE 06160, Phone: 04 93 61 25 15
Specialties: Hi-tech folders with natural furnishings. **Patterns:** Damascus & Mokumes. **Prices:** $500 to 2000. **Remarks:** Full-time maker for last 5 years. **Mark:** G/P in a circle. **Other:** 8 years active.

HEARN, TERRY L, Rt 14 Box 7676, Lufkin, TX 75904, Phone: 936-632-5045

HEASMAN, H. G., 28 St. Mary's Rd., Llandudno, N. Wales U. K. LL302UB, Phone: (UK)0492-876351
Specialties: Miniatures only. **Patterns:** Bowies, daggers and swords. **Technical:** Files from stock high-carbon and stainless steel. **Prices:** $400 to $600. **Remarks:** Part-time maker; first knife sold in 1975. Doing business as Reduced Reality. **Mark:** NA.

HEDRICK, DON, 131 Beechwood Hills, Newport News, VA 23608, Phone: 757-877-8100
Specialties: Working straight knives; period pieces and fantasy knives. **Patterns:** Hunters, boots, Bowies and miniatures. **Technical:** Grinds 440C and commercial Damascus. **Prices:** $150 to $550; some to $1,200.

Remarks: Part-time maker; first knife sold in 1982. **Mark:** First initial, last name in oval logo.

HEFLIN, CHRISTOPHER M, 6013 Jocelyn Hollow Rd, Nashville, TN 37205, Phone: (615) 352-3909

HEGWALD, J. L., 1106 Charles, Humboldt, KS 66748, Phone: 316-473-3523
Specialties: Working straight knives, some fancy. **Patterns:** Makes Bowies, miniatures. **Technical:** Forges or grinds O1, L6, 440C; mixes materials in handles. **Prices:** $35 to $200; some higher. **Remarks:** Part-time maker; first knife sold in 1983. **Mark:** First and middle initials.

HEHN, RICHARD KARL, Lehnmuehler Str. 1, 55444 Dorrebach, GERMANY, Phone: 06724 3152
Specialties: High-tech, full integral working knives. **Patterns:** Hunters, fighters & daggers. **Technical:** Grinds CPM T-440V, CPM T-420V, forges his own stainless Damascus. **Prices:** $1000 to $10,000. **Remarks:** Full-time maker; first knife sold in 1963. **Mark:** Runic last initial in logo.

HEINZ, JOHN, 611 Cafferty Rd, Upper Black Eddy, PA 18972, Phone: (610) 847-8535

HEITLER, HENRY, P. O. Box 15025, Tampa, FL 33684-5025, Phone: 813-933-1645
Specialties: Traditional working and using straight knives of his design and to customer specs. **Patterns:** Fighters, hunters, utility/camp knives and fillet knives. **Technical:** Flat-grinds ATS-34; offers tapered tangs. **Prices:** $135 to $450; some to $600. **Remarks:** Part-time maker; first knife sold in 1990. **Mark:** First initial, last name, city, state circling double "H's.

HELSCHER, JOHN W, 2645 Highway 1, Washington, IA 52353, Phone: (319) 653-7310

HELTON, ROY, Helton Knives, 10812 Dapple Way, Bakersfield, CA 93312, Phone: 661-587-8197

HEMBROOK KNIVES, Ron Hembrook, PO Box 201, Neosho, WI 53059, Phone: 920-625-3607
Specialties: Hunters, working knives. **Technical:** Grinds ATS34, 440C, 01 & Damascus. **Prices:** $125 to $750, some to $1000. **Remarks:** First knife sold in 1980. **Mark:** Hembrook plus a serial number. Part-time maker, makes hunters, daggers, Bowies, folders and miniatures.

HEMPERLEY, GLEN, 21106 Roydencrest, Spring, TX 77388, Phone: 281-350-0283
Specialties: Specializes in hunting knives, does fixed and folding knives.

HENDRICKS, SAMUEL J., 2162 Van Buren Rd., Maurertown, VA 22644, Phone: 703-436-3305
Specialties: Integral hunters and skinners of thin design. **Patterns:** Boots, hunters and locking folders. **Technical:** Grinds ATS-34, 440C and D2. Integral liners and bolsters of N-S and 7075 T6 aircraft aluminum. Does leatherwork. **Prices:** $50 to $250; some to $500. **Remarks:** Full-time maker; first knife sold in 1992. **Mark:** First and middle initials, last name, city and state in football-style logo.

HENDRICKSON, E. JAY, 4204 Ballenger Creek Pike, Frederick, MD 21703, Phone: 301-663-6923
Specialties: Classic collectors and working straight knives of his design. **Patterns:** Bowies, Kukri's, camp, hunters, and fighters. **Technical:** Forges 06, 1084, 5160, 52100, D2, L6 and W2; makes Damascus; offers silver wire inlay. Moran styles on order. **Prices:** $400 to $5,000. **Remarks:** Full-time maker; first knife sold in 1975. **Mark:** Last name, M. S.

HENDRICKSON, SHAWN, 2327 Kaetzel Rd, Knoxville, MD 21758, Phone: 301-432-4306
Specialties: Hunting knives. **Patterns:** Clip points, drop points and trailing point hunters. **Technical:** Forges 5160, 1084 and L6. **Prices:** $175 to $400.

HENDRIX, JERRY, Hendriz Custom Knives, 175 Skyland Dr. Ext., Clinton, SC 29325, Phone: 864-833-2659
Specialties: Traditional working straight knives of all designs. **Patterns:** Hunters, utility, boot, bird and fishing. **Technical:** grinds ATS-34 and 440C. **Prices:** $85-$275. **Remarks:** Full-time maker. **Mark:** Full name in shape of knife. **Other:** Hand stitched, waxed leather sheaths.

HENDRIX, WAYNE, 9636 Burton's Ferry Hwy, Allendale, SC 29810, Phone: 803-584-3825, Fax:803-584-3825
Specialties: Working/using knives of his design. **Patterns:** Hunters and fillet knives. **Technical:** Grinds ATS-34, D2 and 440C. **Prices:** $55 to $300. **Remarks:** Full-time maker; first knife sold in 1985. **Mark:** Last name.

HENNON, ROBERT, 940 Vincent Lane, Ft. Walton Beach, FL 32547, Phone: 904-862-9734

HENRIKSEN, HANS J., Birkegaardsvej 24, DK 3200 Helsinge, DENMARK, Fax:45 4879 4899
Specialties: Zirconia ceramic blades. **Patterns:** Customer designs. **Technical:** Slip-cast zirconia-water mix in plaster mould; offers hidden or full tang. **Prices:** White blades start at $10cm; colored +50 percent. **Remarks:** Part-time maker; first ceramic blade sold in 1989. **Mark:** Initial logo.

HENRY & SON, PETER, 332 Nine Mile Ride, Wokingham, Berkshire, ENGLAND RG40 3NJ, Phone: 0118-9734475
Specialties: Period pieces. **Patterns:** Period pieces only--Scottish dirks, sgian dubhs and Bowies, modern hunters. **Technical:** Grinds O1. **Prices:** £50 to £250 or $80 to $400; Bowies £110 to £120. **Remarks:** Full-time maker; first knife sold in 1974. **Mark:** P. Henry & Son.

HENSLEY, WAYNE, P. O. Box 904, Conyers, GA 30012, Phone: 770-483-8938
Specialties: Period pieces and fancy working knives. **Patterns:** Boots to Bowies, locking folders to miniatures. Large variety of straight knives. **Technical:** Grinds ATS34, 440C, D2 and commercial Damascus. **Prices:** $85 and up. **Remarks:** Full-time maker; first knife sold in 1974. **Mark:** Last name.

HERBST, PETER, Komotauer Strasse 26, 91207 Lauf a. d. Pegn., GERMANY, Phone: 09123-13315, Fax:09123-13379
Specialties: Working/using knives and folders of his design. **Patterns:** Hunters, fighters and daggers; interframe and integral. **Technical:** Grinds CPM-T-440V, UHB-Elmax, ATS-34 and stainless Damascus. **Prices:** $300 to $3,000; some to $8,000. **Remarks:** Full-time maker; first knife sold in 1981. **Mark:** First initial, last name.

HERGERT, BOB, 12 Geer Circle, Port Orford, OR 97465, Phone: 541-332-3010

HERMAN, TIM, 7721 Foster, Overland Park, KS 66204, Phone: 913-649-3860, Fax:913-649-0603
Specialties: Investment-grade folders of his design; interframes and bolster frames. **Patterns:** Interframes and new designs in carved stainless. **Technical:** Grinds ATS-34 and damasteel damascus. Engraves and gold inlays with pearl, jade, lapis and Australian opal. **Prices:** $1,000 to $15,000. **Remarks:** Full-time maker; first knife sold in 1978. **Mark:** Etched signature.

HERMES, DANA E., 39594 Kona Ct., Fremont, CA 94538, Phone: 415-490-0393
Specialties: Fancy and embellished classic straight knives of his design. **Patterns:** Hunters and Bowies. **Technical:** Grinds 440C and D2. **Prices:** $200 to $600; some to $1,000. **Remarks:** Spare-time maker; first knife sold in 1985. **Mark:** Last name.

HERNDON, WM. R. "BILL", 32520 Michigan St., Acton, CA 93510, Phone: 661-269-5860, Fax:661-269-4568
Specialties: Straight knives, plain and fancy. **Technical:** Carbon steel (white and blued), Damascus, stainless steels. **Prices:** Start at $120. **Remarks:** Full-time maker; first knife sold in 1976. **Mark:** Signature and/or helm logo.

HERRING, MORRIS, Box 85 721 W Line St, Dyer, AR 72935, Phone: (501) 997-8861

HERRON, GEORGE, 474 Antonio Way, Springfield, SC 29146, Phone: 803-258-3914
Specialties: High-tech working and using straight knives; some folders. **Patterns:** Hunters, fighters, boots in personal styles. **Technical:** Grinds 154CM, ATS-34. **Prices:** $150 to $1,000; some to $2,000. **Remarks:** Full-time maker; first knife sold in 1963. About 12 year back log. Not excepting orders. No catalog. **Mark:** Last name in script.

HESSER, DAVID, P. O. Box 1079, Dripping Springs, TX 78620, Phone: 512-894-0100
Specialties: High-art daggers and fantasy knives of his design; court weapons of the Renaissance. **Patterns:** Daggers, swords, axes, miniatures and sheath knives. **Technical:** Forges 1065, 1095, O1, D2 and recycled tool steel. Offers custom lapidary work and stone-setting, stone handles and custom hardwood scabbards. **Prices:** $95 to $500; some to $6,000. **Remarks:** Full-time maker; first knife sold in 1989. Doing business as Exotic Blades. **Mark:** Last name, year.

HETHCOAT, DON, Box 1764, Clovis, NM 88101, Phone: 505-762-5721
Specialties: Liner lock-locking and multi-blade folders **Patterns:** Hunters, Bowies. **Technical:** Grinds stainless; forges Damascus. **Prices:**Moderate to upscale. **Remarks:** Part-time maker; first knife sold in 1969. **Mark:** Last name on all.

HIBBEN, WESTLEY G., 14101 Sunview Dr., Anchorage, AK 99515
Specialties: Working straight knives of his design or to customer specs. **Patterns:** Hunters, fighters, daggers, combat knives and some fantasy pieces. **Technical:** Grinds 440C mostly. Filework available. **Prices:** $200 to $400; some to $3,000. **Remarks:** Part-time maker; first knife sold in 1988. **Mark:** Signature.

HIBBEN, DARYL, P. O. Box 172, LaGrange, KY 40031-0172, Phone: 502-222-0983
Specialties: Working straight knives, some fancy to customer specs. **Patterns:** Hunters, fighters, Bowies, short sword, art and fantasy. **Technical:** Grinds 440C, ATS-34, 154CM, Damascus; prefers hollow-grinds. **Prices:**

$175 to $3,000. **Remarks:** Full-time maker; first knife sold in 1979. **Mark:** Etched full name in script.

HIBBEN, GIL, P. O. Box 13, LaGrange, KY 40031, Phone: 502-222-1397, Fax:502-222-2676
Specialties: Working knives and fantasy pieces to customer specs. **Patterns:** Full range of straight knives, including swords, axes and miniatures; some locking folders. **Technical:** Grinds ATS-34, 440C and 154CM. **Prices:** $300 to $2,000; some to $10,000. **Remarks:** Full-time maker; first knife sold in 1957. Maker and designer of *Rambo III* knife; made swords for movie *Marked for Death* and throwing knife for movie *Under Seige* made belt buckle knife and knives for movie *Perfect Weapon;* made knives featured in movie *Star Trek the Next Generation;* designer for United Cutlery Official klingon armourer for *Star Trek,* over 30 movies and TV productions. **Mark:** Hibben Knives, city and state, or signature.

HIBBEN, JOLEEN, P. O. Box 172, LaGrange, KY 40031, Phone: 502-222-0983
Specialties: Miniature straight knives of her design; period pieces. **Patterns:** Hunters, axes and fantasy knives. **Technical:** Grinds Damascus, 1095 tool steel and stainless 440C or ATS-34. Uses wood, ivory, bone, feathers and claws on/for handles. **Prices:** $60 to $200. **Remarks:** Spare-time maker; first knife sold in 1991. **Mark:** Initials or first name.

HIELSCHER, GUY, 6550 Otoe Rd, Alliance, NE 69301, Phone: 308-762-4318
Specialties: Traditional and working straight knives of his design, to customer specs and in standard patterns. **Patterns:** Bowies, fighters, skinners, daggers and hunters. **Technical:** Forges his own Damascus from O1 and 1018 steel. **Prices:** $150 to $225; some to $850. **Remarks:** Part-time maker; first knife sold in 1988. Doing business as G. H. Knives. **Mark:** Initials in arrowhead.

HIGH, TOM, 5474 S. 112. 8 Rd., Alamosa, CO 81101, Phone: 719-589-2108
Specialties: Hunters, some fancy. **Patterns:** Drop-points in several shapes; some semi-skinners. Knives designed by and for top outfitters and guides. **Technical:** Grinds ATS-34; likes hollow-grinds, mirror finishes; prefers scrim able handles. **Prices:** $175 to $8,000. **Remarks:** Full-time maker; first knife sold in 1965. Limited edition wildlife series knives. **Mark:** Initials connected; arrow through last name on fancy knives.

HILKER, THOMAS N., P. O. Box 409, Williams, OR 97544, Phone: 541-846-6461
Specialties: Traditional working straight knives and folders. **Patterns:** Folding skinner in two sizes, Bowies, fork and knife sets, camp knives and interchangeable. **Technical:** Grinds D2, 440C and ATS-34. Heat-treats. **Prices:** $50 to $350; some to $400. Doing business as Thunderbolt Artisans. Only limited production models available; not currently taking orders. **Remarks:** Full-time maker; first knife sold in 1983. **Mark:** Last name.

HILL, HOWARD E., 111 Mission Lane, Polson, MT 59860, Phone: 406-883-3405, Fax:406-883-3486
Specialties: Autos, complete new design, legal in Montana (with permit). **Patterns:** Bowies, daggers, skinners and lockback folders. **Technical:** Grinds 440C; uses micro and satin finish. **Prices:** $150 to $1,000. **Remarks:** Part-time maker; first knife sold in 1981. **Mark:** Persuader.

HILL, STEVE E., 40 Rand Pond Rd, Goshen, NH 03752, Phone: 603-863-4762, Fax:603-863-4762
Specialties: Fancy liner lock folders; some exotic mechanisms, some working grade. **Patterns:** Classic to cool. **Technical:** Grinds Damascus and occasional 440C, D2. Prefers natural handle materials; offers elaborate filework, carving, and inlays. **Prices:** $375 to $5,000; some higher. **Remarks:** Full-time maker; first knife sold in 1978. **Mark:** First initial, last name and handmade. **Other:** Knife maker to Rock 'n' Roll stars.

HILL, RICK, 20 Nassau, Maryville, IL 62062-5618, Phone: 618-288-4370
Specialties: Working knives and period pieces to customer specs. **Patterns:** Hunters, locking folders, fighters and daggers. **Technical:** Grinds D2, 440C and 154CM; forges his own Damascus. **Prices:** $75 to $500; some to $3,000. **Remarks:** Part-time maker; first knife sold in 1983. **Mark:** Full name in hill shape logo.

HILLMAN, CHARLES, 225 Waldoboro Rd, Friendship, ME 04547, Phone: 207-832-4634
Specialties: Working knives of my own or custom design. Heavy Scagel influence. **Patterns:** Hunters, fishing, camp and general utility. Occasional folders. **Technical:** Grinds D2 and 440C. File work, blade and handle carving, engraving. Natural handle materials-antler, bone, leather, wood, horn. Sheaths made to order. **Prices:** $60 to $500. **Remarks:** Part-time maker; first knife sold 1986. **Mark:** Last name in oak leaf.

HINDERER, RICK, 5423 Kister Rd., Wooster, OH 44691, Phone: 216-263-0962
Specialties: Working knives to one-of-a-kind Damascus straight knives and folders. **Patterns:** All. **Technical:** Grinds ATS-34 and D2; forges O1,

W2 and his own nickel Damascus steel. **Prices:** $50 to $3,200. **Remarks:** Part-time maker; first knife sold in 1988. Doing business as Mustang Forge. **Mark:** Initials or first initial, last name.

HINK III, LES, 1599 Aptos Lane, Stockton, CA 95206, Phone: 209-547-1292
Specialties: Working straight knives and traditional folders in standard patterns or to customer specs. **Patterns:** Hunting and utility/camp knives; others on request. **Technical:** Grinds carbon and stainless steels. **Prices:** $80 to $200; some higher. **Remarks:** Part-time maker; first knife sold in 1980. Mark : Last name, or last name 3.

HINMAN, TED, 183 Highland Ave, Watertown, MA 02472

HINSON AND SON, R., 2419 Edgewood Rd., Columbus, GA 31906, Phone: 706-327-6801
Specialties: Working straight knives and folders. **Patterns:** Locking folders, liner locks, combat knives and swords. **Technical:** Grinds 440C and commercial Damascus. **Prices:** $100 to $350; some to $1,500. **Remarks:** Part-time maker; first knife sold in 1983. Son Bob is co-worker. **Mark:** HINSON, city and state.

HINTZ, GERALD M., 5402 Sahara Ct., Helena, MT 59602, Phone: 406-458-5412
Specialties: Fancy, high-art, working/using knives of his design. **Patterns:** Bowies, hunters, daggers, fish fillet and utility/camp knives. **Technical:** Forges ATS-34, 440C and D2. Animal art in horn handles or in the blade. **Prices:** $75 to $400; some to $1,000. **Remarks:** Part-time maker; first knife sold in 1980. Doing business as Big Joe's Custom Knives. Will take custom orders. **Mark:** F. S. or W. S. with first and middle initials and last name.

HIRAYAMA, HARUMI, 4-5-13 Kitamachi, Warabi City, Saitama Pref. 335-0001, JAPAN, Phone: 048-443-2248, Fax:048-443-2248
Specialties: High-tech working knives of her design. **Patterns:** Locking folders, interframes, straight gents and slip-joints. **Technical:** Grinds 440C or equivalent; uses natural handle materials and gold. **Prices:** Start at $700. **Remarks:** Part-time maker; first knife sold in 1985. **Mark:** First initial, last name.

HIROTO, FUJIHARA, , 2-34-7 Koioosako Nishi-ku Hiroshima-city, Hiroshima, JAPAN, Phone: 082-271-8389

HITCHMOUGH, HOWARD, 95 Old Street Road, Peterborough, NH 03458-1637, Phone: 603-924-9646, Fax:603-924-9595
Specialties: High class folding knives. **Patterns:** Lockback folders, liner locks, pocket knives. **Technical:** Uses ATS-34, stainless Damascus, titanium, gold and gemstones. Prefers hand-rubbed finishes and natural handle materials. **Prices:** $850 to $3,500; some to $4,500. **Remarks:** Full-time maker; first knife sold in 1967. **Mark:** Last name.

HOBART, GENE, 100 Shedd Rd, Windsor, NY 13865, Phone: (607) 655-1345

HOCKENBARY, WARREN E, 1806 Vallecito Dr, San Pedro, CA 90732

HOCKENSMITH, DAN, P. O. Box E, Drake, CO 80515, Phone: 970-669-5404
Specialties: Traditional working and using straight knives of his design. **Patterns:** Hunters, Bowies, folders and utility/camp knives. **Technical:** Uses his Damascus, 5160, carbon steel. Hand forged. **Prices:** $150 to $600; some to $1,000. **Remarks:** full-time maker; first knife sold in 1987. **Mark:** Name, town & state, anvil

HODGE, J. B., 1100 Woodmont Ave. SE, Huntsville, AL 35801, Phone: 205-536-8388
Specialties: Fancy working folders. **Patterns:** Slip-joints. **Technical:** Grinds 154CM and ATS-34. **Prices:** Start at $175. **Remarks:** Part-time maker; first knife sold in 1978. Not currently taking orders. **Mark:** Name, city and state.

HODGE III, JOHN, 422 S. 15th St., Palatka, FL 32177, Phone: 904-328-3897
Specialties: Fancy straight knives and folders. **Patterns:** Various. **Technical:** Pattern-welded Damascus--"Southern-style. " **Prices:** To $1,000. **Remarks:** Part-time maker; first knife sold in 1981. **Mark:** JH3 logo.

HODGSON, RICHARD J., 9081 Tahoe Lane, Boulder, CO 80301, Phone: 303-666-9460
Specialties: Straight knives and folders in standard patterns. **Patterns:** High-tech knives in various patterns. **Technical:** Grinds 440C, AEB-L and CPM. **Prices:** $850 to $2,200. **Remarks:** Part-time maker. **Mark:** None.

HOEL, STEVE, P. O. Box 283, Pine, AZ 85544, Phone: 602-476-4278
Specialties: Investor-class folders, straight knives and period pieces of his design. **Patterns:** Folding interframes lockers and slip-joints; straight Bowies, boots and daggers. **Technical:** Grinds 154CM, ATS-34 and commercial Damascus. **Prices:** $600 to $1,200; some to $7,500. **Remarks:** Full-time maker. **Mark:** Initial logo with name and address.

HOFER, LOUIS, Gen Del, Rose Prairie BC, CANADA V0C 2H0, Phone: (250) 630-2513

HOFFMAN, KEVIN L., 14672 Kristenright Lane, Orlando, FL 32826-5305, Phone: 407 207-2643, Fax:407 207-2643
Specialties: High-tech working knives, distinctive folders. **Patterns:** Frame lock folders. **Technical:** Grinds ATS-34, Damascus; titanium folders. Makes Kydex sheaths. **Prices:** $400 to $2,000. **Remarks:** Full-time maker since 1981. **Mark:** KLH.

HOFFMANN, UWE H., P. O. Box 60114, Vancouver, BC, CANADA V5W 4B5, Phone: 604-572-7320 (after 5 p. m.)
Specialties: High-tech working knives, folders and fantasy knives of his design or to customer specs. **Patterns:** Hunters, fishing knives, combat and survival knives, folders and diver's knives. **Technical:** Grinds 440C, ATS-34, D2 and commercial Damascus. **Prices:** $95 to $900; some to $2,000 and higher. **Remarks:** Full-time maker; first knife sold in 1985. **Mark:** Hoffmann Handmade Knives.

HOGAN, THOMAS R, 2802 S. Heritage Av, Boise, ID 83709, Phone: (208) 362-7848

HOGSTROM, ANDERS T., 2130 Valerga Dr #8, Belmont, CA 94002, Phone: 650-592-2989
Specialties: Short Dirks of own design. For select pieces makes wooden display boxes. **Patterns:** Dirks, Daggers, Fighters and an occasional Sword. **Technical:** Grinds 1050 High Carbon, ATS-34, 440C, occasional Damascus and ancient ivories. Does clay tempering and uses exotic hardwoods. **Prices:** Start at $225. Marks: Last name in various typefaces.

HOKE, THOMAS M., 3103 Smith Ln, LaGrange, KY 40031, Phone: 502-222-0350
Specialties: Working/using knives, straight knives. Own designs and customer specs. **Patterns:** Daggers, Bowies, Hunters, Fighters, Short Swords. **Technical:** Grind 440C, Damascus and ATS-34. Filework on all knives. Tooling on sheaths (custom fit on all knives). Any handle material - mostly exotic. **Prices:** $100 to $700; some to $1500. **Remarks:** Full-time maker, first knife sold in 1986. **Mark:** Dragon on banner which says T. M. Hoke.

HOLBROOK, H. L., Rt. #3, Box 585, Olive Hill, KY 41164, Phone: 606-738-6542/606-738-6842 Shop
Specialties: Traditional working using straight knives and folders of his design, to customer specs and in standard patterns. **Patterns:** Hunters, folders. **Technical:** Grinds 440C, ATS-34 and D2. Blades have hand-rubbed satin finish. Uses exotic woods, stag and Micarta. Hand sewn sheath with each straight knife. **Prices:** $90 to $270; some to $400. **Remarks:** Part-time maker; first knife sold in 1983. Doing business as Holbrook knives. **Mark:** Name, city, state.

HOLDEN, LARRY, PO Box 2017, Ridgecrest, CA 93555, Phone: 760-375-7955
Specialties: Sculptured high art, fantasy, and classical fixed blade knives of his design. **Patterns:** Sculptured art knives, fantasy, Bowies, bustier, traditional or non traditional. Will work with customer on designs. **Technical:** Hand grinds modern steels, Boye dendritic blanks, Damascus. Sculpts integrated blade, handle, and sheath designs. Mastodon ivory, natural, and exotic materials. Casts in precious metals. **Prices:** $300 and up. **Remarks:** Full-time maker, first complete knife sold 1995. **Mark:** Dragon logo followed by makers name and city.

HOLDER, D'ALTON, 7148 W. Country Gables Dr., Peoria, AZ 85381, Phone: 623-878-3064, Fax:623-878-3964
Specialties: Deluxe working knives and high-art hunters. **Patterns:** Drop-point hunters, fighters, Bowies, miniatures and locking folders. **Technical:** Grinds 440C and 154CM; uses amber and other materials in combination on stick tangs. **Prices:** $300 to $1,000; some to $2,000. **Remarks:** Full-time maker; first knife sold in 1966. **Mark:** D'HOLDER, city and state.

HOLLAND, JOHN H., 1580 Nassau St, Titusville, FL 32780, Phone: 321-267-4378
Specialties: Traditional and fancy working/using straight knives and folders of his design, to customer specs and in standard patterns. **Patterns:** Hunters, and slip-joint folders. **Technical:** Grinds 440V and 440C. Offers engraving. **Prices:** $200 to $500; some to $1,000. **Remarks:** Part-time maker; first knife sold in 1988. doing business as Holland Knives. **Mark:** First and last name, city, state.

HOLLAR, BOB, 701 2nd Ave SW, Great Falls, MT 59404, Phone: 406-268-8252
Specialties: Working/using straight knives and folders of his design and to customer specs; period pieces. **Patterns:** Fighters, hunters, liners & back lock folders. **Technical:** Forges 52100, 5160, 15N20 & 1084 (Damascus)*. **Prices:** $225 to $650; some to $1,500. **Remarks:** Full-time maker. doing business as Goshawk Knives. **Mark:** Goshawk stamped. **Other:** *Burled woods, stag, ivory; all stabilized material for handles.

HOLLOWAY, PAUL, 714 Burksdale Rd., Norfolk, VA 23518, Phone: 804-588-7071
Specialties: Working straight knives and folders to customer specs. **Patterns:** Lockers and slip-joints; fighters and boots; fishing and push knives, from swords to miniatures. **Technical:** Grinds A2, D2, 154CM, 440C and ATS-34. **Prices:** $125 to $400; some to $1,200. **Remarks:** Part-time maker; first knife sold in 1981. **Mark:** Last name, or last name and city in logo.

HOLMES, ROBERT, 1431 S Eugene St, Baton Rouge, LA 70808-1043, Phone: 504-291-4864
Specialties: Using straight knives and folders of his design or to customer specs. **Patterns:** Bowies, utility hunters, camp knives, skinners, slip-joint and lock-back folders. **Technical:** Forges 1065, 1095 and L6. Makes his own Damascus and cable Damascus. Offers clay tempering. **Prices:** $150 to $1,500. **Remarks:** Part-time maker; first knife sold in 1988. **Mark:** DOC HOLMES, or anvil logo with last initial inside.

HOLUM, MORTEN, Bolerskrenten 28, 0691, Oslo, NORWAY, Phone: 011-47-22-27-69-96
Specialties: Working straight knives. **Patterns:** Traditional Norwegian knives, hunters, fighters, axes. **Technical:** Forges Damascus. Uses his own blades. **Prices:** $200 to $800; some to $1,500. **Remarks:** Part-time maker; first knife sold in 1986. **Mark:** Last name.

HORN, DES, 5 Wenlock Rd, Newlands, 7700 Cape Town, SOUTH AFRICA, Phone: 27 21 671 5795, Fax:27 21 671 5795
Specialties: Folding knives. **Patterns:** Ball release side lock mechanism and interframe automatics. **Technical:** Prefers working in totally stainless materials. **Prices:** $400 to $2000. **Remarks:** Enjoys working in gold, titanium, meteorite, pearl & mammoth. **Mark:** Des Horn.

HORN, JESS, 2526 Lansdown Rd, Eugene, OR 97404, Phone: 541-463-1510
Specialties: Investor-class working folders; period pieces; collectibles. **Patterns:** High-tech design and finish in folders; liner locks, traditional slip-joints and featherweight models. **Technical:** Grinds ATS-34, 154CM. **Prices:** Start at $1000. **Remarks:** Full-time maker; first knife sold in 1968. **Mark:** Full name or last name.

HORNE, GRACE, 182 Crimicar Ln, Sheffield, BRITIAN S10 4EJ
Specialties: Knives of own design including kitchen and utility knives for people with reduced hand use. **Technical:** Working at Sheffield Hallam University researching innovative, contemporary damasks steels using non-traditional methods of manufacture. **Remarks:** Spare time maker/full time researcher. **Mark:** 'gH' & 'Sheffield'.

HORTON, SCOT, P. O. Box 451, Buhl, ID 83316, Phone: 208-543-4222
Specialties: Traditional working stiff knives and folders. **Patterns:** Hunters, skinners, utility and show knives. **Technical:** Grinds ATS-34. Uses stag, abalone and exotic woods. **Prices:** $200 to $2,500. **Remarks:** First knife sold in 1990. **Mark:** Full name in arch underlined with arrow, city, state.

HOSSOM, JERRY, 3585 Schilling ridge, Duluth, GA 30096, Phone: 770-449-7809
Specialties: Working straight knives of his own design. Patterns: Fighters, combat knives, modern bowies and daggers, modern swords, concealment knives for military and LE uses. **Technical:** Grinds 154CM, S30V, CPM-3V and stainless Damascus. Uses natural and synthetic handle materials. **Prices:** $250-1500, some higher. **Remarks:** Full-time maker since 1997. First knife sold in 1983. **Mark:** First initial and last name, includes city and state since 2002.

HOUSE, GARY, 2851 Pierce Rd, Ephrata, WA 98823, Phone: (509) 754-3272
Specialties: Mosaic Damascus bar stock. **Patterns:** Unlimited, SW Indian designs, geometric patterns, using 1084, 15N20 & some nickel. **Prices:** $50 per inch and up. **Remarks:** Some of the finest and most unique patterns available.

HOUSE, LAWRENCE, 932 Eastview Dr, Canyon Lake, TX 78133, Phone: (830) 899-6932

HOWARD, DURVYN M., 4220 McLain St. S., Hokes Bluff, AL 35903, Phone: 256-492-5720
Specialties: Collectible upscale folders; one of kinds, gentlemen's folders. Multiple patents. **Patterns:** Conceptual designs; each unique and different. **Technical:** Uses natural and exotic materials and precious metals. **Prices:** $5,000 to $25,000. **Remarks:** Full-time maker; by commission or available work. **Mark:** Howard: new for 2000; Howard in Garamond Narrow "etched". **Other:** Work displayed at select shows, K. G. Show etc.

HOWE, TORI, 13000 E Stampede Rd, Athol, ID 83801

HOWELL, JASON G, 213 Buffalo Trl, Lake Jackson, TX 77566, Phone: (979) 297-9454
Specialties: Fixed blades and liner lock folders. Makes own Damascus. **Patterns:** Clip & drop point. **Prices:** $150 to $750. **Remarks:** I like making Mosaic Damascus out of the ordinary stuff. Member of TX Knifemakers &

custom knifemakers

Collectors Association; apprentice in ABS; working towards Journeyman Stamp. **Mark:** Name, city, state.

HOWELL, ROBERT L., Box 1617, Kilgore, TX 75663, Phone: 903-986-4364
Specialties: Straight knives and folders of his design. **Patterns:** Hunters and locking folders. **Technical:** Grinds D2 and ATS-34; forges and grinds Damascus. **Prices:** $75 to $200; some to $2,500. **Remarks:** Part-time maker; first knife sold in 1978. Doing business as Howell Knives. **Mark:** Last name.

HOWELL, LEN, 550 Lee Rd. 169, Opelika, AL 36804, Phone: 334-749-1942
Specialties: Traditional and working knives of his design and to customer specs. **Patterns:** Buckskinner, hunters and utility/camp knives. **Technical:** Forges cable Damascus, 1085 and 5160; makes own Damascus. **Mark:** Engraved last name.

HOWELL, TED, 1294 Wilson Rd., Wetumpka, AL 36092, Phone: 205-569-2281, Fax:205-569-1764
Specialties: Working/using straight knives and folders of his design; period pieces. **Patterns:** Bowies, fighters, hunters. **Technical:** Forges 5160, 1085 and cable. Offers light engraving and scrimshaw. **Prices:** $75 to $250; some to $450. **Remarks:** Part-time maker; first knife sold in 1991. Doing business as Howell Co. **Mark:** Last name, Slapout AL.

HOWSER, JOHN C., 54 Bell Ln., Frankfort, KY 40601, Phone: 502-875-3678
Specialties: Slip joint folders (old patterns-multi blades). **Patterns:** traditional slip joint folders, lockbacks, hunters & fillet knives. **Technical:** ATS-34 standard steel, will use D-2, 440V-hand rubbed satin finish natural materials. **Prices:** $100-$400 some to $500. **Remarks:** Part-time maker; first knife sold in 1974. **Mark:** Signature or stamp.

HOY, KEN, 54744 Pinchot Dr., North Fork, CA 93643, Phone: 209-877-7805

HRISOULAS, JIM, 330 S. Decatur Ave., Suite 109, Las Vegas, NV 89107, Phone: 702-566-8551
Specialties: Working straight knives; period pieces. **Patterns:** Swords, daggers and sgian dubhs. **Technical:** Double-edged differential heat treating. **Prices:** $85 to $175; some to $600 and higher. **Remarks:** Full-time maker; first knife sold in 1973. Author of *The Complete Bladesmith, The Pattern Welded Blade* and *The Master Bladesmith* Doing business as Salamander Armory. **Mark:** 8R logo and sword and salamander.

HUCKABEE, DALE, 254 Hwy 260, Maylene, AL 35114
Specialties: Fixed blade hunter & Bowies of my design. **Technical:** Steel used: 5160, 1095, 1084 & some Damascus. **Prices:** Starting at $95 & up, depending on materials used. **Remarks:** Hand forged & stock removal. **Mark:** Stamped HUCKABEE. **Other:** Part-time maker.

HUDSON, ROB, 340 Roush Rd, Northumberland, PA 17857, Phone: 570-473-9588
Specialties: Custom hunters, bowies, daggers, tantos, miniatures, custom orders. **Technical:** Grinds ATS-34, carbon & stainless steel, damascus, hollow grinds or flat. Filework, finger grooves. Engraving and scrimshaw available. **Prices:** $100 to $500. **Remarks:** Part time maker. Business: Rob's Custom Knives. **Mark:** Capital R, Capital H in script.

HUDSON, ROBERT, 3802 Black Cricket Ct., Humble, TX 77396, Phone: 713-454-7207
Specialties: Working straight knives of his design. **Patterns:** Bowies, hunters, skinners, fighters and utility knives. **Technical:** Grinds D2, 440C, 154CM and commercial Damascus. **Prices:** $85 to $350; some to $1,500. **Remarks:** Part-time maker; first knife sold in 1980. **Mark:** Full name, hand-made, city and state.

HUDSON, C. ROBBIN, 22280 Frazier Rd., Rock Hall, MD 21661, Phone: 410-639-7273
Specialties: High-art working knives. **Patterns:** Hunters, Bowies, fighters and kitchen knives. **Technical:** Forges W2, nickel steel, pure nickel steel, composite and mosaic Damascus; makes knives one at a time. **Prices:** 500 to $1200; some to $5,000. **Remarks:** Full-time maker; first knife sold in 1970. **Mark:** Last name and MS.

HUDSON, ANTHONY B, 279 Valley St, Midland, OH 45148, Phone: (937) 783-5822

HUEY, STEVE, 5060 W Port St, Eugene, OR 97402, Phone: 541-484-7344
Specialties: Working straight knives, some one-of-a-kind. **Patterns:** Folders, fixed hunting, fighters, kitchen knives, some one of a kind. **Technical:** D2 and ATS-34 carbon on request. **Prices:** $75 to $600. **Remarks:** Part-time maker; first knife sold in 1981. **Mark:** Last name in rectangle.

HUGHES, DAN, 13743 Persimmon Blvd., West Palm Beach, FL 33411
Specialties: Working straight knives to customer specs. **Patterns:** Hunters, fighters, fillet knives. **Technical:** Grinds 440C and ATS-34. **Prices:**

$55 to $175; some to $300. **Remarks:** Part-time maker; first knife sold in 1984. **Mark:** Initials.

HUGHES, BILL, 110 Royale Dr, Texarkana, TX 75503, Phone: (903) 838-0134

HUGHES, DARYLE, 10979 Leonard, Nunica, MI 49448, Phone: 616-837-6623
Specialties: Working knives. **Patterns:** Buckskinners, hunters, camp knives, kitchen and fishing knives. **Technical:** Forges and grinds W2, O1 and D2. **Prices:** $40 to $100; some to $400. **Remarks:** Part-time maker; first knife sold in 1979. **Mark:** Name and city in logo.

HUGHES, ED, 280 1/2 Holly Lane, Grand Junction, CO 81503, Phone: 970-243-8547
Specialties: Working and art folders. **Patterns:** Folders. **Technical:** Grinds stainless steels. Engraves. **Prices:** $75 to $250; some to $600. **Remarks:** Full-time maker; first knife sold in 1978. **Mark:** Name or initials.

HUGHES, LAWRENCE, 207 W. Crestway, Plainview, TX 79072, Phone: 806-293-5406
Specialties: Working and display knives. **Patterns:** Bowies, daggers, hunters, buckskinners. **Technical:** Grinds D2, 440C and 154CM. **Prices:** $125 to $300; some to $2,000. **Remarks:** Full-time maker; first knife sold in 1979. **Mark:** Name with buffalo skull in center.

HULETT, STEVE, 115 Yellowstone Ave, West Yellowstone, MT 59758, Phone: 888-735-0634
Specialties: Classic, working/using knives, straight knives, folders. Your design, custom specs. **Patterns:** Utility/camp knives, hunters, and liner lock folders. **Technical:** Grinds 440C stainless steel, O1 Carbon, 1095. Shop is retail and knife shop--people watch their knives being made. We do everything in house--"all but smelt the ore, or tan the hide. " **Prices:** $125 to $7,000. **Remarks:** Full-time maker; first knife sold in 1994.

HULL, MICHAEL J., 1330 Hermits Circle, Cottonwood, AZ 86326, Phone: 520-634-2871
Specialties: Period pieces and working knives. **Patterns:** Hunters, fighters, Bowies, camp and Mediterranean knives, etc. **Technical:** Grinds 440C, ATS-34 and BG42 and S30V. **Prices:** $125 to $750; some to $1000. **Remarks:** Full-time maker; first knife sold in 1983. **Mark:** Name, city, state.

HULSEY, HOYT, 379 Shiloh, Attalla, AL 35954, Phone: 256-538-6765
Specialties: Traditional working straight knives and folders of his design. **Patterns:** Hunters and utility/camp knives. **Technical:** Grinds 440C, ATS-34, O1 and A2. **Prices:** $75 to $250. **Remarks:** Part-time maker; first knife sold in 1989. **Mark:** Hoyt Hulsey Attalla AL.

HUMENICK, ROY, P. O. Box 55, Rescue, CA 95672
Specialties: Multiplied folders of his design. **Patterns:** Traditional folders, whittlers and trappers. **Technical:** Grinds ATS-34, BG-42 & Damascus. **Prices:** $300 and up; some to $1,500. **Remarks:** First knife sold in 1984. **Mark:** Last name in ARC.

HUMPHREYS, JOEL, 3260 Palmer Rd, Bowling Green, FL 33834-9801, Phone: 863-773-0439
Specialties: Traditional working/using straight knives and folders of his design and in standard patterns. **Patterns:** Hunters, folders and utility/camp knives. **Technical:** Grinds ATS-34, D2, 440C. All knives have tapered tangs, mitered bolster/handle joints, handles of horn or bone fitted sheaths. **Prices:** $135 to $225; some to $350. **Remarks:** Part-time maker; first knife sold in 1990. Doing business as Sovereign Knives. **Mark:** First name or "H" pierced by arrow.

HUNT, MAURICE, 2492 N 800 E, Winter: 2925 Argyle Rd Venice FL 34293, AVON, IN 46123, Phone: 317 272-2669/Winter: 941-493-4027, Fax:317 272-2159
Patterns: Bowies, hunters, fighters. **Prices:** $200 to $800. **Remarks:** Spare-time maker prior to 1995; Part-time maker after 1995. **Other:** Journeyman smith as of 6/01.

HUNTER, RICHARD D, 7230 NW 200th Terrace, Alachua, FL 32615, Phone: (904) 462-3150
Specialties: Traditional working/using knives of his design or customer suggestions; filework. **Patterns:** Folders of various types, Bowies, hunters, daggers. **Technical:** Traditional blacksmith; hand forges high carbon steel (5160, 1084, 52100) and makes own Damascus; grinds 440C and ATS34. **Prices:** $200 & up. **Remarks:** Part-time maker; first knife sold in 1992. **Mark:** Last name in capital letters.

HUNTER, HYRUM, 285 N. 300 W., P. O. Box 179, Aurora, UT 84620, Phone: 435-529-7244
Specialties: Working straight knives of my design or to customer specs. **Patterns:** Drop and clip, fighters dagger, some folders. **Technical:** Forged from two piece Damascus. **Prices:** Prices are adjusted according to size, complexity and material used. **Remarks:** I will consider any design you have. Part-time maker; first knife sold in 1990. **Mark:** Initials encircled with first initial and last name and city, then state. Some patterns are numbered.

HURST, COLE, 1583 Tedford, E. Wenatchee, WA 98802, Phone: 509-884-9206
Specialties: Fantasy, high-art and traditional straight knives. **Patterns:** Bowies, daggers and hunters. **Technical:** Blades are made of stone; handles are made of stone, wood or ivory and embellished with fancy woods, ivory or antlers. **Prices:** $100 to $300; some to $2,000. **Remarks:** Spare-time maker; first knife sold in 1985. **Mark:** Name and year.

HURST, JEFF, P. O. Box 247, Rutledge, TN 37861, Phone: 865-828-5729
Specialties: Working straight knives and folders of his design. **Patterns:** Tomahawks, hunters, boots, folders and fighters. **Technical:** Forges W2, O1 and his own Damascus. Makes mokume. **Prices:** $175 to $350; some to $500. **Remarks:** Full-time maker; first knife sold in 1984. Doing business as Buzzard's Knob Forge. **Mark:** Last name; partnered knives are marked with Newman L. Smith, handle artisan, and SH in script.

HURT, WILLIAM R., 9222 Oak Tree Cir., Frederick, MD 21701, Phone: 301-898-7143
Specialties: Traditional and working/using straight knives. **Patterns:** Bowies, hunters, fighters and utility knives. **Technical:** Forges 5160, O1 and O6; makes own Damascus. Offers silver wire inlay. **Prices:** $200 to $600; some higher. **Remarks:** Full-time maker; first knife sold in 1989. **Mark:** First and middle initials, last name.

HUSIAK, MYRON, P. O. Box 238, Altona 3018, Victoria, AUSTRALIA, Phone: 03-315-6752
Specialties: Straight knives and folders of his design or to customer specs. **Patterns:** Hunters, fighters, lock-back folders, skinners and boots. **Technical:** forges and grinds his own Damascus, 440C and ATS-34. **Prices:** $200 to $900. **Remarks:** Part-time maker; first knife sold in 1974. **Mark:** First initial, last name in logo and serial number.

HYDE, JIMMY, 5094 Stagecoach Rd., Ellenwood, GA 30049, Phone: 404-968-1951, Fax:404-209-1741
Specialties: Working straight knives of any design; period pieces. **Patterns:** Bowies, hunters and utility knives. **Technical:** Grinds 440C; forges 5160, 1095 & O1. Makes his own Damascus and cable Damascus. **Prices:** $150 to $600; some to $400. **Remarks:** Part-time maker; first knife sold in 1978. **Mark:** First initial, last name.

HYTOVICK, JOE"HY", 14872 SW 111th St., Dunnellon, FL 34432, Phone: 800-749-5339
Specialties: Straight, Folder & Miniature. **Technical:** Blades from Wootz, Damascus and Alloy steel. **Prices:** To $5,000. **Mark:** HY

i

IKOMA, FLAVIO YUJI, R. MANOEL R. TEIXEIRA, 108, 108, Centro Presidente Prudente, SP-19031-220, BRAZIL, Phone: 0182-22-0115
Specialties: Straight knives and folders of all designs. **Patterns:** Fighters, hunters, Bowies, swords, folders, skinners, utility and defense knives. **Technical:** Grinds and forges D6, 440C, high-carbon steels and Damascus. **Prices:** $60 to $350; some to $3,300. **Remarks:** Full-time maker; first knife sold in 1991. All stainless steel blades are ultra sub-zero quenched. **Mark:** Ikoma Knives beside eagle.

IMBODEN II, HOWARD L., 620 Deauville Dr., Dayton, OH 45429, Phone: 513-439-1536
Specialties: One-of-a-kind hunting, flint, steel and art knives. **Technical:** Forges and grinds stainless, high-carbon and Damascus. Uses obsidian, cast sterling silver, 14K and 18K gold guards. Carves ivory animals and more. **Prices:** $65 to $25,000. **Remarks:** Full-time maker; first knife sold in 1986. Doing business as Hill Originals. **Mark:** First and last initials, II.

IMEL, BILLY MACE, 1616 Bundy Ave., New Castle, IN 47362, Phone: 765-529-1651
Specialties: High-art working knives, period pieces and personal cutlery. **Patterns:** Daggers, fighters, hunters; locking folders and slip-joints with interframes. **Technical:** Grinds D2, 440C and 154CM. **Prices:** $300 to $2,000; some to $6,000. **Remarks:** Part-time maker; first knife sold in 1973. **Mark:** Name in monogram.

INMAN III, PAUL R, 3120 B Blake Ave #224, Glenwood Springs, CO 81601, Phone: 970-963-5951
Specialties: Bowies in the Moran style. **Prices:** $300-$1000.

IRIE, MICHAEL L, Mike Irie Handcraft, 1606 Auburn Dr., Colorado Springs, CO 80909, Phone: 719-572-5330
Specialties: Working fixed blade knives and handcrafted blades for the do-it-yourselfer. **Patterns:** Twenty standard designs along with custom. **Technical:** Blades are ATS-34, BG-43, 440C with some outside Damascus. **Prices:** Fixed blades $95 & up, blade work $45 and up. **Remarks:** Formerly dba Wood, Irie & Co. with Barry Wood. Full-time maker since 1991. **Mark:** Name.

IRON WOLF FORGE, SEE NELSON, KEN,

ISAO, OHBUCHI, , 702-1 Nouso Yame-City, Fukuoka, JAPAN, Phone: 0943-23-4439

ISGRO, JEFFERY, 1516 First St, West Babylon, NY 11704, Phone: 631-587-7516
Specialties: File work, glass beading, kydex, leather. **Patterns:** Tactical use knives, skinners, capers, Bowies, camp, hunters. **Technical:** ATS 34, 440C & D2. **Price:** $120 to $600. **Remarks:** Part-time maker. **Mark:** First name, last name, Long Island, NY.

ISHIHARA, HANK, 86-18 Motomachi, Sakura City, Chiba Pref., JAPAN, Phone: 043-485-3208, Fax:043-485-3208
Specialties: Fantasy working straight knives and folders of his design. **Patterns:** Boots, Bowies, daggers, fighters, hunters, fishing, locking folders and utility camp knives. **Technical:** Grinds ATS-34, 440C, D2, 440V, CV-134, COS25 and Damascus. Engraves. **Prices:** $250 to $1,000; some to $10,000. **Remarks:** Full-time maker; first knife sold in 1987. **Mark:** HANK.

j

JACKS, JIM, 344 S. Hollenbeck Ave., Covina, CA 91723-2513, Phone: 626-331-5665
Specialties: Working straight knives in standard patterns. **Patterns:** Bowies, hunters, fighters, fishing and camp knives, miniatures. **Technical:** Grinds Stellite 6K, 440C and ATS-34. **Prices:** Start at $100. **Remarks:** Spare-time maker; first knife sold in 1980. **Mark:** Initials in diamond logo.

JACKSON, DAVID, 214 Oleander Av, Lemoore, CA 93245, Phone: (559) 925-8547
Specialties: Forged steel. **Patterns:** Hunters, camp knives, Bowies. **Prices:** $150 and up. **Mark:** G. D. Jackson - Maker - Lemoore CA.

JACKSON, JIM, 10 Chantry Close, Windsor, Berkshire SL4 5EP, ENGLAND, Phone: 01753-858729, Fax:01753 771986
Specialties: Large Bowies, concentrating on form and balance; collector quality Damascus daggers. **Patterns:** With fancy filework & engraving available. **Technical:** Forges O1, 5160 and CS70 and 15N20 Damascus. **Prices:** From $1,000. **Remarks:** Part-time maker. **Mark:** Jackson England with in a circle M. S. **Other:** All knives come with a custom tooled leather swivel sheath or exotic materials.

JACKSON, CHARLTON R, 6811 Leyland Dr, San Antonio, TX 78239, Phone: (210) 601-5112

JAKSIK JR, MICHAEL, 427 Marschall Creek Rd, Fredericksburg, TX 78624, Phone: (830) 997-1119
Mark: MJ or M. Jaksik

JAMES, PETER, 2549 W. Golf Rd., #290, Hoffman Estates, IL 60194, Phone: 708-310-9113, Fax:708-885-1716
Specialties: Working/using straight knives of his design and in standard patterns. **Patterns:** Bowies, daggers and urban companion knives. **Technical:** Grinds 440C and soligen tool. Makes a variety of sheaths for urban companion series. **Prices:** $48 to $250. **Remarks:** Part-time maker; first knife sold in 1986. doing business as Peter James & Sons. **Mark:** Initials overlapped.

JANIGA, MATTHEW A., 15950 Xenia St. NW, Andover, MN 55304-2346, Phone: 612-427-2510
Specialties: Period pieces, swords, daggers. **Patterns:** Daggers, fighters and swords. **Technical:** Forges 5160, Damascus and 52100. Does own heat treating. Forges own pattern-welded steel. **Prices:** $100 - $1000; some to $5,000. **Remarks:** Spare-time maker; first knife sold in 1991. **Mark:** Interwoven initials.

JARVIS, PAUL M., 30 Chalk St., Cambridge, MA 02139, Phone: 617-547-4355 or 617-666-9090
Specialties: High-art knives and period pieces of his design. **Patterns:** Japanese and Mid-Eastern knives. **Technical:** Grinds Myer Damascus, ATS-34, D2 and O1. Specializes in height-relief Japanese-style carving. Works with silver, gold and gems. **Prices:** $200 to $17,000. **Remarks:** Part-time maker; first knife sold in 1978.

JEAN, GERRY, 25B Cliffside Dr., Manchester, CT 06040, Phone: 860-649-6449
Specialties: Historic replicas. **Patterns:** Survival and camp knives. **Technical:** Grinds A2, 440C and 154CM. Handle slabs applied in unique tongue-and-groove method. **Prices:** $125 to $250; some to $1,000. **Remarks:** Spare-time maker; first knife sold in 1973. **Mark:** Initials and serial number.

JEFFRIES, ROBERT W., Route 2, Box 227, Red House, WV 25168, Phone: 304-586-9780
Specialties: Straight knives and folders. **Patterns:** Hunters, skinners and folders. **Technical:** Uses 440C, ATS-34; makes his own Damascus.

custom knifemakers

Prices: Moderate. **Remarks:** Part-time maker; first knife sold in 1988. **Mark:** NA.

JENSEN, JOHN LEWIS, dba Magnus Design Studio, PO Box 60547, Pasadena, CA 91116, Phone: 626-449-1148, Fax:626-449-1148
Specialties: Designer & fabricator of modern, unique, elegant, innovative, original, one-of-a-kind, hand crafted, custom ornamental edged weaponry. Combines skill, precision, distinction & the finest materials, geared toward the discriminating art collector. **Patterns:** Folding knives & fixed blades, daggers, fighters & swords. **Technical:**High embellishment, BFA 96 Rhode Island School of Design: Jewelry & metalsmithing. Grinds 440C, ATS-34, Damascus. Works with custom made Damascus to his specs. Uses gold, silver, gemstones, pearl, titanium, fossil mastodon & walrus ivories. Carving, file work, soldering, deep etches Damascus, engraving, layers, bevels, blood grooves. **Prices:** Start at $3,500. **Remarks:** Available on a 1st come basis & via commission based on his designs. **Mark:** Maltese cross/butterfly shield.

JENSEN JR., CARL A., 8957 Country Road P-35, Blair, NE 68008, Phone: 402-426-3353
Specialties: Working knives of his design; some customer designs. **Patterns:** Hunters, fighters, boots and Bowies. **Technical:** Grinds A2, D2, O1, 440C, 5160 and ATS-34; recycles old files, leaf springs; heat-treats. **Prices:** $35 to $350. **Remarks:** Part-time maker; first knife sold in 1980. **Mark:** Stamp "BEAR'S CUTLERY" or etch of letters "BEAR" forming silhouette of a Bear.

JERNIGAN, STEVE, 3082 Tunnel Rd., Milton, FL 32571, Phone: 850-994-0802, Fax:850-994-0802
Specialties: Investor-class folders and various theme pieces. **Patterns:** Array of models and sizes in side plate locking interframes and conventional liner construction. **Technical:** Grinds ATS-34, CPM-T-440V and Damascus. Inlays mokume (and minerals) in blades and sculpts marble cases. **Prices:** $650 to $1,800; some to $6,000. **Remarks:** Full-time maker; first knife sold in 1982. Takes orders for folders only. **Mark:** Last name.

JOBIN, JACQUES, 46 St. Dominique, Levis Quebec, CANADA G6V 2M7, Phone: 418-833-0283, Fax:418-833-8378
Specialties: Fancy and working straight knives and folders; miniatures. **Patterns:** Minis, fantasy knives, fighters and some hunters. **Technical:** ATS-34, some Damascus and titanium. Likes native snake wood. Heat-treats. **Prices:** Start at $250. **Remarks:** Full-time maker; first knife sold in 1986. **Mark:** Signature on blade.

JOEHNK, BERND, Posadowskystrasse 22, 24148 Kiel, GERMANY, Phone: 0431-7297705, Fax:0431-7297705
Specialties: One of a kind fancy/embellished and traditional straight knives of his design and to customer specs. **Patterns:** Daggers, fighters, hunters and letter openers. **Technical:** Grinds 440C, ATS-34, commercial Damascus and various stainless and corrosion-resistant steels. Likes filework. Leather sheaths. Offers engraving. **Prices:** Upscale. **Remarks:** Part-time maker; first knife sold in1990. **Mark:** Full name and city.

JOHANNING CUSTOM KNIVES, TOM, 1735 Apex Rd, Sarasota, FL 34240 9386, Phone: 941-371-2104, Fax:941-378-9427

JOHANSSON, ANDERS, Konstvartarevagen 9, S-772 40 Grangesberg, SWEDEN, Phone: 46 240 23204, Fax:+46 21 358778
Specialties: Scandinavian traditional and modern straight knives. **Patterns:** Hunters, fighters and fantasy knives. **Technical:** Grinds stainless steel and makes own Damascus. Prefers water buffalo and mammoth for handle material. **Prices:** Start at $100. **Remarks:** Spare-time maker; first knife sold in 1994. Works together with scrimshander Viveca Sahlin. **Mark:** Stylized initials.

JOHNS, ROB, 1423 S. Second, Enid, OK 73701, Phone: 405-242-2707
Specialties: Classic and fantasy straight knives of his design or to customer specs; fighters for use at Medieval fairs. **Patterns:** Bowies, daggers and swords. **Technical:** Forges and grinds 440C, D2 and 5160. Handles of nylon, walnut or wire-wrap. **Prices:** $150 to $350; some to $2,500. **Remarks:** Full-time maker; first knife sold in 1980. **Mark:** Medieval Customs, initials.

JOHNSON, HAROLD "HARRY" C., 98 Penn St, Trion, GA 30753-1520
Specialties: Working straight knives. **Patterns:** Mostly hunters and large Bowies. **Technical:** Grinds popular steels. Offers leatherwork, sheaths and cases. **Prices:** $125 to $2,000; some higher. **Remarks:** Part-time maker; first knife sold in 1973. **Mark:** First initial, last name, city, state. **Other:** Also makes wood and leather cases for knives and guns.

JOHNSON, JOHN R, 5535 Bob Smith Ave, Plant City, FL 33565, Phone: (813) 986-4478

JOHNSON, RYAN M., 7320 Foster Hixson Cemetery Rd., Hixson, TN 37343, Phone: 615-842-9323
Specialties: Working and using straight knives of his design and to customer specs. **Patterns:** Bowies, hunters and utility/camp knives. **Technical:** Forges 5160, Damascus and files. **Prices:** $70 to $400; some to $800. **Remarks:** Full-time maker; first knife sold in 1986. **Mark:** Sledge-hammer with halo.

JOHNSON, RUFFIN, 215 LaFonda Dr., Houston, TX 77060, Phone: 281-448-4407
Specialties: Working straight knives and folders. **Patterns:** Hunters, fighters and locking folders. **Technical:** Grinds 440C and 154CM; hidden tangs and fancy handles. **Prices:** $200 to $400; some to $1,095. **Remarks:** Full-time maker; first knife sold in 1972. **Mark:** Wolf head logo and signature.

JOHNSON, R. B., Box 11, Clearwater, MN 55320, Phone: 320-558-6128
Specialties: Liner Locks with Titanium - Mosaic Damascus. **Patterns:** Liner lock folders - skeleton hunters - frontier Bowies. **Technical:** Damascus - Mosaic Damascus - A-2, O-1, 1095. **Prices:** $200 and up. **Remarks:** Full-time maker since 1973. Not accepting orders. **Mark:** R B Johnson (signature).

JOHNSON, RANDY, 2575 E. Canal Dr., Turlock, CA 95380, Phone: 209-632-5401
Specialties: Straight knives and folders. **Patterns:** Locking folders. **Technical:** Grinds Damascus. **Prices:** $200 to $300. **Remarks:** Spare-time maker; first knife sold in 1989. Doing business as Puedo Knifeworks. **Mark:** PUEDO

JOHNSON, DAVID A, 1791 Defeated Creek Rd, Pleasant Shade, TN 37145, Phone: (615) 774-3596

JOHNSON, KENNETH R., W3565 Lockington, Mindoro, WI 54644, Phone: 608-857-3035
Specialties: Hunters, clip-points, special orders. **Patterns:** Hunters, utility/camp knives and kitchen knives. **Technical:** Grinds 440C, D2 and O1. Makes sheaths. **Prices:** $65 to $500. **Remarks:** Full-time maker; first knife sold in 1990. doing business as Corken Knives. **Mark:** CORKEN.

JOHNSON, STEVEN R., 202 E. 200 N., P. O. Box 5, Manti, UT 84642, Phone: 801-835-7941, Fax:801-835-8052
Specialties: Investor-class working knives. **Patterns:** Hunters, fighters and boots in clean-lined contemporary patterns. **Technical:** Grinds ATS-34, 440-C, RWL-34. **Prices:** $500 to $5,000. **Remarks:** Full-time maker; first knife sold in 1972. **Mark:** Name, city, state and optional signature mark.

JOHNSON, GORDEN W., 5426 Sweetbriar, Houston, TX 77017, Phone: 713-645-8990
Specialties: Working knives and period pieces. **Patterns:** Hunters, boots and Bowies. **Technical:** Flat-grinds 440C; most knives have narrow tang. **Prices:** $90 to $450. **Remarks:** Full-time maker; first knife sold in 1974. **Mark:** Name, city, state.

JOHNSON, DURRELL CARMON, P. O. Box 594, Sparr, FL 32192, Phone: 352-622-5498
Specialties: Old-fashioned working straight knives and folders of his design or to customer specs. **Patterns:** Bowies, hunters, fighters, daggers, camp knives and Damascus miniatures. **Technical:** Forges 5160, his own Damascus, W2, wrought iron, nickel and horseshoe rasps. Offers filework. **Prices:** $100 to $2,000. **Remarks:** Full-time maker and blacksmith; first knife sold in 1957. **Mark:** Middle name.

JOHNSON, C. E. GENE, 5648 Redwood Ave., Portage, IN 46368, Phone: 219-762-5461
Specialties: Lock-back folders and sprinters of his design or to customer specs. **Patterns:** Hunters, Bowies, survival lock-back folders. **Technical:** Grinds D2, 440C, A18, O1, Damascus; likes filework. **Prices:** $100 to $2,000. **Remarks:** Full-time maker; first knife sold in 1975. **Mark:** "Gene" city, state and serial number.

JOHNSON, RICHARD, W165 N10196 Wagon Trail, Germantown, WI 53022, Phone: 262-251-5772
Specialties: Custom knives and knife repair.

JOHNSTON, DR ROBT, PO Box 9887 1 Lomb Mem Dr, Rochester, NY 14623

JOKERST, CHARLES, 9312 Spaulding, Omaha, NE 68134, Phone: 402-571-2536
Specialties: Working knives in standard patterns. **Patterns:** Hunters, fighters and pocketknives. **Technical:** Grinds 440C, ATS-34. **Prices:** $90 to $170. **Remarks:** Spare-time maker; first knife sold in 1984. **Mark:** Early work marked RCJ; current work marked with last name and city.

JONES, BOB, 6219 Aztec NE, Albuquerque, NM 87110, Phone: 505-881-4472
Specialties: Fancy working knives of his design. **Patterns:** Mountain man/buckskinner-type knives; multi-blade folders, locking folders, and slipjoints. **Technical:** Grinds A2, O1, 1095 and commercial Damascus; uses no stainless steel. Engraves. **Prices:** $100 to $500; some to $1,500. **Remarks:** full-time maker; first knife sold in 1960. **Mark:** Initials on fixed blades; initials encircled on folders.

JONES, CHARLES ANTHONY, 36 Broadgate Close, Bellaire Barnstaple, No. Devon E31 4AL, ENGLAND, Phone: 0271-75328
Specialties: Working straight knives. **Patterns:** Simple hunters, fighters and utility knives. **Technical:** Grinds 440C, O1 and D2; filework offered. Engraves. **Prices:** $100 to $500; engraving higher. **Remarks:** Spare-time maker; first knife sold in 1987. **Mark:** Tony engraved.

JONES, FRANKLIN (FRANK) W., 6030 Old Dominion Rd, Columbus, GA 31909, Phone: 706-563-6051
Specialties: Traditional/working/tactical/period straight knives of his or your design. **Patterns:** Liner lock folders. Hunters, skinners, utility/camp, Bowies, fighters, kitchen, carving sets. **Technical:** Forges all straight knives using 5160, 01, 52100, 1085 and 1095. **Prices:** $150 to $1,000. **Remarks:** Full-time, AM Bladesmith Society (ABS) Journeyman Smith. **Mark:** F. W. Jones, Columbus, GA.

JONES, JOHN A, 779 SW 131 Hwy, Holden, MO 64040, Phone: 816-850-4318
Specialties: Working, using knives. Hunters, skinners & fighters. **Technical:** Grinds D2, 01, 440C, 1095. Prefers forging; creates own Damascus. File working on most blades. **Prices:** $50 to $500. **Remarks:** Part-time maker; first knife sold in 1996. Doing business as Old John Knives. **Mark:** OLDJOHN & serial number.

JONES, ENOCH, 7278 Moss Ln, Warrenton, VA 20187, Phone: (540) 341-0292
Specialties: Fancy working straight knives. **Patterns:** Hunters, fighters, boots and Bowies. **Technical:** Forges and grinds O1, W2, 440C and Damascus. **Prices:** $100 to $350; some to $1,000. **Remarks:** Part-time maker; first knife sold in 1982. **Mark:** First name.

JONES, JOHN, 12 Schooner Circuit, Manly West, QLD 4179, AUSTRALIA, Phone: 07-339-33390
Specialties: Straight knives and folders. **Patterns:** Working hunters, folding lockbacks, fancy daggers and miniatures. **Technical:** Grinds 440C, O1 and L6. **Prices:** $180 to $1200; some to $2,000. **Remarks:** Part-time maker; first knife sold in 1986. **Mark:** Jones

JONES, CURTIS J., 39909 176th St. E., Palmdale, CA 93591, Phone: 805-264-2753
Specialties: Big Bowies, daggers, his own style of hunters. **Patterns:** Bowies, daggers, hunters, swords, boots and miniatures. **Technical:** Grinds 440C, ATS-34 and D2. Fitted guards only; does not solder. Heat-treats. Custom sheaths-hand-tooled and stitched. **Prices:** $125 to $1,500; some to $3,000. **Remarks:** Full-time maker; first knife sold in 1975. Mail orders accepted. **Mark:** Stylized initials on either side of three triangles interconnected.

JONES, BARRY M. AND PHILLIP G., 221 North Ave., Danville, VA 24540, Phone: 804-793-5282
Specialties: Working and using straight knives and folders of their design and to customer specs; combat and self-defense knives. **Patterns:** Bowies, fighters, daggers, swords, hunters and liner lock folders. **Technical:** Grinds 440C, ATS-34 and D2; flat-grinds only. All blades hand polished. **Prices:** $100 to $1000, some higher. **Remarks:** Part-time makers; first knife sold in 1989. **Mark:** Jones Knives, city, state.

JORGENSEN, GERD, Jernbanegata 8, N-3262 Larvik, NORWAY, Phone: (+47) 33 18 66 06, Fax:(+47) 33 18 66 06
Specialties: Scandinavian styles hunters, working/using straight knives of my design, flint knives. **Patterns:** Mild modifications of traditional Scandinavian patterns, hunters, camp knives and fighters/tactical. **Technical:** Grinds Sandvik 12C27, forges own blades collaborates with other Scandinavian blacksmiths. Buys Damascus blades. **Prices:** $150 to $400. **Remarks:** Part-time maker; first knife sold in 1990. **Mark:** First name or initials.

JURGENS, JOHN, 3650 Emerald St Apt Y-1, Torrence, CA 90503, Phone: (310) 542-3985

JUSTICE, SHANE, PO Box 251, Sheridan, WY 82801, Phone: 307-673-4432
Specialties: Fixed blade working knives. **Patterns:** Hunters, skinners and camp knives. Other designs produced on a limited basis. **Technical:** Hand forged 5160 and 52100. **Remarks:** Part-time maker. Sole author. **Mark:** Cross over a Crescent.

k

K B S, KNIVES, RSD 181, North Castlemaine, Vic 3450, AUSTRALIA, Phone: 0011 61 3 54 705864, Fax:0011 61 3 54 706233
Specialties: Bowies, daggers and miniatures. **Patterns:** Art daggers, traditional Bowies, fancy folders and miniatures. **Technical:** Hollow or flat grind, most steels. **Prices:** $200 to $600+. **Remarks:** Full-time maker; first knife sold in 1983. **Mark:** Initials and address in Southern Cross motif.

KACZOR, TOM, 375 Wharncliffe Rd. N., Upper London, Ont., CANADA N6G 1E4, Phone: 519-645-7640

KADASAH, AHMED BIN, P O Box 1969, Jeddah 21441, SAUDI ARABIA, Phone: (26) 913-0082

KAGAWA, KOICHI, 1556 Horiyamashita, Hatano-Shi, Kanagawa, JAPAN
Specialties: Fancy high-tech straight knives and folders to customer specs. **Patterns:** Hunters, locking folders and slip-joints. **Technical:** Uses 440C and ATS-34. **Prices:** $500 to $2,000; some to $20,000. **Remarks:** Part-time maker; first knife sold in 1986. **Mark:** First initial, last name-YOKOHAMA.

KAJIN, AL, P O Box 1047, Forsyth, MT 59327, Phone: 406-356-2442
Specialties: Damascus, utility knives, working knives; make my own Damascus. **Patterns:** All types. **Technical:** Maker since 1989; ABS member. **Prices:** $175 & up. **Remarks:** Like to work with customer on design. **Mark:** AK on forged blades. Stylized Kajin in outline of Montana for stock removal knives.

KALFAYAN, EDWARD N., 410 Channing, Ferndale, MI 48220, Phone: 248-548-4882
Specialties: Working straight knives and lockback folders; some art and fantasy pieces. **Patterns:** Bowies, toothpicks, fighters, daggers, swords and hunters. **Technical:** Grinds ATS-34, 440C, O1, 5160 and Damascus. **Prices:** $150 to $5,000. **Remarks:** Full-time maker; first knife sold in 1973. **Mark:** Last name.

KALUZA, WERNER, Lochnerstr. 32, 90441 Nurnberg, GERMANY, Phone: 0911 666047
Specialties: Fancy high-art straight knives of his design. **Patterns:** Boots and ladies knives. **Technical:** Grinds ATS-34, CPM-T-440V and Schneider Damascus. Engraving available. **Prices:** NA. **Remarks:** Part-time maker. **Mark:** First initial and last name.

KANDA, MICHIO, 7-32-5 Shinzutumi-cho, Shinnanyo-shi, Yamaguchi 746 0033, JAPAN, Phone: 0834-62-1910, Fax:011-81-83462-1910
Specialties: Fantasy knives of his design. **Patterns:** Animal knives. **Technical:** Grinds ATS-34. **Prices:** $300 to $3,000. **Remarks:** Full-time maker; first knife sold in 1985. Doing business as Shusui Kanda. **Mark:** Last name inside "M".

KANKI, IWAO, 14-25 3-Chome Fukui Miki, Hyougo, JAPAN 673-0433, Phone: 07948-3-2555
Specialties: Plane, knife. **Prices:** Not determined yet. **Mark:** Chiyozuru Sadahide. **Other:** Masters of traditional crafts designated by the Minister of International Trade & Industry (Japan).

KARP, BOB, P. O. Box 47304, Phoenix, AZ 85068, Phone: 602 870-1234
602 870-1234, Fax:602 331-0283

KATO, SHINICHI, 3233-27-5-410 Kikko Taikogane, Moriyama-ku, Nagoya 463-0004
Specialties: Flat grind and hand finish. **Patterns:** Bowie, fighter. Hunting knife. **Technical:** Flat grind. **Prices:** $150-$1500. **Remarks:** Part-time maker. First knife sold in 1995. **Mark:** Name.

KATO, KIYOSHI, 4-6-4 Himonya Meguro-ku, Tokyo 152, JAPAN
Specialties: Swords, Damascus knives, working knives and paper knives. **Patterns:** Traditional swords, hunters, Bowies and daggers. **Technical:** Forges his own Damascus and carbon steel. Grinds ATS-34. **Prices:** $260 to $700; some to $4,000. **Remarks:** Full-time maker. **Mark:** First initial, last name.

KATSUMARO, SHISHIDO, , 2-6-11 Kamiseno Aki-ku, Hiroshima, JAPAN, Phone: 090-3634-9054, Fax:082-227-4438

KAUFFMAN, DAVE, 120 Clark Creek Loop, Montana City, MT 59634, Phone: 406-442-9328
Specialties: Field grade & exhibition grade hunting knives & ultra light folders. **Patterns:** Fighters, Bowies and drop-point hunters. **Technical:** ATS-34 and Damascus. **Prices:** $60 to $1,200. **Remarks:** Full-time maker; first knife sold in 1989. On the cover of Knives '94. **Mark:** First and last name, city and state.

KAUFMAN, SCOTT, 302 Green Meadows Cr., Anderson, SC 29624, Phone: 864-231-9201
Specialties: Classic and working/using straight knives in standard patterns. **Patterns:** Fighters, hunters and utility/camp knives. Technical Grinds ATS-34, 440C, O1. **Prices:** $100 to $500. **Remarks:** Part-time maker; first knife sold in 1987. **Mark:** Kaufman Knives with Bible in middle.

KAWASAKI, AKIHISA, 11-8-9 Chome Minamiamachi, Suzurandai Kita-Ku, Kobe, JAPAN, Phone: 078-593-0418, Fax:078-593-0418
Specialties: Working/using knives of his design. **Patterns:** Hunters, kit camp knives. **Technical:** Forges and grinds Molybdenum Panadium. Grinds ATS-34 and stainless steel. Uses Chinese Quince wood, desert ironwood and cow leather. **Prices:** $300 to $800; some to $1,000. **Remarks:** Full-time maker. **Mark:** Last name, first name.

custom knifemakers

KAY, J. WALLACE, 332 Slab Bridge Rd., Liberty, SC 29657

KAZSUK, DAVID, P O Box 39, Perris, CA 92572-0039, Phone: (909) 780-2288

KEARNEY, JAROD, 7200 Townsend Forest Ct, Brown Summit, NC 27214, Phone: (336) 656-4617

KEELER, ROBERT, 623 N Willett St, Memphis, TN 38107, Phone: (901) 278-6538

KEESLAR, JOSEPH F., 391 Radio Rd., Almo, KY 42020, Phone: 270-753-7919, Fax:270-753-7919
Specialties: Classic and contemporary bowies, combat, hunters, daggers & folders. **Patterns:** Decorative filework, engraving and custom leather sheaths available. **Technical:** Forges 5160, 52100 and his own Damascus steel. **Prices:** $300 to $3,000. **Remarks:** Full-time maker; first knife sold in 1976. **Mark:** First and middle initials, last name in hammer, knife and anvil logo, M. S. **Other:** ABS Mastersmith

KEESLAR, STEVEN C., 115 Lane 216, Hamilton, IN 46742, Phone: 219-488-3161, Fax:219-488-3149
Specialties: Traditional working/using straight knives of his design and to customer specs. **Patterns:** Bowies, hunters, utility/camp knives. **Technical:** Forges 5160, files 52100. **Prices:** $100 to $600; some to $1500. **Remarks:** Part-time maker; first knife sold in 1976. **Mark:** First initial, last name.

KEETON, WILLIAM L., 6095 Rehobeth Rd. SE, Laconia, IN 47135-9550, Phone: 812-969-2836
Specialties: Plain and fancy working knives. **Patterns:** Hunters and fighters; locking folders and slip-joints. Names patterns after Kentucky Derby winners. **Technical:** Grinds D2, ATS-34, 440C, 440V and 154CM; mirror and satin finishes. **Prices:** $95 to $2,000. **Remarks:** Full-time maker; first knife sold in 1971. **Mark:** Logo of key.

KEHIAYAN, ALFREDO, Cuzco 1455, Ing. Maschwitz, CP B1623GXU Buenos Aires, ARGENTINA, Phone: 03488-4-42212
Specialties: Functional straight knives. **Patterns:** Utility knives, skinners, hunters and boots. **Technical:** Forges and grinds SAE 52. 100, SAE 6180, SAE 9260, SAE 5160, 440C and ATS-34, titanium with nitride. All blades mirror-polished; makes leather sheath and wood cases. **Prices:** $300 to $500; some to $6000. **Remarks:** Full-time maker; first knife sold in 1983. **Mark:** Name.

KEIDEL, GENE W. AND SCOTT J., 4661 105th Ave. SW, Dickinson, ND 58601
Specialties: Fancy/embellished and working/using straight knives of his design. **Patterns:** Bowies, hunters and miniatures. **Technical:** Grind 440C and O1 tool steel. Offer scrimshaw and filework. **Prices:** $95 to $500. **Remarks:** Full-time makers; first knife sold in1990. Doing business as Keidel Knives. **Mark:** Last name.

KEISUKE, GOTOH, , 105 Cosumo-City Otozu 202 Ohita-city, Ohita, JAPAN, Phone: 097-523-0750

KELLEY, THOMAS P, 4711 E Ashler Hills Dr, Cave Creek, AZ 85331, Phone: (480) 488-3101

KELLEY, GARY, 17485 SW Pheasant Lane, Aloha, OR 97006, Phone: 503-848-9313
Specialties: Primitive knives and blades. **Patterns:** Fur trade era rifleman's knives, patch and throwing knives. **Technical:** Hand-forges and precision investment casts. **Prices:** $25 to $250. **Remarks:** Part-time maker. Staff photographer/writer for *Tactical Knives* magazine; does illustrative knife photography. Doing business as Reproduction Blades. **Mark:** Full name or initials.

KELLOGG, BRIAN R., 19048 Smith Creek Rd, New Market, VA 22844, Phone: 540-740-4292
Specialties: Fancy and working straight knives of his design and to customer specs. **Patterns:** Fighters, hunters and utility/camp knives. **Technical:** Grinds 440C, D2 and A2. Offers filework and fancy pin and cable pin work. Prefers natural handle materials. **Prices:** $75 to $225; some to $350. **Remarks:** Part-time maker; first knife sold in 1983. **Mark:** Last name.

KELLY, LANCE, 1723 Willow Oak Dr., Edgewater, FL 32132, Phone: 904-423-4933
Specialties: Investor-class straight knives and folders. **Patterns:** Kelly style in contemporary outlines. **Technical:** Grinds O1, D2 and 440C; engraves; inlays gold and silver. **Prices:** $600 to $3,500. **Remarks:** Full-time engraver and knife maker; first knife sold in 1975. **Mark:** Last name.

KELSO, JIM, 577 Collar Hill Rd, Worcester, VT 05682, Phone: 802-229-4254, Fax:802-229-0595
Specialties: Fancy high-art straight knives and folders that mix Eastern and Western influences. Only uses own designs, but accepts suggestions for themes. **Patterns:** Daggers, swords and locking folders. **Technical:** Grinds only custom Damascus. Works with top Damascus blade smiths. **Prices:** $3,000 to $8,000; some to $15,000. **Remarks:** Full-time maker; first knife sold in 1980. **Mark:** Stylized initials.

KENNEDY JR., BILL, P. O. Box 850431, Yukon, OK 73085, Phone: 405-354-9150
Specialties: Working straight knives. **Patterns:** Hunters, fighters, minis and fishing knives. **Technical:** Grinds D2, 440C and Damascus. **Prices:** $80 and higher. **Remarks:** Part-time maker; first knife sold in 1980. **Mark:** Last name and year made.

KERBY, MARLIN W, Rt1 Box 114D, Brashear, TX 75420, Phone: (903) 485-6201

KERN, R W, 20824 Texas Trail W, San Antonio, TX 78257-1602, Phone: (210) 698-2549
Specialties: Damascus, straight and folders. **Patterns:** Hunters, Bowies & folders. **Technical:** Grinds ATS-34, 440C & BG42. Forge own Damascus. **Prices:** $200 & up. **Remarks:** First knives 1980; retired; work as time permits. **Mark:** Outline of Alamo with kern over outline. **Other:** Member ABS, Texas Knife maker & Collectors Association.

KESSLER, RALPH A., P. O. Box 61, Fountain Inn, SC 29644-0061
Specialties: Traditional-style knives. **Patterns:** Folders, hunters, fighters, Bowies and kitchen knives. **Technical:** Grinds D2, O1, A2 and ATS-34. Forges 1090 and 1095. **Prices:** $100 to $500. **Remarks:** Part-time maker; first knife sold in 1982. **Mark:** Last name or initials with last name.

KEYES, DAN, 6688 King St., Chino, CA 91710, Phone: 909-628-8329

KHALSA, JOT SINGH, 368 Village St., Millis, MA 02054, Phone: 508-376-8162, Fax:508-376-8081
Specialties: Liner locks, one of a king daggers, swords, and kirpans (Sikh daggers) all original designs. **Technical:** Forges own Damascus, uses others high quality Damascus including stainless, and grinds stainless steels. Uses natural handle materials frequently unusual minerals. Pieces are frequently engraved and more recently carved. **Prices:** Start at $700.

KHARLAMOV, YURI, Oboronnay 46, 2, Tula, 300007, RUSSIA
Specialties: Classic, fancy and traditional knives of his design. **Patterns:** Daggers and hunters. **Technical:** Forges only Damascus with nickel. Uses natural handle materials; engraves on metal, carves on nut-tree; silver and pearl inlays. **Prices:** $600 to $2380; some to $4000. **Remarks:** Full-time maker; first knife sold in 1988. **Mark:** Initials.

KI, SHIVA, 5222 Ritterman Ave., Baton Rouge, LA 70805, Phone: 225-356-7274
Specialties: Fancy working straight knives and folders to customer specs. **Patterns:** Emphasis on personal defense knives, martial arts weapons. **Technical:** Forges and grinds; makes own Damascus; prefers natural handle materials. **Prices:** $135 to $850; some to $1,800. **Remarks:** Full-time maker; first knife sold in 1981. **Mark:** Name with logo.

KIEFER, TONY, 112 Chateaugay Dr., Pataskala, OH 43062, Phone: 740-927-6910
Specialties: Traditional working and using straight knives in standard patterns. **Patterns:** Bowies, fighters and hunters. **Technical:** Grinds 440C and D2; forges D2. Flat-grinds Bowies; hollow-grinds drop-point and trailing-point hunters. **Prices:** $95 to $140; some to $200. **Remarks:** Sparetime maker; first knife sold in 1988. **Mark:** Last name.

KILBY, KEITH, 1902 29th St, Cody, WY 82414, Phone: 307-587-2732
Specialties: Works with all designs. **Patterns:** Mostly Bowies, camp knives and hunters of his design. **Technical:** Forges 52100, 5160, 1095, Damascus and mosaic Damascus. **Prices:** $250 to $3,500. **Remarks:** Part-time maker; first knife sold in 1974. Doing business as Foxwood Forge. **Mark:** Name

KIMBERLEY, RICHARD L, 2370 Hopewell Plantation Dr, Alpharetta, GA 30004, Phone: (770) 751-9118
Remarks: Member ABS.

KIMSEY, KEVIN, 198 Cass White Rd. N. W., Cartersville, GA 30121, Phone: 770-387-0779 & 770-655-8879
Specialties: Tactical fixed blades & folders. **Patterns:** Fighters, folders, hunters and utility knives. **Technical:** Grinds 440C, ATS-34 and D2 carbon. **Prices:** $100 to $400; some to $600. **Remarks:** Three-time "Blade" award winner, Knife maker since 1983. **Mark:** Rafter and stylized KK.

KING, JASON M, Box 151, Eskridge, KS 66423, Phone: 785-449-2638
Specialties: Working and using straight knives of his design and sometimes to customer specs. Some slip joint & lockback folders. **Patterns:** Hunters, Bowies, tacticals, fighters; some miniatures. **Technical:** Grinds D2, 440C and other Damascus. **Prices:** $75 to $200; some up to $500. **Remarks:**Full-time maker since 2000. First knife sold in 1998. **Mark:** JMK. **Other:** Likes to use height quality stabilized wood.

KING, HERMAN, P O Box 122, Millington, TN 38083, Phone: (901) 876-3062

KING, BILL, 14830 Shaw Road, Tampa, FL 33625, Phone: 813-961-3455
Specialties: Folders, lockbacks, liner locks and stud openers. **Patterns:** Wide varieties; folders. **Technical:** ATS-34 and some Damascus; single and double grinds. Offers filework and jewel embellishment; nickel-silver

Damascus and mokume bolsters. **Prices:** $150 to $475; some to $850. **Remarks:** Full-time maker; first knife sold in 1976. All titanium fitting on liner-locks; screw or rivet construction on lock-backs. **Mark:** Last name in crown.

KING, FRED, 430 Grassdale Rd, Cartersville, GA 30120, Phone: 770-382-8478
Specialties: Fancy and embellished working straight knives and folders. **Patterns:** Hunters, Bowies and fighters. **Technical:** Grinds ATS-34 and D2; forges 5160 and Damascus. Offers filework. **Prices:** $100 to $3,500. **Remarks:** Spare-time maker; first knife sold in 1984. **Mark:** Kings Edge.

KING JR., HARVEY G., Box 184, Eskridge, KS 66423-0184, Phone: 785-449-2487
Specialties: Traditional working and using straight knives of his design and to customer specs. **Patterns:** Hunters, Bowies and fillet knives. **Technical:** Grinds O1, A2 and D2. Prefers natural handle materials; offers leatherwork. **Prices:** Start at $70. **Remarks:** 3/4 time maker; first knife sold in 1988. **Mark:** Name and serial number based on steel used, year made and number of knives made that year.

KINKADE, JACOB, 197 Rd. 154, Carpenter, WY 82054, Phone: 307-649-2446
Specialties: Working/using knives of his design or to customer specs; some miniature swords, daggers and battle axes. **Patterns:** Hunters, daggers, boots; some miniatures. **Technical:** Grinds carbon and stainless and commercial Damascus. Prefers natural handle material. **Prices:** Start at $30. **Remarks:** Part-time maker; first knife sold in 1990. **Mark:** Connected initials or none.

KINKER, MIKE, 8755 E County Rd 50 N, Greensburg, IN 47240, Phone: 812-663-5277, Fax:812-662-8131
Specialties: Working/using knives, Straight knives. Starting to make folders. Your design. **Patterns:** Boots, daggers, hunters, skinners, hatchets. **Technical:** Grind 440C & ATS34, others if required. Damascus, Dovetail Bolsters, Jeweled Blade. **Prices:** $125 to 375; some to $1,000. **Remarks:** Part-time maker; first knife sold in 1991. Doing business as Kinker Knives. **Mark:** Kinker and Kinker plus year.

KINNIKIN, TODD, Eureka Forge, 8356 John McKeever Rd., House Springs, MO 63051, Phone: 314-938-6248
Specialties: Mosaic Damascus. **Patterns:** Hunters, fighters, folders and automatics. **Technical:** Forges own mosaic Damascus with tool steel Damascus edge. Prefers natural, fossil and artifact handle materials. **Prices:** $400 to $2,400. **Remarks:** Full-time maker; first knife sold in 1994. **Mark:** Initials connected.

KIOUS, JOE, 1015 Ridge Pointe Rd., Kerrville, TX 78028, Phone: 830-367-2277, Fax:830-367-2286
Specialties: Investment-quality interframe & bolstered folders. **Patterns:** Folder specialist - all types. **Technical:** Both stainless and non stainless damascus. **Prices:** $450 to $3,000; some to $10,000. **Remarks:** Full-time maker; first knife sold in 1969. **Mark:** Last name, city and state or last name only.

KIRK, RAY, P O Box 1445, Tahlequah, OK 74465, Phone: (918) 456-1519
Patterns: Neck knives & small hunters & skinners. **Technical:** Forges 52100 and other high carbon steels; some stock removal. **Prices:** $65 to $800. **Remarks:** Started forging in 1989; makes own Damascus. **Mark:** Stamped "Raker" on blade.

KITSMILLER, JERRY, 67277 Las Vegas Dr., Montrose, CO 81401, Phone: 970-249-4290
Specialties: Working straight knives in standard patterns. **Patterns:** Hunters, boots. **Technical:** Grinds ATS-34 and 440C only. **Prices:** $75 to $200; some to $300. **Remarks:** Spare-time maker; first knife sold in 1984. **Mark:** J&S Knives.

KLINGBEIL, RUSSELL K, 1120 Shaffer Trail, Oviedo, FL 32765, Phone: (407) 366-3223, Fax:407-977-0329
Specialties: Frontier and Sheffield Bowies, gentlemen's fancy folders. **Patterns:** Bowies, daggers & fighters. **Technical:** Forges Damascus & Mosaic as well as straight carbon. **Prices:** $250 to $1,200. **Remarks:** Part-time maker, ABS Journeyman; sold first knife 199 2. **Mark:** R. Klingbeil maker Oviedo, FL dated. **Other:** Steels used: 52100, 5160, 1095, 203E, 0-1.

KNICKMEYER, KURT, 6344 Crosscreek, Cedar Hill, MO 63016, Phone: (314) 274-0481

KNICKMEYER, HANK, 6300 Crosscreek, Cedar Hill, MO 63016, Phone: 314-285-3210
Specialties: Complex mosaic Damascus constructions. **Patterns:** Fixed blades, swords, folders and automatics. **Technical:** Mosaic Damascus with all tool steel Damascus edges. **Prices:** $500 to $2,000; some $3,000 and higher. **Remarks:** Part-time maker; first knife sold in 1989. Doing business as Dutch Creek Forge & Foundry. **Mark:** Initials connected.

KNIGHT, JASON, PO Box 267, Harleyville, SC 29448, Phone: 843-462-7217

KNIPSCHIELD, TERRY, 808 12th Ave. NE, Rochester, MN 55906, Phone: 507-288-7829
Specialties: Working straight and some folding knives in standard patterns. **Patterns:** Lockback and slip-joint knives. **Technical:** Grinds ATS-34. **Prices:** $55 to $350; some to $600. **Remarks:** Part-time maker; first knife sold in 1986. Doing business as Knip Custom Knives. **Mark:** KNIP in Old English with shield logo.

KNIPSTEIN, R. C. (JOE), 731 N. Fielder, Arlington, TX 76012, Phone: 817-265-0573;817-265-2021, Fax:817-265-3410
Specialties: Traditional pattern folders along with custom designs. **Patterns:** Hunters, Bowies, folders, fighters, utility knives. **Technical:** Grinds 440C, D2, 154CM and ATS-34. Natural handle materials and full tangs are standard. **Prices:** Start at $300. **Remarks:** Part-time maker; first knife sold in 1989. **Mark:** Last name.

KNUTH, JOSEPH E., 3307 Lookout Dr., Rockford, IL 61109, Phone: 815-874-9597
Specialties: High-art working straight knives of his design or to customer specs. **Patterns:** Daggers, fighters and swords. **Technical:** Grinds 440C, ATS-34 and D2. **Prices:** $150 to $1,500; some to $15,000. **Remarks:** Full-time maker; first knife sold in 1989. **Mark:** Initials on bolster face.

KOHLS, JERRY, N4725 Oak Rd, Princeton, WI 54968, Phone: 920-295-3648
Specialties: Working knives & period pieces. **Patterns:** Hunters-boots & bowies - your designs or mine. **Technical:** Grinds, ATS 34 440c 154CM & 1095 & commercial Damascus. **Remarks:** Part-time maker. **Mark:** Last Name.

KOJETIN, W., 20 Bapaume Rd., Delville, Germiston 1401, SOUTH AFRICA, Phone: 011 825 6680
Specialties: High-art and working straight knives of all designs. **Patterns:** Daggers, hunters and his own Man hunter Bowie. **Technical:** Grinds D2 and ATS-34; forges and grinds 440B/C. Offers "wrap-around" pava and abalone handles, scrolled wood or ivory, stacked filework and setting of faceted semi-precious stones. **Prices:** $185 to $600; some to $11,000. **Remarks:** Spare-time maker; first knife sold in 1962. **Mark:** Billy K.

KOLITZ, ROBERT, W9342 Canary Rd., Beaver Dam, WI 53916, Phone: 920-887-1287
Specialties: Working straight knives to customer specs. **Patterns:** Bowies, hunters, bird and trout knives, boots. **Technical:** Grinds O1, 440C; commercial Damascus. **Prices:** $50 to $100; some to $500. **Remarks:** Spare-time maker; first knife sold in 1979. **Mark:** Last initial.

KOMMER, RUSS, 9211 Abbott Loop Rd., Anchorage, AK 99507, Phone: 907-346-3339
Specialties: Working straight knives with the outdoorsman in mind. **Patterns:** Hunters, semi-skinners, fighters, folders and utility knives, art knives. **Technical:** Hollow-grinds ATS-34, 440C and 440V. **Prices:** $125 to $850; some to $3,000. **Remarks:** Full-time maker; first knife sold in 1995. **Mark:** Bear paw--full name, city and state or full name and state.

KOPP, TODD M., P. O. Box 3474, Apache Jct., AZ 85217, Phone: 602-983-6143
Specialties: Classic and traditional straight knives. **Patterns:** Bowies, boots, daggers, fighters and hunters. **Technical:** Grinds M1, ATS-34 and 4160. Some engraving and filework. **Prices:** $125 to $400; some to $800. **Remarks:** Part-time maker; first knife sold in 1989. **Mark:** Name, city and state.

KOSTER, STEVEN C, 16251 Birdie Lane, Huntington Beach, CA 92649, Phone: (714) 840-8621
Specialties: Bowies, daggers, skinners, camp knives. **Technical:** Use 5160, 52100, 1084, 1095 steels. **Prices:** $200 to $1000. **Remarks:** Wood & leather sheaths with silver furniture. **Mark:** Koster squeezed between lines. **Other:** ABS apprentice, member California Knives Assoc.

KOUTSOPOULOS, GEORGE, 41491 Biggs Rd., LaGrange, OH 44050, Phone: 216-355-5013
Specialties: Heavy-duty working straight knives and folders. **Patterns:** Traditional hunters and skinners; lockbacks. **Technical:** Grinds 440C, 154CM, ATS-34. **Prices:** $75 to $275; some higher. **Remarks:** Spare-time maker; first knife sold in 1976. **Mark:** Initials in diamond logo.

KOVAL, MICHAEL T., 5819 Zarley St., New Albany, OH 43054, Phone: 614-855-0777
Specialties: Working straight knives of his design; period pieces. **Patterns:** Bowies, boots and daggers. **Technical:** Grinds D2, 440C and ATS34. **Prices:** $95 to $195; some to $495. **Remarks:** Full-time knife maker supply house; spare-time knife maker. **Mark:** Last name.

KOVAR, EUGENE, 2626 W. 98th St., Evergreen Park, IL 60642, Phone: 708-636-3724
Specialties: One-of-a-kind miniature knives only. **Patterns:** Fancy to fantasy miniature knives; knife pendants and tie tacks. **Technical:** Files and

custom knifemakers

grinds nails, nickel-silver and sterling silver. **Prices:** $5 to $35; some to $100. **Mark:** GK.

KOYAMA, CAPTAIN BUNSHICHI, 3-23 Shirako-cho, Nakamura-ku, Nagoya City 453-0817, JAPAN, Phone: 052-461-7070
Specialties: Innovative folding knife. **Patterns:** General purpose one hand. **Technical:** Grinds ATS-34 and Damascus. **Prices:** $400 to $900; some to $1,500. **Remarks:** Part-time maker; first knife sold in 1994. **Mark:** Captain B. Koyama and the shoulder straps of CAPTAIN.

KOZAI, SHINGO, 934 Toyo Oka, Ueki, Kamoto Kumamoto, JAPAN 8611063, Phone: (8196) 272-2988

KRAFT, ELMER, 1358 Meadowlark Lane, Big Arm, MT 59910, Phone: 406-849-5086, Fax:406-883-3056
Specialties: Traditional working/using straight knives of all designs. **Patterns:** Fighters, hunters, utility/camp knives. **Technical:** Grinds 440C, D2. Custom makes sheaths. **Prices:** $125 to $350; some to $500. **Remarks:** Part-time maker; first knife sold in 1984. **Mark:** Last name.

KRAFT, STEVE, 315 S. E. 6th, Abilene, KS 67410, Phone: 785-263-1411
Specialties: Folders, lockbacks, scale release auto, push button auto. **Patterns:** Hunters, boot knives and fighters. **Technical:** Grinds ATS-34, Damascus; uses titanium, pearl, ivory etc. **Prices:** $500 to $2500. **Remarks:** Part-time maker; first knife sold in 1984. **Mark:** Kraft.

KRANNING, TERRY L., 1900 West Quinn, #153, Pocatello, ID 83202, Phone: 208-237-9047
Specialties: Miniature and full-size fantasy and working knives of his design. **Patterns:** Miniatures and some mini straight knives including razors, tomahawks, hunters, Bowies and fighters. **Technical:** Grinds 1095, 440C, commercial Damascus and nickel-silver. Uses exotic materials like meteorite. **Prices:** $40 to $150. **Remarks:** Part-time maker; first knife sold in 1978. **Mark:** Last initial or full initials in eagle head logo.

KRAPP, DENNY, 1826 Windsor Oak Dr., Apopka, FL 32703, Phone: 407-880-7115
Specialties: Fantasy and working straight knives of his design. **Patterns:** Hunters, fighters and utility/camp knives. **Technical:** Grinds ATS-34 and 440C. **Prices:** $85 to $300; some to $800. **Remarks:** Spare-time maker; first knife sold in 1988. **Mark:** Last name.

KRAUSE, ROY W., 22412 Corteville, St. Clair Shores, MI 48081, Phone: 810-296-3995, Fax:810-296-2663
Specialties: Military and law enforcement/Japanese-style knives and swords. **Patterns:** Combat and back-up, Bowies, fighters, boot knives, daggers, tantos, wakazashis and katanas. **Technical:** Grinds ATS-34, A2, D2, 1045, O1 and commercial Damascus; differentially hardened Japanese-style blades. **Prices:** Moderate to upscale. **Remarks:** Full-time maker. **Mark:** Last name on traditional knives; initials in Japanese characters on Japanese-style knives.

KRAVITT, CHRIS, Treestump Leather, HC 31, Box 6484, Ellsworth, ME 04605-9320, Phone: 207-584-3000, Fax:207-584-3000

KREH, LEFTY, 210 Wichersham Way, "Cockeysville", MD 21030

KREIBICH, DONALD L., 6082 Boyd Ct., San Jose, CA 95123, Phone: 408-225-8354
Specialties: Working straight knives in standard patterns. **Patterns:** Bowies, boots and daggers; camp and fishing knives. **Technical:** Grinds 440C, 154CM and ATS-34; likes integrals. **Prices:** $100 to $200; some to $500. **Remarks:** Part-time maker; first knife sold in 1980. **Mark:** First and middle initials, last name.

KRESSLER, D. F., Schloss Odetzhausen, Schlossberg 1-85235, Odetzhausen, GERMANY, Phone: 08134-998 7290, Fax:08134-998 7290
Specialties: High-tech Integral and Interframe knives. **Patterns:** Hunters, fighters, daggers. **Technical:** Grinds new state-of-the-art steels; prefers natural handle materials. **Prices:** Upscale. **Mark:** Name in logo.

KRETSINGER JR., PHILIP W., 17536 Bakersville Rd., Boonsboro, MD 21713, Phone: 301-432-6771
Specialties: Fancy and traditional period pieces. **Patterns:** Hunters, Bowies, camp knives, daggers, carvers, fighters. **Technical:** Forges W2, 5160 and his own Damascus. **Prices:** Start at $200. **Remarks:** Full-time knife maker. **Mark:** Name.

KUBAIKO, HANK, 10765 Northvale, Beach City, OH 44608, Phone: 330-359-2418
Specialties: Reproduce antique Bowies. Distal tapering and clay zone tempering. **Patterns:** Bowies, fighters, fishing knives, kitchen cutlery, lockers, slip-joints, camp knives, axes and miniatures. Also makes American, European and traditional samurai swords and daggers. **Technical:** Grinds 440C, ATS-34 and D2; will use CPM-T-440V at extra cost. **Prices:** Moderate. **Remarks:** Full-time make. Allow three months for sword order fulfillment. **Mark:** Alaskan Maid and name. **Other:** This is my 25th year as a knife maker. I will be making 25 serial numbered knives-folder (liner-locks).

KUBASEK, JOHN A., 74 Northhampton St., Easthampton, MA 01027, Phone: 413-532-3288
Specialties: Left- and right-handed liner lock folders of his design or to customer specs Also new knives made with Ripcord patent. **Patterns:** Fighters, tantos, drop points, survival knives, neck knives and belt buckle knives. **Technical:** Grinds ATS-34 and Damascus. **Prices:** $395 to $1500. **Remarks:** Part-time maker; first knife sold in 1985. **Mark:** Name and address etched.

I

LA GRANGE, FANIE, 22 Sturke Rd., Selborne, Bellville 7530, SOUTH AFRICA, Phone: 27-021-9134199, Fax:27-021-9134199
Specialties: Fancy high-tech straight knives and folders of his design and to customer specs. **Patterns:** Daggers, hunters and locking folders. **Technical:** Grinds Sandvik 12C27 and ATS-34; forges and grinds Damascus. Engraves, enamels and anodizes bolsters. Uses rare and natural handle materials. **Prices:** $250 to $500; some higher. **Remarks:** Full-time maker; first knife sold in 1987. **Mark:** Name, town, country under Table Mountain.

LABORDE, TERRY, 26280 Guthridge Ln, Homeland, CA 92548-9714, Phone: 909-926-6654
Specialties: Polished stone handles; jade to leopard skin, jasper, etc. **Patterns:** Ladder variations. Layer count medium to fine, 200+. **Technical:** Daggers-exotic ethnic creations-integral guards. **Prices:** $1000 & up. **Remarks:** One-of-a-kind, in ladder patterns, inlaid ruby, cats eye stone handles etc. **Mark:** Initials of maker, or preference in stainless Damascus. **Other:** Exotic wood, polished stone handles.

LADD, JIMMIE LEE, 1120 Helen, Deer Park, TX 77536, Phone: 713-479-7186
Specialties: Working straight knives. **Patterns:** Hunters, skinners and utility knives. **Technical:** Grinds 440C and D2. **Prices:** $75 to $225. **Remarks:** First knife sold in 1979. **Mark:** First and middle initials, last name.

LADD, JIM S., 1120 Helen, Deer Park, TX 77536, Phone: 713-479-7286
Specialties: Working knives and period pieces. **Patterns:** Hunters, boots and Bowies plus other straight knives. **Technical:** Grinds D2, 440C and 154CM. **Prices:** $125 to $225; some to $550. **Remarks:** Part-time maker; first knife sold in 1965. **Remarks:** Doing business as The Tinker. **Mark:** First and middle initials, last name.

LAINSON, TONY, 114 Park Ave., Council Bluffs, IA 51503, Phone: 712-322-5222
Specialties: Working straight knives, liner locking folders. **Technical:** Grinds 154CM, ATS-34, 440C buys Damascus. Handle materials include Micarta, carbon fiber G-10 ivory pearl and bone. **Prices:** $95 to $600. **Remarks:** Part-time maker; first knife sold in 1987. **Mark:** Name and state.

LAIRSON SR, JERRY, H C 68 Box 970, Ringold, OK 74754, Phone: (580) 876-3426
Specialties: Fighters and hunters. **Patterns:** Damascus, random, raindrop, ladder, twist & others. **Technical:** All knives hammer forged. **Prices:** Carbon steel $150 to $400; Damascus $600 to $900. **Remarks:** I make any style knife but prefer fighters and hunters.

LAKE, RON, 3360 Bendix Ave., Eugene, OR 97401, Phone: 541-484-2683
Specialties: High-tech working knives; inventor of the modern interframe folder. **Patterns:** Hunters, boots, etc. ; locking folders. **Technical:** Grinds 154CM and ATS-34. Patented interframe with special lock release tab. **Prices:** $2,200 to $3,000; some higher. **Remarks:** Full-time maker; first knife sold in 1966. **Mark:** Last name.

LALA, PAULO RICARDO P. AND LALA, ROBERTO P., R. Daniel Martins, 636, Centro, Presidente Prudente, SP-19031-260, BRAZIL, Phone: 0182-210125
Specialties: Straight knives and folders of all designs to customer specs. **Patterns:** Bowies, daggers fighters, hunters and utility knives. **Technical:** Grinds and forges D6, 440C, high-carbon steels and Damascus. **Prices:** $60 to $400; some higher. **Remarks:** Full-time makers; first knife sold in 1991. All stainless steel blades are ultra sub-zero quenched. **Mark:** Sword carved on top of anvil under KORTH.

LAMB, CURTIS J, 3336 Louisiana Terrace, Ottawa, KS 66067-8996, Phone: (785) 242-6657

LAMBERT, RONALD S., 24 Vermont St., Johnston, RI 02919, Phone: 401-831-5427
Specialties: Traditional working and using straight knives of his design. **Patterns:** Boots, Bowies and hunters. **Technical:** Grinds O1 and 440C; forges 1070. Offers exotic wood handles; sheaths have exotic skin overlay. **Prices:** $100 to $500; some to $850. **Remarks:** Part-time maker; first knife sold in 1991. Doing business as RL Custom Knives. **Mark:** Initials; each knife is numbered.

LAMBERT—LAY

LAMBERT, JARRELL D., 2321 FM 2982, Granado, TX 77962, Phone: 512-771-3744
Specialties: Traditional working and using straight knives of his design and to customer specs. Patterns: Bowies, hunters, tantos and utility/camp knives. Technical: Grinds ATS-34; forges W2 and his own Damascus. Makes own sheaths. Prices: $80 to $600; some to $1000. Remarks: Part-time maker; first knife sold in 1982. Mark: Etched first and middle initials, last name; or stamped last name.

LAMEY, ROBERT M, 15800 Lamey Dr, Biloxi, MS 39532, Phone: (228) 396-9066, Fax:(228) 396-9022
Specialties: Bowies, fighters, hard use knives. Patterns: Bowies, fighters, hunters & camp knives. Technical: Forged and stock removal. Prices: $125 to $350. Remarks: Lifetime reconditioning; will build to customer designs, specializing in hard use, affordable knives. Mark: LAMEY.

LAMPREY, MIKE, 32 Pathfield, Great Torrington, Devon EX38 7BX, ENGLAND, Phone: 01805 601331
Specialties: High-tech locking folders of his design. Patterns: Side lock folders. Technical: Grinds ATS-34, Dendritic 440C, PM stainless Damascus. Linerless handle shells in titanium. Belt clips in ATS-34. Prices: $300 to $750; some to $1,000. Remarks: Part-time maker; first knife sold in 1982. Mark: Signature or Celtic knot.

LAMPSON, FRANK G., 3215 Saddle Bag Circle, Rimrock, AZ 86335, Phone: 928-567-7395
Specialties: Working folders; one of a kinds. Patterns: Folders, hunters, utility knives, fillet knives and Bowies. Technical: Grinds ATS-34, 440C and 154CM. Prices: $100 to $750; some to $3,500. Remarks: Full-time maker; first knife sold in 1971. Mark: Name in fish logo.

LANCASTER, C. G., No 2 Schoonwinkel St., Parys, Free State, SOUTH AFRICA, Phone: 0568112090
Specialties: High-tech working and using knives of his design and to customer specs. Patterns: Hunters, fighters and utility/camp knives. Technical: Grinds Sandvik 12C27, 440C and D2. Offers anodized titanium bolsters. Prices: $450 to $750; some to $1,500. Remarks: Part-time maker; first knife sold in 1990. Mark: Etched logo.

LANCE, BILL, P. O. Box 4427, Eagle River, AK 99577, Phone: 907-694-1487
Specialties: Ooloos and working straight knives; limited issue sets. Patterns: Several ooloo patterns, drop-point skinners. Technical: Uses ATS-34, Vascomax 350; ivory, horn and high-class wood handles. Prices: $85 to $300; art sets to $3,000. Remarks: First knife sold in 1981. Mark: Last name over a lance.

LANDERS, JOHN, 758 Welcome Rd., Newnan, GA 30263, Phone: 404-253-5719
Specialties: High-art working straight knives and folders of his design. Patterns: hunters, fighters and slip-joint folders. Technical: Grinds 440C, ATS-34, 154CM and commercial Damascus. Prices: $85 to $250; some to $500. Remarks: Part-time maker; first knife sold in 1989. Mark: Last name.

LANE, BEN, 4802 Massie St., North Little Rock, AR 72218, Phone: 501-753-8238
Specialties: Fancy straight knives of his design and to customer specs; period pieces. Patterns: Bowies, hunters, utility/camp knives. Technical: Grinds D2 and 154CM; forges and grinds 1095. Offers intricate handle work including inlays and spacers. Prices: $120 to $450; some to $5,000. Remarks: Part-time maker; first knife sold in 1989. Mark: Full name, city, state.

LANG, KURT, 4908 S. Wildwood Dr., McHenry, IL 60050, Phone: 708-516-4649
Specialties: High-art working knives. Patterns: Bowies, utilitarian-type knives with rough finishes. Technical: Forges welded steel in European and Japanese styles. Prices: Moderate to upscale. Remarks: Part-time maker. Mark: "Crazy Eye" logo.

LANG, BUD, 265 S Anita Dr Ste 120, Orange, CA 92868-3310, Phone: (714) 939-9991

LANGLEY, GENE H., 1022 N. Price Rd., Florence, SC 29506, Phone: 843-669-3150
Specialties: Working knives in standard patterns. Patterns: Hunters, boots, fighters, locking folders and slip-joints. Technical: Grinds 440C, 154CM and ATS-34. Prices: $125 to $450; some to $1000. Remarks: Part-time maker; first knife sold in 1979. Mark: Name.

LANKTON, SCOTT, 8065 Jackson Rd. R-11, Ann Arbor, MI 48103, Phone: 313-426-3735
Specialties: Pattern welded swords, krisses and Viking period pieces. Patterns: One of a kind. Technical: Forges W2, L6 nickel and other steels. Prices: $600 to $12,000. Remarks: Part-time bladesmith, full-time smith; first knife sold in 1976. Mark: Last name logo.

LAPEN, CHARLES, Box 529, W. Brookfield, MA 01585
Specialties: Chefs knives for the culinary artist. Patterns: camp knives, Japanese-style swords and wood working tools, hunters. Technical: Forges 1075, car spring and his own Damascus. Favors narrow and Japanese tangs. Prices: $200 to $400; some to $2,000. Remarks: Part-time maker; first knife sold in 1972. Mark: Last name.

LAPLANTE, BRETT, 4545 CR412, McKinney, TX 75071, Phone: 972-838-9191
Specialties: Working straight knives and folders to customer specs. Patterns: Survival knives, Bowies, skinners, hunters. Technical: Grinds D2 and 440C. Heat-treats. Prices: $175 to $600. Remarks: Part-time maker; first knife sold in 1987. Mark: Last name in Canadian maple leaf logo.

LARAMIE, MARK, 181 Woodland St, Fitchburg, MA 01420, Phone: 978-353-6979
Specialties: Fancy and working folders and straight knives. Patterns: Locking folders, hunters. Technical: Grinds 440c, ATS-34, and commercial damascus. Prices: $100. 00 to $1500. 00. Remarks: part-time maker, first knife sold in 2000. Mark: name, city, state or initials.

LARGIN, Kelgin Knives, PO Box 151, Metamora, IN 47030, Phone: 765-969-5012
Remarks: Teach classes across U. S. in mobile knife shop.

LARSON, RICHARD, 549 E. Hawkeye Ave., Turlock, CA 95380, Phone: 209-668-1615
Specialties: Traditional working/using straight knives in standard patterns. Patterns: Bowies, hunters and utility/camp knives. Technical: Grinds ATS-34, 440C, and 154CM. Engraves and scrimshaws holsters and handles. Hand-sews sheaths with tooling. Prices: $150 to $300; some to $1,000. Remarks: Part-time maker; first knife sold in 1986. Doing business as Larson Knives. Mark: Knife logo spelling last name.

LARY, ED, 651 Rangeline Rd., Mosinee, WI 54455, Phone: 715-693-3940
Specialties: Upscale hunters and art knives. Patterns: Hunters, fighters, period pieces. Technical: Grinds all steels, heat treats, fancy file work. Prices: Upscale. Remarks: Since 1974. Mark: Lary.

LAUGHLIN, DON, 190 Laughlin Dr., Vidor, TX 77662, Phone: 409-769-3390
Specialties: Straight knives and folders of his design. Patterns: Hunters, spring-back folders, drop points and trailing points. Technical: Grinds D2, 440C and 154CM; stock removal; makes his own Damascus. Prices: $175 to $250 for stock removal blades; $250 to $800 for Damascus blades. Remarks: Full-time maker; first knife sold in 1973. Mark: DEER or full name.

LAURENT, KERMIT, 1812 Acadia Dr., LaPlace, LA 70068, Phone: 504-652-5629
Specialties: Traditional and working straight knives and folders of his design. Patterns: Bowies, hunters, utilities and folders. Technical: Forges own damascus, plus uses most tool steels & stainless. Specializes in altering patterns. Uses stabilized handle materials, especially select exotic woods. Prices: $100 to $2,500; some to $50,000. Remarks: Full-time maker; first knife sold in 1982. Doing business as Kermit's Knife Works. Favorite material is meteorite Damascus Mark: First name.

LAWLER, TIM, Sabersmith, 11073 S Hartel, Grand Ledge, ME 48837, Phone: 517-281-8327

LAWRENCE, ALTON, 201 W Stillwell, De Queen, AR 71832, Phone: 870-642-7643, Fax:870-642-4023
Specialties: Classic straight knives and folders to customer specs. Patterns: Bowies, hunters, folders and utility/camp knives. Technical: Forges 5160, 1095, 1084, Damascus and railroad spikes. Prices: Start at $100. Remarks: Part-time maker; first knife sold in 1988. Mark: Last name inside fish symbol.

LAY, R J (BOB), Box 122, Falkland BC, CANADA V0E 1W0, Phone: 250-379-2265, Fax:SAME
Specialties: Traditional styled, fancy straight knifes of his design. Specializing in hunters. Patterns: Bowies, fighters and hunters. Technical: Grinds 440C, forges and grinds tool steels. Uses exotic handle and spacer material. File cut, prefers narrow tang. Sheaths available. Price: $200 to $500, some to $1,500. Remarks: Full-time maker, first knife sold in 1976. Doing business as Lay's Custom Knives. Mark: Signature acid etched.

LAY, L. J., 602 Mimosa Dr., Burkburnett, TX 76354, Phone: 817-569-1329
Specialties: Working straight knives in standard patterns; some period pieces. Patterns: Drop-point hunters, Bowies and fighters. Technical: Grinds ATS-34 to mirror finish; likes Micarta handles. Prices: Moderate. Remarks: Full-time maker; first knife sold in 1985. Mark: Name or name with ram head and city or stamp L J Lay.

custom knifemakers

LEACH, MIKE J., 5377 W. Grand Blanc Rd., Swartz Creek, MI 48473, Phone: 810-655-4850
Specialties: Fancy working knives. **Patterns:** Hunters, fighters, Bowies and heavy-duty knives; slip-joint folders and integral straight patterns. **Technical:** Grinds D2, 440C and 154CM; buys Damascus. **Prices:** Start at $150. **Remarks:** Full-time maker; first knife sold in 1952. **Mark:** First initial, last name.

LEAVITT JR., EARL F., Pleasant Cove Rd., Box 306, E. Boothbay, ME 04544, Phone: 207-633-3210
Specialties: 1500-1870 working straight knives and fighters; pole arms. **Patterns:** Historically significant knives, classic/modern custom designs. **Technical:** Flat-grinds O1; heat-treats. Filework available. **Prices:** $90 to $350; some to $1000. **Remarks:** Full-time maker; first knife sold in 1981. Doing business as Old Colony Manufactory. **Mark:** Initials in oval.

LEBATARD, PAUL M., 14700 Old River Rd., Vancleave, MS 39565, Phone: 228-826-4137, Fax:228-826-2933
Specialties: Sound working knives; lightweight folders. **Patterns:** Hunters, fillets, camp and kitchen knives, combat/survival utility knives, Bowies, toothpicks and one- and two-blade folders. **Technical:** Grinds ATS-34, A-2, D-2, 440-C; forges 52100 & 5160. Machines folder frames from aircraft aluminum. **Prices:** $50 to $550. **Remarks:** Part-time maker; first knife sold in 1974. Offers knife repair, restoration and sharpening. **Mark:** Last name. **Other:** Knives are serial numbered.

LEBER, HEINZ, Box 446, Hudson's Hope, BC, CANADA V0C 1V0, Phone: 250-783-5304
Specialties: Working straight knives of his design. **Patterns:** 20 models, form capers to Bowies. **Technical:** Hollow-grinds D2 and M2 steel; mirror-finishes and full tang only. Likes moose, elk, stone sheep for handles. **Prices:** $175 to $1,000. **Remarks:** Full-time maker; first knife sold in 1975. **Mark:** Initials connected.

LEBLANC, JOHN, Rt. 2, Box 22950, Winnsboro, TX 75494, Phone: 903-629-7745

LECK, DAL, Box 1054, Hayden, CO 81639, Phone: 970-276-3663
Specialties: Classic, traditional and working knives of his design and in standard patterns; period pieces. **Patterns:** Boots, daggers, fighters, hunters and push daggers. **Technical:** Forges O1 and 5160; makes his own Damascus. **Prices:** $175 to $700; some to $1,500. **Remarks:** Part-time maker; first knife sold in 1990. Doing business as The Moonlight Smithy. **Mark:** Stamped: hammer & anvil with initials.

LEDBETTER, RANDELL, 60630 River Bend Dr, Bend, OR 97702-8945, Phone: (541) 383-0155

LEDFORD, BRACY R., 3670 N. Sherman Dr., Indianapolis, IN 46218, Phone: 317-546-6176
Specialties: Art knives and fantasy knives; working knives upon request. **Patterns:** Bowies, locking folders and hunters; coil spring action folders. **Technical:** Files and sandpapers 440C by hand; other steels available upon request; likes exotic handle materials. **Prices:** Folders start at $350; fixed blades $225. **Remarks:** Full-time maker; first knife sold in 1983. **Mark:** First and middle initials, last name, city and state.

LEE, RANDY, P. O. Box 1873, St. Johns, AZ 85936, Phone: 928-337-2594, Fax:928-337-5002
Specialties: Traditional working and using straight knives of his design. **Patterns:** Bowies, fighters, hunters, daggers and professional throwing knives. **Technical:** Grinds ATS-34, 440C and D2. Offers sheaths. **Prices:** $235 to $1,500; some to $800. **Remarks:** Part-time maker; first knife sold in 1979. **Mark:** Full name, city, state.

LEET, LARRY W., 14417 2nd Ave. S. W., Burien, WA 98166-1505
Specialties: Heavy-duty working knives. **Patterns:** Hunters, tantos, camp knives and Bowies. **Technical:** Grinds stainless steels; likes filework. **Remarks:** Full-time maker; first knife sold in 1970. **Mark:** Stylized initials.

LELAND, STEVE, 2300 Sir Francis Drake Blvd., Fairfax, CA 94930-1118, Phone: 415-457-0318, Fax:415-457-0995
Specialties: Traditional and working straight knives and folders of his design and to customer specs. Makes straight & locking folder sets. **Patterns:** Boots, hunters, fighters, Bowies. **Technical:** Grinds O1, ATS-34 and 440C. Does own heat treat. Makes nickel silver sheaths. **Prices:** $150 to $550; some to $1,500. **Remarks:** Part-time maker; first knife sold in 1987. Doing business as Leland Handmade Knives. **Mark:** Last name.

LEMCKE, JIM L, 10649 Haddington, Ste 180, Houston, TX 77043, Phone: 888-461-8632, Fax:713-461-8221
Specialties: Large supply of custom ground and factory finished blades; knife kits; leather sheaths; in-house heat treating and cryogenic tempering; exotic handle material (wood, ivory, oosik, horn, stabilized woods); machines & supplies for knife making; polishing and finishing supplies; heat treat ovens; etching equipment; bar, sheet and rod material (brass, stainless steel, nickel silver); titanium sheet material. Catalog. $4.

LEONARD, RANDY JOE, 188 Newton Rd, Sarepta, LA 71071, Phone: (318) 994-2712

LEONE, NICK, 9 Georgetown, Pontoon Beach, IL 62040, Phone: 618-797-1179
Specialties: Working straight knives and art daggers. **Patterns:** Bowies, skinners, hunters, camp/utility, fighters, daggers and primitive knives. **Technical:** Forges 5160, W2, O1, 1098, 52100 and his own Damascus. **Prices:** t$100 to $1,000; some to $3,500. **Remarks:** Full-time maker; first knife sold in 1987. Doing business as Anvil Head Forge. **Mark:** Last name, NL, AHF.

LEPORE, MICHAEL J., 66 Woodcutters Dr., Bethany, CT 06524, Phone: 203-393-3823
Specialties: One of a kind designs to customer specs; mostly handmade. **Patterns:** Fancy working straight knives and folders. **Technical:** Forges and grinds W2, W1 and O1; prefers natural handle materials. **Prices:** Start at $350. **Remarks:** Spare-time maker; first knife sold in 1984. **Mark:** Last name.

LERCH, MATTHEW, N88 W23462 North Lisbon Road, Sussex, WI 53089, Phone: 262-246-6362
Specialties: Gentlemen's working and investment-grade folders. **Patterns:** Interframe and integral folders; lock backs, slip-joints, side locks, button locks. **Technical:** Grinds ATS-34, 1095, 440 and Damascus. Offers filework and embellished bolsters. **Prices:** $400 to $1,000; some to $3,000. **Remarks:** Part-time maker; first knife sold in 1995. **Mark:** Last name.

LEVENGOOD, BILL, 15011 Otto Rd., Tampa, FL 33624, Phone: 813-961-5688
Specialties: Working straight knives and folders. **Patterns:** Hunters, Bowies, folders and collector pieces. **Technical:** Grinds ATS-34, BG-42 and Damascus. **Prices:** $175 to $1,500. **Remarks:** Part-time maker; first knife sold in 1983. **Mark:** Last name, city, state.

LEVERETT, KEN, P. O. Box 696, Lithia, FL 33547, Phone: 813-689-8578
Specialties: High-tech and working straight knives and folders of his design and to customer specs. **Patterns:** Bowies, hunters and locking folders. **Technical:** Grinds ATS-34, Damascus. **Prices:** $100 to $350; some to $1,500. **Remarks:** Part-time maker; first knife sold in 1991. **Mark:** Name, city, state.

LEVIN, JACK, 72-16 Bay Pkwy., Brooklyn, NY 11204, Phone: 718-232-8574

LEVINE, BOB, 101 Westwood Dr., Tullahoma, TN 37388, Phone: 931-454-9943
Specialties: Working left- and right-handed Liner Lock® folders. **Patterns:** Hunters and folders. **Technical:** Grinds ATS-34, 440C, D2, O1 and some Damascus; hollow and some flat grinds. Uses sheep horn, fossil ivory, Micarta and exotic woods. Provides custom leather sheath with each fixed knife. **Prices:** $125 to $500; some higher. **Remarks:** Full-time maker; first knife sold in 1984. Voting member Knife Makers Guild. **Mark:** Name and logo.

LEWIS, K. J., 374 Cook Rd., Lugoff, SC 29078, Phone: 803-438-4343

LEWIS, STEVE, Knife Dealer, PO Box 9056, Woodland Park, CO 80866, Phone: 719-686-1120 or 888-685-2322
Specialties: Buy, sell, trade and consign W. F. Moran and other fine custom-made knives. Mail order and major shows.

LEWIS, TOM R., 1613 Standpipe Rd., Carlsbad, NM 88220, Phone: 505-885-3616
Specialties: Traditional working straight knives and pocketknives. **Patterns:** Outdoor knives, hunting knives and Bowies and pocketknives. **Technical:** Grinds ATS-34 and CPM-T-440V; forges 5168 & 01. Makes wire, pattern welded and chainsaw Damascus. **Prices:** $100 to $650. **Remarks:** Part-time maker; first knife sold in 1980. Doing business as TR Lewis Handmade Knives. **Mark:** Lewis family crest.

LEWIS, MIKE, 21 Pleasant Hill Dr, DeBary, FL 32713, Phone: 386-753-0936
Specialties: Traditional straight knives. **Patterns:** Swords and daggers. **Technical:** Grinds 440C, ATS-34 and 5160. Frequently uses cast bronze and cast nickel guards and pommels. **Prices:** $100 to $750. **Remarks:** Part-time maker; first knife sold in 1988. **Mark:** Dragon Steel and serial number.

LICATA, STEVEN, Licata Custom Knives, 89 Fenner Ave, Clifton, NJ 07013, Phone: 973-523-6964, Fax:Web: www. home. att. net/~Steven. Licata/

LIEBENBERG, ANDRE, 8 Hilma Rd., Bordeauxrandburg 2196, SOUTH AFRICA, Phone: 011-787-2303
Specialties: High-art straight knives of his design. **Patterns:** Daggers, fighters and swords. **Technical:** Grinds 440C and 12C27. **Prices:** $250 to $500; some $4,000 and higher. Giraffe bone handles with semi-precious stones. **Remarks:** Spare-time maker; first knife sold in 1990. **Mark:** Initials.

LIEGEY, KENNETH R., 132 Carney Dr., Millwood, WV 25262, Phone: 304-273-9545
Specialties: Traditional working/using straight knives of his design and to customer specs. **Patterns:** Hunters, utility/camp knives, miniatures. **Technical:** Grinds 440C. **Prices:** $75 to $150; some to $300. **Remarks:** Spare-time maker; first knife sold in 1977. **Mark:** First and middle initials, last name.

LIGHTFOOT, GREG, RR #2, Kitscoty AB, CANADA T0B 2P0, Phone: 780-846-2812
Specialties: Stainless steel and Damascus . **Patterns:** Boots, fighters and locking folders. **Technical:** Grinds BG-42, 440C, D2, CPM steels, Stellite 6K. Offers engraving. **Prices:** $250 to $500; some to $850. **Remarks:** Full-time maker; first knife sold in 1988. Doing business as Lightfoot Knives. **Mark:** Shark with Lightfoot Knives below.

LIKARICH, STEVE, 26075 Green Acres Rd., Colfax, CA 95713, Phone: 530-346-8480
Specialties: Fancy working knives; art knives of his design. **Patterns:** Hunters, fighters and art knives of his design. **Technical:** Grinds ATS-34, 154CM and 440C; likes high polishes and filework. **Prices:** $200 to $2,000; some higher. **Remarks:** Full-time maker; first knife sold in 1987. **Mark:** Name.

LILE HANDMADE KNIVES CORP, 2721 S Arkansas Ave, Russellville, AR 72802, Phone: 501-968-2011, Fax:501-968-4640
Specialties: Fancy working knives. **Patterns:** Bowies, full line of straight knives, button-lock folders. **Technical:** Grinds D2 and 440C. **Prices:** $125 to $800; some higher. **Remarks:** Full-time maker; first knife sold in 1944. Creator of the original *First Blood* and *Rambo* survival knives. **Mark:** Lile with a dot above the name.

LINCOLN, JAMES, 5359 Blue Ridge Pkwy., Bartlett, TN 38134, Phone: 901-372-5577
Specialties: Fancy and embellished automatics with unusual/hidden releases, in standard patterns. **Patterns:** locking folders and automatics. **Technical:** Grinds ATS-34, RWL & Damasteel. Filework on most knives. Most blades and bolsters hand-finished and polished. Prefers pearl and ivory for handle material, occasionally uses precious stones and gold. Offers engraving. **Prices:** $400 to $1,000; some to $1500. **Remarks:** Part-time maker; first knife sold in 1994. Doing business as JBL Knives. **Mark:** Handmade by J. B. Lincoln.

LINDSAY, CHRIS A., 1324 N. E. Locksley Dr., Bend, OR 97701, Phone: 541-389-3875
Specialties: Working knives in standard patterns. **Patterns:** Hunters and camp knives. **Technical:** Hollow- and flat-grinds 440C and ATS-34; offers brushed finishes, tapered tangs. **Prices:** $75 to $160; knife kits $60 to $80. **Remarks:** Part-time maker; first knife sold in 1980. **Mark:** Last name, town and state in oval.

LINKLATER, STEVE, 8 Cossar Drive, Aurora, Ont., CANADA L4G 3N8, Phone: 905-727-8929
Specialties: Traditional working/using straight knives and folders of his design. **Patterns:** Fighters, hunters and locking folders. **Technical:** Grinds ATS-34, 440V and D2. **Prices:** $125 to $350; some to $600. **Remarks:** Part-time maker; first knife sold in 1987. Doing business as Links Knives. **Mark:** LINKS, year and Ontario, Canada.

LISTER JR., WELDON E., 9140 Sailfish Dr., Boerne, TX 78006, Phone: 210-981-2210
Specialties: One-of-a-kind fancy and embellished folders. **Patterns:** Locking and slip-joint folders. **Technical:** Commercial Damascus and O1. All knives embellished. Engraves, inlays, carves and scrimshaws. **Prices:** Upscale. **Remarks:** Spare-time maker; first knife sold in 1991. **Mark:** Last name.

LITTLE, GARY M., HC84 Box 10301, P. O. Box 156, Broadbent, OR 97414, Phone: 503-572-2656
Specialties: Fancy working knives. **Patterns:** Hunters, tantos, Bowies, axes and buckskinners; locking folders and interframes. **Technical:** Forges and grinds O1, L6, 1095; makes his own Damascus; bronze fittings. **Prices:** $85 to $300; some to $2,500. **Remarks:** Full-time maker; first knife sold in 1979. Doing business as Conklin Meadows Forge. **Mark:** Name, city and state.

LITTLE, JIMMY L., P. O. Box 871652, Wasilla, AK 99687, Phone: 907-373-7831
Specialties: Working straight knives; fancy period pieces. **Patterns:** Bowies, bush swords and camp knives. **Technical:** Grinds 440C, 154CM and ATS-34. **Prices:** $100 to $1,000. **Remarks:** Full-time maker; first knife sold in 1984. **Mark:** First and middle initials, last name.

LITTLE, GUY A, 486 West Lincoln Av, Oakhurst, NJ 07755

LIVELY, TIM AND MARIAN, P. O. Box 8784 CRB, Tucson, AZ 85738
Specialties: Multi-cultural primitive knives of their design on speculation. **Patterns:** Neo-tribal one of a kinds. **Technical:** Hand forges using ancient techniques; hammer finish. **Prices:** Moderate. **Remarks:** Full-time makers; first knife sold in 1974. **Mark:** Last name.

LIVINGSTON, ROBERT C., P. O. Box 6, Murphy, NC 28906, Phone: 704-837-4155
Specialties: Art letter openers to working straight knives. **Patterns:** Minis to machetes. **Technical:** Forges and grinds most steels. **Prices:** Start at $20. **Remarks:** Full-time maker; first knife sold in 1988. Doing business as Mystik Knife works. **Mark:** MYSTIK.

LOCKE, KEITH, PO Box 48363, Ft Worth, TX 76148, Phone: 817-514-7272
Technical: Forges carbon steel and handcrafts sheaths for his knives. **Remarks:** Sold first knife in 1996.

LOCKETT, LOWELL C, 66653 Gunderson Rd, North Bend, OR 97459-9210, Phone: 541-756-1614
Specialties: Traditional & working/using knives. **Patterns:** Bowies, hunters, utility/camp knives. **Technical:** Forges 5160, 1095, 1084, 02, L6. Makes own guards & sheaths. **Prices:** Start at $90. **Remarks:** Full-time maker. **Mark:** Script initials & JS for ABS Journeyman Smith, member OKCA

LOCKETT, STERLING, 527 E. Amherst Dr., Burbank, CA 91504, Phone: 818-846-5799
Specialties: Working straight knives and folders to customer specs. **Patterns:** Hunters and fighters. **Technical:** Grinds. **Prices:** Moderate. **Remarks:** Spare-time maker. **Mark:** Name, city with hearts.

LOERCHNER, WOLFGANG, Wolfe Fine Knives, P. O. Box 255, Bayfield, Ont., CANADA N0M 1G0, Phone: 519-565-2196
Specialties: Traditional straight knives, mostly ornate. **Patterns:** Small swords, daggers and stilettos; locking folders and miniatures. **Technical:** Grinds D2, 440C and 154CM; all knives hand-filed and flat-ground. **Prices:** $300 to $5,000; some to $10,000. **Remarks:** Part-time maker; first knife sold in 1983. Doing business as Wolfe Fine Knives. **Mark:** WOLFE.

LONEWOLF, J. AGUIRRE, 481 Hwy 105, Demorest, GA 30535, Phone: 706-754-4660, Fax:706-754-8470
Specialties: High-art working and using straight knives of his design. **Patterns:** Bowies, hunters, utility/camp knives and fine steel blades. **Technical:** Forges Damascus and high-carbon steel. Most knives have hand-carved moose antler handles. **Prices:** $55 to $500; some to $2000. **Remarks:** Full-time maker; first knife sold in 1980. Doing business as Lonewolf Trading Post. **Mark:** Stamp.

LONG, GLENN A., 10090 SW 186th Ave, Dunnellon, FL 34432, Phone: 352-489-4272
Specialties: Classic working and using straight knives of his design and to customer specs. **Patterns:** Hunters, Bowies, utility. **Technical:** Grinds 440C D2 and 440V. **Prices:** $85 to $300; some to $800. **Remarks:** Part-time maker; first knife sold in 1990. **Mark:** Last name inside diamond.

LONGWORTH, DAVE, 1811 SR 774, Hamersville, OH 45130, Phone: 513-876-3637
Specialties: High-tech working knives. **Patterns:** Locking folders, hunters, fighters and elaborate daggers. **Technical:** Grinds O1, ATS-34, 440C; buys Damascus. **Prices:** $125 to $600; some higher. **Remarks:** Part-time maker; first knife sold in 1980. **Mark:** Last name.

LOOS, HENRY C., 210 Ingraham, New Hyde Park, NY 11040, Phone: 516-354-1943
Specialties: Miniature fancy knives and period pieces of his design. **Patterns:** Bowies, daggers and swords. **Technical:** Grinds O1 and 440C. Uses sterling, 18K, rubies and emeralds. All knives come with handmade hardwood cases. **Prices:** $90 to $195; some to $250. **Remarks:** Spare-time maker; first knife sold in 1990. **Mark:** Script last initial.

LORENZI, GIOVANNI ALDO, 9 Via Monte Napoleone, Milano 20121, ITALY

LORO, GENE, 2457 State Route 93 NE, Crooksville, OH 43731, Phone: 740-982-4521, Fax:740-982-1249
Specialties: Hand forged knives. **Patterns:** Damascus, Random, Ladder, Twist, etc. **Technical:** ABS Journeyman Smith. **Prices:** $100 and up. **Remarks:** I do not make folders. **Mark:** Loro. Retired engineer.

LOTT, SHERRY, 1098 Legion Park Rd, Greensburg, KY 42743, Phone: 270-932-2212, Fax:270-932-6442
Specialties: One-of-a-kind, usually carved handles. **Patterns:** Art. **Technical:** Carbon steel, stock removal. **Prices:** Moderate. **Mark:** Sherry Lott. **Other:** First knife sold in 1994.

LOVELESS, R. W., P. O. Box 7836, Riverside, CA 92503, Phone: 909-689-7800
Specialties: Working knives, fighters and hunters of his design. **Patterns:** Contemporary hunters, fighters and boots. **Technical:** Grinds 154CM and ATS-34. **Prices:** $850 to $4,950. **Remarks:** Full-time maker since 1969. **Mark:** Name in logo.

LOVESTRAND, SCHUYLER, 1136 19th St SW, Vero Beach, FL 32962, Phone: 561-778-0282, Fax:561-466-1126
Specialties: Fancy working straight knives of his design and to customer specs; unusual fossil ivories. **Patterns:** Hunters, fighters, Bowies and fish-

custom knifemakers

ing knives. **Technical:** Grinds ATS-34. **Prices:** $150 to $1,095; some higher. **Remarks:** Part-time maker; first knife sold in 1982. **Mark:** Name in logo.

LOZIER, DON, 5394 SE 168th Ave., Ocklawaha, FL 32179, Phone: 352-625-3576
Specialties: Fancy and working straight knives of his design and in standard patterns. **Patterns:** Daggers, fighters, boot knives, and hunters. **Technical:** Grinds ATS-34, 440C & Damascus. Most Pieces are highly embellished by notable artisans. Taking limited number of orders per annum. **Prices:** Start at $250; most are $1,250 to $3,000; some to $12,000. **Remarks:** Full-time maker. **Mark:** Name.

LUBRICH, MARK, P. O. Box 122, Matthews, NC 28106-0122, Phone: 704-567-7692
Specialties: Traditional working and using straight knives of his design and to customer specs. **Patterns:** Hunters and utility/camp knives. Some woodcarving sets. **Technical:** Forges O1, 5160 and 1095; using some cable, brass and silver inlaid handles. Differentially heat-treats; makes sheaths; hardwood/stag or leather/stag handles. **Prices:** $250 to $700. **Remarks:** Part-time maker; first knife sold in 1980. Doing business as Handmade Knives by Mark Lubrich. **Mark:** Etched last name on stock removal; stamped logo on forged blades.

LUCHAK, BOB, 15705 Woodforest Blvd., Channelview, TX 77530, Phone: 281-452-1779
Specialties: Presentation knives; start of The Survivor series. **Patterns:** Skinners, Bowies, camp axes, steak knife sets and fillet knives. **Technical:** Grinds 440C. Offers electronic etching; filework. **Prices:** $50 to $1,500. **Remarks:** Full-time maker; first knife sold in 1983. Doing business as Teddybear Knives. **Mark:** Full name, city and state with Teddybear logo.

LUCHINI, BOB, 1220 Dana Ave, Palo Alto, CA 94301, Phone: (650) 321-8095

LUCIE, JAMES R., 4191 E. Fruitport Rd., Fruitport, MI 49415, Phone: 231-865-6390, Fax:231-865-3170
Specialties: Hand-forges William Scagel-style knives. **Patterns:** Authentic scagel-style knives and miniatures. **Technical:** Forges 5160, 52100 & 1084. **Prices:** Start at $550. **Remarks:** Full-time maker; first knife sold in 1975. Believes in sole authorship of his work. ABS Journeyman Smith. **Mark:** Scagel Kris with maker's name and address.

LUCKETT, BILL, 108 Amantes Ln., Weatherford, TX 76088, Phone: 817-613-9412
Specialties: Uniquely patterned robust straight knives. **Patterns:** Fighters, Bowies, hunters. **Technical:** Grinds 440C and commercial Damascus; makes heavy knives with deep grinding. **Prices:** $275 to $1,000; some to $2,000. **Remarks:** Part-time maker; first knife sold in 1975. **Mark:** Last name over Bowie logo.

LUDWIG, RICHARD O., 57-63 65 St., Maspeth, NY 11378, Phone: 718-497-5969
Specialties: Traditional working/using knives. **Patterns:** Boots, hunters and utility/camp knives. Technical Grinds 440C, ATS-34 and 154CM. File work on guards and handles; silver spacers. Offers scrimshaw. **Prices:** $325 to $400; some to $2,000. **Remarks:** Full-time maker. **Mark:** Stamped first initial, last name, state.

LUI, RONALD M., 4042 Harding Ave., Honolulu, HI 96816, Phone: 808-734-7746
Specialties: Working straight knives and folders in standard patterns. **Patterns:** Hunters, boots and liner locks. **Technical:** Grinds 440C and ATS-34. **Prices:** $100 to $700. **Remarks:** Spare-time maker; first knife sold in 1988. **Mark:** Initials connected.

LUM, ROBERT W., 901 Travis Ave., Eugene, OR 97404, Phone: 541-688-2737
Specialties: High-art working knives of his design. **Patterns:** Hunters, fighters, tantos and folders. **Technical:** Grinds 440C, 154CM and ATS-34; plans to forge soon. **Prices:** $175 to $500; some to $800. **Remarks:** Full-time maker; first knife sold in 1976. **Mark:** Chop with last name underneath.

LUMAN, JAMES R, Clear Creek Trail, Anaconda, MT 59711, Phone: 406-560-1461
Specialties: San Mai and composite end patterns. **Patterns:** Pool and eye Spiro graph southwest composite patterns. **Technical:** All patterns with blued steel; all made by myself. **Prices:** $200 to $800. **Mark:** Stock blade removal. Pattern welded steel. Bottom ricasso JRL.

LUNDSTROM, JAN-AKE, Mastmostigen 8, 66010 Dals-Langed, SWEDEN, Phone: 0531-40270
Specialties: Viking swords, axes and knives in cooperation with handle makers. **Patterns:** All traditional styles, especially swords and inlaid blades. **Technical:** Forges his own Damascus and laminated steel.

Prices: $200 to $1,000. **Remarks:** Full-time maker; first knife sold in 1985; collaborates with museums. **Mark:** Runic.

LUNN, GAIL, 6970 9th Ave N, St Petersburg, FL 33743-8931, Phone: 727-345-7455
Specialties: Fancy folders & double action autos, some straight blades. **Patterns:** One of a kind - All types. **Technical:** Stock removal - Hand made. **Prices:** $300 and up. **Remarks:** Fancy file work, exotic materials, inlays, stone etc. **Mark:** Name in script.

LUNN, LARRY A., 6970 9th Ave N, St Petersburg, FL 33743-8931, Phone: 727-345-7455
Specialties: Fancy folders & double action autos; some straight blades. **Patterns:** All types; my own designs. **Technical:** Stock removal; commercial Damascus. **Prices:** $125 & up. **Remarks:** File work inlays and exotic materials. **Mark:** Name in script.

LUTZ, GREG, 149 Effie Dr., Greenwood, SC 29649, Phone: 864-229-7340
Specialties: Working and using knives and period pieces of his design and to customer specs. **Patterns:** Fighters, hunters and swords. **Technical:** Forges 1095 and O1; grinds ATS-34. Differentially heat-treats forged blades; uses cryogenic treatment on ATS-34. **Prices:** $50 to $350; some to $1,200. **Remarks:** Part-time maker; first knife sold in 1986. Doing business as Scorpion Forge. **Mark:** First initial, last name.

LYLE III, ERNEST L., Lyle Knives, PO Box 1755, Chiefland, FL 32644, Phone: 352-490-6693
Specialties: Fancy period pieces; one of a kind and limited editions. **Patterns:** Arabian/Persian influenced fighters, military knives, Bowies and Roman short swords; several styles of hunters. **Technical:** Grinds 440C, D2 and 154 CM. Engraves. **Prices:** Upscale. **Remarks:** Full-time maker; first knife sold in 1972. **Mark:** Last name in capital letters - LYLE over a much smaller Chief land.

LYONS, WILLIAM R, 1109 Hillside Ct, Ft Collins, CO 80524, Phone: (970) 493-3009

LYTTLE, BRIAN, Box 5697, High River, AB, CANADA T1V 1M7, Phone: 403-558-3638
Specialties: Fancy working straight knives and folders; art knives. **Patterns:** Bowies, daggers, dirks, Sgian Dubhs, folders, dress knives. **Technical:** Forges Damascus steel; engraving; scrimshaw; heat-treating; classes. **Prices:** $200 to $1000; some to $5,000. **Remarks:** Full-time maker; first knife sold in 1983. **Mark:** Last name, country.

m

MACDONALD, JOHN, 9 David Drive, Raymond, NH 03077, Phone: 603-895-0918
Specialties: Working/using straight knives of his design and to customer specs. **Patterns:** Japanese cutlery, bowies, hunters and working knives. **Technical:** Grinds O1, L6 and ATS-34. Swords have matching handles and scabbards with Japanese flair. **Prices:** $70 to $250; some to $500. **Remarks:** Part-time maker; first knife sold in 1988. Wood/glass-topped custom cases. Doing business as Mac the Knife. **Mark:** Initials.

MACDONALD, DAVID, 2824 Hwy 47, Los Lunas, NM 87031, Phone: (505) 866-5866

MACKIE, JOHN, 13653 Lanning, Whittier, CA 90605, Phone: (562) 945-6104
Specialties: Forged. **Patterns:** Bowie & camp knives. **Technical:** Attended ABS Bladesmith School. **Prices:** $75 to $500. **Mark:** JSM in a triangle.

MACKRILL, STEPHEN, P. O. Box 1580, Pinegowrie 2123, Johannesburg, SOUTH AFRICA, Phone: 27-11-886-2893, Fax:27-11-334-6230
Specialties: Art fancy, historical, collectors and corporate gifts cutlery. **Patterns:** Fighters, hunters, camp, custom lock back and liner lock folders. **Technical:** N690, 12C27, ATS-34, silver and gold inlay on handles; wooden and silver sheaths. **Prices:** $330 and upwards. **Remarks:** First knife sold in 1978. **Mark:** Oval with first initial, last name, "Maker" country of origin.

MADISON II, BILLY D., 2295 Tyler Rd., Remlap, AL 35133, Phone: 205-680-6722
Specialties: Traditional working and using straight knives and folders of his design or yours. **Patterns:** Hunters, locking folders, utility/camp knives, and fighters. **Technical:** Grinds 440C, ATS-34, D2 & BG-42; forges some high carbons. Prefers natural handle material. Ivory, bone, exotic woods & horns. **Prices:** $100 to $400; some to $1,000. **Remarks:** Limited part-time maker (disabled machinist); first knife sold in 1978. **Mark:** Last name and year. Offers sheaths. **Other:** Wife makes sheaths. All knives have unconditional lifetime warranty. Never had a knife returned in 23 years.

MADRULLI, MME JOELLE, Residence Ste Catherine B1, Salon De Provence, FRANCE 13330

MAE, TAKAO, 1-119, 1-4 Uenohigashi, Toyonaka, Osaka, JAPAN 560-0013, Phone: 81-6-6852-2758, Fax:81-6-6481-1649 **Distinction stylish in art-forged blades, with lacquered ergonomic handles.**

MAESTRI, PETER A., S11251 Fairview Rd., Spring Green, WI 53588, Phone: 608-546-4481
Specialties: Working straight knives in standard patterns. **Patterns:** Camp and fishing knives, utility green-river styled. **Technical:** Grinds 440C, 154CM and 440A. **Prices:** $15 to $45; some to $150. **Remarks:** Full-time maker; first knife sold in 1981. Provides professional cutler service to professional cutters. **Mark:** CARISOLO, MAESTRI BROS., or signature.

MAIENKNECHT, STANLEY, 38648 S. R. 800, Sardis, OH 43946

MAINES, JAY, Sunrise River Custom Knives, 5584 266th St, Wyoming, MN 55092, Phone: 651-462-5301
Specialties: Heavy duty working, classic and traditional fixed blades. Some high-tech and fancy embellished knives available. **Patterns:** Hunters, skinners, Bowies, Tantos, fillet, fighters, daggers, boot and cutlery sets. **Technical:** Hollow ground, stock removal blades of 440C, ATS34 and CPM S-90V. Prefers natural handle materials, exotic hard woods, and stag, rams and buffalo horns. Offers dovetailed bolsters in brass, stainless steel and nickel silver. Custom sheaths from matching wood or hand-stitched from heavy duty water buffalo hide. **Prices:** Moderate to up-scale. **Remarks:** Part-time maker; first knife sold in 1992. Color brochure available upon request. Doing business as Sunrise River Custom Knives. **Mark:** Full name under a Rising Sun logo. **Other:** Offers fixed blade knives repair and handle conversions.

MAISEY, ALAN, PO Box 197, Vincentia 2540, NSW AUSTRALIA, Phone: 2-4443 7829
Specialties: Daggers, especially krisses; period pieces. **Technical:** Offers knives and finished blades in Damascus and nickel Damascus. **Prices:** $75 to $2,000; some higher. **Remarks:** Part-time maker; provides complete restoration service for krisses. Trained by a Javanese Kris smith. **Mark:** None, triangle in a box, or three peaks.

MAJER, MIKE, 50 Palmetto Bay Rd, Hilton Head, SC 29928, Phone: (843) 681-3483

MAKOTO, KUNITOMO, , 3-3-18 Imazu-cho Fukuymam-city, Hiroshima, JAPAN, Phone: 084-933-5874

MALABY, RAYMOND J, 835 Calhoun Ave, Juneau, AK 99801, Phone: (907) 586-6981

MALLETT, JOHN, 760 E Francis St #N, Ontario, CA 91761, Phone: 800-532-3336/ 909-923-4116, Fax:909-923-9932
Specialties: Complete line of 3/M, Norton and Hermes belts for grinding and polishing 24-2000 grit; also hard core, Bader and Burr King grinders. Baldor motors and buffers. ATS-34, 440C, BG42 and 416 stainless steel.

MALLOY, JOE, P. O. Box 156, 1039 Schwabe St., Freeland, PA 18224, Phone: 570-636-2781
Specialties: Working straight knives and lock back folders-plain and fancy-of his design. **Patterns:** Hunters, utility, Bowie, survival knives, folders. **Technical:** Grinds ATS-34, 440C, D2 and A2 and Damascus. Makes own leather and kyder sheaths. **Prices:** $100 to $1,800. **Remarks:** Part-time maker; first knife sold in 1982. **Mark:** First and middle initials, last name, city and state.

MANABE, MICHAEL K., 3659 Tomahawk Lane, San Diego, CA 92117, Phone: 619-483-2416
Specialties: Classic and high-art straight knives of his design or to customer specs. **Patterns:** Bowies, fighters, hunters, utility/camp knives; all knives one of a kind. **Technical:** Forges and grinds 52100, 5160 and 1095. does multiple quenching for distinctive temper lines. Each blade triple-tempered. **Prices:** Start at $200. **Remarks:** part-time maker; first knife sold in 1994. Mark First and middle initials, last name and J. S. on other side.

MANEKER, KENNETH, RR 2, Galiano Island, B. C., CANADA V0N 1P0, Phone: 604-539-2084
Specialties: Working straight knives; period pieces. **Patterns:** Camp knives and hunters; French chef knives. **Technical:** Grinds 440C, 154CM and Vascowear. **Prices:** $50 to $200; some to $300. **Remarks:** Part-time maker; first knife sold in 1981. Doing business as Water Mountain Knives. **Mark:** Japanese Kanji of initials, plus glyph.

MANKEL, KENNETH, 7836 Cannonsburg Rd, Cannonsburg, MI 49317, Phone: (616) 874-6955

MANLEY, DAVID W, 3270 Six Mile Hwy, Central, SC 29630, Phone: 864-654-1125
Specialties: Working straight knives of his design or to custom specs. **Patterns:** Hunters, boot & fighters. **Technical:** Grinds 440C & ATS34. **Prices:**

$60 to $250. **Remarks:** Part-time maker; first knife sold in 1994. **Mark:** First initial, last name, year and serial number.

MANN, TIM, Bladeworks, P O Box 1196, Honokaa, HI 96727, Phone: (808) 775-0949, Fax:(808)-775-0949
Specialties: Hand-forged knives and swords. **Patterns:** Bowies, Tantos, pesh kabz, daggers. **Technical:** Use 5160, 1050, 1075, 1095 & ATS-34 steels, cable Damascus. **Prices:** $200 to $800. **Remarks:** Just learning to forge Damascus. **Mark:** None yet.

MANN, MICHAEL L., Idaho Knife Works, PO Box 144, Spirit Lake, ID 83869, Phone: 509 994-9394
Specialties: Good working blades-historical reproduction, modern or custom design. **Patterns:** Cowboy Bowies, Mountain Man period blades, old style folders, designer & maker of "The Cliff Knife", hunter and hook knives, hand ax, fish fillet and kitchen knives. **Technical:** High carbon steel blades-hand forged 5160 or grind L6 tool steel. **Prices:** $100 to $630+. **Remarks:** Made first knife in 1965. Full time making knives as Idaho Knife Works since 1986. Functional as well as collectible. Each knife truly unique! **Mark:** Four mountain peaks are his initials MM.

MARAGNI, DAN, R. D. 1, Box 106, Georgetown, NY 13072, Phone: 315-662-7490
Specialties: Heavy-duty working knives, some investor class. **Patterns:** Hunters, fighters and camp knives, some Scottish types. **Technical:** Forges W2 and his own Damascus; toughness and edge-holding a high priority. **Prices:** $125 to $500; some to $1,000. **Remarks:** Full-time maker; first knife sold in 1975. **Mark:** Celtic initials in circle.

MARKLEY, KEN, 7651 Cabin Creek Lane, Sparta, IL 62286, Phone: 618-443-5284
Specialties: Traditional working and using knives of his design and to customer specs. **Patterns:** Fighters, hunters and utility/camp knives. **Technical:** Forges 5160, 1095 and L6; makes his own Damascus; does file work. **Prices:** $150 to $800; some to $2,000. **Remarks:** Part-time maker; first knife sold in 1991. Doing business as Cabin Creek Forge. **Mark:** Last name, JS.

MARKS, CHRIS, RT 2 Box 527, Ava, MO 65608, Phone: 417-683-1065
Specialties: Mosaic Damascus. **Patterns:** Too numerous to list - ever changing. **Technical:** W1, W2, 1095, 203E, Nickel 200. **Prices:** $20 and up. **Mark:** Anvil with name in center.

MARLOWE, DONALD, 2554 Oakland Rd., Dover, PA 17315, Phone: 717-764-6055
Specialties: Working straight knives in standard patterns. **Patterns:** Bowies, fighters, boots and utility knives. **Technical:** Grinds D2 and 440C. **Prices:** $120 to $525. **Remarks:** Spare-time maker; first knife sold in 1977. **Mark:** Last name.

MARSHALL, GLENN, P. O. Box 1099, 1117 Hofmann St, Mason, TX 76856, Phone: 915-347-6207
Specialties: Working knives and period pieces. **Patterns:** Straight and folding hunters, fighters and camp knives. **Technical:** Steel used 440C, D2, CPM & 440V. **Prices:** $90 and up according to options. **Remarks:** Full-time maker; first knife sold in 1932. **Mark:** First initial, last name, city and state with anvil logo.

MARSHALL, STEPHEN R, 975 Harkreader Rd, Mt. Juliet, TN 37122

MARTIN, HAL W, 781 Hwy 95, Morrilton, AR 72110, Phone: (501) 354-1682

MARTIN, JOHN ALEXANDER, 20100 NE 150th, Luther, OK 73054, Phone: (405) 277-3992
Specialties: Inlaid and engraved mother of pearl. **Patterns:** Bowies, fighters, hunters & traditional patterns. **Technical:** Forges 5160 & 1084. **Prices:** Start at $175. **Remarks:** Part-time maker. **Mark:** Initials JAM.

MARTIN, WALTER E, 570 Cedar Flat Rd., Williams, OR 97544, Phone: (541) 846-6755

MARTIN, ROBB, 7 Victoria St., Elmira, Ontario, CANADA N3B 1R9

MARTIN, GENE, P. O. Box 396, Williams, OR 97544, Phone: 541-846-6755
Specialties: Straight knives and folders. **Patterns:** Fighters, hunters, skinners, boot knives, spring back and lock back folders. **Technical:** Grinds ATS-34, 440C, Damascus and 154CM. Forges; makes own Damascus; scrimshaws. **Prices:** $100 TO $1,200, some higher. **Remarks:** Full-time maker; first knife sold in 1993. Doing business as Provision Forge. **Mark:** Name and/or crossed staff and sword.

MARTIN, JIM, 1120 S. Cadiz Ct., Oxnard, CA 93035, Phone: 805-985-9849
Specialties: Fancy and working/using folders of his design. **Patterns:** Automatics, locking folders and miniatures. **Technical:** Grinds 440C, AEB-L, 304SS and Damascus. **Prices:** $350 to $700; some to $1,500. **Remarks:** Full-time maker; first knife sold in 1992. Doing business as Jim Martin Custom Knives.

custom knifemakers

MARTIN, MICHAEL W., Box 572, Jefferson St., Beckville, TX 75631, Phone: 903-678-2161

Specialties: Classic working/using straight knives of his design and in standard patterns. **Patterns:** Hunters. **Technical:** Grinds ATS-34, 440C, O1 and A2. Bead blasted, Parkerized, high polish and satin finishes. Sheaths are handmade. Also hand forges cable Damascus. **Prices:** $145 to $230. **Remarks:** Part-time maker; first knife sold in 1995. Doing business as Michael W. Martin Knives. **Mark:** Name and city, state in arch.

MARTIN, PETER, 28220 N. Lake Dr., Waterford, WI 53185, Phone: 262-895-2815

Specialties: Fancy, fantasy and working straight knives and folders of his design and in standard patterns. **Patterns:** Fighters, hunters, locking folders and liner locks. **Technical:** Forges own Mosaic Damascus, powdered steel and his own Damascus. Prefers natural handle material; offers file work and carved handles. **Prices:** Moderate. **Remarks:** Part-time maker; first knife sold in 1988. Doing business as Martin Custom Products. Uses only natural handle materials. **Mark:** Martin Knives.

MARTIN, RANDALL J., 1477 Country Club Rd., Middletown, CT 06457, Phone: 860-347-1161

Specialties: High-performance using knives. **Patterns:** Neck knives, tactical liner locks, survival, utility and Japanese knives. **Technical:** Grinds BG42, CPMM4, D2 and A2; aerospace composite materials; carbon fiber sheaths. **Prices:** Start at $150. **Remarks:** Part-time maker; first knife sold in 1976. Doing business as Martinsite Knives. **Mark:** First and middle initials, last name.

MARTIN, TONY, 108 S. Main St., PO Box 324, Arcadia, MO 63621, Phone: 573-546-2254

Specialties: Specializes in historical designs. Puko, etc.

MARTIN, BRUCE E., Rt. 6, Box 164-B, Prescott, AR 71857, Phone: 501-887-2023

Specialties: Fancy working straight knives of his design. **Patterns:** Bowies, camp knives, skinners and fighters. **Technical:** Forges 5160, 1095 and his own Damascus. Uses natural handle materials; filework available. **Prices:** $75 to $350; some to $500. **Remarks:** Full-time maker; first knife sold in 1979. **Mark:** Name in arch.

MARZITELLI, PETER, 19929 35A Ave., Langley, BC, CANADA V3A 2R1, Phone: 604-532-8899

Specialties: Specializes in unique functional knife shapes & designs using natural and synthetic handle materials. **Patterns:** Mostly folders, some daggers and art knives. **Technical:** Grinds ATS-34, S/S Damascus & others. **Prices:** $220 to $1000 (average $375). **Remarks:** Full-time maker; first knife sold in 1984. **Mark:** Stylized logo reads "Marz. "

MASON, BILL, 1114 St. Louis, #33, Excelsior Springs, MO 64024, Phone: 816-637-7335

Specialties: Combat knives; some folders. **Patterns:** Fighters to match knife types in book *Cold Steel*. **Technical:** Grinds O1, 440C and ATS-34. **Prices:** $115 to $250; some to $350. **Remarks:** Spare-time maker; first knife sold in 1979. **Mark:** Initials connected.

MASSEY, ROGER, 4928 Union Rd, Texarkana, AR 71854, Phone: 870-779-1018

Specialties: Traditional and working straight knives and folders of his design and to customer specs. **Patterns:** Bowies, hunters, daggers and utility knives. **Technical:** Forges 1084 & 52100, makes his own Damascus. Offers filework and silver wire inlay in handles. **Prices:** $200 to $1500; some to $2500. **Remarks:** Part-time maker; first knife sold in 1991. **Mark:** Last name, M. S.

MASSEY, AL, Box 14, Site 15, RR#2, Mount Uniacke, Nova Scotia, CANADA B0N 1Z0, Phone: 902-866-4754

Specialties: Working knives and period pieces. **Patterns:** Swords and daggers of Celtic to medieval design, bowies. **Technical:** Forges 5160, 1084 and 1095. Makes own Damascus. **Prices:** $100 to $400, some to $900. **Remarks:** Part-time maker, first blade sold in 1988. **Mark:** Initials and JS on Ricasso.

MASSEY, RON, 61638 El Reposo St., Joshua Tree, CA 92252, Phone: 760-366-9239 after 5 p. m., Fax:763-366-4620

Specialties: Classic, traditional, fancy/embellished, high art, period pieces, working/using knives, straight knives, folders, and automatics. Your design, customer specs, about 175 standard patterns. **Patterns:** Automatics, hunters and fighters. All my folders are side locking folder. Unless requested as lock books slip joint I specialize or custom design. **Technical:** ATS-34, 440C, D-2 upon request. Engraving, filework, scrimshaw, most of the exotic handle materials. All aspects are performed by me - inlay work in pearls or stone, hand made Pem' work. **Prices:** $110 to $2,500; some to $6,000. **Remarks:** Part-time maker; first knife sold in 1976.

MATA, LEONARD, 3583 Arruza St, San Deigo, CA 92154, Phone: (619) 690-6935

MATSUSAKI, TAKESHI, Matsusaki Knives, 151 Ono. Sasebo-city, Nagasaki, JAPAN, Phone: 0956-47-2938

MAXEN, MICK, 2 Huggins Lane Welham Green, "Hatfield, Herts", UNITED KINGDOM AL97LR, Phone: 01707 261213

Specialties: Damascus & Mosaic. **Patterns:** Medieval style daggers & Bowies. **Technical:** Forges CS75 & 15N20 / nickel Damascus. **Mark:** Last name with axe above.

MAXFIELD, LYNN, 382 Colonial Ave., Layton, UT 84041, Phone: 801-544-4176

Specialties: Sporting knives, some fancy. **Patterns:** Hunters, fishing, fillet, special purpose: some locking folders. **Technical:** Grinds 440-c, ATS-34, 154-CM, D2, CPM-S60V, S90V, CPM-3, Talonite, and Damascus. **Prices:** $125 to $400; some to $900. **Remarks:** Part-time maker; first knife sold in 1979. **Mark:** Name, city and state.

MAXWELL, DON, 3164 N. Marks, Suite 122, Fresno, CA 93722, Phone: 559-497-8441

Specialties: Fancy working and using straight knives of his design. **Patterns:** Hunters, fighters, utility/camp knives, liner lock folders and fantasy knives. **Technical:** Grinds 440C, ATS-34, D2 and commercial Damascus. **Prices:** $250 to $1000; some to $2,500. **Remarks:** Full-time maker; first knife sold in 1987. **Mark:** Last name, city, state or last name only.

MAYNARD, LARRY JOE, P. O. Box 493, Crab Orchard, WV 25827

Specialties: Fancy and fantasy straight knives. **Patterns:** Big knives; a Bowie with a full false edge; fighting knives. **Technical:** Grinds standard steels. **Prices:** $350 to $500; some to $1,000. **Remarks:** Full-time maker; first knife sold in 1986. **Mark:** Middle and last initials.

MAYNARD, WILLIAM N., 2677 John Smith Rd., Fayetteville, NC 28306, Phone: 910-425-1615

Specialties: Traditional and working straight knives of all designs. **Patterns:** Combat, Bowies, fighters, hunters and utility knives. **Technical:** Grinds 440C, ATS-34 and commercial Damascus. Offers fancy filework; handmade sheaths. **Prices:** $100 to $300; some to $750. **Remarks:** Full-time maker; first knife sold in 1988. **Mark:** Last name.

MAYO JR., TOM, 67-420 Alahaka St., Waialua, HI 96791, Phone: 808-637-6560

Specialties: Presentation grade working knives. **Patterns:** Combat knives, hunters, Bowies and folders. **Technical:** Uses BG-42 & 440V (ATS-34 & 440C upon request). **Prices:** Start at $250. **Remarks:** Part-time maker; first knife sold in 1983. **Mark:** Volcano logo with name and state.

MAYVILLE, OSCAR L., 2130 E. County Rd. 910S., Marengo, IN 47140, Phone: 812-338-3103

Specialties: Working straight knives; period pieces. **Patterns:** Kitchen cutlery, Bowies, camp knives and hunters. **Technical:** Grinds A2, O1 and 440C. **Prices:** $50 to $350; some to $500. **Remarks:** Full-time maker; first knife sold in 1984. **Mark:** Initials over knife logo.

MC CORNOCK, CRAIG, McC Mtn Outfitters, 4775 Rte 212, Willow, NY 12495, Phone: 914-679-9758

MCABEE, WILLIAM, 27275 Norton Grade, Colfax, CA 95713, Phone: 530-389-8163

Specialties: Working/using knives. **Patterns:** Fighters, Bowies, Hunters. **Technical:** Grinds ATS-34. **Prices:** $75 to $200; some to $350. **Remarks:** Part-time maker; first knife sold in 1990. **Mark:** Stylized WM stamped.

MCADAMS, DENNIS, 1709 Ichabod Lane, Chattanooga, TN 37405-2250, Phone: (423) 267-4743

MCBURNETTE, HARVEY, P. O. Box 227, Eagle Nest, NM 87718, Phone: 505-377-6254, Fax:505-377-6218

Specialties: Fancy working folders; some to customer specs. **Patterns:** Front-locking folders. **Technical:** Grinds D2, 440C and 154CM; engraves. **Prices:** $450 to $3,000. **Remarks:** Full-time maker; first knife sold in 1972. **Mark:** Last name, city and state.

MCCALLEN JR, HOWARD H, 110 Anchor Dr, So Seaside Park, NJ 08752

MCCARLEY, JOHN, 4165 Harney Rd, Taneytown, MD 21787

Specialties: Working straight knives; period pieces. **Patterns:** Hunters, Bowies, camp knives, miniatures, throwing knives. **Technical:** Forges W2, O1 and his own Damascus. **Prices:** $150 to $300; some to $1,000. **Remarks:** Part-time maker; first knife sold in 1977. **Mark:** Initials in script.

MCCARTY, HARRY, 1121 Brough Ave., Hamilton, OH 45015

Specialties: Period pieces. **Patterns:** 18th & 19th Century trade knives, bowies and belt knives. **Technical:** Grinds & forges high carbon steel. **Prices:** $125 to $650; some higher. **Remarks:** Part-time maker; first knife sold in 1977. **Mark:** Stylized initials inside shamrock.

MCCLURE, MICHAEL, 803 17th Ave., Menlo Park, CA 94025, Phone: 650-323-2596
Specialties: Working/using straight knives of his design and to customer specs. **Patterns:** Bowies, hunters, skinners, utility/camp, tantos, fillets and boot knives. **Technical:** Hand forging; grinds ATS-34, 440C, D2, and commercial Damascus. Makes sheaths. **Prices:** Start at $100. **Remarks:** Part-time maker; first knife sold in 1991. **Mark:** Mike McClure.

MCCONNELL, CHARLES R., 158 Genteel Ridge, Wellsburg, WV 26070, Phone: 304-737-2015
Specialties: Working straight knives. **Patterns:** Hunters, Bowies, daggers, minis and push knives. **Technical:** Grinds 440C and 154CM; likes full tangs. **Prices:** $65 to $325; some to $800. **Remarks:** Part-time maker; first knife sold in 1977. **Mark:** Name.

MCCONNELL JR., LOYD A., 1710 Rosewood, Odessa, TX 79761, Phone: 915-363-8344
Specialties: Working straight knives and folders, some fancy. **Patterns:** Hunters, boots, Bowies, locking folders and slip-joints. **Technical:** Grinds CPM Steels, ATS-34 and BG-42 and commercial Damascus. **Prices:** $175 to $900; some to $10,000. **Remarks:** Full-time maker; first knife sold in 1975. Doing business as Cactus Custom Knives. **Mark:** Name, city and state in cactus logo.

MCCOUN, MARK, 14212 Pine Dr., DeWitt, VA 23840, Phone: 804-469-7631
Specialties: Working/using straight knives of his design and in standard patterns; custom miniatures. **Patterns:** Locking liners, integrals. **Technical:** Grinds Damascus, ATS-34 and 440C. **Prices:** $150 to $500. **Remarks:** Part-time maker; first knife sold in 1989. **Mark:** Name, city and state.

MCCRACKIN, KEVIN, 3720 Hess Rd, House Springs, MO 63051, Phone: (636) 677-6066

MCCRACKIN AND SON, V. J., 3720 Hess Rd., House Springs, MO 63051, Phone: 636-677-6066
Specialties: Working straight knives in standard patterns. **Patterns:** Hunters, Bowies and camp knives. **Technical:** Forges L6, 5160, his own Damascus, cable Damascus. **Prices:** $125 to $700; some to $1,500. **Remarks:** Part-time maker; first knife sold in 1983. Son Kevin helps make the knives. **Mark:** Last name, M. S.

MCCULLOUGH, JERRY, 274 West Pettibone Rd, Georgiana, AL 36033, Phone: 334-382-7644
Specialties: Standard patterns or custom designs. **Technical:** Forge and grind scrap-tool and Damascus steels. Use natural handle materials & turquoise trim on some. Filework on others. **Prices:** $65 to $250 and up. **Remarks:** Part-time maker. **Mark:** Initials (JM) combined.

MCDERMOTT, MICHAEL, 151 Hwy F, Defiance, MO 63341, Phone: (314) 798-2077

MCDONALD, ROBIN J, 6509 E Jeffrey Dr, Fayettebville, NC 28314
Specialties: Working knives of my design. **Patterns:** Bowies, hunters, camp knives & fighters. **Technical:** Forges primarily 5160. **Prices:** $100 to $500. **Remarks:** Part-time maker; first knife sold in 1999. **Mark:** initials RJM.

MCDONALD, W. J. "JERRY", 7173 Wickshire Cove E., Germantown, TN 38138, Phone: 901-756-9924
Specialties: Classic and working/using straight knives of his design and in standard patterns. **Patterns:** Bowies, hunters kitchen and traditional spring back pocket knives. **Technical:** Grinds ATS 34, 154CM, D2, 440V, BG42 & 440C. **Prices:** $125 to $1,000. **Remarks:** Full-time maker; first knife sold in 1989. **Mark:** First and middle initials, last name, maker, city and state. Some of my knives are stamped McDonald in script.

MCDONALD, RICH, 4590 Kirk Rd., Columbiana, OH 44408, Phone: 330-482-0007, Fax:330-482-0007
Specialties: Traditional working/using and art knives of his design. **Patterns:** Bowies, hunters, folders, primitives and tomahawks. **Technical:** Forges 5160, 1084, 1095, 52100 and his own Damascus. Fancy filework. **Prices:** $200 to $1,500. **Remarks:** Full-time maker; first knife sold in 1994. **Mark:** First and last initials connected.

MCDONALD, ROBERT J., 14730 61 Court N., Loxahatchee, FL 33470, Phone: 561-790-1470
Specialties: Traditional working straight knives to customer specs. **Patterns:** Fighters, swords and folders. **Technical:** Grinds 440C, ATS-34 and forges own Damascus. **Prices:** $150 to $1,000. **Remarks:** Part-time maker; first knife sold in 1988. **Mark:** Electro-etched name.

MCFALL, KEN, P. O. Box 458, Lakeside, AZ 85929, Phone: 928-537-2026, Fax:928-537-8066
Specialties: Fancy working straight knives and some folders. **Patterns:** Daggers, boots, tantos, Bowies; some miniatures. **Technical:** Grinds D2, ATS-34 and 440C. Forges his own Damascus. **Prices:** $200 to $1,200. **Remarks:** Full-time maker; first knife sold in 1984. **Mark:** Name, city and state.

MCFARLIN, ERIC E., P. O. Box 2188, Kodiak, AK 99615, Phone: 907-486-4799
Specialties: Working knives of his design. **Patterns:** Bowies, skinners, camp knives and hunters. **Technical:** Flat and convex grinds 440C, A2 and AEB-L. **Prices:** Start at $200. **Remarks:** Part-time maker; first knife sold in 1989. **Mark:** Name and city in rectangular logo.

MCFARLIN, J. W., 3331 Pocohantas Dr., Lake Havasu City, AZ 86404, Phone: 928-855-8095, Fax:928-855-8095
Technical: Flat grinds, D2, ATS-34, 440C, Thomas & Peterson Damascus. **Remarks:** From working knives to investment. Customer designs always welcome. 100% hand made. **Prices:** $150 to $3,000. **Mark:** Hand written in the blade.

MCGILL, JOHN, P. O. Box 302, Blairsville, GA 30512, Phone: 404-745-4686
Specialties: Working knives. **Patterns:** Traditional patterns; camp knives. **Technical:** Forges L6 and 9260; makes Damascus. **Prices:** $50 to $250; some to $500. **Remarks:** Full-time maker; first knife sold in 1982. **Mark:** XYLO.

MCGOVERN, JIM, 105 Spinnaker Way, Portsmouth, NH 03801-3331
Specialties: Working straight knives and folders. **Patterns:** Hunters and boots. **Technical:** Hollow-grinds 440C, ATS-34; prefers full tapered tangs. Offers filework. **Prices:** Straight knives, $165 to $250; folders start at $325. **Remarks:** Full-time maker; first knife sold in 1985. **Mark:** Name.

MCGOWAN, FRANK E., 12629 Howard Lodge Dr., Sykesville, MD 21784, Phone: 410-489-4323
Specialties: Fancy working knives & folders to customer specs. **Patterns:** Survivor knives, fighters, fishing knives, folders and hunters. **Technical:** Grinds and forges O1, 440C, 5160, ATS-34, 52100, or customer choice. **Prices:** $100 to $1,000; some more. **Remarks:** Full-time maker; first knife sold in 1986. **Mark:** Last name.

MCGRATH, PATRICK T, 8343 Kenyon Av, Westchester, CA 90045, Phone: (310) 338-8764

MCGRODER, PATRICK J., 5725 Chapin Rd., Madison, OH 44057, Phone: 216-298-3405, Fax:216-298-3405
Specialties: Traditional working/using knives of his design. **Patterns:** Bowies, hunters and utility/camp knives. **Technical:** Grinds ATS-34, D2 and customer requests. Does reverse etching; heat-treats; prefers natural handle materials; custom made sheath with each knife. **Prices:** $125 to $250. **Remarks:** Part-time maker. **Mark:** First and middle initials, last name, maker, city and state.

MCGUANE IV, THOMAS F., 410 South 3rd Ave., Bozeman, MT 59715, Phone: 406-522-9739
Specialties: Traditional straight knives and folders of his design. **Patterns:** Tantos, swords and locking folders. **Technical:** Forges 1095 and L6; hand-smelted Japanese style steel. Silk and same handles. **Prices:** $375 to $850; some to $3,000. **Remarks:** Full-time maker; first knife sold in 1988. **Mark:** Last name, city, state.

MCHENRY, WILLIAM JAMES, Box 67, Wyoming, RI 02898, Phone: 401-539-8353
Specialties: Fancy high-tech folders of his design. **Patterns:** Locking folders with various mechanisms. **Technical:** One-of-a-kind only, no duplicates. Inventor of the Axis Lock. Most pieces disassemble and feature top-shelf materials including gold, silver and gems. **Prices:** Upscale. **Remarks:** Full-time maker; first knife sold in 1988. Former goldsmith. **Mark:** Last name or first and last initials.

MCINTOSH, DAVID L., P. O. Box 948, Haines, AK 99827, Phone: 907-766-3673
Specialties: Working straight knives and folders of all designs. **Patterns:** All styles, except swords. **Technical:** Grinds ATS-34 and top name maker Damascus. Engraves; offers tooling on sheaths. Uses fossil ivory. **Prices:** $60 to $800; some to $2,000. **Remarks:** Full-time maker; first knife sold in 1984. **Mark:** Last name, serial number, steel type, city and state.

MCKENZIE, DAVID BRIAN, 2311B Ida Rd, Campbell River B., CANADA V9W-4V7

MCKIERNAN, STAN, 205 E. Park St, Vandalia, MO 63382, Phone: 573-594-6135

MCLENDON, HUBERT W, 125 Thomas Rd, Waco, GA 30182, Phone: 770-574-9796
Specialties: Using knives; my design or customers. **Patterns:** Bowies & hunters. **Technical:** Hand ground or forged ATS-34, 440C & D2. **Prices:** $100 to $300. **Remarks:** First knife sold in 1978. **Mark:** McLendon or Mc.

MCLUIN, TOM, 36 Fourth St., Dracut, MA 01826, Phone: 978-957-4899
Specialties: Working straight knives and folders of his design. **Patterns:** Boots, hunters and folders. **Technical:** Grinds ATS-34, 440C, O1 and Damascus; makes his own mokume. **Prices:** $100 to $400; some to $700. **Remarks:** Part-time maker; first knife sold in 1991. **Mark:** Last name.

custom knifemakers

MCLURKIN, ANDREW, 2112 Windy Woods Dr, Raleigh, NC 27607, Phone: 919-834-4693
Specialties: Collector grade folders, working folders, fixed blades, and miniatures. Knives made to order and to his design. **Patterns:** Locking liner and lock back folders, hunter, working and tactical designs. **Technical:** Using patterned Damascus, Mosaic Damascus, ATS_34, BG-42, and CPM steels. Prefers natural handle materials such as pearl, ancient ivory and stabilized wood. Also using synthetic materials such as carbon fiber, titanium, and G10. Prices:$250 and up. **Mark:** Last name. Mark is often on inside of folders.

MCMANUS, DANNY, 413 Fairhaven Drive, Taylors, SC 29687, Phone: 864-268-9849, Fax:864-268-9699
Specialties: High-tech and traditional working/using straight knives of his design, to customer specs and in standard patterns. **Patterns:** Boots, Bowies, fighters, hunters and utility/camp knives. **Technical:** Forges stainless steel Damascus; grinds ATS-34. Offers engraving and scrimshaw. **Prices:** $300 to $2,000; some to $3,000. **Remarks:** Full-time maker; first knife sold in 1997. Doing business as Stamascus KnifeWorks Corp. **Mark:** Stamascus.

MCNABB, TOMMY, 4015 Brownsboro Rd, Winston-Salem, NC 27106, Phone: 336-759-0640, Fax:336-759-0641
Specialties: Working and using straight knives of his design. **Patterns:** Hunters, fighters and utility/camp knives. **Technical:** Forges his own Damascus; grinds ATS-34. **Prices:** $100 to $1250; some to $2,500. **Remarks:** Full-time maker; first knife sold in 1979. **Mark:** Carolina Custom Knives.

MCNABB, TOMMY, Carolina Custom Knives, 4015 Brownsboro Rd, Winston-Salem, NC 27106, Phone: 336-759-0640, Fax:336-759-0641

MCNEIL, JIMMY, 1175 Mt. Moriah Rd., Memphis, TN 38117, Phone: 901-544-0710 or 901-683-8133
Specialties: Fancy high-art straight knives of his design. **Patterns:** Bowies, daggers and swords. **Technical:** Grinds O1 and Damascus. Engraves, carves and inlays. **Prices:** $50 to $300; some to $2,000. **Remarks:** Spare-time maker; first knife sold in 1993. Doing business as McNeil's Minerals and Knives. **Mark:** Crossed mining picks and serial number.

MCRAE, J MICHAEL, 7750 Matthews-Mint Hill Rd, Mint Hill, NC 28227, Phone: 704-545-2929
Specialties: Scottish dirks and sgian dubhs. **Patterns:** Traditional blade styles with traditional and slightly non-traditional handle treatments. **Technical:** Forges 1095, 5160 and his own Damascus. Prefers Stag and exotic hardwoods for handles, many intricately carved. **Prices:** Starting at $125, some to $2000. **Remarks:**Journeyman Smith in ABS, member of North Carolina Custom Knifemakers Guild and ABANA. Full-time maker, first knife sold in 1982. Doing business as Scotia Metalwork. **Mark:** Last name underlined with a claymore.

MEERDINK, KURT, 120 Split Rock Dr, Barryville, NY 12719, Phone: 845-557-0783
Specialties: Working straight knives. **Patterns:** Hunters, Bowies, tactical & neck knives. **Technical:** Grinds ATS34, 440C, D2, Damascus. **Prices:** $95 to $1100. **Remarks:** Full-time maker, first knife sold in 1994. **Mark:** Meerdink Maker, Rio NY.

MEIER, DARYL, 75 Forge Rd., Carbondale, IL 62901, Phone: 618-549-3234
Specialties: One-of-a-kind knives and swords. **Patterns:** Collaborates on blades. **Technical:** Forges his own Damascus, W1 and A203E, 440C, 431, nickel 200 and clad steel. **Prices:** $250 to $450; some to $6,000. **Remarks:** Full-time smith and researcher since 1974; first knife sold in 1974. **Mark:** Name or circle/arrow symbol or SHAWNEE.

MELIN, GORDON C, 11259 Gladhill Road Unit 4, Whittier, CA 90604, Phone: (562) 946-5753

MELLARD, J R, 17006 Highland Canyon Dr, Houston, TX 77095, Phone: (281) 550-9464

MELLO, JACINTO, Rua Maceiò, 388 Parà de Minas M6 35660-129, BRAZIL, Phone: 55-3732323934
Specialties: Bowies and hunters with natural materials. **Patterns:** Flat ground. **Technical:** Grinds and forges D6 & 52100. **Prices:** $100 to $600. **Remarks:**Stainless fittings and filework are his trademarks. **Mark:**M average.

MELOY, SEAN, 7148 Rosemary Lane, Lemon Grove, CA 91945-2105, Phone: 619-465-7173
Specialties: Traditional working straight knives of his design. **Patterns:** Bowies, fighters and utility/camp knives. **Technical:** Grinds 440C, ATS-34 and D2. **Prices:** $125 to $300. **Remarks:** Part-time maker; first knife sold in 1985. **Mark:** Broz Knives.

MENSCH, LARRY C., RD #3, Box 1444, Milton, PA 17847, Phone: 570-742-9554
Specialties: Custom orders. **Patterns:** Bowies, daggers, hunters, tantos, short swords and miniatures. **Technical:** Grinds ATS-34, carbon and stainless steel Damascus; blade grinds hollow, flat and slack. Filework; bending

guards and fluting handles with finger grooves. Offers engraving and scrimshaw. **Prices:** $100 to $300; some to $1,000. **Remarks:** Part-time maker; first knife sold in 1993. Doing business as Larry's Knife Shop. **Mark:** Connected capital "L" and small "m" in script.

MERCER, MIKE, 149 N. Waynesville Rd., Lebanon, OH 45036, Phone: 513-932-2837
Specialties: Jeweled gold and ivory daggers; multi-blade folders. **Patterns:** 1-1/4" folders, hunters, axes, replicas. **Technical:** Uses O1 Damascus and mokume. **Prices:** $150 to $1,500. **Remarks:** Full-time maker since 1991. **Mark:** Last name in script.

MERCHANT, TED, 7 Old Garrett Ct., White Hall, MD 21161, Phone: 410-343-0380
Specialties: Traditional and classic working knives. **Patterns:** Bowies, hunters, camp knives, fighters, daggers and skinners. **Technical:** Forges W2 and 5160; makes own Damascus. Makes handles with wood, stag, horn, silver and gem stone inlay; fancy filework. **Prices:** $125 to $600; some to $1,500. **Remarks:** Full-time maker; first knife sold in 1985. **Mark:** Last name.

MERZ III, ROBERT L., 20219 Prince Creek Dr., Katy, TX 77450, Phone: 281-492-7337
Specialties: Working straight knives and folders, some fancy, of his design. **Patterns:** Hunters, skinners, fighters and camp knives. **Technical:** Flat-grinds 440C, 154CM, ATS-34, 440V and commercial Damascus. **Prices:** $150 to $450; some to $600. **Remarks:** Part-time maker; first knife sold in 1974. **Mark:** MERZ KNIVES, city and state, or last name in oval.

MESHEJIAN, MARDI, 33 Elm Dr., E. Northport, NY 11731, Phone: 516-757-4541
Specialties: One of a kind fantasy and high-art straight knives of his design. **Patterns:** Swords, daggers, finger knives and other edged weapons. **Technical:** Hand-forged chainsaw and timing chain Damascus. **Prices:** $150 to $2,500; some to $3,000. **Remarks:** Part-time maker; first knife sold in 1996. Doing business as Tooth and Nail Metalworks. **Mark:** Etched stylized "M".

MESSER, DAVID T., 134 S. Torrence St., Dayton, OH 45403-2044, Phone: 513-228-6561
Specialties: Fantasy period pieces, straight and folding, of his design. **Patterns:** Bowies, daggers and swords. **Technical:** Grinds 440C, O1, 06 and commercial Damascus. Likes fancy guards and exotic handle materials. **Prices:** $100 to $225; some to $375. **Remarks:** Spare-time maker; first knife sold in 1991. **Mark:** Name stamp.

METHENY, H. A. "WHITEY", 7750 Waterford Dr., Spotsylvania, VA 22553, Phone: 703-582-3228
Specialties: Working and using straight knives of his design and to customer specs. **Patterns:** Hunters and kitchen knives. **Technical:** Grinds 440C and ATS-34. Offers filework; tooled custom sheaths. **Prices:** $150 to $350. **Remarks:** Spare-time maker; first knife sold in 1990. **Mark:** Initials/full name football logo.

METZ, GREG T, c/o James Ranch HC 83, Cascade, ID 83611, Phone: (208) 382-4336
Specialties: Hunting & utility knives. **Prices:** $300 and up. **Remarks:** Natural handle materials; hand forged blades; 1084 & 1095. **Mark:** METZ (last name).

MICHINAKA, TOSHIAKI, I-679 Koyamacho-nishi, Totton-shi, Tottori 680-0947, JAPAN, Phone: 0857-28-5911

MICHO, KANDA, , 7-32-5 Shinzutsumi-Cho Shinnanyo-City, Yamaguchi, JAPAN, Phone: 0834-62-1910

MILFORD, BRIAN A., RD 2 Box 294, Knox, PA 16232, Phone: 814-797-2595, Fax:814-226-4351
Specialties: Traditional and working/using straight knives of his design or to customer specs. **Patterns:** Fighters, hunters and utility/camp knives. **Technical:** Forges Damascus and 52100; grinds 440C. **Prices:** $50 to $300; some to $750. **Remarks:** Part-time maker; first knife sold in 1991. Doing business as BAM Forge. **Mark:** Full name or initials.

MILITANO, TOM, Custom Knives, 77 Jason Rd, Jacksonville, AL 36265-6655, Phone: 256-435-7132
Specialties: Fixed blade, one of a kind knives. **Patterns:** Bowies, fighters, hunters and tactical knives. **Technical:** Grinds 440C, ATS-34, A2, and Damascus. Hollow grinds, flat grinds, and decorative filework. **Prices:** $150. 00 plus. **Remarks:** Part-time maker. **Mark:** Name, city and state in oval with maker in the center. Sold first knives in the mid to late 1980's. Memberships: Arkansas Knifemakers Association, Mississippi Noisemakers Association and Flint River Knife Club.

MILLARD, FRED G., 5317 N. Wayne, Chicago, IL 60640, Phone: 773-769-5160
Specialties: Working/using straight knives of his design or to customer specs. **Patterns:** Bowies, hunters, utility/camp knives, kitchen/steak knives. **Technical:** Grinds ATS-34, O1, D2 and 440C. Makes sheaths. **Prices:** $80 to $250. **Remarks:** Full-time maker; first knife sold in 1993.

Doing business as Millard Knives. **Mark:** Mallard duck in flight with serial number.

MILLER, MICHAEL E., 1508 Crestwood Dr, Wagoner, OK 74467, Phone: 918-485-6166
Specialties: Traditional working/using knives of his design. **Patterns:** Bowies, hunters and kitchen knives. **Technical:** Grinds ATS-34, CPM 440V; forges Damascus and cable Damascus and 52100. Prefers scrimshaw, fancy pins, basket weave and embellished sheaths. **Prices:** $80 to $300; some to $500. **Remarks:** Part-time maker; first knife sold in 1984. Doing business as Miller Custom Knives. **Mark:** First and middle initials, last name, maker, city and state.

MILLER, RONALD T., 12922 127th Ave. N., Largo, FL 34644, Phone: 813-595-0378 (after 5 p. m.)
Specialties: Working straight knives in standard patterns. **Patterns:** Combat knives, camp knives, kitchen cutlery, fillet knives, locking folders and butterflies. **Technical:** Grinds D2, 440C and ATS-34; offers brass inlays and scrimshaw. **Prices:** $45 to $325; some to $750. **Remarks:** Part-time maker; first knife sold in 1984. **Mark:** Name, city and state in palm tree logo.

MILLER, RICK, 516 Kanaul Rd, Rockwood, PA 15557, Phone: 814-926-2059
Specialties: Working/using straight knives of his design and in standard patterns. **Patterns:** Bowies, daggers, hunters and friction folders. **Technical:** Grinds L6. Forges 5160, L6 and Damascus. Patterns for Damascus are random, twist, rose or ladder. **Prices:** $75 to $250; some to $400. **Remarks:** Part-time maker; first knife sold in 1982. **Mark:** Script stamp "R. D. M. ".

MILLER, MICHAEL K., 28510 Santiam Hwy., Sweet Home, OR 97386, Phone: 541-367-4927
Specialties: Specializes in kitchen cutlery of his design or made to customer specs. **Patterns:** Hunters, utility/camp knives and kitchen cutlery. **Technical:** Grinds ATS-34, AEBL & 440-C. Wife does scrimshaw as well. Makes custom sheaths and holsters. **Prices:** $200. **Remarks:** Full-time maker; first knife sold in 1989. **Mark:** M&M Kustom Krafts.

MILLER, M. A., 8979 Pearl St., Apt. 2005, Thornton, CO 80229, Phone: 303-427-8756
Specialties: Using knives for hunting. 3-1/2"-4" Loveless drop-point. Made to customer specs. **Patterns:** Skinners and camp knives. **Technical:** Grinds 440C, D2, O1 and ATS-34 Damascus miniatures. **Prices:** $225 to $275; miniatures $75. **Remarks:** Part-time maker; first knife sold in 1988. **Mark:** Last name stamped in block letters or first and middle initials, last name, maker, city and state with triangles on either side etched.

MILLER, JAMES P., 9024 Goeller Rd., RR 2, Box 28, Fairbank, IA 50629, Phone: 319-635-2294
Specialties: All tool steel Damascus; working knives and period pieces. **Patterns:** Hunters, Bowies, camp knives and daggers. **Technical:** Forges and grinds 1095, 52100, 440C and his own Damascus. **Prices:** $100 to $350; some to $1,500. **Remarks:** Full-time maker; first knife sold in 1970. **Mark:** First and middle initials, last name with knife logo.

MILLER, HANFORD J., Box 97, Cowdrey, CO 80434, Phone: 970-723-4708
Specialties: Working knives in Moran style; period pieces. **Patterns:** Bowies, fighters, camp knives and other large straight knives. **Technical:** Forges W2, 1095, 5160 and his own Damascus; differential tempers; offers wire inlay. **Prices:** $300 to $800; some to $3,000. **Remarks:** Full-time maker; first knife sold in 1968. **Mark:** Initials or name within Bowie logo.

MILLER, DON, 1604 Harrodsburg Rd., Lexington, KY 40503, Phone: 606-276-3299

MILLER, BOB, 7659 Fine Oaks Pl., Oakville, MO 63129, Phone: 314-846-3851
Specialties: Mosaic Damascus; collector using straight knives and folders. **Patterns:** Hunters, Bowies, utility/camp knives, daggers. **Technical:** Forges own Damascus, mosaic-Damascus and 52100. **Prices:** $125 to $500. **Remarks:** Part-time maker; first knife sold in 1983. **Mark:** First and middle initials and last name, or initials.

MILLER, R. D., 10526 Estate Lane, Dallas, TX 75238, Phone: 214-348-3496
Specialties: One-of-a-kind collector-grade knives. **Patterns:** Boots, hunters, Bowies, camp knives, fishing and bird knives, miniatures. **Technical:** Grinds a variety of steels to include O1, D2, 440C, 154CM and 1095. **Prices:** $65 to $300; some to $900. **Remarks:** Full-time maker; first knife sold in 1984. **Mark:** R. D. Custom Knives with date or bow and arrow logo.

MILLS, LOUIS G., 9450 Waters Rd., Ann Arbor, MI 48103, Phone: 734-668-1839
Specialties: High-art Japanese-style period pieces. **Patterns:** Traditional tantos, daggers and swords. **Technical:** Makes steel from iron; makes his own Damascus by traditional Japanese techniques. **Prices:** $900 to $2,000; some to $8,000. **Remarks:** Spare-time maker. **Mark:** Yasutomo in Japanese Kanji.

MINK, DAN, P. O. Box 861, 196 Sage Circle, Crystal Beach, FL 34681, Phone: 727-786-5408
Specialties: Traditional and working knives of his design. **Patterns:** Bowies, fighters, folders and hunters. **Technical:** Grinds ATS-34, 440C and D2. Blades and tanges embellished with fancy filework. Uses natural and rare handle materials. **Prices:** $125 to $450. **Remarks:** Part-time maker; first knife sold in 1985. **Mark:** Name and star encircled by custom made, city, state.

MINNICK, JIM, 144 North 7th St., Middletown, IN 47356, Phone: 317-354-4108
Specialties: Lever-lock folding art knives, liner-locks. **Patterns:** Stilettos, Persian and one-of-a-kind folders. **Technical:** Grinds and carves Damascus, stainless, and high carbon. **Prices:** $950 to $7,000. **Remarks:** Part-time maker; first knife sold in 1976. **Mark:** Minnick and JMJ. **Other:** Husband & wife team.

MIRABILE, DAVID, 1715 Glacier Av., Juneau, AK 99801, Phone: (907) 463-3404
Specialties: Elegant edged weapons. **Patterns:** Fighters, Bowies, claws, tklinget daggers, executive desk knives. **Technical:** Forged high carbon steels, his own Damascus; uses ancient walrus ivory and prehistoric bone extensively, very rarely uses wood. **Prices:** $350 to $7,000. **Remarks:** Full-time maker. Knives sold through art gallery in Juneau, AK. **Mark:** Last name etched or engraved.

MITCHELL, MAX, DEAN AND BEN, 3803 V. F. W. Rd., Leesville, LA 71440, Phone: 318-239-6416
Specialties: Hatchet and knife sets with folder & belt & holster all match. **Patterns:** Hunters, 200 L6 steel. **Technical:** L6 steel; soft back, hand edge. **Prices:** $300 to $500. **Remarks:** Part-time makers; first knife sold in 1965. Custom orders only; no stock. **Mark:** First names.

MITCHELL, WM. DEAN, 8438 Cty Rd One, Lamar, CO 81052, Phone: 719-336-8807
Specialties: Classic and period knives. **Patterns:** Bowies, hunters, daggers and swords. **Technical:** Forges carbon steel and damascus 52100, 1095, 5160; makes pattern, composite and mosaic Damascus; offers filework. Makes wooden display cases. **Prices:** Mid scale. **Remarks:** Part-time maker since 1986; first knife sold in 1986. Doing business as Pioneer Forge & Woodshop. **Mark:** Full name with anvil, MS.

MITCHELL, JAMES A., P. O. Box 4646, Columbus, GA 31904, Phone: 404-322-8582
Specialties: Fancy working knives. **Patterns:** Hunters, fighters, Bowies and locking folders. **Technical:** Grinds D2, 440C and commercial Damascus. **Prices:** $100 to $400; some to $900. **Remarks:** Part-time maker; first knife sold in 1976. Sells knives in sets. **Mark:** Signature and city.

MITSUYUKI, ROSS, 94-1071 KEPAKEPA ST, C-3, WAIPAHU, HAWAII 96797, Phone: 808-671-3335, Fax:808-671-3335
Specialties: Working straight knives and folders. **Patterns:** Hunting, fighters, utility knives and boot knives. **Technical:** 440C and ATS-34. **Prices:** $100-$500. **Remarks:** Spare-time maker, first knife sold in 1998. **Mark:** Name, state, Hawaiian sea turtle.

MIZE, RICHARD, Fox Creek Forge, 2038 Fox Creek Rd, Lawrenceburg, KY 40342, Phone: 502-859-0602
Specialties: Forges spring steel, 5160, 10xx steels, natural handle materials. **Patterns:** Traditional working knives, period flavor Bowies, rifle knives. **Technical:** Does own heat treating, differential temper. **Prices:** $100 to $1000. **Remarks:** Strongly advocates sole authorship. **Mark:** Letter M stamped, zoomorph stamped.

MOMCILOVIC, GUNNAR, Nordlysv, 16, N-30055 Krokstadelva, NORWAY, Phone: 0111-47-3287-3586

MONCUS, MICHAEL STEVEN, 1803 US 19 NORTH, SMITHVILLE, GA 31787, Phone: (912) 846-2408

MONK, NATHAN P., 1304 4th Ave. SE, Cullman, AL 35055, Phone: 205-737-0463
Specialties: Traditional working and using straight knives of his design and to customer specs; fancy knives. **Patterns:** Bowies, daggers, fighters, hunters, utility/camp knives, bird knives and one of a kinds. **Technical:** Grinds ATS-34, 440C and A2. **Prices:** $50 to $175. **Remarks:** Spare-time maker; first knife sold in 1990. **Mark:** First and middle initials, last name, city, state.

MONTANO, GUS A, 11217 Westonhill Dr, San Diego, CA 92126-1447, Phone: 619-273-5357
Specialties: Traditional working/using straight knives of his design. **Patterns:** Boots, Bowies and fighters. **Technical:** Grinds 1095 and 5160; grinds and forges cable. Double or triple hardened and triple drawn; hand rubbed finish. Prefers natural handle materials. **Prices:** $200 to $400; some to $600. **Remarks:** Spare-time maker; first knife sold in 1997. **Mark:** First initial and last name.

custom knifemakers

MONTEIRO, VICTOR, 31, Rue D'Opprebais, 1360 Maleves Ste Marie, BELGIUM, Phone: 010 88 0441
Specialties: Working and fancy straight knives, folders and integrals of his design. **Patterns:** Bowies, fighters and hunters. **Technical:** Grinds ATS-34, 440C and commercial Damascus, embellishment, filework and domed pins. **Prices:** $300 to $1000, some higher. **Remarks:** Part-time maker; first knife sold in 1989. **Mark:** Logo with initials connected.

MONTJOY, CLAUDE, 706 Indian Creek Rd, Clinton, SC 29325, Phone: 864-697-6160
Specialties: Folders, slip joint, lock, lock liner & inter frame. **Patterns:** Hunters, boots, fighters, some art knives and folders. **Technical:** Grinds ATS-34 and Damascus. Offers inlaid handle scales. **Prices:** $100 to $500. **Remarks:** Full-time maker; first knife sold in 1982. **Mark:** Montjoy. **Other:** Custom orders, no catalog.

MOORE, JAMES B., 1707 N. Gillis, Ft. Stockton, TX 79735, Phone: 915-336-2113
Specialties: Classic working straight knives and folders of his design. **Patterns:** Hunters, Bowies, daggers, fighters, boots, utility/camp knives, locking folders and slip-joint folders. **Technical:** Grinds 440C, ATS-34, D2, L6, CPM and commercial Damascus. **Prices:** $85 to $700; exceptional knives to $1,500. **Remarks:** Full-time maker; first knife sold in 1972. **Mark:** Name, city and state.

MOORE, MARVE, 1216 Paintersville-New Jasper Rd, Xenia, OH 45385, Phone: (937) 256-8235

MOORE, TED, 340 E Willow St, Elizabethtown, PA 17022-1946, Phone: 717-367-3939
Specialties: Damascus folders, cigar cutters. **Patterns:** Locking folders & slip joint. **Technical:** Grinds Damascus, high carbon & stainless; also ATS34 & D2. **Prices:** $250 to $1,500. **Remarks:** Part-time maker; first knife sold 1993. **Mark:** Moore U. S. A.

MOORE, MICHAEL ROBERT, 61 Beaulieu St, Lowell, MA 01850, Phone: 978-459-2163, Fax:978-441-1819

MOORE, BILL, 806 Community Ave., Albany, GA 31705, Phone: 912-438-5529
Specialties: Working and using folders of his design and to customer specs. **Patterns:** Bowies, hunters and locking folders. **Technical:** Grinds ATS-34, forges 5168 and cable Damascus. Filework. **Prices:** $100 to $400. **Remarks:** Part-time maker; first knife sold in 1988. **Mark:** Moore Knives.

MORAN JR., WM. F., P. O. Box 68, Braddock Heights, MD 21714, Phone: 301-371-7543
Specialties: High-art working knives of his design. **Patterns:** Fighters, camp knives, Bowies, daggers, axes, tomahawks, push knives and miniatures. **Technical:** Forges W2, 5160 and his own Damascus; puts silver wire inlay on most handles; uses only natural handle materials. **Prices:** $400 to $7,500; some to $9,000. **Remarks:** Full-time maker. **Mark:** W. F. Moran Jr. Master Smith MS.

MORETT, DONALD, 116 Woodcrest Dr, Lancaster, PA 17602-1300, Phone: (717) 746-4888

MORGAN, TOM, 14689 Ellett Rd., Beloit, OH 44609, Phone: 330-537-2023
Specialties: Working straight knives and period pieces. **Patterns:** Hunters, boots and presentation tomahawks. **Technical:** Grinds O1, 440C and 154CM. **Prices:** Knives, $65 to $200; tomahawks, $100 to $325. **Remarks:** Full-time maker; first knife sold in 1977. **Mark:** Last name and type of steel used.

MORGAN, JEFF, 9200 Arnaz Way, Santee, CA 92071, Phone: 619-448-8430
Specialties: Fancy working straight knives. **Patterns:** Hunters, fighters, boots, miniatures. **Technical:** Grinds D2, 440C and ATS-34; likes exotic handles. **Prices:** $65 to $140; some to $500. **Remarks:** Full-time maker; first knife sold in 1977. **Mark:** Initials connected.

MORRIS, C. H., 1590 Old Salem Rd., Frisco City, AL 36445, Phone: 334-575-7425
Specialties: Liner lock folders. **Patterns:** Interframe liner locks. **Technical:** Grinds 440C and ATS-34. **Prices:** Start at $350. **Remarks:** Full-time maker; first knife sold in 1973. Doing business as Custom Knives. **Mark:** First and middle initials, last name.

MORRIS, DARRELL PRICE, 92 Union, St. Plymouth, Devon, ENGLAND PL1 3EZ, Phone: 0752 223546
Specialties: Traditional Japanese knives, Bowies and high-art knives. **Technical:** Nickel Damascus and mokamame. **Prices:** $1,000 to $4,000. **Remarks:** Part-time maker; first knife sold in 1990. **Mark:** Initials and Japanese name--Kuni Shigae.

MORRIS, ERIC, 306 Ewart Ave., Beckley, WV 25801, Phone: 304-255-3951

MORTENSON, ED, 2742 Hwy. 93 N, Darby, MT 59829, Phone: 406-821-3146, Fax:406-821-3146
Specialties: Period pieces and working/using straight knives of his design, to customer specs and in standard patterns. **Patterns:** Bowies, hunters and kitchen knives. **Technical:** Grinds ATS-34, 5160 and 1095. Sheath combinations - flashlight/knife, hatchet/knife, etc. **Prices:** $60 to $140; some to $300. **Remarks:** Full-time maker; first knife sold in 1993. Doing business as The Blade Lair. **Mark:** M with attached O.

MOSES, STEVEN, 1610 WEST Hemlock Way, Santa Ana, CA 92704

MOSIER, JOSHUA J, Spring Creek Knife Works, PO Box 442/802 6th St, Edgar, NE 68935
Specialties: Working straight and folding knives of my designs with customer specs. **Patterns:** Hunters, utilities, frame lock folders, kitchen and camp knives. **Technical:** Forges and grinds 5160, W2, L6, simple carbon steels and my own Damascus, uses some antique materials, provides a history of the materials used in each knife. **Prices:** $45 and up. **Remarks:** Part-time maker, sold first knife in 1986. **Mark:** SCK with year.

MOSIER, RICHARD, 52 Dapplegray Ln, Rolling Hills Est, CA 90274

MOSSER, GARY E., 11827 NE 102nd Place, Kirkland, WA 98033-5170, Phone: 425-827-2279
Specialties: Working knives. **Patterns:** Hunters, skinners, camp knives, some art knives. **Technical:** Stock removal method; prefers ATS-34. **Prices:** $100 to $250; special orders and art knives are higher. **Remarks:** Part-time maker; first knife sold in 1976. **Mark:** Name.

MOULTON, DUSTY, 135 Hillview Lane, Loudon, TN 37774, Phone: (865) 408-9779
Specialties: Fancy and working straight knives. **Patterns:** Hunters, fighters, fantasy and miniatures. **Technical:** Grinds ATS-34 and Damascus. **Prices:** $300 to $2000. **Remarks:** Full-time maker; first knife sold in 1991. **Mark:** Last name. **Other:** Now doing engraving on own knives as well as other makers.

MOUNT, DON, 4574 Little Finch Ln., Las Vegas, NV 89115, Phone: 702-531-2925
Specialties: High-tech working and using straight knives of his design. **Patterns:** Bowies, fighters and utility/camp knives. **Technical:** Uses 440C and ATS-34. **Prices:** $150 to $300; some to $1,000. **Remarks:** Part-time maker; first knife sold in 1985. **Mark:** Name below a woodpecker.

MOUNTAIN HOME KNIVES, P. O. Box 167, Jamul, CA 91935, Phone: 619-669-0833
Specialties: High-quality working straight knives. **Patterns:** Hunters, fighters, skinners, tantos, utility and fillet knives, Bowies and *san-mai Damascus Bowies.* **Technical:** *Hollow-grind 440C by hand. Feature linen Micarta handles, nickel-silver handle bolts and handmade sheaths.* **Prices:** *$65 to $270.* **Remarks:** *Company owned by Jim English.* **Mark:** *Mountain Home Knives.*

MOYER, RUSS, HC 36 Box 57C, Havre, MT 59501, Phone: 406-395-4423
Specialties: Working knives to customer specs. **Patterns:** Hunters, Bowies and survival knives. **Technical:** Forges W2. **Prices:** $150 to $350. **Remarks:** Part-time maker; first knife sold in 1976. **Mark:** Initials in logo.

MULLER, JODY, P. O. Box 35, Pittsburg, MO 65724, Phone: 417-852-4306
Specialties: Hand engraving, carving and inlays. One of a king personal carry knives with billfold cases, cleavers. **Patterns:** One of a kind fixed blades in all styles. **Technical:** Forges 1095, L6 and Nickel into our own patterned Damascus. **Prices:** $150-$1500. **Remarks:** Son and father team of part-time makes. Jody made first knife at age 12. Now does fien hand-engraving, carving and inlay. **Mark:** Muller Forge in script.

MULLIN, STEVE, 500 Snowberry Lane, Sandpoint, ID 83864, Phone: 208-263-7492
Specialties: Damascus period pieces and folders. **Patterns:** Full range of folders, hunters and Bowies. **Technical:** Forges and grinds O1, D2, 154CM and his own Damascus. Engraves. **Prices:** $100 to $2,000. **Remarks:** Full-time maker; first knife sold in 1975. Sells line of using knives under Pack River Knife Co. **Mark:** Full name, city and state.

MUNROE, DERYK C, P O Box 3454, Bozeman, MT 59772

MURRAY, BILL, 1632 Rio Mayo, Green Valley, AZ 85614

MURSKI, RAY, 12129 Captiva Ct., Reston, VA 22091-1204, Phone: 703-264-1102
Specialties: Fancy working/using folders of his design. **Patterns:** Hunters, slip-joint folders and utility/camp knives. **Technical:** Grinds CPM-3V. **Prices:** $125-$500. **Remarks:** Spare-time maker; first knife sold in 1996. **Mark:** Etched name with serial number under name.

MYERS, PAUL, 614 W. Airwood Dr., E. Alton, IL 62024
Specialties: Fancy working straight knives and folders. **Patterns:** Full range of folders, straight hunters and Bowies; tie tacks; knife and fork sets.

Technical: Grinds D2, 440C, ATS-34 and 154CM. **Prices:** $100 to $350; some to $3,000. **Remarks:** Full-time maker; first knife sold in 1974. **Mark:** Initials with setting sun on front; name and number on back.

n

NATEN, GREG, 1804 Shamrock Way, Bakersfield, CA 93304-3921
Specialties: Fancy and working/using folders of his design. **Patterns:** Fighters, hunters and locking folders. **Technical:** Grinds 440C, ATS-34 and CPM440V. Heat-treats; prefers desert ironwood, stag and mother of pearl. Designs and sews leather sheaths for straight knives. **Prices:** $175 to $600; some to $950. **Remarks:** Spare-time maker; first knife sold in 1992. **Mark:** Last name above battle-ax, handmade.

NAVAGATO, ANGELO, 5 Commercial Apt 2, Camp Hill, PA 17011

NEALEY, IVAN F. (FRANK), Anderson Dam Rd., Box 65, HC #87, Mt. Home, ID 83647, Phone: 208-587-4060
Specialties: Working straight knives in standard patterns. **Patterns:** Hunters, skinners and utility knives. **Technical:** Grinds D2, 440C and 154CM. **Prices:** $90 to $135; some higher. **Remarks:** Part-time maker; first knife sold in 1975. **Mark:** Name.

NEALY, BUD, 1439 Poplar Valley Rd, Stroudsburg, PA 18360, Phone: 570-402-1018, Fax:570-402-1019
Specialties: Original design concealment knives with designer multi-concealment sheath system. **Patterns:** Concealment knives, boots, combat and collector pieces. **Technical:** Grinds ATS-34; uses Damascus. **Prices:** $200 to $2,500. **Remarks:** Full-time maker; first knife sold in 1980. **Mark:** Name, city, state or signature.

NEDVED, DAN, 206 Park Dr., Kalispell, MT 59901, Phone: 406-752-5060
Specialties: Slip joint folders, liner locks, straight knives. **Patterns:** Mostly traditional or modern blend with traditional lines. **Technical:** Grinds ATS34, 440C, 1095 and uses other makers Damascus. **Prices:** $95 and up. Mostly in the $150 to $200 range. **Remarks:** Part-time maker, averages 2 a month. **Mark:** Dan Nedved or Nedved with serial # on opposite side.

NEELY, GREG, 9605 Radio Rd., Houston, TX 77075-2238, Phone: 713-991-2677
Specialties: Traditional patterns and his own patterns for work and/or collecting. **Patterns:** Hunters, Bowies and utility/camp knives. **Technical:** Forges own Damascus, 1084, 5160 and some tool steels. Differentially tempers. **Prices:** $225 to $5,000. **Remarks:** Part-time maker; first knife sold in 1987. **Mark:** Last name or interlocked initials, MS.

NEILSON, J. & TESS, RR 2 Box 16, Wyalusing, PA 18853, Phone: 570-746-4944
Specialties: Working and collectable fixed blade knives; custom sheaths. **Patterns:** Hunter/fighters, bowies, neck knives and historical replicas. **Technical:** Flat grinds, 1095, 516, 440C (beginning to forge Damascus). Tess makes custom sheaths with stamping/carving, exotic inlays, traditional stitching and magnetic neck sheaths. **Prices:** $150-$450. **Remarks:** Full-time maker, first knife sold in 2000. Doing business at Mountain Hollow Blade & Hide Co. **Mark:** Mountain Hollow and full name.

NELSON, TOM, P O Box 2298, Wilropark 1731, Gauteng, SOUTH AFRICA

NELSON, BOB, 21 Glen Rd, Sparta, NJ 07871

NELSON, DR CARL, 2500 N Robison Rd, Texarkana, TX 75501

NELSON, KEN, 11059 Hwy 73, Pittsville, WI 54466, Phone: 715-884-6448
Specialties: Working straight knives, period pieces. **Patterns:** Utility, hunters, dirks, daggers, throwers, hawks, axes, swords, and pole arms. **Technical:** Forges 5160, 52100, W2, 10xx, L6, and own Damascus. Multiple and differential heat treating. **Prices:** $50 to $350, some to $3000. **Remarks:** Part-time maker. First knife sold in 1995. Doing business as Iron Wolf Forge. Member of ABS. **Mark:** Stylized wolf paw print.

NETO JR., NELSON AND DE CARVALHO, HENRIQUE M., R. Joao Margarido, No. 20-V, Guerra, Braganca Paulista, SP-12900-000, BRAZIL, Phone: 011-7843-6889, Fax:011-7843-6889
Specialties: Straight knives and folders. **Patterns:** Bowies, katanas, jambyias and others. **Technical:** Forges high carbon steels. **Prices:** $70 to $3000. **Remarks:** Full-time makers; first knife sold in 1990. **Mark:** H&N.

NEUHAEUSLER, ERWIN, Heiligenangerstrasse 15, 86179 Augsburg, GERMANY, Phone: 0821/81 49 97
Specialties: Using straight knives of his design. **Patterns:** Hunters, boots, Bowies. **Technical:** Grinds ATS-34, RWL-34 and Damascus. **Prices:** $200 to $750. **Remarks:** Spare-time maker; first knife sold in 1991. **Mark:** Etched logo, last name and city.

NEVLING, MARK, Burr Oak Knives, PO Box 9, Hume, IL 61932, Phone: 217-887-2522
Specialties: Straight knives and folders of his own design. **Patterns:** Hunters, fighters, bowies, folders, and small executive knives. **Technical:** Convex grinds, Forges, uses only high carbon and Damascus. **Prices:** $200 - $2000. **Remarks:** Full-time maker, first knife sold 1988.

NEWCOMB, CORBIN, 628 Woodland Ave., Moberly, MO 65270, Phone: 660-263-4639
Specialties: Working straight knives and folders; period pieces. **Patterns:** Hunters, axes, Bowies, folders, buckskinned blades and boots. **Technical:** Hollow-grinds D2, 440C and 154CM; prefers natural handle materials. Makes own Damascus; offers cable Damascus. **Prices:** $100 to $500. **Remarks:** Full-time maker; first knife sold in 1982. Doing business as Corbin Knives. **Mark:** First name and serial number.

NEWHALL, TOM, 3602 E 42nd Stravenue, Tucson, AZ 85713, Phone: (520) 721-0562

NEWTON, RON, 223 Ridge Lane, London, AR 72847, Phone: 479-293-3001
Specialties: Mosaic Damascus folders with accelerated actions. **Patterns:** One-of-a-kind. **Technical:** 1084-15N20 steels used in my mosaic Damascus steels. **Prices:** $1,000 to $5,000. **Remarks:** Also making antique Bowie repros and various fixed blades. **Mark:** All capital letters in NEWTON "Western Invitation" font.

NEWTON, LARRY, 1758 Pronghorn Ct., Jacksonville, FL 32225, Phone: 904-221-2340, Fax:904-220-4098
Specialties: Traditional and slender high grade gentlemen's automatics folders, locking liner type tactical, and working straight knives. **Patterns:** Front release locking folders, interframes, hunters, and skinners. **Technical:** Grinds Damascus, ATS-34, 440C and D2. **Prices:** Folders start at $350, straights start at $150. **Remarks:** Spare-time maker; first knife sold in 1989. **Mark:** Last name.

NICHOLSON, R. KENT, P. O. Box 204, Phoenix, MD 21131, Phone: 410-323-6925
Specialties: Large using knives. **Patterns:** Bowies and camp knives in the Moran style. **Technical:** Forges W2, 9260, 5160; makes Damascus. **Prices:** $150 to $995. **Remarks:** Part-time maker; first knife sold in 1984. **Mark:** Name.

NIELSON, JEFF V., PO Box 365, Monroe, UT 84754, Phone: 801-527-4242
Specialties: Classic knives of his design and to customer specs. **Patterns:** Fighters, hunters, locking folders; miniatures. **Technical:** Grinds 440C stainless & Damascus. **Prices:** $100 to $1200. **Remarks:** Part-time maker; first knife sold in 1991. **Mark:** Name, location.

NIEMUTH, TROY, 3143 North Ave., Sheboygan, WI 53083, Phone: 414-452-2927
Specialties: Period pieces and working/using straight knives of his design and to customer specs. **Patterns:** Hunters and utility/camp knives. **Technical:** Grinds 440C, 1095 and A2. **Prices:** $85 to $350; some to $500. **Remarks:** Full-time maker; first knife sold in 1995. **Mark:** Etched last name.

NISHIUCHI, MELVIN S., 6121 Forest Park Dr., Las Vegas, NV 89116, Phone: 702-438-2327
Specialties: Working knives; collector pieces. **Patterns:** Hunters, fighters, locking liner folders, and some fancy personal knives. **Technical:** Grinds ATS-34; prefers exotic wood and/or semi-precious stone handle materials. **Prices:** $250 to $2,000. **Remarks:** Part-time maker; first knife sold in 1985. **Mark:** Circle with a line above it.

NIX, ROBERT T, 4194 Cadillac, Wayne, MI 48184, Phone: 734-729-6468
Specialties: Hunters, skinners, art, bowie, camp/survival/boot folders. Most are file worked. Custom leather work available also, mainly sheath's/overlays, inlays, tooling, combinations of material/leather, micarta, wood, kydex, nylon. **Technical:** Stock removal, ATS-34, stainless Damascus, 440C, 420V, 440V, BG42, D2, 01, carbon Damascus. Every blade gets Rockwelled. I like the natural handle materials best, but will use anything that's available; ivory, bone, horn, pearl, stabilized woods, micarta. **Prices:** Knives from $125 to $2500. Sheaths from $40 to $400. **Remarks:** Part-time maker, first knife sold in 1993. Make each piece as if it were for me. **Mark:** R. T. Nix in script or Nix in bold face.

NOLEN, R. D. AND STEVE, 1110 Lakeshore Dr., Estes Park, CO 80517-7113, Phone: 970-586-5814, Fax:Fax: 970-586-8827
Specialties: Working knives; display pieces. **Patterns:** Wide variety of straight knives, butterflies and buckles. **Technical:** Grind D2, 440C and 154CM. Offer filework; make exotic handles. **Prices:** $150 to $800; some higher. **Remarks:** Full-time makers; first knife sold in 1968. Steve is third generation maker. **Mark:** NK in oval logo.

custom knifemakers

NORDELL, INGEMAR, Skarpå 2103, 82041 Färila, SWEDEN, Phone: 0651-23347
Specialties: Classic working and using straight knives. **Patterns:** Hunters, Bowies and fighters. **Technical:** Forges and grinds ATS-34, D2 and Sandvik. **Prices:** $120 to $1,500. **Remarks:** Part-time maker; first knife sold in 1985. **Mark:** Initials or name.

NOREN, DOUGLAS E, 14676 Boom Rd, Springlake, MI 49456, Phone: (616) 842-4247
Specialties: Hand forged blades, custom built & made to order. Hand file work, carving & casting. Stag & stacked handles. Replicas of Scagel & Joseph Rogers. Hand tooled custom made sheaths. **Technical:** 5160, 52100 & 1084 steel. **Prices:** Start at $250. **Remarks:** Sole authorship, works in all mediums, ABS member, all knives come with a custom hand tooled sheath Also makes anvils & does gold & silver plaiting. **Other:** I enjoy the challenge & meeting people.

NORFLEET, ROSS W., 3947 Tanbark Rd, Richmond, VA 23235, Phone: 804-276-4169
Specialties: Classic, traditional and working/using knives of his design or in standard patterns. **Patterns:** Hunters and folders. **Technical:** Hollow-grinds 440C and ATS-34. **Prices:** $150 to $550. **Remarks:** Part-time maker; first knife sold in 1992. **Mark:** Last name.

NORRIS, DON, 8861 N Shadow Rock Dr, Tucson, AZ 85743, Phone: 520-744-2494
Specialties: Classic and traditional working/using straight knives and folders of his design, or to customer specs etc. **Patterns:** Bowies, daggers, fighters, hunters and utility/camp knives. **Technical:** Grinds and forges Damascus; grinds ATS-34 and 440C. Cast sterling guards and bolsters on Bowies. **Prices:** $350 to $2,000, some to $3500. **Remarks:** Full-time maker; first knife sold in 1990. Doing business as Norris Custom Knives. **Mark:** Last name.

NORRIS, MIKE, 2115 W Main St, Albermarle, NC 28001, Phone: 704-982-8445

NORTON, DON, 7517 Mountain Quail Dr, Las Vegas, NV 89146, Phone: 703-642-5036
Specialties: Fancy and plain straight knives. **Patterns:** Hunters, small Bowies, tantos, boot knives, fillets. **Technical:** Prefers 440C, Micarta, exotic woods and other natural handle materials. Hollow-grinds all knives except fillet knives. **Prices:** $165 to $1,500; average is $200. **Remarks:** Full-time maker; first knife sold in 1980. **Mark:** Full name, Hsi Shuai, city, state.

NOTT, RON P., P. O. Box 281, Summerdale, PA 17093, Phone: 717-732-2763
Specialties: High-art folders and some straight knives. **Patterns:** Scale release folders. **Technical:** Grinds ATS-34, 416 and nickel-silver. Engraves, inlays gold. **Prices:** $250 to $3,000. **Remarks:** Full-time maker; first knife sold in 1993. Doing business as Knives By Nott, customer engraving. **Mark:** First initial, last name and serial number.

NOWLAND, RICK, 3677 E Bonnie Rd., Waltonville, IL 62894, Phone: 618-279-3170
Specialties: Fancy single blade slip joints & trappers using Damascus & Mokume. **Patterns:** Uses several Remington patterns and also his own designs. **Technical:** Uses ATS-34, 440C; forges his own Damascus; makes mokume. **Prices:** Start at $200. **Remarks:** Part-time maker; first knife sold in 1986. **Mark:** Last name.

NUNN, GREGORY, HC64 Box 2107, Castle Valley, UT 84532, Phone: 435-259-8607
Specialties: High-art working and using knives of his design; new edition knife with handle made from anatomized dinosaur bone - first ever made. **Patterns:** Flaked stone knives. **Technical:** Uses gem-quality agates, jaspers and obsidians for blades. **Prices:** $250 to $2300. **Remarks:** Full-time maker; first knife sold in 1989. **Mark:** Name, knife and edition numbers, year made.

O

OAKES, WINSTON, 431 Deauville Dr, Dayton, OH 45429, Phone: (937) 434-3112
Specialties: Dealer. **Prices:** $200 to $10,000. **Remarks:** Dealer in Jess Horn folders and other high quality hunters.

OBRIEN, GEORGE, 22511 Tullis Trails Ct, Katy, TX 77494-8265

O'CEILAGHAN, MICHAEL, 1623 Benhill Rd., Baltimore, MD 21226, Phone: 410-355-1660, Fax:410-355-1661
Specialties: High-art and traditional straight knives of his design and to customer specs. **Patterns:** Fighters, hunters and utility/camp knives. **Technical:** Forges 5160, O6, 1045 and railroad spikes. Blades are "Hamon" tempered and drawn; handles are either horn or hand-carved wood. **Prices:** $100 to $325; some to $750. **Remarks:** First knife sold in 1992. Doing business as Howling Wolf Forge. **Mark:** Howling Wolf Forge, signed signature, date forged.

OCHS, CHARLES F., 124 Emerald Lane, Largo, FL 33771, Phone: 727-536-3827, Fax:727-536-3827
Specialties: Working knives; period pieces. **Patterns:** Hunters, fighters, Bowies, buck skinners and folders. **Technical:** Forges 52100, 5160 and his own Damascus. **Prices:** $150 to $1,800; some to $2,500. **Remarks:** Full-time maker; first knife sold in 1978. **Mark:** OX Forge.

O'DELL, CLYDE, 176 Ouachita 404, Camden, AR 71701, Phone: (870) 574-2754
Specialties: Working knives. **Patterns:** Hunters, camp knives, tomahawks. **Technical:** Forges 5160 and 1084. **Prices:** Starting at $50. **Remarks:** Spare-time maker. **Mark:** Last name.

ODGEN, RANDY W, 10822 Sage Orchard, Houston, TX 77089, Phone: (713) 481-3601

ODOM, VIC, P O Box 572, North, SC 29112, Phone: (803) 247-5614

OGDEN, BILL, Ogden Knives, PO Box 52, Avis, PA 17721, Phone: 570-753-5568
Specialties: One-of-a-kind, liner-lock folders, hunters, skinners, minis. **Technical:** Grinds ATS-34, 440-C, D2, 52100, Damascus, natural & unnatural handle materials, hand-stitched custom sheaths. **Prices:** $50 and up. **Remarks:** Part-time maker since 1992. Marks: Last name or "OK" stamp (Ogden Knives).

OGLETREE JR., BEN R., 2815 Israel Rd., Livingston, TX 77351, Phone: 409-327-8315
Specialties: Working/using straight knives of his design. **Patterns:** Hunters, kitchen and utility/camp knives. **Technical:** Grinds ATS-34, W1 and 1075; heat-treats. **Prices:** $200 to $400. **Remarks:** Part-time maker; first knife sold in 1955. **Mark:** Last name, city and state in oval with a tree on either side.

OKAYSU, KAZOU, 12-2 1 Chome Higashi Veno, Taito-Ku, Tokyo 110, JAPAN

OLIVE, MICHAEL E, HC 78 Box 442, Leslie, AR 72645, Phone: (870) 363-4452

OLIVER, ANTHONY CRAIG, 1504 Elaine Pl., Ft. Worth, TX 76106, Phone: 817-625-0825
Specialties: Fancy and embellished traditional straight knives of his design. **Patterns:** Hunters, full-size folders, Bowies, daggers and miniatures in stainless and nickel Damascus with tempered blades. **Technical:** Grinds 440C and ATS-34. **Prices:** $40 to $500. **Remarks:** Part-time maker; first knife sold in 1988. **Mark:** Initials and last name.

OLIVER, TODD D, RR5 Box 659, Spencer, IN 47460, Phone: 812-829-1762
Specialties: Damascus hunters and daggers. High carbon as well. **Patterns:** Ladder, twist random. **Technical:** I am the sole author of all my blades. **Prices:** $350 and up. **Remarks:** I learned bladesmithing from Jim Batson at the ABS school & Damascus from Billy Merritt in Indiana. **Mark:** T. D. Oliver Spencer IN. **Other:** Two crossed swords and a battle ax.

OLSON, DARROLD E., P. O. Box 1539, Springfield, OR 97477, Phone: 541-726-8300; 541-726-7503
Specialties: Straight knives and folders of his design and to customer specs. **Patterns:** Hunters, liner locks and locking folders. **Technical:** Grinds 440C, ATS-34 and 154CM. Uses anodized titanium; sheaths wet-molded. **Prices:** $150 to $350. **Remarks:** Part-time maker; first knife sold in 1989. **Mark:** Etched logo, year, type of steel & name.

OLSON, ROD, Box 5973, High River, AB, CANADA T1V 1P6, Phone: 403-652-2744, Fax:403-652-3061
Specialties: Traditional and working/using folders of his design; period pieces. **Patterns:** Locking folders. **Technical:** Grinds ATS-34. Offers filework, sculptured steel frames. **Prices:** $300 to $750. **Remarks:** Part-time maker; first knife sold in 1979. Doing business as Olson Pocket Knives. Mark Last name on blade; country, serial number inside frame.

OLSON, WAYNE C., 890 Royal Ridge Dr, Bailey, CO 80421, Phone: 303-816-9486
Specialties: High-tech working knives. **Patterns:** Hunters to folding lockers; some integral designs. **Technical:** Grinds 440C, 154CM and ATS-34; likes hand-finishes; precision-fits stainless steel fittings--no solder, no nickel silver. **Prices:** $275 to $600; some to $3,000. **Remarks:** Part-time maker; first knife sold in 1979. **Mark:** Name, maker.

OLSZEWSKI, STEPHEN, 1820 Harkney Hill Rd, Coventry, RI 02816, Phone: 401-397-4774
Specialties: Lock back, liner locks, automatics (art knives). **Patterns:** One-of-a-kind art knives specializing in figurals. **Technical:** Damascus steel, titanium file worked liners, fossil ivory & pearl. **Prices:** $1,800 to $6,500. **Remarks:** Will custom build to your specifications. **Other:** Quality work with guarantee. **Mark:** SCO inside fish symbol.

O'MALLEY, DANIEL, 4338 Evanston Ave N, Seattle, WA 98103, Phone: (206) 527-0315
Specialties: Custom chef's knives. **Remarks:** Making knives since 1997.

ONION, KENNETH J., 91-990 Oaniani St., Kapolei, HI 96707, Phone: 808-674-1300, Fax:808-674-1403
Specialties: Straight knives and folders. **Patterns:** Bowies, daggers, tantos, fighters, boots, hunters, utility knives and art knives. **Technical:** ATS-34, 440C, Damascus, 5160, D2. **Prices:** $135 to $1,500. **Remarks:** Part-time maker; first knife sold in 1991. All knives fully guaranteed. Call for availability. **Mark:** Name and state.

ORTEGA, BEN M, 165 Dug Road, Wyoming, PA 18644, Phone: (717) 696-3234

ORTON, RICHARD, P. O. Box 7002, La Verne, CA 91750, Phone: 909-596-8344
Specialties: Collectible folders, using and collectible straight knives. **Patterns:**Wharncliffe, gents, tactical, boot, neck knives, bird & trout, hunters, camp, bowie. **Technical:** Grinds ATS-34, Jim Fergeson Damascus titanium liners, bolsters, anodize, lots of filework, jigged and picked bone, giraffe bone. Scrimshaw on some. **Prices:** Folders $300 to $600; straight $100 to $750. **Remarks:** Full-time maker; first knife sold in 1992. Doing business as Orton Knife Works. Now making folders. **Mark:** Last name, city and state.

OSBORNE, DONALD H, 5840 N McCall, Clovis, CA 93611, Phone: (559) 299-9483, Fax:(559) 298-1751
Specialties: Traditional working and using straight knives of his design. **Patterns:** Working straight knives, hunters, Bowies and camp knives. **Technical:** Forges 5160, 1084, 1095; grinds 440C & 154CM. **Prices:** $150 to $500. **Remarks:** Part-time maker. **Mark:** Last name.

OSBORNE, WARREN, 215 Edgefield, Waxahachie, TX 75165, Phone: 972-935-0899, Fax:972-937-9004
Specialties: Investment grade collectible, interframes, one of a kinds; unique locking mechanisms. **Patterns:** Folders; bolstered and interframes; conventional lockers, front lockers and back lockers; some slip-joints; some high-art pieces; fighters. **Technical:** Grinds ATS-34, 440 and 154; some Damascus and CPM400V. **Prices:** $400 to $2,000; some to $4,000. Interframes $650 to $1,500. **Remarks:** Full-time maker; first knife sold in 1980. **Mark:** Last name in boomerang logo.

OSBORNE, MICHAEL, 585 Timber Ridge Dr., New Braunfels, TX 78132, Phone: 210-609-0118
Specialties: Traditional and working/using straight knives of his design. **Patterns:** Bowies, fighters and hunters. **Technical:** Forges 5160, 52100 and 10. Tempers all blades. Some filework. Embellishes with silver wire inlay. **Prices:** $125 to $500; some to $1,000. **Remarks:** Part-time maker; first knife sold in 1988. **Mark:** Engraved signature and year.

OSTERMAN, DANIEL E., 1644 W. 10th, Junction City, OR 97448, Phone: 541-998-1503
Specialties: One-third scale copies of period pieces, museum class miniatures. **Patterns:** Antique Bowies. **Technical:** Grinds all cutlery grade steels, engraves, etches, inlays and overlays. **Remarks:** Full-time maker; first miniature knife sold in 1975. **Mark:** Initials.

OTT, FRED, 1257 Rancho Durango Rd, Durango, CO 81303, Phone: 970-375-9669
Patterns: Bowies, Camp knives & hunters**Technical:**Forges 1084 Damascus **Prices:** $150 to $800. **Remarks:** Full-time maker. **Mark:** Last name.

OVEREYNDER, T. R., 1800 S. Davis Dr., Arlington, TX 76013, Phone: 817-277-4812, Fax:817-277-4812
Specialties: Highly finished collector-grade knives. **Patterns:** Fighters, Bowies, daggers, locking folders, slip-joints and 90 percent collector-grade interframe knives. **Technical:** Grinds D2, 440C, 440V,154CM, vendor supplied Damascus. Has been making titanium-frame folders since 1977. **Prices:** $500 to $1,500; some to $7,000. **Remarks:** Full-time maker; first knife sold in 1977. Doing business as TRO Knives. **Mark:** T. R. OVEREYNDER KNIVES, city and state.

OWENS, DONALD, 2274 Lucille Ln, Melbourne, FL 32935, Phone: (407) 254-9765

OWENS, JOHN, 14500 CR 270, Nathrop, CO 81236, Phone: 719-395-0870
Specialties: Hunters. **Prices:** $175to $235 Some to $650. **Remarks:** Spare-time maker. **Mark:** Last name.

OWNBY, JOHN C., 3316 Springbridge Ln, Plano, TX 75025
Specialties: Hunters, utility/camp knives. **Patterns:** Hunters, locking folders and utility/camp knives. **Technical:** 440C, D2 & ATS-34. All blades are flat ground. Prefers natural materials for handles--exotic woods, horn and antler. **Prices:** $150 to $350; some to $500. **Remarks:** Part-time maker; first knife sold in 1993. **Mark:** Name, city, state. **Other:** Doing business as John C. Ownby Handmade Knives

OYSTER, LOWELL R., 543 Grant Road, Corinth, ME 04427, Phone: 207-884-8663
Specialties: Traditional and original designed multi-blade slip-joint folders. **Patterns:** Hunters, minis, camp and fishing knives. **Technical:** Grinds O1; heat-treats. **Prices:** $55 to $450; some to $750. **Remarks:** Full-time maker; first knife sold in 1981. **Mark:** A scallop shell.

p

PACHI, FRANCESCO, Via Pometta, 1, 17046 Sassello (SV), ITALY, Phone: 019 720086, Fax:019 720086
Specialties: Fancy and working knives. **Patterns:** Hunters and skinners. **Technical:** Grinds ATS-34 and Damascus. **Prices:** $400 to $2,500. **Remarks:** Full-time maker; first knife sold in 1991. **Mark:** Logo with last name.

PACKARD, BOB, P. O. Box 311, Elverta, CA 95626, Phone: 916-991-5218
Specialties: Traditional working/using straight knives of his design and to customer specs. **Patterns:** Hunters, fishing knives, utility/camp knives. **Technical:** Grinds ATS-34, 440C; Forges 52100, 5168 and cable Damascus. **Prices:** $75 to $225. **Mark:** Engraved name and year.

PADGETT JR., EDWIN L., 340 Vauxhall St, New London, CT 06320-3838, Phone: 860-443-2938
Specialties: Skinners and working knives of any design. **Patterns:** Straight and folding knives. **Technical:** Grinds ATS-34 or any tool steel upon request. **Prices:** $50 to $300. **Mark:** Name.

PADILLA, GARY, P. O. Box 6928, Auburn, CA 95604, Phone: 530-888-6992
Specialties: Native American influenced working and using straight knives of his design. **Patterns:** Hunters, kitchen knives, utility/camp knives and obsidian ceremonial knives. **Technical:** Grinds 440C, ATS-34, O1 and Damascus. **Prices:** $65 to $195; some to $500. **Remarks:** Part-time maker; first knife sold in 1977. Doing business as Bighorn Knifeworks. **Mark:** Stylized initials or name over company name.

PAGE, LARRY, 165 Rolling Rock Rd., Aiken, SC 29803, Phone: 803-648-0001
Specialties: Working knives of his design. **Patterns:** Hunters, boots and fighters. **Technical:** Grinds ATS-34. **Prices:** Start at $85. **Remarks:** Part-time maker; first knife sold in 1983. **Mark:** Name, city and state in oval.

PAGE, REGINALD, 6587 Groveland Hill Rd., Groveland, NY 14462, Phone: 716-243-1643
Specialties: High-art straight knives and one-of-a-kind folders of his design. **Patterns:** Hunters, locking folders and slip-joint folders. **Technical:** Forges O1, 5160 and his own Damascus. Prefers natural handle materials but will work with Micarta. **Remarks:** Spare-time maker; first knife sold in 1985. **Mark:** First initial, last name.

PALAZZO, TOM, 207-30 Jordon Dr, Bayside, NY 11360, Phone: 718-352-2170
Specialties: Fixed blades, custom sheaths, neck knives. **Patterns:** No fixed patterns. **Prices:** $150. 00 and up.

PALMER, TAYLOR, Taylor-Made Scenic Knives Inc, Box 97, Blanding, UT 84511, Phone: 435-678-2523
Specialties: Bronze carvings inside of blade area. **Prices:** $250 and up. **Mark:**Taylor Palmer Utah.

PANKIEWICZ, PHILIP R., RFD #1, Waterman Rd., Lebanon, CT 06249
Specialties: Working straight knives. **Patterns:** Hunters, daggers, minis and fishing knives. **Technical:** Grinds D2, 440C and 154CM. **Prices:** $60 to $125; some to $250. **Remarks:** Spare-time maker; first knife sold in 1975. **Mark:** First initial in star.

PARDUE, MELVIN M., Rt. 1, Box 130, Repton, AL 36475, Phone: 334-248-2447
Specialties: Folders, collectable, combat, utility and tactical. **Patterns:** Lockback, liner lock, pushbutton; all blade and handle patterns. **Technical:** Grinds 154-CM, 440-C, 12-C-27. Forges Mokume and Damascus. Uses Titanium. **Prices:** $400 to $1,600. **Remarks:** Full-time maker; Guild member, ABS member, AFC member. **Mark:** Mel Pardue or Pardue. **Other:** First knife made 1957; first knife sold professionally 1974.

PARK, VALERIE, PO Box 85319, Seattle, WA 98145-1319

PARKER, CLIFF, 6350 Tulip Dr, Zephyrhills, FL 33544, Phone: (813) 973-1682
Specialties: Damascus folders & straight knives. **Patterns:** Skinners & locking liners. **Technical:** Mostly use 1095, 1084, L6, 15N20 & A203E. **Prices:** $300 to $1500. **Remarks:** Making own Damascus & mosaic; first knife sold in 1996. **Mark:** CP. **Other:** Full-time beginning Jan. 2001.

custom knifemakers

PARKER, ROBERT NELSON, 5223 Wilhelm Rd. N. W., Rapid City, MI 49676, Phone: 231-331-6173, Fax:248-545-8211
Specialties: Traditional working and using straight knives of his design. **Patterns:** Hunters, fighters, utility/camp knives; some Bowies. **Technical:** Grinds ATS-34;GB-42, forges 01-516--L6 hollow and flat grinds, full and hidden tangs. Hand-stitched leather sheaths. **Prices:** $225 to $500; some to $1,000. **Remarks:** Part-time maker; first knife sold in 1986. **Mark:** Full name.

PARKER, J. E., 1300 E. Main, Clarion, PA 16214, Phone: 814-226-4837, Fax:814-226-4351
Specialties: Fancy/embellished, traditional and working straight knives of his design and to customer specs. **Patterns:** Bowies, hunters and liner lock folders. **Technical:** Grinds 440C, 440V, ATS-34 and nickel Damascus. Prefers mastodon, oosik, amber and malachite handle material. **Prices:** $90 to $2750. 00**Remarks:** Full-time maker; first knife sold in 1991. Doing business as Custom Knife. **Mark:** J E Parker & Clarion PA stamped in Blade.

PARKS, BLANE C., 15908 Crest Dr., Woodbridge, VA 22191, Phone: 703-221-4680
Specialties: Knives of his design. **Patterns:** Boots, Bowies, daggers, fighters, hunters, kitchen knives, locking and slip-joint folders, utility/camp knives, letter openers and friction folders. **Technical:** Grinds ATS-34, 440C, D2 and other carbon steels. Offers filework, silver wire inlay and wooden sheaths. **Prices:** Start at $250 & up. **Remarks:** Part-time maker; first knife sold in 1993. Doing business as B. C. Parks Knives. **Mark:** First and middle initials, last name.

PARKS, JOHN, 3539 Galilee Church Rd., Jefferson, GA 30549, Phone: 706-367-4916
Specialties: Traditional working and using straight knives of his design. **Patterns:** Trout knives, hunters and integral bolsters. **Technical:** Forges 1095 and 5168. **Prices:** $175 to $450; some to $650. **Remarks:** Part-time maker; first knife sold in 1981. **Mark:** Initials.

PARLER, THOMAS O, 11 Franklin St, Charleston, SC 29401, Phone: (803) 723-9433

PARRISH, ROBERT, 271 Allman Hill Rd., Weaverville, NC 28787, Phone: 828-645-2864
Specialties: Heavy-duty working knives of his design or to customer specs. **Patterns:** Survival and duty knives; hunters and fighters. **Technical:** Grinds 440C, D2, O1 and commercial Damascus. **Prices:** $200 to $300; some to $6,000. **Remarks:** Part-time maker; first knife sold in 1970. **Mark:** Initials connected, sometimes with city and state.

PARRISH III, GORDON A., 940 Lakloey Dr., North Pole, AK 99705, Phone: 907-488-0357
Specialties: Classic and high-art straight knives of his design and to customer specs; working and using knives. **Patterns:** Bowies and hunters. **Technical:** Grinds tool steel and ATS-34. Uses mostly Alaskan handle materials. **Prices:** $125 to $750. **Remarks:** Spare-time maker; first knife sold in 1980. **Mark:** Last name, state.

PARSONS, MICHAEL R., McKee Knives, 1600 S. 11th St, Terre Haute, IN 47802-1722, Phone: 812-234-1679
Specialties: Fancy straight knives; fancy R R Spike knives. **Patterns:** Railroad spike knives and variety of one of a kinds including files. **Technical:** Hand forged from files. Engraves, carves, wire inlays and leather work. All knives one of a kind. **Prices:** $350 to $1,500. **Remarks:** Full-time maker; first knife sold in 1965. **Mark:** Mc with a key-McKee. Michael R Parsons maker.

PASSMORE, JIMMY D, 316 SE Elm, Hoxie, AR 72433, Phone: (870) 886-1922

PATE, LLOYD D., 219 Cottontail Ln., Georgetown, TX 78626, Phone: 512-863-7805
Specialties: Traditional working straight knives. **Patterns:** Hunters, fighters and Bowies. **Technical:** Hollow-grinds D2, 440C and ATS-34; likes mirror-finishes. **Prices:** $75 to $350; some to $500. **Remarks:** Part-time maker; first knife sold in 1983. **Mark:** Last name.

PATRICK, PEGGY, P. O. Box 127, Brasstown, NC 28902, Phone: 828-837-7627
Specialties: Authentic period and Indian sheaths, braintan, rawhide, beads and quill work. **Technical:** Does own braintan, rawhide; uses only natural dyes for quills, old color beads.

PATRICK, WILLARD C., P. O. Box 5716, Helena, MT 59604, Phone: 406-458-6552
Specialties: Working straight knives and one-of-a-kind art knives of his design or to customer specs. **Patterns:** Hunters, Bowies, fish, patch and kitchen knives. **Technical:** Grinds ATS-34, 1095, O1, A2 and Damascus. **Prices:** $85 to $350; some to $600. **Remarks:** Full-time maker; first knife sold in 1989. Doing business as Wil-A-Mar Cutlery. **Mark:** Shield with last name and a dagger.

PATRICK, CHUCK, P. O. Box 127, Brasstown, NC 28902, Phone: 828-837-7627
Specialties: Period pieces. **Patterns:** Hunters, daggers, tomahawks, pre-Civil War folders. **Technical:** Forges hardware, his own cable and Damascus, available in fancy pattern and mosaic. **Prices:** $150 to $1,000; some higher. **Remarks:** Full-time maker. **Mark:** Hand-engraved name or flying owl.

PATRICK, BOB, 12642 24A Ave., S. Surrey, B. C., CANADA V4A 8H9, Phone: 604-538-6214, Fax:604-888-2683
Specialties: Field grade to presentation grade traditional straight knives and period pieces of his design. **Patterns:** Bowies, Pierce-Arrow throwing knives, daggers and more. **Technical:** Prefers D2, 5160, 01 and some Damascus by Devon or Daryl. **Prices:** $160 for a set of P. A. throwers and up. **Remarks:** Full-time maker; first knife sold in 1987. Doing business as Crescent Knife Works. **Mark:** Logo with name and province or Crescent Knife Works.

PATTAY, RUDY, 510 E. Harrison St., Long Beach, NY 11561, Phone: 516-431-0847
Specialties: Fancy and working straight knives of his design. **Patterns:** Bowies, hunters, utility/camp knives. **Technical:** Hollow-grinds ATS-34, 440C, O1. Offers commercial Damascus, stainless steel soldered guards; fabricates guard and butt cap on lathe and milling machine. Heat-treats. Prefers synthetic handle materials. Offers hand-sewn sheaths. **Prices:** $100 to $350; some to $500. **Remarks:** Part-time maker; first knife sold in 1990. **Mark:** First initial, last name in sorcerer logo.

PATTERSON, PAT, Box 246, Barksdale, TX 78828, Phone: (830) 234-3586, Fax:(830) 234-3587
Specialties: Traditional fixed blades & liner lock folders. **Patterns:** Hunters & fighters. **Technical:** Grinds 440C, ATS-34, D2, 01 & Damascus. Prices $250 to $1000. **Remarks:** Full-time maker. First knife sold in 1991. **Mark:** Name & city.

PATTERSON, ALAN W., Rt. 3, Box 131, Hayesville, NC 28904, Phone: 704-389-9103
Specialties: Working straight knives and folders of his design or to customer specs; period pieces. **Patterns:** Forged knives, swords, tomahawks and folders. **Technical:** Damascus, cable and tool steels. Some custom leatherwork; wife offers scrimshaw. **Prices:** $125 to $5,000. **Remarks:** Full-time maker; first knife sold in 1990. **Mark:** Patterson Forge.

PATTON, DICK & ROB, 206-F W. 38th St., Garden City, ID 83714, Phone: 208-395-089(W); 208-377-5704 or 208-327-7641
Specialties: Custom Damascus, hand forged, fighting knives-Bowie & tactical. **Patterns:** Mini Bowie, Merlin Fighter, Mandrita Fighting Bowie. **Prices:** $100 to $2000.

PAULICHECK, GARTH, P O Box 812, Williston, ND 58802-0812, Phone: (701) 774-8803

PAULO, FERNANDES R, Raposo Tavares, no 213, Lencois Paulista, SP, 18680, Sao Paulo, BRAZIL, Phone: 014-263-4281
Specialties: An apprentice of Jose Alberto Paschoarelli, his designs are heavily based on the later designs. **Technical:** Grinds tool steels and stainless steels. Part-time knife maker. **Prices:** Start from $100. Stamp: P. R. F.

PAWLOWSKI, JOHN R, 804 Iron Gate Ct, Newport News, VA 23602, Phone: 757-890-9098
Specialties: Traditional working and using straight knives and folders. **Patterns:**Hunters, Bowies, Fighters and Camp Knives. **Technical:**Stock removal, grinds 440C, ATS34, 154CM and buys Damascus. **Prices:**$150 to $500; some higher. **Remarks:**Part-time maker, first knife sold in 1983. **Mark:**Early mark, Name over attacking Eagle and Alaska. Current mark, Name over attacking Eagle and Virginia.

PEAGLER, RUSS, P. O. Box 1314, Moncks Corner, SC 29461, Phone: 803-761-1008
Specialties: Traditional working straight knives of his design and to customer specs. **Patterns:** Hunters, fighters, boots. **Technical:** Hollow-grinds 440C, ATS-34 and O1; uses Damascus steel. Prefers bone handles. **Prices:** $85 to $300; some to $500. **Remarks:** Spare-time maker; first knife sold in 1983. **Mark:** Initials.

PEASE, W. D., 657 Cassidy Pike, Ewing, KY 41039, Phone: 606-845-0387, Fax:Fax: 606-845-8058
Specialties: Display-quality working folders. **Patterns:** Fighters, tantos and boots; locking folders and interframes. **Technical:** Grinds ATS-34 and commercial Damascus; has own side-release lock system. **Prices:** $500 to $1,000; some to $3,000. **Remarks:** Full-time maker; first knife sold in 1970. **Mark:** First and middle initials, last name.

PEELE, BRYAN, 219 Ferry St., P. O. Box 1363, Thompson Falls, MT 59873, Phone: 406-827-4633
Specialties: Fancy working and using knives of his design. **Patterns:** Hunters, Bowies and fighters. **Technical:** Grinds 440C, ATS-34, D2, O1 and commercial Damascus. **Prices:** $110 to $300; some to $900. **Remarks:** Part-time maker; first knife sold in 1985. **Mark:** The Elk Rack, full name, city, state.

PENDLETON, LLOYD, 24581 Shake Ridge Rd., Volcano, CA 95689, Phone: 209-296-3353, Fax:209-296-3353
Specialties: Contemporary working knives in standard patterns. **Patterns:** Hunters, fighters and boots. **Technical:** Grinds 154CM and ATS-34; mirror finishes. **Prices:** $300 to $700; some to $2,000. **Remarks:** Full-time maker; first knife sold in 1973. **Mark:** First initial, last name logo, city and state.

PENDRAY, ALFRED H., 13950 NE 20th St, Williston, FL 32696, Phone: 352-528-6124
Specialties: Working straight knives and folders; period pieces. **Patterns:** Fighters and hunters, axes, camp knives and tomahawks. **Technical:** Forges Wootz steel; makes his own Damascus; makes traditional knives from old files and rasps. **Prices:** $125 to $1,000; some to $3,500. **Remarks:** Part-time maker; first knife sold in 1954. **Mark:** Last initial in horseshoe logo.

PENNINGTON, C. A., 137 Riverlea Estate Dr., Stewarts Gully, Christchurch 9, NEW ZEALAND, Phone: +64 (3)3237292, Fax:+64 (3)3237292
Specialties: Classic working and collectors knives. Folders a specialty. **Patterns:** Classical styling for hunters and collectors. **Technical:** Forges his own all tool steel Damascus. Grinds D2 when requested. **Prices:** $240 to $2,000. **Remarks:** Full-time maker; first knife sold in 1988. **Mark:** Name, country. **Other:** color brochure $3.

PEPIOT, STEPHAN, 73 Cornwall Blvd., Winnipeg, Man., CANADA R3J-1E9, Phone: 204-888-1499
Specialties: Working straight knives in standard patterns. **Patterns:** Hunters and camp knives. **Technical:** Grinds 440C and industrial hack-saw blades. **Prices:** $75 to $125. **Remarks:** Spare-time maker; first knife sold in 1982. Not currently taking orders. **Mark:** PEP.

PERRY, CHRIS, 1654 W. Birch, Fresno, CA 93711, Phone: 209-498-2342
Specialties: Traditional working/using straight knives of his design. **Patterns:** Boots, hunters and utility/camp knives. **Technical:** Grinds ATS-34 and 416 ss fittings. **Prices:** $190 to $225. **Remarks:** Spare-time maker. **Mark:** Name above city and state.

PERRY, JOHN, 9 South Harrell Rd., Mayflower, AR 72106, Phone: 501-470-3043
Specialties: Investment grade and working folders; some straight knives. **Patterns:** Front and rear lock folders, liner locks and hunters. **Technical:** Grinds CPM440V, D2 and making own Damascus. Offers filework. **Prices:** $375 to $950; some to $2500. **Remarks:** Part-time maker; first knife sold in 1990. Doing business as Perry Custom Knives. **Mark:** Initials or last name in high relief set in a diamond shape.

PERRY, JOHNNY, P O Box 4666, Spartanburg, SC 29305-4666, Phone: (803) 578-3533

PERRY, JIM, Hope Star P O Box 648, Hope, AR 71801

PERSSON, CONNY, PL 605, 820 50 Loos, SWEDEN, Phone: +46 657 10305, Fax:+46 657 413 435
Mosaic Damascus.

PETEAN, FRANCISCO AND MAURICIO, R. Dr. Carlos de Carvalho Rosa, 52, Centro, Birigui, SP-16200-000, BRAZIL, Phone: 0186-424786
Specialties: Classic knives to customer specs. **Patterns:** Bowies, boots, fighters, hunters and utility knives. **Technical:** Grinds D6, 440C and high carbon steels. Prefers natural handle material. **Prices:** $70 to $500. **Remarks:** Full-time maker; first knife sold in 1985. **Mark:** Last name, hand made.

PETERSEN, DAN L., 3015 SW Clark Ct., Topeka, KS 66604
Specialties: Period pieces and forged integral hilts on hunters and fighters. **Patterns:** Texas style Bowies, boots and hunters in high carbon and Damascus steel. **Technical:** Austempers forged high-carbon blades. **Prices:** $200 to $3,000. **Remarks:** First knife sold in 1978. **Mark:** Stylized initials, MS.

PETERSON, LLOYD (PETE) C, 64 Halbrook Rd, Clinton, AR 72031, Phone: (501) 893-2570
Specialties: Miniatures, and mosaic folders. **Prices:** $250 & up. **Remarks:** Lead time is 6-8 months. **Mark:** Pete.

PETERSON, ELDON G., 260 Haugen Heights Rd., Whitefish, MT 59937, Phone: 406-862-2204
Specialties: Fancy and working folders, any size. **Patterns:** Lockback interframes, integral bolster folders, liner locks, and two-blades. **Technical:** Grinds 440C and ATS-34. Offers gold inlay work, gem stone inlays and engraving. **Prices:** $285 to $5,000. **Remarks:** Full-time maker; first knife sold in 1974. **Mark:** Name, city and state.

PETERSON, CHRIS, Box 143, 2175 W. Rockyford, Salina, UT 84654, Phone: 801-529-7194
Specialties: Working straight knives of his design. **Patterns:** Large fighters, boots, hunters and some display pieces. **Technical:** Forges O1 and

meteor. Makes and sells his own Damascus. Engraves, scrimshaws and inlays. **Prices:** $150 to $600; some to $1,500. **Remarks:** Full-time maker; first knife sold in 1986. **Mark:** A drop in a circle with a line through it.

PEYTON III, CLAY C, 4830 Coxey Brown Rd, Frederick, MD 21702, Phone: (301) 293-2403

PFANENSTIEL, DAN, 1824 Lafayette Av, Modesto, CA 95355, Phone: (209) 575-5937
Specialties: Japanese tanto, swords. One of a kind knives. **Technical:** Forges simple carbon steels, some Damascus. **Prices:** $200-$1000. **Mark:** Circle with wave inside.

PHILIPPE, D A, 295 Holmes Rd, Pittsfield, MA 01201, Phone: 413-448-2214
Specialties: Traditional working straight knives. **Patterns:** Hunters, trout & bird, camp knives etc. **Technical:** Grinds ATS-34, 440c, A-2, Damascus, flat and hollow ground. Exotic woods and antler handles. Brass, nickel silver and stainless components. **Prices:** $250 - $600. **Remarks:** Full-time maker, first knife sold in 1984. **Mark:** First initial, last name.

PHILLIPS, RANDY, 759 E. Francis St., Ontario, CA 91761, Phone: 909-923-4381
Specialties: Hunters, collector-grade liner locks and high-art daggers. **Technical:** Grinds D2, 440C and 154CM; embellishes. **Prices:** Start at $200. **Remarks:** Part-time maker; first knife sold in 1981. Not currently taking orders. **Mark:** Name, city and state in eagle head.

PHILLIPS, DENNIS, 16411 West Bennet Rd, Independence, LA 70443, Phone: 985-878-8275
Specialties: Specializes in fixed blade military combat tacticals.

PHILLIPS, JIM, P O Box 168, Williamstown, NJ 08094, Phone: (609) 567-0695

PHILLIPS, SCOTT C, 671 California Rd, Gouverneur, NY 13642, Phone: 315-287-1280
Specialties: Sheaths in leather. Fixed blade hunters, boot knives, Bowies, buck skinners (hand forged & stock removal). **Technical:** 440C, 5160, 1095 & 52100. **Prices:** Start at $125. **Remarks:** Part-time maker; first knife sold in 1993. **Mark:** Before "2000" as above after S Mangus.

PICKENS, SELBERT, Rt. 1, Box 216, Liberty, WV 25124, Phone: 304-586-2190
Specialties: Using knives. **Patterns:** Standard sporting knives. **Technical:** Stainless steels; stock removal method. **Prices:** Moderate. **Remarks:** Part-time maker. **Mark:** Name.

PIENAAR, CONRAD, 19A Milner Rd., Bloemfontein 9300, SOUTH AFRICA, Phone: 051 436 4180, Fax:051 436 7400
Specialties: Fancy working and using straight knives and folders of his design, to customer specs and in standard patterns. **Patterns:** Hunters, locking folders, cleavers, kitchen and utility/camp knives. **Technical:** Grinds 12C27, D2 and ATS-34. Uses some Damascus. Scrimshaws; inlays gold. Knives come with wooden box and custom-made leather sheath. **Prices:** $300 to $1,000. **Remarks:** Part-time maker; first knife sold in 1981. Doing business as C. P. Knife maker. **Mark:** Initials and serial number.

PIERCE, HAROLD L., 106 Lyndon Lane, Louisville, KY 40222, Phone: 502-429-5136
Specialties: Working straight knives, some fancy. **Patterns:** Big fighters and Bowies. **Technical:** Grinds D2, 440C, 154CM; likes sub-hilts. **Prices:** $150 to $450; some to $1,200. **Remarks:** Full-time maker; first knife sold in 1982. **Mark:** Last name with knife through the last initial.

PIERCE, RANDALL, 903 Wyndham, Arlington, TX 76017, Phone: (817) 468-0138

PIERGALLINI, DANIEL E., 4011 N. Forbes Rd., Plant City, FL 33565, Phone: 813-754-3908
Specialties: Traditional and fancy straight knives and folders of my design or to customer's specs. **Patterns:** Hunters, fighters, three-fingered skinners, fillet, working and camp knives. **Technical:** Grinds 440C, O1, D2, ATS-34, some Damascus; forges his own mokume. Uses natural handle material. **Prices:** $250-$600, some to $600;some to $1,600. **Remarks:** Part-time maker; sold first knife in 1994. **Mark:** Last name, city, state or last name in script.

PIESNER, DEAN, 30 King St., St. Jacobs, Ont., CANADA N0B 2N0, Phone: 519-664-3622, Fax:519-664-1828
Specialties: Classic and period pieces of his design and to customer specs. **Patterns:** Bowies, skinners, fighters and swords. **Technical:** Forges 5160, 52100, steel Damascus and nickel-steel Damascus. Makes own mokume gane with copper, brass and nickel silver. Silver wire inlays in wood. **Prices:** Start at $150. **Remarks:** Full-time maker; first knife sold in 1990. **Mark:** First initial, last name, JS.

PIOREK, JAMES S., P. O. Box 733, Lakeside, MT 59922, Phone: 406-844-2620
Specialties: True custom and semi custom production (SCP), specialized concealment blades; advanced sheaths and tailored body harnessing systems. **Patterns:** Tactical/personal defense fighters, swords, utility and cus-

custom knifemakers

tom patterns. **Technical:** Grinds A2 and Talonite®; heat-treats. Sheaths: Kydex or Kydex-lined leather laminated or Kydex-lined with Rigger Coat™. Exotic materials available. **Prices:** $50 to $10,000. **Remarks:** Full-time maker. Doing business as Blade Rigger L. L. C. **Mark:** For true custom: Initials with abstract cutting edge and for SCP: Blade Rigger. **Other:** Martial artist and unique defense industry tools and equipment.

PITMAN, DAVID, P O Drawer 2566, Williston, ND 58802, Phone: (701) 572-3325

PITT, DAVID F., 6812 Digger Pine Ln, Anderson, CA 96007, Phone: 530-357-2393
Specialties: Fixed blade, hunters & hatchets. Flat ground mirror finish. **Patterns:** Hatchets with gut hook, small gut hooks, guards, bolsters or guard less. **Technical:** Grinds A2, 440C, 154CM, ATS-34, D2. **Prices:** $150 to $750. **Remarks:** Guild member since 1982. **Mark:** Bear paw with name David F. Pitt.

PLUNKETT, RICHARD, 29 Kirk Rd., West Cornwall, CT 06796, Phone: 860-672-3419; Toll free: 888-KNIVES-8
Specialties: Traditional, fancy folders and straight knives of his design. **Patterns:** Slip-joint folders and small straight knives. **Technical:** Grinds O1 and stainless steel. Offers many different file patterns. **Prices:** $150 to $450. **Remarks:** Full-time maker; first knife sold in 1994. **Mark:** Signature and date under handle scales.

POAG, JAMES, RR 1, Box 212A, Grayville, IL 62844, Phone: 618-375-7106
Specialties: Working straight knives and folders; period pieces; of his design or to customer specs. **Patterns:** Bowies and camp knives, lockers and slip-joints. **Technical:** Forges and grinds stainless steels and others; provides serious leather; offers embellishments; scrimshaws, engraves and does leather work for other makers. **Prices:** $65 to $1,200. **Remarks:** Full-time maker; first knife sold in 1967. **Mark:** Name.

POGREBA, LARRY, Box 861, Lyons, CO 80540, Phone: 303-823-6691
Specialties: Steel and Damascus lightweight hunters; kitchen knives. **Technical:** Forges, grinds, Damascus since 1978. **Prices:** $40 to $1,000. **Remarks:** Part-time maker; first knife sold in 1976. Doing business as Cadillac Blacksmithing. **Mark:** Initials.

POLK, CLIFTON, 4625 Webber Creek Rd., Van Buren, AR 72956, Phone: 501-474-3828
Specialties: Fancy working straight knives and folders. **Patterns:** Locking folders, slip-joints, two-blades, straight knives. **Technical:** Offers 440C, D2 ATS-34 and Damascus. **Prices:** $150 to $3,000. **Remarks:** Full-time maker. **Mark:** Last name.

POLKOWSKI, AL, 8 Cathy Ct., Chester, NJ 07930, Phone: 908-879-6030
Specialties: High-tech straight knives and folders for adventurers and professionals. **Patterns:** Fighters, side-lock folders, boots and concealment knives. **Technical:** Grinds D2 and ATS-34; features satin and bead-blast finishes; Kydex sheaths. **Prices:** Start at $100. **Remarks:** Full-time maker; first knife sold in 1985. **Mark:** Full name, Handmade.

POLLOCK, WALLACE J., 806 Russet Vly Dr, Cedar Park, TX 78613
Specialties: Using knives, dressed up or not. **Patterns:** Use my own patterns or yours. **Patterns:** Traditional hunters, daggers, fighters, camp knives. **Technical:** Grinds ATS-34, d-2, bg-42, makes own Damascus, dentritic d-2, 440c handles exotic wood, horn, bone, ivory. **Remarks:** Full-time maker, sold first knife 1973. **Prices:** $250. 00 to $2500. 00. **Mark:** last name, maker, city/state.

POLZIEN, DON, 1912 Inler Suite-L, Lubbock, TX 79407, Phone: 806-791-0766
Specialties: Traditional Japanese-style blades; restores antique Japanese swords, scabbards and fittings. **Patterns:** Hunters, fighters, one-of-a-kind art knives. **Technical:** 1045-1050 carbon steels, 440C, D2, ATS-34, standard and cable Damascus. **Prices:** $150 to $2,500. **Remarks:** Full-time maker. First knife sold in 1990. **Mark:** Oriental characters inside square border.

PONZIO, DOUG, 3212 93rd St., Pleasant Prairie, WI 53158, Phone: 262-694-3188
Specialties: Damascus - Jem stone handles. **Mark:** P. F.

POOLE, STEVE L., 200 Flintlock Trail, Stockbridge, GA 30281, Phone: 770-474-9154
Specialties: Traditional working and using straight knives and folders of his design, to customer specs and in standard patterns. **Patterns:** Bowies, fighters, hunters, utility and locking folders. **Technical:** Grinds ATS-34 and 440V; buys Damascus. Heat-treats; offers leatherwork. **Prices:** $85 to $350; some to $800. **Remarks:** Spare-time maker; first knife sold in 1991. **Mark:** Stylized first and last initials.

POOLE, MARVIN O., P. O. Box 5234, Anderson, SC 29623, Phone: 803-225-5970
Specialties: Traditional working/using straight knives and folders of his design and in standard patterns. **Patterns:** Bowies, fighters, hunters, lock-

ing folders, bird and trout knives. **Technical:** Grinds 440C, D2, ATS-34. **Prices:** $50 to $150; some to $750. **Remarks:** Part-time maker; first knife sold in 1980. **Mark:** First initial, last name, year, serial number.

POPLIN, JAMES L., 103 Oak St., Washington, GA 30673, Phone: 404-678-2729
Specialties: Contemporary hunters. **Patterns:** Hunters and boots. **Technical:** Hollow-grinds. **Prices:** Reasonable. **Mark:** POP.

POPP SR., STEVE, 6573 Winthrop Dr., Fayetteville, NC 28311, Phone: 910-822-3151
Specialties: Working straight knives. **Patterns:** Hunters, Bowies and fighters. **Technical:** Forges and grinds his own Damascus, O1, L6 and spring steel. **Prices:** $75 to $600; some to $1,000. **Remarks:** Full-time maker; first knife sold in 1984. **Mark:** Initials and last name.

POSKOCIL, HELMUT, Oskar Czeijastrasse 2, A-3340 Waidhofen/Ybbs, AUSTRIA, Phone: 0043-7442-54519, Fax:0043-7442-54519
Specialties: High-art and classic straight knives and folders of his design. **Patterns:** Bowies, daggers, hunters and locking folders. **Technical:** Grinds ATS-34 and stainless and carbon Damascus. Hardwoods, fossil ivory, horn and amber for handle material; silver wire and gold inlays; silver butt caps. Offers engraving and scrimshaw. **Prices:** $350 to $850; some to $3,500. **Remarks:** Part-time maker; first knife sold in 1991. **Mark:** Name.

POSNER, BARRY E., 12501 Chandler Blvd., Suite 104, N. Hollywood, CA 91607, Phone: 818-752-8005, Fax:818-752-8006
Specialties: Working/using straight knives. **Patterns:** Hunters, kitchen and utility/camp knives. **Technical:** Grinds ATS-34; forges 1095 and nickel. **Prices:** $95 to $400. **Remarks:** Part-time maker; first knife sold in 1987. Doing business as Posner Knives. Supplier of finished mosaic handle pin stock. **Mark:** First and middle initials, last name.

POSTON, ALVIN, 1197 Bass Rd., Pamplico, SC 29583, Phone: 803-493-0066
Specialties: Working straight knives. **Patterns:** Hunters, Bowies and fishing knives; some miniatures. **Technical:** Grinds 154CM and ATS-34. **Prices:** Start at $100. **Remarks:** Part-time maker; first knife sold in 1979. **Mark:** Last name.

POTIER, TIMOTHY F., P. O. Box 711, Oberlin, LA 70655, Phone: 337-639-2229
Specialties: Classic working and using straight knives to customer specs; some collectible. **Patterns:** Hunters, Bowies, utility/camp knives and belt axes. **Technical:** Forges carbon steel and his own Damascus; offers filework. **Prices:** $300 to $1,800; some to $4,000. **Remarks:** Part-time maker; first knife sold in 1981. **Mark:** Last name, MS.

POTOCKI, ROGER, Route 1, Box 333A, Goreville, IL 62939, Phone: 618-995-9502

POTTER, FRANK, 25 Renfrew Ave, Middletown, RI 02842, Phone: 401-846-5352
Specialties: Autos. **Patterns:** Liner lock; my own design. **Technical:** Damascus bolters & blades; ivory & pearl. **Prices:** $1,000 to $3,000. **Remarks:** Full-time maker, first knife sold 1996. **Mark:** Frank Potter

POWELL, JAMES, 2500 North Robison Rd, Texarkana, TX 75501

POWELL, ROBERT CLARK, P O Box 321, 93 Gose Rd, Smarr, GA 31086, Phone: 478-994-5418
Specialties: Composite bar Damascus blades. **Patterns:** Art knives, hunters, combat, tomahawks. **Patterns:** Hand forge all blades. **Prices:** $300 & up. **Remarks:** Member ABS. **Mark:** Powell.

POYTHRESS, JOHN, P. O. Box 585, 625 Freedom St., Swainsboro, GA 30401, Phone: 478-237-9233 day/478-237-9478 night, Fax:912-237-9478
Specialties: Traditional working and using straight knives of his design or to customer specs. **Patterns:** Hunters, liner lock folders, dagger, tanto. **Technical:** Uses 440C, ATS-34 and D2. **Prices:** $150 and up. **Remarks:** Part-time maker; first knife sold in 1983. Member N. C. Customer Knifemaker's Guild. **Mark:** J. W. Poythress Handcrafted.

PRATER, MIKE, Prater and Company, 81 Sanford Ln, Flintstone, GA 30725
Specialties: Variety of horn- and stag-handled belt knives. **Patterns:** Standard patterns in large and small narrow-tang construction. **Technical:** Grind O1, D2 and Damascus. **Prices:** $165 to $10,000. **Remarks:** First knife sold in 1980. **Mark:** Prater Knives.

PRESSBURGER, RAMON, 59 Driftway Rd., Howell, NJ 07731, Phone: 732-363-0816
Specialties: BG-42. I am the only knife maker in USA that has a complete line of affordable hunting knives made from BG-42. **Patterns:** All types hunting styles. **Technical:** Uses all steels; my main steels are D-2 & BG-42. **Prices:** $75 to $500. **Remarks:** Full-time maker; I have been making hunting knives for 30 years. **Mark:** NA. **Other:** I will make knives to your patterning.

PRICE, TIMMY, P. O. Box 906, Blairsville, GA 30514, Phone: 706-745-5111

PRIMOS, TERRY, 932 Francais Dr, Shreveport, LA 71118, Phone: (318) 686-6625
Specialties: traditional forged straight knives. **Patterns:** Hunters, bowies, camp knives, and fighters. **Technical:** Forges primarily 1084 and 5160; also forges Damascus. **Prices:** $250 to $600. **Remarks:** Full-time maker; first knife sold in 1993. **Mark:** Last name.

PRITCHARD, RON, 613 Crawford Ave., Dixon, IL 61021, Phone: 815-284-6005
Specialties: Plain and fancy working knives. **Patterns:** Variety of straight knives, locking folders, interframes and miniatures. **Technical:** Grinds 440C, 154CM and commercial Damascus. **Prices:** $100 to $200; some to $1,500. **Remarks:** Part-time maker; first knife sold in 1979. **Mark:** Name and city.

PROVENZANO, JOSEPH D., 3024 Ivy Place, Chalmette, LA 70043, Phone: 504-279-3154
Specialties: Working straight knives and folders in standard patterns. **Patterns:** Hunters, Bowies, folders, camp and fishing knives. **Technical:** Grinds ATS-34, 440C, 154CM, CPM 4400V, CPM420V and Damascus. Hollow-grinds hunters. **Prices:** $90 to $300; some to $600. **Remarks:** Part-time maker; first knife sold in 1980. **Mark:** Joe-Pro.

PRYOR, STEPHEN L, HC Rt 1, Box 1445, Boss, MO 65440, Phone: 573-626-4838, Fax:same
Specialties: Working & fancy straight knives, some to customer specs. **Patterns:** Bowies, hunting/fishing, utility/camp, fantasy/art. **Technical:** Grinds 440C, ATS34, 1085, some Damascus, and does filework. Stag & exotic hardwood handles. **Prices:** $250 and up. **Remarks:** Full-time maker; first knife sold in 1991. **Mark:** Stylized first initial and last name over city & state.

PUGH, JIM, P. O. Box 711, Azle, TX 76020, Phone: 817-444-2679, Fax:817-444-5455
Specialties: Fancy/embellished limited editions by request. **Patterns:** 5- to 7-inch Bowies, wildlife art pieces, hunters, daggers and fighters; some commemoratives. **Technical:** Multi color transplanting in solid 18K gold, fine gems; grinds 440C and ATS-34. Offers engraving, fancy file etching and leather sheaths for wildlife art pieces. Ivory and coco bolo handle material on limited editions. Designs animal head butt caps and paws or bear claw guards; sterling silver heads and guards. **Prices:** $60,000 to $80,000 each in the Big Five 2000 edition. **Remarks:** Full-time maker; first knife sold in 1970. **Mark:** Pugh (old English).

PUGH, VERNON, 701-525 3rd Ave North, Saskatoon SK, CANADA S7K 2J6, Phone: (306) 652-9274

PULIS, VLADIMIR, Horna Ves 43/B/25, 96 701 Kremnica, SLOVAKIA, Phone: 421-857-6757-x214
Specialties: Fancy and high-art straight knives of his design. **Patterns:** Daggers and hunters. **Technical:** Forges Damascus steel. All work done by hand. **Prices:** $250 to $3,000; some to $10,000. **Remarks:** Full-time maker; first knife sold in 1990. **Mark:** Initials in sixtagon.

PULLEN, MARTIN, 1701 Broken Bow Rd., Granbury, TX 76049, Phone: 817-573-1784
Specialties: Working straight knives; period pieces. **Patterns:** Fighters, Bowies and daggers; locking folders. **Technical:** Grinds D2, 440C, ATS-34 and 154CM. **Prices:** Start at $150. **Remarks:** Full-time maker; first knife sold in 1978. **Mark:** Last name.

PULLIAM, MORRIS C., 560 Jeptha Knob Rd., Shelbyville, KY 40065, Phone: 502-633-2261
Specialties: Working knives; classic Bowies. Cherokee River pattern Damascus. **Patterns:** Bowies, hunters, and 376 tomahawks. **Technical:** Forges L6, W2, 1095, Damascus and nickel-sheet and bar 320 layer Damascus. **Prices:** $165 to $1,200. **Remarks:** Full-time maker; first knife sold in 1974. Makes knives for Native American festivals. Doing business as Knob Hill Forge. Member of Piqua Sept Shawnee of Ohio. **Mark:** Small and large - Pulliam.

PURSLEY, AARON, BOX 1037, , Big Sandy, MT 59520, Phone: 406-378-3200
Specialties: Fancy working knives. **Patterns:** Locking folders, straight hunters and daggers, personal wedding knives and letter openers. **Technical:** Grinds O1 and 440C; engraves. **Prices:** $300 to $600; some to $1,500. **Remarks:** Full-time maker; first knife sold in 1975. **Mark:** Initials connected with year.

PURVIS, BOB & ELLEN, 2416 N Loretta Dr, Tucson, AZ 85716, Phone: 520-795-8290
Specialties: Hunter, skinners, bowies, using knives, gentlemen's folders and collectible knives. **Technical:** Grinds ATS 34, 440C, Damascus, Dama steel, heat-treats and cryogenically quenches. We do gold-plating, salt bluing, scrimshawing, filework and fashion hand made leather sheaths. Materials used for handles include exotic woods, mammoth ivory, mother of pearl, G-10 and micarta. **Prices:** $165 to $800. **Remarks:** Knifemaker

since retirement in 1984. Selling them since 1993. **Mark:** Script or print R. E. Purvis ~ Tucson, AZ or last name only.

PUTNAM, DONALD S., 590 Wolcott Hill Rd., Wethersfield, CT 06109, Phone: 203-563-9718, Fax:203-563-9718
Specialties: Working knives for the hunter and fisherman. **Patterns:** His design or to customer specs. **Technical:** Uses stock removal method, O1, W2, D2, ATS-34, 154CM, 440C and CPM REX 20; stainless steel Damascus on request. **Prices:** NA. **Remarks:** Full-time maker; first knife sold in 1985. **Mark:** Last name with a knife outline.

q

QUAKENBUSH, THOMAS C, 2426 Butler Rd, Ft. Wayne, IN 46808, Phone: (219) 483-0749

QUARTON, BARR, P. O. Box 4335, McCall, ID 83638, Phone: 208-634-3641
Specialties: Plain and fancy working knives; period pieces. **Patterns:** Hunters, tantos and swords. **Technical:** Forges and grinds 154CM, ATS-34 and his own Damascus. **Prices:** $180 to $450; some to $4,500. **Remarks:** Part-time maker; first knife sold in 1978. Doing business as Barr Custom Knives. **Mark:** First name with bear logo.

QUATTLEBAUM, CRAIG, 2 Ridgewood Ln., Searcy, AR 72143
Specialties: Traditional straight knives and one-of-a-kind knives of his design; period pieces. **Patterns:** Bowies and fighters. **Technical:** Forges 5168, 52100 and own Damascus. **Prices:** $100 to $1,200. **Remarks:** Part-time maker; first knife sold in 1988. **Mark:** Stylized initials.

QUICK, MIKE, 23 Locust Ave., Kearny, NJ 07032, Phone: 201-991-6580
Specialties: Traditional working/using straight knives. **Patterns:** Bowies. **Technical:** 440C and ATS-34 for blades; Micarta, wood and stag for handles.

r

R. BOYES KNIVES, N81 W16140 Robin Hood Dr, Menomonee Falls, WI 53051, Phone: 262-255-7341
Specialties: Hunters, working knives. **Technical:** Grinds ATS-34, 440C, 01 tool steel & Damascus. **Prices:** $60 to $500. **Remarks:** First knife sold in 1998. Tom Boyes changed to R. Boyes Knives.

RACHLIN, LESLIE S., 1200 W. Church St., Elmira, NY 14905, Phone: 607-733-6889
Specialties: Classic and working/using straight knives and folders of his design. **Patterns:** Hunters, locking folders and utility/camp knives. **Technical:** Grinds 440C and Damascus. **Prices:** $110 to $200; some to $450. **Remarks:** Spare-time maker; first knife sold in 1989. Doing business as Tinkermade Knives. **Mark:** Stamped initials or Tinkermade, city and state.

RADOS, JERRY F., 7523 E 5000 N Rd., Grant Park, IL 60940, Phone: 815-472-3350, Fax:815-472-3944
Specialties: Deluxe period pieces. **Patterns:** Hunters, fighters, locking folders, daggers and camp knives. **Technical:** Forges and grinds his own Damascus which he sells commercially; makes pattern-welded Turkish Damascus. **Prices:** Start at $900. **Remarks:** Full-time maker; first knife sold in 1981. **Mark:** Last name.

RAGSDALE, JAMES D., 3002 Arabian Woods Dr., Lithonia, GA 30038, Phone: 770-482-6739
Specialties: Fancy and embellished working knives of his design or to customer specs. **Patterns:** Hunters, folders and daggers. **Technical:** Grinds 440C, ATS-34 and A2. **Prices:** $100 to $350; some to $800. **Remarks:** Full-time maker; first knife sold in 1984. **Mark:** Fish symbol with name above, town below.

RAINVILLE, RICHARD, 126 Cockle Hill Rd., Salem, CT 06420, Phone: 860-859-2776
Specialties: Traditional working straight knives. **Patterns:** Outdoor knives, including fishing knives. **Technical:** L6, 400C, ATS-34. **Prices:** $100 to $800. **Remarks:** Full-time maker; first knife sold in 1982. **Mark:** Name, city, state in oval logo.

RALEY, R WAYNE, 825 Poplar Acres Rd, Collierville, TN 38017, Phone: (901) 853-2026

RALPH, DARREL, Briar Knives, 4185 S St Rt 605, Galena, OH 43021, Phone: 740-965-9970
Specialties: Fancy, high-art, high-tech, collectible straight knives and folders of his design and to customer specs; unique mechanisms, some disassemble. **Patterns:** Daggers, fighters and swords. **Technical:** Forges his own Damascus, nickel and high carbon. Uses mokume and Damascus; mosaics and special patterns. Engraves and heat-treats. Prefers pearl, ivory and abalone handle material; uses stones and jewels. **Prices:** $250

custom knifemakers

to six figures. **Remarks:** Full-time maker; first knife sold in 1987. Doing business as Briar Knives. **Mark:** DDR.

RAMEY, LARRY, 1315 Porter Morris Rd, Chapmansboro, TN 37035-5120, Phone: 615-307-4233

RAMEY, MARSHALL F., P. O. Box 2589, West Helena, AR 72390, Phone: 501-572-7436, Fax:501-572-6245
Specialties: Traditional working knives. **Patterns:** Designs military combat knives; makes butterfly folders, camp knives and miniatures. **Technical:** Grinds D2 and 440C. **Prices:** $100 to $500. **Remarks:** Full-time maker; first knife sold in 1978. **Mark:** Name with ram's head.

RAMSEY, RICHARD A, 8525 Trout Farm Rd, Neosho, MO 64850, Phone: (417) 451-1493

RANDALL, GARY, P O Box 1988, Orlando, FL 32802, Phone: (407) 855-8075

RANDALL JR, JAMES W, 11606 Keith Hall Rd, Keithville, LA 71047, Phone: (318) 925-6480, Fax:(318) 925-1709
Specialties: Mosaic Damascus. **Patterns:**Swords. **Technical:** Custom inlay work on handles. **Prices:** $350 and up. **Mark:** J. W. Randall.

RANDALL MADE KNIVES, P. O. Box 1988, Orlando, FL 32802, Phone: 407-855-8075, Fax:407-855-9054
Specialties: Working straight knives. **Patterns:** Hunters, fighters and Bowies. **Technical:** Forges and grinds O1 and 440B. **Prices:** $65 to $250; some to $450. **Remarks:** Full-time maker; first knife sold in 1937. **Mark:** Randall, city and state in scimitar logo.

RANDOW, RALPH, 4214 Blalock Rd, Pineville, LA 71360, Phone: (318) 640-3369

RANKL, CHRISTIAN, Possenhofenerstr. 33, 81476 Munchen, GERMANY, Phone: 089-75967265, Fax:0727-3662679
Specialties: Tail-lock knives. **Patterns:** Fighters, hunters and locking folders. **Technical:** Grinds ATS-34, D2, CPM1440V, RWL 34 also stainless Damascus . **Prices:** $450 to $950; some to $2,000. **Remarks:** Full-time maker; first knife sold in 1989. **Mark:** Electrochemical etching on blade.

RAPP, STEVEN J., 7273 South 245 East, Midvale, UT 84047, Phone: 801-567-9553
Specialties: Gold quartz; mosaic handles. **Patterns:** Daggers, Bowies, fighters and San Francisco knives. **Technical:** Hollow- and flat-grinds 440C and Damascus. **Prices:** Start at $500. **Remarks:** Full-time maker; first knife sold in 1981. **Mark:** Name and state.

RAPPAZZO, RICHARD, 142 Dunsbach Ferry Rd., Cohoes, NY 12047, Phone: 518-783-6843
Specialties: Damascus locking folders and straight knives. **Patterns:** Folders, dirks, fighters and tantos in original and traditional designs. **Technical:** Hand-forges all blades; specializes in Damascus; uses only natural handle materials. **Prices:** $400 to $1,500. **Remarks:** Part-time maker; first knife sold in 1985. **Mark:** Name, date, serial number.

RARDON, ARCHIE F., 1589 SE Price Dr, Polo, MO 64671, Phone: 660-354-2330
Specialties: Working knives. **Patterns:** Hunters, Bowies and miniatures. **Technical:** Grinds O1, D2, 440C, ATS-34, cable and Damascus. **Prices:** $50 to $500. **Remarks:** Part-time maker. **Mark:** Boar hog.

RARDON, A. D., 1589 S. E. Price Dr., Polo, MO 64671, Phone: 660-354-2330
Specialties: Folders, miniatures. **Patterns:** Hunters, buck skinners, Bowies, miniatures and daggers. **Technical:** Grinds O1, D2, 440C and ATS-34. **Prices:** $150 to $2,000; some higher. **Remarks:** Full-time maker; first knife sold in 1954. **Mark:** Fox logo.

RAY, ALAN W., P. O. Box 479, Lovelady, TX 75851, Phone: 936-636-2350
Specialties: Working straight knives of his design. **Patterns:** Hunters, camp knives, steak knives and carving sets. **Technical:** Forges L6 and 5160 for straight knives; grinds D2 and 440C for folders and kitchen cutlery. **Prices:** $200 to $500. **Remarks:** Full-time maker; first knife sold in 1979. **Mark:** Stylized initials.

RED, VERNON, 2020 Benton Cove, Conway, AR 72032, Phone: 501-450-7284
Specialties: Traditional straight knives and folders of my design and special orders. Most are one of a kind. **Patterns:** Hunters, fighters, Bowies, fillet, folders & lock-blades. **Technical:** Hollow Grind 90%; use 440C, D-2, ATS-34, Stamascus and Damascus. Uses natural woods, pakka, pearl, horn, stag, ivory & bone. **Prices:** $125 and up. **Remarks:** Part-time maker; first knife sold in 1992. Do scrimshaw on ivory & micarta. **Mark:** Last name. **Other:** Member Arkansas Knives Assoc. (aka) Custom Made Knives by Vernon Red.

REDDIEX, BILL, 27 Galway Ave., Palmerston North, NEW ZEALAND, Phone: 06-357-0383, Fax:06-358-2910
Specialties: Collector-grade working straight knives. **Patterns:** Traditional-style Bowies and drop-point hunters. **Technical:** Grinds 440C, D2 and O1; offers variety of grinds and finishes. **Prices:** $130 to $750.

Remarks: Full-time maker; first knife sold in 1980. **Mark:** Last name around kiwi bird logo.

REED, DAVE, Box 132, Brimfield, MA 01010, Phone: 413-245-3661
Specialties: Traditional styles. Makes knives from chains, rasps, gears, etc. **Patterns:** Bush swords, hunters, working minis, camp and utility knives. **Technical:** Forges 1075 and his own Damascus. **Prices:** Start at $50. **Remarks:** Part-time maker; first knife sold in 1970. **Mark:** Initials.

REED, JOHN M., 1095 Spalding Cir, Goose Creek, SC 29445, Phone: 843-797-6287
Specialties: Hunter, utility, some survival knives. **Patterns:** Trailing Point, and drop point sheath knves. **Technical:** ATS-34, rockwell 60 exotic wood or natural material handles. **Prices:** $135-$300. Depending on handle material. **Remarks:** I like the stock removal method. "Old Fashioned trainling point blades". **Mark:** "Reed" acid etched on left side of blade. **Other:** Hande made and sewn leather sheaths.

REEVE, CHRIS, 11624 W. President Dr., Ste. B, Boise, ID 83713, Phone: 208-375-0367, Fax:208-375-0368
Specialties: Originator and designer of the One Piece range of fixed blade utility knives and of the Sebenza Integral Lock folding knives made by Chris Reeve Knives. Currently makes only one or two pieces per year himself. **Patterns:** Art folders and fixed blades; one-of-a-kind. **Technical:** Grinds BG-42, Damascus and other materials to his own design. **Prices:** $1000 and upwards. **Remarks:** Full-time in knife business; first knife sold in 1982. **Mark:** Signature and date.

REEVES, WINFRED M., P. O. Box 300, West Union, SC 29696, Phone: 803-638-6121
Specialties: Working straight knives; some elaborate pieces. **Patterns:** Hunters, tantos and fishing knives. **Technical:** Grinds D2, 440C and ATS-34. Does not solder joints; does not use buffer unless requested. **Prices:** $75 to $150; some to $300. **Remarks:** Part-time maker; first knife sold in 1975. **Mark:** Last name, Walhalla, state.

REGGIO JR., SIDNEY J., P. O. Box 851, Sun, LA 70463, Phone: 504-886-5886
Specialties: Miniature classic and fancy straight knives of his design or in standard patterns. **Patterns:** Fighters, hunters and utility/camp knives. **Technical:** Grinds 440C, ATS-34 and commercial Damascus. Engraves; scrimshaws; offers filework. Hollow grinds most blades. Prefers natural handle material. Offers handmade sheaths. **Prices:** $85 to $250; some to $500. **Remarks:** Part-time maker; first knife sold in 1988. Doing business as Sterling Workshop. **Mark:** Initials.

REMINGTON, DAVID W., 12928 Morrow Rd, Gentry, AR 72734-9781, Phone: 501-846-3526
Specialties: Fancy and traditional straight knives of his design and to customer specs. **Patterns:** Bowies, daggers and hunters. **Technical:** Grinds ATS-34, A2 and D2. Makes own twist and random-pattern Damascus. Wholesale D2, A2, stag and ossic sheep horn. Rope and thorn pattern filework; tapered tangs; heat treats. **Prices:** $65 to $250; some to $1,000. **Remarks:** Part-time maker; first knife sold in 1991. **Mark:** First and last name, Custom.

REPKE, MIKE, 4191 N. Euclid Ave., Bay City, MI 48706, Phone: 517-684-3111
Specialties: Traditional working and using straight knives of their design or to customer specs; classic knives; display knives. **Patterns:** Hunters, Bowies, skinners, fighters boots, axes and swords. **Technical:** Grind 440C. Offer variety of handle materials. **Prices:** $99 to $1,500. **Remarks:** Full-time makers. Doing business as Black Forest Blades. **Mark:** Knife logo.

REVERDY, PIERRE, 5 rue de l'egalite', 26100 Romans, FRANCE, Phone: 334 75 05 10 15, Fax:334 75 02 28 40
Specialties: Art knives; legend blades. **Patterns:** Daggers, Bowies, hunters and other large patterns. **Technical:** Forges his Damascus and "poetique Damascus"; works with his own EDM machine to create any kind of pattern inside the steel with his own touch. **Prices:** $2000 and up. **Remarks:** Full-time maker; first knife sold in 1986. Nicole (wife) collaborates with enamels. **Mark:** Initials connected.

REVISHVILI, ZAZA, 2102 Linden Ave, Madison, WI 53704, Phone: 608-243-7927
Specialties: Fancy/embellished and high-art straight knives and folders of his design. **Patterns:** Daggers, swords and locking folders. **Technical:** Uses Damascus; silver filigree; silver inlay in wood; enameling. **Prices:** $1,000 to $9,000; some to $15,000. **Remarks:** Full-time maker; first knife sold in 1987. **Mark:** Initials, city.

REXROAT, KIRK, 527 Sweetwater Circle, Box 224, Wright, WY 82732, Phone: 307-464-0166
Specialties: Using and collectible straight knives and folders of his design or to customer specs. **Patterns:** Bowies, hunters, folders. **Technical:** Forges Damascus patterns, mosaic and 52100. **Prices:** $400 and up. **Remarks:** Part-time maker, Mastersmith in the ABS; first knife sold in 1984. Doing business as Rexroat Knives. **Mark:** Last name.

REYNOLDS, JOHN C., #2 Andover, HC77, Gillette, WY 82716, Phone: 307-682-6076
Specialties: Working knives, some fancy. **Patterns:** Hunters, Bowies, tomahawks and buck skinners; some folders. **Technical:** Grinds D2, ATS34, 440C and I forge my own Damascus and Knifes now. Scrimshaws. **Prices:** $200 to $3,000. **Remarks:** Spare-time maker; first knife sold in 1969. **Mark:** On ground blades JC Reynolds Gillette,Wy, On forged blades, my initials make my mark-JCR.

REYNOLDS, DAVE, Rt. 2, Box 36, Harrisville, WV 26362, Phone: 304-643-2889
Specialties: Working straight knives of his design. **Patterns:** Bowies, kitchen and utility knives. **Technical:** Grinds and forges L6, 1095 and 440C. Heat-treats. **Prices:** $50 to $85; some to $175. **Remarks:** Full-time maker; first knife sold in 1980. Doing business as Terra-Gladius Knives. **Mark:** Mark on special orders only; serial number on all knives.

RHO, NESTOR LORENZO, Primera Junta 589, (6000) Junin, Buenos Aires, ARGENTINA, Phone: (02362) 15670686
Specialties: Classic and fancy straight knives of his design. **Patterns:** Bowies, fighters and hunters. **Technical:** Grinds 420C, 440C and 1050. Offers semi-precious stones on handles, acid etching on blades and blade engraving. **Prices:** $60 to $300 some to $1,200. **Remarks:** Full-time maker; first knife sold in 1975. **Mark:** Name.

RHODES, JAMES D., 205 Woodpoint Ave., Hagerstown, MD 21740, Phone: 301-739-2657
Specialties: Traditional working and using straight knives of his design. **Patterns:** Bowies, fighters, hunters and kitchen knives. **Technical:** Forges 5160, 1085, and 9260; makes own Damascus. Hard edges, soft backs, dead soft tangs. Heat-treats. **Prices:** $150 to $350. **Remarks:** Part-time maker. **Mark:** Last name, JS.

RICARDO ROMANO, BERNARDES, Ruai Coronel Rennò, 1261, Itajuba MG, BRAZIL 37500, Phone: 0055-2135-622-5896
Specialties: Hunters, fighters, bowies. **Technical:** Grinds blades of stainless and tools steels. **Patterns:** Hunters. **Prices:** $100 to $700. **Mark:** Romano.

RICE, STEPHEN E, 11043C Oak Spur Ct, St. Louis, MO 63146, Phone: (314) 432-2025

RICHARD, RON, 4875 Calaveras Ave., Fremont, CA 94538, Phone: 510-796-9767
Specialties: High-tech working straight knives of his design. **Patterns:** Bowies, swords and locking folders. **Technical:** Forges and grinds ATS-34, 154CM and 440V. All folders have dead-bolt button locks. **Prices:** $650 to $850; some to $1400. **Remarks:** Full-time maker; first knife sold in 1968. **Mark:** Full name.

RICHARDS JR., ALVIN C, 2889 Shields Ln, Fortuna, CA 95540-3241, Phone: (707) 725-2526
Specialties: Fixed blade Damascus. One-of-a-kind. **Patterns:** Hunters, fighters. **Prices:** $125 to $500. **Remarks:** Like to work with customers on a truly custom knife. **Mark:** A C Richards or ACR.

RICHARDSON JR., PERCY, P. O. Box 973, Hemphill, TX 75948, Phone: 409-787-2279
Specialties: Traditional and working straight knives and folders in standard patterns and to customer specs. **Patterns:** Bowies, daggers, hunters, automatics, locking folders, slip-joints and utility/camp knives. **Technical:** Grinds ATS-34, 440C and D2. **Prices:** $125 to $600; some to $1,800. **Remarks:** Full-time maker; first knife sold in 1990. Doing business as Lone Star Custom Knives. **Mark:** Lone Star with last name across it.

RICHTER, SCOTT, 516 E. 2nd St., S. Boston, MA 02127, Phone: 617-269-4855
Specialties: Traditional working/using folders. **Patterns:** Locking folders, swords and kitchen knives. **Technical:** Grinds ATS-34, 5160 and A2. High-tech materials. **Prices:** $150 to $650; some to $1,500. **Remarks:** Full-time maker; first knife sold in 1991. Doing business as Richter Made. **Mark:** Last name, Made.

RICHTER, JOHN C., 932 Bowling Green Trail, Chesapeake, VA 23320
Specialties: Hand-forged knives in original patterns. **Patterns:** Hunters, fighters, utility knives and other belt knives, folders, swords. **Technical:** Hand-forges high carbon and his own Damascus; makes mokume gane. **Prices:** $75 to $1,500. **Remarks:** Part-time maker. **Mark:** Richter Forge.

RICKE, DAVE, 1209 Adams, West Bend, WI 53090, Phone: 262-334-5739
Specialties: Working knives; period pieces. **Patterns:** Hunters, boots, Bowies; locking folders and slip-joints. **Technical:** Grinds ATS-34, A2, 440C and 154CM. **Prices:** $75 to $260; some to $1,200. **Remarks:** Part-time maker; first knife sold in 1976. **Mark:** Last name.

RIDER, DAVID M, P O Box 5946, Eugene, OR 97405-0911, Phone: (541) 343-8747

RIEPE, RICHARD A, 17604 East 296 Street, Harrisonville, MO 64701

RIETVELD, BERTIE, P. O. Box 53, Magaliesburg 1791, SOUTH AFRICA, Phone: +2714 577 1294, Fax:014 577 1294
Specialties: Damascus, Persian, art daggers, button-lock folders. **Patterns:** Mostly one-ofs. **Technical:** Work only in own stainless Damascus and other exotics. **Prices:** $500 to $8,000. **Remarks:** First knife made in 1979. Past chairman of SA Knifemakers Guild. Member SA Knifemakers Guild & Knifemakers Guild (USA). Also a member of the Italian Guild. **Mark:** Elephant with last name.

RIGNEY JR., WILLIE, 191 Colson Dr., Bronston, KY 42518, Phone: 606-679-4227
Specialties: High-tech period pieces and fancy working knives. **Patterns:** Fighters, boots, daggers and push knives. **Technical:** Grinds 440C and 154CM; buys Damascus. Most knives are embellished. **Prices:** $150 to $1,500; some to $10,000. **Remarks:** Full-time maker; first knife sold in 1978. **Mark:** First initial, last name.

RINKES, SIEGFRIED, Am Sportpl 2, D 91459, Markterlbach, GERMANY

RIZZI, RUSSELL J., 37 March Rd., Ashfield, MA 01330, Phone: 413-625-2842
Specialties: Fancy working and using straight knives and folders of his design or to customer specs. **Patterns:** Hunters, locking folders and fighters. **Technical:** Grinds 440C, D2 and commercial Damascus. **Prices:** $150 to $750; some to $2,500. **Remarks:** Part-time maker; first knife sold in 1990. **Mark:** Last name, Ashfield, MA.

ROATH, DEAN, 3050 Winnipeg Dr., Baton Rouge, LA 70819, Phone: 225-272-5562
Specialties: Classic working knives; focusing on filet knives for salt water fishermen. **Patterns:** Hunters, filets, canoe/trail, and boating/sailing knives. **Technical:** Grinds 440C. **Prices:** $85 to $500; some to $1,500. **Remarks:** Part-time maker; first knife sold in 1978. **Mark:** Name, city and state.

ROBBINS, HOWARD P., 1407 S. 217th Ave., Elkhorn, NE 68022, Phone: 402-289-4121
Specialties: High-tech working knives with clean designs, some fancy. **Patterns:** Folders, hunters and camp knives. **Technical:** Grinds 440C. Heat-treats; likes mirror finishes. Offers leatherwork. **Prices:** $100 to $500; some to $1,000. **Remarks:** Full-time maker; first knife sold in 1982. **Mark:** Name, city and state.

ROBERTS, E RAY, 191 Nursery Rd, Monticello, FL 32344, Phone: (850) 997-4403
Specialties: High-Carbon Damascus knives & tomahawks.

ROBERTS, MICHAEL, 601 Oakwood Dr., Clinton, MS 39056-4332, Phone: 601-924-3154
Specialties: Working and using knives in standard patterns and to customer specs. **Patterns:** Hunters, Bowies, tomahawks and fighters. **Technical:** Forges 5160, O1, 1095 and his own Damascus. Uses only natural handle materials. **Prices:** $145 to $500; some to $1,100. **Remarks:** Part-time maker; first knife sold in 1988. **Mark:** Last name or first and last name in Celtic script.

ROBERTS, CHUCK, PO Box 7174, Golden, CO 80403, Phone: 303-642-0512
Specialties: Sheffield Bowies; historic styles only. **Patterns:** Bowies and California knives. **Technical:** Grinds 440C, 5160 and ATS-34. Handles made of stag, ivory or mother-of-pearl. **Prices:** Start at $750. **Remarks:** Full-time maker. **Mark:** Last initial or last name.

ROBERTS, GEORGE A., PO Box 31228, 211 Main St, Whitehorse, YT, CANADA Y1A 5P7, Phone: 867-667-7099, Fax:867-667-7099
Specialties: Masadon Ivory, fossil walrus ivory handled knives, scrimshawed or carved. **Patterns:** Side lockers, fancy bird & trout knives, hunters, fillet blades. **Technical:** Grinds stainless Damascus, all surgical steels. **Prices:** Up to $3,500 U. S. **Remarks:** Full-time maker; first knives sold in 1986. Doing business as Bandit Blades. **Mark:** Bandit Yukon with pick & shovel crossed. **Other:** Most recent works have gold nuggets in fossilized Mastodon ivory. Something new using mosaic pins in mokume bolster and in mosaic Damascus it creates a new look

ROBERTSON, LEO D, 3728 Pleasant Lake Dr, Indianapolis, IN 46227, Phone: 317-882-9899
Specialties: Hunting, fillet, bowie, utility, folding (liner lock and lockback), fighters, tantos & art knives. **Patterns:** ATS-34, 154CM, 440C, 1095, 0-1, D-2 and various types of Damascus. **Technical:** Use Mother of Pearl, coral, stag, bone, mammoth ivory, ivory, wildwoods, amber & laminates for handles. Make own sheaths from high grade leather. **Prices:** Fixed sheaths are $100 to $1000 (includes sheath and certificate of authenticity). Folding blades are $300 to $750 (includes certificate of authenticity). **Other:** Made first knife in 1990. Member of American Blade smith Society.

ROBINSON, CHUCK, Sea Robin Forge, 1423 Third Ave, Picayune, MS 39466, Phone: 601-798-0060
Specialties: Deluxe period pieces and working/using knives of his design and to customer specs. **Patterns:** Bowies, RR spike knives, hunters, folders, utility knives and original designs. **Technical:** Forges own Damascus, 52100, 01, L6, 1070 thru 1095, 15N20 and cable. **Prices:** Start at $225. **Remarks:** First knife 1958. Recently transitioned to full-time maker. **Mark:** Dolphin entwined on anchor and initials C. R. **Other:** Makes bladesmithing anvils, hammers & finishing jigs.

ROBINSON, CHUCK, Sea Robin Forge, 1423 Third Ave, Picayune, MS 39466, Phone: 601-798-0060
Specialties: Deluxe period pieces and working / using knives of his design and to customer specs. **Patterns:** Bowies, fighters, hunters, folders, utility knives and original designs. **Technical:** Forges own Damascus, 52100, 01, L6 and 1070 thru 1095. **Prices:** Start At $225. **Remarks:** First knife 1958. Recently transitioned to full-time maker. **Mark:** Fish logo, anchor and initials C. R.

ROBINSON, CHARLES (DICKIE), P. O. Box 221, Vega, TX 79092, Phone: 806-267-2629
Specialties: Classic and working/using knives. **Patterns:** Bowies, daggers, fighters, hunters and camp knives. **Technical:** Forges O1, 5160, 52100 and his own Damascus. **Prices:** $125 to $850; some to $2,500. **Remarks:** Part-time maker; first knife sold in 1988. Doing business as Robinson Knives. **Mark:** Last name, JS.

ROBINSON, ROBERT W., 1569 N. Finley Pt., Polson, MT 59860, Phone: 406-887-2259, Fax:406-887-2259
Specialties: High-art straight knives, folders and automatics of his design. **Patterns:** Hunters and locking folders. **Technical:** Grinds ATS-34, 154CM and 440V. Inlays pearl and gold; engraves sheep horn and ivory. **Prices:** $150 to $500; some to $2,000. **Remarks:** Full-time maker; first knife sold in 1983. Doing business as Robbie Knife. **Mark:** Name on left side of blade.

ROBINSON III, REX R., 10531 Poe St., Leesburg, FL 34788, Phone: 352-787-4587
Specialties: One-of-a-kind high-art automatics of his design. **Patterns:** Automatics, liner locks and lock back folders. **Technical:** Uses tool steel and stainless Damascus and mokume; flat grinds. Hand carves folders. **Prices:** $1,800 to $7,500. **Remarks:** First knife sold in 1988. **Mark:** First name inside oval.

ROCHFORD, MICHAEL R., P. O. Box 577, Dresser, WI 54009, Phone: 715-755-3520
Specialties: Working straight knives and folders. Classic Bowies and Moran traditional. **Patterns:** Bowies, fighters, hunters: slip-joint, locking and liner locking folders. **Technical:** Grinds ATS-34, 440C, 154CM and D-2; forges W2, 5160, and his own Damascus. Offers metal & metal and leather sheaths. Filework and wire inlay. **Prices:** $150 to $1,000; some to $2,000. **Remarks:** Full-time maker; first knife sold in 1984. **Mark:** Name.

RODEBAUGH, JAMES L, 9374 Joshua Rd, Oak Hills, CA 92345

RODEWALD, GARY, 447 Grouse Court, Hamilton, MT 59840, Phone: (406) 363-2192
Specialties: Bowies of my design as inspired from his torical pieces. **Patterns:** Hunters, bowies & camp/combat. Forges 5160 1084 & my own Damascus of 1084, 15N20, field grade hunters AT-34 - 440C, 440V, and BG42. **Prices:** $200-$1500 **Remarks:** Sole author on knives - sheaths done by saddle maker. **Mark:** Rodewald

RODKEY, DAN, 18336 Ozark Dr., Hudson, FL 34667, Phone: 727-863-8264
Specialties: Traditional straight knives of his design and in standard patterns. **Patterns:** Boots, fighters and hunters. **Technical:** Grinds 440C, D2 and ATS-34. **Prices:** Start at $200. **Remarks:** Full-time maker; first knife sold in 1985. Doing business as Rodkey Knives. **Mark:** Etched logo on blade.

ROE JR., FRED D., 4005 Granada Dr., Huntsville, AL 35802, Phone: 205-881-6847
Specialties: Highly finished working knives of his design; period pieces. **Patterns:** Hunters, fighters and survival knives; locking folders; specialty designs like divers' knives. **Technical:** Grinds 154CM, ATS-34 and Damascus. Field-tests all blades. **Prices:** $125 to $250; some to $2,000. **Remarks:** Part-time maker; first knife sold in 1980. **Mark:** Last name.

ROGERS, RODNEY, 602 Osceola St., Wildwood, FL 34785, Phone: 352-748-6114
Specialties: Traditional straight knives and folders. **Patterns:** Fighters, hunters, skinners. **Technical:** Flat-grinds ATS-34 and Damascus. Prefers natural materials. **Prices:** $150 to $1,400. **Remarks:** Full-time maker; first knife sold in 1986. **Mark:** Last name, Handmade.

ROGERS, RICHARD, PO Box 769, Magdalena, NM 87825, Phone: 505-854-2567
Specialties: Sheffield style folders & multi-blade folders. **Patterns:** Folders: various traditional patterns. One-of-a-kind fixed blades. Fixed blades: bowies, daggers, hunters, utility knives. **Technical:** Use various steels, like natural handle materials. **Prices:** $400 on up. **Mark:** Last name.

ROGERS, CHARLES W, RT 1 Box 1552, Douglass, TX 75943, Phone: (409) 326-4496

ROGERS JR., ROBERT P., 3979 South Main St., Acworth, GA 30101, Phone: 404-974-9982
Specialties: Traditional working knives. **Patterns:** Hunters, 4-inch trailing-points. **Technical:** Grinds D2, 154CM and ATS-34; likes ironwood and ivory Micarta. **Prices:** $125 to $175. **Remarks:** Spare-time maker; first knife sold in 1975. **Mark:** Name.

ROGHMANS, MARK, 607 Virginia Ave., LaGrange, GA 30240, Phone: 706-885-1273
Specialties: Classic and traditional knives of his design. **Patterns:** Bowies, daggers and fighters. **Technical:** Grinds ATS-34, D2 and 440C. **Prices:** $250 to $500. **Remarks:** Part-time maker; first knife sold in 1984. Doing business as LaGrange Knife. **Mark:** Last name and/or LaGrange Knife.

ROHN, FRED, 7675 W Happy Hill Rd, Coeur d'Alene, ID 83814, Phone: 208-667-0774
Specialties: Hunters, boot knives, custom patterns. **Patterns:** Drop points, double edge etc. **Technical:** Grinds 440 or 154CM. **Prices:** $85 and up. **Remarks:** Part-time maker. **Mark:** Logo on blade; serial numbered.

ROLLERT, STEVE, P. O. Box 65, Keenesburg, CO 80643-0065, Phone: 303-732-4858
Specialties: Highly finished working knives. **Patterns:** Variety of straight knives; locking folders and slip-joints. **Technical:** Forges and grinds W2, 1095, ATS-34 and his pattern-welded, cable Damascus and nickel Damascus. **Prices:** $300 to $1,000; some to $3,000. **Remarks:** Full-time maker; first knife sold in 1980. Doing business as Dove Knives. **Mark:** Last name in script.

ROLLICK, WALTER D, 2001 Cochran Rd, Maryville, TN 37803, Phone: (423) 681-6105

RONZIO, N JACK, P O Box 248, Fruita, CO 81521, Phone: (970) 858-0921

ROSA, PEDRO GULLHERME TELES, R. das Magnolias, 45 CECAP Presidente Prudente, SP-19065-410, BRAZIL, Phone: 0182-271769
Specialties: Using straight knives and folders to customer specs; some high-art. **Patterns:** Fighters, Bowies and daggers. **Technical:** Grinds and forges D6, 440C, high carbon steels and Damascus. **Prices:** $60 to $400. **Remarks:** Full-time maker; first knife sold in 1991. **Mark:** A hammer over "Hammer. "

ROSE, DEREK W, 14 Willow Wood Rd, Gallipolis, OH 45631, Phone: (740) 446-4627

ROSENFELD, BOB, 955 Freeman Johnson Road, Hoschton, GA 30548, Phone: 770-867-2647
Specialties: Fancy and embellished working/using straight knives of his design and in standard patterns. **Patterns:** Daggers, hunters and utility/camp knives. **Technical:** Forges 52100, A203E, 1095 and L6 Damascus. Offers engraving. **Prices:** $125 to $650; some to $1,000. **Remarks:** Full-time maker; first knife sold in 1984. Also makes folders; ABS journeyman. **Mark:** Last name or full name, Knife maker.

ROSS, GREGG, 4556 Wenhart Rd., Lake Worth, FL 33463, Phone: 407-439-4681
Specialties: Working/using straight knives. **Patterns:** Bowies, hunters and utility/camp knives. **Technical:** Forges and grinds ATS-34, Damascus and cable Damascus. Uses decorative pins. **Prices:** $125 to $250; some to $400. **Remarks:** Part-time maker; first knife sold in 1992. **Mark:** Name, city and state.

ROSS, STEPHEN, 534 Remington Dr., Evanston, WY 82930, Phone: 307-789-7104
Specialties: One-of-a-kind collector-grade classic and contemporary straight knives and folders of his design and to customer specs; some fantasy pieces. **Patterns:** Combat and survival knives, hunters, boots and folders. **Technical:** Grinds stainless; forges spring and tool steel. Engraves, scrimshaws. Makes leather sheaths. **Prices:** $160 to $3,000. **Remarks:** Part-time-time maker; first knife sold in 1971. **Mark:** Last name in modified Roman; sometimes in script.

ROSS, TIM, 3239 Oliver Rd., RR #17, Thunder Bay, ONT, CANADA P7B 6C2, Phone: 807-935-2667
Specialties: Fancy working knives of his design. **Patterns:** Fishing and hunting knives, Bowies, daggers and miniatures. **Technical:** Uses D2, Stellite 6K and 440C; forges 52100 and Damascus. Makes antler handles and sheaths; has supply of whale teeth and moose antlers for trade. Prefers natural materials only. Wife Katherine scrimshaws. **Prices:** $100 to $350; some to $2,100. **Remarks:** Part-time maker; first knife sold in 1975. **Mark:** Last name stamped on tang.

ROSS, D. L., 27 Kinsman St., Dunedin, NEW ZEALAND, Phone: 64 3 464 0239, Fax:64 3 464 0239
Specialties: Working straight knives of his design. **Patterns:** Hunters, various others. **Technical:** Grinds 440C. **Prices:** $100 to $450; some to $700 NZ dollars. **Remarks:** Part-time maker; first knife sold in 1988. **Mark:** Dave Ross, Maker, city and country.

ROSSDEUTSCHER, ROBERT N, 133 S Vail Av, Arlington Hts, IL 60005, Phone: (847) 577-0404
Specialties: Frontier style and historically inspired knives. **Patterns::** Trade knives, Bowies, camp knives & hunting knives. **Technical:** Most knives are hand forged, a few are stock removal. **Prices:** $85 to $600. **Remarks:** Journeyman Smith of the American Bladesmith Society and Neo-Tribal Metalsmiths. **Mark:** Back-to-back "R's", one upside down and backwards, one right side up & forward in an oval. Sometimes with name, town & state; depending on knife style.

ROTELLA, RICHARD A., 643--75th St., Niagara Falls, NY 14304
Specialties: Working knives of his design. **Patterns:** Various fishing, hunting and utility knives; folders. **Technical:** Grinds ATS-34. Prefers hand-rubbed finishes. **Prices:** $65 to $450; some to $900. **Remarks:** Spare-time maker; first knife sold in 1977. Not taking orders at this time; only sells locally. **Mark:** Name and city in stylized waterfall logo.

ROULIN, CHARLES, 113 B Rt. de Soral, 1233 Geneva, SWITZERLAND, Phone: 022-757-4479, Fax:022-757-4479
Specialties: Fancy high-art straight knives and folders of his design. **Patterns:** Bowies, locking folders, slip-joint folders and miniatures. **Technical:** Grinds 440C, ATS-34 and D2. Engraves; carves nature scenes and detailed animals in steel, ivory, on handles and blades. **Prices:** $500 to $3,000; some to $10,000. **Remarks:** Full-time maker; first knife sold in 1988. **Mark:** Symbol of fish with name or name engraved.

ROWE, STEWART G., 8-18 Coreen Court, Mt. Crosby, Brisbane 4306, AUSTRALIA, Phone: Ph: 073-201-0906, Fax:Fax: 073-201-2406
Specialties: Designer knives, reproduction of ancient weaponry, traditional Japanese tantos and edged tools. **Patterns:** "Shark"--blade range. **Technical:** Forges W1, W2, D2; creates own Tamahagne steel and composite pattern-welded billets. Gold, silver and ivory fittings available. **Prices:** $300 to $11,000. **Remarks:** Full-time maker; first knife sold in 1981. Doing business as Stewart Rowe Productions Pty Ltd .

ROWE, KENNY, 1406 W Ave C, Hope, AR 71801, Phone: (870) 777-8216, Fax:(870) 777-2974

ROY, ROBERT F, 16180 Schaeffer St, PO Box 262, Bayview, id 83803, Phone: 208-683-9396

ROZAS, CLARK D, 1436 W "G" Street, Wilmington, CA 90744, Phone: 310-518-0488
Specialties: Hand forged blades. **Patterns:** Pig stickers, toad stabbers, whackers, choppers. **Technical:** Damascus, 52100, 1095, 1084, 5160. **Prices:** $200 to $600. **Remarks:** A. B. S. member; part-time maker since 1995. **Mark:** Name over dagger.

RUANA KNIFE WORKS, Box 520, Bonner, MT 59823, Phone: 406-258-5368
Specialties: Working knives and period pieces. **Patterns:** Variety of straight knives. **Technical:** Forges 5160 chrome alloy for Bowies and 1095. **Prices:** $105 and up. **Remarks:** Full-time maker; first knife sold in 1938. **Mark:** Name.

RUBLEY, JAMES A., 4609 W Nevada Mills Rd, Angola, IN 46703, Phone: 219-833-1255
Specialties: Working American knives and collectibles for hunters, buckskinners and re-enactment groups from Pre-Revolutionary War through the Civil War. **Patterns:** Anything authentic, barring knives. **Technical:** Iron fittings, natural materials; forges files. **Prices:** $175 to $2,500. **Remarks:** Museum consultant and blacksmith for two decades. Offers classes in beginning, intermediate and advanced traditional knife making. **Mark:** Lightning bolt.

RUPERT, BOB, 301 Harshaville Rd., Clinton, PA 15026, Phone: 724-573-4569
Specialties: Wrought period pieces with natural elements. **Patterns:** Elegant straight blades - friction folders. **Technical:** Forges colonial 7; 1095; 5160; diffuse mokume-gane and form Damascus. **Prices:** $150 to $1500; some higher. **Remarks:** Part-time maker; first knife sold in 1980. Evening hours studio since 1980. **Mark:** R etched in Old English. **Other:** Likes simplicity that disassembles.

RUPLE, WILLIAM H., P. O. Box 370, Charlotte, TX 78011, Phone: 830-277-1371
Specialties: Multi blade folders, slip joints, some lock backs. **Patterns:** Like to reproduce old patterns. **Technical:** Grinds 440C, ATS-34, D2 and commercial Damascus. Offers filework on back springs and liners. **Prices:** $300 to $500; some to $1,000. **Remarks:** Full-time maker; first knife sold in 1988. **Mark:** Ruple.

RUSS, RON, 5351 NE 160th Ave., Williston, FL 32696, Phone: 352-528-2603
Specialties: Damascus and Mokume. **Patterns:** Ladder, rain drop and butterfly. **Technical:** Most knives, including Damascus, are forged from 52100-E. **Prices:** $65 to $2,500. **Mark:** Russ.

RUSSELL, A. G., 1920 North 26th St, Lowell, AR 72745-8489, Phone: 800-255-9037 479-631-0130, Fax:479-631-8493
Specialties: A. G. Russell Shopmade™ (handmade, custom) knives made in our own shop using the best tool steels: 154CM, A-2, D-2, 52100, Damascus and Stellite. Morseth™ knives made with Norwegian laminated steels. Hunters, camp knives. Working to our own designs in the finest materials.

RUSSELL, MICK, 4 Rossini Rd., Pari Park, Port Elizabeth 6070, SOUTH AFRICA
Specialties: Art knives. **Patterns:** Working and collectible bird, trout and hunting knives, defense knives and folders. **Technical:** Grinds D2, 440C, ATS-34 and Damascus. Offers mirror or satin finishes. **Prices:** Start at $100. **Remarks:** Full-time maker; first knife sold in 1986. **Mark:** Stylized rhino incorporating initials.

RUSSELL, TOM, 6500 New Liberty Rd., Jacksonville, AL 36265, Phone: 205-492-7866
Specialties: Straight working knives of his design or to customer specs. **Patterns:** Hunters, folders, fighters, skinners, Bowies and utility knives. **Technical:** Grinds D2, 440C and ATS-34; offers filework. **Prices:** $75 to $225. **Remarks:** Part-time maker; first knife sold in 1987. Full-time tool and die maker. **Mark:** Last name with tulip stamp.

RUTH, MICHAEL G, 3101 New Boston Rd, Texarkana, TX 75501, Phone: (903) 832-7166

RYAN, C. O., 902-A Old Wormley Creek Rd., Yorktown, VA 23692, Phone: 757-898-7797
Specialties: Working/using knives. **Patterns:** Hunters, kitchen knives, locking folders. **Technical:** Grinds 440C and ATS-34. **Prices:** $45 to $130; some to $450. **Remarks:** Part-time maker; first knife sold in 1980. **Mark:** Name-C. O. Ryan.

RYBAR JR., RAYMOND B., 277 Stone Church Road, Finleyville, PA 15332, Phone: 412-348-4841
Specialties: Fancy/embellished, high-art and traditional working using straight knives and folders of his design and in standard patterns; period pieces. **Patterns:** Daggers, fighters and swords. **Technical:** Forges Damascus. All blades have etched biblical scripture or biblical significance. **Prices:** $120 to $1,200; some to $4,500. **Remarks:** Full-time maker; first knife sold in 1972. Doing business as Stone Church Forge. **Mark:** Last name or business name.

RYBERG, GOTE, Faltgatan 2, S-562 00 Norrahammar, SWEDEN, Phone: 4636-61678

RYDBOM, JEFF, PO Box 548, Annandale, MI 55302, Phone: 320-274-9639

RYDER, BEN M., P. O. Box 133, Copperhill, TN 37317, Phone: 615-496-2750
Specialties: Working/using straight knives of his design and to customer specs. **Patterns:** Fighters, hunters, utility/camp knives. **Technical:** Grinds 440C, ATS-34, D2, commercial Damascus. **Prices:** $75 to $400. **Remarks:** Part-time maker; first knife sold in 1992. **Mark:** Full name in double butterfly logo.

RYUICHI, KUKI, 504-7 Tokorozawa-Shinmachi Tokorozawa-City, Saitama, JAPAN, Phone: 042-943-3451

RZEWNICKI, GERALD, 8833 S Massbach Rd, Elizabeth, IL 61028-9714, Phone: (815) 598-3239

S

SAINDON, R. BILL, 11 Highland View Rd., Claremont, NH 03743, Phone: 603-542-9418
Specialties: Collector-quality folders of his design or to customer specs. **Patterns:** Latch release, liner lock and lockback folders. **Technical:** Offers limited amount of own Damascus; also uses Damas makers steel. Prefers natural handle material, gold and gems. **Prices:** $500 to $4,000. **Remarks:** Full-time maker; first knife sold in 1981. Doing business as Daynia Forge. **Mark:** Sun logo or engraved surname.

SAKAKIBARA, MASAKI, 20-8 Sakuragaoka, 2-Chome Setagaya-ku, Tokyo 156, JAPAN, Phone: 03-420-0375

SAKMAR, MIKE, 2470 Melvin, Rochester, MI 48307, Phone: 248-852-6775, Fax:248-852-8544
Specialties: Mokume in various patterns and alloy combinations. **Patterns:** Bowies, fighters, hunters and integrals. **Technical:** Grinds ATS-34, Damascus and high-carbon tool steels. Uses mostly natural handle materi-

custom knifemakers

als--elephant ivory, walrus ivory, stag, wildwood, oosic, etc. Makes mokume for resale. **Prices:** $250 to $2,500; some to $4,000. **Remarks:** Part-time maker; first knife sold in 1990. **Mark:** Last name. **Other:** Supplier of Mokume.

SALLEY, JOHN D., 3965 Frederick-Ginghamsburg Rd., Tipp City, OH 45371, Phone: 513-698-4588
Specialties: Fancy working knives and art pieces. **Patterns:** Hunters, fighters, daggers and some swords. **Technical:** Grinds ATS-34, 12C27 and W2; buys Damascus. **Prices:** $85 to $1,000; some to $6,000. **Remarks:** Part-time maker; first knife sold in 1979. **Mark:** First initial, last name.

SAMPSON, LYNN, 381 Deakins Rd., Jonesborough, TN 37659, Phone: 423-348-8373
Specialties: Highly finished working knives, mostly folders. **Patterns:** Locking folders, slip-joints, interframes and two-blades. **Technical:** Grinds D2, 440C and ATS-34; offers extensive filework. **Prices:** Start at $300. **Remarks:** Full-time maker; first knife sold in 1982. **Mark:** Name and city in logo.

SANDERS, A. A., 3850 72 Ave. NE, Norman, OK 73071, Phone: 405-364-8660
Specialties: Working straight knives and folders. **Patterns:** Hunters, fighters, daggers and Bowies. **Technical:** Forges his own Damascus; offers stock removal with ATS-34, 440C, A2, D2, O1, 5160 and 1095. **Prices:** $85 to $1,500. **Remarks:** Full-time maker; first knife sold in 1985. Formerly known as Athern Forge. **Mark:** Name.

SANDERS, BILL, 335 Bauer Ave., P. O. Box 957, Mancos, CO 81328, Phone: 970-533-7223
Specialties: Working straight knives, some fancy and some fantasy, of his design. **Patterns:** Hunters, boots, utility knives, using belt knives. **Technical:** Grinds 440C, ATS-34 and commercial Damascus. Provides wide variety of handle materials. **Prices:** $170 to $350; some to $800. **Remarks:** Full-time maker. **Mark:** Name, city and state.

SANDERS, MICHAEL M., P. O. Box 1106, Ponchatoula, LA 70454, Phone: 225-294-3601
Specialties: Working straight knives and folders, some deluxe. **Patterns:** Hunters, fighters, Bowies, daggers, large folders and deluxe Damascus miniatures. **Technical:** Grinds O1, D2, 440C, ATS-34 and Damascus. **Prices:** $75 to $650; some higher. **Remarks:** Full-time maker; first knife sold in 1967. **Mark:** Name and state.

SANDERSON, RAY, 4403 Uplands Way, Yakima, WA 98908, Phone: 509-965-0128
Specialties: One-of-a-kind Buck knives; traditional working straight knives and folders of his design. **Patterns:** Bowies, hunters and fighters. **Technical:** Grinds 440C and ATS-34. **Prices:** $200 to $750. **Remarks:** Part-time maker; first knife sold in 1984. **Mark:** Sanderson Knives in shape of Bowie.

SANDLIN, LARRY, 4580 Sunday Dr., Adamsville, AL 35005, Phone: 205-674-1816
Specialties: High-art straight knives of his design. **Patterns:** Boots, daggers, hunters and fighters. **Technical:** Forges 1095, L6, O1, carbon steel and Damascus. **Prices:** $200 to $1,500; some to $5,000. **Remarks:** Part-time maker; first knife sold in 1990. **Mark:** Chiseled last name in Japanese.

SARVIS, RANDALL J., 110 West park Ave, Fort Pierre, SD 57532, Phone: 605-223-2772

SAWBY, SCOTT, 480 Snowberry Ln, Sandpoint, ID 83864, Phone: 208-263-4171
Specialties: Folders, working and fancy. **Patterns:** Locking folders, patent locking systems and interframes. **Technical:** Grinds D2, 440C, 154CM, CPM-T-440V and ATS-34. **Prices:** $400 to $1,000. **Remarks:** Full-time maker; first knife sold in 1974. **Mark:** Last name, city and state.

SCARROW, WIL, c/o L&W Mail Service, 6012 Pearce, Lakewood, CA 90712, Phone: 626-286-6069
Specialties: Carving knives, also working straight knives in standard patterns or to customer specs. **Patterns:** Carving, fishing, hunting, skinning, utility, swords & bowies. **Technical:** Forges and grinds: A2, L6, W1, D2, 5160, 1095, 440C, AEB-L, ATS-34 and others on request. Offers some filework. **Prices:** $65 to $850; some higher. Prices include sheath (carver's $40 and up). **Remarks:** Spare-time maker; first knife sold in 1983. Two to eight month construction time on custom orders. Doing business as Scarrow's Custom Stuff and Gold Hill Knife works (in Oregon). **Mark:** SC with arrow and date/year made. **Other:** Carving knives available at the 'Wild Duck' Woodcarvers Supply. Contact at duckstore@aol.com

SCHALLER, ANTHONY BRETT, 5609 Flint Ct. NW, Albuquerque, NM 87120, Phone: 505-899-0155
Specialties: Straight knives and locking-liner folders of his design and in standard patterns. **Patterns:** Boots, fighters, utility knives and folders. **Technical:** Grinds ATS-34, BG42 and stainless Damascus. Offers filework, mirror finishes and full and narrow tangs. Prefers exotic woods or Micarta for handle materials. **Prices:** $60 to $350; some to $500. **Remarks:** Part-time maker; first knife sold in 1990. **Mark:** Last name.

SCHEID, MAGGIE, 124 Van Stallen St., Rochester, NY 14621-3557
Specialties: Simple working straight knives. **Patterns:** Kitchen and utility knives; some miniatures. **Technical:** Forges 5160 high-carbon steel. **Prices:** $100 to $200. **Remarks:** Part-time maker; first knife sold in 1986. **Mark:** Full name.

SCHEMPP, ED, P. O. Box 1181, Ephrata, WA 98823, Phone: 509-754-2963, Fax:509-754-3212
Specialties: Mosaic Damascus and unique folder designs **Patterns:** Primarily folders. **Technical:** Grinds CPM440V; forges many patterns of mosaic using powdered steel. **Prices:** $100 to $400; some to $2,000. **Remarks:** Part-time maker; first knife sold in 1991. Doing business as Ed Schempp Knives. **Mark:** Ed Schempp Knives over five heads of wheat, city and state.

SCHEMPP, MARTIN, P. O. Box 1181, 5430 Baird Springs Rd. N. W., Ephrata, WA 98823, Phone: 509-754-2963, Fax:509-754-3212
Specialties: Fantasy and traditional straight knives of his design, to customer specs and in standard patterns; Paleolithic styles. **Patterns:** Fighters and Paleolithic designs. **Technical:** Uses opal, Mexican rainbow and obsidian. Offers scrimshaw. **Prices:** $15 to $500; some to $250. **Remarks:** Spare-time maker; first knife sold in 1995. **Mark:** Initials and date.

SCHEPERS, GEORGE B., PO Box 395, Shelton, NE 68876-0395
Specialties: Fancy period pieces of his design. **Patterns:** Bowies, swords, tomahawks; locking folders and miniatures. **Technical:** Grinds W1, W2 and his own Damascus; etches. **Prices:** $125 to $600; some higher. **Remarks:** Full-time maker; first knife sold in 1981. **Mark:** Schep.

SCHEURER, ALFREDO E. FAES, Av. Rincon de los Arcos 104, Col. Bosque Res. del Sur, C. P. 16010, MEXICO, Phone: 5676 47 63
Specialties: Fancy and fantasy knives of his design. **Patterns:** Daggers. **Technical:** Grinds stainless steel; casts and grinds silver. Sets stones in silver. **Prices:** $2,000 to $3,000. **Remarks:** Spare-time maker; first knife sold in 1989. **Mark:** Symbol.

SCHILLING, ELLEN, 95 Line Rd, Hamilton Square, NJ 08690, Phone: (609) 448-0483

SCHIPPNICK, JIM, PO Box 326, SANBORN, NY 14132, Phone: 716-731-3715
Specialties: Nordic, early American, rustic. **Mark:** Runic R. **Remarks:** Also import Nordic knives from Norway, Sweden & Finland.

SCHIRMER, MIKE, 28 Biltmore Rd., P. O. Box 534, Twin Bridges, MT 59754, Phone: 406-684-5868
Specialties: Working straight knives of his design or to customer specs; mostly hunters and personal knives. **Patterns:** Hunters, camp, kitchen, bowies and fighters. **Technical:** Grinds O1, D2, A2 and Damascus and Talonoite. **Prices:** Start at $150. **Remarks:** Full-time maker; first knife sold in 1992. Doing business as Ruby Mountain Knives. **Mark:** Name or name & location.

SCHLOMER, JAMES E., 2543 Wyatt Pl, Kissimmee, FL 34741, Phone: 407-348-8044
Specialties: Working and show straight knives. **Patterns:** Hunters, Bowies and skinners. **Technical:** Stock removal method, 440C. Scrimshaws; carves sambar stag handles. Works on corean and Micarta. **Prices:** $150 to $750. **Remarks:** Full-time maker. **Mark:** Name and steel number.

SCHLUETER, DAVID, P. O. Box 463, Syracuse, NY 13209, Phone: 315-485-0829
Specialties: Japanese style swords, handmade fittings, leather wraps, and full mounting services. Prefers difficult projects. **Patterns:** Kozuka to Tachi, also Naginata and Nagimaaki. Preference for large blades with bo-hi and o-kissaki. **Technical:** Sole author, forges and grinds, mostly high carbon steels. All blades are tempered after clay-coated and water-quenched heat treatment. All fittings are original handmade pieces. Carves and wraps handles. Carves and finishes scabbards, including inlays ray skin and pocket scabbards. **Prices:**$800. 00 to $5000. 00 plus. **Remarks:**Full-time maker, doing business as Odd Frog Forge. **Mark:**Full name and date.

SCHMIDT, RICK, P. O. Box 1318, Whitefish, MT 59937, Phone: 406-862-6471, Fax:406-862-6078
Specialties: Traditional working and using straight knives and folders of his design and to customer specs. **Patterns:** Fighters, hunters, cutlery and utility knives. **Technical:** Flat-grinds D2 and ATS-34. Custom leather sheaths. **Prices:** $120 to $250; some to $1,900. **Remarks:** Full-time maker; first knife sold in 1975. **Mark:** Stylized initials.

SCHMITZ, RAYMOND E, P O Box 1787, Valley Center, CA 92082, Phone: (760) 749-4318

SCHMOKER, RANDY, Spirit of the Hammer, HC 63 Box 1085, Slana, AK 99586, Phone: 907-822-3371
Specialties: Hand carved, natural materials, mastodon ivory, moose antler. **Patterns:** Hunter, skinner, bowie, fighter, artistic collectables. **Technical:** Hand forged. **Prices:** $300 to $600. **Remarks:** 01 tool steel, 1095, 5160, 52100. **Mark:** Sheep with an S. **Other:** Custom sheaths, display stands.

SCHNEIDER, CRAIG M., 285 County Rd. 1400 N., Seymour, IL 61875, Phone: 217-687-2651
Specialties: Straight knives of my own design. **Patterns:** Bowies & hunters. **Technical:**Stock removal stainless and forged high carbon steels & Damascus. Uses a wide selection of handle materials and various guard and boster material **Prices:** $75 to $2,000. **Remarks:** Part-time maker; first knife sold in 1985. **Mark:** Stylized initials.

SCHNEIDER, KARL A., 209 N. Brownleaf Rd., Newark, DE 19713, Phone: 302-737-0277
Specialties: Traditional working and using straight knives of his design. **Patterns:** Hunters, kitchen and fillet knives. **Technical:** Grinds ATS-34. Shapes handles to fit hands; uses Micarta, Pakkawood and exotic woods. Makes hand-stitched leather cases. **Prices:** $95 to $225. **Remarks:** Part-time maker; first knife sold in 1984-85. **Mark:** Name, address; also name in shape of fish.

SCHOEMAN, CORRIE, Box 573, Bloemfontein 9300, SOUTH AFRICA, Phone: 027 51 4363528 Cell:027 82-3750789
Specialties: High-tech folders of his design or to customer's specs. **Patterns:** Liner lock folders. **Technical:** ATS-34, Damascus or stainless Damascus with titanium frames; prefers exotic materials for handles. **Prices:** $400 to $800. **Remarks:** Full-time maker; first knife sold in 1984. **Mark:** Etched name logo in knife shape engraved on inside of back bar.

SCHOENFELD, MATTHEW A., RR #1, Galiano Island, B. C., CANADA V0N 1P0, Phone: 250-539-2806
Specialties: Working knives of his design. **Patterns:** Kitchen cutlery, camp knives, hunters. **Technical:** Grinds 440C. **Prices:** $85 to $500. **Remarks:** Part-time maker; first knife sold in 1978. **Mark:** Signature, Galiano Is. B. C., and date.

SCHOENINGH, MIKE, 49850 Miller Rd, North Powder, OR 97867, Phone: (541) 856-3239

SCHOLL, TIM, 1389 Langdon Rd., Angier, NC 27501, Phone: 910-897-2051, Fax:910-897-4742
Specialties: Fancy and working/using straight knives and folders of his design and to customer specs. **Patterns:** tomahawks, swords, tantos, hunters and fantasy knives. **Technical:** Grinds ATS-34 & D2; forges carbon and tool steel and Damascus. Offers filework, engraving and scrimshaw. **Prices:** $85; some to $3,000. **Remarks:** Full-time maker; first knife sold in 1990. Doing business as Tim Scholl Custom Knives. **Mark:** Last name or last initial with arrow.

SCHRADER, ROBERT, 20825 Journey Ave, Bend, OR 97701, Phone: (541) 385-3259

SCHRAP, ROBERT G., Custom Leather Knife Sheath Co, 7024 W. Wells St., Wauwatosa, WI 53213-3717, Phone: 414-771-6472, Fax:414-479-9765
Specialties: Leatherwork. **Prices:** $35 to $100. **Mark:** Schrap in oval.

SCHROEN, KARL, 4042 Bones Rd., Sebastopol, CA 95472, Phone: 707-823-4057, Fax:707-823-2914
Specialties: Using knives made to fit. **Patterns:** Sgian dubhs, carving sets, wood-carving knives, fishing knives, kitchen knives and new cleaver design. **Technical:** Forges A2, ATS-34 and D2. **Prices:** $100 to $800. **Remarks:** Full-time maker; first knife sold in 1968. Author of *The Hand Forged Knife*. **Mark:** Last name.

SCHULTZ, ROBERT W, P O Box 70, Cocolalla, ID 83813-0070

SCHWARZER, STEPHEN, P. O. Box 4, Pomona Park, FL 32181, Phone: 904-649-5026, Fax:904-649-8585
Specialties: Mosaic Damascus & picture mosaic in folding knives. **Patterns:** Folders, axes and buckskinner knives. **Technical:** Specializes in picture mosaic Damascus and powder metal mosaic work. Sole authorship; all work including carving done in-house. Most knives have file work & carving. **Prices:** $1,500 to $5,000, some higher; carbon steel & primitive knives much less. **Remarks:** Full-time maker; first knife sold in 1976, considered by many to be one of the top mosaic Damascus specialists in the world. Mosaic Master level work. **Mark:** Schwarzer + anvil.

SCIMIO, BILL, HC 01 Box 24A, Spruce Creek, PA 16683, Phone: (814) 632-3751

SCOFIELD, EVERETT, 2873 Glass Mill Rd., Chickamauga, GA 30707, Phone: 706-375-2790
Specialties: Historic and fantasy miniatures. **Patterns:** All patterns. **Technical:** Uses only the finest tool steels and other materials. Uses only natural, precious and semi-precious materials. **Prices:** $100 to $1,500. **Remarks:** Full-time maker; first knife sold in 1971. Doing business as Three Crowns Cutlery. **Mark:** Three Crowns logo.

SCORDIA, PAOLO, Via Terralba 143, 00050 Torrimpietra, ROMA, ITALY, Phone: 06-61697231
Specialties: Working and using knives of my own design. **Patterns:** Any pattern. **Technical:** I forge my own Damascus and grind ATS-34, 420C, 440C; use hardwoods & Micarta for handles, brass & nickel-silver for fit-

tings. Makes sheaths. **Prices:** $80 to $500. **Remarks:** Part-time maker; first knife sold in 1988. **Mark:** Initials with sun and moon logo.

SCOTT, AL, HC63 Box 802, Harper, TX 78631, Phone: 830-864-4182
Specialties: High-art straight knives of his design. **Patterns:** Daggers, swords, early European, Middle East and Japanese knives. **Technical:** Uses ATS-34, 440C and Damascus. Hand engraves; does file work cuts filigree in the blade; offers ivory carving and precious metal inlay. **Remarks:** Full-time maker; first knife sold in 1994. Doing business as Al Scott Maker of Fine Blade Art. **Mark:** Name engraved in old English, sometime inlaid in 24K gold.

SCOTT, WINSTON, Rt. 2, Box 62, Huddleston, VA 24104, Phone: 703-297-6130
Specialties: Working knives. **Patterns:** Hunting and fishing knives. **Technical:** Grinds ATS-34, 440C and 154CM; likes full and narrow tangs, natural materials, sterling silver guards. **Prices:** $100 to $200; some to $400. **Remarks:** Part-time maker; first knife sold in 1984. **Mark:** Last name.

SCRIMSHAW BY LYNN BENADE, 2610 Buckhurst Dr, Beachwood, OH 44122, Phone: 216-464-0777

SCROGGS, JAMES A, 108 Murray Hill Dr, Warrensburg, MO 64093, Phone: (660) 747-2568
Specialties: Straight knives, prefers light weight. **Patterns:** Hunters, hideouts, and fighters. **Technical:** Grinds 5160, 01, and 52-100. Prefers handles of walnut in English, bastonge, American black Also uses myrtle, maple, Osage orange. **Prices:** $200-$1000. **Remarks:** 1st knife sold in 1985. Part-time maker, no orders taken. **Mark:** SCROGGS in block or script.

SCULLEY, PETER E, 340 Sunset Dr, Rising Fawn, GA 30738, Phone: (706) 398-0169

SEARS, MICK, 1697 Peach Orchard Rd. #302, Sumter, SC 29154, Phone: 803-499-5074
Specialties: Scots and confederate reproductions; Bowies and fighters. **Patterns:** Bowies, fighters. **Technical:** Grinds 440C and 1095. **Prices:** $50 to $150; some to $300. **Remarks:** Part-time maker; first knife sold in 1975. Doing business as Mick's Custom Knives. **Mark:** First name.

SELENT, CHUCK, P. O. Box 1207, Bonners Ferry, ID 83805-1207, Phone: 208-267-5807
Specialties: Period, art and fantasy miniatures; exotics; one-of-a-kinds. **Patterns:** Swords, daggers and others. **Technical:** Works in Damascus, meteorite, 440C and tool steel. Offers scrimshaw. Offers his own casting and leatherwork; uses jewelry techniques. Makes display cases for miniatures. **Prices:** $75 to $400. **Remarks:** Part-time maker; first knife sold in 1990. **Mark:** Last name and bear paw print logo scrimshawed on handles or leatherwork.

SELF, ERNIE, 950 O'Neill Ranch Rd., Dripping Springs, TX 78620-9760, Phone: 512-858-7133, Fax:512-858-9363
Specialties: Traditional and working straight knives and folders of his design and in standard patterns. **Patterns:** Hunters, locking folders and slip-joints. **Technical:** Grinds 440C, D2, 440V, ATS-34 and Damascus. Offers fancy filework. **Prices:** $125 to $500; some to $1,500. **Remarks:** Full-time maker; first knife sold in 1982. **Mark:** In oval shape - Ernie Self Maker Dripping Springs TX. **Other:** I also customize Buck 110's and 112's folding hunters.

SELLEVOLD, HARALD, S. Kleivesmau:2, PO Box 4134, N5834 Bergen, NORWAY, Phone: 55-310682
Specialties: Norwegian styles; collaborates with other Norse craftsmen. **Patterns:** Distinctive ferrules and other mild modifications of traditional patterns; Bowies and friction folders. **Technical:** Buys Damascus blades; blacksmiths his own blades. Semi-gemstones used in handles; gemstone inlay. **Prices:** $350 to $2,000. **Remarks:** Full-time maker; first knife sold in 1980. **Mark:** Name and country in logo.

SELVIDIO, RALPH, PO Box 1464, Crystal River, FL 34423, Phone: 352-628-1883
Specialties: Collector grade folders with unique mechanisms. **Patterns:** Locking folders. **Technical:** Grinds Damascus. **Prices:** $1000 to $6000. **Remarks:** Full-time maker; first knife sold in 1986. **Mark:** Rattler. **Other:** Doing business as Rattler brand Knives.

SENTZ, MARK C., 4084 Baptist Rd., Taneytown, MD 21787, Phone: 410-756-2018
Specialties: Fancy straight working knives of his design. **Patterns:** Hunters, fighters, folders and utility/camp knives. **Technical:** Forges 1085, 1095, 5160, 5155 and his Damascus. Most knives come with wood-lined leather sheath or wooden presentation sheath. **Prices:** Start at $275. **Remarks:** Full-time maker; first knife sold in 1989. Doing business as M. Charles Sentz Gunsmithing, Inc. **Mark:** Last name.

SERAFEN, STEVEN E., 24 Genesee St., New Berlin, NY 13411, Phone: 607-847-6903
Specialties: Traditional working/using straight knives of his design and to customer specs. **Patterns:** Bowies, fighters, hunters. **Technical:** Grinds ATS-34, 440C, high-carbon steel. **Prices:** $175 to $600; some to $1,200.

custom knifemakers

Remarks: Part-time maker; first knife sold in 1990. **Mark:** First and middle initial, last name in script.

SERVEN, JIM, P. O. Box 1, Fostoria, MI 48435, Phone: 517-795-2255
Specialties: Highly finished unique folders. **Patterns:** Fancy working folders, axes, miniatures and razors; some straight knives. **Technical:** Grinds 440C; forges his own Damascus. **Prices:** $150 to $800; some to $1,500. **Remarks:** Full-time maker; first knife sold in 1971. **Mark:** Name in map logo.

SEVEY CUSTOM KNIFE, 94595 Chandler Rd, Gold Beach, OR 97444, Phone: 541-247-2649
Specialties: Fixed blade hunters. **Patterns:** Drop point, trailing paint, clip paint, full tang hidden tang. **Technical:** D-2, & ATS-34 blades, stock removal. Heat treatment by Paul Bos. **Prices:** $225 and up depending on overall length & grip material. **Mark:** Sevey Custom Knife.

SHADLEY, EUGENE W., 26315 Norway Dr., Bovey, MN 55709, Phone: 218-245-3820, Fax:218-245-1639
Specialties: Classic multi-blade folders. **Patterns:** Whittlers, stockman, sowbelly, congress, trapper, etc. **Technical:** Grinds ATS-34, 416 frames. **Prices:** Start at $300. **Remarks:** Full-time maker; first knife sold in 1985. Doing business as Shadley Knives. **Mark:** Last name.

SHADMOT, BOAZ, Moshav Paran D N, Arava, ISRAEL 86835

SHARRIGAN, MUDD, 111 Bradford Rd, Wiscasset, ME 04578-4457, Phone: 207-882-9820, Fax:207-882-9835
Specialties: Wood carvers knives, custom designs, seaman's knives; repair straight knives, handles and blades on heirloom pieces; custom leather sheaths. **Patterns:** Daggers, fighters, hunters, buckskinner, Indian crooked knives and seamen working knives; traditional Scandinavian styles. **Technical:** Forges 1095, O1. Laminates 1095 and mild steel. **Prices:** $50 to $325; some to $1,200. **Remarks:** Full-time maker; first knife sold in 1982. **Mark:** First name and swallow tail carving.

SHEEHY, THOMAS J, 4131 NE 24th Ave, Portland, OR 97211-6411, Phone: (503) 493-2843
Specialties: Hunting knives and ULUs. **Patterns:** Own or customer designs. **Technical:** 1095/01 and ATS-34 steel. **Prices:** $35 to $200. **Remarks:** Do own heat treating; forged or ground blades. **Mark:** Name.

SHEETS, STEVEN WILLIAM, 6 Stonehouse Rd, Mendham, NJ 07945, Phone: (201) 543-5882

SHELTON, PAUL S., 1406 Holloway, Rolla, MO 65401, Phone: 314-364-3151
Specialties: Fancy working straight knives of his design or to customer specs. **Patterns:** All types from camp knives to miniatures, except folders. **Technical:** Grinds ATS-34 and commercial Damascus. Offers filework, texturing, natural handle materials and exotic leather sheaths. **Prices:** Start at $100. **Remarks:** Part-time maker; first knife sold in 1984. **Mark:** Last name and serial number.

SHIKAYAMA, TOSHIAKI, 259-2 Suka Yoshikawa City, Saitama 342-0057, JAPAN, Phone: 04-89-81-6605, Fax:04-89-81-6605
Specialties: Folders in standard patterns. **Patterns:** Locking and multi-blade folders. **Technical:** Grinds ATS, carbon steel, high speed steel. **Prices:** $400 to $2,500; $4,500 with engraving. **Remarks:** Full-time maker; first knife sold in 1952. **Mark:** First initial, last name.

SHINOSKY, ANDY, 3117 Meanderwood Dr, Canfield, OH 44406, Phone: 330-702-0299
Specialties: Collectible fancy folders and interframes. **Patterns:** Drop points, trailing points and daggers. **Technical:** Grinds ATS-34 and Damascus. Prefers natural handle materials. **Prices:** Start at $450. **Remarks:** Part-time maker; first knife sold in 1992. **Mark:** Name or bent folder logo.

SHIPLEY, STEVEN A, 800 E Campbell Rd Ste 137, Richardson, TX 75081, Phone: 972-644-7981, Fax:972-644-7985
Specialties: Hunters, skinners and traditional straight knives. **Technical:** Hand grinds ATS-34, 440C and Damascus steels. Each knife is custom sheathed by my son, Dan. **Prices:** $175 to $2000. **Remarks:** Part-time maker; like smooth lines and unusual handle materials. **Mark:** S A Shipley

SHOEBOTHAM, HEATHER, Heather's Blacksmith Shop, Private Bag 1890, Gold Reef City 2159 Johannesburg, SOUTH AFRICA, Phone: +27 11 496 1600, Fax:+27 11 835 2932
Specialties: All steel hand forged knives of my own design. **Patterns:** Traditional African weapons, friction folders and by-gone forged styles. **Technical:** Own Damascus, specializing in drive chain and steel wire rope, Meteorite, 420 & Mokume. Also using forged brass, copper and titanium fittings. All work hand-forged using a traditional coal fire. Differential heat-treatment used. **Prices:** $150 to $3,000. **Remarks:** Full-time practicing blacksmith and furrier and part-time bladesmith. First Damascus sold in 1995. First knife sold in 1998. Member of ABS. **Mark:** Knives: Rearing unicorn in horseshoe surround with first name. Damascus: Sold under "Damsel Damascus".

SHOEMAKER, CARROLL, 380 Yellowtown Rd., Northup, OH 45658, Phone: 740-446-6695
Specialties: Working/using straight knives of his design. **Patterns:** Hunters, utility/camp and early American backwoodsmen knives. **Technical:** Grinds ATS-34; forges old files, O1 and 1095. Uses some Damascus; offers scrimshaw and engraving. **Prices:** $100 to $175; some to $350. **Remarks:** Spare-time maker; first knife sold in 1977. **Mark:** Name and city or connected initials.

SHOEMAKER, SCOTT, 316 S. Main St., Miamisburg, OH 45342, Phone: 513-859-1935
Specialties: Twisted, wire-wrapped handles on swords, fighters and fantasy blades; new line of seven models with quick-draw, multi-carry Kydex sheaths. **Patterns:** Bowies, boots and one of a kinds in his design or to customer specs. **Technical:** Grinds A6 and ATS-34. Buys Damascus. Hand satin finish is standard. **Prices:** $100 to $1,500; swords to $8,000. **Remarks:** Part-time maker; first knife sold in 1984. **Mark:** Angel wings with last initial, or last name.

SHOGER, MARK O., 14780 SW Osprey Dr., Suite 345, Beaverton, OR 97007, Phone: 503-579-2495
Specialties: Working and using straight knives and folders of his design; fancy and embellished knives. **Patterns:** Hunters, Bowies, daggers and locking folders. **Technical:** Forges O1, W2 and his own pattern-welded Damascus. **Remarks:** Spare-time maker. **Mark:** Last name or stamped last initial over anvil.

SHORE, JOHN I, Alaska Knifemaker, 2901 Sheldon Jackson St, Anchorage, AK 99508, Phone: 907-272-2253
Specialties: Working straight knives, hatchets, and folders. **Patterns:**Hunters, skinners, Bowies, fighters, working using knives. **Technical:**Prefer using exotic steels, grinds most CPM's, Damasteel, RWL34, BG42 and some ATS34. Prefers exotic hardwoods, stabilized materials, Micarta, and Pearl. **Prices:** Start at $200. **Remarks:** Full-time maker; first knife sold in 1985. **Mark:** Name in script, Anchorage, AK.

SHOSTLE, BEN, 1121 Burlington, Muncie, IN 47302, Phone: 765-282-9073, Fax:765-282-5270
Specialties: Fancy high-art straight knives of his design. **Patterns:** Bowies, daggers and fighters. **Technical:** Uses 440C, ATS-34 and commercial Damascus. All knives and engraved. **Prices:** $900 to $3,200; some to $4,000. **Remarks:** Full-time maker; first knife sold in 1987. Doing business as The Gun Room (T. G. R.). **Mark:** Last name.

SIBRIAN, AARON, 4308 Dean Dr., Ventura, CA 93003, Phone: 805-642-6950
Specialties: Tough working knives of his design and in standard patterns. **Patterns:** Makes a "Viper utility"--a kukri derivative and a variety of straight using knives. **Technical:** Grinds 440C and ATS-34. Offers traditional Japanese blades; soft backs, hard edges, temper lines. **Prices:** $60 to $100; some to $250. **Remarks:** Spare-time maker; first knife sold in 1989. **Mark:** Initials in diagonal line.

SIGMAN, JAMES P., 10391 Church Rd, North Adams, MI 49262, Phone: 517-523-3058
Specialties: High-tech working knives of his design. **Patterns:** Daggers, hunters, fighters and folders. **Technical:** Forges and grinds L6, O1, W2 and his Damascus. **Prices:** $150 to $750. **Remarks:** Part-time maker; first knife sold in 1982. **Mark:** Sig or Sig Forge.

SIGMAN, CORBET R., Rt. 1, Box 260, Liberty, WV 25124, Phone: 304-586-9131
Specialties: Collectible working straight knives and folders. **Patterns:** Hunters, fighters, boots, camp knives and exotics such as sgian dubhs--distinctly Sigman lines; folders. **Technical:** Grinds D2, 154CM, plain carbon tool steel and ATS-34. **Prices:** $60 to $800; some to $4,000. **Remarks:** Full-time maker; first knife sold in 1970. **Mark:** Name or initials.

SIMMONS, H. R., 1100 Bay City Road, Aurora, NC 27806, Phone: 252-322-5969
Specialties: Working/using straight knives of his design. **Patterns:** Fighters, hunters and utility/camp knives. **Technical:** Forges and grinds Damascus and L6; grinds ATS-34. **Prices:** $150 to $250; some to $400. **Remarks:** Part-time maker; first knife sold in 1987. Doing business as HRS Custom Knives, Royal Forge & Trading Company. **Mark:** Initials.

SIMONELLA, GIANLUIGI, 15, via Rosa Brustolo, 33085 Maniago, ITALY, Phone: 01139-427-730350
Specialties: Traditional and classic folding and working/using knives of his design and to customer specs. **Patterns:** Bowies, fighters, hunters, utility/camp knives. **Technical:** Forges ATS-34, D2, 440C. **Prices:** $250 to $400; some to $1,000. **Remarks:** Full-time maker; first knife sold in 1988. **Mark:** Wilson.

SIMONICH, ROB, P. O. Box 278, Clancy, MT 59634, Phone: 406-933-8274
Specialties: Working knives in standard patterns. **Patterns:** Hunters, combat knives, Bowies and small fancy knives. **Technical:** Grinds D2, ATS-34 and 440C; forges own cable Damascus. Offers filework on most knives.

Prices: $75 to $300; some to $1,000. **Remarks:** Spare-time maker; first knife sold in 1984. Not currently taking orders. **Mark:** Last name in buffalo logo.

SIMONS, BILL, 6217 Michael Ln., Lakeland, FL 33811, Phone: 863-646-3783
Specialties: Working folders. **Patterns:** Locking folders, liner locks, hunters, slip joints most patterns; some straight camp knives. **Technical:** Grinds D2, ATS-34 and O1. **Prices:** Start at $100. **Remarks:** Full-time maker; first knife sold in 1970. **Mark:** Last name.

SIMS, JOHN PAUL, RT 1 Box 116B, Dekalb, TX 75559

SIMS, BOB, P. O. Box 772, Meridian, TX 76665, Phone: 254-435-6240, Fax:254-435-6240
Specialties: Traditional working straight knives and folders in standard patterns; banana/sheep foot blade combinations in trapper patterns. **Patterns:** Locking folders, slip-joint folders and hunters. **Technical:** Grinds D2, ATS-34 and O1. Offers filework on some knives. **Prices:** $150 to $275; some to $600. **Remarks:** Part-time maker; first knife sold in 1975. **Mark:** The division sign.

SINCLAIR, J. E., 520 Francis Rd., Pittsburgh, PA 15239, Phone: 412-793-5778
Specialties: Fancy hunters & fighters, liner locking folders. **Patterns:** Fighters, hunters and folders. **Technical:** Flat-grinds & hollow grind, prefers hand rubbed satin finish. Uses natural handle materials. **Prices:** $185 to $800. **Remarks:** Part-time maker; first knife sold in 1995. **Mark:** First and middle initials, last name and maker.

SINNICKSON, JOHN L, P O Box 103, Lyons, CO 80540

SINYARD, CLESTON S., 27522 Burkhardt Dr., Elberta, AL 36530, Phone: 334-987-1361
Specialties: Working straight knives and folders of his design. **Patterns:** Hunters, buckskinners, Bowies, daggers, fighters and all-Damascus folders. **Technical:** Makes Damascus from 440C, stainless steels, D2 and regular high-carbon steel; forges "forefinger pad" into hunters and skinners. **Prices:** In Damascus $450 to $1,500; some $2,500. **Remarks:** Full-time maker; first knife sold in 1980. Doing business as Nimo Forge. **Mark:** Last name, U. S. A. in anvil.

SISEMORE, CHARLES RUSSEL, RR 2 Box 329AL, Mena, AR 71953, Phone: 918-383-1360

SISKA, JIM, 6 Highland Ave., Westfield, MA 01085, Phone: 413-568-9787, Fax:413-568-6341
Specialties: Traditional working straight knives and folders. **Patterns:** Hunters, fighters, Bowies and one of a kinds; folders. **Technical:** Grinds D2 and ATS-34; buys Damascus. Likes exotic woods. **Prices:** $195 to $2,500. **Remarks:** Part-time maker; first knife sold in 1983. **Mark:** Last name in Old English.

SJOSTRAND, KEVIN, 1541 S. Cain St., Visalia, CA 93292, Phone: 209-625-5254
Specialties: Traditional and working/using straight knives and folders of his design or to customer specs. **Patterns:** Bowies, hunters, utility/camp knives, lockback, springbuck and liner lock folders. **Technical:** Grinds ATS-34, 440C and 1095. Prefers high polished blades and full tang. Natural and stabilized hardwoods, Micarta and stag handle material. **Prices:** $75 to $300. **Remarks:** Part-time maker; first knife sold in 1992. Doing business as Black Oak Blades. **Mark:** Oak tree, Black Oak Blades, name, or just last name.

SKELLERN, DR. M. J., P. O. Munster 4278, SOUTH AFRICA, Phone: 03930-92537, Fax:03931-76513
Specialties: Fancy high-tech folders of his design. **Patterns:** Locking and slip-joint folders. **Technical:** Grinds ATS-34 and Sandvick 12C27; uses Damascus. Inlays his stainless steel integral handles; offers rare African handle materials. **Prices:** $200 to $500; some to $700. **Remarks:** Part-time maker; first knife sold in 1986. **Mark:** Last name.

SKETOS, S TED, 5232 County Rd 34, Hartford, AL 36344, Phone: (334) 588-3172

SKOW, H. A. "TEX", Tex Custom Knives, 3534 Gravel Springs Rd, SENATOBIA, MS 38668, Phone: 662-301-1568
Specialties: One of a kind daggers, bowies, boot knives & hunters. **Patterns:** Different Damascus patterns (By Bob Eggerling). **Technical:** 440C, 58, 60 Rockwell hardness. **Prices:** Negotiable. **Remarks:** 30 hunters 10 collector knives per year. **Mark:** TEX.

SLEE, FRED, 9 John St., Morganville, NJ 07751, Phone: 908-591-9047
Specialties: Working straight knives, some fancy, to customer specs. **Patterns:** Hunters, fighters, boots, fancy daggers and folders. **Technical:** Grinds D2, 440C and ATS-34. **Prices:** $125 to $550. **Remarks:** Part-time maker; first knife sold in 1980. **Mark:** Last name in old English.

SLOAN, SHANE, Rt. 1, Box 17, Newcastle, TX 76372, Phone: 817-846-3290
Specialties: Collector-grade straight knives and folders. **Patterns:** Bowies, lockers, slip-joints, fancy folders, fighters and period pieces. **Technical:** Grinds D2 and ATS-34. Uses hand-rubbed satin finish. Prefers rare natural handle materials. **Prices:** $250 to $1,600. **Remarks:** Full-time maker; first knife sold in 1985. **Mark:** Name and city.

SLOBODIAN, SCOTT, 4101 River Ridge Dr., P. O. Box 1498, San Andreas, CA 95249, Phone: 209-286-1980, Fax:209-286-1982
Specialties: Japanese-style knives and swords, period pieces, fantasy pieces and miniatures. **Patterns:** Small kweikens, tantos, wakazashis, katanas, traditional samurai swords. **Technical:** Flat-grinds 1050, commercial Damascus. **Prices:** $800 to $3,500; some to $7,500. **Remarks:** Full-time maker; first knife sold in 1987. **Mark:** Blade signed in Japanese characters and various scripts.

SMALE, CHARLES J., 509 Grove Ave, Waukegan, IL 60085, Phone: (847) 244-8013

SMALL, ED, Rt. 1, Box 178-A, Keyser, WV 26726, Phone: 304-298-4254
Specialties: Working knives of his design; period pieces. **Patterns:** Hunters, daggers, buckskinners and camp knives; likes one of a kinds. **Technical:** Forges and grinds W2, L6 and his own Damascus. **Prices:** $150 to $1,500. **Remarks:** Full-time maker; first knife sold in 1978. Doing business as Iron Mountain Forge Works. **Mark:** Script initials connected.

SMALLWOOD, WAYNE, 146 Poplar Dr, Kalispell, MT 59901

SMART, STEVE, 1 Meadowbrook Cir., Melissa, TX 75454, Phone: 214-837-4216, Fax:214-837-4111
Specialties: Working/using straight knives and folders of his design, to customer specs and in standard patterns. **Patterns:** Bowies, hunters, kitchen knives, locking folders, utility/camp, fishing and bird knives. **Technical:** Grinds ATS-34, D2, 440C and O1. Prefers mirror polish or satin finish; hollow-grinds all blades. All knives come with sheath. Offers some filework. **Prices:** $95 to $225; some to $500. **Remarks:** Spare-time maker; first knife sold in 1983. **Mark:** Name, Custom, city and state in oval.

SMART, STEATEN, 15815 Acorn Circle, Tavares, FL 32778, Phone: 352-343-8423

SMIT, GLENN, 627 Cindy Ct., Aberdeen, MD 21001, Phone: 410-272-2959
Specialties: Working and using straight and folding knives of his design or to customer specs. Customizes and repairs all types of cutlery. Exclusive maker of Dave Murphy Style knives. **Patterns:** Hunters, Bowies, daggers, fighters, utility/camp, folders, kitchen knives and miniatures, Murphy combat, C. H. A. I. K., Little 88 and Tiny 90 styles. **Technical:** Grinds 440C, ATS-34, O1 and A2; reforges commercial Damascus and makes own Damascus, cast aluminum handles. **Prices:** Miniatures start at $20; full-size knives start at $40. **Remarks:** Spare-time maker; first knife sold in 1986. Doing business as Wolf's Knives. **Mark:** G. P. SMIT, with year on reverse side, Wolf's knives-Murphy's way with date.

SMIT, CORN, P. O. Box 31, Darwendale, Zimbabwe, SOUTH AFRICA, Phone: 110-263-69-3107
Specialties: Working/using knives, custom made collectors knives. Your design and customer specs. **Patterns:** Daggers, Bowies, hunters, and exclusive one off designs. **Technical:** Grind 440C stainless and D-2. We photo etch animals, names, logos, etc. on the blades. We do gold plating of etches and scrimshaw on handles. Guards can be brass or sterling sclens or horn. Handles indigenous wood or horns. **Prices:** $150 to $1,000; some to $5,000. **Remarks:** Full-time maker; first knife sold in 1984. We give a limited lifetime guarantee. **Mark:** Blacksmith - Zimbabwe with SMIT underneath.

SMITH, J. D., 516 E. Second St., No. 38, S. Boston, MA 02127, Phone: 617-828-4293
Specialties: Fighters, bowies, Persian, locking folders & swords. **Patterns:** Bowies, fighters and locking folders. **Technical:** Forges and grinds D2, his Damascus, O1, 52100 etc. and wootz-pattern hammer steel. **Prices:** $500 to $2,000; some to $5,000. **Remarks:** Full-time maker; first knife sold in 1987. Doing business as Hammersmith. **Mark:** Last initial alone or in cartouche.

SMITH, W. M., 802 W. Hwy. 90, Bonifay, FL 32425, Phone: 904-547-5935

SMITH, LENARD C, P O Box D68, Valley Cottage, NY 10989, Phone: (914) 268-7359

SMITH, BOBBIE D., 802 W. Hwy. 90., Bonifay, FL 32425, Phone: 904-547-5935
Specialties: Working straight knives and folders. **Patterns:** Bowies, hunters and slip-joints. **Technical:** Grinds 440C and ATS-34; custom sheaths for each knife. **Prices:** $75 to $250. **Remarks:** Part-time maker. **Mark:** NA.

SMITH, D. NOEL, 12018 NE Lonetree Ct, Poulsbo, WA 98370, Phone: 360-697-6992
Specialties: Fantasy art knives of his own design or to standard patterns. **Patterns:** Daggers, hunters and art knives. **Technical:** Grinds O1, D2, 440C stainless and Damascus. Offers natural and synthetic carved handles, engraved and acid etched blades, sculptured guards, butt caps and bases. **Prices:** Start at $250. **Remarks:** Full-time maker; first knife sold in 1990. Doing business as Minds' Eye Metal master. **Mark:** Signature.

SMITH, RICK, Bear Bone Knife Works, 1843 W Evans Creek Rd, Rogue River, OR 97537, Phone: 541-582-4144, Fax:541-582-4151
Specialties: Classic, historical style Bowies for re-enactors and custom sheaths. **Patterns:** Historical style Bowies, varied contemporary knife styles. **Technical:** Mostly made by stock removal method; also forge weld tri-cable Damascus blades. Do own heat treating & tempering using an Even heat digital kiln. Preferred steels are ATS-34, 154CM, 5160, D-2, 1095 and 01 tool & various carbon Damascus. **Prices:** $250 to $1,000. **Remarks:** Full-time maker since 1997 Now forging random pattern Damascus up to 600 layers. Discontinued using BG42 steel. **Mark:** "Bear Bone" over initials "R S" (separated by downward arrow) on blade; initials R S (separated by downward arrow) within a 3/8" circle; 2 shooting stars & a Bowie. Serial numbers appear on ricasso area of blade unless otherwise requested.

SMITH, GREGORY H., 8607 Coddington Ct., Louisville, KY 40299, Phone: 502-491-7439
Specialties: Traditional working straight knives and fantasy knives to customer specs. **Patterns:** Fighters and modified Bowies; camp knives and swords. **Technical:** Grinds O1, 440C and commercial Damascus bars. **Prices:** $55 to $300. **Remarks:** Part-time maker; first knife sold in 1985. **Mark:** JAGED, plus signature.

SMITH, JOHN M., 3450 E Beguelin Rd, Centralia, IL 62801, Phone: 618-249-6444, Fax:618-249-6444
Specialties: Traditional work knives, art knives. **Patterns:** daggers, Bowies, folders. **Technical:** Forges Damascus & hi-carbon. Also uses stainless. **Prices:** $250 to $2,500. **Remarks:** Full-time maker; first knife sold in 1980. **Mark:** Etched signature or logo.

SMITH, JOHN W., 1322 Cow Branch Rd, West Liberty, KY 41472, Phone: 606-743-3599
Specialties: Fancy and working locking folders of his design or to customer specs. **Patterns:** Interframes, traditional and daggers. **Technical:** Grinds 530V and my own Damascus. Offers gold inlay, engraving with gold inlay, hand-fitted mosaic pearl inlay and filework. Prefers hand-rubbed finish. Pearl and ivory available. **Prices:** Utility pieces $375-$650. Art knives $1200 to $10,000 **Remarks:** Full-time maker. **Mark:** Initials engraved inside diamond.

SMITH, JOSH, Box 683, Lincoln, MT 59639, Phone: 406-362-4112, Fax:406-362-4098
Specialties: Hunting knives, Mosaic Damascus. **Patterns:** Hunters, Bowies, fighters etc. **Technical:** Hand-forges 52100 and all types of Damascus. **Prices:** Start at $250. **Mark:** Josh Smith. **Other:** ABS Mastersmith.

SMITH, MICHAEL J., 1418 Saddle Gold Ct, Brandon, FL 33511, Phone: 813-431-3790
Specialties: Fancy high art folders of his design. **Patterns:** Locking locks and automatics. **Technical:** Uses ATS-34, non-stainless & stainless Damascus; hand carves folders, prefers ivory & pearl. Hand-rubbed satin finish. Liners are 6AL4V titanium. **Prices:** $500 to $3,000. **Remarks:** Full-time maker; first knife sold in 1989. **Mark:** Name, city, state.

SMITH, NEWMAN L., 676 Glades Rd., Shop #3, Gatlinburg, TN 37738, Phone: 423-436-3322
Specialties: Collector-grade and working knives. **Patterns:** Hunters, slip-joint and lock-back folders, some miniatures. **Technical:** Grinds O1 and ATS-34; makes fancy sheaths. **Prices:** $110 to $450; some to $1,000. **Remarks:** Full-time maker; first knife sold in 1984. Partners part-time to handle Damascus blades by Jeff Hurst; marks these with SH connected. **Mark:** First and middle initials, last name.

SMITH, RAYMOND L., 217 Red Chalk Rd, Erin, NY 14838, Phone: 607-795-5257
Specialties: Working/using straight knives and folders to customer specs and in standard patterns; period pieces. **Patterns:** Bowies, hunters, slip-joints. **Technical:** Forges 5160, 52100, 1018 Damascus and wire cable Damascus. Filework. **Prices:** $70 to $500 estimates for custom orders. **Remarks:** Part-time maker; first knife sold in 1991. ABS Master Smith. Doing business as The Anvils Edge. **Mark:** Initials in script.

SMITH JR., JAMES B. "RED", Rt. 2, Box 1525, Morven, GA 31638, Phone: 912-775-2844
Specialties: Folders. **Patterns:** Rotating rear-lock folders. **Technical:** Grinds ATS-34, D2 and Vascomax 350. **Prices:** Start at $350. **Remarks:** Full-time maker; first knife sold in 1985. **Mark:** GA RED in cowboy hat.

SMOCK, TIMOTHY E, 1105 N Sherwood Dr, Marion, IN 46952, Phone: (765) 664-0123

SMOKER, RAY, 113 Church Rd., Searcy, AR 72143, Phone: 501-796-2712
Specialties: Working/using fixed blades of his design only. **Patterns:** Hunters, skinners, utility/camp and flat-ground knives. **Technical:** Forges his own Damascus and 52100; makes sheaths. Uses improved multiple edge quench he developed. **Prices:** $140 to $200; price includes sheath. **Remarks:** Full-time maker; first knife sold in 1992. **Mark:** Last name.

SNARE, MICHAEL, 3352 E. Mescal St., Phoenix, AZ 85028

SNELL, JERRY L., 235 Woodsong Dr., Fayetteville, GA 30214, Phone: 770-461-0586
Specialties: Working straight knives of his design and in standard patterns. **Patterns:** Hunters, boots, fighters, daggers and a few folders. **Technical:** Grinds 440C, ATS-34; buys Damascus. **Prices:** $175 to $1,000. **Remarks:** Part-time maker. **Mark:** Last name, or name, city and state.

SNODY, MIKE, 7169 Silk Hope Rd, Liberty, NC 27298, Phone: 888-393-9534
Specialties: High performance straight knives in traditional & Japanese styles. **Patterns:** Skinners, hunters, tactical, Kwaiken &Tantos. **Technical:** Grinds BG-42, ATS-34, 440C & A-2. Offers full or tapered tangs, upgraded handle materials such as fossil ivory, coral and exotic woods. Traditional diamond wrap over stingray on Japanese style knives. Sheaths available in leather or Kydex. **Prices:** $100 to $1,000. **Remarks:** Part-time maker; first knife sold in 1999. **Mark:** Name over knife maker.

SNOW, BILL, 4824 18th Ave., Columbus, GA 31904, Phone: 706-576-4390
Specialties: Traditional working/using straight knives and folders of his design and to customer specs. Offers engraving and scrimshaw. **Patterns:** Bowies, fighters, hunters and folders. **Technical:** Grinds ATS-34, 440V, 440C, 420V, CPM350, BG42, A2, D2, 5160, 52100 and O1; forges if needed. Cryogenically quenches all steels; inlaid handles; some integrals; leather or Kydex sheaths. **Prices:** $125 to $700; some to $3,500. **Remarks:** Full-time maker; first knife sold in 1958. Doing business as Tipi Knife works. **Mark:** Old English scroll "S" inside a tipi.

SNYDER, MICHAEL TOM, P O Box 522, Zionsville, IN 46077-0522, Phone: (317) 873-6807

SOLOMON, MARVIN, 23750 Cold Springs Rd., Paron, AR 72122, Phone: 501-821-3170, Fax:501-821-6541
Specialties: Traditional working and using straight knives of his design and to customer specs also lock back 7 liner lock folders. **Patterns:** Single blade folders. **Technical:** Forges 5160, 1095, O1 and random Damascus. **Prices:** $125 to $1000. **Remarks:** Part-time maker; first knife sold in 1990. Doing business as Cold Springs Forge. **Mark:** Last name.

SONNTAG, DOUGLAS W., 906 N 39 St, Nixa, MO 65714, Phone: 417-693-1640, Fax:(417) 582-1392
Specialties: Working knives; art knives. **Patterns:** Hunters, boots, straight working knives; Bowies, some folders, camp/axe sets. **Technical:** Grinds D-2, ATS-34, forges own Damascus; does own heat treating. **Prices:** $175 to $500; some higher. **Remarks:** Part-time maker; first knife sold in 1986. **Mark:** Etched name in arch.

SONTHEIMER, G. DOUGLAS, 12604 Bridgeton Dr., Potomac, MD 20854, Phone: 301-948-5227
Specialties: Fixed blade knives. **Patterns:**White tale deer, backpackers, camp, claws, filet, fighters. **Technical:** Hollow Grinds. **Price:** $325 and up. **Remarks:** Spare-time maker; first knife sold in 1976. **Mark:** LORD.

SOPPERA, ARTHUR, Morgentalstr. 37, P. O. Box 708, CH-8038 Zurich, SWITZERLAND, Phone: 1-482 86 12, Fax:1-481 62 71
Specialties: High-art, high-tech knives of his design. **Patterns:** Mostly locking folders, some straight knives. **Technical:** Grinds ATS-34 and commercial Damascus. Folders have button lock of his own design; some are fancy folders in jeweler's fashion. Also makes jewelry with integrated small knives. **Prices:** $200 to $1,000; some $2,000 and higher. **Remarks:** Full-time maker; first knife sold in 1986. **Mark:** Stylized initials, name, country.

SORNBERGER, JIM, 25126 Overland Dr., Volcano, CA 95689, Phone: 209-295-7819
Specialties: Collectible straight knives. **Patterns:** Fighters, daggers, Bowies; miniatures; hunters, custom canes, liner locks folders. **Technical:** Grinds 440C, 154CM and ATS-34; engraves, carves and embellishes. **Prices:** $500 to $7,500 & up. **Remarks:** Full-time maker; first knife sold in 1970. **Mark:** First initial, last name, city and state.

SOWELL, BILL, 100 Loraine Forest Ct, Macon, GA 31210, Phone: 478- 994-9863
Specialties: Hunters, boot, Bowies, fighters, tactical. **Patterns:** Makes own Damascus, forges L-6, 5160, 1095. **Technical:** Grinds ATS-34. **Prices:** Starts at $150. **Remarks:** Part-time maker; first knife 1998. **Mark:** Iron Horse Knives; Iron Horse Forge.

SPARKS, BERNARD, PO Box 73, Dingle, ID 83233, Phone: 208-847-1883
Specialties: Maker engraved, working and art knives. Straight knives and folders of his own design. **Patterns:** Locking inner-frame folders, hunters, fighters, one-of-a-kind art knives. **Technical:** Grinds 530V steel, 440-C, 154CM, ATS-34, D-2 and forges by special order; triple temper, cryogenic soak. Mirror or hand finish **Prices:** $300 to $2000. **Remarks:** Full-time maker, first knife sold in 1967. **Mark:** Last name over state with a knife logo on each end of name. Prior 1980 stamp last name.

SPICKLER, GREGORY NOBLE, 5614 Mose Circle, Sharpsburg, MD 21782, Phone: (301) 432-2746

SPINALE, RICHARD, 4021 Canterbury Ct., Lorain, OH 44053, Phone: 440-282-1565
Specialties: High-art working knives of his design. **Patterns:** Hunters, fighters, daggers and locking folders. **Technical:** Grinds 440C, ATS-34 and 07; engraves. Offers gold bolsters and other deluxe treatments. **Prices:** $300 to $1,000; some to $3,000. **Remarks:** Spare-time maker; first knife sold in 1976. **Mark:** Name, address, year and model number.

SPIVEY, JEFFERSON, 9244 W. Wilshire, Yukon, OK 73099, Phone: 405-721-4442
Specialties: The Saber tooth: a combination hatchet, saw and knife. **Patterns:** Built for the wilderness, all are one of a kind. **Technical:** Grinds chromemoly steel. The saw tooth spine curves with a double row of biangular teeth. **Prices:** Start at $300. **Remarks:** First knife sold in 1977. **Mark:** Name and serial number.

SPRAGG, WAYNE E., P. O. Box 508, 1314 3675 East Rd., Ashton, ID 83420
Specialties: Working straight knives, some fancy. **Patterns:** Folders. **Technical:** Forges carbon steel and makes Damascus. **Prices:** $110 to $400; some higher. **Remarks:** All stainless heat-treated by Paul Bos. Carbon steel in shop heat treat. **Mark:** Name, city and state with bucking horse logo.

SPROUSE, TERRY, 1633 Newfound Rd., Asheville, NC 28806, Phone: 704-683-3400
Specialties: Traditional and working straight knives of his design. **Patterns:** Bowies and hunters. **Technical:** Grinds ATS-34, 440C and D2. Makes sheaths. **Prices:** $85 to $125; some to $225. **Remarks:** Part-time maker; first knife sold in 1989. **Mark:** NA.

ST CLAIR, THOMAS K, 12608 Fingerboard Rd, Monrovia, MD 21770, Phone: (301) 482-0264

ST. AMOUR, MURRAY, RR 3, 222 Dicks Rd, Pembroke ON, CANADA K8A 6W4, Phone: 613-735-1061
Specialties: Working fixed blades. **Patterns:** Hunters, fish, fighters, bowies and utility knives. **Technical:** Grinds ATS-34, 154-CM, CPM-440V and Damascus. **Prices:** $75 and up. **Remarks:** Full-time maker; sold first knife in 1992. **Mark:** Last name over Canada.

ST. CYR, H RED, 1218 N Cary Av., Wilmington, CA 90744, Phone: (310) 518-9525

STAFFORD, RICHARD, 104 Marcia Ct., Warner Robins, GA 31088, Phone: 912-923-6372
Specialties: High-tech straight knives and some folders. **Patterns:** Hunters in several patterns, fighters, boots, camp knives, combat knives and period pieces. **Technical:** Grinds ATS-34 and 440C; satin finish is standard. **Prices:** Starting at $75. **Remarks:** Part-time maker; first knife sold in 1983. **Mark:** Last name.

STANCER, CHUCK, 62 Hidden Ranch Rd NW, Calgary AB, CANADA T3A 5S5, Phone: (403) 295-7370

STANLEY, JOHN, 604 Elm Street, Crossett, AR 71635, Phone: (870) 304-3005
Specialties: Hand forged fixed blades with engraving and carving. **Patterns:** Scottish dirks, skeans and fantasy blades. **Technical:** Forge high carbon steel, own Damascus. Prices $70 to $500. **Remarks:** All work is sole authorship. **Mark:** Varies. **Other:** Offer engraving and carving services on other knives and handles.

STAPEL, CRAIG, Box 1617, Glendale, CA 91209, Phone: 213-668-2669
Specialties: Working knives. **Patterns:** Hunters, tantos and fishing knives. **Technical:** Grinds 440C and AEB-L. **Prices:** $80 to $150. **Remarks:** Spare-time maker; first knife sold in 1981. **Mark:** First and middle initials, last name.

STAPEL, CHUCK, Box 1617, Glendale, CA 91209, Phone: 213-66-KNIFE, Fax:213-669-1577
Specialties: Working knives of his design. **Patterns:** Variety of straight knives tantos, hunters, folders and utility knives. **Technical:** Grinds D2, 440C and AEB-L. **Prices:** $185 to $3,000. **Remarks:** Full-time maker; first knife sold in 1974. **Mark:** Last name or last name, U. S. A.

STAPLETON, WILLIAM E, 5425 Country Lane, Merritt Island, FL 32953, Phone: (407) 452-8946

STEFFEN, CHUCK, 504 Dogwood Ave NW, St Michael, MN, Phone: 763-497-6315
Specialties: Custom hunting knives, fixed blades folders, Specializing in exotic materials, Damascus excellent fit form & finishes.

STEGALL, KEITH, 2101 W. 32nd, Anchorage, AK 99517, Phone: 907-276-6002
Specialties: Traditional working straight knives. **Patterns:** Most patterns. **Technical:** Grinds 440C and 154CM. **Prices:** $100 to $300. **Remarks:** Spare-time maker; first knife sold in 1987. **Mark:** Name and state with anchor.

STEGNER, WILBUR G., 9242 173rd Ave. SW, Rochester, WA 98579, Phone: 360-273-0937
Specialties: Working/using straight knives and folders of his design. **Patterns:** Hunters and locking folders. **Technical:** Grinds ATS-34 and other tool steels. Quenches, tempers and hardness tests each blade. **Prices:** $80 to $600; some to $3,000. **Remarks:** Full-time maker; first knife sold in 1979. **Mark:** First and middle initials, last name in bar over shield logo.

STEIGER, MONTE L., Box 186, Genesee, ID 83832, Phone: 208-285-1769
Specialties: Traditional working/using straight knives of all designs. **Patterns:** Hunters, utility/camp knives. **Technical:** Grinds 1095, O1, 440C, ATS-34. Handles of stacked leather, natural wood, Micarta or Pakkawood. Each knife comes with right- or left-handed sheath. **Prices:** $70 to $220. **Remarks:** Spare-time maker; first knife sold in 1988. **Mark:** First initial, last name, city and state.

STEIGERWALT, KEN, P. O. Box 172, Orangeville, PA 17859, Phone: 717-683-5156
Specialties: Fancy classic folders of his design. **Patterns:** Folders, button locks and rear locks. **Technical:** Grinds ATS-34, 440C and commercial Damascus. Experiments with unique filework. **Prices:** $200 to $600; some to $1,500. **Remarks:** Full-time maker; first knife sold in 1981. **Mark:** Initials.

STEINAU, JURGEN, Julius-Hart Strasse 44, Berlin 0-1162, GERMANY, Phone: 372-6452512, Fax:372-645-2512
Specialties: Fantasy and high-art straight knives of his design. **Patterns:** Boots, daggers and switch-blade folders. **Technical:** Grinds 440B, 2379 and X90 Cr. Mo. V. 78. **Prices:** $1,500 to $2,500; some to $3,500. **Remarks:** Full-time maker; first knife sold in 1984. **Mark:** Symbol, plus year, month day and serial number.

STEINBERG, AL, 5244 Duenas, Laguna Woods, CA 92653, Phone: 949-951-2889
Specialties: Fancy working straight knives to customer specs. **Patterns:** Hunters, Bowies, fishing, camp knives, push knives and high end kitchen knives. **Technical:** Grinds O1, 440C and 154CM. **Prices:** $60 to $2,500. **Remarks:** Full-time maker; first knife sold in 1972. **Mark:** Signature, city and state.

STEKETEE, CRAIG A., 871 N. Hwy. 60, Billings, MO 65610, Phone: 417-744-2770
Specialties: Classic and working straight knives and swords of his design. **Patterns:** Bowies, hunters, and Japanese style swords . **Technical:** Forges his own Damascus; bronze, silver and Damascus fittings, offers filework. Prefers exotic and natural handle materials. **Prices:** $200 to $4,000. **Remarks:** Full-time maker. **Mark:** STEK.

STEPHAN, DANIEL, 2201 S. Miller Rd., Valrico, FL 33594, Phone: 813-684-2781

STERLING, MURRAY, 693 Round Peak Church Rd, Mount Airy, NC 27030, Phone: 336-352-5110, Fax:Fax: 336-352-5105
Specialties: Single & dual blade folders. Interframes & integral dovetail frames. **Technical:** Grinds ATS-34 or Damascus by Mike Norris and/or Devin Thomas. **Prices:** $300 & up. **Remarks:** Full-time maker; first knife sold in 1991. **Mark:** Last name stamped.

STEVENS, BARRY B., 901 Amherst, Cridersville, OH 45806, Phone: 419-221-2446
Specialties: Small fancy folders of his design and to customer specs; mini-hunters and fighters. **Patterns:** Fighters, hunters, liner locks, lockback and bolster release folders. **Technical:** Grinds ATS-34, 440C, Damascus and SS Damascus. Prefers hand-rubbed finishes and natural handle materials-horn, ivory, pearls, exotic woods. **Prices:** $300 to $1,000; some to $2,500. **Remarks:** Part-time maker; first knife sold in 1991. Doing business as Bare Knives. **Mark:** First and middle initials, last name.

STEWART, EDWARD L, 4297 Audrain Rd 335, Mexico, MO 65265, Phone: (573) 581-3883
Specialties: Fixed blades, working knives some art. **Patterns:** Hunters, Bowies, Utility/camp knives. **Technical:** Forging 1095-W-2-l-6-52100 makes own Damascus. **Prices:** $85-$500. **Remarks:** Part-time maker first knife sold in 1993. **Mark:** First and last initials-last name.

custom knifemakers

STIDHAM, RHETT & JANIE, P O Box 570, Roseland, FL 32957, Phone: (561) 589-0618

STIMPS, JASON M, 374 S Shaffer St, Orange, CA 92866, Phone: (714) 744-5866

STIPES, DWIGHT, 2651 SW Buena Vista Dr, Palm City, FL 34990, Phone: 561-597-0550
Specialties: Traditional and working straight knives in standard patterns. **Patterns:** Boots, Bowies, daggers, hunters and fighters. **Technical:** Grinds 440C, D2 and D3 tool steel. Handles of natural materials, animal, bone or horn. **Prices:** $75 to $150. **Remarks:** Full-time maker; first knife sold in 1972. **Mark:** Stipes.

STOCKWELL, WALTER, 368 San Carlos Ave, Redwood City, CA 94061, Phone: (650) 363-6069
Specialties: Scottish dirks. **Patterns:** All knives one-of-a-kind. **Technical:** Grinds ATS-34, forges 5160, 52100, L6. **Prices:** $125 - $500. **Remarks:** Part-time maker since 1992; graduate of ABS bladesmithing school. **Mark:** Shooting star over "STOCKWELL". Pre-2000, "WKS".

STODDARD'S, INC., COPLEY PLACE, 100 Huntington Ave, Boston, MA 02116, Phone: 617-536-8688, Fax:617-536-8689
Specialties: Cutlery (kitchen, pocket knives, Randall-made Knives, custom knives, scissors, & manicure tools) Binoculars, low vision aids, personal care items (hair brushes, manicure sets, mirrors.)

STODDART, W. B. BILL, 917 Smiley, Forest Park, OH 45240, Phone: 513-851-1543
Specialties: Sportsmen's working knives and multi-blade folders. **Patterns:** Hunters, camp and fish knives; multi-blade reproductions of old standards. **Technical:** Grinds A2, 440C and ATS-34; makes sheaths to match handle materials. **Prices:** $80 to $300; some to $850. **Remarks:** Part-time maker; first knife sold in 1976. **Mark:** Name, Cincinnati, state.

STOKES, ED, 22614 Cardinal Dr., Hockley, TX 77447, Phone: 713-351-1319
Specialties: Working straight knives and folders of all designs. **Patterns:** Boots, Bowies, daggers, fighters, hunters and miniatures. **Technical:** Grinds ATS-34, 440C and D2. Offers decorative butt caps, tapered spacers on handles and finger grooves, nickel-silver inlays, hand-made sheaths. **Prices:** $185 to $290; some to $350. **Remarks:** Full-time maker; first knife sold in 1973. **Mark:** First and last name, Custom Knives with Apache logo.

STONE, JERRY, P. O. Box 1027, Lytle, TX 78052, Phone: 512-772-4502
Specialties: Traditional working and using folders of his design and to customer specs; fancy knives. **Patterns:** Fighters, hunters, locking folders and slip-joints. **Technical:** Grinds 440C and ATS-34. Offers filework. **Prices:** $125 to $375; some to $700. **Remarks:** Full-time maker; first knife sold in 1973. **Mark:** Initials.

STORCH, ED, R. R. 4 Mannville, Alberta T0B 2W0, CANADA, Phone: 780-763-2214
Specialties: Working knives, fancy fighting knives, kitchen cutlery and art knives. **Patterns:** Working patterns, bowies and folders. **Technical:** Forges his own Damascus. Grinds ATS-34. Builds friction folders. **Prices:** $45 to $750 (US). **Remarks:** Part-time maker; first knife sold in 1984. **Mark:** Last Name.

STORMER, BOB, 10 Karabair Rd, St Peters, MO 63376, Phone: 636-441-6807
Specialties: Straight knives - Using collector grade. **Patterns:** Bowies, skinners, hunters, camp knives. **Technical:** Forges 5160, 1095. **Prices:** $150-$400. **Remarks:** Part-time maker ABS journeyman smith 2001. **Mark:** Setting Sun/Fall trees/Initials.

STOUT, JOHNNY, 1205 Forest Trail, New Braunfels, TX 78132, Phone: 830-606-4067
Specialties: Folders, some fixed blades. Working knives, some fancy. **Patterns:** Hunters, tactical, Bowies, automatics, liner locks and slip-joints. **Technical:** Grinds stainless and carbon steels; forges own Damascus. **Prices:** $450 to $895; some to $3,500. **Remarks:** Full-time maker; first knife sold in 1983. **Mark:** Name and city in logo with serial number.

STOUT, CHARLES, Rt3 178 Stout Rd, Gillham, AR 71841, Phone: (870) 386-5521

STOVER, JAMES K, HC 60 Box 1260, Lakeview, OR 97630, Phone: (541) 947-4008

STOVER, HOWARD, 100 Palmetto Dr Apt7, Pasadena, CA 91105, Phone: (765) 452-3928

STOVER, TERRY "LEE", 1809 N. 300 E., Kokomo, IN 46901, Phone: 765-452-3928
Specialties: Damascus folders with filework; Damascus Bowies of his design or to customer specs. **Patterns:** Lockback folders and Sheffield-style Bowies. **Technical:** Forges 1095, Damascus using O2, 203E or O2, pure nickel. Makes mokume. Uses only natural handle material. **Prices:**

$300 to $1,700; some to $2,000. **Remarks:** Part-time maker; first knife sold in 1984. **Mark:** First and middle initials, last name in knife logo; Damascus blades marked in Old English.

STRAIGHT, KENNETH J, 11311 103 Lane N., Largo, FL 33773, Phone: (813) 397-9817

STRAIGHT, DON, P. O. Box 12, Points, WV 25437, Phone: 304-492-5471
Specialties: Traditional working straight knives of his design. **Patterns:** Hunters, Bowies and fighters. **Technical:** Grinds 440C, ATS-34 and D2. **Prices:** $75 to $125; some to $225. **Remarks:** Spare-time maker; first knife sold in 1978. **Mark:** Last name.

STRANDE, POUL, Soster Svenstrup Byvej 16, Dastrup 4130 Viby Sj., DENMARK, Phone: 46 19 43 05, Fax:46 19 53 19
Specialties: Classic fantasy working knives; Damasceret blade, Nikkel Damasceret blade, Lamineret - Lamineret blade with Nikkel. **Patterns:** Bowies, daggers, fighters, hunters and swords. **Technical:** Uses carbon steel and 15C20 steel. **Remarks:** NA. **Remarks:** Full-time maker; first knife sold in 1985. **Mark:** First and last initials.

STRICKLAND, DALE, 1440 E. Thompson View, Monroe, UT 84754, Phone: 435-896-8362
Specialties: Traditional and working straight knives and folders of his design and to customer specs. **Patterns:** Hunters, folders, miniatures and utility knives. **Technical:** Grinds Damascus and 440C. **Prices:** $120 to $350; some to $500. **Remarks:** Part-time maker; first knife sold in 1991. **Mark:** Oval stamp of name, Maker.

STRONG, SCOTT, 2138 Oxmoor Dr., Beavercreek, OH 45431, Phone: 937-426-9290
Specialties: Working knives, some deluxe. **Patterns:** Hunters, fighters, survival and military-style knives, art knives. **Technical:** Forges and grinds O1, A2, D2, 440C and ATS-34. Uses no solder; most knives disassemble. **Prices:** $75 to $450; some to $1,500. **Remarks:** Spare-time maker; first knife sold in 1983. **Mark:** Strong Knives.

STROYAN, ERIC, Box 218, Dalton, PA 18414, Phone: 717-563-2603
Specialties: Classic and working/using straight knives and folders of his design. **Patterns:** Hunters, locking folders, slip-joints. **Technical:** Forges Damascus; grinds ATS-34, D2. **Prices:** $200 to $600; some to $2,000. **Remarks:** Part-time maker; first knife sold in 1968. **Mark:** Signature or initials stamp.

STUART, STEVE, Box 168, Gores Landing, Ont., CANADA K0K 2E0, Phone: 905-342-5617
Specialties: Straight knives. **Patterns:** Tantos, fighters, skinners, file and rasp knives. **Technical:** Uses 440C, files, Micarta and natural handle materials. **Prices:** $60 to $400. **Remarks:** Part-time maker. **Mark:** Interlocking SS with last name.

SUEDMEIER, HARLAN, RFD 2, Box 299D, Nebraska City, NE 68410, Phone: 402-873-4372
Specialties: Working straight knives. **Patterns:** Hunters, fighters and Bowies. **Technical:** Grinds ATS-34 and 440C; forges 52100. **Prices:** Start at $75. **Remarks:** Part-time maker; first knife sold in 1982. Not currently taking orders. **Mark:** First initial, last name.

SUGIHARA, KEIDOH, 4-16-1 Kamori-Cho, Kishiwada City, Osaka, F596-0042, JAPAN, Fax:0724-44-2677
Specialties: High-tech working straight knives and folders of his design. **Patterns:** Bowies, hunters, fighters, fishing, boots, some pocket knives and liner lock folders. **Technical:** Grinds ATS-34, COS-25, buys Damascus and high carbon steels. Prices $60 to $4000. **Remarks:** Full-time maker, first knife sold in 1980. **Mark:** Initial logo with fish design.

SUGIYAMA, EDDY K., 2361 Nagayu Naoirimachi Naoirigun, Ohita, JAPAN, Phone: 0974-75-2050

SUMMERS, ARTHUR L., 8700 Brigner Rd., Mechanicsburg, OH 43044, Phone: 937-834-3776
Specialties: Collector-grade knives in drop points, clip points or straight blades. **Patterns:** Fighters, hunters, Bowies and personal knives. **Technical:** Grinds 440C, ATS-34, D2 and Damascus. **Prices:** $150 to $650; some to $2,000. **Remarks:** Part-time maker; first knife sold in 1987. **Mark:** Last name and serial number.

SUMMERS, DENNIS K., 827 E. Cecil St., Springfield, OH 45503, Phone: 513-324-0624
Specialties: Working/using knives. **Patterns:** Fighters and personal knives. **Technical:** Grinds 440C, A2 and D2. Makes drop and clip point. **Prices:** $75 to $200. **Remarks:** Part-time maker; first knife sold in 1995. **Mark:** First and middle initials, last name, serial number.

SUMMERS, DAN, 2675 NY Rt. 11, Whitney Pt., NY 13862, Phone: 607-692-2391
Specialties: Period knives and tomahawks. **Technical:** All hand forging. **Prices:** Most $100 to $400.

SUNDERLAND, RICHARD, Box 248, Quathiaski Cove, BC, CANADA V0P 1N0, Phone: 250-285-3038
Specialties: Personal and hunting knives with carved handles in oosic and ivory. **Patterns:** Hunters, Bowies, daggers, camp and personal knives. **Technical:** Grinds 440C, ATS 34 and O1. Handle materials of rosewoods, fossil mammoth ivory and oosic. **Prices:** $150 to $1,000. **Remarks:** Full-time maker; first knife sold in 1983. Doing business as Sun Knife Co. **Mark:** SUN.

SUTTON, S. RUSSELL, 4900 Cypress Shores Dr., New Bern, NC 28562, Phone: 252-637-3963
Specialties: Straight knives and folders to customer specs and in standard patterns. **Patterns:** Boots, hunters, interframes and locking liners. **Technical:** Grinds ATS-34, 440C and stainless Damascus. **Prices:** $185 to $650; some to $950. **Remarks:** Full-time maker; first knife sold in 1992. **Mark:** Etched last name.

SWEAZA, DENNIS, 4052 Hwy 321 E, Austin, AR 72007, Phone: (501) 941-1886

SWEDER, JORAM, Tilaru Metalsmithing, PO Box 4175, Ocala, FL 34470, Phone: 352-546-4438
Specialties: Hand forged one-of-a-kind and custom pieces. **Prices:** $100 and up.

SWEENEY, COLTIN D, 4915 49 St Sw, Great Falls, MT 59404, Phone: (406) 452-9887

SWYHART, ART, 509 Main St., P. O. Box 267, Klickitat, WA 98628, Phone: 509-369-3451
Specialties: Traditional working and using knives of his design. **Patterns:** Bowies, hunters and utility/camp knives. **Technical:** Forges 52100, 5160 and Damascus 1084 mixed with either 15N20 or 0186. Blades differentially heat-treated with visible temper line. **Prices:** $75 to $250; some to $350. **Remarks:** Part-time maker; first knife sold in 1983. **Mark:** First name, last initial in script.

SYMONDS, ALBERTO E, Rambla M Gandhi 485, Apt 901, Montevideo 11300, URUGUAY, Phone: 011 598 2 7103201(Phone & Fax), Fax:011 598 5608207 (Phone & Fax)

SYSLO, CHUCK, 3418 South 116 Ave., Omaha, NE 68144, Phone: 402-333-0647
Specialties: High-tech working straight knives. **Patterns:** Hunters, daggers and survival knives; locking folders. **Technical:** Flat-grinds D2, 440C and 154CM; hand polishes only. **Prices:** $175 to $500; some to $3,000. **Remarks:** Part-time maker; first knife sold in 1978. **Mark:** CISCO in logo.

SZAREK, MARK G, 94 Oakwood Av, Revere, MA 02151, Phone: (781) 289-7102
Specialties: Classic period working & using straight knives and tools. **Patterns:** Hunting knives, American & Japanese woodworking tools. **Technical:** Forges 5160, 1050, Damascus; differentially hardens blades with fireclay. **Prices:** $50 to $750. **Remarks:** Part-time maker; first knife sold in 1989. **Mark:** Last name. **Other:** Produces Japanese alloys for sword fittings and accessories. Custom builds knife presentation boxes and cabinets.

SZILASKI, JOSEPH, 29 Carroll Dr., Wappingers Falls, NY 12590, Phone: 845-297-5397
Specialties: Straight knives, folders and tomahawks of his design, to customer specs and in standard patterns. Many pieces are one of a kind. **Patterns:** Bowies, daggers, fighters, hunters, art knives and early American styles. **Technical:** Forges A2, D2, O1 and Damascus. **Prices:** $450 to $4000; some to $10,000. **Remarks:** Full-time maker; first knife sold in 1990. **Mark:** Snake logo. **Other:** ABS mastersmith and voting member KMG.

t

TAKAHASHI, MASAO, 39-3 Sekine-machi, Maebashi-shi, Gunma 371 0047, JAPAN, Phone: 81 27 234 2223, Fax:81 27 234 2223
Specialties: Working straight knives. **Patterns:** Daggers, fighters, hunters, fishing knives, boots. **Technical:** Grinds ATS-34 & Damascus. **Prices:** $350 to $1000 & up. **Remarks:** Full-time maker; first knife sold in 1982. **Mark:** M. Takahashi.

TAKAHASHI, KAORU, 2506 Toyo Oka Yado Ueki, Kamoto, Kumamoto, JAPAN 861-01, Phone: (8196) 272-6759

TALLY, GRANT C., 14618 Cicotte, Allen Park, MI 48101, Phone: 313-381-0100
Specialties: Straight knives and folders of his design. **Patterns:** Bowies, daggers, fighters. **Technical:** Grinds ATS-34, 440C and D2. Offers filework. **Prices:** $250 to $1000. **Remarks:** Part-time maker; first knife sold in 1985. Doing business as Tally Knives. **Mark:**Tally (last name).

TAMBOLI, MICHAEL, 12447 N. 49 Ave., Glendale, AZ 85304, Phone: 602-978-4308
Specialties: Miniatures, some full size. **Patterns:** Miniature hunting knives to fantasy art knives. **Technical:** Grinds 440C, 154CM and Damascus. **Prices:** $75 to $500; some to $1,000. **Remarks:** Part-time maker; first knife sold in 1978. **Mark:** Initials or last name, city and state.

TASMAN, KERLEY, 9 Avignon Retreat, Pt. Kennedy, 6172, Western Australia, AUSTRALIA, Phone: 61-8-9593-0554
Specialties: Consulting designer for Futed Knives, Commissioned to make a presentation knife for Maeda Asano Ryushin. Design and manufacture of knife/harness/sheath systemd for elite martial artist, body guards and Australian Army personnel with spedific weaponry needs. **Patterns:** Small personal knives including liner lock style folders, hunters, and popular designs for the Australian bush, Sheffield bowies, urban utility knives and occasionally knives to a customers specific design. **Technical:** Blades of ATS_34, 440C, O1, D2.

TAY, LARRY C-G, Siglap P. O. Box 315, Singapore 9145, SINGAPORE, Phone: 65-2419421, Fax:65-2434879
Specialties: Push knives, working and using straight knives and folders of his design; Marble's Safety Knife with stained or albino Asian buffalo horn and bone or rosewood handles. **Patterns:** Fighters and utility/camp knives. **Technical:** Forges and grinds D2, truck leaf springs. **Prices:** $200 to $1,000. **Remarks:** Spare-time maker; first knife sold in 1957. **Mark:** LDA/LAKELL, from 1999 initials L. T.

TAYLOR, SHANE, 18 Broken Bow Ln., Miles City, MT 59301, Phone: 406-232-7175
Specialties: One-of-a-kind fancy Damascus straight knives and folders. **Patterns:** Bowies, folders and fighters. **Technical:** Forges own mosaic and pattern welded Damascus. **Prices:** $450 and up. **Remarks:** ABS mastersmith,full-time maker; first knife sold in 1982. **Mark:** First name.

TAYLOR, SCOTT, 18124 B La Salle Av, Gardena, CA 90248, Phone: (310) 538-8104

TAYLOR, C. GRAY, 560 Poteat Ln, Fall Branch, TN 37656, Phone: 423-348-8304
Specialties: High-art display knives; period pieces. **Patterns:** Fighters, Bowies, daggers, locking folders and interframes. **Technical:** Grinds 440C, 154CM and ATS-34. **Prices:** $350 and up. **Remarks:** Full-time maker; first knife sold in 1975. **Mark:** Name, city and state.

TAYLOR, BILLY, 10 Temple Rd., Petal, MS 39465, Phone: 601-544-0041
Specialties: Straight knives of his design. **Patterns:** Bowies, skinners, hunters and utility knives. **Technical:** Flat-grinds 440C, ATS-34 and 154CM. **Prices:** $60 to $300. **Remarks:** Part-time maker; first knife sold in 1991. **Mark:** Full name, city and state.

TERAUCHI, TOSHIYUKI, 7649-13 219-11 Yoshida, Fujita-Cho Gobo-Shi, JAPAN

TERRILL, STEPHEN, 21363 Rd. 196, Lindsay, CA 93247, Phone: 209-562-4395
Specialties: Deluxe working straight knives and folders. **Patterns:** Fighters, tantos, boots, locking folders and axes; traditional oriental patterns. **Technical:** Forges 440C, 1084 and his Damascus. **Prices:** Moderate. **Remarks:** Part-time maker; first knife sold in 1972. **Mark:** Name, city, state in logo.

TERZUOLA, ROBERT, 3933 Agua Fria St, Santa Fe, NM 87501, Phone: 505-473-1002, Fax:505-438-8018
Specialties: Working folders of his design; period pieces. **Patterns:** High-tech utility, defense and gentleman's folders. **Technical:** Grinds154CM and CPM 530V/odd carbon fiber. Offers titanium and G10 carbon fiber composite for side-lock folders & tactical folders. **Prices:** $375 to $1200, carbon fiber. **Remarks:** Full-time maker; first knife sold in 1980. **Mark:** Mayan dragon head, name.

THAYER, DANNY O, 8908S 100W, Romney, IN 47981, Phone: (765) 538-3105
Specialties: Hunters, fighters, Bowies. **Prices:** $250 and up.

THEIS, TERRY, 21452 FM 2093, Harper, TX 78631, Phone: 830-864-4438
Specialties: All European and American engraving styles. **Prices:** $200 to $2,000. **Remarks:** Engraver only.

THEUNS PRINSLOO KNIVES, PO Box 2263, Bethlehem, 9700, SOUTH AFRICA, Phone: 27 58 3037111, Fax:same
Specialties: Fancy Folders. **Technical:** Own Damascus and Mokume

THEVENOT, JEAN-PAUL, 16 Rue De La Prefecture, Dijon, FRANCE 21000

THILL, JIM, 10242 Bear Run, Missoula, MT 59803, Phone: 406-251-5475
Specialties: Traditional and working/using knives of his design. **Patterns:** Fighters, hunters and utility/camp knives. **Technical:** Grinds D2 and ATS-34; forges 10-95-85, 52100, 5160, 10 series, reg. Damascus-mosaic.

Offers hand cut sheaths with rawhide lace. **Prices:** $145 to $350; some to $1,250. **Remarks:** Full-time maker; first knife sold in 1962. **Mark:** Running bear in triangle.

THOMAS, ROCKY, 1716 Waterside Blvd, Moncks Corner, SC 29461, Phone: 843-761-7761
Specialties: Traditional working and using straight knives in standard patterns. **Patterns:** Hunters and utility/camp knives. **Technical:** Grinds 440C, ATS-34 and commercial Damascus. **Prices:** $85 to $150. **Remarks:** Spare-time maker; first knife sold in 1986. **Mark:** First name in script and/or block.

THOMAS, DANIEL, 142 Club House Dr SW Apt 302, Leesburg, VA 20175-4244, Phone: 703-442-6877
Specialties: Traditional working and using straight knives and folders of his design. **Patterns:** Hunters, slip-joint and locking folders. **Technical:** Grinds ATS-34, D2 and commercial Damascus. Offers fixed blade and folder repair and rebuilding. **Prices:** $125 to $200; some to $350. **Remarks:** Spare-time maker; first knife sold in 1983. **Mark:** Last name, Handcrafted.

THOMAS, KIM, PO Box 531, Seville, OH 44273, Phone: 330-769-9906
Specialties: Fancy and traditional straight knives of his design and to customer specs; period pieces. **Patterns:** Boots, daggers, fighters, swords. **Technical:** Forges own Damascus from 5160, 1010 and nickel. **Prices:** $135 to $1,500; some to $3,000. **Remarks:** Part-time maker; first knife sold in 1986. Doing business as Thomas Iron Works. **Mark:** KT.

THOMAS, BOB G, RR 1 Box 121, Thebes, IL 62990-9718

THOMAS, DEVIN, 90 N. 5th St., Panaca, NV 89042, Phone: 775-728-4363
Specialties: Traditional straight knives and folders in standard patterns. **Patterns:** Bowies, fighters, hunters. **Technical:** Forges stainless Damascus, nickel and 1095. Uses, makes and sells Mokume with brass, copper and nickel-silver. **Prices:** $300 to $1,200. **Remarks:** Full-time maker; first knife sold in 1979. **Mark:** First and last name, city and state with anvil, or first name only.

HASLINGER, THOMAS, 164 Fairview Dr. SE, Calgary, Alberta
Specialties: One-of-a-kind using knives, working knives and art knives. **Patterns:** No fixed patterns, likes to work with customers on design. **Technical:** Grinds BG 42, ATS 34 and Damascus, high end satin finish. Prefers natural handle materials e. g. ancient ivory, stag, pear, abalone, stone and exotic woods. I do inlay work with stone, some sterling silver, niobium and gold wire work. Custom sheaths using matching woods or hand stitched with unique leather like sturgeon, Nile perch or carp. Offers engraving. **Prices:** Starting at $150. 00. **Remarks:** Full-time maker: first knife sold in 1994. Doing business as Haslinger Custom Knives. **Mark:** 2 marks used, high end work uses stylized initials, other uses elk antler with Thomas Haslinger, Canada, handcrafted above.

THOMAS, DAVID E, 8502 Hwy 91, Lillian, AL 36549, Phone: (334) 961-7574
Specialties: Bowies & hunters. **Technical:** Hand forged blades in 5160, 1095 and own Damascus. **Prices:** $400 & up. **Mark:** Stylized DT, maker's last name, serial number.

THOMPSON, TOMMY, 4015 NE Hassalo, Portland, OR 97232-2607, Phone: 503-235-5762
Specialties: Fancy and working knives; mostly liner lock folders. **Patterns:** Fighters, hunters and liner locks. **Technical:** Grinds D2, ATS-34, CPM440V and T15. Handles are either hardwood inlaid with wood banding and stone or shell, or made of agate, jasper, petrified woods, etc. **Prices:** $75 to $500; some to $1,000. **Remarks:** Part-time maker; first knife sold in 1987. Doing business as Stone Birds. **Mark:** First and last name, city and state. **Other:** Knife making temporarily stopped due to family obligations.

THOMPSON, LLOYD, P. O. Box 1664, Pagosa Springs, CO 81147, Phone: 970-264-5837
Specialties: Working and collectible straight knives and folders of his design. **Patterns:** Straight blades, lock back folders & slip joint folders. **Technical:** Hollow-grinds ATS-34, D2 and O1. Uses sambar stag and exotic woods. **Prices:** $150 to upscale. **Remarks:** Full-time maker; first knife sold in 1985. Doing business as Trapper Creek Knife Co. Offers 3 day knife making classes. **Mark:** Name.

THOMPSON, KENNETH, 4887 Glenwhite Dr., Duluth, GA 30136, Phone: 770-446-6730
Specialties: Traditional working and using knives of his design. **Patterns:** Hunters, Bowies and utility/camp knives. **Technical:** Forges 5168, O1, 1095 and 52100. **Prices:** $75 to $1,500; some to $2,500. **Remarks:** Part-time maker; first knife sold in 1990. **Mark:** P/W; or name, P/W, city and state.

THOMPSON, LEON, 45723 S. W. Saddleback Dr, Gaston, OR 97119, Phone: 503-357-2573
Specialties: Working knives. **Patterns:** Locking folders, slip-joints and liner locks. **Technical:** Grinds ATS-34, D2 and 440C. **Prices:** $200 to

$600. **Remarks:** Full-time maker; first knife sold in 1976. **Mark:** First and middle initials, last name, city and state.

THOMSEN, LOYD W., HCR-46, Box 19, Oelrichs, SD 57763, Phone: 605-535-6162
Specialties: High-art and traditional working/using straight knives and presentation pieces of his design and to customer specs; period pieces. Hand carved animals in crown of stag on handles and carved display stands. **Patterns:** Bowies, hunters, daggers and utility/camp knives. **Technical:** Forges and grinds 1095HC, 1084, L6, 15N20, 440C stainless steel, nickel 200; special restoration process on period pieces. Makes sheaths. Uses natural materials for handles. **Prices:** $350 to $1,000. **Remarks:** Full-time maker; first knife sold in 1995. Doing business as Horsehead Creek Knives. **Mark:** Initials and last name over a horse's head.

THOUROT, MICHAEL W., T-814 Co. Road 11, Napoleon, OH 43545, Phone: 419-533-6832, Fax:419-533-3516
Specialties: Working straight knives to customer specs. Designed two-handled skinning ax and limited edition engraved knife and art print set. **Patterns:** Fishing and fillet knives, Bowies, tantos and hunters. **Technical:** Grinds O1, D2, 440C and Damascus. **Prices:** $200 to $5,000. **Remarks:** Part-time maker; first knife sold in 1968. **Mark:** Initials.

THUESEN, ED, 21211 Knolle Rd, Damon, TX 77430, Phone: 979-553-1211, Fax:979-553-1211
Specialties: Working straight knives. **Patterns:** Hunters, fighters and survival knives. **Technical:** Grinds D2, 440C, ATS-34 and Vascowear. **Prices:** $150 to $275; some to $600. **Remarks:** Part-time maker; first knife sold in 1979. Runs knife maker supply business. **Mark:** Last name in script.

THUESEN, KEVIN, 10649 Haddington, Suite 180, Houston, TX 77043, Phone: 713-461-8632
Specialties: Working straight knives. **Patterns:** Hunters, including upswept skinners, and custom walking sticks. **Technical:** Grinds D2, 440C, 154CM and ATS-34. **Prices:** $85 to $125; some to $200. **Remarks:** Part-time maker; first knife sold in 1985. **Mark:** Initials on slant.

TICHBOURNE, GEORGE, 7035 Maxwell Rd. #5, Mississauga, Ont., CANADA L5S 1R5, Phone: 905-670-0200, Fax:905-670-0200
Specialties: Traditional working and using knives as well as unique collectibles. **Patterns:** Bowies, hunters, outdoor, kitchen integrals-art-military folders. **Technical:** Stock removal-440C, Stellite 6K, Damasteel, Mammoth, Meteorite, Mother of Pearl, Mosaic, Abalone, Stag. **Prices:** $40 up to $1800 US dollars. **Remarks:** Full-time maker; first knife sold in 1990. **Mark:** Full name over maple leaf. **Other:** Works in Stellite 6K, Damasteel, Mammuth, Meteorite, Mother of Pear.

TIENSVOLD, ALAN L, P O Box 355, Rushville, NE 69360, Phone: (308) 327-2046
Specialties: Working knives, primitive designs & period pieces. **Patterns:** Bowies, hunters, skinners. **Technical:** Forge own Damascus using 15N20 & 1084. **Prices:** $200 & up. **Remarks:** Have been interested & studying knife making since 1979. **Mark:** Tiensvold Handmade U. S. A. **Other:** Also do all my own engraving & fine work.

TIENSVOLD, JASON, P O Box 795, Rushville, NE 69360, Phone: (308) 327-2046
Specialties: Working & using straight knives of my design; period pieces. **Patterns:** Hunters, skinners, Bowies, fighters, daggers. **Technical:** Forge my own Damascus using 15N20 & 1084, custom file work. **Prices:** $200 & up. **Remarks:** Part-time maker, first knife sold in 1994; doing business under Tiensvold Custom Knives. **Mark:** Tiensvold USA Handmade in a circle.

TIGHE, BRIAN, RR 1, Ridgeville, Ont, CANADA L0S 1M0, Phone: 905-892-2734, Fax:905-892-2734
Specialties: High tech tactical folders. **Patterns:** Boots, daggers, locking and slip-joint folders. **Technical:** CPM 440V & CPM 420V. Prefers natural handle material inlay; hand finishes. **Prices:** $450 to $2000. **Remarks:** Part-time maker; first knife sold in 1989. **Mark:** Etched signature.

TILL, CALVIN E. AND RUTH, 211 Chaping, Chadron, NE 69337
Specialties: Straight knives hunters, bowies no folders **Patterns:** Training point, drop point hunters, bowies. **Technical:** ATS-34 sub zero quench RC-59, 61. **Prices:** $700 to $1200. **Remarks:** I sell only the absolute best knives I can make. **Mark:** RC Till. The R is for my wife Ruth. **Other:** I manufacture every part in my knives.

TILTON, JOHN, 24041 Hwy 383, Iowa, LA 70647, Phone: 337-582-6785
Specialties: Camp knives and skinners. **Technical:** All forged blades. **Prices:** $125 and up. **Mark:** Initials J. E. T. **Other:** ABS Journeyman Smith.

TINDERA, GEORGE, Burning River Forge, 751 Hadcock Rd, Brunswick, OH 44212-2648, Phone: (330) 220-6212
Specialties: Straight knives; my designs. **Patterns:** Personal knives; classic Bowies and fighters. **Technical:** Hand forged high carbon; my own cable and pattern welded Damascus. **Prices:** $100 to $400. **Remarks:** Spare-time maker; sold first knife in 1995. **Other:** Natural handle materials.

TINGLE, DENNIS P, 19390 E Clinton Rd, Jackson, CA 95642, Phone: (209) 223-4586

TODD, RICHARD C, RR 1, Chambersburg, IL 62323, Phone: 217-327-4380
Specialties: Multi blade folders & silver sheaths. **Patterns:** Blacksmithing and tool making. **Mark:** RT with letter R crossing the T.

TOICH, NEVIO, Via Pisacane 9, Rettorgole di Caldogna, Vincenza, ITALY 36030, Phone: 0444-985065, Fax:0444-301254
Specialties: Working/using straight knives of his design or to customer specs. **Patterns:** Bowies, hunters, skinners and utility/camp knives. **Technical:** Grinds 440C, D2 and ATS-34. Hollow-grinds all blades and uses mirror polish. Offers hand-sewn sheaths. Uses wood and horn. **Prices:** $120 to $300; some to $450. **Remarks:** Spare-time maker; first knife sold in 1989. Doing business as Custom Toich. **Mark:** Initials and model number punched.

TOKAR, DANIEL, Box 1776, Shepherdstown, WV 25443
Specialties: Working knives; period pieces. **Patterns:** Hunters, camp knives, buckskinners, axes, swords and battle gear. **Technical:** Forges L6, 1095 and his Damascus; makes mokume, Japanese alloys and bronze daggers; restores old edged weapons. **Prices:** $25 to $800; some to $3,000. **Remarks:** Part-time maker; first knife sold in 1979. Doing business as The Willow Forge. **Mark:** Arrow over rune and date.

TOLLEFSON, BARRY A., 177 Blackfoot Trail, Gunnison, CO 81230-9720, Phone: 970-641-0752
Specialties: Working straight knives, some fancy. **Patterns:** Hunters, skinners, fighters and camp knives. **Technical:** Grinds 440C, ATS-34 and D2. Likes mirror-finishes; offers some fancy filework. Handles made from elk, deer and exotic hardwoods. **Prices:** $75 to $300; some higher. **Remarks:** Part-time maker; first knife sold in 1990. **Mark:** Stylized initials.

TOMES, P J, 594 Highpeak Lane, Shipman, VA 22971, Phone: 434-263-8662, Fax:804-263-4439
Specialties: Lock blade folders, forged scagels and Bowies. **Technical:** MS forges 52100 only. **Mark:** Tomes MS USA on forged blades.

TOMEY, KATHLEEN, 146 Buford Pl, Macon, GA 31204, Phone: 478-746-8454
Specialties: Working hunters, skinners, daily users in fixed blades, plain and embellished. Tactical neck and tanto. Bowies. **Technical:** Grinds 01, 440C, ATS-34, flat or hollow grind filework, satin and mirror polish finishes. High quality sheaths with tooling. Kydex with tactical. **Prices:** $150 to $500. **Remarks:** Almost full-time maker. **Mark:** Last name in diamond.

TOMPKINS, DAN, P. O. Box 398, Peotone, IL 60468, Phone: 708-258-3620
Specialties: Working knives, some deluxe, some folders. **Patterns:** Hunters, boots, daggers and push knives. **Technical:** Grinds D2, 440C, ATS-34 and 154CM. **Prices:** $85 to $150; some to $400. **Remarks:** Part-time maker; first knife sold in 1975. **Mark:** Last name, city, state.

TONER, ROGER, 531 Lightfoot Place, Pickering, Ont., CANADA L1V 5Z8, Phone: 905-420-5555
Specialties: Exotic Sword canes. **Patterns:** Bowies, daggers and fighters. **Technical:** Grinds 440C, D2 and Damascus. Scrimshaws and engraves. Silver cast pommels and guards in animal shapes; twisted silver wire inlays. Uses semi-precious stones. **Prices:** $200 to $2000; some to $3000. **Remarks:** Part-time maker; first knife sold in 1982. **Mark:** Last name.

TOPLISS, M. W. "IKE", 1668 Hermosa Ct., Montrose, CO 81401, Phone: 970-249-4703
Specialties: Working/using straight knives of his design and to customer specs. **Patterns:** Boots, hunters, utility/camp knives. **Technical:** {Prefers ATS-34. Other steels available on request. Likes stabilized wood, natural hardwoods, antler and Micarta. **Prices:** $175 to $300; some to $800. **Remarks:** Part-time maker; first knife sold in 1984. **Mark:** Name, city, state.

TORGESON, SAMUEL L, 25 Alpine Ln, Sedona, AZ 86336-6809

TOSHIFUMI, KURAMOTO, 3435 Higashioda Asakura-Gun, Fukuoka, JAPAN, Phone: 0946-42-4470

TOWELL, DWIGHT L., 2375 Towell Rd., Midvale, ID 83645, Phone: 208-355-2419
Specialties: Solid, elegant working knives; art knives. **Patterns:** Hunters, Bowies, daggers; folders in several weights. **Technical:** Grinds 154CM; some engraving. **Prices:** $250 to $800; some $3,500 and higher. **Remarks:** Part-time maker; first knife sold in 1970. **Mark:** Last name.

TOWNSEND, J. W., PO Box 722, Watson, LA 70786-0722, Phone: 225-665-5779
Specialties: One of a kinds. **Patterns:** Fantasy knives and fighters. **Technical:** Grinds 440C, O1, commercial Damascus and ATS-34. **Prices:** $250 to $2,500; some higher. **Remarks:** Full-time maker; first knife sold in 1985. **Mark:** First and middle initials and last name, or stylized last name.

TOWNSEND, ALLEN MARK, 6 Pine Trail, Texarkana, AR 71854, Phone: (870) 772-8945

TRACY, BUD, 495 Flanders Rd, Reno, NV 8951-4784

TREIBER, LEON, P. O. Box 342, Ingram, TX 78025, Phone: 830-367-2246
Specialties: Folders of his design and to customer specs. **Patterns:** Locking folders. **Technical:** Grinds CPM-T-440V, D2, 440C, Damascus, 420v & ats34. **Prices:** $250 to $1,500. **Remarks:** Part-time maker; first knife sold in 1992. Doing business as Treiber Knives. **Mark:** First initial, last name, city, state.

TREIBER, RANDY, P O Box 244, High Bridge, NJ 08829-0244, Phone: (908) 377-0771

TREML, GLENN, RR #14, Site 11-10, Thunder Bay, Ont., CANADA P7B 5E5, Phone: 807-767-1977
Specialties: working straight knives of his design and to customer specs. **Patterns:** Hunters, kitchen knives and double-edged survival knives. Technical Grinds 440C, ATS-34 and O1; stock removal method. Uses various woods and Micarta for handle material. **Prices:** $60 to $400; some higher. **Mark:** Stamped last name.

TRINDLE, BARRY, 1660 Ironwood Trail, Earlham, IA 50072-8611, Phone: 515-462-1237
Specialties: Engraved folders. **Patterns:** Mostly small folders, classical styles and pocket knives. **Technical:** 440 only. Engraves. Handles of wood or mineral material. **Prices:** Start at $1,00. **Mark:** Name on tang.

TRIPLETT, CRAIG, 3524 Jug Factory Rd, Greer, SC 29651, Phone: (864) 968-0398
Specialties: Working straight knives, some one-of-a-kind; most are Damascus. **Patterns:** Hunters, daggers, letter openers. **Technical:** Forges 1095 and his own Damascus. **Prices:** Start at $150. **Remarks:** Spare-time maker; first knife sold in 1998. **Mark:** OFO; doing business as Old Oak Forge.

TRISLER, KENNETH W, 6256 Federal 80, Rayville, LA 71269, Phone: (318) 728-5541

TRITZ, JEAN JOSE, Schopstrasse 23, 20255 Hamburg, GERMANY, Phone: 040-49 78 21
Specialties: Scandinavian knives, Japanese kitchen knives, friction folders, swords. **Patterns:** Puukkos, Tollekniven, Hocho, friction folders, swords. **Technical:** Forges tool steels, carbon steels, 52100 Damascus Mokume, San Maj. **Prices:** $200 to $2,000; some higher. **Remarks:** Full-time maker; first knife sold in 1989. **Mark:** Initials in monogram. **Other:** Does own leatherwork, prefers natural materials. Sole authorship. Speaks French, German, English, Norwegian.

TRUDEL, PAUL, 525 Braydon Ave, Ottawa ON, CANADA K1G 0W7 **Remarks:** Part-time knife maker.

TRUJILLO, ALBERT MB, 2035 Wasmer Circle, Bosque Farms, NM 87068, Phone: 505-869-0428
Specialties: Working/using straight knives of his design or to customer specs. **Patterns:** Hunters, skinners, fighters, working/using knives. File work offered. **Technical:** Grinds ATS34, D2, 440C. Tapers tangs, all blades cryogenically treated. **Prices:** $75 to $500. **Remarks:** Part-time maker; first knife sold in 1997. **Mark:** First and last name under logo.

TRUJILLO, ADAM, 3001 Tanglewood Dr., Anchorage, AK 99517, Phone: 907-243-6093
Specialties: Working/using straight knives of his design. **Patterns:** Hunters and utility/camp knives. **Technical:** Grinds 440C, ATS-34 and O1; ice tempers blades. Sheaths are dipped in wax and oil base. **Prices:** $200 to $500; some to $1,000. **Remarks:** Spare-time maker; first knife sold in 1995. Doing business as Alaska Knife & Service Co. **Mark:** NA.

TRUJILLO, THOMAS A., 3001 Tanglewood Dr., Anchorage, AK 99517, Phone: 907-243-6093
Specialties: High-end art knives. **Patterns:** Hunters, Bowies, daggers and locking folders. **Technical:** Grinds to customer choice, including rock and commercial Damascus. Inlays jewels and carves handles. **Prices:** $150 to $900; some to $6,000. **Remarks:** Full-time maker; first knife sold in 1976. Doing business as Alaska Knife & Service Co. **Mark:** Alaska Knife and/or Thomas Anthony.

TRUJILLO, MIRANDA, 3001 Tanglewood Dr., Anchorage, AK 99517, Phone: 907-243-6093
Specialties: Working/using straight knives of her design. **Patterns:** Hunters and utility/camp knives. **Technical:** Grinds ATS-34 and 440C. Sheaths are water resistant. **Prices:** $145 to $400; some to $600. **Remarks:** Spare-time maker; first knife sold in 1989. Doing business as Alaska Knife & Service Co. **Mark:** NA.

TSCHAGER, REINHARD, Piazza Parrocchia 7, I-39100 Bolzano, ITALY, Phone: 0471-970642, Fax:0471-970642
Specialties: Classic, high-art, collector-grade straight knives of his design. **Patterns:** Hunters. **Technical:** Grinds ATS-34, D2 and Damascus. Oval pins. Gold inlay. Offers engraving. **Prices:** $500 to $1,200; some to

custom knifemakers

$4,000. **Remarks:** Spare-time maker; first knife sold in 1979. **Mark:** Gold inlay stamped with initials.

TURANSKI, TED, 30 Ladoga Pk, Lansing, NY 14882, Phone: (607) 533-3594

TURCOTTE, LARRY, 1707 Evergreen, Pampa, TX 79065, Phone: 806-665-9369, 806-669-0435
Specialties: Fancy and working/using knives of his design and to customer specs. **Patterns:** Hunters, kitchen knives, utility/camp knives. **Technical:** Grinds 440C, D2, ATS-34. Engraves, scrimshaws, silver inlays. **Prices:** $150 to $350; some to $1,000. **Remarks:** Part-time maker; first knife sold in 1977. Doing business as Knives by Turcotte. **Mark:** Last name.

TURECEK, JIM, 12 Elliott Rd, Ansonia, CT 06401, Phone: 203-734-8406
Specialties: Exotic folders, art knives and some miniatures. **Patterns:** Trout and bird knives with split bamboo handles and one-of-a-kind folders. **Technical:** Grinds and forges stainless and carbon Damascus. **Prices:** $750 to $1,500; some to $3,000. **Remarks:** Full-time maker; first knife sold in 1983. **Mark:** Last initial in script, or last name.

TURNBULL, RALPH A., 14464 Linden Dr, Spring Hill, FL 34609, Phone: 352-688-7089
Specialties: Fancy folders. **Patterns:** Primarily gents pocket knives. **Technical:** Wire EDM work on bolsters. **Prices:** $650 and up. **Remarks:** Full-time maker; first knife sold in 1973. **Mark:** Signature or initials.

TURNER, KEVIN, 17 Hunt Ave., Montrose, NY 10548, Phone: 914-739-0535
Specialties: Working straight knives of his design and to customer specs; period pieces. **Patterns:** Daggers, fighters and utility knives. **Technical:** Forges 5160 and 52100. **Prices:** $90 to $500. **Remarks:** Part-time maker; first knife sold in 1991. **Mark:** Acid-etched signed last name and year.

TWO KNIFE GUYS, PO Box 24477, Chattanooga, TN 37422, Phone: 423-894-6640

TYCER, ART, 23820 N Cold Springs Rd, Paron, AR 72122, Phone: 501-821-4487
Specialties: Fancy working/using straight knives of his design, to customer specs and standard patterns. **Patterns:** Boots, Bowies, daggers, fighters, hunters, kitchen and utility knives. **Technical:** Grinds ATS-34, 440C, 52100 & carbon steel. Uses exotic woods with spacer material, stag and water buffalo. Offers filework. **Prices:** $125 & up depending on size & embellishments. **Remarks:** Making and using my own Damascus and other Damascus also. **Mark:** Flying "T" over first initial inside an oval. **Other:** Full-time maker.

TYSER, ROSS, 1015 Hardee Court, Spartanburg, SC 29303, Phone: 864-585-7616
Specialties: Traditional working and using straight knives and folders of his design and in standard patterns. **Patterns:** Bowies, hunters and slip-joint folders. **Technical:** Grinds 440C and commercial Damascus. Mosaic pins; stone inlay. Does filework and scrimshaw. Offers engraving and cutwork and some inlay on sheaths. **Prices:** $45 to $125; some to $400. **Remarks:** Part-time maker; first knife sold in 1995. Doing business as RT Custom Knives. **Mark:** Stylized initials.

u

UCHIDA, CHIMATA, 977-2 Oaza Naga Shisui Ki, Kumamoto, JAPAN 861-1204

UEKAMA, NOBUYUKI, 3-2-8-302 Ochiai, Tama City, Tokyo, JAPAN

v

VAGNINO, MICHAEL, P. O. Box 67, Visalia, CA 93279, Phone: 559-528-2800
Specialties: Working & fancy straight knives & folders of his design & to customer specs. **Patterns:** Hunters, bowies, camp, kitchen & folders:lockinguners, slip joint, lock back & doubleaction autos. **Technical:** Forges 52100, A2, 1084 & 15N20 Damascus and grinds stainless. **Prices:** $150 to $1000 plus.

VALLOTTON, SHAWN, 621 Fawn Ridge Dr., Oakland, OR 97462, Phone: 503-459-2216
Specialties: Left-hand knives. **Patterns:** All styles. **Technical:** Grinds 440C, ATS-34 and Damascus. Uses titanium. Prefers bead-blasted or anodized finishes. **Prices:** $250 to $1,400. **Remarks:** Full-time maker. **Mark:** Name and specialty.

VALLOTTON, RAINY D., 1295 Wolf Valley Dr, Umpqua, OR 97486, Phone: 541-459-0465
Specialties: Folders, one-handed openers and art pieces. **Patterns:** All patterns. **Technical:** Stock removal all steels; uses titanium liners and bolsters; uses all finishes. **Prices:** $350 to $3500. **Remarks:** Full-time maker. **Mark:** Name.

VALLOTTON, BUTCH AND AREY, 621 Fawn Ridge Dr., Oakland, OR 97462, Phone: 541-459-2216, Fax:541-459-7473
Specialties: Quick opening knives w/complicated mechanisms. **Patterns:** Tactical, fancy, working, and some art knives. **Technical:** Grinds all steels, uses others Damascus. Uses Spectrum Metal. **Prices:** From $350 to $4,500. **Remarks:** Full-time maker since 1984; first knife sold in 1981. **Mark:** Name w/viper head in the "V". **Other:** Co/designer, Appelgate Fairbarn folding w/Bill Harsey

VALLOTTON, THOMAS, 621 Fawn Ridge Dr, Oakland, OR 97462, Phone: 541-459-2216
Specialties: Custom autos. **Patterns:** Tactical, fancy. **Technical:** File work, uses Damascus, uses Spectrum Metal. **Prices:** From $350 to $700. **Remarks:** Full-time maker. **Mark:** T and a V mingled. **Other:** Maker of Protégé 3 canoe.

VALOIS, A. DANIEL, 3552 W. Lizard Ck. Rd., Lehighton, PA 18235, Phone: 717-386-3636
Specialties: Big working knives; various sized lock-back folders with new safety releases. **Patterns:** Fighters in survival packs, sturdy working knives, belt buckle knives, military-style knives, swords. **Technical:** Forges and grinds A2, O1 and 440C; likes full tangs. **Prices:** $65 to $240; some to $600. **Remarks:** Full-time maker; first knife sold in 1969. **Mark:** Anvil logo with last name inside.

VAN CLEVE, STEVE, Box 372, Sutton, AK 99674, Phone: (907) 745-3038

VAN DE MANAKKER, THIJS, Koolweg 34, 5759 px Helenaveen, HOLLAND, Phone: 0493539369
Specialties: Classic high-art knives. **Patterns:** Swords, utility/camp knives and period pieces. **Technical:** Forges soft iron, carbon steel and Bloomery Iron. Makes own Damascus, Bloomery Iron and patterns. **Prices:** $20 to $2,000; some higher. **Remarks:** Full-time maker; first knife sold in 1969. **Mark:** Stylized "V".

VAN DEN ELSEN, GERT, Purcelldreef 83, 5012 AJ Tilburg, NETHERLANDS, Phone: 013-4563200
Specialties: Fancy, working/using, miniatures and integral straight knives of the maker's design or to customer specs. **Patterns:** Bowies, fighters, hunters and Japanese style blades. **Technical:** Grinds ATS-34 and 440C; forges Damascus. Offers filework, differentially tempered blades and some mokume-gane fittings. **Prices:** $350 to $1000; some to $4000. **Remarks:** Part-time maker; first knife sold in 1982. Doing business as G-E Knives. **Mark:** Initials GE in lozenge shape.

VAN EIZENGA, JERRY W, 14227 Cleveland, Nunica, MI 49448, Phone: (616) 842-2699
Specialties: Hand forged blades, Scagel patterns and other styles. **Patterns:** Camp, hunting, bird, trout, folders, axes, miniatures. **Technical:** 5160, 52100, 1084. **Prices:** Start at $250. **Remarks:** Part-time maker, sole author of knife and sheath. **Mark:** Interconnecting letters spelling VAN, city and state. **Other:** First knife made early 1970s. ABS member who believes in the beauty of simplicity.

VAN ELDIK, FRANS, Ho Flaan 3, 3632BT Loenen, NETHERLANDS, Phone: 0031 294 233 095, Fax:0031 294 233 095
Specialties: Fancy collector-grade straight knives and folders of his design. **Patterns:** Hunters, fighters, boots and folders. **Technical:** Forges and grinds D2, 154CM, ATS-34 and stainless Damascus. **Prices:** Start at $225. **Remarks:** Spare-time maker; first knife sold in 1979. **Mark:** Lion with name and Amsterdam.

VAN HOY, ED & TANYA, 1826 McCallum Road, Candor, NC 27229, Phone: 910-974-7933
Specialties: Traditional and working/using straight knives of his design, make folders. **Patterns:** Fighters, straight knives, folders, hunters and art knives. **Technical:** Grinds ATS-34 and 440V; forges D2. Offers filework, engraves, acid etching, mosaic pins, decorative bolsters and custom fitted English bridle leather sheaths. **Prices:** $250 to $3,000. **Remarks:** Full-time maker; first knife sold in 1977. Wife also engraves. Doing business as Van Hoy Custom Knives. **Mark:** Acid etched last name.

VAN RIJSWIJK, AAD, Avr Knives, Arij Koplaan 16B, 3132 AA Vlaardingen, THE NETHERLANDS, Phone: +31 10 2343227, Fax:+31 10 2343648
Specialties: High-art interframe folders of his design and in shaving sets. **Patterns:** Hunters and locking folders. **Technical:** Uses semi precious stones, mammoth, ivory, walrus ivory, iron wood. **Prices:** $550 to $3800. **Remarks:** Full-time maker; first knife sold in 1993. **Mark:** NA.

VAN RIPER, JAMES N, PO Box 7045, Citrus Heights, CA 95621-7045, Phone: (916) 721-0892

VAN SCHAIK, BASTIAAN, Post Box 75269, 1070 AG, Amsterdam, NETHERLANDS, Phone: 31-20-633-80-25, Fax:same as phone # **Specialties:** Working/using straight knives and axes of his design. **Patterns:** Daggers, fighters, push daggers and battle axes. **Technical:** Grinds ATS-34 and 440C; forges high-carbon steel. Uses Damascus and high-tech coatings. **Prices:** $400 to $1,500; some to $2,000. **Remarks:** Full-time maker; first knife sold in 1993. Doing business as Licorne Edged Creations. **Mark:** Unicorn head.

VANDERFORD, CARL G., Rt. 9, Box 238B, Columbia, TN 38401, Phone: 615-381-1488 **Specialties:** Traditional working straight knives and folders of his design. **Patterns:** Hunters, Bowies and locking folders. **Technical:** Forges and grinds 440C, O1 and wire Damascus. **Prices:** $60 to $125. **Remarks:** Part-time maker; first knife sold in 1987. **Mark:** Last name.

VANDEVENTER, TERRY L, 3274 Davis Rd, Terry, MS 39170-9750, Phone: (601) 371-7414 **Specialties:** Camp knives, Bowies, friction folders. **Technical:** 1095, 1084, L-6, Damascus & Mokume; natural handles. **Prices:** $250 to $1,200. **Remarks:** Sole author; makes everything here. **Mark:** T L Vandeventer (with silhouette of snake), handcrafted knives. **Other:** Part-time since 1994. ABS Journeyman Smith.

VASQUEZ, JOHNNY DAVID, 1552 7th St, Wyandotte, MI 48192, Phone: (734) 281-2455

VAUGHAN, IAN, 351 Doe Run Rd, Manheim, PA 17545-9368, Phone: (717) 665-6949

VEATCH, RICHARD, 2580 N. 35th Pl., Springfield, OR 97477, Phone: 541-747-3910 **Specialties:** Traditional working and using straight knives of his design and in standard patterns; period pieces. **Patterns:** Daggers, hunters, swords, utility/camp knives and minis. **Technical:** Forges and grinds his own Damascus; uses L6 and O1. Prefers natural handle materials; offers leatherwork. **Prices:** $50 to $300; some to $500. **Remarks:** Full-time maker; first knife sold in 1991. **Mark:** Stylized initials.

VEIT, MICHAEL, 3289 E. Fifth Rd., LaSalle, IL 61301, Phone: 815-223-3538 **Specialties:** Damascus folders. **Technical:** Engraver-Sole author. **Prices:** $2,500 to $6,500. **Remarks:** Part-time maker; first knife sold in 1985. **Mark:** Name in script.

VELARDE, RICARDO, 7240 N Greefield Dr, Park City, UT 84098, Phone: 801-360-1413, Fax:801-375-2742 **Specialties:** Investment grade integrals and interframs. **Patterns:** Boots, fighters and hunters; hollow grind. **Technical:** BG on Integrals. **Prices:** Start at $650. **Remarks:** First knife sold in 1992. **Mark:** First initial, last name on blade; city, state, U. S. A. at bottom of tang.

VENSILD, HENRIK, Gl Estrup, Randersvei 4, DK-8963 Auning, DENMARK, Phone: +45 86 48 44 48 **Specialties:** Classic and traditional working and using knives of his design; Scandinavian influence. **Patterns:** hunters and using knives. **Technical:** Forges Damascus. Hand makes handles, sheaths and blades. **Prices:** $350 to $1,000. **Remarks:** Part-time maker; first knife sold in 1967. **Mark:** Initials.

VIALLON, HENRI, Les Belins, 63300 Thiers, FRANCE, Phone: 04-73-80-24-03, Fax:04 73-51-02-02 **Specialties:**Folders and complex Damascus **Patterns:**My draws. **Technical:** Forge **Prices:** $1000-$5000. **Mark:** H. Viallon.

VIELE, H. J., 88 Lexington Ave., Westwood, NJ 07675, Phone: 201-666-2906 **Specialties:** Folding knives of distinctive shapes. **Patterns:** High-tech folders. **Technical:** Grinds 440C and ATS-34. **Prices:** Start at $475. **Remarks:** Full-time maker; first knife sold in 1973. **Mark:** Last name with stylized throwing star.

VIKING KNIVES (SEE JAMES THORLIEF ERIKSEN)

VILLA, LUIZ, R. Com. Miguel Calfat, 398 Itaim Bibi, Sao Paulo, SP-04537-081, BRAZIL, Phone: 011-8290649 **Specialties:** One-of-a-kind straight knives and jewel knives of all designs. **Patterns:** Bowies, hunters, utility/camp knives and jewel knives. **Technical:** Grinds D6, Damascus and 440C; forges 5160. Prefers natural handle material. **Prices:** $70 to $200. **Remarks:** Part-time knife sold in 1990. **Mark:** Last name and serial number.

VILLAR, RICARDO, Al. Dos Jasmins, 243, Mairipora, S. P. 07600-000, BRAZIL, Phone: 011-4851649 **Specialties:** Straight working knives to customer specs. **Patterns:** Bowies, fighters and utility/camp knives. **Technical:** Grinds D6, ATS-34 and 440C stainless. **Prices:** $80 to $200. **Remarks:** Part-time knife sold in 1993. **Mark:** Percor over sword and circle.

VISTE, JAMES, Edgewize Forge, 13401 Mt Elliot, Detroit, MI 48212, Phone: (313) 664-7455 **Mark:** EWF touch mark.

VISTNES, TOR, N-6930 Svelgen, NORWAY, Phone: 047-57795572 **Specialties:** Traditional and working knives of his design. **Patterns:** Hunters and utility knives. **Technical:** Grinds Uddeholm Elmax. Handles made of rear burls of different Nordic stabilized woods. **Prices:** $300 to $1100. **Remarks:** Part-time maker; first knife sold in 1988. **Mark:** Etched name and deer head.

VOGT, DONALD J, 9007 Hogans Bend, Tampa, FL 33647, Phone: 813 973-3245 **Specialties:** Art knives, folders, automatics, large fixed blades. **Technical:** Uses Damascus steels for blade and bolsters, filework, hand carving on blade bolsters and handles. Other materials used - jewels, gold, stainless steel, mokume. Prefers to use natural handle materials. **Prices:** $800 to $5000. **Remarks:** Part-time maker; first knife sold in 1997. **Mark:** Last name.

VOGT, PATRIK, KUNGSVAGEN 83, S-30270 HALMSTAD, SWEDEN, Phone: 46-35-30977 **Specialties:** Working straight knives. **Patterns:** Bowies, hunters & fighters. **Technical:** Forges carbon steel and own Damascus. **Prices:** From $100. **Remarks:** Not currently making knives. **Mark:** Initials or last name.

VOORHIES, LES, 14511 Lk Mazaska Tr, Faribault, MN 55021, Phone: 507-332-0736 **Specialties:** Steels. **Technical:** ATS-34 Damascus. **Prices:** $75-$450.

VOSS, BEN, 362 Clark St., Galesburg, IL 61401, Phone: 309-342-6994 **Specialties:** Fancy working knives of his design. **Patterns:** Bowies, fighters, hunters, boots and folders. **Technical:** Grinds 440C, ATS-34 and D2. **Prices:** $35 to $1,200. **Remarks:** Part-time maker; first knife sold in 1986. **Mark:** Name, city and state.

VOTAW, DAVID P., Box 327, Pioneer, OH 43554, Phone: 419-737-2774 **Specialties:** Working knives; period pieces. **Patterns:** Hunters, Bowies, camp knives, buckskinners and tomahawks. **Technical:** Grinds O1 and D2. **Prices:** $100 to $200; some to $500. **Remarks:** Part-time maker; took over for the late W. K. Kneubuhler. Doing business as W-K Knives. **Mark:** WK with V inside anvil.

VOWELL, DONALD J, 815 Berry Dr, Mayfield, KY 42066, Phone: (270) 247-2157

VUNK, ROBERT, 3166 Breckenridge Dr, Colorado Springs, CO 80906, Phone: 719-576-5505 **Specialties:** Working knives, some fancy; period pieces. **Patterns:** Variety of tantos, fillet knives, kitchen knives, camp knives and folders. **Technical:** Grinds O1, 440C and ATS-34; provides mountings, cases, stands. **Prices:** $55 to $1,300. **Remarks:** Part-time maker; first knife sold in 1985. Doing business as RV Knives. **Mark:** Initials.

W

WADA, YASUTAKA, Fujinokidai 2-6-22, Nara City, Nara prefect 631-0044, JAPAN, Phone: 0742 46-0689 **Specialties:** Fancy and embellished one-of-a-kind straight knives of his design. **Patterns:** Bowies, daggers and hunters. **Technical:** Grinds ATS-34, Cowry X and Cowry X L-30 laminate. **Prices:** $400 to $2,500: some higher. **Remarks:** Part-time maker; first knife sold in 1990. **Mark:** Owl eyes with initial and last name underneath.

WAGAMAN, JOHN K., 903 Arsenal Ave., Fayetteville, NC 28305, Phone: 910-485-7860 **Specialties:** Fancy working knives. **Patterns:** Bowies, miniatures, hunters, fighters and boots. **Technical:** Grinds D2, 440C, 154CM and commercial Damascus; inlays mother-of-pearl. **Prices:** $110 to $2,000. **Remarks:** Part-time maker; first knife sold in 1975. **Mark:** Last name.

WAHLSTER, MARK DAVID, 1404 N. Second St., Silverton, OR 97381, Phone: 503-873-3775 **Specialties:** Automatics, antique and high tech folders in standard patterns and to customer specs. **Patterns:** Hunters, fillets and combat knives. **Technical:** Flat grinds 440C, ATS-34, D2 and Damascus. Uses titanium in folders. **Prices:** $100 to $1,000. **Remarks:** Full-time maker; first knife sold in 1981. **Mark:** Name, city and state or last name.

WALDROP, MARK, 14562 SE 1st Ave. Rd., Summerfield, FL 34491, Phone: 352-347-9034 **Specialties:** Period pieces. **Patterns:** Bowies and daggers. **Technical:** Uses stock removal. Engraves. **Prices:** Moderate to upscale. **Remarks:** Part-time maker; first knife sold in 1978. **Mark:** Last name.

custom knifemakers

WALKER, JIM, 22 Walker Lane, Morrilton, AR 72110, Phone: 501-354-3175
Specialties: Period pieces and working/using knives of his design and to customer specs. **Patterns:** Bowies, fighters, hunters, camp knives. **Technical:** Forges 5160, O1, L6, 52100, 1084, 1095. **Prices:** Start at $250. **Remarks:** Full-time maker; first knife sold in 1993. **Mark:** Three arrows with last name/MS.

WALKER, JOHN W., 10620 Moss Branch Rd., Bon Aqua, TN 37025, Phone: 931-670-4754
Specialties: Straight knives, daggers and folders; sterling rings, 14K gold wire wrap; some stone setting. **Patterns:** Hunters, boot knives, others. **Technical:** Grinds 440C, ATS-34, L6, etc. Buys Damascus. **Prices:** $150 to $500 some to $1500. **Remarks:** Part-time maker; first knife sold in 1982. **Mark:** Hohenzollern Eagle with name, or last name.

WALKER, GEORGE A., PO Box 3272, 483 Aspen Hills, Alpine, WY 83128-0272, Phone: 307-883-2372, Fax:307-883-2372
Specialties: Deluxe working knives. **Patterns:** Hunters, boots, fighters, Bowies and folders. **Technical:** Forges his own Damascus and cable; engraves, carves, scrimshaws. Makes sheaths. **Prices:** $125 to $750; some to $1,000. **Remarks:** Full-time maker; first knife sold in 1979. Partners with wife. **Mark:** Name, city and state.

WALKER, BILL, 431 Walker Rd, Stevensville, MD 21666, Phone: (410) 643-5041

WALKER, DON, 3236 Halls Chapel Rd, Burnsville, NC 28714, Phone: (828) 675-9716

WALKER, MICHAEL L., P. O. Box 1924, Rancho de Taos, NM 87571, Phone: 505-737-3086, Fax:505-751-0284
Specialties: Innovative knife designs and locking systems; Titanium and SS furniture and art. **Patterns:** Folders from utility grade to museum quality art; others upon request. **Technical:** State-of-the-art materials; titanium, stainless Damascus, gold, etc. **Prices:** $3500 and above. **Remarks:** Designer/MetalCrafts; Full-time professional knife maker since 1980; Four U. S. Patents; Invented Liner Lock® and was awarded Registered U. S. Trademark No. 1,585,333. **Mark:** Early mark MW, Walker's Lockers by M. L. Walker; current M. L. Walker or Michael Walker.

WALKER III, JOHN WADE, 2595 Hwy 1647, Paintlick, KY 40461, Phone: (606) 792-3498

WALLACE, ROGER L., 4902 Collins Lane, Tampa, FL 33603, Phone: 813-239-3261
Specialties: Working straight knives, Bowies and camp knives to customer specs. **Patterns:** Hunters, skinners and utility knives. **Technical:** Forges high-carbon steel. **Prices:** Start at $75. **Remarks:** Part-time maker; first knife sold in 1985. **Mark:** First initial, last name.

WALLINGFORD JR, CHARLES W, 9024 US 42, Union, KY 41091, Phone: 606-384-4141
Specialties: 18th & 19th century styles - Patch knives, Rifleman knives. **Technical:** 1084 & 5160 forged blades. **Prices:** $125 to $300. **Mark:** CW.

WALTER, BREND, 56 Benton Farm Rd, Walterboro, SC 29488, Phone: 843-538-8256

WALTERS, A. F., P. O. Box 523, 275 Crawley Rd., Tyty, GA 31795, Phone: 912-528-6207
Specialties: Working knives, some to customer specs. **Patterns:** Locking folders, straight hunters, fishing and survival knives. **Technical:** Grinds D2, 154CM and 13C26. **Prices:** Start at $200. **Remarks:** Part-time maker. Label: "The jewel knife" **Mark:** "J" in diamond and knife logo.

WARD, J. J., 7501 S. R. 220, Waverly, OH 45690, Phone: 614-947-5328
Specialties: Traditional and working/using straight knives and folders of his design. **Patterns:** Hunters and locking folders. **Technical:** Grinds ATS-34, 440C and Damascus. Offers handmade sheaths. **Prices:** $125 to $250; some to $500. **Remarks:** Spare-time maker; first knife sold in 1980. **Mark:** Etched name.

WARD, CHUCK, 1010 E. North St., Benton, AR 72015, Phone: 501-778-4329
Specialties: Traditional working and using straight knives and folders of his design. **Technical:** Grinds 440C, D2, A2, ATS34 and O1; uses natural and composite handle materials. **Prices:** $90 to $400, some higher. **Remarks:** Part-time maker; first knife sold in 1990. **Mark:** First initial, last name.

WARD, RON, 409 Arrowhead Trails, Loveland, OH 45140, Phone: 513-683-8729
Specialties: Classic working and using straight knives, fantasy knives. **Patterns:** Bowies, hunters, fighters, and utility/camp knives. **Technical:** Grinds 440C, 154CM, ATS-34 uses composite and natural handle materials, makes sheaths. **Prices:** $85 to $200, some to $500. **Remarks:** Part-time maker; first knife sold in 1992. Doing business as Ron Ward Blades. **Mark:** Ron Ward Blades, Loveland OH.

WARD, KEN, 5122 Lake Shastina Blvd, Weed, CA 96094, Phone: 530-938-9720
Specialties: Working knives, some to customer specs. **Patterns:** Straight and folding hunters, axes, Bowies, buckskinners and miniatures. **Technical:** Grinds ATS-34, Damascus and Stellite 6K. **Prices:** $100 to $700. **Remarks:** Part-time maker; first knife sold in 1977. **Mark:** Name.

WARD, W. C., 817 Glenn St., Clinton, TN 37716, Phone: 615-457-3568
Specialties: Working straight knives; period pieces. **Patterns:** Hunters, Bowies, swords and kitchen cutlery. **Technical:** Grinds O1. **Prices:** $85 to $150; some to $500. **Remarks:** Part-time maker; first knife sold in 1969. He styled the Tennessee Knife Maker. **Mark:** TKM.

WARDELL, MICK, 20, Clovelly Rd, Bideford, N Devon EX39 3BU, ENGLAND, Phone: 01237 475312, Fax:01237 475312
Specialties: Folders of his design. **Patterns:** Locking and slip-joint folder, hunters and Bowies. **Technical:** Grinds ATS-34, D2 and Damascus. Heat-treats. **Prices:** $200 to $700. **Remarks:** Full-time maker; first knife sold in 1986. **Mark:** M. Wardell - England

WARDEN, ROY A., 275 Tanglewood Rd., Union, MO 63084, Phone: 314-583-8813
Specialties: Complex mosaic designs of "EDM wired figures" and " Stack up" patterns and "Lazer Cut" and "Torch cut" and "Sawed" patterns combined. **Patterns:** Mostly "all mosaic" folders, automatics, fixed blades. **Technical:** Mosaic Damascus with all tool steel edges. **Prices:** $500 to $2000 and up. **Remarks:** Part-time maker; first knife sold in 1987. **Mark:** WARDEN stamped or initials connected.

WARDIAN, PAUL G., 460 SW Halsey Loop, Troutdale, OR 97060, Phone: 503-661-4324
Specialties: Artful straight knives and miniatures. **Patterns:** Bowies, daggers, period. **Technical:** Grinds 440C, 5160 & Damascus. **Prices:** $120; some to $4500. **Remarks:** Part-time maker; first knife sold in 1988. Doing business as One Of A Kind Knives. **Mark:** Engraved logo.

WARE, TOMMY, P. O. Box 488, Datil, NM 87821, Phone: 505-772-5817
Specialties: Traditional working and using straight knives, folders and automatics of his design and to customer specs. **Patterns:** Hunters, automatics and locking folders. **Technical:** Grinds ATS-34, 440C and D2. Offers engraving and scrimshaw. **Prices:** $275 to $575; some to $1,000. **Remarks:** Full-time maker; first knife sold in 1990. Doing business as Wano Knives. **Mark:** Last name inside oval, business name above, city and state below, year on side.

WARENSKI, BUSTER, P. O. Box 214, Richfield, UT 84701, Phone: 435-896-5319
Specialties: Investor-class straight knives. **Patterns:** Daggers, swords. **Technical:** Grinds, engraves and inlays; offers surface treatments. All engraved by Julie Warenski. **Prices:** Upscale. **Remarks:** Full-time maker. **Mark:** Warenski (hand engraved on blade).

WARREN, DANIEL, 571 Lovejoy Rd, Canton, NC 28716, Phone: 828-648-7351
Specialties: Using knives. **Patterns:** Drop point hunters. **Prices:** $200 to $500. **Mark:** Warren-Bethel NC.

WARREN, AL, 1423 Sante Fe Circle, Roseville, CA 95678, Phone: 916-784-3217/Cell Phone 916-257-5904
Specialties: Working straight knives and folders, some fancy. **Patterns:** Hunters, Bowies, daggers, short swords, fillets, folders and kitchen knives. **Technical:** Grinds D2, ATS-34 and 440C, 440V. **Prices:** $110 to $1100 some to $3700. **Remarks:** Part-time maker; first knife sold in 1978. **Mark:** First and middle initials, last name.

WARREN (SEE DELLANA) DELLANA

WARTHER, DALE, 331 Karl Ave., Dover, OH 44622, Phone: 216-343-7513
Specialties: Working knives; period pieces. **Patterns:** Kitchen cutlery, daggers, hunters and some folders. **Technical:** Forges and grinds O1, D2 and 440C. **Prices:** $250 to $7,000. **Remarks:** Full-time maker; first knife sold in 1967. Takes orders only at shows or by personal interviews at his shop. **Mark:** Warther Originals.

WASHBURN, ARTHUR D, ADW Custom Knives, 10 Hinman St/POB 625, Pioche, NV 89043, Phone: 775-962-5463
Specialties: Locking liner folders. **Patterns:** Slip joint folders (single & multiplied), lock back folders, some fixed blades. Do own heat-treating; Rockwell test each blade. **Technical:** Carbon & stainless Damascus, some 1084, 1095, ATS-34. **Prices:** $200 to $1000 and up. **Remarks:** Sold first knife in 1997. Part-time maker. **Mark:** ADW enclosed in an oval or ADW.

WASHBURN JR, ROBERT LEE, 244 Lovett Scott Rd, Adrian, GA 31002, Phone: (475) 275-7926, Fax:(475) 272-6849
Specialties: Hand-forged period, Bowies, tactical, boot & hunters. **Prices:** $200 to $800. **Mark:** Washburn Knives W of Dublin GA.

WATANABE, WAYNE, P. O. Box 3563, Montebello, CA 90640, Phone: 323-728-6867
Specialties: Straight knives in Japanese styles. One of a kind designs; welcomes customer designs. **Patterns:** Tantos to katanas, Bowies. **Technical:** Flat grinds A2, O1 and ATS-34. Offers hand-rubbed finishes and wrapped handles. **Prices:** Start at $200. **Remarks:** Part-time maker. **Mark:** Name in characters with flower.

WATERS, GLENN, 11 Shinakawa Machi, Hirosaki City 036-8183, JAPAN, Phone: 172-33-8881
Specialties: One of a kind collector grade highly embellished art knives. Folders fixed blades and automatics. **Patterns:** Locking liner folders, automatics and fixed art knives. **Technical:** Grinds blades from Damasteel, and selected Damascus makers, mostly stainless. Does own engraving gold inlaying and stone setting, filework, carving. Gold and Japanese precious metal fabrication. Prefers exotic material, high karat gold, silver, Shyaku Dou, Shibu Ichi Gin, precious gemstones. **Prices:** Upscale. **Remarks:** Designs and make some of a king highly embellished art knives often fully engraved handles and blades. A jeweler by trade for 20 years before starting to make knives. Full-time since 1999, first knife sold in 1994. **Mark:** Glenn Waters maker Japan, G. Waters or Glen in Japanese writing.

WATERS, LU, 2516 Regency, Magnolia, AR 71753, Phone: 870-234-5409

WATERS, HERMAN HAROLD, 2516 Regency, Magnolia, AR 71753, Phone: (870) 234-5409

WATSON, BERT, P. O. Box 26, Westminster, CO 80036-0026, Phone: 303-426-7577
Specialties: Working/using straight knives of his design and to customer specs. **Patterns:** Hunters, utility/camp knives. **Technical:** Grinds O1, ATS-34, 440C, D2, A2 and others. **Prices:** $50 to $250. **Remarks:** Part-time maker; first knife sold in 1974. Doing business as Game Trail Knives. **Mark:** GTK stamped or etched, sometimes with first or last name.

WATSON, TOM, 1103 Brenau Terrace, Panama City, FL 32405, Phone: 850-785-9209, Fax:850-763-6034
Specialties: Liner lock folders. **Patterns:** Tactical, utility and art investment pieces. **Technical:** Flat-grinds ATS-34, 440-V, Damascus. **Prices:** Tactical start at $250, investment pieces $500 & up. **Remarks:** In business since 1978. **Mark:** Name and city.

WATSON, PETER, 66 Kielblock St., La Hoff 2570, SOUTH AFRICA, Phone: 018-84942
Specialties: Traditional working and using straight knives and folders of his design. **Patterns:** Hunters, locking folders and utility/camp knives. **Technical:** Sandvik and 440C. **Prices:** $120 to $250; some to $1500. **Remarks:** Part-time maker; first knife sold in 1989. **Mark:** Buffalo head with name.

WATSON, BILLY, 440 Forge Rd., Deatsville, AL 36022, Phone: 334-365-1482
Specialties: Working and using straight knives and folders of his design; period pieces. **Patterns:** Hunters, Bowies and utility/camp knives. **Technical:** Forges and grinds his own Damascus, 1095, 5160 and 52100. **Prices:** $25 to $1500. **Remarks:** Full-time maker; first knife sold in 1970. Doing business as Billy's Blacksmith Shop. **Mark:** Last name.

WATSON, DANIEL, 350 Jennifer Ln., Driftwood, TX 78619, Phone: 512-847-9679
Specialties: One-of-a-kind knives and swords. **Patterns:** Hunters, daggers, swords. **Technical:** Hand-purify and carbonize his own high-carbon steel, pattern-welded Damascus, cable and carbon-induced crystalline Damascus. European and Japanese tempering. **Prices:** $125 to $25,000. **Remarks:** Full-time maker; first knife sold in 1979. **Mark:** "Angel Sword" on forged pieces; "Bright Knight" for stock removal.

WATT III, FREDDIE, P. O. Box 1372, Big Spring, TX 79721, Phone: 915-263-6629
Specialties: Working straight knives, some fancy. **Patterns:** Hunters, fighters and Bowies. **Technical:** Grinds A2, D2, 440C and ATS-34; prefers mirror finishes. **Prices:** $150 to $350; some to $750. **Remarks:** Full-time maker; first knife sold in 1979. **Mark:** Last name, city and state.

WATTELET, MICHAEL A., P. O. Box 649, 125 Front, Minocqua, WI 54548, Phone: 715-356-3069
Specialties: Working and using straight knives of his design and to customer specs; fantasy knives. **Patterns:** Daggers, fighters and swords. **Technical:** Grinds 440C and L6; forges and grinds O1. Silversmith. **Prices:** $75 to $1,000; some to $5,000. **Remarks:** Full-time maker; first knife sold in 1966. Doing business as M & N Arts Ltd. **Mark:** First initial, last name.

WATTS, WALLY, 9560 S. Hwy. 36, Gatesville, TX 76528, Phone: 254-487-2866
Specialties: Unique traditional folders of his design. **Patterns:** One- to five-blade folders and single-blade gents in various blade shapes. **Technical:** Grinds ATS-34; D2 and 440C on request. **Prices:** $150 to $250; some

to $500. **Remarks:** Full-time maker; first knife sold in 1986. **Mark:** Last name.

WEBER, FRED E., 517 Tappan St., Forked River, NJ 08731, Phone: 609-693-0452
Specialties: Working knives in standard patterns. **Patterns:** Hunters, slip-joint and lock-back folders, Bowies and various-sized fillets. **Technical:** Grinds D2, 440V and ATS-34. **Prices:** $125 to $250; some to $500. **Remarks:** Full-time maker; first knife sold in 1973. **Mark:** First and middle initials, last name.

WEDDLE JR., DEL, 2703 Green Valley Rd., St. Joseph, MO 64505, Phone: 816-364-1981
Specialties: Working knives; some period pieces. **Patterns:** Hunters, fighters, locking folders, push knives. **Technical:** Grinds D2 and 440C; can provide precious metals and set gems. Offers his own forged wire-cable Damascus in his finished knives. **Prices:** $80 to $250; some to $2,000. **Remarks:** Full-time maker; first knife sold in 1972. **Mark:** Signature with last name and date.

WEHNER, RUDY, 297 William Warren Rd, Collins, MS 39428, Phone: 601-765-4997
Specialties: Reproduction antique Bowies and contemporary Bowies in full and miniature. **Patterns:** Skinners, camp knives, fighters, axes and Bowies. **Technical:** Grinds 440C, ATS-34, 154CM and Damascus. **Prices:** $100 to $500; some to $850. **Remarks:** Full-time maker; first knife sold in 1975. **Mark:** Last name on Bowies and antiques; full name, city and state on skinners.

WEILAND JR, J REESE, PO Box 2337, Riverview, FL 33568, Phone: 813-671-0661
Specialties: Hawk bills; tactical to fancy folders. **Patterns:** Hunters, tantos, bowies, fantasy knives, spears and some swords. **Technical:** Grinds ATS-34, 154CM, 440C, D2, 01, A2, Damascus. Titanium hardware on locking liners and button locks. **Prices:** $150 to $4000. **Other:** Full time maker, first knife sold in 1978. Knifemakers Guild member since 1988.

WEILER, DONALD E., P. O. Box 1576, Yuma, AZ 85366-9576, Phone: 928-782-1159
Specialties: Working straight knives; period pieces. **Patterns:** Strong springbuck folders, blade & spring ATS-34. **Technical:** Forges O1, W2, 5160, ATS-34, D2 and cable Damascus. Makes his own high-carbon steel Damascus. **Prices:** $80 to $1,000. **Remarks:** Full-time maker; first knife sold in 1952. **Mark:** Last name, city.

WEINAND, GEROME M., 14440 Harpers Bridge Rd., Missoula, MT 59802, Phone: 406-543-0845
Specialties: Working straight knives. **Patterns:** Bowies, fishing and camp knives, large special hunters. **Technical:** Grinds O1, 440C, ATS-34, 1084 and L6; makes all-tool steel Damascus; Dendritic D2 from powdered steel. Heat-treats. **Prices:** $30 to $100; some to $500. **Remarks:** Full-time maker; first knife sold in 1982. **Mark:** Last name.

WEINSTOCK, ROBERT, Box 39, 520 Frederick St., San Francisco, CA 94117, Phone: 415-731-5968
Specialties: Fancy and high-art straight knives of his design. **Patterns:** Daggers, folders, poignards and miniatures. **Technical:** Grinds A2, O1 and 440C. Chased and hand-carved blades and handles. **Prices:** $1,000 to 5,000+. **Remarks:** Full-time maker; first knife sold in1994. **Mark:** Last name carved.

WEISS, CHARLES L., 18847 N. 13th Ave., Phoenix, AZ 85027, Phone: 623-582-6147
Specialties: High-art straight knives and folders; deluxe period pieces. **Patterns:** Daggers, fighters, boots, push knives and miniatures. **Technical:** Grinds 440C, 154CM and ATS-34. **Prices:** $300 to $1,200; some to $2,000. **Remarks:** Full-time maker; first knife sold in 1975. **Mark:** Name and city.

WELCH, WILLIAM H., 8232 W. Red Snapper Dr., Kimmell, IN 46760, Phone: 219-856-3577
Specialties: Working knives; deluxe period pieces. **Patterns:** Hunters, tantos, Bowies. **Technical:** Grinds ATS-34, D2 and 440C. **Prices:** $100 to $600. **Remarks:** Part-time maker; first knife sold in 1976. **Mark:** Last name.

WERNER JR., WILLIAM A., 336 Lands Mill, Marietta, GA 30067, Phone: 404-988-0074
Specialties: Fantasy and working/using straight knives. **Patterns:** Bowies, daggers, fighters. **Technical:** Grinds 440C stainless, 10 series carbon and Damascus. **Prices:** $150 to $400; some to $750. **Remarks:** Part-time maker. Doing business as Werner Knives. **Mark:** Last name.

WERTH, GEORGE W., 5223 Woodstock Rd., Poplar Grove, IL 61065, Phone: 815-544-4408
Specialties: Period pieces, some fancy. **Patterns:** Straight fighters, daggers and Bowies. **Technical:** Forges and grinds O1, 1095 and his Damascus, including mosaic patterns. **Prices:** $200 to $650; some higher. **Remarks:** Full-time maker. Doing business as Fox Valley Forge. **Mark:** Name in logo or initials connected.

custom knifemakers

WESCOTT, CODY, 5330 White Wing Rd., Las Cruces, NM 88012, Phone: 505-382-5008
Specialties: Fancy and presentation-grade working knives. **Patterns:** Hunters, locking folders and Bowies. **Technical:** Hollow-grinds D2 and ATS-34; all knives file worked. Offers some engraving. Makes sheaths. **Prices:** $80 to $300; some to $950. **Remarks:** Full-time maker; first knife sold in 1982. **Mark:** First initial, last name.

WEST, PAT, P. O. Box 9, Charlotte, TX 78011, Phone: 830-277-1290
Specialties: Classic working and using straight knives and folders. **Patterns:** Hunters, kitchen knives, slip-joint folders. **Technical:** Grinds ATS-34, D2 and Vascowear. Offers filework and decorates liners on folders. **Prices:** $300 to $600. **Remarks:** Spare-time maker; first knife sold in 1984. **Mark:** Name.

WEST, CHARLES A., 1315 S. Pine St., Centralia, IL 62801, Phone: 618-532-2777
Specialties: Classic, fancy, high tech, period pieces, traditional and working/using straight knives and folders. **Patterns:** Bowies, fighters and locking folders. **Technical:** Grinds ATS-34, O1 and Damascus. Prefers hot blued finishes. **Prices:** $100 to $1,000; some to $2,000. **Remarks:** Full-time maker; first knife sold in 1963. Doing business as West Custom Knives. **Mark:** Name or name, city and state.

WESTBERG, LARRY, 305 S. Western Hills Dr., Algona, IA 50511, Phone: 515-295-9276
Specialties: Traditional and working straight knives of his design and in standard patterns. **Patterns:** Bowies, hunters, utility knives and miniatures. **Technical:** Grinds 440C, D2 and 1095. Heat-treats. Uses natural handle materials. **Prices:** $85 to $600; some to $1,000. **Remarks:** Part-time maker; first knife sold in 1987. **Mark:** Last name-town & state.

WHEELER, ROBERT, 289 S Jefferson, Bradley, IL 60915, Phone: 815-932-5854

WHETSELL, ALEX, 1600 Palmetto Tyrone Rd, Sharpsburg, GA 30277, Phone: 770-463-4881
Specialties: Knifekits. com a source for fold locking liner type, and straight knife kits. Our kits are industry standard for folding knife kits. **Technical:** Many selections of colored G10 carbon fiber, and wood handle material for our kits and well as bulk sizes for the custom knife maker, heat treated folding knife pivots, screws, bushings. Etc.

WHIPPLE, WESLEY A., P. O. Box 3771, Kodiak, AK 99615, Phone: 907-486-6737
Specialties: Working straight knives, some fancy. **Patterns:** Hunters, Bowies, camp knives, fighters. **Technical:** Forges high carbon steels, Damascus, offers relief carving & silver wire inlay. **Prices:** $150 to $450; some higher. **Remarks:** Part-time maker; first knife sold in 1989. **Mark:** Last name/JS. **Other:** A. K. A. Wilderness knife and forge Box 3771 Kodiak, AK 99615 907-486-6737

WHITE, GENE E., 6620 Briarleigh Way, Alexandria, VA 22315, Phone: 703-924-1268
Specialties: Small utility/gents knives. **Patterns:** Eight standard hunters; most other patterns on commission basis. Currently no swords, axes and fantasy knives. **Technical:** Stock removal 440C and D2; others on request. Mostly hollow grinds; some flat grinds. Prefers natural handle materials. Makes own sheaths. **Prices:** Start at $85. **Remarks:** Part-time maker; first knife sold in 1971. **Mark:** First and middle initials, last name.

WHITE, ROBERT J., RR 1, 641 Knox Rd. 900 N., Gilson, IL 61436, Phone: 309-289-4487
Specialties: Working knives, some deluxe. **Patterns:** Bird and trout knives, hunters, survival knives and locking folders. **Technical:** Grinds A2, D2 and 440C; commercial Damascus. Heat-treats. **Prices:** $125 to $250; some to $600. **Remarks:** Full-time maker; first knife sold in 1976. **Mark:** Last name in script.

WHITE, BRYCE, 1415 W Col. Glenn Rd, Little Rock, AR 72210, Phone: 501-821-2956
Specialties: Hunters, fighters, makes Damascus, file work, handmade only. **Technical:** L6, 1075, 1095, 01 steels used most. **Patterns:** I will do any pattern or use my own. **Prices:** $200 to $300. Sold first knife in 1995. **Mark:** White.

WHITE, LOU, 7385 Red Bud Rd NE, Ranger, GA 30734, Phone: 706-334-2273

WHITE, RICHARD T, 359 Carver St., Grosse Pointe Farms, MI 48236, Phone: 313-881-4690

WHITE JR., ROBERT J. BUTCH, RR 1, Gilson, IL 61436, Phone: 309-289-4487
Specialties: Folders of all sizes. **Patterns:** Hunters, fighters, boots and folders. **Technical:** Forges Damascus; grinds tool and stainless steels. **Prices:** $500 to $1,800. **Remarks:** Full-time maker; first knife sold in 1980. **Mark:** Last name in block letters.

WHITENECT, JODY, Elderbank, Halifax County, Nova Scotia, CANADA B0N 1K0, Phone: 902-384-2511
Specialties: Fancy and embellished working/using straight knives of his design and to customer specs. **Patterns:** Bowies, fighters and hunters. **Technical:** Forges 1095 and O1; forges and grinds ATS-34. Various filework on blades and bolsters. **Prices:** $200 to $400; some to $800. **Remarks:** Part-time maker; first knife sold in 1996. **Mark:** Longhorn stamp or engraved.

WHITLEY, L WAYNE, 1675 Carrow Rd, Chocowinity, NC 27817-9495, Phone: 252-946-5648

WHITLEY, WELDON G., 6316 Jebel Way, El Paso, TX 79912, Phone: 915-584-2274
Specialties: Working knives of his design or to customer specs. **Patterns:** Hunters, folders and various double-edged knives. **Technical:** Grinds 440C, 154CM and ATS 34. **Prices:** $150 to $1250. **Mark:** Name, address, road-runner logo.

WHITMAN, JIM, 21044 Salem St., Chugiak, AK 99567, Phone: 907-688-4575, Fax:907-688-4278
Specialties: Working straight knives and folders; some art pieces. **Patterns:** Hunters, skinners, Bowies, camp knives, working fighters, swords and hatchets. **Technical:** Grinds AEB-L Swedish, 440C, 154CM, ATS-34, and Damascus in full convex. Prefers exotic hardwoods, natural and native handle materials--whale bone, antler, ivory and horn. **Prices:** Start at $150. **Remarks:** Full-time maker; first knife sold in 1983. **Mark:** Name, city, state.

WHITMIRE, EARL T., 725 Colonial Dr., Rock Hill, SC 29730, Phone: 803-324-8384
Specialties: Working straight knives, some to customer specs; some fantasy pieces. **Patterns:** Hunters, fighters and fishing knives. **Technical:** Grinds D2, 440C and 154CM. **Prices:** $40 to $200; some to $250. **Remarks:** Full-time maker; first knife sold in 1967. **Mark:** Name, city, state in oval logo.

WHITTAKER, RANDY, 6930 Burruss Mill Rd, Cummings, GA 30131, Phone: 770-889-5263

WHITTAKER, ROBERT E., P. O. Box 204, Mill Creek, PA 17060
Specialties: Using straight knives. Has a line of knives for buckskinners. **Patterns:** Hunters, skinners and Bowies. **Technical:** Grinds O1, A2 and D2. Offers filework. **Prices:** $35 to $100. **Remarks:** Part-time maker; first knife sold in 1980. **Mark:** Last initial or full initials.

WHITTAKER, WAYNE, 2900 Woodland Ct., Metamore, MI 48455, Phone: 810-797-5315
Specialties: Folders, hunters on request. **Patterns:** Bowies, daggers and hunters. **Technical:** ATS-34 S. S. and Damascus **Prices:** $300 to $500; some to $2,000. **Remarks:** Full-time maker; first knife sold in 1985. **Mark:** Etched name on one side.

WHITWORTH, KEN J., 41667 Tetley Ave., Sterling Heights, MI 48078, Phone: 313-739-5720
Specialties: Working straight knives and folders. **Patterns:** Locking folders, slip-joints and boot knives. **Technical:** Grinds 440C, 154CM and D2. **Prices:** $100 to $225; some to $450. **Remarks:** Part-time maker; first knife sold in 1976. **Mark:** Last name.

WICKER, DONNIE R., 2544 E. 40th Ct., Panama City, FL 32405, Phone: 904-785-9158
Specialties: Traditional working and using straight knives of his design or to customer specs. **Patterns:** Hunters, fighters and slip-joint folders. **Technical:** Grinds 440C, ATS-34, D2 and 154CM. Heat-treats and does hardness testing. **Prices:** $90 to $200; some to $400. **Remarks:** Part-time maker; first knife sold in 1975. **Mark:** First and middle initials, last name.

WIGGINS, HORACE, 203 Herndon, Box 152, Mansfield, LA 71502, Phone: 318-872-4471
Specialties: Fancy working knives. **Patterns:** Straight and folding hunters. **Technical:** Grinds O1, D2 and 440C. **Prices:** $90 to $275. **Remarks:** Part-time maker; first knife sold in 1970. **Mark:** Name, city and state in diamond logo.

WILCHER, WENDELL L., RR 6 Box 6573, Palestine, TX 75801, Phone: 903-549-2530
Specialties: Fantasy, miniatures and working/using straight knives and folders of his design and to customer specs. **Patterns:** Fighters, hunters, locking folders. **Technical:** Hand works (hand file and hand sand knives), not grind. **Prices:** $75 to $250; some to $600. **Remarks:** Part-time maker; first knife sold in 1987. **Mark:** Initials, year, serial number.

WILE, PETER, RR 3, Bridgewater, Nova Scotia, CANADA B4V 2W2, Phone: 902-543-1373
Specialties: Collector grade one of a kind file worked folders. **Patterns:** Folders or fixed blades of his design or to customers specs. **Technical:** Grinds ATS-34, carbon and stainless Damascus. Does intricate filework on blades, spines and liners. Carves. Prefers natural handle materials. Does own heat treating. **Prices:** $350. 00 to $2000. 00 some to $4000. 00.

Remarks: Part-time maker: sold first knife in 1985; doing business as Wile Knives. **Mark:** Wile

WILKINS, MITCHELL, 15523 Ralson Chapel Rd, Montgomery, TX 77316, Phone: 409-588-2696

WILLEY, W. G., R. D. 1, Box 235-B, Greenwood, DE 19950, Phone: 302-349-4070
Specialties: Fancy working straight knives. **Patterns:** Small game knives, Bowies and throwing knives. **Technical:** Grinds 440C and 154CM. **Prices:** $225 to $600; some to $1,500. **Remarks:** Part-time maker; first knife sold in 1975. Owns retail store. **Mark:** Last name inside map logo.

WILLIAM E, STAPLETON, Buffalo 'b' Forge, 5425 Country Ln, Merritt Island, FL 32953
Specialties: Classic and traditional knives of my design and customer spec. **Patterns:** Hunters and using knives. **Technical:** Forges, 01 and L-6 Damascus, cable Damascus and 5160; stock removal on request. **Prices:** $150 to $1,000. **Remarks:** Part-time maker, first knife sold 1990. Doing business as Buffalo "B" Forge. **Mark:** Anvil with S initial in center of anvil.

WILLIAMS, MICHAEL L., Rt. 4, P. O. Box 64-1, Broken Bow, OK 74728, Phone: 405-494-6326
Specialties: Plain to fancy working and dress knives. **Patterns:** Hunters, Bowies, camp knives and others. **Technical:** Forges 1084, L6, 52100 and pattern-welded steel. **Prices:** $295 and up. **Remarks:** Part-time maker; first knife sold in 1989. ABS Mastersmith. **Mark:** Williams.

WILLIAMS, A L, 4950 Lake Pierce Dr, Lake Wales, FL 33853, Phone: 941-439-1906

WILLIAMS, JASON L., P. O. Box 67, Wyoming, RI 02898, Phone: 401-539-8353, Fax:401-539-0252
Specialties: Fancy & high tech folders of his design, co-inventor of the Axis Lock. **Patterns:** Fighters, locking folders, automatics and fancy pocket knives. **Technical:** Forges Damascus and other steels by request. Uses exotic handle materials and precious metals. Offers inlaid spines and gemstone thumb knobs. **Prices:** $1,000 and up. **Remarks:** Full-time maker; first knife sold in 1989. **Mark:** First and last initials on pivot.

WILLIAMS JR., RICHARD, 1440 Nancy Circle, Morristown, TN 37814, Phone: 615-581-0059
Specialties: Working and using straight knives of his design or to customer specs. **Patterns:** Hunters, dirks and utility/camp knives. **Technical:** Forges 5160 and uses file steel. Hand-finish is standard; offers filework. **Prices:** $80 to $180; some to $250. **Remarks:** Spare-time maker; first knife sold in 1985. **Mark:** Last initial or full initials.

WILLIAMSON, TONY, Rt. 3, Box 503, Siler City, NC 27344, Phone: 919-663-3551
Specialties: Flint knapping--knives made of obsidian flakes and flint with wood, antler or bone for handles. **Patterns:** Skinners, daggers and flake knives. **Technical:** Blades have width/thickness ratio of at least 4 to 1. Hafts with methods available to prehistoric man. **Prices:** $58 to $160. **Remarks:** Student of Errett Callahan. **Mark:** Initials and number code to identify year and number of knives made.

WILLIS, BILL, RT 7 Box 7549, Ava, MO 65608, Phone: 417-683-4326
Specialties: Forged blades, Damascus & carbon steel. **Patterns:** Cable, random or ladder lamented. **Technical:** Professionally heat treated blades. **Prices:** $75 to $600. **Remarks:** Lifetime guarantee on all blades against breakage. **Mark:** WF. **Other:** All work done by myself; including leather work.

WILLSON, HARLAN M., P. O. Box 2113, Lompoc, CA 93436, Phone: 805-735-0085, Fax:805-735-0085
Specialties: Working, fantasy and art straight knives of his design and to customer specs. **Patterns:** Various styles. **Technical:** Grinds ATS-34, 440C, 1095 and O1. Prefers bone and natural handle materials; some exotic woods. Carves custom handle designs. **Prices:** $200 to $500; some to $1,000. **Remarks:** Full-time maker; first knife sold in 1990. Doing business as Harlan Willson Custom Cutlery. **Mark:** Initials and last name or heart within bear paw.

WILLSON, WAYNE O, 11403 Sunflower Ln, Fairfax, VA 22030-6031, Phone: 703-278-8000

WILSON, PHILIP C., Seamount Knifeworks, PO Box 846, Mountain Ranch, CA 95246, Phone: 209-754-1990
Specialties: Working knives; emphasis on salt water fillet knives and utility hunters of his design. **Patterns:** Fishing knives, hunters, kitchen knives. **Technical:** Grinds CPM S-30V, CPM10V, S-90V and 154CM. Heat-treats and Rockwell tests all blades. **Prices:** Start at $280. **Remarks:** First knife sold in 1985. Doing business as Sea-Mount Knife Works. **Mark:** Signature.

WILSON, JAMES R, PO Box 1285, Westcliffe, CO 81252, Phone: 719-331-4995
Specialties: Collectible, traditional functional knives. **Patterns:** Bowies, fighters, hunters and folders. **Technical:** Forges 5160, 1095 &

my own Damascus. **Prices:** $150 to $1000. **Remarks:** Limited production fine knives; first knife sold in 1994. **Mark:** J and last name.

WILSON, JAMES R., Rt. 2 Box 175HC, Seminole, OK 74868, Phone: 405-382-7230
Specialties: Traditional working knives. **Patterns:** Bowies, hunters, skinners, fighters and camp knives. **Technical:** Forges 5160, 1095, O1 and his Damascus. **Prices:** Start at $125. **Remarks:** Part-time maker; first knife sold in 1994. **Mark:** First initial, last name.

WILSON, R. W., P. O. Box 2012, Weirton, WV 26062, Phone: 304-723-2771
Specialties: Working straight knives; period pieces. **Patterns:** Bowies, tomahawks and patch knives. **Prices:** $85 to $175; some to $1,000. **Technical:** Grinds 440C; scrimshaws. **Remarks:** Part-time maker; first knife sold in 1966. Knife maker supplier. Offers free knife making lessons. **Mark:** Name in tomahawk.

WILSON, JAMES G., P. O. Box 4024, Estes Park, CO 80517, Phone: 303-586-3944
Specialties: Bronze Age knives; Medieval and Scottish styles; tomahawks. **Patterns:** Bronze knives, daggers, swords, spears and battle axes; 12-inch steel Misericorde daggers, sgian dubhs, "his and her" skinners, bird and fish knives, capers, boots and daggers. **Technical:** Casts bronze; grinds D2, 440C and ATS-34. **Prices:** $49 to $400; some to $1,300. **Remarks:** Part-time maker; first knife sold in 1975. **Mark:** WilsonHawk.

WILSON, JON J., 1826 Ruby St., Johnstown, PA 15902, Phone: 814-266-6410
Specialties: Miniatures & full size. **Patterns:** Bowies, daggers and hunters. **Technical:** Grinds Damascus, 440C and O1. Scrimshaws and carves. **Prices:** $75 to $500; some higher. **Remarks:** Full-time maker; first knife sold in 1988. **Mark:** First and middle initials, last name.

WILSON, RON, 2639 Greenwood ave, Morro Bay, CA 93442, Phone: 805-772-3381
Specialties: Classic and fantasy straight knives of his design. **Patterns:** Daggers, fighters, swords and axes--mostly all miniatures. **Technical:** Forges and grinds Damascus and various tool steels; grinds meteorite. Uses gold, precious stones and exotic woods. **Prices:** Vary. **Remarks:** Part-time maker; first knife sold in 1995. **Mark:** Stamped first and last initials.

WILSON, MIKE, 1416 McDonald Rd, Hayesville, NC 28904, Phone: 828-389-8145
Specialties: Fancy working and using straight knives of his design or to customer specs, folders. **Patterns:** Hunters, Bowies, utility knives, gut hooks, skinners, fighters and miniatures. **Technical:** Hollow-grinds 440C, L-6, 01 and D2. Mirror finishes are standard. Offers filework. **Prices:** $50 to $600. **Remarks:** Full-time maker; first knife sold in 1985. **Mark:** Last name.

WILSON (SEE SIMONELLA, GIANLUIGI)

WILSON, III, GEORGE H., 150-6 Dreiser Loop #6-B, Bronx, NY 10475

WIMPFF, CHRISTIAN, P. O. Box 700526, 70574 Stuttgart 70, GERMANY, Phone: 711 7206 749, Fax:711 7206 749
Specialties: High-tech folders of his design. **Patterns:** Boots, locking folders and liners locks. **Technical:** Grinds CPM-T-440V, ATS-34 and Schneider stainless Damascus. Offers meteorite bolsters and blades. **Prices:** $1,000 to $2,800; some to $4,000. **Remarks:** Full-time maker; first knife sold in 1984. **Mark:** First initial, last name.

WINBERG, DOUGLAS R, 19720 Hiway 78, Ramona, CA 92076, Phone: (760) 788-8304

WINGO, GARY, 240 Ogeechee, Ramona, OK 74061, Phone: 918-536-1067
Specialties: Folder specialist. Steel 44OC, D2, others on request. Handle bone-stag, others on request. **Patterns:** Trapper-three blade stockman, 4 blade congress, single and 2 blade barlows. **Prices:** 150 to $400. **Mark:** First knife sold 1994. Steer head with Wingo Knives or Straight line Wingo Knives.

WINGO, PERRY, 22 55th St., Gulfport, MS 39507, Phone: 228-863-3193
Specialties: Traditional working straight knives. **Patterns:** Hunters, skinners, Bowies and fishing knives. **Technical:** Grinds 440C. **Prices:** $75 to $1,000. **Remarks:** Part-time maker; first knife sold in 1988. **Mark:** Last name.

WINKLER, DANIEL, P. O. Box 2166, Blowing Rock, NC 28605, Phone: 828-295-9156, Fax:828-295-0673
Specialties: Forged cutlery styled in the tradition of an era past. **Patterns:** Fixed blades, friction folders, axes/tomahawks and war clubs. **Technical:** Forges and grinds carbon steels and his own Damascus. **Prices:** $200 to $4,000. **Remarks:** Full-time maker since 1988. Exclusively offers leatherwork by Karen Shook. **Mark:** Initials connected. **Other:**ABS MasterSmith; Knifemakers Guild voting member.

custom knifemakers

WINN, TRAVIS A., 558 E. 3065 S., Salt Lake City, UT 84106, Phone: 801-467-5957
Specialties: Fancy working knives and knives to customer specs. **Patterns:** Hunters, fighters, boots, Bowies and fancy daggers, some miniatures, tantos and fantasy knives. **Technical:** Grinds D2 and 440C. Embellishes. **Prices:** $125 to $500; some higher. **Remarks:** Part-time maker; first knife sold in 1976. **Mark:** TRAV stylized.

WINSTON, DAVID, 1671 Red Holly St., Starkville, MS 39759, Phone: 601-323-1028
Specialties: Fancy and traditional knives of his design and to customer specs. **Patterns:** Bowies, daggers, hunters, boot knives and folders. **Technical:** Grinds 440C, ATS-34 and D2. Offers filework; heat-treats. **Prices:** $40 to $750; some higher. **Remarks:** Part-time maker; first knife sold in 1984. Offers lifetime sharpening for original owner. **Mark:** Last name.

WINTER, GEORGE, 5940 Martin Hwy, Union City, TN 38261

WIRTZ, ACHIM, Mittelstrasse 58, Wuerselen, D-52146, GERMANY, Phone: (4924) 056-7455
Specialties: Period pieces, Scandinavian style knives. **Technical:** Forges 5160, 52100 and own Damascus. **Prices:** Start at $50. **Remarks:** Spare-time maker. First knife sold in 1997. **Mark:** Stylized initials.

WISE, DONALD, 304 Bexhill Rd., St. Leonardo-On-Sea, East Sussex, TN3 8AL, ENGLAND
Specialties: Fancy and embellished working straight knives to customer specs. **Patterns:** Hunters, Bowies and daggers. **Technical:** Grinds Sandvik 12C27, D2 D3 and O1. Scrimshaws. **Prices:** $110 to $300; some to $500. **Remarks:** Full-time maker; first knife sold in 1983. **Mark:** KNIFECRAFT.

WITSAMAN, EARL, 3957 Redwing Circle, Stow, OH 44224, Phone: 330-688-4208
Specialties: Straight and fantasy miniatures. **Patterns:** Wide variety--Randalls to D-guard Bowies. **Technical:** Grinds O1, 440C and 300 stainless; buys Damascus; highly detailed work. **Prices:** $85 to $300. **Remarks:** Part-time maker; first knife sold in1974. **Mark:** Initials.

WOLF, BILL, 4618 N. 79th Ave., Phoenix, AZ 85033, Phone: 623-846-3585, Fax:623-846-3585
Specialties: Investor-grade folders and straight knives. **Patterns:** Lockback, slip joint and side lock interframes. **Technical:** Grinds ATS-34 and 440C. **Prices:** $400 to $1,800. **Remarks:** Full-time maker; first knife sold in 1989. **Mark:** Name.

WOLF JR, WILLIAM LYNN, 4006 Frank Rd, Lagrange, TX 78945, Phone: (409) 247-4626

WOOD, WILLIAM W., P. O. Box 606, Seymour, TX 76380, Phone: 817-888-5832
Specialties: Exotic working knives with Middle-East flavor. **Patterns:** Fighters, boots and some utility knives. **Technical:** Grinds D2 and 440C; buys Damascus. Prefers hand-rubbed satin finishes; uses only natural handle materials. **Prices:** $300 to $600; some to $2,000. **Remarks:** Full-time maker; first knife sold in 1977. **Mark:** Name, city and state.

WOOD, ALAN, Greenfield Villa, Greenhead, Carlisle, CA6 7HH, ENGLAND, Phone: 016977-47303
Specialties: High-tech working straight knives of his design. **Patterns:** Hunters, utility/camp and woodcraft knives. **Technical:** Grinds Sandvik 12C27, D2 and O1. Blades are cryogenic treated. **Prices:** $150 to $400; some to $750. **Remarks:** Full-time maker; first knife sold in 1979. **Mark:** First initial, last name and country.

WOOD, OWEN DALE, P. O. Box 515, Honeydew 2040 (Transvaal), SOUTH AFRICA, Phone: 011-958-1789
Specialties: Fancy working knives. **Patterns:** Hunters and fighters; variety of big knives; sword canes. **Technical:** Forges and grinds 440C, 154CM and his own Damascus. Uses rare African handle materials. **Prices:** $280 to $450; some to $3,000. **Remarks:** Full-time maker; first knife sold in 1976. **Mark:** Initials.

WOOD, WEBSTER, 22041 Shelton Trail, Atlanta, MI 49709, Phone: 989-785-2996
Specialties: Work mainly in stainless; art knives, Bowies, hunters and folders. **Remarks:** Full-time maker; first knife sold in 1980. Guild member since 1984. All engraving done by maker. **Mark:** Initials inside shield and name.

WOOD, LARRY B., 6945 Fishburg Rd., Huber Heights, OH 45424, Phone: 513-233-6751
Specialties: Fancy working knives of his design. **Patterns:** Hunters, buckskinners, Bowies, tomahawks, locking folders and Damascus miniatures. **Technical:** Forges 1095, file steel and his own Damascus. **Prices:** $125 to $500; some to $2,000. **Remarks:** Full-time maker; first knife sold in 1974. Doing business as Wood's Metal Studios. **Mark:** Variations of last name, sometimes with blacksmith logo.

WOODARD, WILEY, 4527 Jim Mitchell W., Colleyville, TX 76034
Specialties: Straight knives, Damascus carbon and stainless, all natural material.

WOODCOCK, DENNIS "WOODY", PO Box 416, Nehalem, OR 97131, Phone: 503-368-7511
Specialties: Working knives. **Patterns:** Hunters, Bowies, skinners, hunters. **Technical:** Grinds ATS-34, D2, 440C, 440V. Offers filework; makes sheaths. **Prices:** $50 to $500. **Remarks:** Full-time maker; first knife sold in 1982. Doing business as Woody's Custom Knives. **Mark:** Nickname, last name, city, state.

WOODIWISS, DORREN, P O Box 396, Thompson Falls, MT 59873-0396, Phone: (406) 827-0079

WOODWARD, WILEY, 4517 Jim Mitchell W, Colleyville, TX 76034, Phone: (817) 267-3277

WOOTTON, RANDY, 83 Lafayette 254, Stamps, AR 71860, Phone: (870) 533-2472

WORRELL, MORRIS C, 5625 S 25 W, Lebanon, IN 46052-9766
Specialties: Bowies daggers, Japanese, Tantos, art knives, tactical, Viking knives. **Patterns:** Prefers ivory handles, filework & engraving, gemstone. **Technical:** Forges 1050, 1084, 5160, 1095, 01, grinds ATS-34, 440C, 420C. **Prices:** $250 to $2000. **Remarks:** Makes classic blades from all cultures. **Mark:** Worrell stamp, 3 sizes or WORRELL MAKER logo. **Other:** Makes own Damascus from L-6 and 1095.

WORTHEN, BILL, 200 E 3rd, Little Rock, AR 72201-1608, Phone: (501) 324-9351

WRIGHT, TIMOTHY, P. O. Box 3746, Sedona, AZ 86340, Phone: 928-282-4180
Specialties: High-tech folders and working knives. **Patterns:** Interframe locking folders, non-inlaid folders, straight hunters and kitchen knives. **Technical:** Grinds BG-42, AEB-L, K190 and Cowry X; works with new steels. All folders can disassemble and are furnished with tools. **Prices:** $150 to $1,800; some to $3,000. **Remarks:** Full-time maker; first knife sold in 1975. **Mark:** Last name and type of steel used.

WRIGHT, KEVIN, 671 Leland Valley Rd. W, Quilcene, WA 98376-9517, Phone: 360-765-3589
Specialties: Fancy working or collector knives to customer specs. **Patterns:** Hunters, boots, buckskinners, miniatures. **Technical:** Forges and grinds L6, 1095, 440C and his own Damascus. **Prices:** $75 to $500; some to $2,000. **Remarks:** Part-time maker; first knife sold in 1978. **Mark:** Last initial in anvil.

WRIGHT, RICHARD S, PO Box 201, 111 Hilltop Dr, Carolina, RI 02812, Phone: 401-364-3579
Specialties: Bolster release switchblades. **Patterns:** Folding fighters, gents pocket knives, one-of-a-kind high-grade automatics. **Technical:** Reforges and grinds various makers Damascus. Uses a variety of tool steels. Uses natural handle material such as ivory & pearl, extensive filework on most knives. **Prices:** $2000 and up. **Remarks:** Part-time knife maker with background as a gunsmith. Made first folder in 1991. **Mark:** RSW on blade, all folders are serial numbered.

WUERTZ, TRAVIS, 2487 E. Hwy 287, Casa Grande, AZ 85222, Phone: (520) 723-4432

WYATT, WILLIAM R., Box 237, Rainelle, WV 25962, Phone: 304-438-5494
Specialties: Classic and working knives of all designs. **Patterns:** Hunters and utility knives. **Technical:** Forges and grinds saw blades, files and rasps. Prefers stag handles. **Prices:** $45 to $95; some to $350. **Remarks:** Part-time maker; first knife sold in 1990. **Mark:** Last name in star with knife logo.

WYMAN, MARC L, 5320 SW 28th Terrace, Ft Lauderdale, FL 33312, Phone: (954) 985-3863, Fax:(954) 964-4418
Remarks: Part-time maker.

y

YASHINSKI, JOHN L, 207 N Platt, PO Box 1284, Red Lodge, MT 59068, Phone: 406-446-3916
Specialties: Native American Beaded sheathes. **Prices:** Vary.

YEATES, JOE A., 730 Saddlewood Circle, Spring, TX 77381, Phone: 281-367-2765
Specialties: Bowies and period pieces. **Patterns:** Bowies, toothpicks and combat knives. **Technical:** Grinds 440C, D2 and ATS-34. **Prices:** $400 to $2,000; some to $2,500. **Remarks:** Full-time maker; first knife sold in 1975. **Mark:** Last initial within outline of Texas; or last initial.

YESKOO, RICHARD C, 76 Beekman Rd, Summit, NJ 07901

YORK, DAVID C., PO Box 3166, Chino Valley, AZ 86323, Phone: 520-636-1709
Specialties: Working straight knives and folders. **Patterns:** Prefers small hunters and skinners; locking folders. **Technical:** Grinds D2 and 440C; buys Damascus. **Prices:** $75 to $300; some to $600. **Remarks:** Full-time maker; first knife sold in 1975. **Mark:** Last name.

YOSHIHARA, YOSHINDO, 8-17-11 Takasago, Katsushi, Tokyo, JAPAN

YOSHIKAZU, KAMADA, , 540-3 Kaisaki Niuta-cho, Tokushima, JAPAN, Phone: 0886-44-2319

YOSHIO, MAEDA, 3-12-11 Chuo-Cho Tamashima Kurashiki-City, Okayama, JAPAN, Phone: 086-525-2375

YOUNG, RAYMOND L, Cutler/Bladesmith, 2922 Hwy 188E, Mt Ida, AR 71957, Phone: (870) 867-3947
Specialties: Cutler-Bladesmith, Sharpening service. **Patterns:** Hunter, skinners, fighters, no guard, no ricasso, chef tools. **Technical:** Edge tempered 1095, 516C, Mosiac handles, water buffalo and exotic woods. **Prices:** $100 and up. **Remarks:** Federal contractor since 1995. Surgical steel sharpening. **Mark:** R/

YOUNG, BUD, Box 336, Port Hardy, BC, CANADA V0N 2P0, Phone: 250-949-6478
Specialties: Fixed blade, working knives, some fancy. **Patterns:** Drop-points to skinners. **Technical:** Hollow or flat grind, 5160, 440-C, mostly ATS-34, satin finish. **Prices:** $150 to $500 CDN. **Remarks:** Spare-time maker; making knives since 1962; first knife sold in 1985. **Mark:** Name. **Other:** Not taking orders at this time, sell as produced.

YOUNG, PAUL A., 168 Elk Ridge Rd., Boone, NC 28607, Phone: 704-264-7048
Specialties: Working straight knives and folders of his design or to customer specs; some art knives. **Patterns:** Small boot knives, skinners, 18th century period pieces and folders. **Technical:** Forges O1 and file steels. Full-time embellisher--engraves and scrimshaws. Prefers floral designs; any design accepted. Does not engrave hardened metals. **Prices:** Determined by type and design. **Remarks:** Full-time maker; first knife sold in 1978. **Mark:** Initials in logo.

YOUNG, CLIFF, Fuente De La Cibeles No. 5, Atascadero, San Miguel De Allende, GTO., MEXICO, Phone: 37700, Fax:011-52-415-2-57-11
Specialties: Working knives. **Patterns:** Hunters, fighters and fishing knives. **Technical:** Grinds all; offers D2, 440C and 154CM. **Prices:** Start at $250. **Remarks:** Part-time maker; first knife sold in 1980. **Mark:** Name.

YOUNG, ERROL, 4826 Storey Land, Alton, IL 62002, Phone: 618-466-4707
Specialties: Traditional working straight knives and folders. **Patterns:** Wide range, including tantos, Bowies, miniatures and multi-blade folders. **Technical:** Grinds D2, 440C and ATS-34. **Prices:** $75 to $650; some to $800. **Remarks:** Part-time maker; first knife sold in 1987. **Mark:** Last name with arrow.

YOUNG, GEORGE, 713 Pinoak Dr., Kokomo, IN 46901, Phone: 765-457-8893
Specialties: Fancy/embellished and traditional straight knives and folders of his design and to customer specs. **Patterns:** Hunters, fillet/camp knives and locking folders. **Technical:** Grinds 440C, CPM440V, and Stellite 6K. Fancy ivory, black pearl and stag for handles. Filework--all Stellite construction (6K and 25 alloys). Offers engraving. **Prices:** $350 to $750; some $1,500 to $3,000. **Remarks:** Full-time maker; first knife sold in 1954. Doing business as Young's Knives. **Mark:** Last name integral inside Bowie.

YURCO, MIKE, P. O. Box 712, Canfield, OH 44406, Phone: 330-533-4928
Specialties: Working straight knives. **Patterns:** Hunters, utility knives, Bowies and fighters, push knives, claws and other hideouts. **Technical:** Grinds 440C, ATS-34 and 154CM; likes mirror and satin finishes. **Prices:** $20 to $500. **Remarks:** Part-time maker; first knife sold in 1983. **Mark:** Name, steel, serial number.

Z

ZACCAGNINO JR., DON, 2256 Bacom Point Rd, Pahokee, FL 33476-2622, Phone: 407-924-7844
Specialties: Working knives and some period pieces of their designs. **Patterns:** Heavy-duty hunters, axes and Bowies; a line of light-weight hunters, fillets and personal knives. **Technical:** Grinds 440C and 17-4 PH--highly finished in complex handle and blade treatments. **Prices:** $165 to $500;

some to $2,500. **Remarks:** Part-time maker; first knife sold in 1969 by Don Zaccagnino Sr. **Mark:** ZACK, city and state inside oval.

ZAHM, KURT, 488 Rio Casa, Indialantic, FL 32903, Phone: 407-777-4860
Specialties: Working straight knives of his design or to customer specs. **Patterns:** Daggers, fancy fighters, Bowies, hunters and utility knives. **Technical:** Grinds D2, 440C; likes filework. **Prices:** $75 to $1,000. **Remarks:** Part-time maker; first knife sold in 1985. **Mark:** Last name.

ZAKABI, CARL S., P. O. Box 893161, Mililani Town, HI 96789-0161, Phone: 808-626-2181
Specialties: Working and using straight knives of his design. **Patterns:** Fighters, hunters and utility/camp knives. **Technical:** Grinds 440C and ATS-34. **Prices:** $55 to $200. **Remarks:** Spare-time maker; first knife sold in 1988. Doing business as Zakabi's Knifeworks. **Mark:** Last name and state.

ZAKHAROV, CARLOS, R. Pernambuco175, Rio Comprido Jacarei, SP-12305-340, BRAZIL, Phone: 55 12 3958 4027, Fax:55 12 3958 4103
Specialties: Using straight knives of his design. **Patterns:** Hunters, kitchen, utility/camp and barbecue knives. **Technical:** Grinds his own "secret steel. " **Prices:** $30 to $200. **Remarks:** Full-time maker. **Mark:** Arkhip Special Knives.

ZBORIL, TERRY, RT 4 Box 318, Caldwell, TX 77836, Phone: 979-535-4157
Specialties: ABS Journey man smith.

ZEMBKO III, JOHN, 140 Wilks Pond Rd, Berlin, CT 06037, Phone: 860-828-3503
Specialties: Working knives of his design or to customer specs. **Patterns:** Likes to use stabilized high figured woods. **Technical:** Grinds ATS-34, A-2, D-2; forges O-1, 1095; grinds Damasteel. **Prices:** $50 to $400; some higher. **Remarks:** First knife sold in 1987. **Mark:** Name.

ZEMITIS, JOE, 14 Currawong Rd., Cardiff Hts., 2285 Newcastle, AUSTRALIA, Phone: 0249549907
Specialties: Traditional working straight knives. **Patterns:** Hunters, Bowies, tantos, fighters and camp knives. **Technical:** Grinds O1, D2, W2 and 440C; makes his own Damascus. Embellishes; offers engraving and scrimshaw. **Prices:** $150 to $3,000. **Remarks:** Full-time maker; first knife sold in 1983. **Mark:** First initial, last name and country, or last name.

ZIMA, MICHAEL F., 732 State St., Ft. Morgan, CO 80701, Phone: 970-867-6078
Specialties: Working straight knives and folders. **Patterns:** Hunters; utility, locking and slip-joint folders. **Technical:** Grinds D-2, 440C, ATS-34, and Specialty Damascus. **Prices:** $150 to $300; some higher. **Remarks:** Full-time maker; first knife sold in 1982. **Mark:** Last name.

ZINKER, BRAD, BZ KNIVES, 1591 NW 17 St, Homestead, FL 33030, Phone: 305-216-0404
Specialties: Fillets, folders & hunters. **Technical:** Uses ATS-34 and stainless Damascus. **Prices:** $200-$600. **Remarks:** Voting member of knifemakrs guild & Floria knifemakers association. **Mark:** Offset connected initials BZ.

ZIRBES, RICHARD, Neustrasse 15, D-54526 Niederkail, GERMANY, Phone: 0049 6575 1371
Specialties: Fancy embellished knives with engraving and self-made scrimshaw (scrimshaw made by himself). High-tech working knives and high-tech hunters, boots, fighters and folders. All knives made by hand. **Patterns:** Boots, fighters, folders, hunters. **Technical:** I use only the best steels for blade material like CPM-T 440V, CPM-T 420V, ATS-34, D2, C440, stainless Damascus or steel according to customer's desire. **Prices:**Working knives & hunters: $200 to $600. Fancy embellished knives with engraving and/or scrimshaw: $800 to $3000. **Remarks:** Part-time maker; first knife sold in 1991. Member of the German Knife maker Guild. **Mark:** Zirbes or R. Zirbes.

ZOWADA, TIM, 4509 E. Bear River Rd, Boyne Falls, MI 49713, Phone: 231-348-5446
Specialties: Working knives, some fancy. **Patterns:** Hunters, camp knives, boots, swords, fighters, tantos and locking folders. **Technical:** Forges O2, L6, W2 and his own Damascus. **Prices:** $150 to $1,000; some to $5,000. **Remarks:** Full-time maker; first knife sold in 1980.

ZSCHERNY, MICHAEL, 1840 Rock Island Dr., Ely, IA 52227, Phone: 319-848-3629
Specialties: Quality folding knives. **Patterns:** Liner lock and lock back folders in titanium, working straight knives. **Technical:** Grinds 440 and commercial Damascus, prefers natural materials such as pearls and ivory. **Prices:** Starting at $200. **Remarks:** Full-time maker; first knife sold in 1978. **Mark:** Last name, city and state; folders, last name with stars inside folding knife.

alabama

Andress, Ronnie	Satsuma
Batson, James	Madison
Bowles, Chris	Reform
Bullard, Bill	Andalusia
Coffman, Danny	Jacksonville
Conn Jr., C.t.	Attalla
Connell, Steve	Adamsville
Cutchin, Roy D.	Seale
Daniels, Alex	Town Creek
Di Marzo, Richard	Birmingham
Durham, Kenneth	Cherokee
Elrod, Roger R	Enterprise
Fikes, Jimmy L.	Jasper
Fogg, Don	Jasper
Fowler, Ricky & Susan	Silverhill
Fronefield, Daniel	Hampton Cove
Gilbreath, Randall	Dora
Green, Mark	Graysville
Hammond, Jim	Arab
Hodge, J.B.	Huntsville
Howard, Durvyn M.	Hokes Bluff
Howell, Len	Opelika
Howell, Ted	Wetumpka
Huckabee, Dale	Maylene
Hulsey, Hoyt	Attalla
Madison II, Billy D.	Remlap
Mccullough, Jerry	Georgiana
Militano, Tom	Jacksonville
Monk, Nathan P.	Cullman
Morris, C.h.	Frisco City
Pardue, Melvin M.	Repton
Roe Jr., Fred D.	Huntsville
Russell, Tom	Jacksonville
Sandlin, Larry	Adamsville
Sinyard, Cleston S.	Elberta
Sketos, S Ted	Hartford
Thomas, David E	Lillian
Watson, Billy	Deatsville

alaska

Barlow, Jana Poirier	Anchorage
Brennan, Judson	Delta Junction
Breuer, Lonnie	Wasilla
Broome, Thomas A.	Kenai
Bucholz, Mark A.	Eagle River
Button-inman, Dee	Anchorage
Cannon, Raymond W.	Homer
Cawthorne, Christopher A	Wrangell
Chamberlin, John A.	Anchorage
Clark, Peter	Anchorage
Dempsey, Gordon S.	N. Kenai
Dufour, Arthur J.	Anchorage
England, Virgil	Anchorage
Flint, Robert	Anchorage
Gouker, Gary B.	Sitka
Grebe, Gordon S.	Anchor Point
Hibben, Westley G.	Anchorage
Kommer, Russ	Anchorage
Lance, Bill	Eagle River
Little, Jimmy L.	Wasilla
Malaby, Raymond J	Juneau
McFarlin, Eric E.	Kodiak
Mcintosh, David L.	Haines
Mirabile, David	Juneau
Parrish III, Gordon A.	North Pole
Schmoker, Randy	Slana
Shore, John I	Anchorage
Stegall, Keith	Anchorage
Trujillo, Adam	Anchorage
Trujillo, Miranda	Anchorage
Trujillo, Thomas A.	Anchorage
Van Cleve, Steve	Sutton
Whipple, Wesley A.	Kodiak
Whitman, Jim	Chugiak

arizona

Ammons, David C	Tucson
Bennett, Glen C	Tucson
Boye, David	Dolan Springs
Bryan, Tom	Gilbert
Cheatham, Bill	Laveen
Choate, Milton	Somerton
Craft III, John M.	Peoria
Evans, Vincent K. & Grace	Show Low
Fuegen, Larry	Prescott
Goo, Tai	Tucson
Guignard, Gib	Quartzsite
Gundersen, D.f. "Doc"	Tempe
Hancock, Tim	Scottsdale
Hankins, R	Tempe
Hoel, Steve	Pine
Holder, D'Alton	Peoria
Hull, Michael J.	Cottonwood
Karp, Bob	Phoenix
Kelley, Thomas P	Cave Creek
Kopp, Todd M.	Apache Jct.
Lampson, Frank G.	Rimrock
Lee, Randy	St. Johns
Lively, Tim and Marian	Tucson
Mcfall, Ken	Lakeside
Mcfarlin, J.W.	Lake Havasu City
Murray, Bill	Green Valley
Newhall, Tom	Tucson
Norris, Don	Tucson
Purvis, Bob & Ellen	Tucson
Snare, Michael	Phoenix
Tamboli, Michael	Glendale
Torgeson, Samuel L	Sedona
Weiler, Donald E.	Yuma
Weiss, Charles L.	Phoenix
Wolf, Bill	Phoenix
Wright, Timothy	Sedona
Wuertz, Travis	Casa Grande
York, David C.	Chino Valley

arkansas

A.G., Russell	Lowell
Alexander, Jered	Dierks
Anders, David	Center Ridge
Anders, Jerome	Center Ridge
Ardwin, Corey	North Little Rock
Barnes, Eric	Mountain View
Barnes Jr, Cecil C	Center Ridge
Birdwell, Ira Lee	Bagdad
Brown, Jim	Little Rock
Browning, Steven W	Benton
Bullard, Tom	Flippin
Burnett, Max	Paris
Cabe, Jerry (Buddy)	Hattieville
Connelley, Larry	Little Rock
Cook, James R.	Nashville
Copeland, Thom	Nashville
Crawford, Pat & Wes	West Memphis
Crowell, James L.	Mtn. View
Dozier, Bob	Springdale
Duvall, Fred	Benton
Echols, Roger	Nashville
Edge, Tommy	Cash
Ferguson, Lee	Hindsville
Fisk, Jerry	Lockesburg
Fitch, John S	Clinton
Flournoy, Joe	El Dorado
Foster, Ronnie E	Morrilton
Foster, Timothy L	El Dorado
Frizzell, Ted	West Fork
Gadberry, Emmet	Hattieville
Gaston, Bert	North Little Rock
Greenaway, Don	Fayetteville
Hartgrove, Wm Anthony	Eagle River
Herring, Morris	Dyer
Lane, Ben	North Little Rock
Lawrence, Alton	De Queen
Lile Handmade Knives Corp,	Russellville
Martin, Bruce E.	Prescott
Martin, Hal W	Morrilton
Massey, Roger	Texarkana
Newton, Ron	London
O'Dell, Clyde	Camden
Olive, Michael E	Leslie
Passmore, Jimmy D	Hoxie
Perry, Jim	Hope
Perry, John	Mayflower
Peterson, Lloyd (Pete) C	Clinton
Polk, Clifton	Van Buren
Quattlebaum, Craig	Searcy
Ramey, Marshall F.	West Helena
Red, Vernon	Conway
Remington, David W.	Gentry
Rowe, Kenny	Hope
Sisemore, Charles Russel	Mena
Smoker, Ray	Searcy
Solomon, Marvin	Paron
Stanley, John	Crossett
Stout, Charles	Gillham
Sweaza, Dennis	Austin
Townsend, Allen Mark	Texarkana
Tycer, Art	Paron
Walker, Jim	Morrilton
Ward, Chuck	Benton
Waters, Herman Harold	Magnolia
Waters, Lu	Magnolia
White, Bryce	Little Rock
Wootton, Randy	Stamps
Worthen, Bill	Little Rock
Young, Raymond L	Mt Ida

california

Abegg, Arnie	Huntington Beach
Abernathy, Paul J.	Eureka
Adkins, Richard L	Mission Viejo
Aldrete, Bob	Lomita
Barnes, Gregory	Altadena
Barney, Richard	Mt. Shasta
Barron, Brian	San Mateo
Benson, Don	Escalon
Berger, Max A.	Carmichael
Biggers, Gary	Ventura
Blum, Chuck	Brea
Bost, Roger E	Palos Verdes
Boyd, Francis	Berkeley
Brack, Douglas D.	Camirillo
Breshears, Clint	Manhattan Beach
Brooks, Buzz	Los Angles
Browne, Rick	Upland
Brunetta, David	Laguna Beach
Butler, Bart	Ramona
Cabrera, Sergio B	Harbor City
Cantrell, Kitty D	Ramona

Chelquist, Cliff	Arroyo Grande	Luchini, Bob	Palo Alto
Cohen, Terry A.	Laytonville	Mackie, John	Whittier
Collins, A.J.	Arleta	Mallett, John	Ontario
Combs, Roger	Anaheim	Manabe, Michael K.	San Diego
Comus, Steve	Anaheim	Martin, Jim	Oxnard
Connolly, James	Oroville	Massey, Ron	Joshua Tree
Davis, Charlie	Santee	Mata, Leonard	San Deigo
Davisson, Cole	Hemet	Maxwell, Don	Fresno
De Maria Jr, Angelo	Carmel Valley	McAbee, William	Colfax
Dion, Greg	Oxnard	McClure, Michael	Menlo Park
Dixon Jr., Ira E.	Ventura	McGrath, Patrick T	Westchester
Donovan, Patrick	San Jose	Melin, Gordon C	Whittier
Doolittle, Mike	Novato	Meloy, Sean	Lemon Grove
Driscoll, Mark	La Mesa	Montano, Gus A	San Diego
Dugan, Brad M	San Marcos	Morgan, Jeff	Santee
Eaton, Al	Clayton	Moses, Steven	Santa Ana
Ellis, Dave/ABS Mastorsmith	San Diego	Mosier, Richard	Rolling Hills Est
Ellis, William Dean	Fresno	Mountain Home Knives	Jamul
Ellis, ABS, Mastersmith, David	San Diego	Naten, Greg	Bakersfield
Emerson, Ernest R.	Torrance	Orton, Richard	La Verne
English, Jim	Jamul	Osborne, Donald H	Clovis
Essegian, Richard	Fresno	Packard, Bob	Elverta
Felix, Alexander	Torrance	Padilla, Gary	Auburn
Ferguson, Jim	Temecula	Pendleton, Lloyd	Volcano
Fisher, Theo (Ted)	Montague	Perry, Chris	Fresno
Flores, Henry	Santa Clara	Pfanenstiel, Dan	Modesto
Forrest, Brian	Descanso	Phillips, Randy	Ontario
Fox, Jack L.	Citrus Heights	Pitt, David F.	Anderson
Fraley, D B	Dixon	Posner, Barry E.	N. Hollywood
Francis, Vance	Alpine	Richard, Ron	Fremont
Fred, Reed Wyle	Sacramento	Richards Jr., Alvin C	Fortuna
Freer, Ralph	Seal Beach	Rodebaugh, James L	Oak Hills
Fulton, Mickey	Willows	Rozas, Clark D	Wilmington
Gamble, Frank	Fremont	Scarrow, Wil	Lakewood
George, Tom	Magalia	Schmitz, Raymond E	Valley Center
Gofourth, Jim	Santa Paula	Schroen, Karl	Sebastopol
Golding, Robin	Lathrop	Sibrian, Aaron	Ventura
Green, Russ	Lakewood	Sjostrand, Kevin	Visalia
Guarnera, Anthony R	Quartzhill	Slobodian, Scott	San Andreas
Guidry, Bruce	Murrieta	Sornberger, Jim	Volcano
Hall, Jeff	Los Alamitos	St.cyr, H Red	Wilmington
Hardy, Scott	Placerville	Stapel, Chuck	Glendale
Harris, Jay	Redwood City	Stapel, Craig	Glendale
Hartsfield, Phill	Newport Beach	Steinberg, Al	Laguna Woods
Hayes, Dolores	Los Angeles	Stimps, Jason M	Orange
Helton, Roy	Bakersfield	Stockwell, Walter	Redwood City
Hermes, Dana E.	Fremont	Stover, Howard	Pasadena
Herndon, Wm. R. "Bill"	Acton	Taylor, Scott	Gardena
Hink III, Les	Stockton	Terrill, Stephen	Lindsay
Hockenbary, Warren E	San Pedro	Tingle, Dennis P	Jackson
Hogstrom, Anders T.	Belmont	Vagnino, Michael	Visalia
Holden, Larry	Ridgecrest	Van Riper, James N	Citrus Heights
Hoy, Ken	North Fork	Ward, Ken	Weed
Humenick, Roy	Rescue	Warren, Al	Roseville
Jacks, Jim	Covina	Watanabe, Wayne	Montebello
Jackson, David	Lemoore	Weinstock, Robert	San Francisco
Jensen, John Lewis	Pasadena	Willson, Harlan M.	Lompoc
Johnson, Randy	Turlock	Wilson, Philip C.	Mountain Ranch
Jones, Curtis J.	Palmdale	Wilson, Ron	Morro Bay
Jurgens, John	Torrence	Winberg, Douglas R	Ramona
Kazsuk, David	Perris		
Keyes, Dan	Chino		

colorado

Anderson, Mel	Cedaredge
Appleton, Ray	Byers
Barrett, Cecil Terry	Colorado Springs
Booco, Gordon	Hayden
Brandon, Matthew	Denver
Brock, Kenneth L.	Allenspark
Campbell, Dick	Conifer
Davis, Don	Loveland

Koster, Steven C	Huntington Beach
Kreibich, Donald L.	San Jose
Laborde, Terry	Homeland
Lang, Bud	Orange
Larson, Richard	Turlock
Leland, Steve	Fairfax
Likarich, Steve	Colfax
Lockett, Sterling	Burbank
Loveless, R.W.	Riverside

Dawson, Barry	Durango
Dawson, Lynn	Durango
Delong, Dick	Aurora
Dennehy, Dan	Del Norte
Dill, Robert	Loveland
Ewing, Wyman	Pueblo
High, Tom	Alamosa
Hockensmith, Dan	Drake
Hodgson, Richard J.	Boulder
Hughes, Ed	Grand Junction
Inman III, Paul R	Glenwood Springs
Irie, Michael L	Colorado Springs
Kitsmiller, Jerry	Montrose
Leck, Dal	Hayden
Lewis, Steve	Woodland Park
Lyons, William R	Ft Collins
Miller, Hanford J.	Cowdrey
Miller, M.A.	Thornton
Mitchell, Wm. Dean	Lamar
Nolen, R.D. and Steve	Estes Park
Olson, Wayne C.	Bailey
Ott, Fred	Durango
Owens, John	Nathrop
Pogreba, Larry	Lyons
Roberts, Chuck	Golden
Rollert, Steve	Keenesburg
Ronzio, N Jack	Fruita
Sanders, Bill	Mancos
Sinnickson, John L	Lyons
Thompson, Lloyd	Pagosa Springs
Tollefson, Barry A.	Gunnison
Topliss, M.W. "Ike"	Montrose
Vunk, Robert	Colorado Springs
Watson, Bert	Westminster
Wilson, James G.	Estes Park
Wilson, James R	Westcliffe
Zima, Michael F.	Ft. Morgan

connecticut

Barnes, William	Middlefield
Buebendorf, Robert E.	Monroe
Chapo, William G.	Wilton
Coughlin, Michael M	Woodbury
Framski, Walter P	Prospect
Jean, Gerry	Manchester
Lepore, Michael J.	Bethany
Martin, Randall J.	Middletown
Padgett Jr., Edwin L.	New London
Pankiewicz, Philip R.	Lebanon
Plunkett, Richard	West Cornwall
Putnam, Donald S.	Wethersfield
Rainville, Richard	Salem
Turecek, Jim	Ansonia
Zembko III, John	Berlin

delaware

Antonio Jr., William J.	Newark
Daland, B. MacGregor	Harbeson
Schneider, Karl A.	Newark
Willey, W.G.	Greenwood

florida

Adams, Les	Hialeah
Angell, Jon	Hawthorne
Atkinson, Dick	Wausau
Bacon, David R	Bradenton
Barry III, James J.	West Palm Beach
Bartrug, Hugh E.	St. Petersburg
Beers, Ray	Lake Wales

Benjamin Jr., George	Kissimmee	Ross, Gregg	Lake Worth
Birnbaum, Edwin	Miami	Russ, Ron	Williston
Blackton, Andrew E.	Bayonet Point	Schlomer, James E.	Kissimmee
Bosworth, Dean	Key Largo	Schwarzer, Stephen	Pomona Park
Bradley, John	Pomona Park	Selvidio, Ralph	Crystal River
Bray Jr., W. Lowell	New Port Richey	Simons, Bill	Lakeland
Brown, Harold E.	Arcadia	Smart, Steaten	Tavares
Butler, John	Havana	Smith, Bobbie D.	Bonifay
Chase, Alex	DeLand	Smith, Michael J.	Brandon
Cole, Dave	Satellite Beach	Smith, W.M.	Bonifay
Cooper, Todd A	Crystal River	Stapleton, William E	Merritt Island
Davenport, Jack	Dade City	Stephan, Daniel	Valrico
Dietzel, Bill	Middleburg	Stidham, Rhett & Janie	Roseland
Doggett, Bob	Brandon	Stipes, Dwight	Palm City
Dotson, Tracy	Baker	Straight, Kenneth J	Largo
Ellerbe, W.B.	Geneva	Sweder, Joram	Ocala
Enos III, Thomas M	Orlando	Turnbull, Ralph A.	Spring Hill
Essman, Justus P	St Petersburg	Vogt, Donald J	Tampa
Fagan, James A	Lake Worth	Waldrop, Mark	Summerfield
Ferrara, Thomas	Naples	Wallace, Roger L.	Tampa
Ferris, Bill	Palm Beach Garden	Watson, Tom	Panama City
Fowler, Charles R	Ft McCoy	Weiland Jr, J Reese	Riverview
Gamble, Roger	St. Petersburg	Wicker, Donnie R.	Panama City
Garcia, Tony	West Palm Beach	William E, Stapleton	Merritt Island
Garner Jr., William O.	Pensacola	Williams, A L	Lake Wales
Gibson, James Hoot	Bunnell	Wyman, Marc L	Ft Lauderdale
Goers, Bruce	Lakeland	Zaccagnino Jr., Don	Pahokee
Griffin Jr., Howard A.	Davie	Zahm, Kurt	Indialantic
Grospitch, Ernie	Orlando	Zinker, Brad	Homestead
Harris, Ralph Dewey	Brandon		

georgia

Heitler, Henry	Tampa	Adams, Bill	Conyers
Hennon, Robert	Ft. Walton Beach	Arrowood, Dale	Sharpsburg
Hodge III, John	Palatka	Ashworth, Boyd	Powder Springs
Hoffman, Kevin L.	Orlando	Barker, Robert G.	Bishop
Holland, John H.	Titusville	Bentley, C L	Albany
Hughes, Dan	West Palm Beach	Bish, Hal	Jonesboro
Humphreys, Joel	Bowling Green	Black, Scott	Covington
Hunter, Richard D	Alachua	Bradley, Dennis	Blairsville
Hytovick, Joe"HY"	Dunnellon	Buckner, Jimmie H.	Putney
Jernigan, Steve	Milton	Carey Jr., Charles W.	Griffin
Johanning Custom Knives, Tom	Sarasota	Cash, Terry	Canton
Johnson, Durrell Carmon	Sparr	Chamblin, Joel	Concord
Johnson, John R	Plant City	Cofer, Ron	Loganville
Kelly, Lance	Edgewater	Cole, Welborn I.	Atlanta
King, Bill	Tampa	Cosby, E. Blanton	Columbus
Klingbeil, Russell K	Oviedo	Crockford, Jack	Chamblee
Krapp, Denny	Apopka	Davis, Steve	Powder Springs
Levengood, Bill	Tampa	Dempsey, David	Macon
Leverett, Ken	Lithia	Dunn, Charles K.	Shiloh
Lewis, Mike	Debary	Feigin, B	Marietta
Long, Glenn A.	Dunnellon	Frost, Dewayne	Barnesville
Lovestrand, Schuyler	Vero Beach	Gaines, Buddy	Commerce
Lozier, Don	Ocklawaha	Glover, Warren D	Cleveland
Lunn, Gail	St Petersburg	Greene, David	Covington
Lunn, Larry A.	St Petersburg	Halligan, Ed	Sharpsburg
Lyle III, Ernest L.	Chiefland	Hardy, Douglas E	Franklin
McDonald, Robert J.	Loxahatchee	Harmon, Jay	Woodstock
Miller, Ronald T.	Largo	Hawkins, Rade	Fayetteville
Mink, Dan	Crystal Beach	Haynie, Charles	Toccoa
Newton, Larry	Jacksonville	Hensley, Wayne	Conyers
Ochs, Charles F.	Largo	Hinson and Son, R.	Columbus
Owens, Donald	Melbourne	Hossom, Jerry	Duluth
Parker, Cliff	Zephyrhills	Hyde, Jimmy	Ellenwood
Pendray, Alfred H.	Williston	Johnson, Harold "Harry" C.	Trion
Piergallini, Daniel E.	Plant City	Jones, Franklin (Frank) W.	Columbus
Randall, Gary	Orlando	Kimberley, Richard L	Alpharetta
Randall Made Knives,	Orlando	Kimsey, Kevin	Cartersville
Roberts, E Ray	Monticello	King, Fred	Cartersville
Robinson III, Rex R.	Leesburg	Landers, John	Newnan
Rodkey, Dan	Hudson		
Rogers, Rodney	Wildwood		

Lonewolf, J. Aguirre	Demorest		
McGill, John	Blairsville		
McLendon, Hubert W	WACO		
Mitchell, James A.	Columbus		
Moncus, Michael Steven	Smithville		
Moore, Bill	Albany		
Parks, John	Jefferson		
Poole, Steve L.	Stockbridge		
Poplin, James L.	Washington		
Powell, Robert Clark	Smarr		
Poythress, John	Swainsboro		
Prater, Mike	Flintstone		
Price, Timmy	Blairsville		
Ragsdale, James D.	Lithonia		
Rogers Jr., Robert P.	Acworth		
Roghmans, Mark	Lagrange		
Rosenfeld, Bob	Hoschton		
Scofield, Everett	Chickamauga		
Sculley, Peter E	Rising Fawn		
Smith Jr., James B. "Red"	Morven		
Snell, Jerry L.	Fayetteville		
Snow, Bill	Columbus		
Sowell, Bill	Macon		
Stafford, Richard	Warner Robins		
Thompson, Kenneth	Duluth		
Tomey, Kathleen	Macon		
Walters, A.F.	Tyty		
Washburn Jr, Robert Lee	Adrian		
Werner Jr., William A.	Marietta		
Whetsell, Alex	Sharpsburg		
White, Lou	Ranger		
Whittaker, Randy	Cummings		

hawaii

Dolan, Robert L.	Kula
Fujisaka, Stanley	Kaneohe
Gibo, George	Hilo
Guild, Don	Paia
Lui, Ronald M.	Honolulu
Mann, Tim	Honokaa
Mayo Jr., Tom	Waialua
Mitsuyuki, Ross	Waipahu
Onion, Kenneth J.	Kapolei
Zakabi, Carl S.	Mililani Town

idaho

Alderman, Robert	Sagle
Alverson, Tim (R.V.)	Orofino
Andrews, Don	Coeur D'alene
Burke, Bill	Salmon
Eddy, Hugh E	Caldwell
Hatch, Ken	Kooskia
Hawk, Gavin	Idaho City
Hawk, Grant	Idaho City
Hogan, Thomas R	Boise
Horton, Scot	Buhl
Howe, Tori	Athol
Kranning, Terry L.	Pocatello
Mann, Michael L.	Spirit Lake
Metz, Greg T	Cascade
Mullin, Steve	Sandpoint
Nealey, Ivan F. (Frank)	Mt. Home
Patton, Dick & Rob	Garden City
Quarton, Barr	Mccall
Reeve, Chris	Boise
Rohn, Fred	Coeur D'alene
Roy, Robert F	Bayview
Sawby, Scott	Sandpoint
Schultz, Robert W	Cocolalla
Selent, Chuck	Bonners Ferry

Sparks, Bernard	Dingle
Spragg, Wayne E.	Ashton
Steiger, Monte L.	Genesee
Towell, Dwight L.	Midvale

illinois

Abbott, William M.	Chandlerville
Bloomer, Alan T.	Maquon
Caudell, Richard M.	Lawrenceville
Cook, Louise	Ozark
Cook, Mike	Ozark
Detmer, Phillip	Breese
Eaker, Allen L.	Paris
Hawes, Chuck	Weldon
Hill, Rick	Maryville
James, Peter	Hoffman Estates
Knuth, Joseph E.	Rockford
Kovar, Eugene	Evergreen Park
Lang, Kurt	Mchenry
Leone, Nick	Pontoon Beach
Markley, Ken	Sparta
Meier, Daryl	Carbondale
Millard, Fred G.	Chicago
Myers, Paul	E. Alton
Nevling, Mark	Hume
Nowland, Rick	Waltonville
Poag, James	Grayville
Potocki, Roger	Goreville
Pritchard, Ron	Dixon
Rados, Jerry F.	Grant Park
Rossdeutscher, Robert N	Arlington Hts
Rzewnicki, Gerald	Elizabeth
Schneider, Craig M.	Seymour
Smale, Charles J.	Waukegan
Smith, John M.	Centralia
Thomas, Bob G	Thebes
Todd, Richard C	Chambersburg
Tompkins, Dan	Peotone
Veit, Michael	Lasalle
Voss, Ben	Galesburg
Werth, George W.	Poplar Grove
West, Charles A.	Centralia
Wheeler, Robert	Bradley
White, Robert J.	Gilson
White Jr., Robert J. Butch	Gilson
Young, Errol	Alton

indiana

Ball, Ken	Mooresville
Barrett, Rick L (Toshi Hisa)	Goshen
Bose, Reese	Shelburn
Bose, Tony	Shelburn
Chaffee, Jeff L.	Morris
Claiborne, Jeff	Franklin
Damlovac, Sava	Indianapolis
Darby, Jed	Greensburg
Fitzgerald, Dennis M.	Fort Wayne
Fraps, John	Indianapolis
Hunt, Maurice	Avon
Imel, Billy Mace	New Castle
Johnson, C.E. Gene	Portage
Keeslar, Steven C.	Hamilton
Keeton, William L.	Laconia
Kinker, Mike	Greensburg
Largin,	Metamora
Ledford, Bracy R.	Indianapolis
Mayville, Oscar L.	Marengo
Minnick, Jim	Middletown
Oliver, Todd D	Spencer
Parsons, Michael R.	Terre Haute

Quakenbush, Thomas C	Ft. Wayne
Robertson, Leo D	Indianapolis
Rubley, James A.	Angola
Shostle, Ben	Muncie
Smock, Timothy E	Marion
Snyder, Michael Tom	Zionsville
Stover, Terry "Lee"	Kokomo
Thayer, Danny O	Romney
Welch, William H.	Kimmell
Worrell, Morris C	Lebanon
Young, George	Kokomo

iowa

Brooker, Dennis	Derby
Brower, Max	Boone
Clark, Howard F.	Runnells
Cockerham, Lloyd	Denham Springs
Helscher, John W	Washington
Lainson, Tony	Council Bluffs
Miller, James P.	Fairbank
Trindle, Barry	Earlham
Westberg, Larry	Algona
Zscherny, Michael	Ely

kansas

Battle Axe, The,	Wichita
Bradburn, Gary	Wichita
Chard, Gordon R.	Iola
Courtney, Eldon	Wichita
Craig, Roger L.	Topeka
Culver, Steve	Meriden
Darpinian, Dave	Olathe
Dawkins, Dudley L.	Topeka
Dugger, Dave	Westwood
Dunn, Melvin T.	Rossville
George, Les	Wichita
Hegwald, J.l.	Humboldt
Herman, Tim	Overland Park
King, Jason M	Eskridge
King Jr., Harvey G.	Eskridge
Kraft, Steve	Abilene
Lamb, Curtis J	Ottawa
Petersen, Dan L.	Topeka

kentucky

Barr, A.T.	Nicholasville
Baskett, Lee Gene	Eastview
Bodner, Gerald "Jerry"	Louisville
Bybee, Barry J.	Cadiz
Carson, Harold J. "Kit"	Vine Grove
Clay, J.D.	Greenup
Coil, Jimmie J.	Owensboro
Corbit, Gerald E.	Elizabethtown
Downing, Larry	Bremen
Dunn, Steve	Smiths Grove
Edwards, Mitch	Glasgow
Finch, Ricky D.	West Liberty
Fister, Jim	Simpsonville
France, Dan	Cawood
Frederick, Aaron	West Liberty
Gevedon, Hanners (Hank)	Crab Orchard
Greco, John	Greensburg
Hibben, Daryl	Lagrange
Hibben, Gil	Lagrange
Hibben, Joleen	Lagrange
Hoke, Thomas M.	Lagrange
Holbrook, H.l.	Olive Hill
Howser, John C.	Frankfort
Keeslar, Joseph F.	Almo

Lott, Sherry	Greensburg
Miller, Don	Lexington
Mize, Richard	Lawrenceburg
Pease, W.D.	Ewing
Pierce, Harold L.	Louisville
Pulliam, Morris C.	Shelbyville
Rigney Jr., Willie	Bronston
Smith, Gregory H.	Louisville
Smith, John W.	West Liberty
Vowell, Donald J	Mayfield
Walker III, John Wade	Paintlick
Wallingford Jr, Charles W	Union

louisiana

Barker, Reggie	Springhill
Blaum, Roy	Covington
Caldwell, Bill	West Monroe
Calvert Jr, Robert W (Bob)	Rayville
Capdepon, Randy	Carencro
Capdepon, Robert	Carencro
Chauvin, John	Scott
Culpepper, John	Monroe
Dake, C.M.	New Orleans
Dake, Mary H	New Orleans
Diebel, Chuck	Broussard
Durio, Fred	Opelousas
Elkins, R. Van	Bonita
Faucheaux, Howard J.	Loreauville
Fontenot, Gerald J	Mamou
Forstall, Al	Pearl River
Gorenflo, Gabe	Baton Rouge
Gorenflo, James T. (JT)	Baton Rouge
Graffeo, Anthony I.	Chalmette
Holmes, Robert	Baton Rouge
Ki, Shiva	Baton Rouge
Laurent, Kermit	Laplace
Leonard, Randy Joe	Sarepta
Mitchell, Max, Dean and Ben	Leesville
Phillips, Dennis	Independence
Potier, Timothy F.	Oberlin
Primos, Terry	Shreveport
Provenzano, Joseph D.	Chalmette
Randall Jr, James W	Keithville
Randow, Ralph	Pineville
Reggio Jr., Sidney J.	Sun
Roath, Dean	Baton Rouge
Sanders, Michael M.	Ponchatoula
Tilton, John	Iowa
Townsend, J.W.	Watson
Trisler, Kenneth W	Rayville
Wiggins, Horace	Mansfield

maine

Coombs Jr., Lamont	Bucksport
Corrigan, David P	Bingham
Courtois, Bryan	Saco
Gray, Daniel	Brownville
Hillman, Charles	Friendship
Kravitt, Chris	Ellsworth
Lawler, Tim	Grand Ledge
Leavitt Jr., Earl F.	E. Boothbay
Oyster, Lowell R.	Corinth
Sharrigan, Mudd	Wiscasset

maryland

Bagley, R Keith	White Plains
Barnes, Aubrey G.	Hagerstown
Barnes, Gary L.	New Windsor
Beers, Ray	Monkton

Bouse, D. Michael — Waldorf
Carnahan, Charles A — Germantown
Cohen, N.J. (Norm) — Baltimore
Dement, Larry R. — Prince Fredrick
Freiling, Albert J. — Finksburg
Fuller, Jack A. — New Market
Hart, Bill — Pasadena
Hendrickson, E. Jay — Frederick
Hendrickson, Shawn — Knoxville
Hudson, C. Robbin — Rock Hall
Hurt, William R. — Frederick
Kreh, Lefty — "Cockeysville,"
Kretsinger Jr., Philip W. — Boonsboro
McCarley, John — Taneytown
McGowan, Frank E. — Sykesville
Merchant, Ted — White Hall
Moran Jr., Wm. F. — Braddock Heights
Nicholson, R. Kent — Phoenix
O'Ceilaghan, Michael — Baltimore
Peyton III, Clay C — Frederick
Rhodes, James D.
Sentz, Mark C. — Taneytown
Smit, Glenn — Aberdeen
Sontheimer, G. Douglas — Potomac
Spickler, Gregory Noble — Sharpsburg
St Clair, Thomas K — Monrovia
Walker, Bill — Stevensville

massachusetts

Aoun, Charles — Wakefield
Daconceicao, John M. — Rehoboth
Dailey, G.e. — Seekonk
Ellis, Willy B — Methuen
Entin, Robert — Boston
Frankl, John M — Cambridge
Gaudette, Linden L. — Wilbraham
Grossman, Stewart — Clinton
Hinman, Ted — Watertown
Jarvis, Paul M. — Cambridge
Khalsa, Jot Singh — Millis
Kubasek, John A. — Easthampton
Lapen, Charles — W. Brookfield
Laramie, Mark — Fitchburg
Mcluin, Tom — Dracut
Moore, Michael Robert — Lowell
Philippe, D A — Pittsfield
Reed, Dave — Brimfield
Richter, Scott — S. Boston
Rizzi, Russell J. — Ashfield
Siska, Jim — Westfield
Smith, J.D. — S. Boston
Stoddard's, Inc., Copley Place — Boston
Szarek, Mark G — Revere

michigan

Ackerson, Robin E — Buchanan
Andrews, Eric — Grand Ledge
Behnke, William — Lake City
Bethke, Lora Sue — Grand Haven
Booth, Philip W. — Ithaca
Bruner, Rick — Jenison
Buckbee, Donald M. — Grayling
Canoy, Andrew B — Byron
Carlisle, Frank — Detroit
Carr, Tim — Muskegon
Carroll, Chad — Grant
Cashen, Kevin R. — Hubbardston
Cook, Mike A. — Portland
Costello, Dr. Timothy L — Farmington Hills

Cousino, George — Onsted
Cowles, Don — Royal Oak
Dilluvio, Frank J. — Warren
Ealy, Delbert — Indian River
Erickson, Walter E. — Atlanta
Gordon, Larry B. — Farmington Hills
Gottage, Dante — Clinton Twp.
Gottage, Judy — Clinton Twp.
Harm, Paul W — Attica
Hartman, Arlan (Lanny) — N. Muskegon
Hughes, Daryle — Nunica
Kalfayan, Edward N. — Ferndale
Krause, Roy W. — St. Clair Shores
Lankton, Scott — Ann Arbor
Leach, Mike J. — Swartz Creek
Lucie, James R. — Fruitport
Mankel, Kenneth — Cannonsburg
Mills, Louis G. — Ann Arbor
Nix, Robert T — Wayne
Noren, Douglas E — Springlake
Parker, Robert Nelson — Rapid City
Repke, Mike — Bay City
Rydbom, Jeff — Annandale
Sakmar, Mike — Rochester
Serven, Jim — Fostoria
Sigman, James P. — North Adams
Tally, Grant C. — Allen Park
Van Eizenga, Jerry W — Nunica
Vasquez, Johnny David — Wyandotte
Viste, James — Detroit
White, Richard T — Grosse Pointe Farms
Whittaker, Wayne — Metamore
Whitworth, Ken J. — Sterling Heights
Wood, Webster — Atlanta
Zowada, Tim — Boyne Falls

minnesota

Fiorini, Bill — Dakota
Goltz, Warren L. — Ada
Griffin, Thomas J. — Windom
Hagen, Philip L. — Pelican Rapids
Hansen, Robert W. — Cambridge
Janiga, Matthew A. — Andover
Johnson, R.B. — Clearwater
Knipschield, Terry — Rochester
Maines, Jay — Wyoming
Shadley, Eugene W. — Bovey
Steffen, Chuck — St Michael
Voorhies, Les — Faribault

mississippi

Black, Scott — Picayune
Boleware, David — Carson
Craft, Richard C. — Jackson
Davis, Jesse W. — Sarah
Evans, Bruce A — Booneville
Hand M.D., James E. — Gloster
Lamey, Robert M — Biloxi
LeBatard, Paul M. — Vancleave
Roberts, Michael — Clinton
Robinson, Chuck — Picayune
Robinson, Chuck — Picayune
Skow, H. A. "Tex" — Senatobia
Taylor, Billy — Petal
Vandeventer, Terry L — Terry
Wehner, Rudy — Collins
Wingo, Perry — Gulfport
Winston, David — Starkville

missouri

Ames, Mickey L. — Monett
Andrews II, E R (Russ) — Sugar Creek
Bolton, Charles B. — Jonesburg
Burrows, Stephen R. — Kansas City
Conner, Allen L — Fulton
Cover, Raymond A. — Mineral Point
Cox, Colin J. — Raymore
Davis, W.c. — Raymore
Dippold, Al — Perryville
Driskill, Beryl — Braggadocio
Duvall, Larry E. — Gallatin
Ehrenberger, Daniel Robert — Shelbyville
Engle, William — Boonville
Hanson III, Don L — Success
Harris, Jeffery A — St. Louis
Harrison, James — St Louis
Harrison, Jim (Seamus) — St.louis
Jones, John A — Holden
Kinnikin, Todd — House Springs
Knickmeyer, Hank — Cedar Hill
Knickmeyer, Kurt — Cedar Hill
Marks, Chris — Ava
Martin, Tony — Arcadia
Mason, Bill — Excelsior Springs
McCrackin, Kevin — House Springs
McCrackin and SON, V.J. — House Springs
McDermott, Michael — Defiance
McKiernan, Stan — Vandalia
Miller, Bob — Oakville
Muller, Jody — Pittsburg
Newcomb, Corbin — Moberly
Pryor, Stephen L — Boss
Ramsey, Richard A — Neosho
Rardon, A.D. — Polo
Rardon, Archie F. — Polo
Rice, Stephen E — St. Louis
Riepe, Richard A — Harrisonville
Scroggs, James A — Warrensburg
Shelton, Paul S. — Rolla
Sonntag, Douglas W. — Nixa
Steketee, Craig A. — Billings
Stewart, Edward L — Mexico
Stormer, Bob — St Peters
Warden, Roy A. — Union
Weddle Jr., Del — St. Joseph
Willis, Bill — Ava

montana

Barnes, Jack — Whitefish
Barnes, Wendell — Missoula
Barth, J D — Alberton
Beam, John R. — Kalispell
Beaty, Robert B — Missoula
Becker, Steve — Conrad
Bizzell, Robert — Butte
Brooks, Steve R. — Walkerville
Caffrey, Edward J. — Great Falls
Carlisle, Jeff — Simms
Christensen, Jon P. — Shepherd
Colter, Wade — Colstrip
Conklin, George L. — Ft. Benton
Crowder, Robert — Thompson Falls
Des Jardins, Dennis — Plains
Dunkerley, Rick — Lincoln
Eaton, Rick — Shepherd
Ellefson, Joel — Manhattan
Fassio, Melvin G. — Lolo
Forthofer, Pete — Whitefish

Gallagher, Barry	Lewistown
Harkins, J.A.	Conner
Hill, Howard E.	Polson
Hintz, Gerald M.	Helena
Hollar, Bob	Great Falls
Hulett, Steve	West Yellowstone
Kajin, Al	Forsyth
Kauffman, Dave	Montana City
Kraft, Elmer	Big Arm
Luman, James R	Anaconda
McGuane IV, Thomas F.	Bozeman
Mortenson, Ed	Darby
Moyer, Russ	Havre
Munroe, Deryk C	Bozeman
Nedved, Dan	Kalispell
Patrick, Willard C.	Helena,
Peele, Bryan	Thompson Falls
Peterson, Eldon G.	Whitefish
Piorek, James S.	Lakeside
Pursley, Aaron	Big Sandy
Robinson, Robert W.	Polson
Rodewald, Gary	Hamilton
Ruana Knife Works,	Bonner
Schirmer, Mike	Twin Bridges
Schmidt, Rick	Whitefish
Simonich, Rob	Clancy
Smallwood, Wayne	Kalispell
Smith, Josh	Lincoln
Sweeney, Coltin D	Great Falls
Taylor, Shane	Miles City
Thill, Jim	Missoula
Weinand, Gerome M.	Missoula
Woodiwiss, Dorren	Thompson Falls
Yashinski, John L	Red Lodge

nebraska

Hielscher, Guy	Alliance
Jensen Jr., Carl A.	Blair
Jokerst, Charles	Omaha
Mosier, Joshua J	Edgar
Robbins, Howard P.	Elkhorn
Schepers, George B.	Shelton
Suedmeier, Harlan	Nebraska City
Syslo, Chuck	Omaha
Tiensvold, Alan L	Rushville
Tiensvold, Jason	Rushville
Till, Calvin E. and Ruth	Chadron

nevada

Barnett, Van	Reno
Beasley, Geneo	Wadsworth
Blanchard, G.R. (Gary)	Las Vegas
Cameron, Ron G.	Logandale
Defeo, Robert A.	Henderson
Dellana,	Reno
Duff, Bill	Virginia City
Hrisoulas, Jim	Las Vegas
Mount, Don	Las Vegas
Nishiuchi, Melvin S.	Las Vegas
Norton, Don	Las Vegas
Thomas, Devin	Panaca
Tracy, Bud	Reno
Washburn, Arthur D	Pioche

new hampshire

Classic Cutlery	Franklin
Gunn, Nelson L.	Epping
Hill, Steve E.	Goshen
Hitchmough, Howard	Peterborough

MacDonald, John	Raymond
McGovern, JIM	Portsmouth
Saindon, R. Bill	Claremont

new jersey

Eden, Thomas	Cranbury
Grussenmeyer, Paul G.	Cherry Hill
Licata, Steven	Clifton
Little, Guy A	Oakhurst
McCallen Jr, Howard H	So Seaside Park
Nelson, Bob	Sparta
Phillips, Jim	Williamstown
Polkowski, Al	Chester
Pressburger, Ramon	Howell
Quick, Mike	Kearny
Schilling, Ellen	Hamilton Square
Sheets, Steven William	Mendham
Slee, Fred	Morganville
Treiber, Randy	High Bridge
Viele, H.J.	Westwood
Weber, Fred E.	Forked River
Yeskoo, Richard C	Summit

new mexico

Beckett, Norman L.	Farmington
Black, Tom	Albuquerque
Cherry, Frank J	Albuquerque
Coleman, Keith E.	Albuquerque
Cordova, Joseph G.	Peralta
Cumming, R.J.	Cedar Crest
Digangi, Joseph M.	Santa Cruz
Duran, Jerry T.	Albuquerque
Dyess, Eddie	Roswell
Fisher, Jay	Magdalena
Goode, Bear	Navajo Dam
Gunter, Brad	Tijeras
Hethcoat, Don	Clovis
Jones, Bob	Albuquerque
Lewis, Tom R.	Carlsbad
MacDonald, David	Los Lunas
McBurnette, Harvey	Eagle Nest
Rogers, Richard	Magdalena
Schaller, Anthony Brett	Albuquerque
Terzuola, Robert	Santa Fe
Trujillo, Albert MB	Bosque Farms
Walker, Michael L.	Rancho De Taos
Ware, Tommy	Datil
Wescott, Cody	Las Cruces

new york

Baker, Wild Bill	Boiceville
Berg, Steven	Brooklyn
Champagne, Paul	Mechanicville
Cute, Thomas	Cortland
Davis, Barry L.	Castleton
Farr, Dan	Rochester
Faust, Dick	Rochester
Hobart, Gene	Windsor
Isgro, Jeffery	West Babylon
Johnston, Dr Robt	Rochester
Levin, Jack	Brooklyn
Loos, Henry C.	New Hyde Park
Ludwig, Richard O.	Maspeth
Maragni, Dan	Georgetown
Mc Cornock, Craig	Willow
Meerdink, Kurt	Barryville
Meshejian, Mardi	E. Northport
Page, Reginald	Groveland
Palazzo, Tom	Bayside

Pattay, Rudy	Long Beach
Phillips, Scott C	Gouverneur
Rachlin, Leslie S.	Elmira
Rappazzo, Richard	Cohoes
Rotella, Richard A.	Niagara Falls
Scheid, Maggie	Rochester
Schippnick, Jim	Sanborn
Schlueter, David	Syracuse
Serafen, Steven E.	New Berlin
Smith, Lenard C	Valley Cottage
Smith, Raymond L.	Erin
Summers, Dan	Whitney Pt.
Szilaski, Joseph	Wappingers Falls
Turanski, Ted	Lansing
Turner, Kevin	Montrose
Wilson, III, George H.	Bronx

north carolina

Baker, Herb	Eden
Bauchop, Peter	Cary
Boxer, Rex	Sylva
Britton, Tim	Winston-Salem
Busfield, John	Roanoke Rapids
Chastain, Wade	Horse Shoe
Clark, Dave	Andrews
Coltrain, Larry D	Buxton
Comar, Roger N	Marion
Daniel, Travis E.	Chocowinity
Draw, Gerald	Asheville
Edwards, Fain E.	Topton
Fox, Paul	Claremont
Gaddy, Gary Lee	Washington
Goguen, Scott	Newport
Greene, Chris	Shelby
Gross, W.W.	High Point
Gurganus, Carol	Colerain
Gurganus, Melvin H.	Colerain
Guthrie, George B.	Bassemer City
Harless, Walt	Stoneville
Hazen, Mark	Charlotte
Kearney, Jarod	Brown Summit
Livingston, Robert C.	Murphy
Lubrich, Mark	Matthews
Maynard, William N.	Fayetteville
McDonald, Robin J	Fayettebville
McLurkin, Andrew	Raleigh
McNabb, Tommy	Winston-salem
McNabb, Tommy	Winston-salem
McRae, J Michael	Mint Hill
Norris, Mike	Albermarle
Parrish, Robert	Weaverville
Patrick, Chuck	Brasstown
Patrick, Peggy	Brasstown
Patterson, Alan W.	Hayesville
Popp Sr., Steve	Fayetteville
Scholl, Tim	Angier
Simmons, H.R.	Aurora
Snody, Mike	Liberty
Sprouse, Terry	Asheville
Sterling, Murray	Mount Airy
Sutton, S. Russell	New Bern
Van Hoy, Ed & Tanya	Candor
Wagaman, John K.	Fayetteville
Walker, Don	Burnsville
Warren, Daniel	Canton
Whitley, L Wayne	Chocowinity
Williamson, Tony	Siler City
Wilson, Mike	Hayesville
Winkler, Daniel	Blowing Rock
Young, Paul A.	Boone

north dakota

Keidel, Gene W. and Scott J.	Dickinson
Paulicheck, Garth	Williston
Pitman, David	Williston

ohio

Babcock, Raymond G.	Vincent
Bailey, Ryan	Galena
Bendik, John	Olmsted Falls
Busse, Jerry	Wauseon
Click, Joe	Liberty Center
Collins, Harold	West Union
Collins, Lynn M.	Elyria
Cottrill, James I.	Columbus
Downing, Tom	Cuyaho Falls
Downs, James F.	Londonderry
Etzler, John	Grafton
Foster, R.L. (Bob)	Mansfield
Franklin, Mike	Aberdeen
Geisler, Gary R.	Clarksville
Gittinger, Raymond	Tiffin
Glover, Ron	Mason
Greiner, Richard	Green Springs
Guess, Raymond L.	Mechanicstown
Hinderer, Rick	Wooster
Hudson, Anthony B	Midland
Imboden II, Howard L.	Dayton
Kiefer, Tony	Pataskala
Koutsopoulos, George	Lagrange
Koval, Michael T.	New Albany
Kubaiko, Hank	Beach City
Longworth, Dave	Hamersville
Loro, Gene	Crooksville
Maienknecht, Stanley	Sardis
McCarty, Harry	Hamilton
McDonald, Rich	Columbiana
McGroder, Patrick J.	Madison
Mercer, Mike	Lebanon
Messer, David T.	Dayton
Moore, Marve	Xenia
Morgan, Tom	Beloit
Oakes, Winston	Dayton
Ralph, Darrel	Galena
Rose, Derek W	Gallipolis
Salley, John D.	Tipp City
Scrimshaw by Lynn Benade,	Beachwood
Shinosky, Andy	Canfield
Shoemaker, Carroll	Northup
Shoemaker, Scott	Miamisburg
Spinale, Richard	Lorain
Stevens, Barry B.	Cridersville
Stoddart, W.B. Bill	Forest Park
Strong, Scott	Beavercreek
Summers, Arthur L.	Mechanicsburg
Summers, Dennis K.	Springfield
Thomas, Kim	Seville
Thourot, Michael W.	Napoleon
Tindera, George	Brunswick
Votaw, David P.	Pioneer
Ward, J.J.	Waverly
Ward, Ron	Loveland
Warther, Dale	Dover
Witsaman, Earl	Stow
Wood, Larry B.	Huber Heights
Yurco, Mike	Canfield

oklahoma

Baker, Ray	Sapulpa

Barngrover, Jerry	Afton
Brown, Troy L.	Park Hill
Burke, Dan	Edmond
Crenshaw, Al	Eufaula
Darby, David T	Cookson
Dill, Dave	Bethany
Englebretson, George	Oklahoma City
Fletcher, Michael J	Tulsa
Gepner, Don	Norman
Griffith, Lynn	Glenpool
Johns, Rob	Enid
Kennedy Jr., Bill	Yukon
Kirk, Ray	Tahlequah
Lairson Sr, Jerry	Ringold
Martin, John Alexander	Luther
Miller, Michael E.	Wagoner
Sanders, A.A.	Norman
Spivey, Jefferson	Yukon
Williams, Michael L.	Broken Bow
Wilson, James R.	Seminole
Wingo, Gary	Ramona

oregon

Bell, Michael	Coquille
Bochman, Bruce	Grants Pass
Brandt, Martin W	Springfield
Buchman, Bill	Bend
Buchner, Bill	Idleyld Park
Clark, Nate	Oakland
Coon, Raymond C.	Gresham
Corrado, Jim	Glide
Davis, Terry	Sumpter
Dowell, T.M.	Bend
Ferdinand, Don	Shady Cove
Fox, Wendell	Springfield
Frank, Heinrich H.	Seal Rock
Goddard, Wayne	Eugene
Harsey, William H.	Creswell
Hergert, Bob	Port Orford
Hilker, Thomas N.	Williams
Horn, Jess	Eugene
Huey, Steve	Eugene
Kelley, Gary	Aloha
Lake, Ron	Eugene
Ledbetter, Randell	Bend
Lindsay, Chris A.	Bend
Little, Gary M.	Broadbent
Lockett, Lowell C	North Bend
Lum, Robert W.	Eugene
Martin, Gene	Williams
Martin, Walter E	Williams
Miller, Michael K.	Sweet Home
Olson, Darrold E.	Springfield
Osterman, Daniel E.	Junction City
Rider, David M	Eugene
Schoeningh, Mike	North Powder
Schrader, Robert	Bend
Sevey Custom Knife,	Gold Beach
Sheehy, Thomas J	Portland
Shoger, Mark O.	Beaverton
Smith, Rick	Rogue River
Stover, James K	Lakeview
Thompson, Leon	Gaston
Thompson, Tommy	Portland
Vallotton, Butch And Arey	Oakland
Vallotton, Rainy D.	Umpqua
Vallotton, Shawn	Oakland
Vallotton, Thomas	Oakland
Veatch, Richard	Springfield

Wahlster, Mark David	Silverton
Wardian, Paul G.	Troutdale
Woodcock, Dennis "Woody"	Nehalem

pennsylvania

Amor Jr., Miguel	Lancaster
Anderson, Gary D.	Spring Grove
Anderson, Tom	Manchester
Besedick, Frank E.	Ruffsdale
Candrella, Joe	Warminster
Chavar, Edward V	Bethlehem
Clark, D.E. (Lucky)	Mineral Point
Corkum, STEVE	Littlestown
D'andrea, JOHN	East Stroudsberg
Darby, Rick	Levittown
Evans, Ronald B	Middleton
Frey Jr., W. Frederick	Milton
Goldberg, David	Blue Bell
Goldberg, Metalsmith, David	Blue Bell
Goodling, Rodney W	York Springs
Gottschalk, Gregory J.	Carnegie
Heinz, John	Upper Black Eddy
Hudson, Rob	Northumberland
Malloy, Joe	Freeland
Marlowe, Donald	Dover
Mensch, Larry C.	Milton
Milford, Brian A.	Knox
Miller, Rick	Rockwood
Moore, Ted	Elizabethtown
Morett, Donald	Lancaster
Navagato, Angelo	Camp Hill
Nealy, Bud	Stroudsburg
Neilson, J. & Tess	Wyalusing
Nott, Ron P.	Summerdale
Ogden, Bill	Avis
Ortega, Ben M	Wyoming
Parker, J.e.	Clarion
Rupert, Bob	Clinton
Rybar Jr., Raymond B.	Finleyville
Scimio, Bill	Spruce Creek
Sinclair, J.e.	Pittsburgh
Steigerwalt, Ken	Orangeville
Stroyan, Eric	Dalton
Valois, A. Daniel	Lehighton
Vaughan, Ian	Manheim
Whittaker, Robert E.	Mill Creek
Wilson, Jon J.	Johnstown

rhode island

Bardsley, Norman P.	Pawtucket
Burak, Chet	E Providence
Dickison, Scott S.	Portsmouth
Lambert, Ronald S.	Johnston
Mchenry, William James	Wyoming
Olszewski, Stephen	Coventry
Potter, Frank	Middletown
Williams, Jason L.	Wyoming
Wright, Richard S	Carolina

south carolina

Barefoot, Joe W.	Liberty
Beatty, Gordon H.	Seneca
Branton, Robert	Awendaw
Bridwell, Richard A.	Taylors
Campbell, Courtnay M	Columbia
Cannady, Daniel L.	Allendale
Cox, Sam	Gaffney
Defreest, William G.	Barnwell
Denning, Geno	Gaston

Easler Jr., Russell O.	Woodruff
Fecas, Stephen J.	Anderson
Gainey, Hal	Greenwood
Gaston, Ron	Woodruff
George, Harry	Aiken
Gregory, Michael	Belton
Hendrix, Jerry	Clinton
Hendrix, Wayne	Allendale
Herron, George	Springfield
Kaufman, Scott	Anderson
Kay, J. Wallace	Liberty
Kessler, Ralph A.	Fountain Inn
Knight, Jason	Harleyville
Langley, Gene H.	Florence
Lewis, K.J.	Lugoff
Lutz, Greg	Greenwood
Majer, Mike	Hilton Head
Manley, David W	Central
Mcmanus, Danny	Taylors
Montjoy, Claude	Clinton
Odom, Vic	North
Page, Larry	Aiken
Parler, Thomas O	Charleston
Peagler, Russ	Moncks Corner
Perry, Johnny	Spartanburg
Poole, Marvin O.	Anderson
Poston, Alvin	Pamplico
Reed, John M.	Goose Creek
Reeves, Winfred M.	West Union
Sears, Mick	Sumter
Thomas, Rocky	Moncks Corner
Triplett, Craig	Greer
Tyser, Ross	Spartanburg
Walter, Brend	Walterboro
Whitmire, Earl T.	Rock Hill

south dakota

Boysen, Raymond A	Rapid City
Ferrier, Gregory K	Rapid City
Sarvis, Randall J.	Fort Pierre
Thomsen, Loyd W.	Oelrichs

tennessee

Bailey, Joseph D.	Nashville
Baker, Vance	Riceville
Breed, Kim	Clarksville
Broyles-sebenick, Lisa	Chattanooga
Byrd, Wesley L	Evansville
Canter, Ronald E.	Jackson
Casteel, Dianna	Monteagle
Casteel, Douglas	Monteagle
Centofante, Frank	Madisonville
Claiborne, Ron	Knox
Clay, Wayne	Pelham
Conley, Bob	Jonesboro
Coogan, Robert	Smithville
Copeland, George Steve	Alpine
Corby, Harold	Johnson City
Dickerson, Gordon S	Hohenwald
Elder Jr, Perry B	Clarksville
Ewing, John H.	Clinton
Harju, Gary	Franklin
Harley, Larry W.	Bristol
Heflin, Christopher M	Nashville
Hurst, Jeff	Rutledge
Johnson, David A	Pleasant Shade
Johnson, Ryan M.	Hixson
Keeler, Robert	Memphis
King, Herman	Millington
Levine, Bob	Tullahoma

Lincoln, James	Bartlett
Marshall, Stephen R	Mt. Juliet
Mcadams, Dennis	Chattanooga
McDonald, W.J. "Jerry"	Germantown
McNeil, Jimmy	Memphis
Moulton, Dusty	Loudon
Raley, R Wayne	Collierville
Ramey, Larry	Chapmansboro
Rollick, Walter D	Maryville
Ryder, Ben M.	Copperhill
Sampson, Lynn	Jonesborough
Smith, Newman L.	Gatlinburg
Taylor, C. Gray	Fall Branch
Two Knife Guys,	Chattanooga
Vanderford, Carl G.	Columbia
Walker, John W.	Bon Aqua
Ward, W.C.	Clinton
Williams Jr., Richard	Morristown
Winter, George	Union City

texas

Adams, William D.	Houston
Alexander, Eugene	Ganado
Allen, Mike "Whiskers"	Malakoff
Ashby, Douglas	Dallas
Bailey, Kirby C.	Lytle
Barnes, Marlen R	Atlanta
Barr, Judson C	Irving
Batts, Keith	Hooks
Benfield Jr, Robert O	Forney
Blasingame, Robert	Kilgore
Blum, Kenneth	Brenham
Boatright, Basel	New Braunfels
Bradshaw, Bailey	Dallas
Bratcher, Brett	Plantersville
Brightwell, Mark	Leander
Broadwell, David	Wichita Falls
Brooks, Michael	Lubbock
Bullard, Randall	Canyon
Burden, James	Burkburnett
Cairnes Jr, Carroll B	Palacios
Callahan, F. Terry	Boerne
Cannon, Dan	Dallas
Carpenter, Ronald W	Jasper
Carter, Fred	Wichita Falls
Champion, Robert	Amarillo
Chase, John E.	Aledo
Churchman, T.w.	San Antonio
Clark, Roger	Rockdale
Cole, James M	Bartonville
Connor, John W	Odessa
Connor, Michael	Winters
Cosgrove, Charles G.	Arlington
Costa, Scott	Spicewood
Crain, Jack W.	Granbury
Darcey, Chester L	College Station
Davis, Vernon M.	Waco
Dean, Harvey J.	Rockdale
Dietz, Howard	New Braunfels
Dominy, Chuck	Colleyville
Dyer, David	Granbury
Edwards, Lynn	W. Columbia
Eldridge, Allan	Ft Worth
Elishewitz, Allen	New Braunfels
Epting, Richard	College Station
Eriksen, James Thorlief	Garland
Evans, Carlton	Aledo
Fant Jr, George	Atlanta
Ferguson, Jim	San Angelo
Fortune Products, Inc.,	Marble Falls

Foster, Al	Magnolia
Foster, Norvell C	San Antonio
Fowler, Jerry	Hutto
Fritz, Jesse	Slaton
Fuller, Bruce A.	Baytown
Gardner, Rob	Port Aransas
Garner, Larry W	Tyler
Gault, Clay	Lexington
Glasscock, John	Cypress
Goytia, Enrique	El Paso
Graham, Gordon	New Boston
Green, Bill	Garland
Green, Roger M.	Joshua
Griffin, Rendon And Mark	Houston
Hamlet Jr., Johnny	Clute
Hand, Bill	Spearman
Hawkins, Buddy	Texarkana
Hayes, Scotty	Texarkana
Hays, Mark	Austin
Hearn, Terry L	Lufkin
Hemperley, Glen	Spring
Hesser, David	Dripping Springs
House, Lawrence	Canyon Lake
Howell, Jason G	Lake Jackson
Howell, Robert L.	Kilgore
Hudson, Robert	Humble
Hughes, Bill	Texarkana
Hughes, Lawrence	Plainview
Jackson, Charlton R	San Antonio
Jaksik Jr, Michael	Fredericksburg
Johnson, Gorden W.	Houston
Johnson, Ruffin	Houston
Kerby, Marlin W	Brashear
Kern, R W	San Antonio
Kious, Joe	Kerrville
Knipstein, R.C. (JOE)	Arlington
Ladd, JIM S.	Deer Park
Ladd, Jimmie Lee	Deer Park
Lambert, Jarrell D.	Granado
Laplante, Brett	Mckinney
Laughlin, Don	Vidor
Lay, L.J.	Burkburnett
LeBlanc, John	Winnsboro
Lemcke, Jim L	Houston
Lister Jr., Weldon E.	Boerne
Locke, Keith	Ft Worth
Luchak, Bob	Channelview
Luckett, Bill	Weatherford
Marshall, Glenn	Mason
Martin, Michael W.	Beckville
McConnell Jr., Loyd A.	Odessa
Mellard, J R	Houston
Merz III, Robert L.	Katy
Miller, R.D.	Dallas
Moore, James B.	Ft. Stockton
Neely, Greg	Houston
Nelson, Dr Carl	Texarkana
Obrien, George	Katy
Odgen, Randy W	Houston
Ogletree Jr., Ben R.	Livingston
Oliver, Anthony Craig	Ft. Worth
Osborne, Michael	New Braunfels
Osborne, Warren	Waxahachie
Overeynder, T.R.	Arlington
Ownby, John C.	Plano
Pate, Lloyd D.	Georgetown
Patterson, Pat	Barksdale
Pierce, Randall	Arlington
Pollock, Wallace J.	Cedar Park
Polzien, Don	Lubbock
Powell, James	Texarkana

Pugh, Jim	Azle
Pullen, Martin	Granbury
Ray, Alan W.	Lovelady
Richardson Jr., Percy	Hemphill
Robinson, Charles (Dickie)	Vega
Rogers, Charles W	Douglass
Ruple, William H.	Charlotte
Ruth, Michael G	Texarkana
Scott, Al	Harper
Self, Ernie	Dripping Springs
Shipley, Steven A	Richardson
Sims, Bob	Meridian
Sims, John Paul	Dekalb
Sloan, Shane	Newcastle
Smart, Steve	Melissa
Stokes, Ed	Hockley
Stone, Jerry	Lytle
Stout, Johnny	New Braunfels
Theis, Terry	Harper
Thuesen, Ed	Damon
Thuesen, Kevin	Houston
Treiber, Leon	Ingram
Turcotte, Larry	Pampa
Watson, Daniel	Driftwood
Watt III, Freddie	Big Spring
Watts, Wally	Gatesville
West, Pat	Charlotte
Whitley, Weldon G.	El Paso
Wilcher, Wendell L.	Palestine
Wilkins, Mitchell	Montgomery
Wolf Jr, William Lynn	Lagrange
Wood, William W.	Seymour
Woodard, Wiley	Colleyville
Woodward, Wiley	Colleyville
Yeates, Joe A.	Spring
Zboril, Terry	Caldwell

utah

Allred, Bruce F	Layton
Baum, Rick	Lehi
Black, Earl	Salt Lake City
Davis, Greg	Fillmore
Ence, Jim	Richfield
Ennis, Ray	Ogden
Erickson, L.m.	Liberty
Groesbeck, Brad	American Fork
Harris, Tedd	Cedar Hills
Hunter, Hyrum	Aurora
Johnson, Steven R.	Manti
Maxfield, Lynn	Layton
Nielson, Jeff V.	Monroe
Nunn, Gregory	Castle Valley
Palmer, Taylor	Blanding
Peterson, Chris	Salina
Rapp, Steven J.	Midvale
Strickland, Dale	Monroe
Velarde, Ricardo	Park City
Warenski, Buster	Richfield
Winn, Travis A.	Salt Lake City

vermont

Haggerty, George S.	Jacksonville
Kelso, Jim	Worcester

virginia

Arbuckle, James M	Yorktown
Ballew, Dale	Bowling Green
Barber, Robert E.	Charlottesville
Batley, Mark S	Wake

Batson, Richard G.	Rixeyville
Beverly II, Larry H.	Spotsylvania
Callahan, Errett	Lynchburg
Catoe, David R	Norfolk
Chamberlain, Charles R.	Barren Springs
Compton, William E.	Sterling
Conkey, Tom	Nokesville
Davidson, Edmund	Goshen
Douglas, John J.	Lynch Station
Frazier, Ron	Powhatan
Harris, Cass	Bluemont
Hawk, Jack L.	Ceres
Hawk, Joey K.	Ceres
Hedrick, Don	Newport News
Hendricks, Samuel J.	Maurertown
Holloway, Paul	Norfolk
Jones, Barry M. and Phillip G.	Danville
Jones, Enoch	Warrenton
Kellogg, Brian R.	New Market
Mccoun, Mark	Dewitt
Metheny, H.a. "Whitey"	Spotsylvania
Murski, Ray	Reston
Norfleet, Ross W.	Richmond
Parks, Blane C.	Woodbridge
Pawlowski, John R	Newport News
Richter, John C.	Chesapeake
Ryan, C.O.	Yorktown
Scott, Winston	Huddleston
Thomas, Daniel	Leesburg
Tomes, P J	Shipman
White, Gene E.	Alexandria
Willson, Wayne O	FAIRFAX

washington

Amoureux, A.W.	Northport
Baldwin, Phillip	Snohomish
Ber, Dave	San Juan Island
Berglin, Bruce D.	Mount Vernon
Bloomquist, R Gordon	Olympia
Boguszewski, Phil	Lakewood
Boyer, Mark	Bothell
Bromley, Peter	Spokane
Brothers, Robert L.	Colville
Brown, Dennis G	Shoreline
Brunckhorst, Lyle	Bothell
Bump, Bruce D	Walla Walla
Butler, John R	Shoreline
Chamberlain, John B.	Wenatchee
Chamberlain, Jon A.	E. Wenatchee
Conti, Jeffrey D.	Port Orchard
Crain, Frank	Spokane
Crossman, Daniel C	Blakely Island
Crowthers, Mark F	Rolling Bay
D'angelo, Laurence	Vancouver
Davis, John	Selah
Diskin, Matt	Freeland
Drouin, Joseph D	Bremerton
Ferry, Tom	Auburn
Frey, Steve	Snohomish
Gallagher, Sean	Monroe
Goertz, Paul S.	Renton
Gray, BOB	Spokane
Greenfield, G.O.	Everett
Hansen, Lonnie	Spanaway
House, Gary	Ephrata
Hurst, Cole	E. Wenatchee
Leet, Larry W.	Burien
Mosser, Gary E.	Kirkland
O'malley, Daniel	Seattle
Park, Valerie	Seattle

Sanderson, Ray	Yakima
Schempp, Ed	Ephrata
Schempp, Martin	Ephrata
Smith, D. Noel	Poulsbo
Stegner, Wilbur G.	Rochester
Swyhart, Art	Klickitat
Wright, Kevin	Quilcene

west virginia

Bowen, Tilton	Baker
Dent, Douglas M.	S. Charleston
Derr, Herbert	St Albans
Drost, Jason D.	French Creek
Drost, Michael B.	French Creek
Elliott, Jerry	Charleston
Jeffries, Robert W.	Red House
Liegey, Kenneth R.	Millwood
Maynard, Larry Joe	Crab Orchard
McConnell, Charles R.	Wellsburg
Morris, Eric	Beckley
Pickens, Selbert	Liberty
Reynolds, Dave	Harrisville
Sigman, Corbet R.	Liberty
Small, Ed	Keyser
Straight, Don	Points
Tokar, Daniel	Shepherdstown
Wilson, R.W.	Weirton
Wyatt, William R.	Rainelle

wisconsin

Brandsey, Edward P.	Milton
Bruner Jr, Fred, Bruner Blades	Fall Creek
Delarosa, Jim	Mukwonago
Garrity., Timothy P	Waukesha
Genske, Jay	Fond Du Lac
Haines, Jeff, Haines Custom Knives	Wauzeka
Hembrook Knives,	Neosho
Johnson, Kenneth R.	Mindoro
Johnson, Richard	Germantown
Kohls, Jerry	Princeton
Kolitz, Robert	Beaver Dam
Lary, Ed	Mosinee
Lerch, Matthew	Sussex
Maestri, Peter A.	Spring Green
Martin, Peter	Waterford
Nelson, Ken	Pittsville
Niemuth, Troy	Sheboygan
Ponzio, Doug	Pleasant Prairie
R. Boyes Knives,	Menomonee Falls
Revishvili, Zaza	Madison
Ricke, Dave	West Bend
Rochford, Michael R.	Dresser
Schrap, Robert G.	Wauwatosa
Wattelet, Michael A.	Minocqua

wyoming

Alexander, Darrel	Ten Sleep
Ankrom, W.E.	Cody
Archer, Ray & Terri	Medicine Bow
Banks, David L.	Riverton
Bartlow, John	Sheridan
Bennett, Brett C	Cheyenne
Draper, Audra	Riverton
Draper, Mike	Riverton
Fowler, Ed A.	Riverton
Friedly, Dennis E.	Cody
Justice, Shane	Sheridan
Kilby, Keith	Cody
Kinkade, Jacob	Carpenter

Rexroat, Kirk — Wright
Reynolds, John C. — Gillette
Ross, Stephen — Evanston
Walker, George A. — Alpine

foreign countries

argentina

Ayarragaray, Cristian L. — (3100) Parana-Entre Rios
Kehiayan, Alfredo — CPB1623GXU Buenos Aires
Rho, Nestor Lorenzo — Buenos Aires

australia

Bennett, Peter — Engadine N.S.W. 2233
Crawley, Bruce R. — Croydon 3136 Victoria
Del Raso, Peter — Mt. Waverly, Victoria, 3149
Gerus, Gerry — Qld. 4870
Giljevic, Branko — N.S.W.
Green, William (Bill) — View Bank Vic.
Husiak, Myron — Victoria
Jones, John — Manly West, QLD 4179
K B S, Knives — Vic 3450
Rowe, Stewart G. — Brisbane 4306
Tasman, Kerley — Western Australia
Zemitis, Joe — 2285 Newcastle

austria

Poskocil, Helmut — A-3340 Waidhofen/YBBS

belgium

Dox, Jan — B 2900 Schoten
Monteiro, Victor — 1360 Maleves Ste Marie

brazil

Bodolay, Antal — Belo Horizonte Mg-31730-700
Campos, Ivan — Tatui, Sp
De Castro, Marco A M — Sao Paulo Sp
Gaeta, Angelo — Sp-17201-310
Gaeta, Roberto — 05351 Sao Paulo, S.p.
Garcia, Mario Eiras — Sao Paulo Sp-05516-070
Ikoma, Flavio Yuji,
R. Manoel R. Teixeira, 108 — Sp-19031-220
Lala, Paulo Ricardo P.
and Lala, Roberto P. — Sp-19031-260
Mello, Jacinto — 388 Parà De Minas M6 35660-129
Neto Jr., Nelson and
De Carvalho, Henrique M. — Sp-12900-000
Paulo, Fernandes R — Sao Paulo
Petean, Francisco and Mauricio — Sp-16200-000
Ricardo Romano, Bernardes — Itajuba Mg
Rosa, Pedro Gullherme Teles — Sp-19065-410
Villa, Luiz — Sao Paulo, Sp-04537-081
Villar, Ricardo — S.p. 07600-000
Zakharov, Carlos — Sp-12305-340

britian

Horne, Grace — Sheffield

canada

Arnold, Joe — London, Ont.
Beauchamp, Gaetan — Stoneham, PQ
Beets, Marty — Williams Lake, BC
Bell, Donald — Bedford, Nova Scotia
Berg, Lothar — Kitchener ON
Bold, Stu — Sarnia, Ont.,
Boos, Ralph — Edmonton, Alberta
Bourbeau, Jean Yves — Ile Perrot, Quebec
Bradford, Garrick — Kitchener ON
Dallyn, Kelly — Calgary AB
DeBRAGA, Jose C. — Cardinal Villeneuve Quebec

Deringer, Christoph — Sherbrooke, Quebec
Doiron, Donald — Messines PQ
Doussot, Laurent — Montreal, Quebec
Downie, James T. — Port Franks, Ont.
Dublin, Dennis — Enderby, BC
Freeman, John — Cambridge, Ont.
Frigault, Rick — Niagara Falls ON
Garvock, Mark W — Balderson, Ontario
Grenier, Roger — Saint Jovite, Que.
Harildstad, Matt — Edmonton, AB, T5T 2M8
Haslinger, Thomas — Calgary AB
Hayes, Wally — Orleans, Ont.
Hofer, Louis — Rose Prairie BC
Hoffmann, Uwe H. — Vancouver, BC
Jobin, Jacques — Levis Quebec
Kaczor, Tom — Upper London, Ont.
Lay, R J (Bob) — Falkland BC
Leber, Heinz — Hudson's Hope, BC
Lightfoot, Greg — Kitscoty AB
Linklater, Steve — Aurora, Ont.
Loerchner, Wolfgang — Bayfield, Ont.
Lyttle, Brian — High River, AB
Maneker, Kenneth — Galiano Island, B.C.
Martin, Robb — Elmira, Ontario
Marzitelli, Peter — Langley, BC
Massey, Al — Mount Uniacke, Nova Scotia
McKenzie, David Brian — Campbell River B.
Olson, Rod — High River, AB
Patrick, Bob — S. Surrey, B.C.
Pepiot, Stephan — Winnipeg, Man.
Piesner, Dean — St. Jacobs, Ont.
Pugh, Vernon — Saskatoon SK
Roberts, George A. — Whitehorse, YT
Ross, Tim — Thunder Bay, ONT
Schoenfeld, Matthew A. — Galiano Island, B.C.
St. Amour, Murray — Pembroke ON
Stancer, Chuck — Calgary AB
Storch, Ed — Alberta T0B 2W0
Stuart, Steve — Gores Landing, Ont.
Sunderland, Richard — Quathiaski Cove, BC
Tichbourne, George — Mississauga, Ont.
Tighe, Brian — Ridgeville, Ont
Toner, Roger — Pickering, Ont.
Treml, Glenn — Thunder Bay, Ont.
Trudel, Paul — Ottawa ON
Whitenect, Jody — Nova Scotia
Wile, Peter — Bridgewater, Nova Scotia
Young, Bud — Port Hardy, BC

denmark

Andersen, Henrik Lefolii — 3480, Fredensborg
Anso, Jens — 116, 8472 Sporvp
Carlsson, Marc Bjorn — 1112 Copenhagen K
Dyrnoe, Per — DK 3400 Hilleroed
Henriksen, Hans J. — DK 3200 Helsinge
Strande, Poul — Dastrup 4130 Viby Sj.
Vensild, Henrik — DK-8963 Auning

england

Boden, Harry — Derbyshire DE4 2AJ
Farid R., Mehr — Kent
Hague, Geoff — Wilton Marlborough, Wiltshire
Harrington, Roger — East Sussex
Henry & Son, Peter — Wokingham, Berkshire
Jackson, Jim — Berkshire SL4 5EP
Jones, Charles Anthony — No. Devon E31 4AL
Lamprey, Mike — Devon EX38 7BX
Morris, Darrell Price — Devon
Wardell, Mick — N Devon EX39 3BU
Wise, Donald — East Sussex, TN3 8AL
Wood, Alan — Carlisle, CA6 7HH

france

Bennica, Charles — 34190 Moules et Baucels
Bertholus, Bernard — Antibes
Doursin, Gerard — Pernes les Fontaines
Ganster, Jean-pierre — F-67000 Strasbourg
Graveline, Pascal
and Isabelle — 29350 Moelan-sur-Mer
Headrick, Gary — Juan Les Pins
Madrulli, Mme Joelle — Salon De Provence
Reverdy, Pierre
Thevenot, Jean-paul — Dijon
Viallon, Henri

germany

Balbach, Markus — 35789 Weilmunster-Laubuseschbach/Ts.
Becker, Franz — 84533, Marktl/Inn
Boehlke, Guenter — 56412 Grossholbach
Borger, Wolf — 76676 Graben-Neudorf
Dell, Wolfgang — D-73277 Owen-Teck
Faust, Joachim — 95497 Goldkronach
Fruhmann, Ludwig — 84489 Burghausen
Greiss, Jockl — 73252, Gutenberg
Hehn, Richard Karl — 55444 Dorrebach
Herbst, Peter — 91207 Lauf a.d. Pegn.
Joehnk, Bernd — 24148 Kiel
Kaluza, Werner — 90441 Nurnberg
Kressler, D.F. — Odetzhausen
Neuhaeusler, Erwin — 86179 Augsburg
Rankl, Christian — 81476 Munchen
Rinkes, Siegfried — Markterlbach
Steinau, Jurgen — Berlin 0-1162
Tritz, Jean Jose — 20255 Hamburg
Wimpff, Christian — 70574 Stuttgart 70
Wirtz, Achim — D -52146
Zirbes, Richard — D-54526 Niederkail

great britain

Elliott, Marcus — Llandudno Gwynedd

greece

Filippou, Ioannis-minas — Athens 17122

holland

Van De Manakker, Thijs — 5759 px Helenaveen

israel

Shadmot, Boaz — Arava

italy

Albericci, Emilio — 24100, Bergamo
Ameri, Mauro — 16010 Genova
Ballestra, Santino — 18039 Ventimiglia (IM)
Bertuzzi, Ettore — 24068 Seriate (Bergamo)
Bonassi, Franco — Pordenone 33170
Extreme Ratio S.A.S, — 59100 PRATO
Fogarizzu, Boiteddu — 07016 Pattada
Giagu, Salvatore and
Deroma Maria Rosaria — 07016 Pattada (SS)
Lorenzi, Giovanni Aldo — Milano 20121
Pachi, Francesco — 17046 Sassello (SV)
Scordia, Paolo — Roma
Simonella, Gianluigi — 33085 Maniago
Toich, Nevio — Vincenza
Tschager, Reinhard — I-39100 Bolzano

japan

Aida, Yoshihito — Itabashi-ku, Tokyo 175-0094
Akahori, Yoichiro — 426-0006
Carter, Murray M — Kumamoto
Ebisu, Hidesaku — Hiroshima City
Fujikawa, Shun — Osaka 597 0062
Fukuta, Tak — Seki-City, Gifu-Pref
Hara, Kouji — Gifu-Pref. 501-32

Hirayama, Harumi	Saitama Pref. 335-0001
Hiroto, Fujihara	Hiroshima
Isao, Ohbuchi	Fukuoka
Ishihara, Hank	Chiba Pref.
Kagawa, Koichi	Kanagawa
Kanda, Michio	Yamaguchi 746 0033
Kanki, Iwao	Hyougo
Kato, Kiyoshi	Tokyo 152
Katsumaro, Shishido	Hiroshima
Kawasaki, Akihisa	Kobe
Keisuke, Gotoh	Ohita
Koyama, Captain Bunshichi	Nagoya City 453-0817
Kozai, Shingo	Kamoto Kumamoto
Mae, Takao	Toyonaka, Osaka
Makoto, Kunitomo	Hiroshima
Matsusaki, Takeshi	Nagasaki
Michinaka, Toshiaki	Tottori 680-0947
Micho, Kanda	Yamaguchi
Okaysu, Kazou	Tokyo 110
Ryuichi, Kuki	Saitama
Sakakibara, Masaki	Tokyo 156
Shikayama, Toshiaki	Saitama 342-0057
Sugihara, Keidoh	Osaka, F596-0042
Sugiyama, Eddy K.	Ohita
Takahashi, Kaoru	Kamoto, Kumamoto
Takahashi, Masao	Gunma 371 0047
Terauchi, Toshiyuki	Fujita-Cho Gobo-Shi
Toshifumi, Kuramoto	Fukuoka
Uchida, Chimata	Kumamoto
Uekama, Nobuyuki	Tokyo
Wada, Yasutaka	Nara prefect 631-0044
Waters, Glenn	Hirosaki City 036-8183
Yoshihara, Yoshindo	Tokyo
Yoshikazu, Kamada	Tokushima
Yoshio, Maeda	Okayama

mexico
Scheurer, Alfredo E. Faes	C.P. 16010
Young, Cliff	San Miguel De Allende, GTO.

new zealand
Pennington, C.A.	Christchurch 9
Reddiex, Bill	Palmerston North
Ross, D.L.	Dunedin

n. wales u.k.
Heasman, H.G.	Llandudno

nagoya
Kato, Shinichi	Moriyama-ku

netherlands
Van Den Elsen, Gert	5012 AJ Tilburg
Van Eldik, Frans	3632BT Loenen
Van Schaik, Bastiaan	Amsterdam

norway
Bache-Wiig, Tom	Eivindvik
Holum, Morten	Oslo
Jorgensen, Gerd	N-3262 Larvik
Momcilovic, Gunnar	N-30055 Krokstadelva
Sellevold, Harald	N5834 Bergen
Vistnes, Tor	

nsw australia
Cross, Robert	Tamworth 2340
Maisey, Alan	Vincentia 2540

russia
Kharlamov, Yuri	300007

s.p. brazil
Bossaerts, Carl	14051-110, Ribeirao Preto

saudi arabia
Kadasah, Ahmed Bin	Jeddah 21441

singapore
Tay, Larry C-G	Singapore 9145

slovakia
Bojtos, Arpa D	98403 Lucenec
Pulis, Vladimir	96 701 Kremnica

south africa
Bauchop, Robert	Kwazulu-Natal 4278
Beukes, Tinus	Vereeniging 1939
Bezuidenhout, Buzz	Malvern, Queensburgh, Natal 4093
Boardman, Guy	New Germany 3619
Brown, Rob E.	Port Elizabeth
Burger, Fred	Kwa-Zulu Natal
De Villiers, Andre & Kirsten	Cascades 3202
Dickerson, Gavin	Petit 1512
Fellows, Mike	Velddrie 7365
Frankland, Andrew	Wilderness 6560
Grey, Piet	Naboomspruit 0560
Harvey,	Johannesburg
Harvey, Heather & Kevin	Belfast
Horn, Des	7700 Cape Town

Kojetin, W.	Germiston 1401
La Grange, Fanie	Selborne, Bellville 7530
Lancaster, C.G.	Free State
Liebenberg, Andre	Bordeauxrandburg 2196
Mackrill, Stephen	Johannesburg
Nelson, Tom	Gauteng
Pienaar, Conrad	Bloemfontein 9300
Rietveld, Bertie	Magaliesburg 1791
Russell, Mick	Port Elizabeth 6070
Schoeman, Corrie	Bloemfontein 9300
Shoebotham, Heather	Gold Reef City 2159 Johannesburg
Skellern, Dr. M.J.	
Smit, Corn	Zimbabwe
Theuns Prinsloo Knives,	Bethlehem, 9700
Watson, Peter	La Hoff 2570
Wood, Owen Dale Honeydew 2040 (Transvaal)	

sweden
Bergh, Roger	83070 NRA
Billgren, Per	
Eklund, Maihkel	S-820 41 Farila
Embretsen, Kaj	S-82821 Edsbyn
Johansson, Anders	S-772 40 Grangesberg
Lundstrom, Jan-Ake	66010 Dals-Langed
Nordell, Ingemar	82041 Färila
Persson, Conny	820 50 Loos
Ryberg, Gote	S-562 00 Norrahammar
Vogt, Patrik	S-30270 Halmstad

switzerland
Gagstaetter, Peter	9306 Freidorf TG
Roulin, Charles	1233 Geneva
Soppera, Arthur	CH-8038 Zurich

the netherlands
Van Rijswijk, Aad	3132 AA Vlaardingen

united kingdom
Maxen, Mick	"Hatfield, Herts"

uruguay
Gonzalez, Leonardo Williams	CP 20000
Symonds, Alberto E	Montevideo 11300

western australia
Gerner, Thomas	
Harvey, Max	Perth 6155

zimbabwe
Burger, Pon	Bulawayo

knifemakers membership lists

Not all knifemakers are organization-types, but those listed here are in good standing with these organizations.

the knifemakers' guild

2003 voting membership

a Les Adams, Yoshihito Aida, Mike "Whiskers" Allen, R.V. Alverson, Michael Anderson, W.E. Ankrom, Joe Arnold, Boyd Ashworth, Dick Atkinson

b Joseph D. Bailey, Norman Bardsley, A.T. Barr, Van Barnett, James Barry III, John Bartlow, Gene Baskett, James Batson, Gaetan Beauchamp, Raymond Beers, Charlie Bennica, Tom Black, Andrew Blackton, Gary Blanchard, Alan Bloomer, Arpad Bojtos, Philip Boguszewski, Wolf Borger, Tony Bose, Dennis Bradley, Edward Brandsey, W. Lowell Bray Jr., Judson Brennan, Clint Breshears, Tim Britton, David Broadwell, David Brown, Harold Brown, Rick Browne, John Busfield

c Bill Caldwell, Errett Callahan, Daniel Cannady, Ronald Canter, Harold J. "Kit" Carson, Fred Carter, Dianna Casteel, Douglas Casteel, Frank Centofante, Joel Chamblin, William Chapo, Alex Chase, William Cheatham, Howard F. Clark, Wayne Clay, Lowell Cobb, Keith Coleman, Vernon Coleman, Alex Collins, Blackie Collins, Bob Conley, Harold Corby, Joe Cordova, Gerald Corbit, Jim Corrado, George Cousino, Raymond Cover, Colin Cox, John Craft III, Pat Crawford, John M. Cross, Bob Crowder, James Crowell, Dan Cruze, Roy Cutchin

d George Dailey, Charles M. Dake, Alex Daniels, Jack Davenport, Edmund Davidson, Barry Davis, Terry Davis, Vernon M. Davis, W.C. Davis, Harvey Dean, Robert DeFeo, Bill DeFreest, Dan Dennehy, William Dietzel, Robert Dill, Frank Dilluvio, Charles Dintruff, Allen Dippold, T.M. Dowell, Larry Downing, Tom Downing, Bob Dozier, Bill Duff, Melvin Dunn, Steve Dunn, Jerry Duran

e Russell & Paula K. Easler, Al Eaton, Rick Eaton, Fain Edwards, Allen Elishewitz, Joel Ellefson, Jim Elliott, David Ellis, Kaj Embretsen, Brad Embry, Ernest Emerson, Jim Ence, Virgil England, William Engle, James T. Eriksen

f Stephen Fecas, Lee Ferguson, Thomas M. Ferrara, Bill Fiorini, Jay Fisher, Jerry Fisk, Joe Flournoy, Pete Forthofer, Ricky Flowler, Paul Fox, Henry Frank, Michael H. Franklin, Ron Frazier, Ralph Freer, Dennis Friedly, Larry Fuegen, Shun Fujikawa, Stanley Fujisaka, Tak Fukuta, Shiro Furukawa

g Frank Gamble, Roger Gamble, Robert Garbe, William Garner, Ronald Gaston, Clay Gault, Harry George, James "Hoot" Gibson Sr., Bruce Goers, David Goldberg, Warren Goltz, Greg Gottschalk, Roger M. Green, Jockl Greiss, Carol Gurganus, Melvin Gurganus, Kenneth Guth

h Philip L. "Doc" Hagen, Ed Halligan & Son, Jim Hammond, Tim Hancock, James E. Hand, M.D., Travis Hanson, Kouji Hara, Jeffrey Harkins, Walt Harless, Larry Harley, Jay Harmon, Ralph Harris, Rade Hawkins, Richard Hehn, Henry Heitler, Earl Jay Hendrickson, Wayne Hendrix, Wayne Hensley, Peter Herbst, Tim Herman, George Herron, Don Hethcoat, Thomas S. Hetmanski, Gil Hibben, Howard Hill, Steven Hill, R. Hinson & Son, Harumi Hirayama, Howard Hitchmough, Steve Hoel, Kevin Hoffman, D'Alton Holder, Jess Horn, Durvyn Howard, Arthur Hubbard, Rob Hudson, Daryle Hughes, Joel Humphreys, Joseph Hytovick

i Billy Mace Imel

j Jim Jacks, Paul Jarvis, Steve Jernigan, Tom Johanning, Brad Johnson, Ronald Johnson, Ruffin Johnson, Steve Johnson, W.C. Johnson, Enoch D. Jones, Robert Jones

k Edward N. Kalfayan, Dave Kauffman, William Keeton, Bill Kennedy Jr., Jot Khalsa, Keith Kilby, Bill King, Joe Kious, Russell Klingbeil, Terry Knipschield, R.C. Knipstein, Michael Koval, Dennis G. Krapp, Roy Krause, D.F. Kressler

l Ron Lake, Jarrell Lambert, Frank Lampson, Edward Lary, Kermit Laurent, Mike Leach, Randy Lee, Tommy Lee, William Letcher, Bill Levengood, Bob Levine, Yakov Levin, Steve Linklater, Wolfgang Loerchner, Juan A. Lonewolf, R.W. Loveless, Schuyler Lovestrand, Don Lozier, Bob Luchak, Robert Lum, Ernest Lyle, Brian Lyttle

m Joe Malloy, Dan Maragni, Peter Martin, Randall J. Martin, Zollan McCarty, Charles McConnell, Loyd McConnell, Robert J. McDonald, W. J. McDonald, Ken McFall, Frank McGowan, W.J. McHenry, David McIntosh, Tommy McNabb, Mike Mercer, Ted Merchant, Robert Merz III, James Miller, Steve Miller, Louis Mills, Dan Mink, Jim Minnick, Gunnar Momcilovic, James B. Moore, Jeff Morgan, C.H. Morris, Dusty Moulton, Paul Myers

n Bud Nealy, Corbin Newcomb, Larry Newton, R.D. & George Nolen, Ross Norfleet, Don Norton

o Charles Ochs, Ben R. Ogletree Jr., Warren Osborne, T.R. Overeynder, John Owens

p Larry Page, Robert Papp, Melvin Pardue, Bob Patrick, W.D. Pease, Alfred Pendray, John L. Perry, Eldon Peterson, Kenneth Pfeiffer, David Pitt, Leon Pittman, Clifton Polk, Al Polkowski, Joe Prince, Jim Pugh, Martin Pullen, Morris Pulliam

r Jerry Rados, James D. Ragsdale, Steven Rapp, A.D. Rardon, Chris Reeve, John Reynolds, Ron Richard, David Ricke, Bertie Rietveld, Willie Rigney, Dean Roath, Howard Robbins, Rex Robinson III, Robert Robinson, Fred Roe, Rodney Rogers, Charles Roulin, Ronald Russ, A.G. Russell, Gote Ryberg

s Bill Saindon, Masaki Sakakibara, Mike Sakmar, Hiroyuki Sakurai, John Salley, Scott Sawby, Michael Schirmer, James Schmidt, Herman Schneider, Maurice & Alan Schrock, Steve Schwarzer, Al Scott, Mark C. Sentz, Eugene W. Shadley, Ben Shostle, Bill Simons, R.J. Sims, Cleston Sinyard, Jim Siska, Fred Slee, Scott Slobodian, J.D. Smith, John Smith, John W. Smith, Michael J. Smith, Ralph Smith, Jerry Snell, Marvin Solomon, Arthur Soppera, Jim Sornberger, Harry Stalter, Ken Steigerwalt, Jurgen Steinau, Daniel Stephan, Murray Sterling, Barry Stevens, Johnny Lee Stout, Keidoh Sugihara, Arthur Summers, Greg Sutherland, S. Russell Sutton, Charles Syslo, Joseph Szilaski

t
Grant Tally, David A. Taylor, Gray Taylor, Robert Terzuola, Leon Thompson, Brian Tighe, P.J. Tomes, Dan Tompkins, John Toner, Dwight Towell, Leon Treiber, Barry Trindle, Reinhard Tschager, Jim Turecek, Ralph Turnbull

v
Yvon Vachon, Frans Van Eldik, Edward T. Van Hoy, Aad Van Rijswijk, Michael Veit, Howard Viele

w
John W. Walker, George Walker, Michael Walker, Charles Ward, Tommy Ware, Buster Warenski, Dellana Warren, Dale Warther, Thomas J. Watson, Charles Weeber, Reese Weiland, Robert Weinstock, Charles Weiss, Wayne Whittaker, Weldon Whitley, Donnie R. Wicker, Jason Williams, Gordon Wilson, R.W. Wilson, Daniel Winkler, Earl B. Witsaman, Frank Wojtinowski, William Wolf, Owen Wood, Wood, Irie & Company, Webster Wood, Tim Wright

y
Joe Yeates, Yoshindo Yoshihara, George Young, Mike Yurco

z
Brad Zinker, Tim Zowada

american bladesmith society

a
Robin E. Ackerson,Charles L. Adkins, Anthony "Tony" Aiken, Yoichiro Akahori, Douglas A. Alcorn , David Alexander, Mike Alexander, Eugene Alexander, Daniel Allison, Chris Amos, David Anders, Jerome Anders, Gary D. Anderson, Ronnie A. Andress Sr, E. R. (Russ) Andrews Ii, James M Arbuckle, Doug Asay, Boyd Ashworth, Ron Austin

b
David R. Bacon, Robert Keith Bagley, Marion Bagwell, Brent Bailey, Larry Bailey, Stephen A. Baker, Bruce Baker, Dwayne Bandy, Mark D. Banfield, David L. Banks, Robert G. Barker, Reggie Barker, Gary Barnes, Marlen R. Barnes, Cecil C. Barnes Jr., Aubrey G. Barnes Sr., Van Barnett Barnett International, Judson C. Barr, Rick L. Barrett, Michael Barton, Hugh E. Bartrug, Paul C. Basch, James L. Batson, R. Keith Batts, Michael R. Bauer, Rick Baum, Dale Baxter, Geneo Beasley, Jim Beaty, Robert B. Beaty, Steve Becker, Bill Behnke, Don Bell, John Bendik, Robert O. Benfield Jr., George Benjamin Jr., Rae Bennett, Brett Bennett, Bruce D. Berglin, Brent Beshara, Lora Sue Bethke, Gary Biggers, Ira Lee Birdwell, Hal Bish, William M. Bisher, Robert Bizzell, Scott Black, Randy Blair, Dennis Blankenheim, R. Gordon Bloomquist, Josh Blount, Otto Bluntzer, David Boone, Roger E. Bost, Raymond A. Boysen, Bailey Bradshaw, Sanford (Sandy) Bragman, Martin W. Brandt, Brett Bratcher, W. Lowell Bray Jr., Steven Brazeale, Charles D. Breme, Arthur Britton, Peter Bromley, Charles E. Brooks, Dennis G. Brown, Troy L. Brown, Mark D. Brown, Steven W. Browning, C. Lyle Brunckhorst, Jimmie H. Buckner, Bruce D. Bump, Larry Bundrick, Paul A. Burke, Bill Burke, Stephen R. Burrows, John Butler, John R. Butler, Wesley L. Byrd

c
Jerry (Buddy) Cabe, Sergio B. Cabrera, Ed Caffrey, Larry Cain, F. Terry Callahan, Robt W. Calvert Jr., Craig Camerer, Ron Cameron, Courtnay M. Campbell, Dan Cannon, Andrew B. Canoy, Jeff Carlisle, Ronald W. Carpenter, James V. Carriger, Chad Carroll, Murray M. Carter, George Carter, Terry Cash, Kevin R. Cashen, P. Richard Chastain, Milton Choate, Jon Christensen, Howard F. Clark, Joe Click, Charles Cole , Frank Coleman, Wade Colter, Larry D. Coltrain, Roger N. Comar, Roger Combs, Wm. E. (Bill) Compton, Larry Connelley, John W. Connor, Michael Connor, James R. Cook, Robert Cook, Charles W. Cook, III, Ted Cooper, James Roscoe Cooper, Jr., Joseph G. Cordova, David P. Corrigan, Dr. Timothy L. Costello, William Courtney, Collin Cousino, Gregory G. Covington, Dawnavan M. Crawford, George Crews, Jim Crowell, Steve Culver, George Cummings

d
George E. Dailey, Mary H. Dake, B. MacGregor "Daland, FSA Scot", Kelly Dallyn, Sava Damlovac, David T. Darby, Chester L. Darcey, David Darpinian, Jim Davidson, Barry Davis, John Davis, Dudley L. Dawkins, Michael De Gruchy, Angelo De Maria Jr., Harvey J. Dean, Anthony Del Giorno, Josse Delage, Clark B. Delong, William Derby, Christoph Deringer, Dennis E. Des Jardins, Chuck Diebel, Bill Dietzel, Al Dippold, Matt Diskin, Michael Distin, Patrick J. Downey, Audra L. Draper, Mike Draper, Joseph D. Drouin, Paul Dubro, Ron Duncan, Calvin Duniphan, Rick Dunkerley, Steve Dunn, Eric Durbin, Kenneth Durham, Fred Durio, David Dyer

e
Rick Eaton, Roger Echols, Mike Edelman, Thomas Eden, Gregory K. Edmonson, Randel Edmonson, Mitch Edwards, Lynn Edwards, Daniel Robert Ehrenberger, Fred Eisen, Perry B. Elder Jr., Allen Elishewitz, R. Van Elkins, Rickie Ellington, Gordon Elliott, Carroll Ellis, Dave Ellis, Roger R. Elrod, Kaj Embretsen, Edward Engarto, Richard Epting, David Etchieson, Ronald B. Evans, Vincent K. Evans, Greg Evans, Bruce E. Evans, Wyman Ewing

f
John E. Faltay, George Fant Jr., Daniel Farr, Alexander Felix, Gregory K. Ferrier, Robert Thomas Ferry III, Michael J. Filarski, Ioannis-Minas Filippou, Sean W. Finlayson, William Fiorini, Jerry Fisk, James O. Fister, John S. Fitch, Dawn Fitch, Mike Fletcher, Joe Flournoy, Charles Fogarty, Don Fogg, Burt Foster, Ronnie E. Foster, Edward K. Foster, Timothy L. Foster, Norvell C. Foster, Jerry Fowler, C. Ronnie Fowler, Ed Fowler, Walter P. Framski, John M. Frankl, John R. Fraps, Steve Frey, Rolf Friberg, Daniel Fronefield, Dewayne Frost, Larry D. Fuegen, Jack A. Fuller, Bruce A. Fuller, Richard Furrer

g
Barry Gallagher, Jacques Gallant, Jesse Gambee, Tommy Gann, Tommy Gann, Rodney Gappelberg, Jim L. Gardner, Larry W. Garner, Timothy P. Garrity, Mark W. Garvock, Bert Gaston, Darrell Geisler, Thomas Gerner, James Gibson, Joel Gist, Wayne Goddard, Jim Gofourth, Scott K. Goguen, David Goldberg, Rodney W. Goodling, Tim Gordon, Thomas L. Gore, James T. Gorenflo, Gabe Gorenflo, Greg Gottschalk, Rayne Gough, Paul J. Granger, Don Greenaway, Michael S. Griffin, Anthony R. Guarnera, Bruce Guidry, Christian Guier, Garry Gunderson, Johan Gustafsson,

h
Cyrus Haghjoo, Ed Halligan, N. Pete Hamilton, Timothy J. Hancock, Bill Hand, Don L. Hanson III, Douglas E. Hardy, Larry Harley, Sewell C. Harlin, Paul W. Harm, Brent Harper-Murray, Tedd Harris, Cass Harris, Jeffrey A. Harris, Bill Hart, Kevin Harvey, Heather Harvey, Buddy Hawkins, Rade Hawkins, Wally Hayes, Charlie E. Haynes, Gary Headrick, Dion Hedges, Win Heger, Daniel Heiner, John Heinz, E. Jay Hendrickson, Bill Herndon, Harold Herron, Don Hethcoat, John M. Hill , Donald R. Hinton, Dan

Hockensmith, Thomas R. Hogan, Troy Holland, Mark B. Honea, Michael Honey, John F. Hood, John Horrigan, Lawrence House, Gary House, Michael Houston, Jason G Howell, F. Dale Huckabee, C. Robbin Hudson, Anthony B. Hudson, Bill Hughes, Daryle Hughes, Tony Hughes, Brad Humelsine, Maurice Hunt, Raymon E. Hunt, Richard D. Hunter, William R. Hurt, Joe Hytovick

j David Jackson, Jim L. Jackson, Chuck Jahnke, Jr., Karl H. Jakubik, Melvin Jennings Jr., John Lewis Jensen, Mel "Buz" Johns, Ray Johnson, John R. Johnson, David A. Johnson, Thomas Johnson , Dr. Robt. Johnston, John Jones, Franklin W. Jones, Enoch Jones, Roger W. Jones, Terry J. Jordan, Shane Justice

k Charles Kain, Al J. Kajin, Gus Kalanzis, David Kazsuk, Jarod Kearney, Robert Keeler, Joseph F. Keeslar, Dale Kempf, R. W. Kern, Joe Kertzman, Lawrence Keyes, Charles M. Kilbourn, Jr., Keith Kilby, Richard L. Kimberley, Herman King, David R. King, Fred J. King, Harvey G. King Jr., Frederick D. Kingery, Donald E. Kinkade, Todd Kirk, Ray Kirk, Brad Kliensmid, Russell K. Klingbeil, Hank Knickmeyer, Kurt Knickmeyer, Jason Knight, Steven C. Koster, Bob Kramer, Lefty Kreh, Phil Kretsinger

l Jerry Lairson Sr., Curtis J. Lamb, J. D. Lambert, Robert M. Lamey, Leonard D. Landrum, Warren H. Lange, Paul Lansingh, Rodney Lappe, Kermit J. Laurent, Alton Lawrence, Randell Ledbetter, Denis H. Lefranc, Jim L. Lemcke, Wayne Levin, Bernard Levine, Steve Lewis, Tom Lewis, Guy A. Little, Tim Lively, Keith Locke, Lowell C. Lockett , Anthony P. Lombardo, Phillip Long, Jonathan A. Loose, Eugene Loro, Sherry Lott, Jim Lovelace, Steven Lubecki, Bob Luchini, James R. Lucie, James R. Luman, William R. Lyons

m John Mackie, Madame Joelle Madrulli, Takao Mae, Mike Majer, Raymond J. Malaby, John Mallett, Bob Mancuso, Kenneth Mankel, Matt Manley, James Maples, Dan Maragni, Ken Markley, J. Chris Marks, Stephen R. Marshall, Tony Martin, John Alexander Martin, Hal W. Martin, Alan R. Massey, Roger D. Massey, Mick Maxen, Daniel McBrearty, Howard H. McCallen Jr, Michael McClure, Frederick L. MCcoy, Kevin McCrackin, Victor J. McCrackin, Robert J. McDonald, Richard McDonald, Robin J. McDonald, Frank McGowan, Patrick T. McGrath, Donald McGrath, Neil H. McKee, David Brian McKenzie, Hubert W. McLendon, Tommy McNabb, J. Michael McRae, David L. Meacham, J. R. Mellard, Walter Merrin, Mardi Meshejian, Ged Messinger, Hanford J. Miller, Bob Miller, Michael Mills, David Mirabile, Wm. Dean Mitchell , Jim Molinare, Michael Steven Moncus, Shawn Robert Moore, Marve Moore, Michael Robert Moore, William F Moran Jr., Jim Moyer, Russell A. Moyer, James W. Mueller, Jody Muller, Deryk C. Munroe, Ron Myers

n Angelo Navagato, Bob Neal , Gregory T. Neely, Thomas Conor Neely, Lars Nelson, Corbin Newcomb, Ron Newton, Douglas E. Noren, Paul T. Norris, William North

o Charles F. Ochs III, Clyde O'Dell, Vic Odom, Michael O'Herron, Todd D. Oliver, Joe Olson, Richard Oneill, Philip D. Osattin, Warren Osborne, Donald H. Osborne, Fred Ott, Mac Overton, Donald Owens

p Anthony P. Palermo, Rik Palm, Paul Papich, Cliff Parker, Earl Parker, John Parks, Jimmy D. Passmore, Rob Patton, Gary Payton, Michael Peck, Alfred Pendray, Christopher

A. Pennington, Johnny Perry, John L. Perry, Conny Persson, Dan L. Petersen, Lloyd Pete C. Peterson, Dan Pfanenstiel, Jim Phillips, Benjamin P. Piccola, Ray Pieper III, Diane Pierce, Dean Piesner, Dietmar Pohl, Jon R. "Pop" Poplawski, Timothy Potier, James Powell, Robert Clark Powell, Houston Price, Terry Primos, Gerald Puckett, Martin Pullen

q Thomas C. Quakenbush

r John R. Radford Jr., R. Wayne Raley, Darrel Ralph, Richard A. Ramsey, Gary Randall, James W. Randall Jr., David L. Randolph, Ralph Randow, Mike Reagan, George R. Rebello, Lee Reeves, Roland R. "Rollie" Remmel, Zaza Revishvili, Kirk Rexroat, Scott Reyburn, Stephen E. Rice, Alvin C. Richards Jr., James Richardson, David M. Rider, Richard A. Riepe, Dennis Riley, E. Ray Roberts, Jim Roberts, Leo D. Robertson, Charles R. Robinson, Michael Rochford, James L. Rodebaugh, Gary Rodewald, Charles W. Rogers, Richard Rogers, Willis "Joe" Romero, N. Jack Ronzio, Robert Rosenfeld, Robert N. Rossdeutscher, Charles Roulin, Kenny Rowe, Clark D. Rozas, Ronald S. Russ, Michael G. Ruth, Brad Rutherford, Raymond B. Rybar Jr., Gerald Rzewnicki

s William Sahli, Paul Sarganis, James P. Saviano, Ed Schempp, Ellen Schilling, Tim Scholl, Robert Schrader, Stephen C. Schwarzer, James A. Scroggs, Bert Seale, Turner C. Seale, Jr., David D. Seaton, Steve Seib, Mark C. Sentz, Rodrigo Menezes Sfreddo, Steve Shackleford, Gary Shaw, James F. Shull, Ken Simmons, Charles Russel Sisemore, Charles J. Smale, Joshua J. Smith, Clifford Lee Smith, J. D. Smith, Carel Smith, Raymond L. Smith, Lenard C. Smith, Timothy E. Smock, Michael Tom Snyder, Max Soaper, John E. Soares, Arthur Soppera, Bill Sowell, David R. Sparling, H. Red St. Cyr, Chuck Stancer, Craig Steketee, Edward L. Stewart, Rhett & Janie Stidham, Jason M. Stimps, Walter Stockwell, Bob Stormer, Charles Stout, Johnny L. Stout, John K. Stout Jr., Robert E. Stumphy Jr., Harlan Suedmeier, John Switzer, Arthur Swyhart, Mark G. Szarek, Joseph Szilaski

t Scott Taylor, Shane Taylor, Danny O. Thayer, Jean-Paul Thevenot, Brian Thie, David E. Thomas, Scott Thomas, Alan L. Tiensvold, Jason Tiensvold, John Tilton, George Tindera, Dennis P. Tingle, P. J. Tomes, Kathleen C. Tomey, Mark Torvinen, Joe E. Travieso III, James J. Treacy, Craig Triplett, Kenneth W Trisler, James Turpin, Ross Tyser

v Michael V. Vagnino, Jr, , Steve Van Cleve, Jerry W. Van Eizenga, Terry L. Vandeventer, Michael Viehman, Ricardo Vilar, Mace Vitale, Patrik Vogt, Bruce Voyles

w Steve "Doc" Wacholz, Lawrence M. Wadler, Adam Waldon, Bill Walker, Don Walker, James L. Walker, Carl D. Ward, Jr., Ken Warner, Robert Lee Washburn Jr., Herman Harold Waters, Lu Waters, Charles G. Weeber, Ronald Welling, Eddie Wells, Elsie Westlake, Jim Weyer, Nick Wheeler, Wesley Whipple, Richard T. White, Lou White, John Paul White, L. Wayne Whitley, Randy Whittaker, Timothy L. Wiggins, William Burton Wiggins, Jr., Scott Wiley, Dave Wilkes, Michael L. Williams, A. L. Williams, George H. Wilson, III, Daniel Winkler, Randy Winsor, George Winter, Morris C. Worrell, Bill Worthen, Terry Wright

z Mark D. Zalesky, Kenneth Zarifes, Terry Zboril, Karl Zimmerman

directory

miniature knifemaker's society

Paul Abernathy, Joel Axenroth, Blade Magazine, Dennis Blaine, Gerald Bodner, Gary Bradburn, Brock Custom Knives, Ivan Campos, Mitzi Cater, Don Cowles, Creations Yvon Vachon, Dennis Cutburth, David Davis, Robert Davis, Gary Denms, Dennis Des Jardins, Eisenberg Jay Publishers, Allen Eldridge, Peter Flores, David Fusco, Eric Gillard, Wayne Goddard, Larah Gray, Gary Greyraven, Tom & Gwen Guinn, Karl Hallberg, Ralph Harris, Richard Heise, Laura Hessler, Wayne Hensley, Tom Hetmanski, Howard Hosick, Albert Izuka, Garry Kelley, Knife World Publishers, R F Koebbeman, Terry Kranning, Gary Lack, John LeBlanc, Mike Lee, Les Levinson, Jack Lewis, Mike Ley, Ken Liegey, Henry Loos, Jim Martin, Howard Maxwell, McMullen & Yee Publishing, Ken McFall, Mal Mele, Paul Meyers, Toshiaki Michinaka, Allen G Miller, Wayne & June Morrison, Mullinnix & Co, National Knife Collectors Assoc., Allen Olsen, Charles Ostendorf, Mike Pazos, Jim Pear, Gordon Pivonka, Jim Pivonka, Prof. Knifemakers Assoc, Jim Pugh, Roy Quincy, John Rakusan, A D Rardon, Dawin Richards, Stephen Ricketts, Mark Rogers, Alex Rose, Hank Rummell, Helen Rummell, Sheffield Knifemakers Supply, Sporting Blades, Harry Stalter, Udo Stegemann, Mike Tamboli, Hank Rummell, Paul Wardian, Ken Warner, Michael Wattelet, Ken Wichard Jr. Charles Weiss, Jim Whitehead, Steve Witham, Shirley Whitt, G T Williams, Ron Wilson, Dennis Windmiller, Carol Winold, Earl Witsaman, James Woods

professional knifemaker's association

Mike 'Whiskers' Allen, John Anthon , Ray Archer, Eddie Baca, Cecil Barret, John Bartlow, Paul Basch, Brett Bennett, Nico Bernard, Kenneth Brock, Craig Camerer, Tim Cameron, Rod Carter, Roger Craig, Bob Cumming, Dave Darpinian, Mike Draper, Audra Draper, Ray Ennis, Jim Eriksen , Sal Glesser , Marge Hartman, Guy Hielscher, Terrill Hoffman, Mike Irie, Donald Jones, Harvey King, Jason King, Steve Kraft, Jim Largent, Jim Lemcke (Texas Knifemakers Supply), WSSI (Mike Ludeman), Jim Magee, Daniel May, Jerry McClure, Mac McLaughlin, Larry McLaughlin, Clayton Miller, Mark Molnar, Ty Montell, Mike Mooney, Bill Noehren , Steve Nolen, Fred Ott, Rob Patton, PKA, Pop Knives, David Wattenberg, Rocky Mtn Blade Collectors, Steve Rollert, Clint Sampson, Charles Sauer, Jerry Schroeder, Craig Steketee, Loyd Thomsen , James Thrash, Chuck Trice, Louis Vinquist, Bill Waldrup, Tommy Ware, Joe Wheeler, Owen Wood, Owen Wood, Mike Zima, Daniel Zvonek

state/regional association

alaska knifemakers association
A.W. Amoureux, John Arnold, Bud Aufdermauer, Robert Ball, J.D. Biggs, Lonnie Breuer, Tom Broome, Mark Bucholz, Irvin Campbell, Virgil Campbell, Raymond Cannon, Christopher Cawthorne, John Chamberlin, Bill Chatwood, George Cubic, Bob Cunningham, Gordon S. Dempsey, J.L. Devoll, James Dick, Art Dufour, Alan Eaker, Norm Grant, Gordon Grebe, Dave Highers, Alex Hunt, Dwight Jenkins, Hank Kubaiko, Bill Lance, Bob Levine, Michael Miller, John Palowski, Gordon Parrish, Mark W. Phillips, Frank Pratt, Guy Recknagle, Ron Robertson, Steve Robertson, Red Rowell, Dave Smith, Roger E. Smith, Gary R. Stafford, Keith Stegall, Wilbur Stegner, Norm Story, Robert D. Shaw, Thomas Trujillo, Ulys Whalen, Jim Whitman, Bob Willis

arizona knifemakers association
D. "Butch" Beaver, Bill Cheatham, Dan Dagget, Tom Edwards, Anthony Goddard, Steve Hoel, Ken McFall, Milford Oliver, Jerry Poletis, Merle Poteet, Mike Quinn, Elmer Sams, Jim Sornberger, Glen Stockton, Bruce Thompson, Sandy Tudor, Charles Weiss

arkansas knifemakers association
David Anders, Auston Baggs, Don Bailey, Reggie Barker, Marlen R. Barnes, Paul Charles Basch, Lora Sue Bethke, James Black, R.P. Black, Joel Bradford, Gary Braswell, Paul Brown, Shawn Brown, Troy L. Brown, Jim Butler, Buddy Cabe, Allen Conner, James Cook, Thom Copeland, Gary L. Crowder, Jim Crowell, David T Darby, Fred Duvall, Rodger Echols, David Etchieson, Lee Ferguson, Jerry Fisk, John Fitch, Joe & Gwen Flournoy, Dewayne Forrester, John Fortenbury, Ronnie Foster, Tim Foster, Emmet Gadberry, Larry Garner, Ed Gentis, Paul Giller, James T. Gilmore, Terry Glassco, D.R. (Rick) Gregg, Lynn Griffith, Arthur J. Gunn, Jr., David Gunnell, Morris Herring, Don "Possum" Hicks, Jim Howington, B. R. Hughes, Ray Kirk, Douglas Knight, Lile Handmade Knives, Jerry Lairson Sr., Claude Lambert, Alton Lawrence, Jim Lemcke, Michael H. Lewis, Willard Long, Dr. Jim Lucie, Hal W Martin, Tony Martin, Roger D. Massey, Douglas Mays, Howard McCallen Jr., Jerry McClure, John McKeehan, Joe McVay, Bart Messina, Thomas V. Militano, Jim Moore, Jody Muller, Greg Neely, Ron Newton, Douglas Noren, Keith Page, Jimmy Passmore, John Perry, Lloyd "Pete" Peterson, Cliff Polk, Terry Primos, Paul E Pyle Jr, Ted Quandt, Vernon Red, Tim Richardson, Dennis Riley, Terry Roberts, Charles R. Robinson, Kenny Rowe, Ken Sharp, Terry Shurtleff, Roy Slaughter, Joe D. Smith, Marvin Solomon, Hoy Spear, Charles Stout, Arthur Tycer, Ross Tyser, James Walker, Chuck Ward, Herman Waters, Bryce White, Tillmon T Whitley III, Mike Williams, Rick Wilson, Terry Wright, Ray Young

australian knifemakers guild inc.
Tim Anson, Peter Bald, Wayne Barrett, Alf Bennett, Peter Bennett, Wayne Bennett, Wally Bidgood, Peter Binns, David Brodziak, Stuart Burdett, Mike Carroll, Neil Charity, Bruce Crawley, John Creedy, Mark Crowley, Les Curry, Lance Davison, Steve Dawson, Malcolm Day, Jim Deering, Peter Del Raso, Robert Di Martino, Glen Duncan, Chris Erickson, Marcus Everett, Michael Fechner, Thomas Gerner, Branko Giljevic, Eric Gillard, Russ Gillard, Peter Gordon, Stephen Gregory-Jones, Frank Harbottle, Lloyd Harding, Rod Harris, Max Harvey, Glen Henke, Barry

Hosking, Michael Hunt, Myron Husiak, Raymond Jenkins, Ross Johnston, John Jones, Jason Jonker, Simeon Jurkijevic, Wolf Kahrau, Peter Kandavnieks, Peter Kenney, Tasman Kerley, John Kilby, Mitchell Lowe, Greg Lyell, Paul Maffi, Maurice McCarthy, Ray Mende, Dave Myhill, Adam Parker, John Pattison, Chris Pennington, Mike Petersen, Greg Reader, Peter Reardon, David Ross, Murray Shanaughan, Gary Siemer, Kurt Simmonds, Jim Steele, Rod Stines, David Strickland, Kelvin Thomas, Doug Timbs, Len Van Dongen, Robert Venturin, David Walford, Hardy Wangemann, Brendon Ware, Glen Waters, Bob Wilhelm, Angleo Xepapas, Ross Yeats, Joe Zemitis, David Zerbe

california knifemakers association

Arnie Abegg, George J. Antinarelli, Elmer Art, Gregory Barnes, Mary Michael Barnes, Hunter Baskins, Gary Biggers, Roger Bost, Clint Breshears, Buzz Brooks, Steven E. Bunyea, Peter Carey, Joe Caswell, Frank Clay, Richard Clow, T.C. Collins, Richard Corbaley, Stephanie Engnath, Alex Felix, Jim Ferguson, Dave Flowers, Logwood Gion, Peter Gion, Joseph Girtner, Tony Gonzales, Russ Green, Tony Guarnera, Bruce Guidry, Dolores Hayes, Bill Herndon, Neal A. Hodges, Richard Hull, Jim Jacks, Lawrence Johnson, David Kazsuk, James P. Kelley, Richard D. Keyes, Michael P. Klein, Steven Koster, John Kray, Bud Lang, Tomas N. Lewis, R.W. Loveless, John Mackie, Thomas Markey, James K. Mattis, Toni S. Mattis, Patrick T. McGrath, Larry McLean, Jim Merritt, Greg Miller, Walt Modest, Russ Moody, Emil Morgan, Gerald Morgan, Mike Murphy, Thomas Orth, Tom Paar, Daniel Pearlman, Mel Peters, Barry Evan Posner, John Radovich, James L. Rodebaugh, Clark D. Rozas, Ron Ruppe, Brian Saffran, Red St. Cyr, James Stankovich, Bill Stroman, Tony Swatton, Gary Tamms, James P. Tarozon, Scott Taylor, Tru-Grit Inc., Tommy Voss, Jessie C. Ward, Wayne Watanabe, Charles Weiss, Steven A. Williams, Harlan M. Willson, Steve Wolf, Barry B. Wood

florida knifemaker's association

Les Adams, Dick Atkinson, James Barry III, Ray Beers, Robert E. Bess, Howard Bishop, Andy Blackton, Neil Blackwood, Stephen A. Bloom, Dean Bosworth, Craig Bozorth, W. Lowell Bray Jr., Harold Brown, Doug Buck, Dave Burns, Patrick R. Burris, Peter Channell, Mark Clark, Lowell Cobb, David Cole, Mark Condron, T. Cooper, Dan Cruze, Ralph F. D'Elia, Alex Daniels, Jack Davenport, Susan Davenport, Kenny Davis, J. D. Davis, Bill Dietzel, John B. Durham, Jim Elliot, Tom Enos, Bob Ferring, Roger Gamble, Tony Garcia, William O. Garner, James "Hoot" Gibson, Pedro Gonzalez, Howard A. Griffin Jr., Ernie Grospitch, Ralph D. Harris, Henry Heitler, Ray Hickman, John Hodge, Kevin Hoffman, Edward Holloway, Gail Humel, Joel Humphreys, Joe Hytovick, Steve Jernigan, Raymond C. Johnson, Bill King, F.D. Kingery, Russ Klingbeil, John E. Klingensmith, William S. Letcher, Bill Levengood, Glenn A. Long, Larry Lunn, Ernie Lyle, Mark MacFarlan, Bob Mancuso, R.J. McDonald, Faustina Mead, Maxie Mahaffey, Steve Miller, Dan Mink, Steven Morefield, Eric Morris, Martin L. Murphy, Charles Ochs, Cliff Parker, Larry Dale Patterson, Dan Piergallini, Martin Prudente, Carlo Raineri, Ray Roberts, Rex Robinson, Dan Rodkey, Rodney Rogers, Albert Rubio, David Semones, Ann & Paul Sheffield, Brad Shepherd, Bill Simons, Louis Vallet, Donald Vogt, Roger L. Wallace, Tom Watson, Reese Weiland Jr., Brad Zinker

knifemakers' guild of southern africa

George Baartman, Francois Basson, Peter Bauchop, Arno Bernard, Gert Bezuidenhout, Wolf Borger, Peet Bronkhorst, Rob Brown, Fred Burger, William Burger, Jacobus De Wet Coetzee, Z. André De Beer, André De Villiers, Gavin Dickerson, Roy H. Dunseith, Charl Du Plooy, J.M. Du Plooy, Dries Esterhuizen, Leigh Fogarty, Andrew Frankland, Ettoré Gianferrari, John Grey, Piet Grey, J.C. Greyling, Kevin Harvey, Howard Hitchmough, Des Horn, Ben Kleynhans, Willibald Kojetin, Mark Kretschmer, Fanie LaGrange, Garry Lombard, Steve Lombard, Theo Martins, Francois Massyn, Edward G. Mitchell, Willie Paulsen, Conrad Pienaar, David Schalk Pienaar, Jan Potgieter, Neels Pretorius, Hilton Purvis, Derek Rausch, Chris Reeve, Bertie Rietveld, Dean Riley, John Robertson, Mick Russel, Corrie Schoeman, Elke Schönert, Michael J. Skellern, Toi Skellern, Carel Smith, Ken Smythe, Brent E. Sandow, Graham Sparks, J.H. Stander, André E. Thorburn, Fanie Van Der Linde, Marius Van Der Vyver, Boekoe Van Rensburg, Marlene Van Schalkwyk, Sias Van Schalkwyk, Danie Van Wyk, Shalk Van Wyk, Ben Venter, Willie Venter, Gert Vermaak, René Vermeulen, Tony Victor, Peter Watson, Ted Whitfield, John Wilmot, Armin Winkler, Wollie Wolfaardt, Owen Wood

midwest knifemakers association

E.R. Andrews III, Frank Berlin, Charles Bolton, Tony Cates, Mike Chesterman, Ron Duncan, Larry Duvall, Bobby Eades, Jackie Emanuel, James Haynes, John Jones, Mickey Koval, Ron Lichlyter, George Martoncik, Gene Millard, William Miller, Corbin Newcomb, Chris Owen, A.D. Rardon, Archie Rardon, Max Smith, Ed Stewart, Charles Syslo, Melvin Williams

montana knifemaker's association

Chuck Anderson, Bill Amoureux, Lyle Bainbridge, Wendell Barnes, James Barth, Bob Beaty, Bob Bizzell, Peter Bromley, Bruce Bump, Ed Caffrey, C Camper, Rocco Chicaralli, Jack Cory, Bob Crowder, Dennis Des Jardins, Rick Dunkerley, Mel and Darlene Fassio, Gary Flohr, Vern Ford, Wendell Fox, Barry Gallagher, Doc Hagen, Tedd Harris, Gerald Hintz, Warren Hodges, Tori Howe, Bob Hollar, Al Inman, Jerry Kurzenbaum, Doug Klaudt, Dan Kendrick, James Luman, Mel Long, Mike Mann, W E Martin, Neil McKee, Gerald Morgan, Louis Morton, Ed Mortenson, Deryk Munroe, David Neagle, Dan Nedved, Charles Ochs, Joe Olson, Patton Knives, Brian Peele, Eldon Peterson, Robert Porter, Jim Raymond, Kirk Rexroat, Lori Ristinen, James Rodebaugh, Gary Rodewald, Robert Roy, Charles Sauer, Dean Schroeder, Mel Sorge, Fred St. Pierre, Terry Stiegers, James Stover, Art Swyhart, Justin Tanner, Shane Taylor, Jim Thill, Frank Towsley, Bill and Lori Waldrup, Michael Wattelet, Darlene and Gerome Weinand, Donna and Dan Westlind, Michael Young, Fred Zaloudek

new england bladesmiths guild

Phillip Baldwin, Gary Barnes, Paul Champagne, Jimmy Fikes, Don Fogg, Larry Fuegen, Rob Hudson, Midk Langley, Louis Mills, Dan Maragni, Jim Schmidt, Wayne Valachovic and Tim Zowada

new mexico

Robert J Cummings

north carolina custom knifemakers' guild

David C. Baker, Herbert M. Baker, Robert E. Barber, Dr. James Batson, Donald R. Beamon, William M. Bisher, Dave Breme, Wayne Bernauer, Tim Britton, Richard

Brown, Doug Burns, John (Jack) H. Busfield, Max M. Butcher, Terry Cash, R. C. Chopra, Thomas Clegg, John Conn, Joe Corbin, Robert (Bob) J. Cumming, Travis Daniel, David Dempsey, Geno Denning, Dexter Ewing, Don Fogg, Alan Folts, Norman A. Gervais, Scott Goguen, Mark Gottesman, Nelson Gimbert, Carol & Melvin Gurganus, Ed Halligan, Mark Hazen, George Herron, Terrill Hoffman, Robert M. Horrigan, B. R. Hughes, Jack Hyer, Tommy Johnson, Barry & Phillip Jones, Tony Kelly, Robert Knight, Tom Matthews, W. N. (Bill) Maynard, Tommy McNabb, John McPhearson Jr., J. Michael McRae, Tom Militano, Charlie & Maureen Monroe, Bill Moran, Ron Newton, Charles Ostendorf, Richard C. Overman, Bill Pate, James Poplin, John W. Poythress, Darrel Ralph, Henry Clay Runion, Bruce M. Ryan, Robert J. Schmidt, Tim Scholl, Danks Seel, Cecil H. Self, Jr., Daryl Shelby, J. Wayne Short, Harland R. Simmons, Chuck Staples, Murray Sterling, Russ Sutton, Kathleen Tomey, Bruce Turner, Kaiji & Miki Uchida, Wayne Whitley, James A. Williams, Daniel Winkler, Dave Vail, Edward & Tanya VanHov, Kelly Yates

ohio knifemakers association

Raymond Babcock, Van Barnett, Harold A. Collins, Larry Detty, Tom Downing, Jim Downs, Patty Ferrier, Jeff Flannery, James Fray, Bob Foster, Raymond Guess, Scott Hamrie, Rick Hinderer, Curtis Hurley, Ed Kalfayan, Michael Koval, Judy Koval, Larry Lunn, Stanley Maienknecht, Dave Marlott, Mike Mercer, David Morton, Patrick McGroder, Charles Pratt, Darrel Ralph, Roy Roddy, Carroll Shoemaker, John Smith, Clifton Smith, Art Summers, Jan Summers, Donald Tess, Dale Warther, John Wallingford, Earl Witsaman, Joanne Yurco, Mike Yurco

south carolina association of knifemakers

Ritchie Batchelor, Bobby Branton, Dan Cannady, Wayne Childress, John Conn, Charles S. Cox, William DeFreest, Geno Denning, Charlie Douan, Hal Gainey, Harry George, Wayne Hendrix, George Herron, T.J. Hucks, Johnny Johnson, Ralph Kessler, Col. Thomas D. Kreger, Gene Langley, David Manley, Claude Montjoy, Larry Page, Russ Peagler, Timothy O. Peake, Joe Prince, Ralph Smith, S. David Stroud, Rocky Thomas, Woodrow W. Walker, Charlie Webb

tennessee knifemakers association

John Bartlow, Doug Casteel, Harold Crisp, Larry Harley, John W. Walker, Harold Woodward, Harold Wright

knife photo index

knives 2003

directory

engravers

etchers/carvers

leatherworkers/sheathmakers

scrimshanders

sporting cutlers

The firms listed here are special in the sense that they make or market special kinds of knives made in facilities they own or control either in the U.S. or overseas. Or they are special because they make knives of unique design or function. The second phone number listed is the fax number.

A.G. RUSSELL KNIVES INC
1920 North 26th St.
Lowell, AR 72745-8489
479-631-013 • 800-255-9034 • 749-631-8493
ag@agrussell.com • www.agrussell.com
The oldest knife mail-order company, highest quality. Free catalog available. In these catalogs you will find the newest and the best. If you like knives, this catalog is a must.

AHERN GROUP, THE/EXECUTIVE EDGE
3462 Cascade Ive Drive
Buford, GA 30519
678-482-8116 or 800-334-3790
6784829421 • 800-334-3790
tahern@bellsouth.net • www.executiveedge.com
Pen style shirt pocket knives ideal for carry or gift giving. Several sizes and style available.

AL MAR KNIVES
P.O. Box 2295
Tualatin, OR 97062-2295
503-670-9080 • 503-639-4789
www.almarknives.com
Featuring our Ultrlight Series of knives weighing from less then one oz. to two ozs., and blade lengths from 2-3/4 to 4 inches.

ALCAS COMPANY
1116 E State St.
Olean, NY 14760
716-372-3111 • 716-373-6155
plaine@kabar.com • www.cutco.com
Household cutlery / sport knives.

ANZA KNIVES
C Davis
Dept BL. 12, P.O. Box 710806
Santee, CA 92072
619-561-9445
619-390-6283
sales@anzaknives.com • www.anzaknives.com

B&D TRADING CO.
3935 Fair Hill Rd.
Fair Oaks, CA 95628

BARTEAUX MACHETES, INC.
1916 S.E. 50th St.
Portland, OR 97215
503-233-5880
barteaux@machete.com
www.machete.com
Manufacture of machetes, saws, garden tools.

BEAR MGC CUTLERY
1111 Bear Blvd. SW
Jacksonville, AL 36265
256-435-2227 • 256-435-9348
Lockback, commemorative, multi tools, high tech & hunting knives.

BECK'S CUTLERY & SPECIALTIES
McGregor Village Center
107 Edinburgh South Dr
Cary, NC 27511
919-460-0203 • 919-460-7772
beckscutlery@mindspring.com
www.beckscutlery.com

BENCHMADE KNIFE CO. INC.
300 Beaver Creek Rd.
Oregon City, OR 97045
503-655-6004 • 503-655-6223
info@benchmade.com • www.benchmade.com
Sports, utility, law enforcement, military, gift and semi custom.

BERETTA U.S.A. CORP.
17601 Beretta Dr.
Accokeek, MD 20607
301-283-2191
www.berettausa.com
Full range of hunting & specialty knives.

BLACKJACK KNIVES
P.O. Box 3
Greenville, WV 24945

BLUE GRASS CUTLERY CORP
20 E Seventh St., P.O. Box 156
Manchester, OH 45144
937-549-2602 • 937-549-2709 or 2603
sales @bluegrasscutlery.com

www.bluegrasscutlery.com
Manufacturer of Winchester Knives, John Primble Knives and many contract lines.

BOKER USA INC
1550 Balsam St
Lakewood, CO 80215-3117
303-462-0662 • 303-462-0668
sales@bokerusa.com • www.bokerusa.com
Wide range of fixed blade and folding knives for hunting, military, tactical and general use.

BROWNING
One Browning Pl.
Morgan, UT 84050
801-876-2711 • 801-876-3331
www.browning.com
Outdoor hunting & shooting products.

BUCK KNIVES INC
1900 Weld Blvd.
El Cajon, CA 92020
800-735-2825 • 800-733-2825
www.buckknives.com
Sports cutlery.

BULLDOG BRAND KNIVES
P.O. Box 23852
Chattanooga, TN 37422
423-894-5102 • 423-892-9165
Fixed blade and folding knives for hunting and general use.

BUSSE COMBAT KNIFE CO.
11651 Co Rd 12
Wauseon, OH 43567
419-923-6471 • 419-923-2337
www.bussecombat.com
Simple & very strong straight knife designs for tactical & expedition use.

CAMILLUS CUTLERY CO.
54 Main St.
Camillus, NY 13031
315-672-8111 • 315-672-8832
camcut2@aol.com • www.camillusknives.com

CAS IBERIA INC
650 Industrial Blvd.
Sale Creek, TN 37373
423-332-4700 • 423-332-7248
www.casiberia.com
Extensive variety of fixed-blade and folding knives for hunting, diving, camping, military and general use.

CASE CUTLERY
W R & Sons
Owens Way
Bradford, PA 16701
800-523-6350 • 814-368-1736
consumer-relations@wrcase.com
www.wrcase.com
Folding pocket knives.

CHICAGO CUTLERY CO.
1536 Beech St.
Terre Haute, IN 47804

CHRIS REEVE KNIVES
11624 W President Dr.No.B
Boise, ID 83713
208-375-0367 • 208-375-0368
crknifo@chrisreeve.com • www.chrisreeve.com
Semi-custom fixed blade survival, hunting, skinning knives and high-tech locking folders.

COAST CUTLERY CO
2045 SE Ankeny St.
Portland, OR 97214
800-426-5858 • 503-234-4545 • 503-234-4422
www.coastcutlery.com
Variety of fixed-blade and folding knives and multi-tools for hunting, camping and general use.

COLD STEEL INC
3036 Seaborg Ave. Suite A
Ventura, CA 93003
800-255-4716 • 805-650-8481 • 805-642-9727
custsvc@spyderco.com • www.coldsteel.com
Wide variety of folding lockbacks and fixed-blade hunting, fishing and neck knives, as well as bowies, kukris, tantos, throwing knives and kitchen knives.

COLONIAL CUTLERY INTERNATIONAL
Steve Paolantonio
P.O. Box 960
North Scituate, RI 02857
866-934-3888 • 401-934-1771
stevep780@aol.com
Custom design, sport and camp knives.

COLONIAL KNIFE CO. INC
287 Agnes At Magnolia St
Providence, RI 02909-0327
800-556-7824 • 401-421-2047
ckc191@aol.com
www.colonialknife.com
Fixed-blade and folding knives for hunting, military and general use.

COLUMBIA RIVER KNIFE & TOOL
9720 S.W. Hillman Ct.
Wilsonville, OR 97070
800-891-3100 • 503-682-9680
Fixed-blade and folding knives for hunting, fishing, camping, tactical and general use.

CRAWFORD KNIVES
205 N Center
West Memphis, AR 72301
870-732-2452
Semi-production folding knives for tactical and general use.

CRIPPLE CREEK KNIVES
RT. 1, Box 501B
Oldfort, TN 37362

DAVID BOYE KNIVES
P.O. Box 1238
Dolan Springs, AZ 86441
800-853-1617 • 520-767-4273 • 520-767-3030
www.boyeknives.com
Semi-production fixed-blade and folding knives for hunting and general use.

DELTA Z KNIVES, INC
P.O. Box 1112
Studio City, CA 91614
818-786-9488 • 818-787-8560
sales@deltaz-knives.com
www.deltaz-knives.com
Wide range of folders and fixed-blade designs.

EMERSON KNIVES, INC.
P.O. Box 4180
Torrance, CA 90510-4180
310-212-7455 • 310-212-7289
www.emersonknives.com
Hard use tactical knives; folding & fixed blades.

FALLKNIVEN
P.O.Box 204
S-961 23 Boden
SWEDEN
540-783-6143
info@fallkniven.se • ww.fallkkniven.com
Fixed-blade hunting and survival knives with some traditional Swedish designs.

FROG TOOL CO
P.O. Box 600
Getzville, NY 14068-0600
716-877-2200 • 716-877-2591
gatco@buffnet.net • www.frogtool.net
Precision multi tools.

FROST CUTLERY CO
P.O. Box 22636
Chattanooga, TN 37422
800-251-7768 • 423-894-6079 • 423-894-9576
www.frostcutleryco.com
Wide range of fixed-blade and folding knives with a multitude of handle materials.

GATCO SHARPENERS
P.O. Box 600
Getzville, NY 14068
716-877-2200 • 716-877-2591
gatcosharpeners.com
Precision sharpening systems, diamond sharpening systems, ceramic sharpening systems, carbide sharpening systems, natural Arkansas stones.

directory

Sporting Cutlers, continued

GENUINE ISSUE INC.
949 Middle Country Rd.
Selden, NY 11784
631-696-3802 • 631-696-3803
New, old knives & swords.

GERBER LEGENDARY BLADES
14200 SW 72nd Ave.
Portland, OR 97223
503-639-6161
www.gerberblades.com
Knives, multi-tools, axes, saws, outdoor products.

GIGAND USA
701 Penhoun Ave
Secaucus, NJ 07094
201-583-5968
Imports designed by Fred C.

GROHMANN KNIVES LTD.
P.O. Box 40
Pictou Nova Scotia B0K 1H0
CANADA
888-756-4837 • 902-485-4224 • 902-485-5872
Fixed-blade belt knives for hunting and fishing, folding pocketknives for hunting and general use.

GT KNIVES
7734 Arjons Dr.
San Diego, CA 92126
858-530-8766 • 858-530-8798
gtknives@gtknives.com • www.gtknives.com
Law enforcement & military automatic knives.

GUTMANN CUTLERY INC
P.O. Box 2219
Bellingham, WA 98227
800-288-5379
Junglee knives, Smith & Wesson tools and optics, Walther knives and optics.

H&B FORGE CO.
235 Geisinger Rd.
Shiloh, OH 44878
419-895-1856
Tomahawks & throwing knives.

HISTORIC EDGED WEAPONRY
1021 Saddlebrook Dr Dept. BT
Hendersonville, NC 28739
828-692-0323 • 828-692-0600
Antique knives from around the world; importer of puukko and other knives from Norway, Sweden, Finland and Lapland.

HONEYCUTT MARKETING, INC., DAN
3165 C-4 S Campbell
Springfield MO 65807
417-886-2288 • 417-887-2635
ozk_knife_gun@hotmail.com
All kinds of cutlery, military, Randalls.

IMPERIAL SCHRADE CORP.
7 Schrade Ct.
Ellenville, NY 12428
800-2-Schrade
www.schradeknives.com

JOY ENTERPRISES-FURY CUTLERY
1104 53rd Court South
West Palm Beach, FL 33407
800-500-3879 • 561-863-3205 • 561-863-3277
mail@joyenterprises.com
www.joyenterprises.com • www.furycutlery.com
Extensive variety of fixed-blade and folding knives for hunting, fishing, diving, camping, military and general use; novelty key-ring knives.

KA-BAR KNIVES INC
1125 E State St
Olean, NY 14760
800-282-0130
www.info@ka-bar.com

KATZ KNIVES, INC.
P.O. Box 730
Chandler, AZ 85224-0730
480-786-9334 • 480-786-9338
katzkn@aol.com • www.katzknives.com

KELLAM KNIVES CO.
902 S Dixie Hwy
Lantana, FL 33462
800-390-6918 • 561-588-3185 • 561-588-3186
info@kellamknives.com • www.kellamknives.com
Largest selection of Finnish knives; handmade & production.

KERSHAW/KAI CUTLERY CO.
25300 SW Parkway
Wilsonville, OR 97070

KLOTZLI
CH 3400
Burgdorf, Switzerland
800-922-3537 • 800-255-9034
info@klotzli.com • www.klotzli.com
High-tech folding knives for tactical and general use.

KNIFEWARE INC
P.O. Box 3
Greenville, WV 24945

KNIGHTS EDGE LTD.
5696 N Northwest Highway
Chicago, IL 60646-6136
773-775-3888 • 773-775-3339
sales@knightsedge.com
www.knightsedge.com
Medieval weaponry, swords, suits of armor, katanas, daggers.

KNIVES OF ALASKA, INC.
Charles Or Jody
3100 Airport Dr.
Denison, TX 75020 8623
903-786-7366 • 800-752-0980 • 903-786-7371
info@knivesofalaska.com
www.knivesofalaska.com
High quality hunting & outdoorsmen knives.

KNIVES OF ALASKA, INC.
P.O. Box 675
Cordova, AK 99574

KUTMASTER KNIVES
Div Of Utica Cutlery Co
820 Noyes St.
Utica, NY 13502
315-733-4663 • 315-733-6602
www.kutmaster.com
Manufacturer and importer of pocket, lockback, tool knives and multi-purpose tools.

LAKOTA (BRUNTON USA)
620 E Monroe
Riverton, WY 24945
307-856-6559 • 307-856-1840
AUS 8-A high-carbon stainless steel blades.

LEATHERMAN TOOL GROUP, INC.
P.O. Box 20595
Portland, OR 97294
503-253-7826 • 503-253-7830
mktg@leatherman.com • www.leatherman.com
Multi-tools.

MARBLE'S OUTDOORS
420 Industrial Park
Gladstone, MI 49837
906-428-3710 • 906-428-3711
marble@up.net • www.marblesoutdoors.com

MASTERS OF DEFENSE KNIFE CO
1941 Camp Branch Rd
Waynesville, NC 28786
828-452-4158 • 828-452-4158
www.mastersofdefense.com
Fixed-Blade and folding knives for tactical and general use.

MEYERCO MANUFACTURING
4481 Exchange Service Dr
Dallas, TX 75236
214-467-8949 • 214-467-9241
www.meyercousa.com
Folding tactical, rescue and speed-assisted pocketknives; fixed-balde hunting and fishing designs; multi-function camping tools and machetes.

MCCANN INDUSTRIES
132 S 162nd, P.O. Box 641
Spanaway, WA 98387
253-537-6919 • 253-537-6993
McCann.machine@worldnet.att.net
www.mccannindustries.com

MICRO TECHNOLOGY
932 36th Ct. SW
Vero Beach, FL 32968
772-569-3058 • 772-569-7632
sales@microtechknives.com
www.microtechknives.com
Manufacturers of the highest quality production knives.

MISSION KNIVES & TOOLS, INC.
P.O. Box 1616
San Juan Capistrano, CA 92693

MORTY THE KNIFE MAN, INC.
4 Manorhaven Blvd
Pt Washington, NY 11050
516-767-2357 • 516-767-7058

MUSEUM REPLICAS LTD.
P.O. Box 840, Dept PQ
Conyers, GA 30012
800-883-8838
www.museumreplicas.com
Historically accurate & battle-ready swords & daggers.

MYERCHIN MARINE CLASSICS
14185 Regina Dr Ste G
Rancho Cucamonga, CA 91739
909-463-6741 • 909-463-6751
myerchin@myerchin.com • www.myerchin.com
Rigging/ Police knives.

NATIONAL KNIFE DISTRIBUTORS
P.O. Box 188
Forest City, NC 28043
800-447-4342 • 828-245-4321 • 828-245-5121
Benchmark pocketknives form Solingen Germany.

NORMARK CORP
10395 Yellow Circle Dr
Minnetonka, MN 55343
800-874-4451 • 612-933-0046
Hunting knives, game shears and skinning ax.

ONTARIO KNIFE CO.
26 Empire St.
Franklinville, NY 14737
800-222-5233 • 800-299-2618
salesokc@aol.com • www.ontarioknife.com
Fixed blades, tactical folders, military & hunting knives, machetes.

OUTDOOR EDGE CUTLERY CORP.
6395 Gunpark Dr, Unit Q
Boulder, CO 80301
303-530-7667 • 303-530-7020
outdooredge@plinet.com
www.outdooredge.com

PARAGON CUTLERY CO.
2015 Asheville Hwy.
Hendersonville, NC 28791
828-697-8833 • 828-697-5005
www.paragonweb.com
Knifemaking furnaces.

PILTDOWN PRODUCTIONS
Errett Callahan
2 Fredonia Ave.
Lynchburg, VA 24503

QUEEN CUTLERY COMPANY
P.O. Box 500
Franklinville, NY 14737
800-222-5233 • 800-299-2618
salesokc@aol.com • www.queencutlery.com
Pocket knives, collectibles, Schatt & Morgan, Robeson, club knives.

QUIKUT
P.O. Box 29
Airport Industial Park
Walnut Ridge, AR 72476
870-886-6774 • 870-886-9162

RANDALL MADE KNIVES
P.O. Box 1988
Orlando, FL 32802-1988
407-855-8075 • 407-855-9054
grandall@randallknives.com
www.randallknives.com
Handmade fixed-blade knives for hunting, fishing, diving, military and general use.

Sporting Cutlers, continued

REMINGTON ARMS CO., INC.
870 Remington Drive
P.O. Box 700
Madison, NC 27025

RICHARTZ USA
1825 Walnut Hill Lane Suite 120
Irving, TX 78038
800-859-2029 • 972-331-2566
info@richartz.com • www.richartz.com
German-made, multi-balde folding knives for hunting, camping and general use.

ROUND EYE KNIFE & TOOL
P.O. Box 818
Sagel, ID 83860
208-265-8858 • 208-263-0848
roundeye@nidlink.com • www.roundeye.com
Folding and fixed-blade knives for hunting and general use.

SANTA FE STONEWORKS
3790 Cerrillos Rd.
Santa Fe, NM 87505
800-257-7625 • 505-471-0036
knives@rt66.com • www.santafestoneworks.com
Gem stone handles.

SARCO CUTLERY LLC
115 Fairground Rd
Florence, AL 35630
256-766-8099 • 256-766-7246
sarco@hiwaay.net
www.sarcoproducts.com
Fixed-blade camping knife.

SOG SPECIALTY KNIVES & TOOLS, INC.
6521 212th St. S.w.
Lynwood, WA 98036
425-771-7689 • 425-771-7681
info@sofknives.com • www.sogknives.com
ARC-LOCK advantage, automatic tools. Specialized fixed blades, folding knives, multi-tools.

SPYDERCO, INC.
P.O. Box 800
Golden, CO 80402-0800
800-525-7770 • 303-278-2229
sales@spyderco.com • www.spyderco.com
Knives and sharpeners.

STIDHAM'S KNIVES
P.O. Box 570
Roseland, FL 32957
0570 561-589-0618 • 561-589-3162
rstidham@gate.net
www.randallknifesociety.com
Randall, Loveless, Scagel, custom and antique knives.

STODDARD'S, INC.
Copley Place
100 Huntington Ave.
Boston, MA 02116
617-536-8688 • 617-536-8689
Cutlery (Kitchen, pocket knives, Randall-made knives, custom knives, scissors & manicure tools) Binoculars, lwo vision aids, personal care items (hair brushes, manicure sets mirrors).

SWISS ARMY BRANDS INC.
P.O. Box 874
One Research Dr
Shelton, CT 06484-0874
800-243-4045 • 800-243-4006
www.swissarmy.com
Folding multi-blade designs and multi-tools for hunting, fishing, camping, hiking, golfing and general use. One of the original brands (Victorinox) of Swiss Army Knives.

TAYLOR CUTLERY
1736 N Eastman Rd
P.O. Box 1638
Kingsport, TN 37662-1638
800-251-0254 • 423-247-2406 • 423-247-5371
taylor@preferred.com • www.taylorcutlery.com
Fixed-blade and folding knives for tactical, rescue, hunting and general use.

TIMBERLINE KNIVES
P.O. Box 600
Getzville, NY 14068-0600
716-877-2200 • 716-877-2591
gatco@buffnet.net • timberlineknives.com
High Technology production knives for professionals, sporting, tradesmen & kitchen use.

TINIVES
1725 Smith Rd
Fortson, GA 31808
888-537-9991 • 706-322-9892
info@tinives.com • www.tinives.com
High-tech folding knives for tactical, law enforcement and general use.

TRU-BALANCE KNIFE CO.
P.O. Box 140555
Grand Rapids, MI 49514

TURNER, P.J., KNIFE MFG., INC.
P.O. Box 1549
Afton, WY 83110
307-885-0615
pjtkm@silverstar.com • www.eknife.net

UTICA CUTLERY CO
820 Noyes St
Utica, NY 13503-1537
800-888-4223 • 315-733-6602
sales@kutmaster.com
Wide range of folding and fixed-blade designs, multi-tools and steak knives.

WENGER NORTH AMERICA
15 Corporate Dr
Orangeburg, NY 10962
800-431-2996 • 845-365-3500 • 845-365-3558
www.wengerna.com
One of the official makers of folding multi-blade Swiss Army knives.

WILD BOAR BLADES
1701 Broadway, PMB 282
Vancouver, WA 98663
888-735-8483 • 360-735-0570 • 360-735-0390
www.wildboarblades.com
Fixed-blade and folding hunting and general-use knives.

WILLIAM HENRY FINE KNIVES
2125 Delaware Ave Suite c
Santa Cruz, CA 95060
831-454-9409 • 831-454-9309
www.williamhenryknives.com
Semi-custom folding knives for hunting and general use; some limited editions.

WORLD SURVIVAL INSTITUTE
C Janowsky
Dept BL 12 Box 394
Tok, AK 99780
907-883-4243

WUU JAU CO INC
2600 S Kelly Ave
Edmond, OK 73013
800-722-5760 • 405-359-5031
877-256-4337 • 405-340-5965
www.wuujau.com
Wide variety of imported fixed-blade and folding knives for hunting, fishing, camping, and general use.

WYOMING KNIFE CORP.
101 Commerce Dr.
Ft. Collins, CO 80524

importers & foreign cutlers

A. G. RUSSELL KNIVES INC.
1920 North 26th St.
Lowell, AR 72745-8489
479-631-0130 • 800-255-9034 • 479-631-8493
ag@agrussell.com • www.agrussell.com
The oldest knife mail-order company, highest quality. Free catalog available. In these catalogs you will find the newest and the best. If you like knives, this catalog is a must.

ADAMS INTERNATIONAL KNIFEWORKS
8710 Rosewood Hills
Edwardsville, IL 62025
Importers & foreign cutlers.

AITOR-CUCHILLERIA DEL NORTE, S.A.
P.O. Box No. 1 48260
Ermua (Vizcaya) Spain

ATLANTA CUTLERY CORP.
2143 Gees Mill Rd. Box 839FD
Conyers, GA 30207
770-922-3700 • 770-388-0246
www.atlantacutlery.com

BAILEY'S
P.O. Box 550
Laytonville, CA 95454

BELTRAME, FRANCESCO
Flli Beltrame F&C SNA
Via dei Fabbri AS/3 33085
Maniago PN Italy
switches@iol.it www.italianstiletto.com

BOKER USA, INC.
1550 Balsam St.
Lakewood, CO 80215-3117
303-462-0662 • 303-462-0668
sales@bokerusa.com • www.bokerusa.com
Ceramic blades.

C.A.S. IBERIA, INC.
650 Industrial Blvd.
Sale Creek, TN 37373
423-332-4700 • 423-332-7248
cas@casiberia.com • www.casiberia.com
Paul Chen/Hanwei Swords, Muela, Ajtor, Replica weaponry.

CAMPOS, IVAN DE ALMEIDA
Custom and Old Knives Trader
R. Stelio M. Loureiro
206 Centro, Tatui Brazil

CATOCTIN CUTLERY
P.O. Box 188
Smithsburg, MD 21783

CLASSIC INDUSTRIES
1325 Howard Ave., Suite 408
Burlingame, CA 94010

COAST CUTLERY CO.
2045 SE Ankeny St.
Portland, OR 97214

COLUMBIA PRODUCTS CO.
P.O. Box 1333
Sialkot 51310
Pakistan

COLUMBIA PRODUCTS INT'L
P.O. Box 8243
New York, NY 10116-8243
201-854-8504 • 201-854-7058
nycolumbia@aol.com
http://columbiaproducts.homestead.com/cat/html
Pocket, hunting knives and swords.

COMPASS INDUSTRIES, INC.
104 E. 25th St.
New York, NY 10010

CONAZ COLTELLERIE
Dei F.lli Consigli-Scarperia
Via G. Giordani
20 50038 Scarperia (Firenze) Italy
conaz@dada.it www.conaz.com

CONFEDERATE STATES ARMORY
2143 Gees Mill Rd. Box 839XZ
Conyers, GA 30207

CONSOLIDATED CUTLERY CO., INC.
696 NW Sharpe St.
Port St. Lucie, FL 34983

directory

Importers & Foreign Cutlers, continued

CRAZY CROW TRADING POST
P.O. Box 847 Dept 96
Pottsboro, TX 75020
903-786-2287 • 903-786-9059
info@crazycrow.com • www.crazycrow.com
Solingen blades, knife making parts & supplies.

DER FLEISSIGEN BEAVER
(THE BUSY BEAVER)
Harvey Silk
P.O. Box 1166
64343 Griesheim
Germany 49 6155 2231 • 49 6155 2433
Der.Biber@t-online.de

EMPIRE CUTLERY CORP.
12 Kruger Ct.
Clifton, NJ 07013

EXTREME RATIO SAS
Mauro Chiostri Maurizio Castrat, Viale
Montegrappa 298 59100 Prato Italy
0039 0574 58 4639 • 0039 0574 581312
chios@iol.itwww.extremaratio.com
Tactical & military knives manufacturing.

FALLKNIVEN AB
Havrevagen 10 S-96142 Boden
Sweden 46 92154422 4692154433
info@fallkniven.se • www.fallkniven.com
High Quality knives.

FREDIANI COLTELLI FINLANDESI
Via Lago Maggiore 41
I-21038 Leggiuno Italy

GIESSER MESSERFABRIK GMBH, JOHANNES
Raiffeisenstr 15 D-71349
Winnenden, Germany
49-7195-18080 • 49-7195-64466
info@giesser.de • www.giesser.de
Professional butchers and chef's knives.

HIMALAYAN IMPORTS
3495 Lake Side Dr.
Reno, NV 89509
775-825-2279 himimp@aol.com
httpillmembers.aol.com/himinp/index.html

IVAN DE ALMEIDA
CAMPOS-KNIFE DEALER
R. XI De Agosto 107,
Centro, Tatui, SP 18270 Brazil
55-15-2518092 • 55-15-251-4896
campos@bitweb.com.br
Custom knives from all Brazilian knifemakers.

JOY ENTERPRISES
1104-53rd Court
South West Palm Beach, FL 33407
561-863-3205 • 800-500-3879 • 561-863-3277
mail@joyenterprises.com
www.joyenterprises.com
Fury™, Mustang™, Hawg Knives, Muela.

KELLAM KNIVES CO.
902 S Dixie Hwy
Lantana, FL 33462
561-588-3185 • 800-390-6918 • 561-588-3186
info@kellamknives.com • www.kellamknives.com
Knives from Finland; own line of knives.

KNIFE IMPORTERS, INC.
P.O. Box 1000
Manchaca, TX 78652
800-561-5301 • 800-266-2373
Wholesale only.

KNIGHTS EDGE
5696 N Northwest Hwy
Chicago, IL 60646
773-775-3888 • 773-775-3339
*Exclusive designers of our Rittersteel,
Stagesteel and Valiant Arms lines of
weaponry.*

LEISURE PRODUCTS CORP.
P.O. Box 1171
Sialkot-51310
Pakistan

LINDER, CARL
Nachf. Erholungstr. 10 42699
Solingen Germany
212 330856 • 212 337104
info@linder.de • www.linder.de

MARTTIINI KNIVES
P.O. Box 44 (Marttiinintie 3)
96101 Rovaniemi Finland

MATTHEWS CUTLERY
4401 Sentry Dr., Suite K
Tucker, GA 30084

MESSER KLÖTZLI
P.O. Box 104
Hohengasse 3, CH-3402
Burgdorf Switzerland
034 422 2378 • 034 422 7693
info@klotzli.com • www.klotzli.com

MURAKAMI, ICHIRO
Knife Collectors Assn.
Japan Tokuda Nishi
4 Chome, 76 Banchi,
Ginanchohashimagun, Gifu Japan
81 58 274 1960 • 81 58 273 7369
www.gix.orjp/~n-resin/

MUSEUM REPLICAS LIMITED
2143 Gees Mill Rd., Box 839 XZ
Conyers, GA 30207

NICHOLS CO.
P.O. Box 473, #5
The Green Woodstock, VT 05091
802-457-3970 • 802-457-2051
janjesse@sover.net
*Import & distribute knives from EKA (Sweden),
Helle (Norway), Brusletto (Norway), Roselli
(Finland). Also market Zippo products.*

NORMARK CORP.
Craig Weber
10395 Yellow Circle Drive
Minnetonka, MN 55343

PRECISE INTERNATIONAL
15 Corporate Dr.
Orangeburg, NY 10962
845-365-3500 • 800-431-2996 • 845-425-4700
www.wengerma.com
Swiss army knives.

PRO CUT
9718 Washburn Rd
Downey, CA 90241
562-803-8778 • 562-803-4261
sales@procutdist.com
*Wholesale only. Full service distributor of
domestic & imported brand name cutlery.
Exlusive US importer for both Marto Swords
and Battle Ready Valiant Armory edged
weapons.*

PRODUCTORS AITOR, S.A.
Izelaieta 17 48260 Ermua SPAIN
943-170850 • 943-170001
info@aitor.com
Sporting knives.

PUUKKO CUTLERY
17533 Co Hwy 38
Frazee, MN 56544
icrist@wcta.net
*Scandinavian cutlery custom/factory/new/
antique.*

REFLECTIONS OF EUROPE
Peter Ward
151 Rochelle Ave.
Rochelle Park, NJ 07662
201-845-8120 • 201-843-8419
jward51886@aol.com
Gold hamster Schaaf knives.

SCANDIA INTERNATIONAL INC.
5475 W Inscription Canyon Dr
Prescott, AZ 86305
928-442-0140 • 928-442-0342
frosts@cableone.net • www.frosts-scandia.com
Frosts Knives of Sweden.

STAR SALES CO., INC.
1803 N. Central St., P.O. Box 1503
Knoxville, TN 37901

SVORD KNIVES
Smith Rd., Rd 2 Waiuku,
South Auckland, New Zealand

SWISS ARMY BRANDS LTD.
The Forschner Group, Inc.
One Research Drive
Shelton, CT 06484
203-929-6391 • 203-929-3786
www.swissarmy.com

TAYLOR CUTLERY
P.O. Box 1638
1736 N. Eastman Rd.
Kingsport, TN 37662
*Colman Knives along with Smith & Wesson,
Cuttin Horse, John Deere, Zoland knives.*

UNITED CUTLERY CORP.
1425 United Blvd.
Sevierville, TN 37876
800-548-0835 orders only
865-428-2532 • 865-428-2667
order@unitedcutlery.com
www.unitedcutlery.com
*Harley-Davidson ™, Colt ™, Stanley ™
hunting, camping, fishing, collectible & fantasy
knives.*

UNIVERSAL AGENCIES INC.
4690 S Old Peachtree Rd., Ste C
Norcross, GA 30071-1517
678-969-9147 • 678-969-9148 • 678-969-9169
info@uai.org www.knifesupplies.com
www.thunderforged.com • www.uai.org
*Serving the cutlery industry with the finest
selection of India Stag, Buffalo Horn,
Thurnderforged ™ Damascus. Mother of
Pearl, Knife Kits and more.*

VALOR CORP.
1001 Sawgrass Corp. Pkwy.
Sunrise, FL 33323-2811
954-377-4925 • 954-377-4941
www.valorcorp.com
Wide variety of imported & domestic knives.

WILD BOAR BLADES
1701 Broadway, PMB 282
Vancouver, WA 98663
888-735-8483 • 360-687-5138
www.wildboarblades.com
Knives & cutlery from Poland.

ZWILLING J.A.
Henckels Inc.
171 Saw Mill River Rd.
Hawthorne, NY 10532

knifemaking supplies

AFRICAN IMPORT CO.
ALAN ZANOTTI
20 BRAUNECKER RD.
PLYMOUTH, MA 02360

ALASKAN ANTLERCRAFT & IVORY
ROLAND AND KATHY QUIMBY
BOX 3175-RB
CASA GRANDE, AZ 85222

AMERICAN SIEPMANN CORP.
65 PIXLEY INDUSTRIAL
PARKWAY
ROCHESTER, NY 14624

ART JEWEL ENTERPRISES, LTD.
460 RANDY RD.
CAROL STREAM, IL 60188

ATLANTA CUTLERY CORP.
2143 GEES MILL RD.
BOX 839XE
CONYERS, GA 30207

BATAVIA ENGINEERING
P.O. BOX 53
MAGALIESBURG, 2805
SOUTH AFRICA

Knifemaking Supplies, continued

BILL'S CUSTOM CASES
P.O. BOX 2
DUNSMUIR, CA 96025

BLADEMASTER GRINDERS
P.O. BOX 812
CROWLEY, TX 76036

BLADES "N" STUFF
1019 E. PALMER AVE.
GLENDALE, CA 91205

BOONE TRADING CO., INC.
BOX BB
BRINNON, WA 98320

BORGER, WOLF
BENZSTRASSE 8
76676 GRABEN-NEUDORF
GERMANY

BOYE KNIVES
P.O. BOX 1238
DOLAN SPRINGS, AZ 86441

BRIAR KNIVES
DARREL RALPH
7032 E. LIVINGSTON AVE.
RENOLDSBURG, OH 43068

BRONK'S KNIFEWORKS
C. LYLE BRUNCKHORST
23716 BOTHELL-EVERETT HWY.
COUNTRY VILLAGE, SUITE B
BOTHELL, WA 98021

CHRISTOPHER MFG., E.
P.O. BOX 685
UNION CITY, TN 38281

CUSTOM FURNACES
P.O. BOX 353
RANDVAAL, 1873
SOUTH AFRICA

CUSTOM KNIFEMAKER'S SUPPLY
BOB SCHRIMSHER
P.O. BOX 308
EMORY, TX 75440

CUSTOM KRAFT
14919 NEBRASKA AVE.
TAMPA, FL 33613

CUTLERY SPECIALTIES
DENNIS BLAINE
22 MORRIS LN.
GREAT NECK, NY 11024-1707

DAMASCUS-USA
149 DEANS FARM RD.
TYNER, NC 27980-9718

DAN'S WHETSTONE CO., INC.
130 TIMBS PLACE
HOT SPRINGS, AR 71913

DIAMOND MACHINING TECHNOLOGY, INC.
85 HAYES MEMORIAL DR.
MARLBOROUGH, MA 01752

DIXIE GUN WORKS, INC.
P.O. BOX 130
UNION CITY, TN 38281

EKLUND
P.O. BOX 483
NOME, AK 99762-0483

EZE-LAP DIAMOND PRODUCTS
3572 ARROWHEAD DR.
CARSON CITY, NV 89706

FIELDS, RICK B.
26401 SANDWICH PL.
MT. PLYMOUTH, FL 32776

FLITZ INTERNATIONAL, LTD.
821 MOHR AVE.
WATERFORD, WI 53185

FORTUNE PRODUCTS, INC.
HC 04, BOX 303
HWY. 1431 E. (SMITHWICK)
MARBLE FALLS, TX
78654

GILMER WOOD CO.
2211 NW ST. HELENS RD.
PORTLAND, OR 97210

GOLDEN AGE ARMS CO.
115 E. HIGH ST.
P.O. BOX 366
ASHLEY, OH 43003

GRS CORP.
DON GLASER
P.O. BOX 1153
900 OVERLANDER ST.
EMPORIA, KS 66801

HALPERN TITANIUM
LESLIE HALPERN
14 MAXWELL ROAD
MONSON, MA 01057

HARMON, JOE T.
8014 FISHER DRIVE
JONESBORO, GA 30236

HAWKINS CUSTOM KNIVES & SUPPLIES
110 BUCKEYE RD.
FAYETTEVILLE, GA 30214

HAYDU, THOMAS G.
2507 BIMINI LANE
FT. LAUDERDALE, FL 33312

HILTARY INDUSTRIES
7117 THIRD AVE.
SCOTTSDALE, AZ 85251

HOUSE OF TOOLS LTD.
#136, 8228 MACLEOD TR. S.E.
CALGARY, AB CANADA
T2H 2B8

HOV KNIVES & SUPPLIES
BOX 8005
S-700 08 OREBRO
SWEDEN

INDIAN JEWELERS SUPPLY CO.
P.O. BOX 1774
GALLUP, NM 87305-1774

INTERAMCO INC.
5210 EXCHANGE DR.
FLINT, MI 48507

JANTZ SUPPLY
P.O. BOX 584-GD
DAVIS, OK 73030-0584

JOHNSON, R.B.
I.B.S. INT'L. FOLDER SUPPLIES
BOX 11
CLEARWATER, MN 55320

JOHNSON WOOD PRODUCTS
34968 CRYSTAL RD.
STRAWBERRY POINT, IA 52076

K&G FINISHING SUPPLIES
P.O. BOX 980
LAKESIDE, AZ 85929

KNIFE & CUTLERY PRODUCTS, INC.
4122 N. TROOST AVE.
KANSAS CITY, MO 64116

KNIFE AND GUN FINISHING SUPPLIES
P.O. BOX 458
LAKESIDE, AZ 85929

KNIVES, ETC.
2522 N. MERIDIAN
OKLAHOMA CITY, OK 73107

KOVAL KNIVES, INC.
5819 ZARLEY ST.
NEW ALBANY, OH 43054

KWIK-SHARP
350 N. WHEELER ST.
FT. GIBSON, OK 74434

LINDER-SOLINGEN KNIFE PARTS
4401 SENTRY DR., SUITE K
TUCKER, GA 30084

LITTLE GIANT POWER HAMMER
420 4TH CORSO
NEBRASKA CITY, NE 68410

LIVESEY, NEWT
202 RAINES RD.
SILOAM SPRINGS, AR 72761

LOGISTICAL SOLUTION
P.O. BOX 211961
AUGUSTA, GA 30917

LOHMAN CO., FRED
3405 N.E. BROADWAY
PORTLAND, OR 97232

MARKING METHODS, INC.
LAURA JIMENEZ
301 S. RAYMOND AVE.
ALHAMBRA, CA 91803-1531

MASECRAFT SUPPLY CO.
170 RESEARCH PKWY #3
P.O. BOX 423
MERIDEN, CT 06450

MEIER STEEL
DARYL MEIER
75 FORGE RD.
CARBONDALE, IL 62901

MOTHER OF PEARL CO.
D.A. CULPERPER
P.O. BOX 445, 401 OLD GA RD.
FRANKLIN, NC 28734

NICHOLAS EQUIPMENT CO.
730 E. WASHINGTON ST.
SANDUSKY, OH 44870

NORTHWEST KNIFE SUPPLY
525-L S.W. CALAPOOIA AVE.
SUTHERLIN, OR 97479

OREGON ABRASIVE & MFG. CO.
11303 NE 207TH AVE.
BRUSH PRAIRIE, WA 98606

OZARK KNIFE
3165 S. CAMPBELL
SPRINGFIELD, MO 65807

PAPAI, ABE
5013 N. 800 E.
NEW CARLISLE, IN 46552

PARAGON INDUSTRIES, INC.
2011 SOUTH TOWN EAST BLVD.
MESQUITE, TX 75149-1122

POPLIN, JAMES/POP KNIVES & SUPPLIES
103 OAK ST.
WASHINGTON, GA 30673

PUGH, JIM
P.O. BOX 711
AZLE, TX 76098

RADOS, JERRY
P.O. BOX 531
7523E 5000 N. RD.
RANT PARK, IL 60940

REACTIVE METALS STUDIO,INC.
P.O. BOX 890
CLARKDALE, AZ 86324

REAL WOOD
36 FOURTH ST.
DRACUT, MA 01826

REPRODUCTION BLADES
17485 SW PHEASANT LN.
BEAVERTON, OR 97006

RIVERSIDE KNIFE & FORGE SUPPLY
205 W. STILLWELL
DEQUEEN, AR 71832

ROCKY MOUNTAIN KNIVES
GEORGE L. CONKLIN
P.O. BOX 902, 615
FRANKLIN
FT. BENTON, MT 59442

RUMMELL, HANK
10 PARADISE LANE
WARWICK, NY 10990

SANDPAPER, INC. OF ILLINOIS
270 EISENHOWER LN. N.
UNIT 5B
LOMBARD, IL 60148

SCHELL, CLYDE M.
4735 N.E. ELLIOTT CIRCLE
CORVALLIS, OR 97330

SCHEP'S FORGE
BOX 83
CHAPMAN, NE 68827

SHEFFIELD KNIFEMAKERS SUPPLY, INC.
P.O. BOX 741107
ORANGE CITY, FL 32774-1107

Knifemaking Supplies, continued

SHINING WAVE METALS
P.O. BOX 563
SNOHOMISH, WA 98290-0563

SMITH ABRASIVES, INC.
1700 SLEEPY VALLEY RD.
HOT SPRINGS, AR 71901

SMITH WHETSTONE, INC.
1700 SLEEPY VALLEY RD.
HOT SPRINGS, AR 71901

SMOLEN FORGE, INC.
NICK SMOLEN
RT. 2, BOX 191A
WESTBY, WA 54667

STOVER, JEFF
P.O. BOX 43
TORRANCE, CA 90507

STRANDE, POUL
SOSTER SVENSTRUP BYVEJ 16
DASTRUP 4130 VIBY SJ
DENMARK

TEXAS KNIFEMAKERS SUPPLY
10649 HADDINGTON, SUITE 180
HOUSTON, TX 77043

TRU-GRIT, INC.
760 E. FRANCIS ST. #N
ONTARIO, CA 91761

WASHITA MOUNTAIN
WHETSTONE CO.
P.O. BOX 378
LAKE HAMILTON, AR 71951

WILD WOODS
JIM FRAY
P.O. BOX 104
MONCLOVA, OH 43542

WILSON, R.W.
113 KENT WAY
WEIRTON, WV 26062

WOOD CARVERS SUPPLY, INC.
P.O. BOX 7500-K
ENGLEWOOD, FL 34295-7500

WYVERN INDUSTRIES
P.O. BOX 1564
SHADY COVE, OR 97539-1564

ZOWADA CUSTOM KNIVES
TIM ZOWADA
4509 E. BEAR RIVER RD.
BOYNE FALLS, MI 49713

mail order sales

A.G. RUSSELL KNIVES INC.

1920 North 26th St.
Lowell, AR 72745-8489
479-631-0130 • 479-631-8493
ag@agrussell.com • www.agrussell.com

The oldest knife mail-order company, highest quality. Free catalog available. In these catalogs you will find the newest and the best. If you like knives, this catalog is a must.

ARIZONA CUSTOM KNIVES

Jay and Karen Sadow
8617 E. Clydesdale
Scottsdale, AZ 85258 480-951-0699
sharptalk@aol.com • www.arizona
customknives.com

Color catalog $5 U.S. / $7 Foreign.

ATLANTA CUTLERY CORP.

2143 Gees Mill Rd., Box 839DY
Conyers, GA 30207
800-883-0300
www.atlantacutlery.com

Special knives & cutting tools.

ATLANTIC BLADESMITHS/PETER STEBBINS

32 Bradford St.
Concord, MA 01742
978-369-3608
info@atlanticbladesmith.com
www.atlanticbladesmiths.com

Sell, trade, buy; carefully selected handcrafted, benchmade and factory knives.

BALLARD CUTLERY

1495 Brummel Ave.
Elk Grove Village, IL 60007

BARRETT-SMYTHE, LTD.

30E 81st Grd Floor
New York, NY 10028
212-249-5500 • 212-249-
5550bsmythe1@ix.netcom.com
www.barrett-smythe.com

BECK'S CUTLERY SPECIALTIES

MacGregor Village #109
107 Edinburgh
S Cary, NC 27511
919-460-0203
www.beckscutlery.com

Knives.

BLAIRS BLADES & ACCESSORIES

531 Main St., Suite 651
El Segundo, CA 90245

BLUE RIDGE KNIVES

166 Adwolfe Rd
Marion, VA 24354-9351
276-783-6143 • 276-783-9298
www.blueridgeknives.com

Wholesale distributor of knives.

BOB NEAL CUSTOM KNIVES

P.O. BOX 20923
Atlanta, GA 30320
770-914-7794 • 770-914-7796
knives@peoplepc.com
www.bobnealcustomknives.com

Exclusive limited edition custom knives-sets & single.

BOONE TRADING CO., INC.

P.O. Box 669
Brinnon, WA 98320
800-423-1945
www.boonetrading.com

Ivory scrimshaw horns.

CARMEL CUTLERY

Dolores & 6th; P.O. Box 1346
Carmel, CA 93921
831-624-6699 • 831-624-6780
ccutlery@ix.net
com.comwww.carmelcutlery.com

Quality custom and a variety of production pocket knives, swords; kitchen cutlery; personal grooming items.

CORRADO CUTLERY

Otto Pomper
26 N. Clark St.
Chicago, IL 60602
312-368-8450 • 312-368-8451
www.corradocutlery.com

Knives, Nippers, Scissors, Gifts, Optical Goods.

CREATIVE SALES & MFG.

Box 111
Whitefish, MT 59937
406-849-5174 • 406-849-5130
www.creativesales.com

CUTLERY SHOPPE

357 Steelhead Way
Boise, ID 83704
800-231-1272 • 208-672-8588
www.cutleryshoppe.com

Discount pricing on top quality brands.

CUTTING EDGE, THE

1920 North 26th St.
Lowell, AR 72745-8489
479-631-0055 • 479-631-
8734editor@cuttinedge.com
www.cuttinedge.com

After-market knives since 1968. We offer about 1,000 individual knives for sale each month. Subscription by first class mail, in U.S. $20 per year, Canada or Mexico by air mail, $25 per year. All overseas by air mail, $40 per year.

DENTON, J.W.

102 N. Main St., Box 429
Hiawassee, GA 30546
706-896-2292 • 706-896-1212
jwdenton@alltel.net

Loveless knives.

EDGE CO. KNIVES

17 Kit St.
Keene, NH 03431-7125
603-357-9390 edgeco.com

FAZALARE, ROY

P.O. Box 1335
Agoura Hills, CA 91376
818-879-6161 after 7pm
ourfaz@aol.com

Handmade multiblades; older case; Fight'n Rooster; Bulldog brand & Cripple Creek.

FROST CUTLERY CO.

P.O. Box 22636
Chattanooga, TN 37422

GENUINE ISSUE, INC.

949 Middle Country Rd.
Selden, NY 11784
516-696-3802 • 516-696-3803
g.i._cutlery.com

All knives.

GODWIN, INC., G. GEDNEY

2139 Welsh Valley Rd.
Valley Forge, PA 19481
610-783-0670 • 610-783-6083
www.gggodwin.com

18th century reproductions.

HAWTHORN GALLERIES, INC.

P.O. Box 6071
Branson, MO 65616
417-335-2170 • 417-335-2011
hg_inc@hotmail.com

HERITAGE ANTIQUE KNIVES

Bruce Voyles
P.O. Box 22171
Chattanooga, TN 37422
423-894-8319 • 423-892-7254
bruce@jbrucevoyles.com
www.jbrucevoyles.com

Knives, knife auctions.

HOUSE OF TOOLS LTD.

#136, 8228 Macleod Tr.
Se Calgary, Alberta, Canada T2H 2B8

HUNTER SERVICES

Fred Hunter
P.O. Box 14241
Parkville, MD 64152

JENCO SALES, INC.

P.O. Box 1000
Manchaca, TX 78652
800-531-5301 • 800-266-2373

Wholesale only.

KELLAM KNIVES CO.

902 S Dixie Hwy
Lantana, FL 33462
561-588-3185 • 800-390-6918 • 561-588-3186
info@kellamknives.com • www.kellamknives.com

Largest selection of Finnish knives; own line of folders.

KNIFEART.COM

13301 Pompano Dr.
Little Rock, AR 72211

Mail Order Sales, continued

KNIFE & CUTLERY PRODUCTS, INC.
P.O. Box 12480
North Kansas City, MO 64116

KNIFE IMPORTERS, INC.
P.O. Box 1000
Manchaca, TX 78652

KNIFEMASTERS CUSTOM KNIVES/J&S FEDERPO
Box 208
Westport, CT 06881
203-226-5211 • 203-226-5312
Investment grade custom knives.

KNIVES PLUS
2467 I 40
West Amarillo TX 79109
800-687-6202
Retail cutlery and cutlery accessories since 1987.

KRIS CUTLERY
P.O. Box 133KN
Pinole, CA 94564
510-223-8968
kriscutlery@home.net
Japanese, medieval, Chinese & Philippine.

LDC CUSTOM KNIVES
P.O. Box 20923
Atlanta, GA 30320
770-914-7794 • 770-914-7796
knives@peoplepc.com
Exclusive limited edition custom knives - sets & single.

LES COUTEAUX CHOISSIS DE ROBERTS RON ROBERTS
P.O. Box 273
Mifflin, PA 17058

LONE STAR WHOLESALE
P.O. Box 587
Amarillo TX 79105
806-356-9540 • 806-359-1603
Wholesale only; major brands and accessories.

MATTHEWS CUTLERY
4401 Sentry Dr., Suite K
Tucker, GA 30084

MORTY THE KNIFE MAN, INC.
4 Manorhaven Blvd.
Port Washington, NY 11050

MUSEUM REPLICAS LTD.
2143 Gees Mill Rd., Box 840PQ
Conyers, GA 30207
800-883-8838
www.museumreplicas.com
Historically accurate and battle ready swords & daggers.

NORDIC KNIVES
1634CZ Copenhagen Dr.
Solvang, CA 93463
805-688-3612
info@nordicknives.com • www.nordicknives.com
Custom and Randall knives.

PARKER'S KNIFE COLLECTOR SERVICE
6715 Heritage Business Court
Chattanooga, TN 37422
423-892-0448 • 423-892-0448
bbknife@bellsouth.net

PEN AND THE SWORD LTD., THE
P.O. Box 290741
Brooklyn, NY 11229-0741
718-382-4847 • 718-376-5745
info@pensword.com
Custom folding knives, engraving, scrimshaw, Case knives, English fruit knives, antique pocket knives.

PLAZA CUTLERY, INC.
3333 S. Bristol St., South Coast Plaza
Costa Mesa, CA 92626

ROBERTSON'S CUSTOM CUTLERY
P.O. Box 1367
Evans,GA 30809-1367
706-650-0252 • 706-860-1623
rccedge@csranet.com
www.robertsoncustomcutlery.com
Limited edition exclusive designs, Vanguard knives.

ROBINSON, ROBERT W.
1569 N. Finley Pt.
Polson, MT 59860

SHAW, GARY
24 Central Ave.
Ridgefield Park, NJ 07660
201-641-8801 • 201-641-0872
gshaw@carroll.com
Investment grade custom knives.

SMOKY MOUNTAIN KNIFE WORKS
2320 Winfield Dunn Pkwy
Sevierville, TN 37876
865-453-5871 • 800-251-9306
info@smkw.comwww.eknifeworks.com
The world's largest knife showplace, catalog and website.

STIDHAM'S KNIVES
P.O. Box 570
Roseland, FL 32957-0570
561-589-0618 • 561-589-3162
rstidham@gate.net
www.randallknifesociety.com
Randall, Loveless, Scagel, custom and antique knives.

STODDARD'S, INC.
Copley Place
100 Huntington Ave.
Boston, MA 02116
617-536-8688 • 617-536-8689
Cutlery (Kitchen, pocket knives, Randall-made knives, custom knives, scissors & manicure tools) Binoculars, lwo vision aids, personal care items (hair brushes, manicure sets mirrors).

knife services

custom grinders

Dozier, Bob, Dozier Knives & Grinders, PO Box 1941, Springdale, AR, 72765, 888-823-0023, 501-756-9139

High, Tom, Rocky Mountain Scrimshaw & Arts, 5474 S. 112.8 Rd., Alamosa, CO, 81101

Ingle, Ralph W., 112 Manchester Ct., Centerville, GA, 31028

Lamprey, Mike, Rose Cottage, Peters Marland, Torrington, Devon EX38 8QH, ENGLAND, 01805 601331

McLuin, Tom, 36 Fourth St., Dracut, MA, 01826, 978-957-4899, tmcluin@mediaone.net, www.people.ne.mediaone.net/tmcluin

Peele, Bryan, The Elk Rack, 215 Ferry St. P.O. Box 1363, Thompson, Falls, MT, 59873, Wilson, R.W., P.O. Box 2012, Weirton, WV, 26062

custom handle artisans

Bill's Custom Cases, P.O. Box 2, Dunsmuir, CA, 96025, 530-235-0177, 530-235-4959, billscustomcases@mindspring.com, Knife cases (cordura & leather)

Cooper, Jim, 2148 Cook Pl., Ramona, CA, 92065-3214, 760-789-1097, 760-788-7992, jamcooper@aol.com,

Eccentric Endeavors, Michel Santos and Peggy Quinn, P.O. Box 97, Douglas Flat, CA, 95229

Grussenmeyer, Paul G., 101 S. White Horse Pike, Lindenwold, NJ 08021-2304, 856-435-1500, 856-435-3786, pgrussentne@home.com

High, Tom, Rocky Mountain Scrimshaw & Arts, 5474 S. 112.8 Rd. Alamosa, CO, 81101

Holden, Larry, PO Box 2017, Ridgecrest, CA, 93556-2017, 760-375-7955, lardog44@yahoo.com

Holland, Dennis K., 4908-17th Pl., Lubbock, TX, 79416

Imboden II, Howard L., hi II Originals, 620 Deauville Dr., Dayton, OH, 45429

Ingle, Ralph W., 112 Manchester Ct., Centerville, GA, 31028

Kelley, Gary, 17485 SW Pheasant Lane, Aloha, OR, 97006, 503-848-9313, Custom buckle knives

Kelso, Jim, 577 Collar Hill Rd, Worcester, VT, 05682, 802-229-4254, 802-223-0595

Krogman, Pam, 838 Merlarkkey St., Winnemucca, NV, 89445

Lee, Ray, 209 Jefferson Dr., Lynchburg, VA, 24502

Lott Greco, Sherry, 100 Mattie Jones Rd., Greensburg, KY, 42743, 270-932-3335, 270-932-2225

Marlatt, David, 67622 Oldham Rd., Cambridge, OH, 43725, 740-432-7549

Mead, Dennis, 2250 E. Mercury St., Inverness, FL, 34453- 0514

Miller, Robert, 216 Seminole Ave., Ormond Beach, FL, 32176

Myers, Ron, 6202 Marglenn Ave., Baltimore, MD, 21206, 410-866-6914

Sayen, Murad, P.O. Box 127, Bryant Pond, ME, 04219

Schlott, Harald, Zingster Str. 26, 13051 Berlin, GERMANY, 03 01 929 33 46, 03 01 929 33 46, www.harald-schlott@t-online.de

Schönert, Elke, 18 Lansdowne Pl., Central, Port Elizabeth, SOUTH AFRICA

Smith, D. Noel, PO Box 702, Port Orchard, WA, 98366, knife2@kktv.com

Smith, Glenn, PO Box 54, Roscoe, MT, 59071

Snell, Barry A.,4801 96th St. N., St. Petersburg, FL, 33708- 3740

Vallotton, A., 621 Fawn Ridge Dr., Oakland, OR, 97462

Williams, Gary, (GARBO), 221 Autumn Way, Elizabethtown, KY, 42701

Willson, Harlan M., P.O. Box 2113, Lompoc, CA, 93438, hwillson@gte.net

display cases and boxes

Bill's Custom Cases, P.O. Box 2, Dunsmuir, CA, 96025, 530-235-0177, 530-235-4959, billscustomcases@mindspring.com, Knife cases (cordura & leather)

Brooker, Dennis, Rt. 1, Box 12A, Derby, IA, 50068

Clements', Custom, Leathercraft, Chas, 1741 Dallas St., Aurora, CO, 80010-2018, 303-364-0403, gryphons@home.com

Congdon, David, 1063 Whitchurch Ct., Wheaton, IL, 60187

Gimbert, Nelson, P.O. Box 787, Clemmons, NC, 27012

Haydu, Thomas, G., Tomway Products, 750 E Sahara Ave, Las Vegas, NV, 89104, 888 4 Tomway, 702-366-0626, tom@tomway.com, tomway.com

Mesa Case, Arne, Mason, 125 Wimer St., Ashland, OR, 97520, 541-482-2260, 541-482-7785

Miller, Michael K., M&M Kustom Krafts, 28510 Santiam Highway, Sweet Home, OR, 97386

Retichek, Joseph L., W9377 Co. TK. D, Beaver Dam, WI, 53916

Robbins, Wayne, 11520 Inverway, Belvidere, IL, 61008

S&D Enterprises, 20 East Seventh St., Manchester, OH, 45144, 937-549-2602, (937)-549-2602 or 2603, sales@s-denterprises.com, www.s-denterprises.com

Schlott, Harald, Zingster Str. 26, 13051 Berlin, GERMANY, 03 01 929 33 46, 03 01 929 33 46, www.harald-schlott@t-online.de

Schönert, Elke, 18 Lansdowne Pl., Central, Port Elizabeth, SOUTH AFRICA

engravers

Adlam, Tim, 1705 Witzel Ave., Oshkosh, WI, 54902, 920-235-4589, 920-235-4589

Alfano, Sam, 36180 Henry Gaines Rd., Pearl River, LA, 70452, 504-863-5120, sam@masterengraver.com, www.masterengraver.com

Allard, Gary, 2395 Battlefield Rd., Fishers Hill, VA, 22626

Allred, Scott, 2403 Lansing Blvd., Wichita Falls, TX

Alpen, Ralph, 7 Bentley Rd., West Grove, PA, 1939

Aoun, Charles, Galeb Knives, 69 Nahant St, Wakefield, MA, 01880, 781-224-3353, 781-224-3353

Baron, Technology Inc., David, David Baron, 62 Spring Hill Rd., Trumbull, CT, 06611, 203-452-0515, btinc@connix.com, "Polishing, plating, inlays, artwork"

Bates, Billy, 2302 Winthrop Dr. SW, Decatur, AL, 35603

Beaver, Judy, 48835 N. 25 Ave., Phoenix, AZ, 85027

Becker, Franz, Am Kreuzberg 2, 84533 Marktl/Inn, GERMANY

Bettenhausen, Merle L., 17358 Ottawa, Tinley Park, IL, 60477

Blair, Jim, P.O. Box 64, 59 Mesa Verde, Glenrock, WY, 82637, 307463-8115

Bleile, C. Roger, 5040 Ralph Ave., Cincinnati, OH, 45238

Bonshire, Benita, 1121 Burlington, Muncie, IN, 47302

Boster, A.D., 3744 Pleasant Hill Dr., Gainesville, GA, 30504

Bratcher, Dan, 311 Belle Aire Pl., Carthage, MO, 64836

Brooker, Dennis B., Rt. 1 Box 12A, Derby, IA, 50068

Churchill, Winston, G., RFD Box 29B, Proctorsville, VT, 05153

Collins, David, Rt. 2 Box 425, Monroe, VA, 24574

Collins, Michael, Rt. 3075, Batesville Rd., Woodstock, GA, 30188

Cupp, Alana, P.O. Box 207, Annabella, UT, 84711

Dashwood, Jim, 255 Barkham Rd., Wokingham, Berkshire RG11 4BY, ENGLAND

Davidson, Jere, 104 Fox Creek Dr, Goode, VA, 24556, 540-586-5150, JereDavidson@centralva.net

Dean, Bruce, 13 Tressider Ave., Haberfield, N.S.W. 2045, AUSTRALIA

DeLorge, Ed, 6734 W Main St, Houma, LA, 70360, 504-223-0206

Dickson, John W., P.O. Box 49914, Sarasota, FL, 34230

Dolbare, Elizabeth, P.O. Box 222, Sunburst, MT, 59482

Downing, Jim, P.O. Box 4224, Springfield, MO, 65808, 417-865-5953, www.thegunengraver.com

Drain, Mark, SE 3211 Kamilche Pt. Rd., Shelton, WA, 98584

Duarte, Carlos, 108 Church St., Rossville, CA, 95678

Dubben, Michael, 414 S. Fares Ave., Evansville, IN, 47714

Dubber, Michael, W., 8205 Heather Pl, Evansville, IN, 47710-4919, 812-476-0651, mwdub@aol.com

Eklund, Maihkel, Föne 1111, S-82041 Färila, SWEDEN, +46 6512 4192, maihkel.eklund@swipnet.se, http:// euroedge. net/maihkeleklund/hems.shtml

Engel, Terry, (Flowers), P.O. Box 96, Midland, OR, 97634

Eyster, Ken, 6441 Bishop Rd., Centerburg, OH, 43011

Flannery, Engraving Co., Jeff, 11034 Riddles Run Rd., Union, KY, 41091, 606-384-3127, 606-384-2222, engraving@fuse.net, http://home.fuse.net engraving/

Foster, Enterprises, Norvell, Foster, P.O. Box 200343, San Antonio, TX, 78220

Fountain Products, 492 Prospect Ave., West, Springfield, MA, 01089

French, James, Ronald, 1745 Caddo Dr., Irving, TX, 75060-5837

George, Tim and Christy, 3608 Plymouth Pl., Lynchburg, VA, 24503

Gipe, Sandi, Rt. 2, Box 1090A, Kendrick, ID, 83537

Glimm, Jerome C., 19 S. Maryland, Conrad, MT, 59425

Gournet, Geoffroy, 820 Paxinosa Ave., Easton, PA, 18042, 610-559-0710

Hands, Barry Lee, 26192 E. Shore Rte., Bigfork, MT, 59911

Harrington, Fred A., Winter: 3725 Citrus, St. James City, FL, 33956, 941-283-0721

Harrington, Fred A., Summer: 2107 W. Frances Rd, Mt. Morris, MI, 48458-8215, 810-686-3008

Henderson, Fred D., 569 Santa Barbara Dr., Forest Park, GA, 30297, 770-968-4866

Hendricks, Frank, HC03, Box 434, Dripping, Springs, TX, 78620

Holder, Pat, 7148 W. Country Gables Dr., Peoria, AZ, 85381

Hudson, Tommy, PO Box 1457, Yuba City, CA, 95992, 530-841-2966, 530-741-1670

Ingle, Ralph W., 112 Manchester Ct., Centerville, GA, 31028

Jiantonio, Robert, P.O. Box 986, Venice, FL, 34284

Johns, Bill, 6 Ptarmigan Drive, Cody, WY, 82414, 82414, 307-587-5090, Custom silver & gold handle inlays.

Kelly, Lance, 1723 Willow Oak Dr., Edgewater, FL, 32132

Kelso, Jim, RD 1, Box 5300, Worcester, VT, 05682

Koevenig, Eugene and Eve, Rabbit Gulch, Box 55, Hill City, SD, 57745-0055

Kostelnik, Joe and Patty, RD #4, Box 323, Greensburg, PA, 15601

Kudlas, John M., HC 66 Box 22680, Barnes, WI, 54873, 715-795-2031, jkudlas@www.bright.net

Lee, Ray, 209 Jefferson Dr., Lynchburg, VA, 24502

Limings Jr., Harry, 959 County Rd. 170, Marengo, OH, 43334- 9625

Lindsay, Steve, 3714 West Cedar Hills Drive, Kearney, NE, 68847

Lyttle, Brian, Box 5697, High River AB CANADA, T1V 1M7

Lytton, Simon M., 19 Pinewood Gardens, Hemel Hempstead, Herts. HP1 1TN, ENGLAND, 01 442 25542

McCombs, Leo, 1862 White Cemetery Rd., Patriot, OH, 45658

McDonald, Dennis, 8359 Brady St., Peosta, IA, 52068

McFadden, John, PO Box 462, Coeur d'Alene, ID, 83816, 208-762-3090

McKenzie, Lynton, 6940 N. Alvernon Way, Tucson, AZ, 85718

Meyer, Chris, 39 Bergen Ave., Wantage, NJ, 07461, 973-875-6299

Morgan, Tandie, P.O. Box 693, 30700 Hwy. 97, Nucla, CO, 81424

Morton, David A., 1110 W. 21st St., Lorain, OH, 44052

Moschetti, Mitch, 1435 S. Elizabeth, Denver, CO, 80210

Nelida, Toniutti, via G. Pasconi 29/c, Maniago 33085 (PN), ITALY

Norton, Jeff, 2009 65th St., Lubbock, TX, 79412

Nott, Ron, Box 281, Summerdale, PA, 17093

Parsons, Michael, R., McKee Knives, 1600 S. 11th St., Terre Haute, IN, 47802-1722, 812-234-1679

Patterson, W.H., P.O. Drawer DK, College Station, TX, 77841

Perdue, David L., Rt. 1 Box 657, Gladys, VA, 24554

Peri, Valerio, Via Meucci 12, Gardone V.T. 25063, ITALY

Pilkington Jr., Scott, P.O. Box 97, Monteagle, TN, 37356

Poag, James, RR1, Box 212A, Grayville, IL, 62844

Potts, Wayne, 912 Poplar St., Denver, CO, 80220

Rabeno, Martin, Spook Hollow Trading Co., 92 Spook Hole Rd., Ellenville, NY, 12428

Raftis, Andrew, 2743 N. Sheffield, Chicago, IL, 60614

Roberts, J.J., 7808 Lake Dr., Manassas, VA, 22111, 703- 330-0448, james.roberts@angelfire.com, www.angelfire.com/va2/engraver

Robidoux, Roland J., DMR Fine Engraving, 25 N. Federal Hwy., Studio 5, Dania, FL, 33004

Robyn, Jon, Ground Floor, 30 E. 81st St., New York, NY, 10028

Rosser, Bob, Hand Engraving, 1824 29th Ave. South, Suite 214, Birmingham, AL, 35209

Rudolph, Gil, 386 Mariposa Dr., Ventura, CA, 93001, 805-643-4005, 805-643-6416, gtraks@west.net

Rundell, Joe, 6198 W. Frances Rd., Clio, MI, 48420

Schickl, L., Ottingweg 497, A-5580 Tamsweg, AUSTRIA, 0043 6474 8583

Schlott, Harald, Zingster Str. 26, 13051 Berlin, GERMANY, 03 01 929 33 46, 03 01 929 33 46, www.harald-schlott@t-online.de

Schönert, Elke, 18 Lansdowne Pl., Central, Port Elizabeth, SOUTH AFRICA

Shaw, Bruce, P.O. Box 545, Pacific Grove, CA, 93950, 831-646-1937, 831-644-0941

Shostle, Ben, 1121 Burlington, Muncie, IN, 47302

Sinclair, W.P., 3, The Pippins, Warminster, Wiltshire BA12 8TH, ENGLAND

Smith, Jerry, 7029 East Holmes Rd., Memphis, TN, 38125

Smith, Ron, 5869 Straley, Ft. Worth, TX, 76114

Smith, Peggy, 676 Glades Rd., #3, Gatlinburg, TN, 37738

Smitty's Engraving, 800 N. Anderson Rd., Choctaw, OK, 73020

Snell, Barry A.,4801 96th St. N., St. Petersburg, FL, 33708- 3740

Spode, Peter, Tresaith Newland, Malvern, Worcestershire WR13 5AY, ENGLAND

Steduto, Giovanni, Gardone, V.T., ITALY

Swartley, Robert D., 2800 Pine St., Napa, CA, 94558

Takeuchi, Shigetoshi, 21-14-1-Chome kamimuneoka, Shiki shi, 353 Saitama, JAPAN

Valade, Robert B., 931 3rd Ave., Seaside, OR, 97138, 503-738-7672

Waldrop, Mark, 14562 SE 1st Ave. Rd., Summerfield, FL, 34491, 352-347-9034

Wallace, Terry, 385 San Marino, Vallejo, CA, 94589

Warenski, Julie, 590 East 500 N., Richfield, UT, 84701

Warren, Kenneth, W., P.O. Box 2842, Wenatchee, WA, 98807-2842, 509-663-6123, 509-663-6123

Whitehead, James D., 204 Cappucino Way, Sacramento, CA, 95838

Whitmore, Jerry, 1740 Churchill Dr., Oakland, OR, 97462

Williams, Gary, 221 Autumn Way, Elizabeth, KY, 42701

Winn, Travis A., 558 E. 3065 S., Salt Lake City, UT, 84106

Wood, Mel, P.O. Box 1255, Sierra Vista, AZ, 85636, melnan@dakotacom.net

Zietz, Dennis, 5906 40th Ave., Kenosha, WI, 53144

Baron Technology Inc., David Baron, 62 Spring Hill Rd., Trumbull, CT, 06611

Fountain Products, 492 Prospect Ave., West, Springfield, MA, 01089

Hayes, Dolores, P.O. Box 41405, Los Angeles, CA, 90041

Holland, Dennis, 4908 17th Pl., Lubbock, TX, 79416

Kelso, Jim, RD1, Box 5300, Worcester, VT, 05682

Larstein, Francine, David Boye Knives Gallery, 111-B Marine View, Davenport, CA, 95017, 831-426-6046, 831-426-6048, francine@boyeknivesgallery.com, www.boyeknivesgallery.com

Lefaucheux, Jean-Victor, Saint-Denis-Le-Ferment, 27140 Gisors, FRANCE

Leibowitz, Leonard, 1025 Murrayhill Ave., Pittsburgh, PA, 15217

MacBain, Kenneth, C., 30 Briarwood Ave., Norwood, NJ, 07648

Myers, Ron, 6202 Marglenn Ave., Baltimore, MD, 21206

Sayen, Murad, P.O. Box 127, Bryant Pond, ME, 04219

Smith, Glen, 1307 Custer Ave., Billings, MT, 59102

Vallotton, A., Northwest Knife Supply, 621 Fawn Ridge Dr., Oakland, OR, 97462

heat-treaters

Aoun, Charles, Galeb Knives, 69 Nahant St, Wakefield, MA, 01880, 781-224-3353, 781-224-3353

Bay State Metal Treating Co., 6 Jefferson Ave., Woburn, MA, 01801

Bodycote, Thermal, Processing, Tom, Tom Sidney, 710 Burns St., Cincinnati, OH, 45204, www.bodycote-na.com

Bos Heat, Treating, Paul, Shop: 1900 Weld Blvd., El Cajon, CA, 92020, 619-562-2370 / 619-445-4740 eves., paulbos@buckknives.com

El Monte Steel, 355 SE End Ave., Pomona, CA, 91766

Levine, Bernard, P.O. Box 2404, Eugene, OR, 97402, 541-484-0294, brlevine@ix.netcom.com, www.knife-expert.com/, Expert witness

Hauni Richmond Inc., 2800 Charles City Rd., Richmond, VA, 23231

Holt, B.R., 1238 Birchwood Drive, Sunnyvale, CA, 94089

Ingle, Ralph W., 112 Manchester Ct., Centerville, GA, 31028

O&W Heat Treat Inc., One Bidwell Rd., South Windsor, CT, 06074, 860-528-9239, 860-291-9939, owhti@aol.com

Texas Heat Treating Inc., 303 Texas Ave., Round Rock, TX, 78664

Texas Knifemakers Supply, 10649 Haddington, Suite 180, Houston, TX, 77043

The Tinker Shop, 1120 Helen, Deer Park, TX, 77536

Valley Metal Treating Inc., 355 S. East End Ave., Pomona, CA, 91766

Wilson, R.W., P.O. Box 2012, Weirton, WV, 26062

knife appraisers

Baker, Don and Kay, 5950 Foxfire Dr., Zanesville, OH, 43701

Levine, Bernard, P.O. Box 2404, Eugene, OR, 97402, 541-484-0294, brlevine@ix.netcom.com, www.knife-expert.com/, Expert witness

directory

Russell, A.G., 1705 Hwy. 71 North, Springdale, AR, 72764
Vallini, Massimo, Via Dello Scalo 2/3, 40131 Bologna, ITALY

leatherworkers

Alfano, Sam, 36180 Henery Gaines Rd., Pearl River, LA, 70452
Baker, Don and Kay, 5950 Foxfire Dr., Zanesville, OH, 43701
Cheramie, Grant, 4260 West Main, Rt. 3, Box 940, Cut Off, LA, 70345
Clements', Custom, Leathercraft, Chas, 1741 Dallas St., Aurora, CO, 80010-2018, gryphons@home.com
Congdon, David, 1063 Whitchurch Ct., Wheaton, IL, 60187
Cooper, Harold, 136 Winding Way, Frankfort, KY, 40601
Cooper, Jim, 2148 Cook Pl., Ramona, CA, 92065-3214
Cow Catcher Leatherworks, 3006 Industrial Dr., Raleigh, NC, 27609, 919-833-8262, cowcatcher1@msn.com
Cubic, George, GC Custom Leather Co., 10561 E. Deerfield Pl., Tucson, AZ, 85749, 520-760-5988, gcubic@aol.com
Dawkins, Dudley, 221 N. Broadmoor, Topeka, KS, 66606-1254
Evans, Scott V, Edge Works Mfg, 1171 Halltown Rd, Jacksonville, NC, 28546, 910-455-9834, 910-346-5660, edgeworks@coastalnet.com, www.tacticalholsters.com
Fannin, David A., 2050 Idle Hour Center #191, Lexington, KY, 40502
Foley, Barney, 3M Reler Lane, Somerset, NJ, 08873
Genske, Jay, 2621/2 Elm St., Fond du Lac, WI, 54935
Gimbert, Nelson, P.O. Box 787, Clemmons, NC, 27012
Harris, Tom, 519 S. 1st St., Mount Vernon, WA, 98273
Hawk, Ken, Rt. 1, Box 770, Ceres, VA, 24318-9630
Hendryx Design, Scott, 5997 Smokey Way, Boise, ID, 83714, 208-377-8044, 208-377-2601, Kydex knife sheath maker
Homyk, David N., 8047 Carriage Ln., Wichita Falls, TX, 76306
K&J Leatherworks, P.O. Box 609, Watford, ON, N0M, 2S0, CANADA
Kravitt, Chris, HC 31 Box 6484, Rt 200, Ellsworth, ME, 04605-9805, 207-584-3000, sheathmkr@aol.com, www.treestumpleather.com, Reference: Tree Stump Leather
Larson, Richard, 549 E. Hawkeye, Turlock, CA, 95380
Lay, Robert J, Lay's Custom Knives, Box 122, Falkland, BC, V0J 3A0, CANADA V0E, 1W0, 250-379-2265
Layton, Jim, 2710 Gilbert Avenue, Portsmouth, OH, 45662
Lee, Randy, P.O. Box 1873, St. Johns, AZ, 85936, 520-337-2594, 520-337-5002, www.carizona.com/knives, Custom knifemaker
Marlatt, David, 67622 Oldham Rd., Cambridge, OH, 43725, 740-432-7549
Mason, Arne, 125 Wimer St., Ashland, OR, 97520, 541-482-2260, www.arnemason.com
McGowan, Liz, 12629 Howard Lodge Dr., Sykesville, MD, 21784, 410-489-4323
Metheny, H.A., "Whitey", 7750 Waterford Dr., Spotsylvania, VA, 22553
Miller, Michael K., 28510 Santiam Highway, Sweet Home, OR, 97386
Mobley, Martha, 240 Alapaha River Road, Chula, GA, 31733
Morrissey, Martin, 4578 Stephens Rd., Blairsville, GA, 30512
Niedenthal, John, Andre, Beadwork & Buckskin, Studio 3955 NW 103 Dr., Coral Springs, FL, 33065-1551, 954-345-0447, a_niedenthal@hotmail.com, Native American beaded knife sheaths
Patterson, W.H., P.O. Drawer DK, College Station, TX, 77841
Poag, James H., RR #1 Box 212A, Grayville, IL, 62844
Red's Custom, Leather, Ed Todd, 9 Woodlawn Rd., Putnam Valley, NY, 10579
Riney, Norm, 6212 S. Marion Way, Littleton, CO, 71801
Rowe, Kenny, dba Rowe's Leather, 1406 W. Ave. C, Hope, AR, 71801, 870-777-8216, 870-777-2974, knifeart.com, rowesleather@yahoo.com
Ruiz Industries Inc., 1513 Gardena Ave., Glendale, CA, 53213-3717
Schrap, Robert G., 7024 W. Wells St., Wauwatosa, WI, 53213, 414-771-6472, 262-784-2996, rschrap@aol.com
Spragg, Wayne E., P.O. Box 508, Ashton, ID, 26241
Strahin, Robert, 401 Center Ave., Elkins, WV,
Stuart, V. Pat, Rt. 1, Box 447-S, Greenville, VA, 24440
Stumpf, John R., 523 S. Liberty St., Blairsville, PA, 15717
Tierney, Mike, 447 Rivercrest Dr., Woodstock ON CANADA, N4S 5W5
Turner, Kevin, 17 Hunt Ave., Montrose, NY, 10548
Velasquez, Gil, 7120 Madera Dr., Goleta, CA, 93117
Walker, John, 17 Laver Circle, Little Rock, AR, 72209, 501-455-0239
Watson, Bill, #1 Presidio, Wimberly, TX, 78676

Wegner, Tim, 8818-158th St. E., Puyallup, WA, 98373
Whinnery, Walt, 1947 Meadow Creek Dr., Louisville, KY, 40218
Williams, Sherman, A., 1709 Wallace St., Simi Valley, CA, 93065

photographers

Adlam, Tim, 1705 Witzel Ave., Oshkosh, WI, 54902, 920-235-4589, 920-234-4589
Alfano, Sam, 36180 Henery Gaines Rd., Pearl River, LA, 70452
Allen, John, Studio One, 3823 Pleasant Valley Blvd., Rockford, IL, 61114
Berisford, Bob, 505 West Adams St., Jacksonville, FL, 32202
Bilal, Mustafa, Turk's Head Productions, 908 NW 50th St., Seattle, WA, 98107-3634, 206-782-4164, 206-783-5677, turksheadp@aol.com, www.turkshead.com, "Graphic design, marketing & advertising"
Bittner, Rodman, 3444 North Apache Circle, Chandler, AZ, 85224
Bloomer, Peter L., Horizons West, 427 S. San Francisco, St., Flagstaff, AZ, 86001
Bogaerts, Jan, Regenweg 14, 5757 Pl., Liessel, HOLLAND
Box, Photography, Doug, 1804 W Main St, Brenham, TX, 77833-3420
Brown, Tom, 6048 Grants Ferry Rd., Brandon, MS, 39042- 8136
Buffaloe, Edwin, 104 W. Applegate, Austin, TX, 78753
Butman, Steve, P.O. Box 5106, Abilene, TX, 79608
Calidonna, Greg, 205 Helmwood Dr., Elizabethtown, KY, 42701
Campbell, Jim, 7935 Ranch Rd., Port Richey, FL, 34668
Catalano, John D., 56 Kingston Ave., Hicksville, NY, 11801
Chastain, Christopher, B&W Labs, 1462 E. Michigan St., Orlando, FL, 32806
Clark, John W., 604 Cherry St., Des Moines, IA, 50309
Clark, Ryerson, P.O. Box 1193, Dartmouth NS CANADA, B2Y 4B8
Cotton, William A., 749 S. Lemay Ave. A3-211, Fort Collins, CO, 80524
Courtice, Bill, P.O. Box 1776, Duarte, CA, 91010-4776
Crosby, Doug, RFD 1, Box 1111, Stockton Springs, ME, 04981
Danko, Michael, 3030 Jane Street, Pittsburgh, PA, 15203
Davis, Marshall, B., P.O. Box 3048, Austin, TX, 78764
Dikeman, Lawrence, 2169 Arbor Ave., Muskegon, MI, 49441
Durant, Ross, 316 E. 1st Ave., Vancouver BC CANADA, V5T 1A9
Earley, Don, 1241 Ft. Bragg Rd., Fayetteville, NC, 28305
Ehrlich, Linn M., 2643 N. Clybourn Ave., Chicago, IL, 60614
Ellison, Troy, P.O. Box 94393, Lubbock, TX, 79493, tellison@hiplains.net
Etzler, John, 11200 N. Island Rd., Grafton, OH, 44044
Fahrner, Dave, 1623 Arnold St., Pittsburgh, PA, 15205
Faul, Jan W., 903 Girard St. NE, Rr. Washington, DC, 20017
Fedorak, Allan, 28 W. Nicola St., Amloops BC CANADA, V2C 1J6
Fisher, Jay, 104 S. Main St., P.O. Box 267, Magdlena, NM, 87825, 509-854-2118, 505-854-2118, www.jayfisher.com
Fisher, Jay, P.O. Box 267, Magdalena, NM, 87825
Fitzgerald, Dan, P.O. Box 198, Beverly Hills, CA, 90213
Forster, Jenny, 1112 N. McAree, Waukegan, IL, 60085
Fox, Daniel, Lumina Studios, 6773 Industrial Parkway, Cleveland, OH, 44070, 440-734-2118, 440-734-3542, lumina@en.com
Gardner, Chuck, 116 Quincy Ave., Oak Ridge, TN, 37830
Gawryla, Don, 1105 Greenlawn Dr., Pittsburgh, PA, 15220
Godby, Ronald E., 204 Seven Hollys Dr., Yorktown, VA, 23692
Goffe Photographic, Associates, 3108 Monte Vista Blvd., NE, Albuquerque, NM, 87106
Graham, James, 7434 E Northwest Hwy, Dallas, TX, 75231, 214-341-5138, 214-341-5216, jags2dos@onramp.net
Graley, Gary W., RR2 Box 556, Gillett, PA, 16925
Griggs, Dennis, 118 Pleasant Pt Rd., Topsham, ME, 04086, 207-725-5689
Hanusin, John, 3306 Commercial, Northbrook, IL, 60062
Hardy, Scott, 639 Myrtle Ave., Placerville, CA, 95667
Hodge, Tom, 7175 S US Hwy 1 Lot 36, Titusville, FL, 32780-8172
Hoffman, Terrill, 7839 Old North Ct, Charlotte, NC, 28270, 704-364-0249
Holter, Wayne V., 125 Lakin Ave., Boonsboro, MD, 21713, 301-416-2855, mackwayne@hotmail.com
Jiantonio, Robert, P.O. Box 986, Venice, FL, 34284
Kelley, Gary, 17485 SW Pheasant Lane, Aloha, OR, 97006, 503-848-9313, Custom buckle knives
Kerns, Bob, 18723 Birdseye Dr., Germantown, MD, 20874
LaFleur, Gordon, 111 Hirst, Box 1209, Parksville BC CANADA, V0R 270

Landis, George E., 16 Prospect Hill Rd., Cromwell, CT, 06416

Lautman, Andy, 4906 41st N.W., Washington, DC, 20016

Lear, Dale, 6450 Cora Mill Rd, Gallipolis, OH, 45631, 740-245-5499, dalelear@yahoo.com, www.learz.com, Web page designer

LeBlanc, Paul, No. 3 Meadowbrook Cir., Melissa, TX, 75454

Lenz Photography, 939 S. 48th St., Suite 206, Tempe, AZ, 85281

Lester, Dean, 2801 Junipero Ave Suite 212, Long Beach, CA, 90806-2140

Leviton, David A., A Studio on the Move, P.O. Box 2871, Silverdale, WA, 98383, 360-697-3452

Long, Gary W., 3556 Miller's Crossroad Rd., Hillsboro, TN, 37342

Long, Jerry, 402 E. Gladden Dr., Farmington, NM, 87401

Lum, Billy, 16307 Evening Star Ct., Crosby, TX, 77532

McCollum, Tom, P.O. Box 933, Lilburn, GA, 30226

Moake, Jim, 18 Council Ave., Aurora, IL, 60504

Moya Inc., 4212 S. Dixie Hwy., West Palm Beach, FL, 33405

Mumford Photography, Phil, 2368 E Floyd Pl., Englewood, CO, 80110, 303-788-0384, 303-788-0384, Fotophil5 @aol.com

Newton, Thomas, D., 136 1/2 W. 2nd St., Reno, NV, 89501

Norman's Studio, 322 S. 2nd St., Vivian, LA, 71082

Owens, William T., Box 99, Williamsburg, WV, 24991

Palmer Studio, 2008 Airport Blvd., Mobile, AL, 36606

Parker, T.C., 1720 Pacific, Las Vegas, NV, 89104

Parsons, 15 South Mission, Suite 3, Wenatchee, WA, 98801

Parsons, Michael R, 1600 S 11th St, Terry Haute, IN, 47802-1722, 812-234-1679

Patterson, W.H., P.O. Drawer DK, College Station, TX, 77841

Payne, Robert G., P.O. Box 141471, Austin, TX, 78714

Peterson Photography, Kent, 230 Polk St., Eugene, OR, 97402, kdp@pond.net, www.pond.net/kdp

Pigott, John, 231 Heidelberg Drive, Loveland, OH, 45140, 513-683-4875

Point Seven Inc., Eric, Eric R. Eggly, 810 Seneca St., Toledo, OH, 43608, 877-787-3836

Rasmussen, Eric L., 1121 Eliason, Brigham City, UT, 84302

Reinders, Rick, 1707 Spring Place, Racine, WI, 53404

Rhoades, Cynthia J., Box 195, Clearmont, WY, 82835

Rice, Tim, 310 Wisconsin Ave., Whitefish, MT, 59937

Richardson, Kerry, 2520 Mimosa St., Santa Rosa, CA, 95405, 707-575-1875, kerry@sonic.net, www.sonic.net/~kerry

Robertson, Kathy, Impress by Design, PO Box 211961, Augusta, GA, 30917, 706-650-0982, 706-860-1623, rccedge@csranet.com, Advertising/ graphic designer

Ross, Bill, 28364 S. Western Ave. Suite 464, Rancho Palos, Verdes, CA, 90275

Rubicam, Stephen, 14 Atlantic Ave., Boothbay, Harbor, ME, 04538-1202

Ruby, Tom, Holiday Inn University, 11200 E. Goodman Rd., Olive Branch, MS, 38654

Rush, John D., 2313 Maysel, Bloomington, IL, 61701

Schreiber, Roger, 429 Boren Ave. N., Seattle, WA, 98109, 206-622-3525

Semmer, Charles, 7885 Cyd Dr., Denver, CO, 80221

Silver Images Photography, 21 E. Aspen Ave., Flagstaff, AZ, 86001

Sims Photography, Bob, 3040 Andora Dr SW, Marietta, GA, 30064-2458

Slobodian, Scott, 4101 River Ridge Dr., P.O. Box 1498, San Andreas, CA, 95249, 209-286-1980, 209-286- 1982, www.slobodianswords.com

Smith, Randall, 1720 Oneco Ave., Winter Park, FL, 32789

Stenzel Photography, P.O. Box 1504, Bozeman, MT, 59771

Storm Photo, 334 Wall St., Kingston, NY, 12401

Surles, Mark, P.O. Box 147, Falcon, NC, 28342

Tardiolo, 9381 Wagon Wheel, Yuma, AZ, 85365

Third Eye Photos, 140 E. Sixth Ave., Helena, MT, 59601

Thurber, David, P.O. Box 1006, Visalia, CA, 93279

Tighe, Brian, RR 1, Ridgeville ON CANADA, L0S 1M0, 905-892-2734, www.tigheknives.com, Knifemaker

Towell, Steven L., 3720 N.W. 32nd Ave., Camas, WA, 98607

Troutman, Harry, 107 Oxford Dr., Lititz, PA, 17543

Valley Photo, 2100 Arizona Ave., Yuma, AZ, 85364

Vara, Lauren, 4412 Waples Rd., Granbury, TX, 76049

Verhoeven, Jon, 106 San Jose Dr., Springdale, AR, 72764-2538

Verno Studio, Jay, 3030 Jane Street, Pittsburgh, PA, 15203

Wells, Carlene L., 1060 S. Main Sp. 52, Colville, WA, 99114

Weyer International, 2740 Nebraska Ave., Toledo, OH, 43607, 800-448-8424, 419-534-2697, law-weyer.international@msn.com, Books

Wise, Harriet, 242 Dill Ave., Frederick, MD, 21701

Worley, Holly, 6360 W David Dr., Littleton, CO, 80128-5708

scrimshanders

Adlam, Tim, 1705 Witzel Ave., Oshkosh, WI, 54902, 920-235-4589, 920-234-4589

Anderson, Terry Jack, 10076 Birnamwoods Way, Riverton, UT, 84065-9073

Arnold, Joe, 47 Patience Cres., London ON, CANADA, N6E 2K7

Bailey, Mary W., 3213 Jonesboro Dr., Nashville, TN, 37214

Baker, Duane, 2145 Alum Creek Dr., Cambridge Park Apt. #10, Columbus, OH, 43207

Barndt, Kristen A., RR3, Box 72, Kunkletown, PA, 18058

Barrows, Miles, 524 Parsons Ave., Chillicothe, OH, 45601

Beauchamp, Gaetan, 125 de la Riviere, Stoneham, PQ, G0A 4P0, CANADA, 418-848-1914, 418-848-6859, gaetanbeauchamp@uldectron.ca, www.pages.infinit.net/couteau/, "Custom grinder, custom handle artisan

Beaver, Judy, 48835 N. 25 Ave., Phoenix, AZ, 85027

Bellet, Connie, PO Box 151, Palermo, ME, 04354, 207- 993-2327, pwhitehawk@juno.com or @palermo.org

Bonshire, Benita, 1121 Burlington Dr., Muncie, IN, 47302

Boone Trading Co. Inc., PO Box 669, Brinnon, WA, 98320, 360-796-4330, 360-796-4511

Bowles, Rick, 556 Pheasant Run, Virginia Beach, VA, 23452-8017

Brady, Sandra, P.O. Box 104, Monclova, OH, 43542, 419-866-0435, 419-867-0656

Bryan, Bob, 1120 Oak Hill Rd., Carthage, MO, 64836

Byrne, Mary Gregg, 1018 15th St., Bellingham, WA, 98225-6604

Cable, Jerry, 332 Main St., Mt. Pleasant, PA, 15666

Caudill, Lyle, 7626 Lyons Rd., Georgetown, OH, 45121

Collins, Michael, Rt. 3075, Batesville Rd., Woodstock, GA, 30188

Conover, Juanita Rae, P.O. Box 70442, Eugene, OR, 97401, 541-747-1726 or 543-4851

Courtnage, Elaine, Box 473, Big Sandy, MT, 59520

Cover Jr., Raymond, A., Rt. 1, Box 194, Mineral Point, MO, 63660

Cox, J. Andy, 116 Robin Hood Lane, Gaffney, SC, 29340

Davenport, Susan, 36842 Center Ave., Dade City, FL, 33525

DeYoung, Brian, 1448 Glen Haven Dr., Ft Collins, CO, 80526-2408

Dietrich, Roni, Wild Horse Studio, 1257 Cottage Dr., Harrisburg, PA, 17112, 717-469-0587, ronimd@aol.com

DiMarzo, Richard, 2357 Center Place, Birmingham, AL, 35205

Dolbare, Elizabeth, P.O. Box 222, Sunburst, MT, 59482

Drain, Mark, SE 3211 Kamilche Pt. Rd., Shelton, WA, 98584

Eklund, Maihkel, Föne 1111, S-82041 Färila, SWEDEN, +46 6512 4192, maihkel.eklund@swipnet.se, http:// euroedge.net/maihkeleklund

Eldridge, Allan, 1424 Kansas Lane, Gallatin, TN, 37066

Evans, Rick M., 2717 Arrowhead Dr., Abilene, TX, 79606

Fisk, Dale, Box 252, Council, ID, 83612

Foster Enterprises, Norvell Foster, P.O. Box 200343, San Antonio, TX, 78220

Fountain Products, 492 Prospect Ave., West Springfield, MA, 01089

Garbe, Sandra, 1246 W. Webb, DeWitt, MI, 48820

Gill, Scott, 925 N. Armstrong St., Kokomo, IN, 46901

Halligan, Ed, 14 Meadow Way, Sharpsburg, GA, 30277, ehkiss@bellsouth.net

Hands, Barry Lee, 26192 East Shore Route, Bigfork, MT, 59911

Hargraves Sr., Charles, RR 3 Bancroft, Ontario CANADA, K0L 1C0

Harless, Star, c/o Arrow Forge, P.O. Box 845, Stoneville, NC, 27048-0845

Harrington, Fred A., Summer: 2107 W Frances Rd, Mt Morris MI 48458 8215 Winter: 3725 Citrus, St. James City, FL, 33956, Winter 941-283-0721,Summer 810-686-3008

Henderson, Fred D., 569 Santa Barbara Dr., Forest Park, GA, 30297, 770-968-4866

Henry, Michael K., Rte. 2, Box 161-J, Robbinsville, NC, 28771

Hielscher, Vickie, PO Box 992, 6550 Otoe Rd, Alliance, NE, 69301, 308-762-4318, hielscher@premaonline.com

High, Tom, 5474 S. 112.8 Rd., Alamosa, CO, 81101

Himmelheber, David R., 11289 40th St. N., Royal Palm Beach, FL, 33411

Holland, Dennis K., 4908-17th Place, Lubbock, TX, 79416

Hoover, Harvey, 5750 Pearl Dr., Paradise, CA, 95969-4829

Houser, Jesse, P.O. Box 993, Biscoe, NC, 27209

Imboden II, Howard L., 620 Deauville Dr., Dayton, OH, 45429, 937-439-1536, Guards by the "Last Wax Technic"

Johnson, Corinne, W3565 Lockington, Mindora, WI, 54644

Johnston, Kathy, W. 1134 Providence, Spokane, WA, 99205

Karst, Linda K., 402 Hwy. 27 E., Ingram, TX, 78025-3315, 830-896-4678,

Kelso, Jim, 577 Collar Hill Rd, Worcester, VT, 05682

Kirk, Susan B., 1340 Freeland Rd., Merrill, MI, 48637

Koevenig, Eugene and Eve, Koevenig's Engraving Service Rabbit Gulch, Box 55, Hill City, SD, 57745-0055

Kostelnik, Joe and Patty, RD #4, Box 323, Greensburg, PA, 15601

Kudlas, John M., HC 66 Box 22680, Barnes, WI, 54873, 715-795-2031, jkudlas@win.bright.net

Land, John W., P.O. Box 917, Wadesboro, NC, 28170

Lee, Ray, 209 Jefferson Dr., Lynchburg, VA, 24502

Lemen, Pam, 3434 N. Iroquois Ave., Tucson, AZ, 85705

Letschnig, Franz, RR1, Martintown ON, CANADA

Martin, Diane, 28220 N. Lake Dr., Waterford, WI, 53185

McDonald, René Cosimini-, 14730 61 Court N., Loxahatchee, FL, 33470

McGowan, Frank, 12629 Howard Lodge Dr., Sykesville, MD, 21784

McGrath, Gayle, 12641 Panasoffkee, N Ft Myers, FL, 33903

McLaran, Lou, 603 Powers St., Waco, TX, 76705

McWilliams, Carole, P.O. Box 693, Bayfield, CO, 81122

Mead, Faustina L., 2550 E. Mercury St., Inverness, FL, 34453-0514, 352-344-4751, scrimsha@citrus.infi.net, scrimshaw-by-faustina.com, Etcher (acid)

Minnick, Joyce, 144 N. 7th St., Middletown, IN, 47356

Mitchell, James, 1026 7th Ave., Columbus, GA, 31901

Moore, James B., 1707 N. Gillis, Stockton, TX, 79735

Ochonicky, Michelle "Mike", 31 High Trail, Eureka, MO, 63025, www.bestofmissourihands.com

Ochs, Belle, 124 Emerald Lane, Largo, FL, 33771, 727- 530-3826, chuckandbelle@juno.com, www.oxforge.com

Pachi, Mirella, Via Pometta 1, 17046 Sassello (SV), ITALY, 019 720086, WWW.PACHI-KNIVES.COM

Pankova-Clark, Inna, P.O. Box 597, Andrews, NC, 28901

Parish, Vaughn, 103 Cross St., Monaca, PA, 15061

Peck, Larry H., 4021 Overhill Rd., Hannibal, MO, 63401

Peterson, Lou, 514 S. Jackson St., Gardner, IL, 60424

Poag, James H., RR #1 Box 212A, Grayville, IL, 62844

Polk, Trena, 4625 Webber Creek Rd., Van Buren, AR, 72956

Purvis, Hilton, P.O. Box 371, Noordhoek, 7985, REP. OF SOUTH AFRICA

Ramsey, Richard, 8525 Trout Farm Rd, Neosho, MO, 64850

Rece, Charles V., 2499 Pebble Creek Ct., Lincolntown, NC, 28092-6115

Riffe, Glen, 4430 See Saw Cir., Colorado Springs, CO, 80917, skrimmer@hotmail.com

Ristinen, Lori, 14256 Cty Hwy 45, Menahga, MN, 56464, 218-538-6608, grist@wcta.net, www.digitmaster.com/ mnpro/lori/index-html

Roberts, J.J., 7808 Lake Dr., Manassas, VA, 22111

Robidoux, Roland J., DMR Fine Engraving, 25 N. Federal Hwy., Studio 5, Dania, FL, 33004

Rodkey, Sheryl, 18336 Ozark Dr., Hudson, FL, 34667

Rundell, Joe, 6198 W. Frances Rd., Clio, MI, 48420

Saggio, Joe, 1450 Broadview Ave. #12, Columbus, OH, 43212, jvsag@webtv.net

Sahlin, Viveca, Lövhagsgatan 39, S-724 71 Västerås, SWEDEN, + 46 21 358778, viveca@scrimart.u.se, www.scrimart.u.se

Satre, Robert, 518 3rd Ave. NW, Weyburn SK CANADA, S4H 1R1

Schlott, Harald, Zingster Str. 26, 13051 Berlin, GERMANY, 03 01 929 33 46, 03 01 929 33 46, www.harald-schlott@t-online.de

Schönert, Elke, 18 Lansdowne Pl., Central, Port Elizabeth, SOUTH AFRICA

Schulenburg, E.W., 25 North Hill St., Carrollton, GA, 30117

Schwallie, Patricia, 4614 Old Spartanburg Rd. Apt. 47, Taylors, SC, 29687

Selent, Chuck, P.O. Box 1207, Bonners Ferry, ID, 83805

Semich, Alice, 10037 Roanoke Dr., Murfreesboro, TN, 37129

Sherwood, George, 46 N. River Dr., Roseburg, OR, 97470

Shostle, Ben, 1121 Burlington, Muncie, IN, 47302

Sinclair, W.P., 3, The Pippins, Warminster, Wiltshire BA12 8TH, ENGLAND

Smith, D. Noel, PO Box 702, Port Orchard, WA, 98366, knife2@kktv.com

Smith, Jerry, 8770 Hunters Run, Olive Branch, TN, 38654, 662-890-5533, jsmith2098@aol.com

Smith, Peggy, 676 Glades Rd., #3, Gatlinburg, TN, 37738

Smith, Ron, 5869 Straley, Ft. Worth, TX, 76114

Snell, Barry A., 4801 96th St. N., St. Petersburg, FL, 33708- 3740

Stahl, John, Images In Ivory, 2049 Windsor Rd., Baldwin, NY, 11510, 516-223-5007

Steigerwalt, Jim, RD#3 Sunbury, PA, 17801

Stuart, Stephen, 15815 Acorn Circle, Tavares, FL, 32778, 352-343-8423, 352-343-8916, scrim@cde.com

Talley, Mary, Austin, 2499 Countrywood Parkway, Cordova, TN, 38018

Thompson, Larry D., 23040 Ave. 197, Strathmore, CA, 93267

Tong, Jill, P.O. Box 572, Tombstone, AZ, 85638

Toniutti, Nelida, Via G. Pascoli, 33085 Maniago-PN, ITALY

Tucker, Steve, 3518 W. Linwood, Turlock, CA, 95380

Tyser, Ross, 1015 Hardee Court, Spartanburg, SC, 29303

Velasquez, Gil, Art of Scrimshaw, 7120 Madera Dr., Goleta, CA, 93117

Walker, Karen, PO Box 3272, Alpine, WY, 83128-0272, gwknives@silverstar.com

Warren, Al, 1423 Santa Fe Circle, Roseville, CA, 95678, warrenives@juno.com

Williams, Gary, (Garbo), 221 Autumn Way, Elizabethtown, KY, 42701

Winn, Travis A., 558 E. 3065 S., Salt Lake City, UT, 84106

Young, Mary, 4826 Storeyland Dr., Alton, IL, 62002

Zima, Russell, 7291 Ruth Way, Denver, CO, 80221

carvers

Marlatt, David, 67622 Oldham Rd., Cambridge, OH, 43725, 740-432-7549

DiMarzo, Richard, 2357 Center Place, Birmingham, AL, 35205

writers

Kelley, Gary, 17485 SW Pheasant Lane, Aloha, OR, 97006, 503-848-9313, Custom buckle knives

etchers

Baron Technology Inc., David Baron, 62 Spring Hill Rd., Trumbull, CT, 06611

Kostelnik, Joe and Patty, RD #4, Box 323, Greensburg, PA, 15601

Schlott, Harald, Zingster Str. 26, 13051 Berlin, GERMANY, 03 01 929 33 46, 03 01 929 33 46, www.harald-schlott@t-online.de

Schönert, Elke, 18 Lansdowne Pl., Central, Port Elizabeth, SOUTH AFRICA

Snell, Barry A., 4801 96th St. N., St. Petersburg, FL, 33708- 3740

hand-forged fancy knives

Patterson, W.H., P.O. Drawer DK, College Station, TX, 77841

knife videos

Congdon, David, 1063 Whitchurch Ct., Wheaton, IL, 60187

Gimbert, Nelson, P.O. Box 787, Clemmons, NC, 27012

antique knife dealers

Congdon, David, 1063 Whitchurch Ct., Wheaton, IL, 60187

Gimbert, Nelson, P.O. Box 787, Clemmons, NC, 27012

organizations & publications

organizations

AMERICAN BLADESMITH SOCIETY
PO Box 1481, Cypress, TX 77410-1481; (281) 225-9159
info@americanbladesmith.com www.americanbladesmith.com
If you're interested in the forged blade, you are welcome here. The Society has a teaching program, East and West, and awards stamps to Journeymen and Master smiths after they pass tests--tough tests at a hot forge. You don't have to make knives to belong.

AMERICAN EDGED PRODUCTS MANUFACTURERS ASSOCIATION
112-J Elden St., Herndon, VA 20170, 703-709-8253; 703-709-1036
aepma@erols.com mailto:aepma@erols.com, http://www.aepma.org

AMERICAN KNIFE THROWERS ALLIANCE
c/o Bobby Branton, 4976 Seewee Rd., Awendaw, SC 29429

ART KNIFE COLLECTOR'S ASSOCIATION
c/o Mitch Weiss, Pres., 2211 Lee Road, Suite 104, Winter Park, FL 32789
The high-grade knife on the Internet with Web sites for everyone interested--makers and collectors.

AUSTRALIAN KNIFEMAKERS GUILD INC.
P.O. Box 659, Belgrave 3160, Victoria, AUSTRALIA
The guild was formed by a group of dedicated custom knifemakers in 1984, with the express purpose of fostering the design, manufacture, sale and use of Australian made custom knives.

CALIFORNIA KNIFEMAKERS GUILD
c/o Barry Evan Posner, Mbrshp. Chairman, 5222 Beeman Ave., N. Hollywood, CA 91607, (818) 980-7689

CANADIAN KNIFEMAKERS GUILD
c/o Paul Johnston, Sec./Treas., 8 Forest Dr. RR #4,
Smith Falls ON CANADA, K7A 4S5, (613) 284-2197 freeman@golden.net; www.ckg.org

JAPANESE SWORD SOCIETY OF THE U.S.
P.O. Box 712, Breckenridge, TX 76424
They publish a newsletter bi-monthly and a bulletin once a year.

KNIFEMAKERS GUILD, THE
c/o Alfred Pendray, 13950 NE 20th St, Williston, FL 32696, (352) 528-6124, (352) 528-6124, www.kmg.org
This one continues to be the big one. The Guild has prospered, as have its members. It screens prospects to ensure they are serious craftsmen; and it runs a big show in New Orleans in July through year 2001, where over 250 guild members show their best work, all in one room. Not all good knifemakers belong; some joined and later left for their own reasons; the Guild drops some for cause now and again. The Knifemakers Guild is an organization with a function.

KNIFEMAKERS GUILD OF SOUTHERN AFRICA, THE
c/o Bertie Rietveld, Chairman, P.O. Box 53, Magaliesburg, SOUTH AFRICA

MIDWEST KNIFEMAKERS ASSOCIATION
c/o Corbin Newcomb, Pres., 628 Woodland Ave., Moberly, MO 65270
The MKA currently has a membership of 49 makers from 10 states in the Midwest.

MONTANA KNIFEMAKERS ASSOCIATION, THE
2608 Central Ave. W, Great Falls, MT 59404 (406) 727-9102

NEO-TRIBAL METALSMITHS
PO Box 44095, Tucson AZ 85773-4095
The Neo-Tribal, approach to metalsmithing combines ancient and modern tools, materials and techniques. It relies heavily on salvaged and recycled materials and the efficient use of both. The emphasis is on high quality and traditional hand craftsmanship.

NORTH CAROLINA CUSTOM KNIFEMAKERS GUILD
c/o Tommy McNabb, Pres., 4015 Brownsboro Rd., Winston-Salem, NC 27106

PROFESSIONAL KNIFEMAKERS ASSOCIATION
Willard Patrick, 2905 N. Montana Ave., Ste 30027, Helena, MT 59601, (406) 458-6552, wilamar@ixi.net, www.web2.com/pka

REGIONAL ASSOCIATIONS
There are a number of state and regional associations with goals possibly more directly related to promotion of their members' sales than the Guild and the ABS. Among those known to us are the Arizona Knifemakers Association; the Arkansas Knifemakers Association; the South Carolina Association of Knifemakers; the New England Bladesmiths Guild; Ohio Knifemakers Association; and the Association of Southern Knifemakers.

UNITED KINGDOM BLADE ASSOCIATION (UKBA)
P.O. Box 1, Brampton, CA6 7GD, ENGLAND
Promotes the study of knives as a sensible and fascinating pastime.

publications

BLADE MAGAZINE
Krause Publications, 700 E. State St., Iola, WI 54990, (800) 272-5233
Editor: Steve Shackleford. Monthly. Official magazine of the Knifemakers Guild. $3.25 on newsstand; $19.95 per year. Also publishes Blade Trade, a cutlery trade magazine; Dream Teams; Tek-Knives; Knives of Europe and knife books.

KRAUSE PUBLICATIONS
700 E. State St., Iola, WI 54990, (715) 445-2214; (715) 445-4087
In addition to this Knives annual, Krause and its DBI Books division publish many knife books, including American Premium Guide to Knives and Razors by Jim Sargent; IBCA Price Guide to Antique Knives by J. Bruce Voyles; Levine's Guide to Knives and Their Values by Bernard Levine; The Wonder of Knifemaking by Wayne Goddard; How To Make Knives by Richard W. Barney and Robert W. Loveless; The Tactical Folding Knife by Bob Terzuola; How to Make Folding Knives by Ron Lake, Frank Centofante and Wayne Clay; Complete Book of Pocketknife Repair by Ben Kelly Jr.; Knife Talk by Ed Fowler; Collins Machetes and Bowies 1845-1965 by Daniel E. Henry; and Collecting Indian Knives by Lar Hothem.

KNIFE WORLD
P.O. Box 3395, Knoxville, TN 37927, (800) 828-7751
Editor: Mark Zalesky. Monthly. Tabloid size on newsprint. Covers custom knives, knifemakers, collecting, old factory knives, etc. General coverage for the knife enthusiast. Subscription $15 year.

KNIVES ILLUSTRATED
265 S. Anita Dr., Ste. 120, Orange, CA 92868, (714) 939-9991
Editor: Bruce Voyles. $3.99 on newsstands; $16.95 for six issues. Bi-monthly; plenty of four-color, all on cutlery; concentrates on handmade knives.

RESOURCE GUIDE AND NEWSLETTER / AUTOMATIC KNIVES
2269 Chestnut St., Suite 212, San Francisco, CA 94123, (415) 731-0210; 415-664-2105 for 24/hr. ordering info.
Editor: Sheldon Levy. In its 10th year as a quarterly. Deep coverage of automatic folders. $30 year by mail.

TACTICAL KNIVES
Harris Publications, 1115 Broadway, New York, NY 10010, (212) 807-7100; (212) 627-4678
Editor: Steve Dick. Aimed at emergency-service knife designs and users, this new publication has made a great start. Price $5.95; $14.95 for six issues. On newsstands.

TRIBAL NOW!
Neo-Tribal Metalsmiths, P.O. Box 44095, Tucson, AZ 85733-4095
Editor: Bill Randall. (See Neo-Tribal Metalsmith under Organizations.) Price: $10 per year for four issues with two- to four-page supplements sent out on a regular basis.

UK BLADE
United Kingdom Blade Associations, P.O. Box 1, Brampton CA67GD, ENGLAND

WEYER INTERNATIONAL BOOK DIVISION
2740 Nebraska Ave., Toledo, OH 43607-3245, (800) 448-8424; (419) 534-2020; (419) 534-2697
law-weyerinternational@msn.com www.weyerinternational.com
Publishers of the Knives: Points of Interest series. Sells knife-related books at attractive prices; has other knife-publishing projects in work.

Additional References You Shouldn't Be Without

2003 Sporting Knives
2nd Edition
edited by Joe Kertzman
More than 60 cutlery companies reveal over 300 models of available sporting knives, complete with large, clear photos and detailed specifications and retail prices. The catalog covers knives from commercial sporting cutlery companies such as Browning, Buck, Case, Columbia River, and Spyderco. Enjoy new feature articles and reports from the field on knife trends, the latest blade materials, and the newest commercial knife designs. An updated reference directory lets you directly contact manufacturers and dealers. Often described as the factory version of the Knives annual, this is a perfect companion to Knives 2002, which showcases custom knives.
Softcover • 8-1/2 x 11 • 256 pages
700 b&w photos
Item# DGK02 • $22.95

Wayne Goddard's $50 Knife Shop
by Wayne Goddard
Outfitting a knifemaking shop doesn't have to cost a fortune and Wayne Goddard shows you how to do it on a budget. This book expands on information from his popular column in Blade magazine to help you create helpful gadgets and obtain useful supplies. You will learn how to acquire the tools you need to make a knife shop for less than the cost of some knives.
Softcover • 8-1/2 x 11 • 160 pages
75 b&w photos • 8-page color section
Item# WGBW • $19.95

100 Legendary Knives
by Gérard Pacella
Feast your eyes on these beautiful, full-color views of the most magnificent custom knives available from European and American knifemakers. A short biography of each knifemaker describes factors influencing their design and favorite knifemaking styles. Trace the evolution of knives from prehistoric times to the military combat models and general use knives of today, with coverage of straight blades, folders, and multi-tools. Explains common knifemaking terms, and includes an index to easily locate specific knife models.
Hardcover • 9-1/2 x 11-3/8 • 144 pages
300+ color photos
Item# LEGKN • $29.95

The Wonder of Knifemaking
by Wayne Goddard
Do you want to know how to make a knife? Wayne Goddard has the answers to your questions. As a columnist for Blade magazine, Goddard has been answering real questions from real knifemakers for the past eight years. With its question-and-answer format, this book gives you the answers to real-world problems like heat-treating, choosing the best steel and finding the right tools for your knifemaking shop.
Softcover • 8-1/2 x 11 • 160 pages
150 b&w photos • 16-page color section
Item# WOKN • $19.95

Levine's Guide to Knives & Their Values
5th Edition
by Bernard Levine, Edited by Bud Lang
Numerous additions, significant pricing revisions and updated sections continue to make this the bible for knife collectors - an invaluable resource for anyone interested in collectible knives. Inside you'll find thirty-two additional pages to accommodate the expansion of current chapters and the all-new chapters on the modern folding knife, modern plier/knife multi-tool and a further chronicling of the pioneers of modern handmade knives.
Softcover • 8-1/2 x 11 • 544 pages
2,000+ b&w photos and illustrations
Item# LGK5 • $29.95

The Official Price Guide to Collector Knives
by C. Houston Price
This essential sourcebook details knives from all major manufacturers, plus specialty and custom knife makers. This revised and expanded guide lists more than 13,000 knife prices and provides valuable information on grading, buying, selling, age determination, and how to spot fakes.
Softcover • 5-1/2 x 8-1/4 • 584 pages
500+ b&w photos • 8-page color section
Item# PGCK13 • $17.95

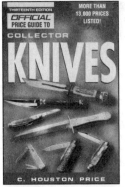

The Tactical Folding Knife
A Study Of The Anatomy And Construction Of The Liner-Locked Folder
by Bob Terzuola
Tactical folding knives are hot. Now you can build your own with the help of an expert as the author guides you through every step of the process with skillful directions and outstanding photos. If you've ever felt like you wanted to build your own masterpiece of a knife, this book is for you. Everything you need to craft your own knife is right here.
Softcover • 8-1/2 x 11 • 160 pages
200 b&w photos
Item# TACTF • $16.95

The Standard Knife Collector's Guide
4th Edition
by Roy Ritchie and Ron Stewart
The guide presents a common sense system for "total appraisal" using the RBR scales; overviews of all the major knife companies; notes on commemoratives, reproductions, and limited editions; knife clubs and organizations; numbering systems used by companies; and current collector values.
Softcover • 5-1/2 x 8-1/2 • 688 pages
800+ line drawings • Full-color section
Item# SKCG4 • $14.95a